Cambridge Handbook of Qualitative Digital Research

Big data and algorithmic decision-making have been touted as game-changing developments in management research, but they have their limitations. Qualitative approaches should not be cast aside in the age of digitalization, since they facilitate understanding of quantitative data and the questioning of assumptions and conclusions that may otherwise lead to faulty implications being drawn, and – crucially – inaccurate strategies, decisions and actions. This handbook comprises three parts: Part I highlights many of the issues associated with 'unthinking digitalization', particularly concerning the over-reliance on algorithmic decision-making and the consequent need for qualitative research. Part II provides examples of the various qualitative methods that can be usefully employed in researching various digital phenomena and issues. Part III introduces a range of emergent issues concerning practice, knowing, datafication, technology design and implementation, data reliance and algorithms, and digitalization.

BOYKA SIMEONOVA is Associate Professor of Innovation at the University of Leicester School of Business. Boyka is an expert in innovation, digitalization, knowledge and strategic management, has published in leading journals in these topics, and is a co-editor of the book, *Strategic Information Management: Theory and Practice*, 5th Edition.

ROBERT D. GALLIERS is the University Distinguished Professor Emeritus and former Provost, Bentley University, and Professor Emeritus and former Dean, Warwick Business School. He received the AIS LEO Award for exceptional lifetime achievement in Information Systems in 2012 and was the founding editor-in-chief of *The Journal of Strategic Information Systems*. His work on research methods has been particularly well cited.

Cambridge Handbook of Qualitative Digital Research

Edited by

BOYKA SIMEONOVA
University of Leicester, UK

ROBERT D. GALLIERS
Bentley University, USA
and

Warwick Business School, UK

CAMBRIDGE
UNIVERSITY PRESS

Shaftesbury Road, Cambridge CB2 8EA, United Kingdom

One Liberty Plaza, 20th Floor, New York, NY 10006, USA

477 Williamstown Road, Port Melbourne, VIC 3207, Australia

314–321, 3rd Floor, Plot 3, Splendor Forum, Jasola District Centre, New Delhi – 110025, India

103 Penang Road, #05–06/07, Visioncrest Commercial, Singapore 238467

Cambridge University Press is part of Cambridge University Press & Assessment,
a department of the University of Cambridge.

We share the University's mission to contribute to society through the pursuit of education,
learning and research at the highest international levels of excellence.

www.cambridge.org
Information on this title: www.cambridge.org/9781009098878

DOI: 10.1017/9781009106436

First published 2023

A catalogue record for this publication is available from the British Library.

Library of Congress Cataloging-in-Publication Data
Names: Simeonova, Boyka, editor. | Galliers, Robert D., 1947– editor.
Title: Cambridge handbook of qualitative digital research / edited by Boyka Simeonova, University
    of Leicester, Robert D. Galliers, Bentley University and Warwick Business School.
Description: 1 Edition. | New York, NY : Cambridge University Press, 2023. | Includes
    bibliographical references and index.
Identifiers: LCCN 2022060708 (print) | LCCN 2022060709 (ebook) | ISBN 9781009098878
    (hardback) | ISBN 9781009102780 (paperback) | ISBN 9781009106436 (epub)
Subjects: LCSH: Qualitative research–Methodology. | Big data. | Digital media.
Classification: LCC H62 .C33633 2023 (print) | LCC H62 (ebook) | DDC 300.72–dc23/eng/
    20221219
LC record available at https://lccn.loc.gov/2022060708
LC ebook record available at https://lccn.loc.gov/2022060709

ISBN 978-1-009-09887-8 Hardback

Contents

Figures

Tables

Contributors

Saeed Akhlaghpour is a senior lecturer in business information systems at the UQ Business School, University of Queensland. Previously, he held academic positions at Middlesex University London (UK) and McGill University (Canada) – where he also obtained his PhD. Saeed conducts research on digital health transformation and data protection. He has published in *American Journal of Sociology*, *Journal of the Association for Information Systems*, *Journal of Information Technology*, *Information and Organization*, *Journal of the American Medical Informatics Association* and the *Best Paper Proceedings of Academy of Management*. He is currently a chief investigator in an Australian Research Council (ARC) funded project studying digital transformation of health services in Queensland.

Jonas Valbjørn Andersen is an associate professor of digital research methods and data in organizations at the IT University of Copenhagen. His research aims to contribute to insights on strategy, management and organizing related to digitally distributed information systems such as Blockchain, Internet of Things (IoT), algorithmic decision-making and digitally distributed organizations through digital trace data analysis, as well as complex systems modelling and simulation. He holds a PhD in Information Systems and Management from Warwick Business School, University of Warwick, UK.

Marie-Claude (Marie) Boudreau is Associate Professor and Head of the Department of Management Information Systems at the University of Georgia's Terry College of Business. Her research interests revolve around the organizational change induced by information technology, primarily leveraging qualitative approaches. More specifically, she focuses on how IT can transform social systems in the particular context of the workplace. She also has a keen interest in the role played by information systems to support environmental sustainability, and has co-developed the concept of Energy Informatics. Dr Boudreau received a PhD degree in Computer Information Systems from Georgia State University, a Diplôme d'Enseignement Supérieur Spécialisé from l'École Supérieure des Affaires de Grenoble (France) and an MBA from l'Université Laval in Quebec (Canada). She has published in many journals, including *Organization Science*, *Information Systems Research*, *MIS Quarterly*, *Journal of Management Information Systems*, *The Academy of Management Executive*, *Journal of the AIS*, and other journal outlets and conference proceedings.

Andrew Burton-Jones is a professor of Business Information Systems at the UQ Business School, University of Queensland. He has a Bachelor of Commerce (Hons 1) and a Master of Information Systems from the University of Queensland and a PhD from Georgia State University. Prior to his appointment at UQ, he was an associate professor at the Sauder School, UBC, Canada. He conducts research on systems analysis and design, the effective use of information systems and several methodological topics. He serves as Editor-in-Chief of *MIS Quarterly* and has served on the editorial boards of several other journals. For the past five years, he has been conducting an in-depth longitudinal study of the digital transformation of public hospitals. Prior to his academic career, he was a senior consultant in a big-4 accounting/consulting firm.

Hameed Chughtai is an ethnographer and Senior Lecturer (Associate Professor) at Lancaster University, UK. His research lies at the intersection of information systems and critical social theory and ethnographically explores the everyday practices of digital work, body, gender, place and power. His current research interests include decolonial approaches to research and studying the ways in which marginalized populations such as Indigenous Peoples engage with, adapt and use information technologies in their practices. His research has appeared in journals such as the *European Journal of Information Systems*, *Journal of Contemporary Ethnography*, *Information Systems Journal*, *Computers in Human Behavior* and *Communications of the Association for Information Systems*, and in various conference proceedings. He currently serves as a guest associate editor of *Information Systems Journal*'s special issue on Sustainable Visitor Economy and as Secretary of the International Federation of Information Processing (IFIP) Working Group 9.5 'Our Digital Lives'.

David Coghlan is Professor Emeritus and Fellow Emeritus at the Trinity Business School, Trinity College Dublin, Ireland. He is author of over 200 articles and book chapters. Recent books include *Collaborative Inquiry for Organization Development and Change* (2021) and *Doing Action Research in Your Own Organization*, 5th Edition (2019). He is co-editor of *The Sage Encyclopedia of Action Research* (2014).

Paul Coughlan is Professor in Operations Management at Trinity Business School, Trinity College Dublin, Ireland. His research explores collaborative strategic improvement of operations through network action learning.

Nicola Ens is a PhD fellow at the department of digitalization, Copenhagen Business School.

She works at the intersections of IS, organization theory and sociologies of work, using ethnographic methods to investigate the changing nature of work on digital labour platforms. She is currently conducting an ethnography of fashion resellers drawing on both traditional and digital ethnographic methods. She has presented her work at top conferences, including the European Group for Organizational Studies and the International Conference on Information Systems.

Samer Faraj is a professor at McGill University's Desautels Faculty of Management, where he holds the Canada Research Chair in Technology, Innovation, and Organizing. His current research focuses on complex collaboration and on how emergent technologies are allowing new forms of coordination and organizing to emerge. He has published in outlets such as *Organization Science*, *Management Science*, *MIS Quarterly*, *Academy of Management Journal* and *Annals of Emergency Medicine*.

Guy Fitzgerald is Emeritus Professor of Information Systems (IS) at Loughborough University. Previously he has worked at Brunel, Birkbeck, Oxford and Warwick universities. He has also been a practitioner with companies such as British Telecom, Mitsubishi and CACI Inc., International. His research interests are concerned with the effective management and development of IS, undertaking research in the areas of IS development methodologies, IS strategy, outsourcing, flexibility and agility, publishing widely in these areas. Guy was elected an AIS (Association for Information Systems) Fellow in 2014 and is a member of the AIS College of Senior Scholars. He is co-founder and was for twenty-five years joint Editor-in-Chief of the *Information Systems Journal*. He is the author (with David Avison) of a major text titled *Information Systems Development: Methodologies, Techniques and Tools*. He has been President of UKAIS and Vice-President (Publications) of AIS. He was a Research Evaluation Exercise sub-panel member responsible for IS (2014–2020).

Robert D. Galliers is the University Distinguished Professor Emeritus and former Provost, Bentley University, and Professor Emeritus and former Dean, Warwick Business School. He has received the Association of Information Systems AIS LEO Award for exceptional lifetime achievement in Information Systems in 2012 and was the founding Editor-in-Chief of *The Journal of Strategic Information Systems* until December 2018. He has published in excess of 100 journal articles and fourteen books and his work on research methods is particularly well cited.

Lakshmi Goel is a professor of Information Systems at the Coggin College of Business, University of North Florida. She received her PhD in Decision and Information Sciences from the University of Houston. Her research works are published in various conferences such as International Conference on Information Systems, Americas Conference on Information Systems, Academy of Management, Hawaii International Conference on System Sciences and European Conference on Information Systems; and journals such as *Management Information Systems Quarterly*, *Journal of the Association of Information Systems*, *Decision Support Systems*, *Information and Management*, *Information and Organization* and *Information Systems Journal*.

Wendy Arianne Günther is a researcher at the KIN Center for Digital Innovation, Vrije University Amsterdam (VU). She holds a Bachelor's degree in Computer Science from the University of Amsterdam, a Master's diploma in ICT in Business from Leiden University and a PhD from the VU, School of Business and Economics. Her research focuses on how organizations can successfully leverage data as strategic resources. This includes studying how organizations develop and implement data-driven strategies; how traditional organizations transform into data-driven organizations, and how organizations can develop, manage and integrate data-driven solutions effectively and responsibly.

Rudy A. Hirschheim (PhD, University of London; Dr hc University of Oulu; University of Bern) is the Ourso Family Distinguished Professor of Information Systems at Louisiana State University. He has previously been on the faculties of the University of Houston, the London School of Economics and Templeton College of the University of Oxford. He is past Senior Editor for *Information and Organization* and *Journal of the Association for Information Systems*. He is on the editorial boards of *Journal of Management Information Systems*, *Information Systems Journal*, *Journal of Information Technology* and *Journal of Strategic Information Systems*. He was the LEO Award for lifetime achievement recipient in 2013 and Fellow of the Association for Information Systems in 2007.

Philipp Hukal is an assistant professor at Copenhagen Business School, Denmark. His research examines digitally enabled innovation within and across organizations, covering topics such as digital platforms, open source software development and digital ventures. He holds a PhD in Information Systems and Management from Warwick Business School, University of Warwick, UK.

Tina Blegind Jensen is a professor at the department of digitalization, Copenhagen Business School. Her research focuses on organizational and managerial issues of information systems, with a particular interest in the impact of digital technology on people in organizations. She has published articles in leading journals and frequently presents her work at major conferences on topics such as digital transformation of work, people analytics, sense-making practices and institutional structures. Tina is an editorial board member of leading IS journals and serves in various organizing capacities for major international conferences on management information systems.

Matthew Jones is a reader in Information Systems at the Judge Business School and the Department of Engineering at the University of Cambridge. He previously held postdoctoral positions at the University of Reading and the University of Cambridge, where he was involved in the development of computer-based models for public policy decision-making. His current research interests are concerned with the relationship between information systems and social and organizational change and theoretical and methodological issues in information systems research.

Mayur P. Joshi is an assistant professor (lecturer) in FinTech at Alliance Manchester Business School, University of Manchester, UK, and he recently finished his PhD in business administration from Ivey Business School, Western University, Canada. His research examines the phenomenon of organizing for – and in – the digital age, with a focus on data science, AI-enabled analytics tools and other digital innovations in the context of financial and information technology industries. He worked as a banker for several years prior to joining academia, where he was engaged with functions and initiatives such as technology implementation, process improvement and branch banking operations.

Iris Junglas is the Noah T. Leask Distinguished Professor of Information Management and Innovation in the Department of Supply Chain and Information Management at the College of Charleston. Over her twenty-five-year career, she has worked for a variety of consulting firms, as well as academia. Her research sits at the intersection of technology innovation and business analytics. Iris has published more than fifty refereed journal articles in outlets, including *European Journal of Information Systems*, *Information Systems Journal*, *Journal of the Association of Information Systems*, *Journal of Strategic Information Systems* and *Management Information Systems Quarterly*.

Stefan Klein is Professor for Interorganizational Systems at the School of Business and Economics, University of Münster, Germany, where he is Vice Dean for Internationalization. His current research areas are information infrastructures, network governance, digitization and

risk, and transformation of work. He studies practices of technology use and organizational transformation from an individual to an industry level. Previously he held teaching or research positions at University College Dublin, Ireland; University of Linz, Austria; University of Koblenz-Landau, Germany; University St Gallen, Switzerland; Harvard University; the German Research Center for Computer Science; and University of Cologne, Germany.

Allen S. Lee is Professor Emeritus of Information Systems at Virginia Commonwealth University. He served as Editor-in-Chief of *MIS Quarterly* and as a founding senior editor of *MIS Quarterly Executive*. His research programme has involved showing not only how qualitative research can be done rigorously and scientifically, but also how quantitative research equally needs to live up to the requirements of science. He is a fellow of the Association for Information Systems, a LEO Award recipient and a member of the Circle of Compadres of the Information Systems Doctoral Students Association of the KPMG PhD Project.

Joe McDonagh is Associate Professor of Business at Trinity Business School, Trinity College Dublin, Ireland. His research, teaching and advisory work focus on the process of leading large-scale strategic, organizational and technological change programmes in civil and public service organizations.

Nathalie Mitev, after thirty years in several UK universities, and for seventeen years at the London School of Economics, now teaches workshops on qualitative research methods, thesis writing, epistemology and technology management to doctoral students in various universities and institutes in Europe. Dr Mitev evaluates research programmes in management for funding agencies and articles for academic journals and conferences, and participates in doctoral supervision and assessment. She has published in a range of management and information systems journals and conferences, and has edited several books on sociomateriality and management based on the Organizations, Artefacts and Practices workshops, and a handbook on research methods.

Josh Morton is a lecturer in Strategy and Innovation at Leeds University Business School, University of Leeds, UK, and the programme director for the school's MSc in Global Strategy and Innovation Management. He teaches strategy and innovation at different levels of study, including to business leaders. His research focuses on the work of strategists and top managers in organizations, with a particular interest in strategic agility, open forms of strategy and digital innovation.

Michael D. Myers is Professor of Information Systems at the University of Auckland Business School, New Zealand. His research interests are in the areas of digital transformation, the social, organizational and cultural aspects of digital technologies, and qualitative research methods in information systems. He won the Best Paper award (with Heinz Klein) in *MIS Quarterly* in 1999 and the Best Paper Award (with Simon Chanias and Thomas Hess) in *Journal of Strategic Information Systems* in 2019. Michael served as a senior editor of *MIS Quarterly* from 2001 to 2005 and as a senior editor of *Information Systems Research* from 2008 to 2010. He also served as President of the Association for Information Systems (AIS) in 2006 and 2007 and as Chair of International Federation of Information Processing Working Group 8.2 from 2006 to 2008. He currently serves as Editor-in-Chief of *European Journal of Information Systems*. Michael is a fellow and LEO Award winner of AIS.

Stavros Polykarpou is Lecturer (Assistant Professor) in Science, Innovation, Technology and Entrepreneurship at the University of Exeter Business School and Initiative for the Digital Economy (INDEX). His research lies at the intersection of technology, digital innovation, work and organizing. He examines the broader question of how to organize for emerging and algorithmic technologies along with associated societal and organizational implications for creating value in the digital age. Methodologically, he employs ethnographic, in-depth qualitative methods to explore these topics. His research was awarded the 2020 Organizational Communications and Information Systems Division Best Paper Award, at the Academy of Management Conference (Vancouver, Canada; held virtually), for his ethnographic study of implementing 3D printing in healthcare. Stavros's research has been published in *Information and Organization* and conditionally accepted at *Information Systems Research*.

M. N. Ravishankar is Professor and Dean of the Management School, Queen's University. He works with a range of start-ups, multinational companies and public sector organizations globally. He has published peer-reviewed articles on the management of digital innovations, social entrepreneurship and global technology sourcing. His research has appeared in scholarly journals such as *Information Systems Research*, *Journal of World Business*, *Information Systems Journal*, *European Journal of Information Systems* and *Journal of Strategic Information Systems*.

Sven-Volker Rehm is an associate professor of Information Systems at EM Strasbourg, the business school of the University of Strasbourg. He held previous positions at WHU – Otto Beisheim School of Management. He holds a diploma in cybernetics and a doctorate in engineering sciences from the University of Stuttgart, along with a habilitation degree in business administration from WHU. His research sits at the intersection of communication, technology and organizing, with a focus on digital platforms and business ecosystems. He has published in journals such as *Information and Management*, *Information and Organization*, *Journal of the AIS* and *MIS Quarterly Executive*.

Hani Safadi is an associate professor at Terry College of Business, University of Georgia. He received his PhD from the Desautels Faculty of Management, McGill University. He is interested in online communities, social media, healthcare information technology, mixed-methods research and the application of computational linguistics in studying qualitative data. His research is published in outlets such as *MIS Quarterly*, *Information Systems Research*, *Organization Science* and *Journal of Medical Internet Research*.

Suprateek Sarker is a Rolls-Royce Commonwealth Commerce professor (Information Technology) at the McIntire School of Commerce, University of Virginia. He currently teaches courses on data management and business intelligence, and global immersion in India and the United Arab Emirates. He is interested in applying different qualitative research approaches to study IS phenomena. He has published in many high-quality journals and has served on editorial boards of journals such as *MIS Quarterly*, *Information Systems Research*, *Journal of MIS*, *Information & Organization*, *Decision Sciences*, *IEEE Transactions on Engineering Management* and *Journal of the AIS*. He is a fellow of the AIS. He is also a former student of the first author of Chapter 2, Allen Lee.

Stefan Schellhammer is Tenured Lecturer and currently serves as Vice Dean for Teaching and Learning at the School of Business and Economics at the University of Münster, Germany. He received his PhD from the University of Münster in the subject area of Interorganizational Information Systems. His research focuses on studying the emergence of information infrastructures, as well as the implications of the changing nature of work to the well-being of individuals. His research has appeared in various books and conferences, and in *MIS Quarterly*.

Boyka Simeonova is Associate Professor of Innovation at the University Leicester School of Business. Boyka is an expert in innovation, digitalization, knowledge and strategic management, has published in leading journals in these topics, and is a co-editor of the book, *Strategic*

Information Management: Theory and Practice, 5th Edition (2020).

Mari-Klara Stein is a professor at the Department of Business Administration, TalTech, and an associate professor at the Department of Digitalization, Copenhagen Business School. Mari-Klara holds a doctoral degree from Bentley University (USA). Her research is focused on digital transformation of work. She has published her work in top management and IS journals (e.g., *MIS Quarterly*, *Journal of Management Studies*). Mari-Klara is the recipient of the European Research Paper of the Year award from CIONET, as well as the recipient of the Association for Information Systems (AIS) Early Career Award.

Mark Thompson is Professor of Digital Economy within the Initiative for the Digital Economy in Exeter (INDEX), part of Exeter Business School. His research interests include digital platforms and the public sector, and the affective dimension within organizational practice. Mark has undertaken technology policy development roles on a pro bono basis for a range of organizations, such as the UK National Audit Office, the Cabinet Office and the Scottish government, and is a board member of technology trade association TechUK. Mark combines his academic work with running London-based digital transformation organization Methods Group.

Gongtai Wang is Assistant Professor at the Smith School of Business, Queen's University. He earned his PhD from Warwick Business School, University of Warwick, and worked as a postdoctoral researcher at the UQ Business School, University of Queensland. His research focuses on the fundamental rethinking and strategic redesign of traditional products, services and business models with emerging digital technologies such as IoT, mixed reality, AI and blockchain. His research has been published in *MIS Quarterly*, the *Journal of Product Innovation Management* and proceedings of flagship Information Systems conferences.

David Whitchurch currently serves as the Business Analytics Manager at the Center for Analytics and Research in Transportation Safety at Louisiana State University, where he manages the development, updates and maintenance of data analytics applications, visualizations and reporting services solutions for a variety of highway safety stakeholders. He also works with clients as an analytics consultant for both US federal and state projects related to highway safety. He previously worked in the private sector in a variety of roles, including operations, human resource development, information technology and business application development. He received his MS Analytics from Louisiana State University and is currently pursuing a PhD in Information Systems and Decision Sciences.

Edgar A. Whitley is an associate professor in Information Systems in the Department of Management at the London School of Economics and Political Science. Edgar has a BSc (Econ.) and PhD in Information Systems, both from the LSE. He is the co-editor of *Information Technology and People*, Senior Editor for the *Journal of Information Technology* and *AIS Transactions of Replication Research*. He has served as research co-chair for the European Conference on Information Systems and track co-chair for the International Conference on Information Systems, and was previously an associate editor for the *European Journal of Information Systems* and *MIS Quarterly*.

Alex Wilson is a reader at the Management School, Queen's University, has been Chartered Association of Business Schools Research Fellow, and has held visiting roles as Lim Kim San Research Fellow at Singapore Management University.

Preface

Rationale and Overview

Academic interest in the digitalization phenomenon is pervasive and growing. Programmes dealing with the technical aspects of the topic, such as in Data Analytics and Data Science, are now commonplace, being provided the world over by higher education institutions and major commercial companies and consultancies alike. Similarly, research output and scholarly publications abound, and have been growing for a decade or so (e.g., Waller and Fawcett, 2013; Chen et al., 2016). The management, societal and ethical implications of digitalization have as yet to be considered to the same degree, however, although researchers in the Information Systems, Organization Studies, Strategic Management and cognate fields are considering these topics and issues (e.g., Constantiou and Kallinikos, 2015; Erevelles et al., 2016; Galliers et al., 2017; Legner et al., 2017; Stein et al., 2019) – broader methodological considerations, especially concerning the use of qualitative methods in this domain, are largely missing given the heightened interest in (quantitative) data analytics (Ardito et al., 2019).

Given the rapid expansion in research on various aspects of digitalization, this handbook is set to be of considerable interest within these research communities, taking as it does a transdisciplinary perspective (Galliers, 2004). Importantly, and increasingly, as the issues – negative as well as positive (Newell and Marabelli, 2015) – and impacts (Günther et al., 2017) become apparent, questions of research *method*, as well as specific emergent topics, will increasingly arise. Given the need for a more critical approach to our research (cf. Howcroft and Trauth, 2005), the emphasis of this handbook is thus on research that applies qualitative methods set alongside the more commonplace data-analytical, quantitative approaches.

Handbook Structure

The book is divided into three parts that in turn provide a theoretical foundation, consider methodological approaches and implications and reflect on illustrative and emergent issues.

Part I deals with *Philosophical, Epistemological and Theoretical Considerations*, setting the scene for the remainder of the handbook. Many of the issues associated with digitalization are highlighted, particularly concerning the over-reliance on algorithmic decision-making and the consequent need for qualitative research. The various contributions provide a critique of 'big data' empiricism and introduce theoretical considerations that open up opportunities for the qualitative researcher by assisting in the identification of a range of limitations associated with data analytics, most importantly with regard to understanding what those data are actually demonstrating. Broader societal issues are also considered (e.g., Loebecke and Pinot, 2015).

As presaged above, Part II deals with *Methodological Considerations*. It provides examples of the various qualitative methods that can usefully be employed in researching various digitalization phenomena and issues. Included in this section are chapters concerning hermeneutics, the use of multi-methods, mixed-methods, text mining and visualization, revisiting the case study approach in the current era, ethnographic approaches and action research. It also includes a comparison of qualitative, quantitative and algorithmic research approaches.

Part III discusses a number of *Illustrative Examples and Emergent Issues*. While by no means comprehensive, the chapters in this section of the handbook delve into the subject matter by introducing a range of issues concerning, inter alia, practice, knowing, implementation, rich facets of digital trace data, data reliance and data sharing. Implications for theory and practice (cf. Smith, 2006; Mingers et al., 2013) and society (cf. Loebecke and Pinot, 2015) are also highlighted.

Target Audiences

The pervasive nature of the digitalization phenomenon, and the transdisciplinary nature of the research that is and will (need to) be undertaken, mean that the handbook has been designed to be accessible to researchers in a variety of academies. While the handbook's contributors are, for the most part, from the international Information Systems (IS) field, the content is entirely relevant for these other communities. Thus, while our chapter authors have particular interests and expertise in qualitative research methods as applied to IS topics, those from cognate fields such as, inter alia, Organization Studies, Strategic Management, Marketing, Engineering Management, Finance, Operational Research and Operations Management, have strong and growing interests in the subject matter and the means by which the phenomena in which they are interested may be appropriately studied – mixed, pluralistic or complementary approaches being a key consideration (cf. Galliers et al., 1997; Mingers, 2001). Indeed, colleagues in other fields of study, such as Strategy, are also calling for research collaborations with the IS community (e.g., Whittington, 2017) – it is, therefore, not a 'one way street'.

Given that we are attempting to deal with these broader and emergent issues, researchers from these fields of study who take a more holistic, critical stance and who consider different epistemological and methodological approaches would doubtless find the handbook of particular interest. Doctoral and Master level students in Business Schools and Faculties of Social Science and Engineering may also find the book to be a key reference source, not just those taking courses on research methods (cf. Galliers and Huang, 2012).

Contributors

As noted above, we have invited contributions from experts in applying qualitative methods to digital phenomena. These contributions were originally sought in 2020 so that, in certain instances (as noted, for example, in Chapter 14), more recent publications of relevance to the subject matter have appeared in the literature. The contributors hail from universities located in Europe, North America and the Asian Pacific region. Each was invited not just for their undoubted expertise and considerable experience in researching and teaching in this domain, but also for their open, questioning, critical and flexible approaches to undertaking research on emerging digital phenomena. Brief biographical summaries can be found before this Preface.

References

Ardito, L., Scuotto, V., Del Giudice, M. and Messeni Petruzzelli, A. (2019). A bibliometric analysis of research on big data analytics for business and management. *Management Decision*, 57(8), 1993–2009.

Chen, Y., Chen, H., Gorkhali, A., Lu, Y., Ma, Y. and Li, L. (2016). Big data analytics and big data science: A survey. *Journal of Management Analytics*, 3(1), 1–42.

Constantiou, I. and Kallinikos, J. (2015). New games, new rules: Big data and the changing context of strategy. *Journal of Information Technology*, 30(1), 44–57.

Erevelles, S., Fukawa, N. and Swayne, L. (2016). Big data consumer analytics and the transformation of marketing. *Journal of Business Research*, 68(2), 897–904.

Galliers, R. D. (2004). Trans-disciplinary research in Information Systems. *International Journal of Information Management*, 24(1), 99–106.

Galliers, R. D. and Huang, J. (2012). The teaching of qualitative research methods in Information Systems: An explorative study utilising learning theory. *European Journal of Information Systems*, 21(2), 119–134.

Galliers, R. D., Jackson, M. C. and Mingers, J. (1997). Organization theory and systems thinking: The benefits of partnership. *Organization*, 4(2), 268–278.

Galliers, R. D., Newell, S., Shanks, G. and Topi, H. (2017). Datification and its human, organizational and societal effects: The strategic opportunities and challenges of algorithmic decision-making. *Journal of Strategic Information Systems*, 26(3), 187–190.

Günther, W. A., Rezazade Mehrizi, M. H., Huysman, M. and Feldberg F. (2017). Debating big data: A literature review on realizing value from big data. *Journal of Strategic Information Systems*, 26(3), 191–209.

Howcroft, D. and Trauth, E. M. (eds). (2005). *Handbook of Critical Information Systems Research: Theory and Application*. Cheltenham, UK and Northampton, MA: Edward Elgar.

Legner, C., Eymann, T., Hess, T., Matt, C., Böhmann, T., Drews, P., Mädche, A., Urbach, N. and Ahlemann, F. (2017). Digitalization: Opportunity and challenge for the business and information systems engineering community. *Business & Information Systems Engineering*, 59(4), 301–308.

Loebecke, C. and Pinot, A. (2015). Reflections on societal and business model transformation arising from digitization and big data analytics: A research agenda. *Journal of Strategic Information Systems*, 24(3), 149–157.

Mingers, J. (2001). Combining IS research methods: Towards a pluralist methodology. *Information Systems Research*, 12(3), 240–259.

Mingers, J., Mutch, A. and Willcocks, L. (2013). Critical realism in information systems research. *MIS Quarterly*, 37(3), 795–802.

Newell, S. and Marabelli, M. (2015). Strategic opportunities (and challenges) of algorithmic decision-making: A call for action on the long-term societal effects of 'datification'. *Journal of Strategic Information Systems*, 24(1), 3–14.

Smith, M. L. (2006). Overcoming theory-practice inconsistencies: Critical realism and information systems research. *Information & Organization*, 16(3), 191–211.

Stein, M. K., Wagner, E., Tierney, P., Newell, S. and Galliers, R. D. (2019). Datification and the pursuit of meaningfulness in work. *Journal of Management Studies*, 56(3), 685–717.

Waller, M. A. and Fawcett, S. E. (2013). Data science, predictive analytics, and big data: A revolution that will transform supply chain design and management. *Journal of Business Logistics*, 34(2), 77–84.

Whittington, R. (2017). Information systems strategy and strategy-as-practice: A joint agenda. *Journal of Strategic Information Systems*, 23(1), 87–91.

PART I

Philosophical, Epistemological and Theoretical Considerations

Introduction

The Need for Qualitative Research in the Age of Digitalization

ROBERT D. GALLIERS and BOYKA SIMEONOVA

1.1 Introduction

As noted in the Preface, we aim in this handbook to delve into the digitalization phenomenon and to go some way to answer the calls for more critical research on the topic (as mentioned, inter alia, by Newell and Marabelli (2015), Galliers et al. (2015, 2017) and Grover et al. (2020)). We do so in light of our increasingly digitized world and the reliance being placed on algorithmic decision-making by organizations (and society more generally) – but also because of our concern that there may well be *over*-reliance being placed on digitalization,[1] not just in practice, but in academic research too. More qualitative approaches would appear to be required given these concerns (cf. Van Maanen, 1979).

While recognizing the growing literature on the topic (e.g., Frické, 2015; Günther et al., 2017; Vial, 2019; Grover, 2020; Hirschheim, 2021), we aim here not only to address in some small way society's apparent taken-for-granted and unknowing acquiescence to this increasingly prevalent phenomenon (Markus and Topi, 2015), but also – and more specifically for the purposes of this handbook – to provide an alternative account of the *means* by which we might most usefully research the topic. Indeed, this is the primary purpose of this handbook: to investigate the rationale for and the role of qualitative research methods in the age of digitalization.

1.2 Opportunities and Issues

As an example of some of the opportunities and issues such research may consider, Vial (2019: 137–138) notes that:

> As digital technologies afford more information, computing, communication, and connectivity, they enable new forms of collaboration among distributed networks of diversified actors. In doing so, they also create dependencies among actors whose interests may not fully be aligned. This new reality offers tremendous potential for innovation and performance in organizations, and extends beyond the boundaries of the firm to affect individuals, industries, and society … future research may … investigate … under which conditions an organizational design performs better than another … or explore under-researched relationships …

So, while transformational opportunities may well arise, new complexities and dependencies do also. Further, there are other considerations that require careful study. For example, Jones (2019: 3) makes the following critical point concerning the data themselves – in his terms, 'data in principle' as compared with 'data in practice':

> Rather than being a referential, natural, foundational, objective and equal representation of the world … data are partial and contingent and are brought into being through situated practices of conceptualization, recording and use. Big data are also not as revolutionary voluminous, universal or exhaustive as they are often presented.

Further, Newell and Marabelli (2015) raise an ethical argument that requires serious consideration when pointing to the fact that 'the many digital

---

[1] Also called 'datification' (e.g., Galliers et al., 2017) or 'datafication' (e.g., in Lycett, 2013; Hansen, 2015; Mai, 2016).

devices that are increasingly in continuous use are capable of enabling the monitoring of "the minutiae of an individual's everyday life". Such data are often processed by predetermined algorithms that lead to decisions that follow on directly without further human intervention (often with the claim that the decisions are for the individual's benefit).' While the strategic value of such data for organizations can be considerable and is doubtless growing, as Vial notes, the implications for individuals and wider society are less clear and are debatable. Also, as Newell and Marabelli indicate, most often they remain 'unaware of how the data they [digital devices] produce are being used, and by whom and with what consequences'.

In their consideration of 'big data', Newell and Marabelli (2015) note the vast amounts of 'digital trace data [that] are collected through digitized devices (captured, for example, via social networks, online shopping, blogs, ATM withdrawals and the like) and through in-built sensors. As such, they fall under the "big data" umbrella (Hedman et al., 2013; Wu and Brynjolfsson, 2009)'. Having said that, they do not discount 'little data' in their discussion either. In their words, 'this targeting can now be taken further when data are used not to predict group trends but to predict the behavior of a specific individual'. Thus, 'little data' is based on 'big data', but has its focus on individuals, using the vast computing capacity that is available today to collect and analyze what is extremely granular data (Munford, 2014). In a nutshell, then, a major concern of theirs with 'datification' (whether in relation to 'big' or 'little' data) – one which we share – is that 'somebody else may . . . use the data . . . often with purposes different from those originally intended'.

Regarding such considerations, Bholat (2015), for example, argues for a more balanced approach which considers human intelligence and decision-making along with algorithmic and data analytics. Those who point to the benefits associated with algorithmic means – Madsen (2015) and Van der Vlist (2016), among others – cite the emergent nature of such intelligence, the innovative concepts thus derived and the avoidance of preconceptions. Those who place greater emphasis on human intelligence – Sharma et al. (2014) and Seddon et al. (2017) , among others – express concerns about the 'unknowing' and

'out of context' nature of what might be termed the 'blind' dependence on the algorithmic approach.

1.3 Some Implications for Research

In light of this background, and as a result of a comprehensive literature review, Günther et al. (2017) identify three different levels of analysis for future research. These relate to tensions occurring at the work-practice, organizational and supra-organizational levels. At the work-practice level, tensions that Günther and colleagues identify relate to (1) inductive versus deductive approaches and (2) algorithmic versus human-based intelligence. Key issues identified include the collection of data without a predefined purpose that, in their words, promotes 'a bottom-up approach to big data collection, exploration and analysis'. Such inductive approaches as these are meant to lead to the identification of 'previously unknown patterns or distinctions'. Deductive, hypothesis-driven approaches 'where data are collected, processed, and visualized for specific purposes' (Tan et al., 2015) provide an alternative avenue. The risks inherent in the former concern data being potentially used out of context, while confirmation bias may arise with the latter.

Whatever the strengths and weaknesses of either stance, Günther et al. (2017) argue for more research on actual practices (cf. Peppard et al., 2014; Whittington, 2014), especially given the number of conceptual rather than empirical studies that have thus far been conducted. For example, actors in the study conducted by Shollo and Galliers (2015) argue that 'data should be supplemented with human experience, common sense, and contextual knowledge that are hard to capture by data [alone]'.[2] One of the dangers of over-

---

[2] Shollo and Galliers (2015) make the point that big data analytics is a similar concept to the older and more familiar concept of business intelligence that has been studied for over a decade (e.g., Power, 2002; Rouiba and Ould-ali, 2002; Thomsen, 2003; Negash, 2004), with the difference that, in the big data context, the sources and types of data are significantly more varied and often gain greater relevance for real-time processing.

reliance on algorithms is the potential of relevant tacit knowledge being lost or replaced – an aspect already noted by Markus (2015) and Newell and Marabelli (2015). Günther and colleagues conclude: 'As of yet, it remains unclear under what particular conditions organizational actors are able to generate insights through inductive or deductive approaches, or a combination of both. Nor is it clear what specific contributions human and algorithmic intelligence add to the creation of insights in different situations (e.g., stable and routine practices versus emergent and temporal situations).'

The tensions identified by Günther et al. (2017) at the organizational level refer to centralized versus decentralized big data capability structures and business model improvement, as against more radical innovations. Capabilities with regard to organizations developing and leveraging technical and human resources (cf. Peppard and Ward, 2004) have been a subject of considerable research over the years (e.g., Daniel et al., 2014; Huang et al., 2015). With regard to big data analytics, 'organizations face questions regarding not only how to acquire or develop [these] resources (Brinkhues et al., 2015; Tambe, 2014), but also how to structure them in teams or departments'. Arguments for the development of centralized competency centres tend to be focused on the (current) shortage of analytical skills (e.g., Davenport et al., 2010 in Sharma et al., 2014). Counter-arguments that highlight concerns about the potential of damaging communication between and limiting involvement with other organizational actors have also been raised. This has led to the identification of 'synergistic benefits of centralized capability structures … [alongside] specific expertise associated with decentralizing' (Sidorova and Torres, 2014). Importantly, Günther and colleagues point out that literature is still scarce regarding what is appropriate and how such data capability may be achieved in practice. While examples of centralized capability have appeared, such as in Bholat (2015), 'it is often not clear how these structures are put in place, how they interact with business units, or how they produce value'. Likewise, little empirical evidence exists to support a more decentralized approach. Similarly, the tension between incremental and radical approaches to innovation is seen as a further

research topic (cf. Loebbecke and Picot, 2015; Woerner and Wixom, 2015). Here, again, Günther and colleagues note a lack of empirical studies, with few cases having been published concerning 'improvements in or innovations to business models based on big data (Gartner, 2013)'.

At the supra-organizational level, Günther et al. (2017) identify two tensions concerning 'how organizations manage data access, and how they deal with stakeholder interests such as ethical concerns and regulation'. The tensions relate to controlled versus open access to big data and to minimizing or simply neglecting the social risks associated with realizing value from data. By social risks, they mean the potential of (inadvertently) revealing personal, sensitive information, in terms of, for example, 'privacy, identity theft, illegal discrimination, unjust classification' (see also Markus, 2015). Regarding the tension between controlled versus open access to big data, they highlight the literature that points to organizations relying on effective data exchange across their network (Malgonde and Bhattacherjee, 2014) and engaging in practices of data disclosure and screening in doing so (Jia et al., 2015). Two concerns arise relating to privacy and security (Chatfield et al., 2015) and the potential negative impacts of sharing proprietary or competitive information that may negatively impact an organization's strategic placement (e.g., Jagadish et al., 2014; Greenaway et al., 2015). Citing Van den Broek and Van Veenstra (2015), Günther and colleagues describe that some organizations have tried to 'square the circle' by controlling and opening data access, based on trust (e.g., Xu et al., 2016; McKnight et al., 2017), although formal agreements and clear communication channels are considered crucial by others (e.g., Kim et al., 2014).

Digitalization could increase control to communication and information channels which may create information asymmetries (Lightfoot and Wisniewski, 2014). However, digitalization could lead to empowerment (Leong et al., 2015). Therefore, understanding issues of power and digitalization is increasingly important. Power, knowledge, digitalization, learning and empowerment need theorization and research in the digital era (Simeonova, 2018; Simeonova et al., 2020, 2022).

A further dimension to this 'problematique' may be discerned. It can reasonably be argued that the question of the changing nature of professional work in the twenty-first century as a result of digitalization is something to which we as a research community can (and should) make a contribution (cf. Grant and Parker, 2009; Stein et al., 2013, 2016; Forman et al., 2014; Baptista et al., 2020). The nature of professional work is changing, as is the management of professional workers. Evidence-based management (Pfeffer and Sutton, 2006) and data-driven approaches to managing workers (e.g., Waber, 2013; Bersin, 2015) are already becoming prevalent in many organizations in modern society (Fecheyr-Lippens et al., 2015). Thus, these are topics that also require research and collaboration with colleagues in cognate fields such as Organization Studies and Strategic Management, given the complexities and nuances of the subject matter – a plea that has been made over the years (e.g., Galliers, 1995; Galliers et al., 1997; Whittington, 2014), but which has often remained unheeded in our quest for disciplinary purity.

In sum, aspects of the digitalization phenomenon – its issues, impacts and implications – that require further study include (based largely on Günther et al., 2017), in our view, a plurality of research methods (cf. Mingers, 2001) that incorporate qualitative research (cf. Van Maanen, 1979; Walsham, 2006):

- the practices and outcomes of inductive and deductive approaches to algorithmic decision-making, in isolation or in combination;
- effects of algorithmic and human-based intelligence – both positive and negative – on professional work practices, skill requirements and organizational performance;
- organizational capabilities and alternative management structures – their development and consequences;
- examples of datafication initiatives involving incremental change vis-à-vis more radical innovations;
- inter-organizational access to and exchange of big data – implications, risks and effects;
- ethical considerations and the social risks associated with datafication, including but not limited to privacy and security;

- further investigation and extension of various datafication patterns in different contexts;
- capturing richness in the digital traces of social interactions; and
- sociotechnical and sociomaterial design considerations for algorithmic decision systems.

1.4 Further Foundational Considerations

Contributors to this handbook provide further foundational considerations of the research methods that might be applied in the context of digitalization. In Chapter 2, 'A Philosophical Perspective on Qualitative Research in the Age of Digitalization', Allen Lee and Suprateek Sarker consider the place of the digitalization of qualitative research in its philosophical context. More specifically, they consider the following key themes: 'Induction, on which current rationales for the digitalization of qualitative research depend, deserves attention given that it can be helpful in the building of a theory while being flawed as a means for justifying a theory … How justifying a theory is indeed carried out, through deduction, deserves and … receive[s] … equal attention. Meaning, which is arguably the central object of attention in interpretive research, merits attention because the digitalization of qualitative research in IS has, so far, largely not effectively addressed it'.

In Chapter 3, Matthew Jones returns to the issue of the veracity – or otherwise – of the data themselves. His contribution, titled 'Data as a Contingent Performance and the Limitations of Big Data', outlines that there is a commonly held assumption among data scientists, consultancies and organizations (public and private) alike, that data represent some form of 'reality' and that 'understanding of the world can therefore be gained through their analysis alone'. He begs to differ, and demonstrates that 'this was never the case, [not] even in the pre-digital era [and that this] … is not altered by the contemporary abundance of data, perhaps *especially of the digital variety*' (emphasis added). He argues that data 'are not, as is often claimed, a natural resource … that pre-exist their collection. Nor do they stand in a direct relationship with the phenomena they are considered as representing. Rather, they are the product of situated practices that provide a selective and potentially inaccurate representation of phenomena.' The chapter considers the implications of this argumentation for research methods, specifically in the field of Information Systems, but also for organizational studies more generally.

In the chapter that follows, Rudy Hirschheim and David Whitchurch provide a complementary tale of caution, noting that both the academic and practitioner fields of Information Systems have been replete with hyperbolic claims concerning the transformative powers of new information technologies, going back to the mid-1980s (e.g., Porter and Millar, 1985), if not beyond. In Chapter 4, they 'examine a number of the underlying assumptions associated with the supposed big data revolution . . . highlight[ing] some of the fallacies and misconceptions that lie behind big data, and how these assumptions can lead to unintended and dysfunctional consequences'. Their chapter has the apposite title, 'Big Data, Little Understanding'. Their central thesis is that 'while big data provides correlations and patterns of the behaviours of large populations, it does not yield understanding/insight'. Questioning whether such behaviour patterns can properly be considered 'knowledge', they contend that 'the big data community have mistakenly adopted the view that what they produce is knowledge and moreover, it is the same as understanding'. They argue that the academic and practitioner communities alike 'continue to make the same mistakes, continue to embrace erroneous assumptions about what they should be doing with their research, what the products of the research should be and how we can help drive practice'.

In Chapter 5, Boyka Simeonova and Bob Galliers note: 'While knowledge sharing processes are of significant importance to organizations, they remain a challenge.' In their chapter, 'Power, Knowledge, and Digitalization: A Qualitative Research Agenda', they provide a qualitative theorization of power, knowledge and digitalization. The authors explain that 'scholars emphasize that science needs theory and explanations not data . . . particularly for studying complex social

phenomenon and hidden factors, where it is important to understand behaviours, actions, processes and the effects of power which are not directly observable'. They question: 'What is unique about human knowing which cannot be replaced or replicated by intelligent machines? What are the impacts of intelligent machines on organizational learning, knowing and power? How might power dynamics influence digitalization and knowledge sharing and vice versa?' The chapter develops a power-knowledge-digitalization framework to theorize the different forms of power, the role of technology, digitalization, and knowledge and their dynamics. The theorized framework includes the quadrants: power as possession; power as asymmetries; power as empowerment; and power as practice. The role of technology and digitalization is theorized within these quadrants and a research agenda for qualitative research is outlined.

Following on from this consideration of power, in Chapter 6, Boyka Simeonova and M. N. Ravishankar describe how the development of new digital technologies, such as intelligent machines and learning algorithms, has had negative as well as positive impacts at societal, organizational and individual levels. They note the contrasting experiences and outcomes with these technologies that may arise from, inter alia, fault lines of power. The chapter is titled 'Information Technology and Power'. In the chapter, Simeonova and Ravishankar theorize that power mechanisms have an important role in the digitalization context and develop a power-IT framework outlining the different power mechanisms. The framework can guide IT implementation and utilization with the associated power mechanisms and their fault lines.

But what of the methods we might employ in undertaking research that takes into account the above issues and topics? Having set something of a foundation by raising some of the philosophical, epistemological and theoretical considerations that might inform our consideration of the subject matter, we go on, in Part II of the handbook, to consider a range of qualitative research methods that might appropriately be employed when considering digitalization phenomena and their impacts.

1.5 Research Methods

We begin Part II of the handbook with Chapter 7 by Hameed Chughtai and Michael Myers, titled, 'Human Values in a Digital-First World: The Implications for Qualitative Research'. The question of human values is key not only because they are 'always inscribed into our apps and devices (whether intentionally or unintentionally)', but they are 'also inscribed into our research methods'. The authors reiterate that human values 'include ethical, moral, cultural, political, aesthetics and social values ... [and] are attached to things, technologies and places, as well as [being] held by people'. Chapter 7 focuses on the implications for qualitative researchers by first considering how 'digital technologies impact human values in a digital society (and vice versa) ... followed by a brief discussion of the current thinking and trends ... [and concluding with the identification of a number of] implications and suggestions for integrating human values into qualitative research and IS research more generally'.

Chapter 8, by Hani Safadi, Marie-Claude Boudreau and Samer Faraj, is titled, 'One Picture to Study One Thousand Words: Visualization for Qualitative Research in the Age of Digitalization'. The authors note that, '[w]hile the availability of trace data and the advancement of computational methods ... allow researchers to test new hypotheses and validate theories, the exploration and inductive understanding of social phenomena are more challenging and require new tools and apparatus'. Noting that this is particularly so 'when questions are not well defined and data are unstructured', they question whether quantification and computing is as appropriate as is often thought. They go on to argue: 'Researchers trained in the qualitative tradition are familiar with the difficulties, challenges and efforts involved in gaining a deep understanding of qualitative data ... These challenges are only exacerbated when analyzing trace data in digitalized contexts such as in social media and virtual worlds'. Noting the advances made in qualitative methods over the years, particularly in the Information Systems field, Safadi and colleagues argue for further advances in this day and age 'by creating tools to investigate digital traces of digital phenomena'. Focusing on large-scale textual data sets, they illustrate how 'interactive visualization can be used to augment qualitative researchers' capabilities to theorize from trace data ... and show how tasks enabled by visualization systems can be synergistically integrated with the qualitative research process'.

Chapter 9 introduces the concept of 'hybrid ethnographic' approaches to researching digital phenomena. Titled, 'Demystifying the Digital: A Case for Hybrid Ethnography in IS', the chapter is authored by Nicola Ens, Mari-Klara Stein and Tina Blegind Jensen. The authors, following Hine (2017), note that to 'understand ... digitally mediated worlds ... research designs which draw on multiple sources of digital and non-digital data present great opportunity'. In questioning how IS researchers might 'capture the ongoing sociotechnical entanglements that occur in ... online and offline spaces', they present a research approach based on the hybrid concept, with researchers immersing themselves in the field in line with prior ethnographic studies (cf. Van Maanen, 2011). What is being recommended is thus not a radical departure from what has come before, but it does present what is argued to be a more balanced approach to ethnographic research whether related to online or offline working environments – thereby mirroring the realities of much of today's working life.

In Chapter 10, 'Case Study Research Revisited', Boyka Simeonova and Guy Fitzgerald reflect on the case studies research method, particularly in the field of Information Systems. Focusing on the interpretivist case study method, the authors consider the benefits and the common critiques of case study research. Following a reprise of illustrative cases, they provide recent examples of the case study method utilization and examples of different case studies that utilize digital trace data. The chapter concludes by reintroducing the notion of mixed-method and multi-method research that can usefully utilize the case studies research, digital trace data and different qualitative or quantitative methods, 'advocating this as a powerful way of making balanced contributions to the discipline' (Mingers, 2001).

Chapter 11, by Alex Wilson, Josh Morton and Boyka Simeonova, provides 'Social Media

Qualitative Research Vignettes'. Referring to McKenna et al. (2017), the chapter explains that qualitative studies using social media are limited, and 'that qualitative methodologies for research using social media have not yet been established, which creates a significant barrier to using social media in qualitative research', which provides a considerable agenda for qualitative researchers to interpret data and research designs. The chapter also considers the question of 'how' social media is used for qualitative research and 'what' social media helps qualitative researchers to understand. It provides social media vignettes that help to demonstrate the opportunities and challenges at different levels of analysis.

With regard to strategic considerations and action research, Joe McDonagh, David Coghlan and Paul Coughlan focus 'on the theory and practice of action research as a Mode 2 approach [cf. Starkey and Madon, 2001] to knowledge production' as managers co-inquire into the practice of strategizing (cf. Galliers, 2011). In Chapter 12, 'Co-Inquiring in a Digital Age: Enhancing the Practice of Strategy Work in Government Organizations through Action Research', McDonagh and colleagues base their argument on the premise that 'good practice informs research and good research informs practice'. They 'pay particular attention to the action researcher ... and explore both the case for and process of inquiring together into the practice of strategizing' (cf. Whittington, 2014). In this light, they discuss 'the practice of action research, enhancing the practice of strategy and the outcomes of co-inquiry ... [concluding] by reaffirming the central role of action research in knowledge production and emphasizing how the practice of action research is ... transformed by enabling digital technologies'.

1.6 Illustrative Examples and Emergent Issues

Part III of this handbook builds on the theoretical foundations introduced in Part I and the methodological considerations outlined in Part II. Chapter 13, titled, 'Observing Artifacts: How Drawing Distinctions Creates Agency and Identity', by Sven-Volker Rehm, Lakshmi Goel and Iris Junglas, raises questions and offers new perspectives for qualitative empirical research in the field of Information Systems (IS). They argue that: 'As technologies become increasingly complex, malleable and continuously co-created by users and software engineers, they test the limits of our observability [thereby raising] major concerns' for the qualitative IS research community. They suggest 'abandoning the traditional concept of identity in lieu of the concept of distinctions ... achieved through the Laws of Form notation ... [and adopting] a more emancipated and self-reflective perspective ... that better mirror[s] emergent, evolving, or transformative processes ... [questioning the very notion of] what "IT artifacts" mean to us'.

Chapter 14 is authored by Wendy Günther, Mark Thompson, Mayur Joshi and Stavros Polykarpou and is titled, 'Algorithms as Co-Researchers: Exploring Meaning and Bias in Qualitative Research'. Their contribution begins by noting: 'Augmenting traditional qualitative methods with advanced algorithmic tools ... raises important epistemological and methodological questions for researchers'. Building on Jones (2016, 2019) – see also Chapter 3 – and in evaluating the use of algorithms, they consider that the 'qualitative researchers' reflexive relationship with the process of selecting, forming, processing and interpreting data is necessarily synthetic, or even creative', in that 'these activities inflect, and are in turn inflected by, the data themselves'. Using Jones (2019) as a foundation and noting the 'illusion' of the objectivity of data (analytics), Günther and colleagues investigate the fascinating notion of the 'reflexive dance'[3] – 'the inseparability of algorithms and the researchers who apply those algorithms in qualitative research', and extend the 'logic of epistemological relativity – hitherto applied in the context of studies *of* technologies – to the phenomenon of studies *with* technologies, where researchers employ algorithmic tools in undertaking their qualitative research' (emphasis in the original).

---

[3] With a nod perhaps to Cook and Brown (1999).

'Sensemaking about HRV Data of High-Performing Individuals: Crafting a Mixed-Methods Study' is the title of Chapter 15. Written by Stefan Klein, Stefan Schellhammer and Nathalie Mitev, the chapter reinforces earlier argumentation for pluralistic or mixed methods (Mingers, 2001) raised in Part II of this handbook. Their contribution is, to quote, 'an example of careful orchestrating and configuring the research process in order to validate, augment and complement [the] data'. The authors 'borrow and extend the notion of "crafting research" ... [(Prasad, 2017), which] ... includes configuring the different steps and components of the research, the equipment, the methods and the analysis approaches'. Engaging with interviewees is key in interpreting the data so that they become *co-producers of meaning*.

This point mirrors, to a certain extent at least, the views expressed by McDonagh and colleagues in Chapter 12. The chapter considers an action research case, which attempts to 'illuminate the practice of co-inquiry ... [to enable the participants] to co-create and co-own the future'. Thus, this chapter adds to our discussion by demonstrating the contribution qualitative methods have – not only in validating and interpreting data, but also in ensuring that our research has practical *impact*.

Chapter 16 is titled, 'The Rich Facets of Digital Trace Data', and is written by Jonas Valbjørn Andersen and Philipp Hukal. In it, the authors aim to 'demonstrate how IS researchers can leverage the richness captured in the digital traces of social interactions within digital environments ... an approach to qualitative computational analysis based on "faceting" of digital trace data'. They describe 'three "facets" inherent to digital trace data', namely, 'social structures (relational facet), sequences (processual facet) and meaning (semantic facet)'. Utilizing these as a basis for their qualitative research, the authors demonstrate the richness of the analysis and of the digital trace data themselves. They argue that: 'Recognizing these rich facets of digital trace data ... offers a methodological vocabulary for the generation of research questions that working with digital trace data is well suited to answer'.

In Chapter 17, Gongtai Wang, Andrew Burton-Jones and Saeed Akhlaghpour introduce the concept of 'datafication momentum'. The chapter is titled, 'Balancing the Momentum of Datafication with Qualitative Researchers as Design Thinkers'. Echoing the kinds of concerns raised in Part I of this handbook in particular, Wang and colleagues highlight the potential 'dark side' of datafication systems and call on qualitative researchers to combat the risk of such downsides with the attitudes of the designers. More specifically and by referring to the history of IT in addition, they recommend '"datafication momentum" as a concept referring to the tendency of datafication systems ... to receive more influence from social systems in their young stage and exert more influence on social systems in their mature stage'. They note: 'This concept highlights that datafication systems are never neutral, but are always subject to potential biases and constraints'. They introduce three social forces driving datafication – expertise, pragmatics and cognitive – in parallel with technical forces, thereby reinforcing the need for qualitative perspectives to be taken. The '*expertise force* refers to the higher influence of people with credible and authentic research and work experience, skills, knowledge and education backgrounds ... *pragmatics force* refers to the tendency that people ... make design decisions with an emphasis on practical efficiency and effectiveness ... *cognition force* refers to [the view that] data and data structures that fit with established cognitive patterns [are] more likely to be accepted than those that do not'. Implications for both research and practice are highlighted in their reflections on the concept they develop.

Chapter 18 is titled, 'What Data Sharing in Government Tells Us about the Digitalization of Government Services: Lessons from the UK Digital Economy Act', and is authored by Edgar A. Whitley. In it, Whitley reflects on his experiences in working with the UK government's recent activities that are aimed at improving data sharing across government departments, in particular, concerning activities associated with the 2017 Digital Economy Act. Data sharing across departments (whether in intra- or inter-organizational contexts) is complex and fraught with difficulties, as noted, for example, by Marabelli and Newell (2012).

While echoing some of the issues raised by McDonagh and colleagues in Chapter 12 – particularly those concerning the uniqueness of particular contexts – he argues that '[a]ssessing both the successful and less successful results of these activities from a qualitative perspective [can lead to] a better understanding of the state of digitalization [not only] in the UK government', but globally, since governments around the world 'are among the largest creators and collectors of data about their citizens, often holding the definitive records … in data centres associated with different functional areas of government bureaucracy'. In reflecting on his work, he provides useful guidance as to the use of qualitative methods in the digital age not just in organizations, but also across organizations, not just in the commercial sphere, but also in the public sector, and not just organizationally, but also societally.

1.7 Conclusion

As noted in the Preface, this handbook is an attempt not just to raise concerns about the potential over-reliance on data analytics in the age of digitalization, but also to present means by which the qualitative researcher may add value in working *with* data scientists in interpreting the results of their analysis and confirming once again the importance of qualitative approaches in Information Systems research. In many ways, the handbook can be seen as a foundation for ongoing research concerning the many key concerns that society faces in the digital age. Key implications are raised – not least for the new generations of IS academics (cf. Galliers and Huang, 2012) working within and between the relevant academies and with and for those in the world of practice.

References

Baptista, J., Stein, M., Klein, S., Watson-Manheim, M. and Lee, J. (2020). Digital work and organisational transformation: Emergent digital/human work configurations in modern organisations. *Journal of Strategic Information Systems*, 29(2), Article 101627.

Bersin, J. (2015). The geeks arrive in HR: People analytics is here. *Forbes Magazine*. www.forbes.com/.

Bholat, D. (2015). Big data and central banks. *Big Data & Society*, 2(1), 1–6.

Brinkhues, R., Da Silva Freitas Jr, J. C. and Maçada, A. C. G. (2015). Information management capability as competitive imperfection in the strategic factor market of big data. Americas Conference on Information Systems, Puerto Rico.

Chatfield, A., Reddick, C. and Al-Zubaidi, W. (2015). Capability challenges in transforming government through open and big data: Tales of two cities. International Conference on Information Systems, Fort Worth, TX.

Cook, S. D. N. and Brown, J. S. (1999). Bridging epistemologies: The generative dance between organizational knowledge and organizational knowing. *Organization Science*, 10(4), 381–400.

Daniel, E. M., Ward, J. M. and Franken, A. (2014). A dynamic capabilities perspective of IS project portfolio management. *Journal of Strategic Information Systems*, 23(2), 95–111.

Davenport, T. H., Harris, J. H. and Morison, R. (2010). *Analytics at Work: Smarter Decisions, Better Results*. Boston, MA: Harvard Business School Press.

Fecheyr-Lippens, B., Schaninger, B. and Tanner, K. (2015). Power to the new people analytics. *McKinsey Quarterly*, www.mckinsey.com/capabilities/people-and-organizational-performance/our-insights/power-to-the-new-people-analytics.

Finlay, L. (2002). 'Outing' the researcher: The provenance, process, and practice of reflexivity. *Qualitative Health Research*, 12(4), 531–545.

Forman, C., King, J. L. and Lyytinen, K. (2014). Special section introduction: Information, technology, and the changing nature of work. *Information Systems Research*, 25(4), 789–795.

Frické, M. (2015). Big data and its epistemology. *Journal of the Association for Information Science and Technology*, 66(4), 651–661.

Galliers, R. D. (2011). Further developments in information systems strategising: Unpacking the concept. In R. D. Galliers and W. L. Currie (eds), *The Oxford Handbook of Management Information Systems: Critical Perspectives and New Directions*. Oxford: Oxford University Press, pp. 329–345.

Galliers, R. D. (1995). A manifesto for information management research. *British Journal of Management*, 6(S1), S45–S52.

Galliers, R. D. and Huang, J. (2012). The teaching of qualitative research methods in Information Systems: An explorative study utilising learning theory. *European Journal of Information Systems*, 21(2), 119–134.

Galliers, R. D., Jackson, M. C. and Mingers, J. (1997). Organization theory and systems thinking: The benefits of partnership. *Organization*, 4(2), 268–278.

Galliers, R. D., Newell, S., Shanks, G. and Topi, H. (2017). Datification and its human, organizational and societal effects: The strategic opportunities and challenges of algorithmic decision-making. *Journal of Strategic Information Systems*, 26(3), 185–190.

Galliers, R. D., Newell, S., Shanks, G. and Topi, H. (2015). Call for papers the *Journal of Strategic Information Systems* special issue: The challenges and opportunities of 'datification' strategic impacts of 'big' (and 'small') and real time data – for society and for organizational decision makers. *Journal of Strategic Information Systems*, 24(2), II–III.

Gartner. (2013). Gartner predicts business intelligence and analytics will remain top focus for CIOs through 2017. Gartner Newsroom. www.gartner.com/newsroom/id/2637615.

Grant, A. M. and Parker, S. K. (2009). Redesigning work design theories: The rise of relational and proactive perspectives. *Academy of Management Annals*, 3(1), 317–375.

Greenaway, K. E., Chan, Y. E. and Robert, E. C. (2015). Company information privacy orientation: A conceptual framework. *Information Systems Journal*, 25(6), 579–606.

Grover, V. (2020). Do we need to understand the world to know it? Knowledge in a big data world. *Journal of Global Information Technology Management*, 23(1), 1–4.

Grover, V., Lindberg, A., Benbasat, I. and Lyytinen, K. (2020). The perils and promises of big data research in information systems. *Journal of the Association for Information Systems*, 21(2), 268–291.

Günther, W. A., Mehrizi, M. H. R., Feldberg, F. and Huysman, M. H. (2017). Debating big data: A literature review on realizing value from big data. *Journal of Strategic Information Systems*, 26(3), 191–209.

Hansen, H. K. (2015). Numerical operations, transparency illusions and the datafication of governance. *European Journal of Social Theory*, 18(2), 203–220.

Hedman, J., Srinivasan, N. and Lindgren, R. (2013). Digital traces or information systems: Sociomateriality made researchable. International Conference on Information Systems, Milan, Italy.

Hine, C. (2017). From virtual ethnography to the embedded, embodied, everyday internet. In L. Hjorth, H. Horst, A. Galloway and G. Bell (eds), *The Routledge Companion to Digital Ethnography*. Abingdon, UK and New York, NY: Routledge, pp. 21–28.

Hirschheim, R. (2021). The attack on understanding: How big data and theory have led us astray – a comment on Gary Smith's Data Mining Fool's Gold. *Journal of Information Technology*, 36(2), 176–183.

Huang, J., Baptista, J. and Newell, S. (2015). Communicational ambidexterity as a new capability to manage social media communication within organizations. *Journal of Strategic Information Systems*, 24(2), 49–64.

Jagadish, H. V., Gehrke, J., Labrinidis, A., Papakonstantinou, Y., Patel, J. M., Ramakrishnan, R. and Shahabi, C. (2014). Big data and its technical challenges. *Communications of the ACM*, 57(7), 86–94.

Jia, L., Hall, D. and Song, J. (2015). The conceptualization of data-driven decision making capability. Americas Conference on Information Systems, Puerto Rico.

Jones, M. (2019). What we talk about when we talk about (big) data. *Journal of Strategic Information Systems*, 28(1), 3–16.

Jones, S. (2016). *Roberto Busa S. J. and the Emergence of Humanities Computing: The Priest and the Punched Cards*. London: Routledge.

Kim, S., Lee, G., Sakata, N. and Billinghurst, M. (2014). Improving co-presence with augmented visual communication cues for sharing experience through video conference. IEEE International Symposium on Mixed and Augmented Reality (ISMAR), Munich, Germany.

Leong, C., Pan, S., Ractham, P. and Kaewkitipong, L. (2015). ICT-enabled community empowerment in crisis response: Social media in Thailand flooding 2011. *Journal of the Association for Information Systems*, 16(3), 174–212.

Lightfoot, G. and Wisniewski, P. (2014). Information asymmetry and power in a surveillance society. *Information and Organization*, 24(4), 214–235.

Loebbecke, C. and Picot, A. (2015). Reflections on societal and business model transformation arising from digitization and big data analytics: A research agenda. *Journal of Strategic Information Systems*, 24(3), 149–157.

Lycett, M. (2013). 'Datafication': Making sense of (big) data in a complex world. *European Journal of Information Systems*, 22(4), 381–386.

Madsen, A. K. (2015). Between technical features and analytic capabilities: Charting a relational affordance space for digital social analytics. *Big Data & Society*, 2(1), 1–15.

Mai, J.-E. (2016). Big data privacy: The datafication of personal information. *Information Society: An International Journal*, 32(3), 192–199.

Malgonde, O. and Bhattacherjee, A. (2014). Innovating using big data: A social capital perspective. Americas Conference on Information Systems, Georgia, USA.

Marabelli, M. and Newell, S. (2012). Knowledge risks in organizational networks: The practice perspective. *Journal of Strategic Information Systems*, 21(1), 18–30.

Markus, M. L. (2015). New games, new rules, new scoreboards: The potential consequences of big data. *Journal of Information Technology*, 30(1), 58–59.

Markus, M. L. and Topi, H. (2015). Big data, big decisions for science, society, and business. NSF Project Outcomes Report. Bentley University, Waltham, MA, http://dl.acm.org/citation.cfm?id=2849516.

McKenna, B., Myers, M. D. and Newman, M. (2017). Social media in qualitative research: Challenges and recommendations. *Information and Organization*, 27(2), 87–99.

McKnight, D. H., Lankton, N. K., Nicolaou, A. and Price, J. (2017). Distinguishing the effects of B2B information quality, system quality, and service outcome quality on trust and distrust. *Journal of Strategic Information Systems*, 26(2), 118–141.

Mingers, J. (2001). Combining IS research methods: Towards a pluralist methodology. *Information Systems Research*, 12(3), 240–259.

Munford, M. (2014). Rule changes and big data revolutionise Caterham F1 chances. *The Telegraph*, www.telegraph.co.uk/technology/technology-topics/10654658/Rule-changes-and-big-data-revolutionise-Caterham-F1-chances.html.

Negash, S. (2004). Business intelligence. *Communications of the Association for Information Systems*, 13, article 15, http://aisel.aisnet.org/cais/vol13/iss1/15.

Newell, S. and Marabelli, M. (2015). Strategic opportunities (and challenges) of algorithmic decision-making: A call for action on the long-term societal effects of 'datification'. *Journal of Strategic Information Systems*, 24(1), 3–14.

Peppard, J., Galliers, R. D. and Thorogood, A. (2014). Information systems strategy as practice: Micro strategy and strategizing for IS. *Journal of Strategic Information Systems*, 23(1), 1–10.

Peppard, J. and Ward, J. (2004). Beyond strategic information systems: Toward an IS capability. *Journal of Strategic Information Systems*, 13(2), 167–194.

Pfeffer, J. and Sutton, R. I. 2006). Evidence-based management. *Harvard Business Review*, 84(1), 63–74.

Porter, M. E. and Millar, V. E. (1985). How information technology gives you competitive advantage. *Harvard Business Review*, 63(2), 149–160.

Power, D. J. (2002). *Decisions Support Systems: Concepts and Resources for Managers*. Westport, CT: Quorum Books.

Prasad, P. (2017). *Crafting Qualitative Research: Working in the Postpositivist Traditions*, 2nd edition. London and Armonk, NY: Routledge and M. E. Sharpe.

Rouibah, K. and Ould-ali, S. (2002). Puzzle: A concept and prototype for linking business intelligence to business strategy. *Journal of Strategic Information Systems*, 11(2), 133–152.

Seddon, P. B., Constantinidis, D., Tamm, T. and Dod, H. (2017). How does business analytics contribute to business value? *Information Systems Journal*, 27(3), 237–268.

Sharma, R., Mithas, S. and Kankanhalli, A. (2014). Transforming decision-making processes: A research agenda for understanding the impact of business analytics on organisations. *European Journal of Information Systems*, 23(4), 433–441.

Shollo, A. and Galliers, R. D. (2015). Towards an understanding of the role of business intelligence systems in organisational knowing. *Information Systems Journal*, 26(4), 339–367.

Sidorova, A. and Torres, R. R. (2014). Business intelligence and analytics: A capabilities dynamization view. *Americas Conference on Information Systems*, Georgia, USA.

Simeonova, B. (2018). Transactive memory systems and Web 2.0 in knowledge sharing: A conceptual model based on activity theory and critical realism. *Information Systems Journal*, 28(4), 592–611.

Simeonova, B., Galliers, R. D. and Karanasios, S. (2022). Power in organisations: The role of information systems. *Information Systems Journal*, 32(2), 233–241.

Simeonova, B., Galliers, R. D. and Karanasios, S. (2020). Strategic information systems and organisational power dynamics. In R. D. Galliers, D. E. Leidner and B. Simeonova (eds), *Strategic Information Management: Theory and Practice*, 5th edition. London and New York, NY: Routledge, pp. 221–238.

Starkey, K. and Madan, P. (2001). Bridging the relevance gap: Aligning stakeholders in the future of management research. *British Journal of Management*, 12(1), 3–26.

Stein, M., Newell, S., Galliers, R. D. and Wagner, E. L. (2013). Classification systems, their digitization and consequences for data-driven decision making: Understanding representational quality. *International Conference on Information Systems*, Milan, Italy.

Stein, M., Newell, S., Wagner, E. L. and Galliers, R. D. (2016). Crafting the 'quantified professional': Systems of accountability and job crafting. *International Workshop on The Changing Nature of Work: The Impact of Digital Innovation on Work*, IFIP WG 9.1, Dublin, Ireland.

Tambe, P. (2014). Big data investment, skills, and firm value. *Management Science*, 60(6), 1452–1468.

Tan, C., Sun, L. and Liu, K. (2015). Big data architecture for pervasive healthcare: A literature review. *European Conference on Information Systems*, Münster, Germany.

Thomsen, E. (2003). BI's promised land. *Intelligent Enterprise*, 6(4), 21–25.

Van den Broek, T. and Van Veenstra, A. F. (2015). Modes of governance in inter-organizational data collaborations. *European Conference on Information Systems*, Münster, Germany.

Van der Vlist, F. N. (2016). Accounting for the social: Investigating commensuration and big data practices at Facebook. *Big Data & Society*, 3(1), 1–16.

Van Maanen, J. (2011). Ethnography as work: Some rules of engagement. *Journal of Management Studies*, 48(1), 218–234.

Van Maanen, J. (1979). Reclaiming qualitative methods for organizational research: A preface. *Administrative Science Quarterly*, 24(4), 520–526.

Vial, G. (2019). Understanding digital transformation: A review and a research agenda. *Journal of Strategic Information Systems*, 28(2), 118–144.

Waber, B. (2013). *People Analytics: How Social Sensing Technology Will Transform Business and What It Tells Us about the Future of Work*. Upper Saddle River, NJ: Pearson Education.

Walsham, G. (2006). Doing interpretive research. *European Journal of Information Systems*, 15(3), 320–330.

Whittington, R. (2014). Information systems strategy and strategy-as-practice: A joint agenda. *Journal of Strategic Information Systems*, 23(1), 87–91.

Woerner, S. L. and Wixom, B. H. (2015). Big data: Extending the business strategy toolbox. *Journal of Information Technology*, 30(1), 60–62.

Wu, L. and Brynjolfsson, E. (2009). The future of prediction: How Google searches foreshadow housing prices and quantities. *International Conference on Information Systems*, Phoenix, AZ.

Xu, J., Cenfetelli, R. T. and Aquino, K. (2016). Do different kinds of trust matter? An examination of the three trusting beliefs on satisfaction and purchase behavior in the buyer–seller context. *Journal of Strategic Information Systems*, 25(1), 15–31.

A Philosophical Perspective on Qualitative Research in the Age of Digitalization

ALLEN S. LEE and SUPRATEEK SARKER*

2.1 Introduction

In the academic discipline of information systems (IS), there are signs that the 'big data' movement has arrived in qualitative research. Vast quantities of 'digital trace data', generated as a result of the rapid digitalization of business organizations and of society, have proved irresistible to qualitative researchers championing inductive approaches to theory building. Specifically, the use of computational methods has emerged as a key innovation in connection with the analysis of digital trace data (Berente et al., 2019; Nelson, 2020). Indeed, impressive research results – both methodological and substantive – have already been delivered by scholars in the IS discipline (e.g., Lindberg et al., 2013; Vaast et al., 2017; Berente et al., 2019; Lindberg, 2020).

Yet, this digitalization of qualitative research raises questions. Is its growing popularity nothing more than a bandwagon effect or is it going to become a permanent fixture in how qualitative IS research is conducted? And if it is the latter, will digitalization become the *sine qua non* of qualitative IS research or will it merely take its place as just another qualitative research approach? Even more provocative are the questions of whether current methods being proposed and discussed are qualitative research at all and, more importantly, does this move of introducing new computational approaches spell the end of qualitative, especially interpretive, research as we have known it in the IS discipline? To address these questions in this chapter, we will take a philosophical stance.

First, we will provide an overview of what we mean by the digitalization of qualitative research. Following that, we will place the digitalization of qualitative research in its philosophical context; we will devote a section of the chapter to each of the following key themes: induction, deduction and meaning. Induction, on which current rationales for the digitalization of qualitative research depend, deserves attention given that it can be helpful in the building of a theory while being flawed as a means for justifying a theory. How justifying a theory is indeed carried out, through deduction, deserves and will receive from us equal attention. Meaning, which is arguably the central object of attention in interpretive research, merits attention because the digitalization of qualitative research in IS has, so far, largely not effectively addressed it. After discussing these key themes, we will end this chapter by reflecting on some nascent myths about the digitalization of qualitative research.

2.2 Defining the Digitalization of Qualitative Research

Numerous terms have been used to denote what we refer to as the digitalization of qualitative research. Such terms include 'data-driven inductive research' (Vaast et al., 2017: 1185), 'a general, computationally intensive approach to the inductive generation of theory' (Berente et al., 2019: 50), 'computational social science' (Lindberg et al., 2013: 1, 4, 14) and the use of 'computational tools' (Lindberg, 2020: 90, 91), where these terms are used in the context of *how to analyze qualitative 'digital trace data'*. Digital trace data, in turn, can be defined as 'the digital records of activity and events that involve information technologies

* We appreciate the comments of Suranjan Chakraborty to an earlier draft, and also valuable inputs provided by Ola Henfridsson.

(Howison et al., 2011)' (Berente et al., 2019: 50). Howison, Wiggins and Crowston (2011) discuss three important characteristics of trace data: First, trace data are 'found' data, not generated deliberately for research. They note that 'Wikipedia was not designed to test theories about knowledge production, nor are corporate email systems designed to collect research data' (p. 769), yet they are valuable sources of trace data. Second, trace data are 'event-based' (p. 770) electronic records, and not a summary of what happened based on the recall of an individual. An example might be someone befriending someone else on social media. Third, trace data tend to be 'longitudinal' (p. 770). A common example is that of a visitor to an e-store. All activities of the visitor in the store are available as trace data, including which links she clicked on, which products she took interest in, how long the visit took, when she came back to the store, etc.

We can see that there are many reasons why data resulting from digitalization are valuable. The advantages include: trace data represent 'real-time' interactions, are available in vast quantities, can be collected very quickly with minimal effort, and provide access to processes and individuals/groups that may have been difficult or not even possible to access in a pre-digitalization era (Cesare et al., 2018). Even more importantly, such data evoke less concern about 'recall bias' and 'social desirability' playing a role in its creation, given that they present an 'unsolicited documentation of individuals' opinions and interactions' (Cesare et al., 2018: 1981).

However, there is also the issue of how, in this new era of digitalization in business organizations and in society, such data serve to influence research thinking (and analysis), which includes induction, deduction and the interpretation of meaning. We discuss these important themes below.

2.3 Key Themes

2.3.1 Induction and the Digitalization of Qualitative Research

Digitalization of organizations and societies often produces 'big data' that are attractive to many scholars interested in inductive theory-building

(Grover et al., 2020). This is because of the widely held belief that more data is better; however, flying in the face of this is Hume's problem of induction (Lee and Baskerville, 2003: 224–226). It turns out that more data which are consistent with a theory does not better justify the theory.

In addition to the task of determining whether or not a theory is true is the task of building the theory in the first place. Data have value as an input to the latter task. However, *no theory is ever true on the basis of how it is built*. A theory could have been built by correctly following whatever theory-building methodology, even involving induction from large quantities of data, but none of this would contribute to making the theory true. *No amount of data – not even 'big data' – from which a theory is induced may ever result in the theory's being true.* The only way to determine the truth of a theory is to deductively test it, against new data, after it has been built.

The preceding argument is based in part on Hume's problem of induction. What exactly is Hume's problem of induction and what are its ramifications for the digitalization of qualitative research?

Hume's problem of induction establishes that inductive inference is not a legitimate way to establish that a theory is true. The fact that induction is useless for justifying a theory is well established and was introduced to the IS research literature by Lee and Baskerville (2003: 224): 'Hume, an 18th century Scottish philosopher, "is almost universally credited with discovering the problem of induction" (Rosenberg, 1993: 75). . . . The problem of induction is about how to establish induction itself as a valid method for empirical inquiry.' For a succinct description of Hume's problem of induction, Lee and Baskerville quote Rosenberg (1993: 75):

> Hume recognized that inductive conclusions could only be derived deductively from premises (such as the uniformity of nature) that themselves required inductive warrant, or from arguments that were inductive in the first place. The deductive arguments are no more convincing than their most controversial premises and so generate a regress, while the inductive ones beg the question. Accordingly, claims that transcend available data, in particular predictions and general laws, remain unwarranted.

Rosenberg's dense text is fleshed out by Lee and Baskerville (2003: 224–225), who re-explain it in terms provided by Wood (2000). The main ramification of this for how a researcher uses data (whether qualitative or otherwise) is that the inductive practice of marshalling data or additional data to support a theory does not prove or better prove the theory to be true. At best, in inductive inference, data may only suggest what a theory should cover when it is being built and then may only be said to be consistent with the theory. These points do not appear to have been recognized in IS articles that advocate for the inductive use of big data in the digitalization of qualitative research.

Implicit in the preceding discussion, but worthy of being made explicit, is the point that data, and additional data, can always be marshalled to support a questionable or even false theory. Popper explicates this point (1968: 35, emphasis in the original):

> The most characteristic element in this situation seemed to me the incessant stream of confirmations, of observations which 'verified' the theories in question; and this point was constantly emphasized by their adherents. A Marxist could not open a newspaper without finding on every page confirming evidence for his interpretation of history; not only in the news, but also in its presentation – which revealed the class bias of the paper – and especially of course in what the paper did *not* say. The Freudian analysts emphasized that their theories were constantly verified by their 'clinical observations.' As for Adler, I was much impressed by a personal experience. Once, in 1919, I reported to him a case which to me did not seem particularly Adlerian, but which he found no difficulty in analysing in terms of his theory of inferiority feelings, although he had not even seen the child. Slightly shocked, I asked him how we could be so sure. 'Because of my thousandfold experience,' he replied; whereupon I could not help saying: 'And with this new case, I suppose, your experience has become thousand-and-one-fold.'

Thus, induction, in the manner of a thousandfold or thousand-and-one-fold experience characteristic of big data, may always 'verify' a theory, even one that is not true. In other words, *induction with larger volumes of data is not necessarily more effective than with smaller volumes of data*. This also means that the proper role of data in induction is limited to one of *merely suggesting*, not verifying, what a theory may cover.

The limited role that data may play in inductive inference and theory building, however, is offset by the different and powerful role that data may play in deductive inference and the justification of a theory. We turn our attention to this in the next section.

2.3.2 Deduction and the Digitalization of Qualitative Research

Qualitative research is often associated with theory building, but qualitative research is also capable of justifying theories (e.g., Markus, 1983; Sarker and Lee, 2002; Dibbern et al., 2008). Exactly what role may data play in justifying a theory?

Lee and Hubona (2009) summarize the deductive logic by which justifying a theory takes place; it is an application of *modus tollens*. Lee (2017) focuses on *modus tollens* as used in qualitative research. In general, the major premise, minor premise and conclusion of *modus tollens* are, respectively, 'if p is true, then q is true', 'q is not true' and 'therefore, p is not true'. In theory testing, 'p' stands for the general statements making up a theory, and 'q' stands for the statements describing an observable consequence of the theory applied in a particular setting. (One example of the statements making up 'q' are the statements describing a prediction that follows from the theory being tested.) Data may play the role of indicating whether or not q is true. If the data indicate that 'q is not true', then it follows that 'therefore, p is not true' or, in other words, the theory is rejected. The logic of *modus tollens* applies in positivist, interpretive, action and design research (Lee and Hubona, 2009: 238–244).

There is no requirement that the data indicating 'q is not true' need be big data. Consider the theory p, 'all swans are white', and the prediction q, 'the next swan to be observed in the lake is white'. Accepting the observation that the next swan is black would be sufficient to reject the theory. Note, however, that the single observation of a black swan would be a case of *small data*, not big data. In other words, big data is not necessary for the scientific testing or justification of a theory. Thus, the earlier-mentioned motivation behind 'big data', which is that more data is better, does not necessarily hold in theory testing.

Also worth considering is the situation where data indicate that 'q is true' instead of, as above, 'q is not true'. In this situation, may the conclusion be 'therefore, p is true'? In other words, does the reasoning change from 'if p is true, then q is true', 'q is not true' and 'therefore, p is not true' to 'if p is true, then q is true', 'q is true' and 'therefore, p is true'? The answer is emphatically *no*. The latter line of reasoning is known as the fallacy of affirming the consequent. For an illustration, consider 'if it is raining, then the street is wet', 'the street is wet' and 'therefore, it is raining'; this reasoning is not valid because the street could be wet for reasons other than rain and 'therefore, it is raining' does not logically follow from the premises. This is another reason (in addition to the one given under inductive reasoning) that even big data (here, innumerable instances of 'q is true') may never prove a theory to be true.

2.3.3 Meaning and the Digitalization of Qualitative Research

In addition to the testing or justification of theory, there is another major aspect of inquiry that has not received sufficient, if any, attention from the digitalization of qualitative research in IS: It is the objectively existing entity in social settings that some interpretive researchers refer to as *meaning*. What is 'meaning'? What are the ramifications of meaning for the digitalization of qualitative research?

The *Oxford English Dictionary* defines meaning as '[t]hat which is indicated or expressed by a (supposed) symbol or symbolic action'.[1] Consider the human beings whom a researcher observes in an organization or other social setting and who create

and share meanings with one another in that setting. Such meanings exist as part and parcel of the empirical reality that the researcher observes, and builds and tests theories about. The existence of meaning can be both a complicating and enriching factor in social science; Schutz states (1962: 59):

> The world of nature, as explored by the natural scientist, does not 'mean' anything to molecules, atoms, and electrons. But the observational field of the social scientist – social reality – has a specific meaning and relevance structure for the human beings living, acting, and thinking within it. By a series of commonsense constructs they have preselected and pre-interpreted this world which they experience as the reality of their daily lives. It is these thought objects of theirs which determine their behavior by motivating it. The thought objects constructed by the social scientist, in order to grasp this social reality, have to be founded upon the thought objects constructed by the common-sense thinking of men, living their daily life within their social world. Thus, the constructs of the social sciences are, so to speak, constructs of the second degree, that is, constructs of the constructs made by the actors on the social scene, whose behavior the social scientist has to observe and to explain in accordance with the procedural rules of his science.

The same action, object or situation can have different meanings for different people – hence the importance, for the social scientist, of determining the meaning(s) an action, object or situation has, where the meaning makes a difference to the theory that the social scientist builds and tests. Schutz (1962: 54) offers an example of the difference that different meanings can make: 'The same overt behavior (say a tribal pageant as it can be captured by the movie camera) may have an entirely different meaning to the performers. What interests the social scientist is merely whether it is a war dance, a barter trade, the reception of a friendly ambassador, or something else of this sort.' Clearly, a difference in what the people themselves mean by their 'overt behaviour' can make a difference to how the observing social scientist theorizes about it.

For the social scientist who seeks to understand the meaning that an action, object or situation has,

---

[1] 'Meaning, n.2', *OED Online*, Oxford University Press, www.oed.com/view/Entry/115465.

the process of reaching that understanding is called *interpretation* and is found at the core of *interpretive research*. What does that process involve? In the context of anthropology and ethnography, Sanday (1979: 528) states:

> When anthropologists explain their craft they often claim that 'the anthropologist is the main instrument of observation' (see Mead, 1959a: 38; Mead, 1959b; Pelto, 1970; Wolcott, 1975). Fieldworkers learn to use themselves as the principal and most reliable instrument of observation, selection, coordination, and interpretation. Ethnography, as Mead (1959b: iii) says, 'depends on this highly trained ability to respond – and to respect that response – as a whole person.'

Thus, 'the researcher as instrument' (Sanday, 1979: 527) is central to the process by which the interpretation of meaning takes place. It is as yet unclear what, if anything, the digitalization of qualitative research offers that can supplant the 'researcher as instrument' for the interpretation of meaning.

Digital traces, such as the thousands of emails generated in an organization or the thousands of tweets generated in an online community, pose challenges and opportunities for the interpretation of meaning. Such emails and tweets would not, in themselves, be meanings, but would be the symbols or symbolic actions that indicate meanings. The digitalization of trace data presumes that there would be an advantage to access thousands of symbols or symbolic actions, but is this necessarily the case?

Returning to Schutz's example, would thousands of observations of overt behaviour (and the corresponding thousands of interpretations of meaning of the overt behaviour) be needed? Probably not even hundreds of such observations would be needed. Conceivably, a smaller number of observations would suffice to determine whether the overt behaviour is a war dance, a barter trade, the reception of a friendly ambassador or something else of this sort. There is no inherent reason that a larger number of observations is necessarily better than a smaller number of observations. A large quantity of digital trace data can certainly be helpful in many research

situations, but would not be the *sine qua non* of interpretive research.

We are sceptical that the digitalization of qualitative research will someday yield methods that can supplant the 'researcher as instrument' for the interpretation of meaning, but we are open to the development of methods that can potentially support a researcher in this endeavour. There is already such work under way in hermeneutics (e.g., Mohr et al., 2015; Romele et al., 2020), ethnography (e.g., Lohmeier, 2014; Abramson et al., 2018) and grounded theory (e.g., Nelson, 2020).

Worthy of note is a term that Charles Taylor coined in his essay, 'Interpretation and the Sciences of Man' (1971): the term is 'brute data'. In the essay, Taylor argued against a purely positivist (he called it 'empiricist') approach to the social sciences (in particular, political science) – an approach which admits of no interpretation of meaning. By Taylor's definition, a brute datum is 'a unit of information which is not the deliverance of a judgment, which has by definition no element in it of reading or interpretation' (p. 7). Thus, the term 'brute data' does not necessarily refer to the quantity of data (although Taylor notes the role of induction in empiricism), but it does refer to data serving as the bedrock foundation to the verification of theory. Whereas we hasten to add that our own view is that there is value in data, where the data are complemented by interpretation of meaning, we also take the view that digital trace data, if un-interpreted, can be brute data that can lead to 'knowing without understanding' (Andrejevic, 2013, quoted in Kitchin, 2014: 133).

In the next section, we revisit some of the preceding issues, reflecting on some of the nascent myths about the digitalization of qualitative research.

2.4 Some Nascent Myths about the Digitalization of Qualitative Research

We will examine four nascent myths. The myths may not necessarily be considered false by all scholars, but they need careful reflection and examination.

2.4.1 The Nascent Myth that 'Digital Traces' Are Data

So far, the discussion has examined how induction, deduction and meaning are related to the digitalization of qualitative research, but this discussion has, so far, taken for granted the conception of data itself. What is meant by 'data' and, in particular, 'trace data'?

Consider the usage of the term 'trace data' in the following (Berente et al., 2019: 50):

> The abundant and ever-increasing digital trace data now widely available offer boundless opportunities for a computationally intensive social science (DiMaggio, 2015; Lazer et al., 2009). By 'trace data' we refer to the digital records of activity and events that involve information technologies (Howison et al., 2011). Given the ubiquitous digitization of so many phenomena, some expect the widespread availability of a variety of trace data to do nothing less than revolutionize the social sciences and challenge established paradigms (Lazer et al., 2009).

However, unlike Berente et al. and other authors writing about 'trace data', we believe that there is a need to distinguish between *traces*, which exist as empirical phenomena in the real world that is the subject matter of the researcher's inquiry, and *data*, which are statements that the researcher makes up to measure or otherwise describe the empirical phenomena. This is somewhat consistent with the statement 'data are never simply data; how data are conceived and used varies between those who capture, analyze, and draw conclusions from them' (Kitchin, 2014: 4). Further, Kitchin highlights the perspective that 'data do not simply represent the reality of the world; *they are constructions about the world*' (p. 20, emphasis added). Thus, by our reckoning, 'the digital records of activity and events that involve information technologies' are not trace data, but actual traces. Likewise, the 'ubiquitous digitization of so many phenomena' is *not* the same thing as 'the widespread availability of a variety of trace data'; instead, the 'ubiquitous digitization of so many phenomena' is the widespread availability of traces that, only if a researcher so chooses, could be measured or otherwise described so as to yield data, whether

qualitative or otherwise. In other words, ontologically speaking, a phenomenon and the data describing it are different and distinct things.

Existing work about digitalization of qualitative research, however, has treated a phenomenon not only as a phenomenon, but also as the data measuring or describing it. Such an ontology would require a new epistemology – one that is different from the epistemologies in use in natural and social science and in positivist and interpretive IS research. And the new epistemology would, in turn, require new methodologies and methods. We await the innovation and the explicit articulation of the new epistemology, methodology and methods.

Until then, we note that the ubiquitous digitization of phenomena is different from the ubiquitous appearance of data. More phenomena can mean more data, but the appearance of data would not occur automatically. The production of data would require deliberate and calculated constructions on the part of the researcher.

2.4.2 The Nascent Myth that Big Data Is Becoming Essential for Qualitative Research

The digitalization of business organizations and of society often comes with the promise of big volumes of data, or big data. Given the often-held assumption among researchers that *more data is better* and that big data tends to claim 'N = all', thereby promising to provide 'exhaustive' data pertaining to a given phenomenon (Kitchin 2014; Johnson et al., 2019), there is an expectation that knowledge derived from such data is necessarily valid. Such data are considered especially valuable since they may not have been easily accessible in the pre-digitalization era. Not to be left behind in engaging with such data, qualitative researchers have rightfully started to explore new opportunities afforded by the digitalization of data and the technologies available to analyze digital data. Such explorations, however, should be carried out with caution.

At a very basic level, big data is known to have high volume, great variety, high velocity with regard to its creation, collection and analysis needs, and, finally, low veracity (e.g., Abbasi et al., 2016). Of particular interest to us are volume and veracity.

With regard to volume, we first mention that, while qualitative researchers in the pre-digitalization era have not been known to work with data sets of the order of big data, it is not as if qualitative research approaches have eschewed large volumes of data in the past, especially in ethnographies and grounded theory methodology (GTM) studies. In fact, Berente et al. (2019: 52) state: 'Traditional manual GTM begins with the world's biggest data set – the world itself – and reduces this data set by sampling from the world in an area of interest.' That is, mechanisms such as 'theoretical sampling' and 'saturation' are frequently used to keep the volume of data manageable for in-depth human processing (Strauss and Corbin, 1990). Moreover, as we have argued above, analysis in the form of induction and deduction does not necessarily, if at all, become more effective with increasing volumes of data. Digital technologies have been used to improve storage, manage codes and linkages among them, manage access and visualize data as the volume of data has increased; however, in the past, the grasping of the meanings and the interpretive understanding of the data have been developed not by digital technologies, but by the mind of the researcher (e.g., Ghazawneh and Henfridsson, 2013).

With regard to veracity, we note that it is ensured in qualitative research, particularly interpretive research, through personal responsibility, which is not easy to do with big data. As mentioned, a qualitative researcher is the key instrument of observation. The instrument is honed over many years of reading, reflecting and practising. Using devices of mind such as the hermeneutic circle, methodological techniques such as triangulation and member-checking, and a number of guidelines such as the principle of suspicion and the principle of contextualization (Klein and Myers, 1999), qualitative researchers deal with the trustworthiness (or validity) question of data, as well as of the interpretations. It is not clear how, if at all, these approaches would be applied in the context of qualitative analysis of big data where the trustworthiness of data is often suspect, since the data sources are varied and sometimes the real

origins and motivations behind sources are unknown.

Moreover, there are significant ethical issues related to big data. Eck and Uebernickel (2016: 4, emphasis in the original), for example, raise at least two important concerns, characterizing them as being 'of hitherto unknown magnitude':

> Due to the very nature of digital trace data, we can safely assume that people did not consent to any analyses unrelated to their immediate interaction with the digital artifact. Furthermore, due to the amount and granularity of available data, any compromise of personal rights will likely incur high damages. Second, digital trace data typically is *incomplete* ... Digital artifacts are susceptible to change and unintended use, which makes full coverage, consistent data extraction, and correct interpretation challenging.

These concerns are related to some of the ethical considerations that interpretive researchers must confront, highlighted by Walsham (2006: 327) based on past literature, that include 'harm to participants, lack of informed consent, invasion of privacy, and deception'. While Walsham acknowledges that 'there are many grey areas', it is clear that ethical issues related to big data and its use must be carefully examined and debated before such data become an essential element of qualitative research.

Our conclusion, then, is that while big data, in different forms, can be potentially useful to both qualitative and quantitative research, there are questions about how and to what extent big data can be considered *essential* to qualitative research. Importantly, in much of qualitative research, what matters is the interpretation, and neither more data nor computational approaches necessarily improve the interpretation. Thus, one cannot simply conclude that big data is necessarily good or essential for qualitative, especially interpretive, research.

2.4.3 The Nascent Myth that Computational Approaches Are Becoming Essential for Analysis in Qualitative Research

The digitalization of qualitative research entails (1) the use of *digital data*, involving digital traces, in large volumes; and (2) the *analysis of data* using computational approaches. We have already discussed digital data; we now take a closer look at analysis.

A number of approaches have been proposed by scholars to help in inductively building theory using computational approaches. We examine Nelson (2020) as a case. Nelson proposes a three-step process for developing what she calls a 'computational grounded theory' that is 'fully reproducible' and 'scientifically valid': (1) the 'pattern detection' step, using unsupervised text classification approaches such as topic modelling; (2) the pattern refinement or 'deep reading' step, performed by a human, to develop an interpretive understanding of the thematically classified texts; and (3) the 'pattern confirmation' step, involving deduction wherein the understanding developed from the first two steps is validated, using methods such as supervised machine learning, to ensure that the theory 'is generalizable to the entire corpus' of data in all the documents used in the analysis.

A few comments are in order. First, unsupervised text classification techniques, including topic modelling, seek to detect patterns in the data such as co-occurrence of words in the corpus of data, and thus *do not lend themselves well to the creative development of concepts*, where such conceptualization goes beyond the data; indeed, such imaginative and 'reflexive' conceptualizations may be considered a hallmark of good interpretive research (Alvesson and Skoldberg, 2000). In other words, this automated step has little scope for enabling the interpretive guess or mental leap often associated with interpretation. Nor are these approaches particularly capable of identifying unique ideas that may be embedded in infrequent patterns, since techniques such as topic modelling tend to highlight 'representative' texts (Nelson, 2020). Further, the topics generated through topic modelling may or may not be relevant to the research question or to the domain of interest; human intervention is required for framing and labelling the topic. Still, this step can lead to efficiency gains in the research process in that it 'uses computational methods to reduce messy and complicated text to interpretable groups of words ...' (p. 9), and can 'simplify and reveal patterns in data of almost infinite size without much added work on the part of the researcher' (p. 25).

Second, the deep reading step involves the human reader's (the researcher's) attachment of meanings to the topics, and the reader makes interpretive guesses regarding what the topics are and the linkages among them. This process can be far less burdensome following the first step because such reading is done on classified text that is less voluminous than the original corpus, and the reading is guided using metrics assessing how prevalent certain texts are to a given topic (Nelson, 2020), although there is some risk that important concepts do not get identified based on how the algorithm in the earlier step works. This step of deep reading 'translates the computational output into sociologically meaningful concepts to enable researchers to draw more abstract conclusions about the social world that produced the data' (Nelson, 2020: 30). In other words, considering the first two steps in the analysis, *what makes the analysis meaningful is human interpretation, not computational analysis*.

Finally, the third step, involving deductive validation through supervised machine learning, is valuable, but may be applicable to only certain kinds of concepts and their interrelationships. While validation is fundamental to the process of interpretation and theorizing, not all types of qualitative approaches use validation in a way that is necessarily compatible with computational techniques. For example, in the context of hermeneutics, which is fundamental to most interpretive studies, Sarker and Lee (2006: 134, emphasis added) quote Ricoeur (1991: 159–160) to explain what 'validation' entails:

> As concerns the procedures of validation with which we test our guesses ... To show that an interpretation is more probable in the light of what is known [i.e., validation] is something other than showing that a conclusion is true [i.e., verification] ... *Validation is an argumentative discipline comparable to juridical procedures of legal interpretation*. It is a logic of uncertainty and of qualitative probability.
>
> ... validation allows us to move between the two limits of dogmatism and skepticism.

In light of the above discussion, we make three points. First, computational approaches can complement but not supplant human interpretation in qualitative research since it is the human labelling and interpretation that endows patterns with meaning. In fact, Nelson (2020) herself notes that researchers who ask 'questions from their data that require interpretation' may not be satisfied with such methods, since 'computers have not yet been successfully programmed to accomplish [interpretive tasks] that are concerned with meanings' (p. 34). Second, qualitative research, except for content analytic approaches and positivistic approaches, relies not only on induction, but also on creative leaps or interpretive guesses; computational approaches do not, as of yet, have the capability to do so. Third, while machine-learning capabilities are improving each day, and machine learning can be used to validate some types of knowledge, it is questionable if it is able to undertake validation that we describe as 'argumentative discipline comparable to juridical procedures of legal interpretation' that involves the 'logic of uncertainty and of qualitative probability'.

Perhaps there will be a time in the future when we will see computational approaches that are able to interpret digital texts as human researchers do today, but until then, digital methods will need to be seen as augmenting, not replacing, the interpretive act of researchers, primarily by supporting researchers in handling (i.e., recording, storing, sorting, accessing, linking and exploring) a high volume of data without being overburdened by it. We should recall, from our earlier discussion, that a higher volume of data does not make either induction or deduction necessarily more effective. Thus, we are confident in saying that qualitative, especially interpretive, research is not going to become wholly computational any time soon. However, we can certainly see situations when *computational approaches can profitably complement interpretive work, leading to interesting streams of mixed-method studies.*

2.4.4 The Nascent Myth that the Digitalization of Qualitative Research Is Becoming the Future of All Qualitative Research

There is no doubt that digitalization is occurring all around us, as products, services and entire organizations and even societies undergo rapid digitalization. Many organizations are even being born digital. This suggests that the study of digital traces, which may be thought of as capturing social interactions and behaviours comprehensively, often in natural settings, can offer an in-depth understanding of the world around us, whether by qualitative or quantitative approaches (Cesare et al., 2018). While we agree that digital traces do allow researchers a view into the phenomenon of interest through real-time, longitudinal and often hard-to-obtain access to certain stakeholders, there are a number of concerns associated with over-emphasizing digitalization in research that can be very pertinent to qualitative research.

2.4.4.1 Being Vulnerable to the So-called 'Streetlight Effect'

According to Rai (2017: v; cf. Kaplan, 1964: 11), the 'streetlight effect [refers to the situation] where a drunkard decides to search for his/her lost wallet under a street lamp because the bright illumination makes it easier to search at that location relative to a darker location where the wallet was likely dropped'. There are at least two different implications of the streetlight effect. First, even the brightest of lamps lights up only certain areas while leaving other areas in the dark. In our context, even though we may have high volumes of digital traces available, we tend to forget that not all processes can be digitalized; therefore, the 'trace data', even if very large in volume, are not necessarily *representative*. Qualitative research has often been concerned with ensuring that marginalized voices are not silenced; yet, a focus on the study of digital traces could lead to excluding a large proportion of stakeholder groups and their behaviours from being part of the conversation that feeds into the knowledge-creation process. Such exclusion potentially raises ethical concerns related to generating biased knowledge. Second, there is the need to acknowledge the point of view that the answer to many important problems/questions relevant to our (or any) discipline may not be related to (or found in) the available digital traces. Thus, we run the danger of seeking answers to questions using the wrong data, over-emphasizing questions that can be answered using the available traces and/

or under-emphasizing or avoiding questions that are critical for the discipline but are not answerable using traces. This issue is not only a concern for qualitative research, but also for quantitative research, both of which are increasingly moving towards the analysis of digital traces.

2.4.4.2 Not Representing Qualitative Research in Its Entirety

The qualitative research arena has much variety that allows different methodologies and approaches to capture different slices of reality and to help in creating an authentic image of a given phenomenon of interest. Do computational approaches accommodate such diversity in ontological and epistemological positions? We are doubtful of this. According to Cesare et al. (2018: 1984):

> ... researchers have noted the difficulty of engaging in qualitative research using digital trace data. The large scale of digital traces (e.g., hundreds of millions of social media posts) prevents the use of many traditional qualitative methods that require human inspection of each data element. Some researchers have used automated analysis strategies, such as topic modeling ... although convenient, these methods do raise concerns.

First of all, we need to clarify what qualitative research means. For many scholars, qualitative research includes scholarly inquiry that might start with qualitative data, even if the data are subsequently quantified and then statistical analysis is undertaken (e.g., Venkatesh et al., 2016); others require qualitative data and qualitative analysis. Sarker et al. (2018) point to a number of qualitative approaches ('genres') that are mapped on a two-dimensional space, with two axes (imagination-centric to data-centric, and inductive to deductive). Methodologies and their variations could include, among others, Straussian grounded theory methodology (Strauss and Corbin, 1990), positivist case studies (Eisenhardt, 1989; Lee, 1989; Dubé and Paré, 2003), interpretive case studies (Walsham, 1995, 2006; Klein and Myers 1999), realist and impressionist ethnography (Van Maanen, 1988), and validation hermeneutics (Hirsch, 1967) and phenomenological hermeneutics (Ricoeur, 1991; Lee, 1994).

Computational approaches, in our opinion, can largely be placed into the inductive, data-centric quadrant, and perhaps also in the deductive, data-centric quadrant, where they may be used to deductively validate certain hypotheses in the data. Thus, computational approaches are largely absent in two of the four quadrants. That is, approaches that deal with disciplined imagination, with mental leaps, are, at least at the present time, not within the purview of the computational techniques. Nor are the approaches that involve experience-near studies and immersion into the context that allow grasping the meaning of symbols specific to a given community.

Adding to our earlier discussion on veracity and truth, we also wish to highlight the fact that different approaches to qualitative research also seek truth in different forms. In fact, the standards and interpretation of veracity are different across diverse qualitative traditions. In some traditions of qualitative research, veracity may be related to the discovery of *the truth* about a phenomenon represented in the data; in other traditions, qualitative researchers may pursue *multiple truths*. Some qualitative studies may also be seeking a truth that is plausible, yet others may be seeking to transform the truth as understood by the audience by taking a particular ideological perspective on the data, or by making a difference through certain pragmatic outcomes. Genres such as 'impressionist' ethnography (Van Maanen, 1988) might use partial or imprecise images of reality to produce meaningful narratives and rich concepts (Boswell and Corbett, 2015) and, in fact, another type of qualitative study, 'scientifiction', deliberately blends reality and imagination to reveal more profound truths (Latour, 1996). It is also worth reiterating the fact that many qualitative researchers intensively study exceptions to discern insights, and such insights tend to get lost when studying a large volume of data and focusing on central tendencies or frequently occurring themes.

Based on the above, our position is that the digitalization of research can be valuable, but at this time, it cannot substitute for all qualitative research, especially interpretive research, which focuses on immersion, a relatively small number of subjects or contexts, meaning and an emic under-the-surface view of a phenomenon, all of which serve to reveal plausible, sometimes counter-intuitive accounts that allow us to see the phenomenon in a different light, rather than necessarily seek to present certain causal relationships with a high degree of confidence. We suggest that computational approaches be combined with qualitative, interpretive approaches, where possible and when meaningful, and some approaches towards that end have been put forth in the IS literature (e.g., Berente et al., 2019). That is the way to the future in the digitalized world, by incorporating new approaches into our research work *when useful*, rather than assuming that the new computational tradition will supplant centuries of thought underlying qualitative research traditions, or that qualitative approaches *must* be combined with computational approaches to be valid or valuable.

2.5 Conclusion

The digitalization of business organizations and of society, in general, has opened the possibility of researching behaviours using large volumes of digital traces and electronic texts that capture behaviours and attitudes in a broad range of natural settings. Because such digitalization is likely to proceed unabated and even to accelerate, the research taking advantage of digital traces and electronic texts is no less likely to proceed with full force. Many researchers see such digital traces as authentic data because the traces are not 'provoked' through researcher interventions or questions, but are created naturally as a result of human actions, thereby minimizing concerns regarding social desirability and recall bias in the data. Further, the large volume of digital traces creates (improperly, we have argued) an expectation among researchers and research audiences that analysis, whether in the form of induction or deduction, will result in more valid findings. In addition, the use of computational approaches promises to make the results more reproducible (Nelson, 2020), a desirable quality for some but not all types of qualitative research. In light of these presumed advantages, qualitative researchers may wonder whether qualitative research is experiencing fundamental changes and

whether qualitative research would mean computational analysis of non-quantitative digital data. We see the growing popularity of the digitalization of qualitative research as more than just a bandwagon effect; it will likely take its place as a permanent fixture in the constellation of different research approaches. However, the digital data and computational approaches will not become the *sine qua non* of qualitative IS research because: first, not all forms of qualitative research – particularly, interpretive research – are amenable to digitalization; second, not all phenomena are necessarily captured by digital traces, electronic texts or other forms of big data; and, third, to avoid becoming merely 'brute data', digital data will require human intervention in the form of researchers' creativity and judgements. Computational approaches have a place and are surely welcome, particularly in the form of mixed-method studies in conjunction with qualitative, interpretive studies, but will hardly spell the end of such research as we have known it in the IS discipline.

References

Abbasi, A., Sarker, S. and Chiang, R. (2016). Big data research in information systems: Toward an inclusive research agenda. *Journal of the Association for Information Systems*, 17(2), i–xxxii.

Abramson, C. M., Joslyn, J., Rendle, K. A., Garrett, S. B. and Dohan, D. (2018). The Promises of computational ethnography: Improving transparency, replicability, and validity for realist approaches to ethnographic analysis. *Ethnography*, 19(2), 254–284.

Alvesson, M. and Skoldberg, K. (2000). *Reflexive Methodology: New Vistas for Qualitative Research*. London: Sage.

Andrejevic, M. (2013). *Infoglut: How Too Much Information Is Changing the Way We Think and Know*. London and New York, NY: Routledge.

Berente, N., Seidel, S. and Safadi, H. (2019). Research commentary: Data-driven computationally intensive theory development. *Information Systems Research*, 30(1), 50–64.

Boswell, J. and Corbett, J. (2015). Embracing impressionism: Revealing the brush strokes of interpretive research. *Critical Policy Studies*, 9(2), 216–225.

Cesare, N., Lee, H., McCormick, T., Spiro, E. and Zagheni, E. (2018). The promises and pitfalls of using digital traces for demographic research. *Demography*, 55(5), 1979–1999.

Dibbern, J., Winkler, J. and Heinzl, A. (2008). Explaining variations in client extra costs between software projects offshored to India. *MIS Quarterly*, 32(2), 333–366.

DiMaggio, P. (2015). Adapting computational text analysis to social science (and vice versa). *Big Data & Society*, 2(2), 1–5.

Dubé, L. and Paré, G. (2003). Rigor in information systems positivist case research: Current practices, trends, and recommendations. *MIS Quarterly*, 27(4), 597–636.

Eck, A. and Uebernickel, F. (2016). Reconstructing open source software ecosystems: Finding structure in digital traces. International Conference on Information Systems, Dublin, Ireland.

Eisenhardt, K. M. (1989). Building theories from case study research. *Academy of Management Review*, 14(4), 532–550.

Ghazawneh, A. and Henfridsson, O. (2013). Balancing platform control and external contribution in third-party development: The boundary resources model. *Information Systems Journal*, 23(2), 173–192.

Grover, V., Lindberg, A., Benbasat, I. and Lyytinen, K. (2020). The perils and promises of big data research in information systems. *Journal of the Association for Information Systems*, 21(2), 268–293.

Hirsch, E. D. (1967). *Validity in Interpretation*. New Haven, CT: Yale University Press.

Howison, J., Wiggins, A. and Crowston, K. (2011). Validity issues in the use of social network analysis with digital trace data. *Journal of the Association for Information Systems*, 12(12), 767–797.

Johnson, S. L., Gray, P. and Sarker, S. (2019). Revisiting IS research practice in the era of big data. *Information and Organization*, 29(1), 41–56.

Kaplan, A. (1964). *The Conduct of Inquiry: Methodology for Behavioral Science*. New York, NY: Chandler Publishing.

Kitchin, R. (2014). *The Data Revolution: Big Data, Open Data, Data Infrastructures and Their Consequence*. London: Sage.

Klein, H. K. and Myers, M. D. (1999). A set of principles for conducting and evaluating interpretive field studies in information systems. *MIS Quarterly*, 23(1), 67–93.

Latour, B. (1996). *Aramis or the Love of Technology*. Cambridge, MA: Harvard University Press.

Lazer, D., Pentland, A. S., Adamic, L., Aral, S., Barabasi, A.-L., Brewer, D. et al. (2009). Life in the network: The coming age of computational social science. *Science*, 323(5915), 721–723.

Lee, A. S. (2017). Philosophy and method: Making interpretive research interpretive. In R. D. Galliers and M.-K. Stein (eds), *The Routledge Companion to Management Information Systems*. New York, NY: Routledge, pp. 30–46.

Lee, A. S. (1994). Electronic mail as a medium for rich communication: An empirical investigation using hermeneutic interpretation. *MIS Quarterly*, 18(2), 143–157.

Lee, A. S. (1989). A scientific methodology for MIS case studies. *MIS Quarterly*, 13(1), 33–50.

Lee, A. S. and Baskerville, R. (2003). Generalizing generalizability in information systems research. *Information Systems Research*, 14(3), 221–243.

Lee, A. S. and Hubona, G. S. (2009). A scientific basis for rigor in information systems research. *MIS Quarterly*, 33(2), 237–262.

Lindberg, A. (2020). Developing theory through human and machine pattern recognition. *Journal of the Association for Information Systems*, 21(1), 90–116.

Lindberg, A., Berente, N., Gaskin, J., Lyytinen, K. and Yoo, Y. (2013). Computational approaches for analyzing latent social structures in open source organizing. International Conference on Information Systems, Milan, Italy.

Lohmeier, C. (2014). The researcher and the never-ending field: Reconsidering big data and digital ethnography. In M. Hand and S. Hillyard (eds), *Big Data? : Qualitative Approaches to Digital Research*. Bingley, UK: Emerald, pp. 75–89.

Markus, M. L. (1983). Power, politics, and MIS implementation. *Communications of the ACM*, 26(6), 430–444.

Mead, M. (1959a). Apprenticeship under Boas. In W. Goldschmidt (ed.), *The Anthropology of Franz Boas*. Washington, DC: American Anthropological Association, Memoir 89, pp. 29–45.

Mead, M. (1959b). Introduction. In R. Benedict, *An Anthropologist at Work*. London and New York, NY: Routledge, pp. xv–xxii.

Mohr, J. W., Wagner-Pacifici, R. and Breiger, R. (2015). Toward a computational hermeneutics. *Big Data & Society*, 2(2), 1–8.

Nelson, L. (2020). Computational grounded theory: A methodological framework. *Sociological Methods & Research*, 49(1), 3–42.

Pelto, P. J. (1970). *Anthropological Research: The Structure of Inquiry*. New York, NY: Harper & Row.

Popper, K. (1968). *Conjectures and Refutations: The Growth of Scientific Knowledge*. New York, NY: Harper Torchbooks.

Rai, A. (2017). Avoiding type III errors: Formulating IS research problems that matter. *MIS Quarterly*, 41(2), iii–vii.

Ricoeur, P. (1991). The model of the text: Meaningful action considered as a text. In *From Text to Action: Essays in Hermeneutics, II*. Evanston, IL: Northwestern University Press, pp. 144–167.

Romele, A., Severo, M. and Furia, P. (2020). Digital hermeneutics: From interpreting with machines to interpretational machines. *AI & Society*, 35(1), 73–86.

Rosenberg, A. (1993). Hume and the philosophy of science. In D. Norton (ed.), *The Cambridge Companion to Hume*. New York, NY: Cambridge University Press, pp. 64–89.

Sanday, P. (1979). The ethnographic paradigm(s). *Administrative Science Quarterly*, 24(4), 527–538.

Sarker, S. and Lee, A. S. (2006). Does the use of computer-based BPC tools contribute to redesign effectiveness? Insights from a hermeneutic study. *IEEE Transactions on Engineering Management*, 53(1), 130–145.

Sarker, S. and Lee, A. S. (2002). Using a positivist case research methodology to test three competing practitioner theories-in-use of business process redesign. *Journal of the Association for Information Systems*, 2(1), 1–74.

Sarker, S., Xiao, X, Beaulieu, T. and Lee, A. S. (2018). The practice of qualitative research in the IS discipline: An evolutionary view and some implications for authors and evaluators (Part I). *Journal of the AIS*, 19(8), 752–774.

Schutz, A. (1962). Concept and theory formation in the social sciences. In M. Natanson (ed.), *Alfred Schutz: Collected Papers 1*. Boston, MA: Kluwer Academic Publishers, pp. 48–66.

Strauss, A. and Corbin, J. M. (1990). *Basics of Qualitative Research: Grounded Theory Procedures and Techniques*. Beverly Hills, CA: Sage.

Taylor, C. (1971). Interpretation and the sciences of man. *Review of Metaphysics*, 25(1), 3–51.

Vaast, E., Safadi, H., Lapointe, L., and Negoita, B. (2017). Social media affordances for connective action: An examination of microblogging use during the Gulf of Mexico oil spill. *MIS Quarterly*, 41(4), 1179–1205.

Van Maanen, J. (1988). *Tales of the Field: On Writing Ethnography*. Chicago, IL: University of Chicago Press.

Venkatesh, V., Brown, S. A. and Sullivan, Y. W. (2016). Guidelines for conducting mixed-methods research: An extension and illustration. *Journal of the Association for Information Systems*, 17(7), 435–494.

Walsham, G. (2006). Doing interpretive research. *European Journal of Information Systems*, 15(3), 320–330.

Walsham, G. (1995). Interpretive case studies in IS research: Nature and method. *European Journal of Information Systems*, 4(2), 74–81.

Wolcott, H. (1975). Criteria for an ethnographic approach to research in schools. *Human Organization*, 34(2), 111–128.

Wood, A. (2000). Hume: The problem of induction. Stanford University. www.stanford.edu/~allenw/Phil102/Hume%20-%20Induction.doc.

Data as a Contingent Performance and the Limitations of Big Data

MATTHEW JONES

3.1 Introduction

The proliferation of digital data, we are told, enables a revolution in research methods that is typically seen as being to the detriment of qualitative methods. Although there are a number of different views on what form this revolution will take, they generally share a common assumption that data instrument reality and that understanding of the world can therefore be gained through their analysis alone. In this chapter, I will seek to show that this was never the case, even in the pre-digital era, and that this situation is not altered by the contemporary abundance of data, perhaps especially of the digital variety.

Data, it will be argued, are not, as is often claimed, a natural resource ('the new oil', as some would have it) that pre-exist their collection. Nor do they stand in a direct relationship with the phenomena they are considered as representing. Rather, they are the product of situated practices that provide a selective and potentially inaccurate representation of phenomena. The implications of such a conceptualization of data for research methods in information systems and organizational research will be considered.

3.2 Three Views on Big Data and Research Methods

There would seem to be at least three different views on how big data[1] will revolutionize research

---

[1] Following Boyd and Crawford (2012), the term big data refers to a phenomenon rather than to data sets of a particular size. As Kitchin and McArdle (2016) show, big data are not always especially voluminous.

methods, even if individual authors may not always make their arguments exclusively from one position. The first such view, generally associated with a 2008 article in *Wired* magazine by Chris Anderson, may be described as the 'end of theory' argument. This proposed that, in the face of the volume of data available in the 'Petabyte age', the traditional, deductive, scientific method is becoming obsolete. Rather than testing hypotheses derived from theoretical models, statistical algorithms can simply be applied to massive scientific or organizational data sets to find patterns without any guiding theory. 'Correlation supersedes causation', Anderson argued, 'and science can advance even without coherent models, unified theories, or really any mechanistic explanation at all' (Anderson, 2008).

Although some have questioned whether Anderson's article was ever intended as more than a provocation (Mazzocchi, 2015), the idea that big data require a new, purely inductive, mode of science has been enthusiastically promoted by a number of authors (e.g., Prensky, 2009; Cukier and Mayer-Schönberger, 2013) and has attracted considerable popular interest. Rather than being theory-driven, it is argued, research should become data-driven. For Cukier and Mayer-Schönberger (2013), this is a necessary response to the changing character of data brought about by digitalization, which they describe in terms of three shifts: from some to all; from clean to messy; and from causation to correlation. Big data, they argue, mean that research need no longer be constrained by data scarcity. Sampling is unnecessary as we can capture and analyze data on the population as a whole. This may involve some loss of accuracy and precision, but this will be offset by the richness of the insights that can be obtained. Citing the example of Google search or the Amazon recommendation system, it is argued that we don't necessarily need to know why something happens, correlation will be enough. 'Sometimes', Cukier and Mayer-Schönberger (2013) argue, 'we just need to let the data speak', or, as Anderson (2008) puts it, 'with enough data, the numbers speak for themselves'.

The claim that big data will lead to the abandonment of the traditional hypothetico-deductive scientific method in favour of a purely inductive search for correlations has been robustly challenged, however, by philosophers and both natural and social scientists (Callebaut, 2012; Frické, 2015; Kitchin, 2014a; Leonelli, 2014; Mazzocchi, 2015; Coveney et al., 2016). Big data, it is argued, are necessarily theory-laden – even if those using the data may not be aware of this or have the means to know what theories their data have been shaped by. Search unguided by theory is likely to be inefficient and will not necessarily yield new insights. Nor can correlations by themselves explain – theory is needed to interpret them. To accept these criticisms, though, does not mean the abandonment of a claim for the revolutionary effects of big data on research. Rather, the claim now shifts from a transformation of the logic of scientific method to an expansion of the domain of science. Big data, it is argued, open new realms of research, in the social sciences especially, to the scientific method. 'This is the time', Wenzel and Van Quaquebeke (2018: 576, emphasis in the original) proclaim, 'to think about properly wielding the big data sword to transform organizational *research* into organizational *science*'.

This view is often associated with claims made in leading scientific journals such as *Science* (Lazer et al., 2009), that big data are leading to the emergence of a new discipline of 'computational social science', in which, as Conte et al. (2012: 327) propose, 'social and behavioural scientists, cognitive scientists, agent theorists, computer scientists, mathematicians and physicists cooperate side-by-side to come up with innovative and theory-grounded models' of social phenomena. This is made possible because, as Mayer-Schönberger and Cukier (2013) argue, datafication is quantifying the world at an ever-accelerating pace. Reality is being instrumented. Indeed, Pentland (2009: 80)

describes his research on the 'digital breadcrumbs' that individuals leave behind as they use mobile phones as 'reality mining'.

Such views have their adherents in the management and organizational literature too, especially among those who would identify themselves as 'quantitatively minded scientist-practitioners' (Tonidandel et al., 2018). Chang et al. (2014: 77), for example, argue that digital traces capture fundamental features of social interaction and can lead to a paradigm shift in management research in which control, realism and generality can be maximized simultaneously. This, George et al. (2016) propose, will enable researchers to understand organizational trends, behaviours and actions in entirely new ways, to achieve better answers to existing questions and to explore entirely new questions through the introduction of new constructs or the operationalization of old constructs in new ways.

For proponents of computational social science, big data thus represent a decisive turning point in social research. Datafication, they argue, with varying degrees of fervour, opens the whole social world to quantitative analysis at hitherto inconceivable levels of detail and comprehensiveness. No longer will researchers need to rely on proxy measures or individuals' reports of their behaviour, they can have direct, unobtrusive access to the phenomenon itself in close to real time. What need is there, then, for qualitative research, when the whole world has been turned into numbers and quantitative research can provide definitive answers to every question?

Not surprisingly, such arguments have received a less positive response from qualitative researchers, a number of whom have sought to stress the continuing relevance of their methods. Strong (2014), for example, proposes that qualitative researchers are needed in big data research as generators of hypotheses and defenders of complex explanations. Other qualitative researchers emphasize the complementarity of qualitative and quantitative data (Mills, 2018) or argue that insights from ethnography can inform data science (Elish and Boyd, 2018).

A third view of big data and research methods is therefore to see them as a resource for, rather than a threat to, qualitative research. If big data do not speak for themselves, and any understanding of them necessarily involves interpretation, an activity central to the qualitative researchers' practice, as authors such as Van Maanen (1979) argue, then they should not reject big data out of hand as fundamentally inimical to their worldview, but embrace the opportunity that big data provides to enrich our understanding of organizational phenomena. Even if big data are not viewed as offering an unmediated representation of social phenomena, they may nevertheless expand enormously the quantity and variety of evidence to which interpretation may be applied. Not that quantity and variety per se will necessarily lead to better interpretation, but to the extent that qualitative methods are considered to be constrained by the availability of data, then big data may potentially make a difference.

These three views would seem to present very different perspectives on big data and their implications for research methods, seeing them as presaging either: a transformation of the logic of research from deduction to induction; an epistemological revolution as datafication opens more, some might say all, social phenomena to quantitative analysis; or an expanded resource for all methods. They nevertheless share a number of common assumptions about data in general and about big data more specifically (Jones, 2019a). Thus, discussion of data, even among qualitative researchers, typically views data as: referential (they stand for something that exists independently of them); natural (they have a real existence independent of their use); foundational (they are the bedrock on which information, knowledge and wisdom are built); and objective (they precede interpretation). Furthermore, big data are assumed to be: revolutionary (necessarily precipitating change); distinctively voluminous (encouraging a focus on quantity as their primary characteristic); universal (representing the entirety of natural and social existence); and exhaustive (approaching, if not achieving, $n = $ all). Similarly, Kitchin (2014b: 3) talks about a 'pre-factual' perspective on data that views them as 'abstract, discrete, aggregative ... and meaningful independent of format, medium, language, producer and context'. In the next section, however, an alternative, performative conception of data will be presented that calls these assumptions into question.

3.3 Data as Contingent Performance

Much of the language used about data promotes the view that they are a natural resource. There is talk of 'raw data', 'data mining', and data 'streams', 'pools' and 'lakes'. Yet, if we take a closer look at what it is that we take to be data, it becomes apparent that data are far from natural. In order for something to be considered data, it needs first to be designated as such. The world is not naturally digitized. It does not present itself to us in discrete states that change at regular intervals, but rather we impose these states and transitions on the ongoing flow of phenomena.

Gitelman and Jackson (2013: 3) compare data to events, arguing that both are 'imagined and enunciated against the seamlessness' of the world. This does not mean that the identification of events or data is arbitrary, but that it involves active selection (perhaps not at the point of writing history or collecting data, but at some point it will have been necessary to choose what will be counted as events, or as data). Often, this process is so taken for granted that we overlook their construction. Research on the productivity paradox, say, tends to focus on which of the available measures should be considered the best indicators of productivity, rather than examining how these measures are produced.

As the reference to 'available' measures indicates, moreover, the identification of data does not necessarily mean that we inevitably record phenomena in the way that best represents them for the purposes that we might consider them to be data for. Not all features of a phenomenon may be recordable and not all of what is recordable may actually be recorded (or retained, such that they are available at the point when data are being looked for). Rather, we may often be choosing from among what can be, and already has been, designated as data about a phenomenon, the measure(s) that we believe provides the best (or maybe least bad) representation of the phenomenon.

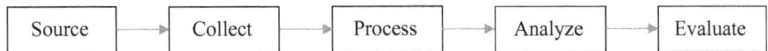

Figure 3.1 Idealized data processing pipeline
Source: Based on Olteanu et al. (2017).

Even where the phenomena that data are taken as reporting on are discretized, such as the numbers of users of an information system, their existence as data is not spontaneous. Rather, as Gitelman and Jackson (2013: 3) argue, they 'need to be imagined as data to exist as such'. The number of users is not data until there is a reason to want to record them. In the case of much IS-related data, this act of imagination is, moreover, the cause of the phenomenon that they are taken as representing. Data are the product of actions, usually intended but sometimes unintended, of the system's developers. A 'like' as a unit of appreciation, for example, is not a natural occurrence, but comes into being through its design as a token within a particular social media system.

Data, therefore, do not precede their designation. Nor are they the primordial soup from which information and knowledge emerge, as much IS literature assumes. Contrary to IS textbooks that define data as 'raw facts that describe a particular phenomenon' (Haag and Cummings, 2013: 508) or 'raw facts that can be processed into accurate and relevant information' (Turban, 2006: G-3), seeing data as facts depends on prior knowledge. 'There are no "isolated pieces of simple facts"', Tuomi (1999: 107) argues, 'unless someone has created them using his or her knowledge'. Following Fleck (2012), this knowledge is always social, agreed upon within a specific 'thought collective' that comprehends a phenomenon in a particular way, and may be instantiated in technological devices that produce a particular sort of record of the phenomenon. What comes to be counted as data, Jones et al. (2019: 243) argue, therefore, is not something that was 'out there' waiting to be found, but 'what is found when they are looked for'. This looking, moreover, is always from a particular point of view.

The data that are 'found' in the world, however, are still not yet the data that will be used by a researcher. Many challenges may need to be overcome to get them into a state in which they can be used in research. The 'idealised data processing pipeline' of Olteanu et al. (2017), as depicted in Figure 3.1, provides a framework that may be used for analyzing these challenges (while recognizing that the process may not be so linear in practice). Although their focus is specifically on social data (defined as 'digital traces produced by or about users, with an emphasis on content explicitly written with the intent of communicating or interacting with others' [Olteanu et al., 2017: 1]), these challenges would seem common to many other forms of research data.

At each stage of this pipeline there is the potential for data loss or distortion. Thus, if we consider the possible set of data that might be looked for to address a research question: only a, potentially unrepresentative, subset of these may be available to be sourced; of these, not all will be possible to collect; processing the collected data into a form that can be analyzed may introduce further losses and distortions; analysis may be biased; and evaluation may not detect or may misinterpret problems with the data. The conclusions we reach from the data may therefore not provide an accurate picture of the phenomenon that the data are taken as representing.

This is not a problem unique to digital data or to big data. Questions of validity and reliability of data, whether quantitative or qualitative, are a perennial concern in discussion of research methods. What is perhaps different, or more evident, in relation to digital and big data is the difficulty of identifying and detecting these challenges in complex data generation and collection processes, large parts of which may be opaque to the researcher. This opacity may be technical, either because the researcher, or even a skilled data scientist, may not have the ability to fully understand the process (a particular concern in relation to machine learning techniques [Burrell, 2016]) or because of commercial constraints on access to proprietary data sets.

Compared to a researcher who is directly involved in the sourcing and gathering of data themselves, it would seem much more difficult for a researcher reliant on data provided by a third party to assess their potential limitations.

The volume of data involved in big data studies may be a further deterrent to critical investigation. Even if the claims of big data proponents such as Cukier and Mayer-Schönberger (2013) that questions of validity and representativeness become moot at such scale are not accepted, the difficulties of identifying and evaluating the potential biases in massive data sets, the provenance of which may not be well-documented, seem likely to make significant scrutiny of any stage of the data pipeline impractical.

A further implication of this view of data that is potentially a major issue for the use of digital and big data in research is the contingent character of the processes of constituting and using data. Data are not stable entities that exist in the world and that can be effortlessly collected in ways that do not change them at all. Rather, data are performed, brought into being by social and technical processes that enact particular representations of phenomena. These representations may then be modified, to a greater or lesser extent, by the further social and technical processes that bring data into use in organizational practices. These processes may vary in their relative influence over time so the outcome will be contingent. This is not to say that the variation in the representation of the phenomenon provided by the data will necessarily be significant for organizational practices, but we should be alert to the processes that may have shaped the representation of the world that they offer.

3.4 A Performative Perspective on Data and Research Methods

Taking this understanding of data as a contingent performance, we can now revisit the debate on data and research methods. Starting first with the 'end of theory' argument, it would seem a necessary assumption of this position that data represent the world as it is. If this were not to be the case, then that of which the numbers speak, as Anderson would have it, would not be the world, but only themselves. Similarly, correlations found in the data could not be assumed to be evidence of the same relationship between the phenomena that the data are seen as representing.

It might be argued that, as Milton Friedman (1953) proposed in relation to positive economics, whether data describe the world correctly is of no importance. All that matters is the 'precision, scope and conformity with experience of the predictions it yields'. This is to assume, however, that conformity with experience is a binary variable that only ever has a single value: predictions either conform, or not. As the Google Flu Trends case (at one time cited as evidence for the end of theory [Cukier and Mayer-Schönberger, 2013] and of the potential of simple models applied to big data [McAfee and Brynjolfsson, 2012]) illustrates, though, predictive accuracy at one time is not necessarily evidence that a correlation correctly characterizes a phenomenon. Having, for a number of years, outperformed, it was said, predictions from the Centers for Disease Control and Prevention (CDC), Google Flu Trends was found to persistently overestimate flu prevalence (Lazer et al., 2014). Even consistent accuracy is not sufficient evidence of the verisimilitude of representation since it is not possible to show definitively that a correlation is not spurious.

Perhaps, then, the absolute conformity of predictions with experience might be considered too demanding a criterion on which to judge the merits of inductive methods applied to big data. All that is needed is that predictions are better than those provided by other methods. Not only, however, is this a test that Google Flu Trends would also have failed, it also does not necessarily tell us anything about whether data represent the world as it is, just that there are possibly worse representations.

This argument is often taken even further in management literature that makes the case for the significance of big data in terms of their effects on company performance. McAfee and Brynjolfsson (2012: 64), for example, propose that big data will revolutionize management, basing their claim on interviews with 330 executives at North American companies, from which they conclude that 'the more companies characterized themselves as data-driven, the better they performed on objective measures of financial and operational results'. By this measure, however, any claim regarding the relationship between data and phenomenon becomes highly tenuous. No more than in the story, related by Weick (1995) in *Sensemaking in Organizations* of soldiers lost in the snow in the Alps who make their way to safety using a map that subsequently turns out to be of the Pyrenees, can we argue that the insight derived from data follows from their correspondence to reality (other than perhaps in the broad sense that getting down from mountains in poor conditions involves finding safe routes of descent whether you are in the Alps or Pyrenees or that successful decisions may involve the analysis of data). It is the outcome of the use of the map/data that is taken as important, not whether the map/data accurately represent the phenomenon. It is just assumed that the outcomes are evidence that this is the case.

Interestingly, this position may be seen as not so different from that advanced in this chapter, in that, for both, the significance of data is seen as being constituted through the practices they are considered as giving rise to. Whether proponents of what Kitchin (2014a) and Johnson et al. (2019) describe as big data empiricism would welcome the comparison, however, seems debatable. With their focus on 'producing actionable, pragmatic knowledge from large datasets' (Johnson et al., 2019: 45), they would seem likely to have little time for claims that data are other than 'raw facts' that objectively represent reality. The two positions also differ fundamentally, in where they locate agency. For the management scholars who champion big data, agency is attributed to the data as the cause of the outcomes, enabling the superior decision-making that leads to better performance. From a performative perspective, on the other hand, outcomes emerge through the entanglement of social and material, some might say sociomaterial, agencies that constitute both the data and the effects that they are seen as giving rise to.

Another claim of 'end of theory' proponents that is less easy to reconcile with a performative view of data is that we are 'approaching n = all'. There are two problems, at least, with this: how can we know what 'all' is and does n ever actually approach 'all' in practice? Thus, while it may be the case that Amazon tracks customers' interactions with their websites in very great detail, the specific elements that they track will be those that have been identified as significant for guiding, facilitating and carrying out purchases and whatever other activities Amazon seeks to acquire data on. N, for Amazon, may therefore approach all for these elements (assuming no loss of data at any point), but there may be other elements of customer interaction that are not considered relevant, appropriate or possible to track. N = all therefore applies to only that part of customer interaction that has been identified and instrumented by Amazon as constituting the activity. Other elements of the activity may exist but not be tracked because they are not seen as significant or because there is some technical, legal or practical constraint on doing so. So n only selectively approaches all.

From Amazon's point of view, this is not a problem. They do not need the data they gather to represent the activity completely. The data just need to represent it in enough detail to enable them to carry out their business. As Zuboff (2019) argues, the scope of what they consider as necessary to enable them to carry out their business may go considerably beyond facilitating and carrying out purchases, but this does not mean that the data they gather does, or has to, constitute a complete representation of phenomena of interest.

If this is the case with the data held by Amazon, in relation to an environment that they designed and control, then n = all would seem scarcely tenable as a description of data held about any social phenomenon 'in the wild'. As has been argued, phenomena are not naturally digitized: we need to decide what constitutes data about them. Nor do whatever data we choose to collect necessarily provide a complete, accurate or representative picture of the phenomenon (indeed, it is quite possible that they don't because, for example, we are engaged in exploratory research about the phenomenon, so we don't know what exactly it is that we are looking at). It would therefore seem a strong claim that we have collected all the data there could be about a phenomenon or even that such data that we have collected will be sufficient to represent the phenomenon correctly.

From the perspective of a performative conception of data, therefore, we can identify several, potentially fatal, flaws in the 'end of theory' claims that big data will lead to a new scientific paradigm that relies solely on induction. Such an argument overstates the exhaustiveness of data and the fidelity of their representation of phenomena. Moreover, in privileging pragmatic and relativist validation criteria (e.g., do our analyses of data yield better predictions than alternatives?), it implicitly assigns agency to data since, as natural and objective representations of reality the status of which we can have no reason, or potentially means, to question, these can be the only cause of the relationships found. This would not seem to provide a sound basis on which to model digital research methods, even assuming it was ever seriously intended as such.

There can be little doubt, on the other hand, about the seriousness of the claims made by proponents of computational social science regarding the representation of phenomena by data. If data are to enable the more accurate estimation of effect sizes (George et al., 2016), to yield 'robust inferences through meticulous observations and analyses' (Wenzel and Van Quaquebeke, 2018), or to uncover the 'laws of society' (Conte et al., 2012), then they must report directly, as Pentland (2009) implies, on reality. No amount of computation will be able to uncover the laws of society if the data being analyzed do not represent society accurately. Some accommodation may be possible if the variability in the way that data are performed is assumed to be too small to make a difference in practice, but the idea that data do not pre-exist their collection or that the representation of the world that data provide may not reflect how the world actually is would seem to put into question the whole enterprise.

Pragmatically, it might be argued that what is being sought is not necessarily the true laws of society, but rather laws that are better (more accurate? broader in scope? more parsimonious?) than those that were previously available. This would be philosophically defensible in the falsificationist tradition of Popper, but this argument is not typically made. Indeed, in their invocation of 'reality' as being what data represent, proponents of computational social science would seem to be asserting claims to the truth of their findings.

This view is not universally held among advocates of computational social science, however. Chang et al. (2014: 72), for example, explicitly differentiate their position from that of what they describe as 'the sociotechnical tradition of research, [that] emphasize[s] research as a process to establish the truth about different technology-related phenomena of the real and social worlds'. Rather, they suggest that their methods 'yield the most interesting results for the new decision support and e-commerce issues, and other social science problems of interest' (2014: 72), which would seem closer to the stance of 'end of theory' proponents who argue that it is more important that the results of research are useful than that they are true.

Whether computational social science is seen to deliver truth or just better answers, arguments that big data make a methodological revolution in social research necessary or even inevitable tend to come down to a question of numbers. One version of this argument posits social research as historically constrained by a shortage of data and/or by the inability to operationalize key phenomena. Both these constraints are now seen to be lifted, thanks to big data, and social research can now realize its true potential and take its place alongside the natural sciences in the highest rank of human knowledge. Another, rather less high-flown, version is based on what we might call, following George Mallory, the Everest principle – big data invite a methodological revolution 'because they are there'. Being fortunate enough to have such an unimaginable cornucopia of data available, it would be remiss not to make use of them (whatever our reservations might be about their provenance, quality, etc.). Whether inspired to realize Comte's vision of a social physics or simply because we can, quantitative data at scale would seem to hold a seductive allure for many researchers.

Not all researchers, of course, are so swayed by the sight of lots of numbers. Nevertheless, for many qualitative researchers too, big data constitute a resource that should be engaged with. Some of these, at least, view these data in a not dissimilar way to proponents of computational social science – big (quantitative) data are to be combined with qualitative data in 'mixed-method' studies that will bring enhanced insight through triangulation, synthesis and complementarity (cf. Tashakkori and Teddlie, 2009).

If big data are to be combined with qualitative data, however, the two types need to be based on shared assumptions, otherwise the data will be incommensurable. As Boyd and Crawford (2012) and Rieder and Simon (2016) discuss, though, literature promoting big data tends to present them as objective reports of an independent reality, untainted by subjectivity or interpretation. Significant traditions in qualitative research, in contrast, would view data as 'our own constructions of other people's constructions of what they and their compatriots are up to' (Geertz, 1973: 9) or describe qualitative research as 'an array of interpretive techniques which seek to describe, decode, translate and otherwise come to terms with the meaning, not the frequency, of certain more or less naturally-occurring phenomena in the social world' (Van Maanen, 1979). It would seem hard to see how these perspectives could be reconciled such that data collected with one set of assumptions could contribute directly to research based on the other. Perhaps it might be possible to view data of one sort in terms of the other, to conceptualize big data as subjective or qualitative data as objective, in order to achieve some sort of rapprochement, but the very different ways in which the perspectives understand what data are and what they tell us about the world make this seem like an exercise in mental gymnastics that risks being inconsistent with both.

Even if we do not see big data as directly combining with qualitative data, there may be other ways in which big data may contribute to qualitative research. Thus, it is not necessarily the case that all big data are quantitative. Tweets, blog posts or web pages, for example, constitute voluminous data resources that may be subject to qualitative analysis. As public expressions of views produced for particular audiences, however, the insights they offer on their authors' thinking may be questioned and the scale at which such data may be collected may make them unsuited to traditional intensive analysis techniques. Nevertheless, they still offer a novel and rich source of data that it might be seen as a mistake for qualitative researchers to ignore simply because they have been produced in ways that have not traditionally been the norm in qualitative research (Powell et al., 2016).

Viewing big (qualitative) data as more of the same, however, does not require the adoption of a performative perspective on data. Just as it is not the case that qualitative researchers are necessarily reflective about the construction of that which they consider as constituting their data, so the expansion in the scale of these data does not necessarily lead to greater awareness of their construction. Indeed, with big data, scale and the detachment from the processes of data creation would seem likely to make this reflection more difficult. Consider, for example, the difference in the relationship to their data of one researcher analyzing hundreds, or maybe thousands, of Tweets (that will have been curated, to a greater or lesser degree, by Twitter), and another who has a handful of interviews that they carried out themselves. In the first case, lacking any access to the process of their production, the researcher has to take on trust that the data tell them what they think they do. The researcher conducting their own interviews, in contrast, will have direct experience of the contingencies of data production and may acquire additional insight from the interview process (from body language, for example, or tone of voice) that could inform their interpretations. The second researcher may therefore be expected to have a rich appreciation of how their relatively small volume of data have come about, while the first researcher has to treat their data as givens, whose status is not open to question.

There is certainly no consensus among qualitative researchers about the status of their data and there are significant constituencies who would argue that qualitative research should aspire to a place, if it has not already achieved this, among the sciences (Flick, 2009) and/or seek to contribute to evidence-based policy and practice (Hammersley, 2008). For such researchers, the performative perspective and its problematization of data as a representation of reality might be viewed as a threat to the hard-won credibility of qualitative research and a self-indulgent distraction from the real task of research. As the next section will seek to demonstrate, however, the performative perspective on data opens up a rich and varied agenda for qualitative researchers that need not detract from pursuit of other goals, but can enhance our appreciation of the phenomena we wish to study.

3.5 A Research Agenda for a Performative Perspective on Data

From the performative perspective, data are not natural givens that exist 'out there' in the world awaiting collection, but come to be identified as representing some phenomenon at the point that we seek to find data on the phenomenon. There may therefore be what Jones et al. (2019) call 'data in principle' which are recorded (quite possibly automatically), but are never used, either because there is never a cause to do so (the data are not seen as relevant to a possible practice) or because attempts to retrieve them fail (due to technical breakdowns, for example, or because knowledge of how to access them, or permission to do so, is not available). Such data may influence practice, as Foucault (1977) argues, through their disciplinary effects on individual behaviour. Such effects, however, do not necessarily depend on the accuracy of the data as a representation of the phenomenon, but on the subject's perceptions of what they may make visible.

A potential focus of research would therefore be to study how data come to be identified as such. What are the beliefs about a phenomenon that lead to particular items of data being considered as evidence of it? How does a person talking in an interview, say, or numbers reported in a company's accounts, come to be viewed as an adequate representation of a particular phenomenon?

If we try to do this by talking to researchers about how they understand what they take to be data as telling them about the phenomena they study, however, this creates a problem of infinite regress – we would need to ask ourselves how we consider their talk to be evidence of their

understanding of data. Such inquiry cannot, therefore, definitively identify the processes of data construction, but may help to unsettle the taken-for-grantedness of data and promote reflection on the nature of what it is that we consider to be data.

An alternative approach to address this issue could be to start with the data and to try to trace its 'biography'. This would be a similar process to that proposed by Fleck in *The Genesis and Development of a Scientific Fact* (Fleck, 1981), in which the arguments used to position particular items of data as evidence in 'classic' IS papers might be investigated. This would not be a re-analysis of the data to question whether they support the findings, such as offered by Hunter (2010) in relation to Barley's 'same technology, different outcome' study of Computed Tomography scanners (Barley, 1986), but a more detailed investigation of the data that Barley uses to support his argument, to the extent that this is possible at such a remove. Barley identifies evidence of 'phases of structuring', for example, from the arrival of the scanners and from alterations in the scanner's staffing patterns. The purpose here is not to question whether the staff members were correct in identifying these as 'major disjunctures' in the organization of the radiology departments at the two hospitals, as Barley argues, but to consider how these events might have been identified from Barley's observations and how these data relate to others, such as the quantitative centralization profile, as evidence of phasing. This would not be a search for a magic formula for constructing top-tier journal data, but an investigation of the assumptions, rather than the rhetorics (Golden-Biddle and Locke, 1993), that are involved in positioning data constructed from sources such as the researcher's observations, solicited interpretations of participants or coding of decisions, as convergent evidence of structuring processes.

Such analysis could, in principle, be applied to any paper, or, indeed, to any piece of research as it is in process. In practice, it would seem unlikely that the resources required could be justified for any other than significant, influential papers. The influence of papers is something that can only really be judged in retrospect, however, by which time access to the phenomenon, and potentially to the researchers, to investigate how data were constructed may be difficult, if not impossible. Nevertheless, it may be a salutary process to examine 'classic' papers, as far as this is possible, to investigate the solidity of the data foundations on which knowledge in the field is said to be built.

Some assessment of what is presented as data in a paper and their adequacy as a representation of the phenomenon of interest will also usually be part of the peer review process. Reviewers, however, have a limited ability to interrogate data sources and are necessarily reliant on the authors' claims of the data's suitability as a representation of the phenomenon. Greater attention to the construction of data, perhaps especially of digital data where this process may often be hidden to the researcher, would seem desirable if judgement is to be made on more than the persuasiveness of rhetoric.

If there are significant challenges in the retrospective investigation of the construction of data, then a second strand of research associated with a performative perspective of data might be studies of the performativity of data. How do data bring about phenomena? While this is a question that may be seen as having acquired particular pertinence in the age of big data, it may be applied with equal relevance to historic forms of data. Revellino and Mouritsen (2015), for example, discuss the performativity of accounting, a practice which dates back to the fifteenth century. Similarly, the operations management mantra, quoted approvingly by McAfee and Brynjolfsson (2012) in relation to big data, that 'you can't manage what you don't measure', may be seen as another example of the creation of a phenomenon through data. That which is to be managed is that which data makes visible, so if we cannot, or choose not to, measure something, it will not form part of the phenomenon we manage. Other discourses in which data are seen to play a significant role in organizations, Jones et al. (2019a) argue, include evidence-based management (Pfeffer and Sutton, 2006) and the audit society (Power, 1997).

Big data potentially amplifies these effects in three ways. First, with the claim that n = all (Cukier and Mayer-Schönberger, 2013), the domain that data are considered as representing is expanded to encompass the entire world. By implication, therefore, anything that is not represented by data does not exist (or, at least, is not important enough to need to pay attention to). Second, the ever-expanding datafication of phenomena creates what is presented as a ready-made resource. This may become for some, perhaps many, researchers their starting point when studying a phenomenon. Why spend time and effort gathering your own data, or even thinking about what might be data about the phenomenon you are interested in, when this immense stockpile is said to be just sitting there waiting to be used? The question for the researcher then becomes not 'what might be data that could provide insight on the phenomenon I am studying?', but rather 'what phenomenon could it be claimed that these data provide insight on?' There is therefore even less incentive to investigate how it is that data come to be seen as representing a phenomenon, even if that were possible, lest we discover something that might undermine our claims. Thus, as Moritz (2016) and Grover (2020) warn, big data research may be particularly susceptible to the 'streetlight effect', where studies are designed on the basis of what data are available rather than on the data's suitability as a representation of the phenomenon. The performative perspective on data offers a corrective to such tendencies.

Third, even if researchers wish to investigate big data sources to understand what representation of the phenomenon they offer, this may not be possible. Many of the sources that might be used in social or organizational research, such as social media data, emails or weblogs, are proprietary and access will be subject to the companies', continually evolving, policies. Even if it were possible to gain access to the whole data set, many questions may still be raised about their validity and representativeness and about what we may legitimately infer from them, for which there may be no clear answers. As Tufekci (2014) discusses in relation to social media data, for example, there are issues of: reliance on a small number of platforms, the structural biases of which may not be adequately recognized; selection on dependent variables; unclear or unrepresentative samples; neglect of the wider ecology of interaction; and inference from what is recorded of online inter-actions to the practices that give rise to them. However impeccable the analysis of such data may be, the applicability of any findings derived from them to anything other than the particular population of users (some of whom may be bots) who happen to be captured in the available data set would seem debatable. The data may be quantita-tive, voluminous and systematically gathered, but, in practice, they may be no more representative of the phenomenon in the population as a whole than a single case study. Big data, and digital data to the extent that it detaches the researcher from the pro-cess of data creation, therefore make it harder to trace the relationship between data and the phe-nomena they are seen as representing, but it makes the task no less important.

The implications of a performative perspective on data, however, go beyond examining the nature of data employed in our research: they should also encourage us to give greater recognition to the differences in the understanding of phenomena within different research traditions. While these understandings are not exclusively dependent on the types of data that a researcher uses (often referred to by the shorthand of quantitative or qualitative), the performative perspective does highlight the very different assumptions that researchers may hold about data that may be con-sequential for claims about the effects of digital data on the future of qualitative research.

Thus, even if it were to be the case that digital data, whether these are considered to be big data or not, were to lead to an increasing proportion of organizational and IS research employing quanti-tative methods (whether for reasons of conveni-ence, or because the data are seen as offering new opportunities for research), this would not mean that qualitative methods should wither away. As the performative perspective on data indicates, no methods have exclusive access to insight on social and organizational phenomena. Rather, these insights are shaped by the assumptions about data that the researcher holds. A methodological mono-culture would therefore necessarily impoverish our understanding, narrowing the range of perspectives and suppressing debate that might challenge the orthodoxy and encourage new thinking.

Although some authors, such as Donaldson (1995), have sought to discredit research, typically qualitative, which they consider to be unscientific and 'anti-management', arguments (e.g., Pfeffer, 1993; Benbasat and Weber, 1996) for greater methodological homogeneity in organizational and IS research (understood, usually, as involving a shift towards quantitative methods) have largely been based on pragmatic considerations of effi-ciency of research progress, and the cohesion and credibility of the discipline rather than claims that qualitative research is illegitimate. These argu-ments were forcefully rebutted at the time by quali-tative researchers such as Van Maanen (1995) and Robey (1996), who questioned both the desirabil-ity and the feasibility of any moves to suppress diversity. The subsequent continuing methodo-logical heterogeneity of organizational and IS research would seem to suggest that efforts to discourage the use of qualitative methods have, as yet, achieved little practical effect. Nor, for similar reasons, should we expect this to be any different in the case of big data and digital data.

Methodological pluralism has been such a long-standing, if not universally cherished, tradition in IS research (Jones, 2019c) that it would seem per-verse to abandon it simply because new data resources are available. The reasons why research-ers employ qualitative methods is rarely, if ever, because quantitative data are not available (in suf-ficient quantities) to study the phenomena they are interested in. Rather, it is because they consider qualitative data as providing distinctive and signifi-cant insight on phenomena that no amount of quantitative data can replace. There may well be situations in which digital data expand our under-standing of organizational phenomena, but this does not supplant the insights that qualitative methods can offer.

Nor is it necessarily the case that the understand-ing of phenomena from quantitative and qualitative data will be, or should be considered, convergent, such that they form part of a common research endeavour. Each offers its own perspective that may not be reconcilable with the other. The pre-factual and performative perspectives on data, for example, would seem to share little common ground and offer very different understandings of what data are and how they relate to the world. This does not mean that no dialogue is possible between perspectives, however, but this may be more in the form of challenge and provocation rather than harmonization and mutual adjustment. Any increase in quantitative research in response to digital data does not invalidate continuing qualitative inquiry.

In three respects at least, indeed, the performative perspective on data suggests an important continuing role for intensive, qualitative research. The first follows from the contingency of the enactment of data and invites investigation of the conditions of production of particular data sets. These could take many forms, such as training data sets for machine learning, electronic medical records, consultants' timesheets or website metrics. The focus here would be on understanding the processes that lead to the particular data being recorded and an awareness of how they might have been otherwise. These might be observational studies of the creation and use of data sets as they happen or interviews with those involved in the design and adoption of data sets about the choices that were made.

The second potential focus of intensive qualitative research would be the phenomenon of big data itself. A performative perspective suggests that big data are not a natural category, but are designated as such for a variety of reasons, the investigation of which would seem an important project in demystifying the 'magic' ascribed to them (Elish and Boyd, 2018). Complementing Elish and Boyd (2018), who direct most of their attention to AI and practices of data analysis, there would seem a need to examine how data come to be identified as Big in the first place. This would seem a particularly pertinent topic in organizational settings (in contrast to the scientific research settings studied by authors such as Leonelli [2014]), where the volume of nominally 'Big' data sets would often not meet the common definition of big data of being 'beyond the ability of typical database software tools to capture, store, manage and analyze' (Manyika et al., 2011: 1). Thus, we might explore how particular data come to be labelled as 'Big' and how this affects the way in which they are perceived and used.

The existence of big data is not just a matter of labelling, though: it also depends on upstream processes of transforming, editing, cleaning and assembling of data such that they can be stored, managed and analyzed (Passi and Jackson, 2018; Jones, 2019b; Leonelli and Tempini, 2020). A third focus for intensive qualitative research would thus be on this mundane but essential work (Lohr [2014] reports that it may take up more than half of data scientists' time) that is often overlooked in studies of data science that prefer to focus on the more glamorous analysis that follows once the data set has been assembled. This 'data wrangling', 'data munging', 'data janitor work' or 'materialization work' (Lohr, 2014; Jones, 2019b), is critical, though, both in terms of constituting the specific 'data in practice' (Jones et al., 2019) that are available for analysis and in shaping the characteristics of the resulting data set. Such attention to the judgements involved in the production of data would seem important in its own right, but may also provide a useful counterweight to claims of the objectivity of subsequent analyses. The point is not that the data sets are pure invention that bears no relation to the phenomena they are considered to represent, but that they are necessarily partial, both in the sense of being incomplete (the map is not the territory, it is an inevitably selective representation) and in the sense of being biased (the selectivity distorts the representation, maybe not intentionally or significantly in terms of the uses to which the data will be put, but to some extent). Qualitative researchers can make an important contribution to big data research in shedding light on these practices.

3.6 Conclusions

In this chapter, I have not sought to address the implications of what might be considered as the distinctive qualities of digital data, such as editability, expansibility and transfigurability (Kallinikos et al., 2013) for qualitative research. While these may be significant, they beg the question of what data are in the first place. I have therefore rather sought to address the nature of data in general as a basis for exploring the continuing relevance of qualitative research. This would seem all the more important as we enter an era of data abundance, where influential discourses encourage us to focus on what we can do with these data, without paying attention to where they come from. Although these discourses vary in their prescriptions, whether arguing for a transformation of the logic of research from deduction to induction, an epistemological shift towards computational (hence implicitly quantitative) social science, or an expanded resource for all methods, I propose that they share some common assumptions about these new digital data.

This chapter has sought to offer a critical analysis of the nature of data that questions these assumptions and to present an alternative, performative perspective on data. This perspective, it is argued, suggests a continuing agenda for qualitative research in studying the constitution of data in practice. Such research does not seek to discredit digital data, especially at scale, as a source of insight on organizational phenomena, but to draw attention to some caveats about the representations of these phenomena that they offer.

References

Anderson, C. (2008). The end of theory: The data deluge makes the scientific method obsolete. *Wired*.

Barley, S. R. (1986). Technology as an occasion for structuring: Evidence from observations of CT scanners and the social order of radiology departments. *Administrative Science Quarterly*, 31(1), 78–108.

Benbasat, I. and Weber, R. (1996). Research commentary: Rethinking 'diversity' in information systems research. *Information Systems Research*, 7(4), 389–399.

Boyd, D. and Crawford, K. (2012). Critical questions for big data: Provocations for a cultural, technological, and scholarly phenomenon. *Information, Community, & Society*, 15(5), 662–679.

Burrell, J. (2016). How the machine 'thinks': Understanding opacity in machine learning algorithms. *Big Data & Society*, 3(1), 1–12.

Callebaut, W. (2012). Scientific perspectivism: A philosopher of science's response to the challenge of big data biology. *Studies in History and Philosophy of Science Part C: Studies in History and Philosophy of Biological and Biomedical Sciences*, 43(1), 69–80.

Chang, R. M., Kauffman, R. J. and Kwon, Y. (2014). Understanding the paradigm shift to computational social science in the presence of big data. *Decision Support Systems*, 63, 67–80.

Conte, R., Gilbert, N., Bonelli, G., Cioffi-Revilla, C., Deffuant, G., Kertesz, J. et al. (2012). Manifesto of computational social science. *European Physical Journal Special Topics*, 214(1), 325–346.

Coveney, P. V., Dougherty, E. R. and Highfield, R. R. (2016). Big data need big theory too. *Philosophical Transactions of the Royal Society A: Mathematical, Physical and Engineering Sciences*, 374(2080), 20160153.

Cukier, K. and Mayer-Schönberger, V. (2013). The rise of big data: How it's changing the way we think about the world. *Foreign Affairs*, 92(3), 28–40.

Donaldson, L. (1995). *American Anti-Management Theories of Organization: A Critique of Paradigm Proliferation*. Cambridge: Cambridge University Press.

Elish, M. C. and Boyd, D. (2018). Situating methods in the magic of big data and AI. *Communication Monographs*, 85(1), 57–80.

Fleck, L. (1981). *Genesis and Development of a Scientific Fact*. London and Chicago, IL: University of Chicago Press.

Flick, U. (2009). *An Introduction to Qualitative Research*, 4th edition. London: Sage.

Foucault, M. (1977). *Discipline and Punish: The Birth of the Prison*. London: Allen Lane.

Frické, M. (2015). Big data and its epistemology. *Journal of the Association for Information Science and Technology*, 66(4), 651–661.

Friedman, M. (1953). *Essays in Positive Economics*. London and Chicago, IL: University of Chicago Press.

Geertz, C. (1973). *The Interpretation of Cultures*. New York, NY: Basic Books.

George, G., Osinga, E. C., Lavie, D. and Scott, B. A. (2016). Big data and data science methods for management research. *Academy of Management Journal*, 59(5), 1493–1507.

Gitelman, L. and Jackson, V. (2013). Introduction. In L. Gitelman (ed.), *Raw Data Is an Oxymoron*. Cambridge, MA: MIT Press, pp. 1–14.

Golden-Biddle, K. and Locke, K. (1993). Appealing work: An investigation of how ethnographic texts convince. *Organization Science*, 4(4), 595–616.

Grover, V. (2020). Do we need to understand the world to know it? Knowledge in a big data world. *Journal of Global Information Technology Management*, 23(1), 1–4.

Haag, S. and Cummings, M. (2013). *Management Information Systems for the Information Age*, 9th edition. New York, NY: McGraw-Hill Irwin.

Hammersley, M. (2008). *Questioning Qualitative Inquiry: Critical Essays*. London: Sage.

Hunter, S. D. (2010). Same technology, different outcome? Reinterpreting Barley's technology as an occasion for structuring. *European Journal of Information Systems*, 19(6), 689–703.

Johnson, S. L., Gray, P. and Sarker, S. (2019). Revisiting IS research practice in the era of big data. *Information and Organization*, 29(1), 41–56.

Jones, M. (2019a). What we talk about when we talk about (big) data. *Journal of Strategic Information Systems*, 28(1), 3–16.

Jones, M. (2019b). Examining materialisation work in data reuse in critical care. EGOS Colloquium: Enlightening the Future: The Challenge for Organizations. Edinburgh, UK.

Jones, M. (2019c). Beyond convergence: Rethinking pluralism in IS research. International Conference on Information Systems, Munich, Germany.

Jones, M., Blackwell, A., Prince, K., Meakins, S., Simpson, A. and Vuylsteke, A. (2019). Data as process: From objective resource to contingent performance. In T. Reay, T. Silber, A. Langley and H. Tsoukas (eds), *Institutions and Organizations: A Process View*. Oxford: Oxford University Press, pp. 227–250.

Kallinikos, J., Aaltonen, A. and Marton, A. (2013). The ambivalent ontology of digital artifacts. *Management Information Systems Quarterly*, 37(2), 357–370.

Kitchin, R. (2014a). Big data, new epistemologies and paradigm shifts. *Big Data & Society*, 1(1), 1–12.

Kitchin, R. (2014b). *The Data Revolution: Big Data, Open Data, Data Infrastructures and Their Consequences*. London: Sage.

Kitchin, R. and McArdle, G. (2016). What makes big data, big data? Exploring the ontological characteristics of 26 datasets. *Big Data & Society*, 3(1), 1–10.

Lazer, D., Kennedy, R., King, G. and Vespignani, A. (2014). The parable of Google Flu: Traps in big data analysis. *Science*, 343(6176), 1203–1205.

Lazer, D., Pentland, A., Adamic, L., Aral, S., Barabási, A. L., Brewer, D. et al. (2009). Computational social science. *Science*, 323(5915), 721–723.

Leonelli, S. (2014). What difference does quantity make? On the epistemology of big data in biology. *Big Data & Society*, 1(1), 1–11.

Leonelli, S. and Tempini, N. (2020). *Data Journeys in the Sciences*. Cham, Switzerland: Springer International.

Lohr, S. (2014). For big-data scientists, 'janitor work' is key hurdle to insights. *The New York Times*.

Manyika, J., Chui, M., Brown, B., Bughin, J., Dobbs, R., Roxburgh, C. and Hung Byers, A. (2011). *Big Data: The Next Frontier for Innovation, Competition, and Productivity*. McKinsey Global Institute.

Mayer-Schönberger, V. and Cukier, K. (2013). *Big Data: A Revolution that Will Transform How We Live, Work and Think*. London: John Murray.

Mazzocchi, F. (2015). Could big data be the end of theory in science? *EMBO Reports*, 16(10), 1250–1255.

McAfee, A. and Brynjolfsson, E. (2012). Big data: The management revolution. *Harvard Business Review*, 90(10), 60–68.

Mills, K. A. (2018). What are the threats and potentials of big data for qualitative research? *Qualitative Research*, 18(6), 591–603.

Moritz, M. (2016). Big data's 'streetlight effect': Where and how we look affects what we see. *The Conversation*, http://theconversation.com/big-datas-streetlight-effect-where-and-how-we-look-affects-what-we-see-58122.

Olteanu, A., Castillo, C., Diaz, F. and Kiciman, E. (2017). Social data: Biases, methodological pitfalls, and ethical boundaries. *Frontiers in Big Data*, 2(13), 1–33.

Passi, S. and Jackson, S. J. (2018). Trust in data science: Collaboration, translation, and accountability in corporate data science projects. *Proceedings of the ACM on Human-Computer Interaction*, 2(CSCW), 136, 1–28.

Pentland, A. (2009). Reality mining of mobile communications: Toward a new deal on data. In S. Dutta and I. Mia (eds), *The Global Information Technology Report 2008–2009*. Geneva, Switzerland: World Economic Forum, pp. 75–80.

Pfeffer, J. (1993). Barriers to the advance of organizational science: Paradigm development as a dependent variable. *Academy of Management Review*, 18(4), 599–620.

Pfeffer, J. and Sutton, R. I. (2006). Evidence-based management. *Harvard Business Review*, 84(1), 62.

Powell, W. W., Horvath, A. and Brandtner, C. (2016). Click and mortar: Organizations on the web. *Research in Organizational Behavior*, 36, 101–120.

Power, M. (1997). *The Audit Society: Rituals of verification*. Oxford: Oxford University Press.

Prensky, M. (2009). H. sapiens digital: From digital immigrants and digital natives to digital wisdom. *Innovate: Journal of Online Education*, 5(3), online article.

Revellino, S. and Mouritsen, J. (2015). Accounting as an engine: The performativity of calculative practices and the dynamics of innovation. *Management Accounting Research*, 28, 31–49.

Rieder, G. and Simon, J. (2016). Datatrust: Or, the political quest for numerical evidence and the epistemologies of big data. *Big Data & Society*, 3(1), 1–6.

Robey, D. (1996). Research commentary – Diversity in information systems research: Threat, promise, and responsibility. *Information Systems Research*, 7(4), 400–408.

Strong, C. (2014). The challenge of 'big data': What does it mean for the qualitative research industry? *Qualitative Market Research*, 17(4), 336–342.

Tashakkori, A. and Teddlie, C. (2009). Integrating qualitative and quantitative approaches to research. In L. Bickman and D. Rog (eds), *The SAGE Handbook of Applied Social Research Methods*. Thousand Oaks, CA: Sage, pp. 283–317.

Tonidandel, S., King, E. B. and Cortina, J. M. (2018). Big data methods: Leveraging modern data analytic techniques to build organizational science. *Organizational Research Methods*, 21(3), 525–547.

Tufekci, Z. (2014). Big questions for social media big data: Representativeness, validity and other methodological pitfalls. Proceedings of the Eighth International AAAI Conference on Weblogs and Social Media, Ann Arbor, MI.

Tuomi, I. (1999). Data is more than knowledge. *Journal of Management Information Systems*, 16(3), 107–121.

Turban, E. (2006). *Information Technology for Management: Transforming Organizations in the Digital Economy*, 5th edition. Hoboken, NJ: Wiley.

Van Maanen, J. (1995). Fear and loathing in organization studies. *Organization Science*, 6(6), 687–692.

Van Maanen, J. (1979). Reclaiming qualitative methods for organizational research: A preface. *Administrative Science Quarterly*, 24(4), 520–526.

Weick, K. E. (1995). *Sensemaking in Organizations*. London: Sage.

Wenzel, R. and Van Quaquebeke, N. (2018). The double-edged sword of big data in organizational and management research: A review of opportunities and risks. *Organizational Research Methods*, 21(3), 548–591.

Zuboff, S. (2019). *The Age of Surveillance Capitalism: The Fight for a Human Future at the New Frontier of Power*. London: Profile Books.

Big Data, Little Understanding

RUDY A. HIRSCHHEIM and DAVID WHITCHURCH*

Big data is a vague term for a massive phenomenon that has rapidly become an obsession with entrepreneurs, scientists, governments and the media. (Harford, 2014)

4.1 Introduction

There has been much written about 'big data' (measured in petabytes, exabytes and zettabytes, and in the future yottabytes) and 'big data analytics' (embodying the algorithms and quantitative tools that are applied to the data)[1] and how these will transform business. Both the popular and academic literature is replete with stories and claims about how big data has revolutionized and will continue to revolutionize how organizations operate, how they compete, and how individuals and society will be affected – both positively and negatively. Big data analytics and its sister technologies 'machine learning' and 'artificial intelligence' are touted as the next wave of technological advancement which will obviate the need for humans to deal with repetitive processes (they will be automated through robotic process automation – RPA), while traditional (and non-traditional) organizational decision-making, operations and jobs will be transformed. The ability to analyze the seemingly endless mountains of textual, numeric, audio and visual data coming from not only traditional company sources but from immensely rich social media platforms makes big data the *sine qua non* of future business and society. Clearly, the world has been inexorably transformed and things will never be the same. Or so it is claimed.

For those of us who have been around for a long time and heard and lived through the numerous technological revolutions, these big data assertions sound suspiciously like prior technological waves which were also promoted as 'revolutionary' and 'transformative'. Is this different? If one believes Tom Davenport (2014) and his book *Big Data @ Work*, one is left accepting that big data is truly different; it is not just hype. Perhaps. But like so many of the other technological innovations which were hyped to death, which promised revolutionary changes, were so-called 'game changers', the big data bandwagon shares a number of similar characteristics. First, there are reportedly existing cases which used big data to great effect – for example, Amazon, Google, Netflix, Zillow, Facebook and Uber (cf. Bernard Marr's (2016) book *Big Data in Practice*). Second, there appears to be no end to the number of consultants, business executives, journalists and academics who write and speak about the importance of big data and the need for organizations to develop a big data strategy. Third, there is a level of 'believability' in their claims. They 'make sense', at least on the surface. Fourth, and more importantly, there are some critics who caution that big data can have significant dysfunctional consequences. This is eloquently documented in, for example, Shoshana Zuboff's (2019) book *The Age of Surveillance Capitalism*. So it seems appropriate to take a look 'under the Big Data covers' as it were to see if big data is truly revolutionary (whatever revolutionary means) or if it is just the next iteration of the technology hype cycle. And that is what we propose to do.

---

* This chapter is based on and is an extension of Hirschheim's (2020) journal article: The attack on understanding: How big data and theory have led us astray.

[1] Although 'big data' and 'big data analytics' are separate but related notions, where big data is the data set used and big data analytics comprise the algorithms, methods and tools used to undertake the analysis of the data, we will typically treat them using one term – 'big data'. See Gandomi and Haider (2015) for a more detailed discussion of these terms.

In this chapter, we wish to examine a number of the underlying assumptions associated with the supposed big data revolution. Our analysis will highlight some of the fallacies and misconceptions that lie behind big data, and how these assumptions can lead to unintended and dysfunctional consequences. In particular, we wish to explore how these dysfunctions might manifest themselves when it comes to organizational knowledge and practice. While there has also been no shortage of books and papers both promoting big data and offering examples of successful big data use; there have concomitantly been others who have questioned this hype and optimism, raising concerns about dystopian data collection and the loss of privacy and identity. What seems to be lacking, however, is a more in-depth analysis of how big data relates to the broader notion of 'understanding' and then how this links to practice. It is this three-part relationship which is the focus of this chapter.

Our thesis is that while big data provides correlations and patterns of the behaviours of large populations, it does not yield understanding/insight. These behaviour patterns are considered 'knowledge', but are they? We contend that the big data community have mistakenly adopted the view that what they produce is knowledge and, moreover, it is the same as understanding. Knowledge may be the product of research, but this is not the same as understanding, which is how to use that knowledge in practice. We argue that academics (and practitioners) involved in big data research continue to make the same mistakes, continue to embrace erroneous assumptions about what they should be doing with their research, what the products of the research should be and how we can help drive practice. Big data is just the latest in a series of waves of technological advancements which will supposedly change what we do and how we do it. But we question whether this is indeed the case. And if it is, what are its likely implications? We are hopeful that this chapter will help bring these issues to the fore, and possibly allow for critical reflection which would then lead to meaningful dialogue taking place. The chapter is structured as follows. First, we review the case for big data – why it is revolutionary and how organizations, society and individuals can benefit from its application. Next,

we look at some of the underlying assumptions adopted by those promoting big data use. We examine whether these assumptions are valid and in what circumstances. We next examine whether the results of big data analytics lead to understanding in its broadest sense, and how understanding informs practice. We then offer a case study which embraces the tenets of big data and explore what the results of adopting big data were in this case. It offers a cautionary tale of the reality of big data use – that is, it is far from a panacea. We then reflect on what we have learned and offer our thoughts on the implications of adopting big data, for better or worse. Our analysis leads us to conclude that while big data offers promise, the hype surrounding it has obscured the potential dangers in its use. Hopefully, our critical appraisal can help the field take a more nuanced view of this new technology, putting safeguards in place to ensure that big data use (including big data analytics, machine learning, artificial intelligence and the algorithms that they develop) does not lead to dysfunction.

4.2 Big Data and the Belief in Its Value in Generating Knowledge

Big data has been defined by many authors using different notions of what 'big data' actually entails. Goes (2014), for example, states: 'Big data has been defined by the 4 V's: volume, velocity, variety, and veracity. The new paradigm comes by combining these dimensions.' Harford (2014) suggests that big data is of interest specifically because it is what he calls 'found data' – that is, 'the digital exhaust of web searches, credit card payments and mobiles pinging the nearest phone mast'. In essence, it is not just the volume which makes it attractive, but rather the source of this data. Grover et al. (2020) seem to capture the essence of what big data is when they define it as:

> . . . involving large and often heterogeneous datasets represented in multiple formats (qualitative, quantitative, video, image, audio, etc.). These datasets are obtained mainly from the digital traces left behind by various groups of users (including bots and other relatively autonomous software or hardware agents) interacting with online

platforms. These data traces are mainly noninvoked, capture naturally occurring interactions, and are therefore collected for purposes unrelated to academic research … Importantly, such data corpora are reflective of the contemporary explosion in the volume, variety, and velocity of the data available … This can be contrasted with 'small' data studies that use either structured (e.g., survey instruments) or nonstructured data (e.g., interviews), mostly collected by the researchers themselves from primary or secondary sources.

It is important to note that the data that are used typically come from digital traces left behind by participants who may or may not be human. The data involve the activities these participants engage in on various online platforms. They typically include software 'bots' and other types of agents. Thus, the 'data' have properties which are new and somewhat different from the past. Some argue that this big data is actually 'better' or more 'accurate' than traditional data sources. For example, Stephens-Davidowitz (2017) claims that data scraped from Google searches provides a much richer base by which to interpret people's 'real' beliefs and intentions. His provocatively titled book *Everybody Lies* implies that asking people questions via, for example, surveys, will only elicit responses which the respondents think are the proper or 'acceptable' answers to give. Shifting the questions so that answers can be given anonymously will provide what people truly believe. This assumed 'anonymous source' is the Google search engine. Stephens-Davidowitz presents a variety of large population behaviours which are gleaned by looking at millions of Google searches. Many of his results run counter to the 'accepted wisdom', which he then uses to support his contention that perceived anonymity leads to better data, which lead to better results.[2]

---

[2] Whether this data is 'better' or not is certainly subject to debate, but one thing is clear: while big data offers the ability to develop 'results', it is important to realize that it cannot 'explain' why the results are what they are. Behaviour is just behaviour. As Lee and Sobol (2012, emphasis in the original) note: 'Data … reveals *what* people do, but not *why* they do it. And understanding the why is critical for innovation.'

One reason for the interest in big data is that it offers the illusion of objectivity, accuracy, knowledge, better science, legitimacy and progress – progress for understanding the world better and making the world better (cf. Bell et al., 2009; Galliers et al., 2017). And there are many good stories about how big data has led to cost savings, increased profitability and the like. Walker (2015), in his book *From Big Data to Big Profits*, documents a variety of companies, including Uber, Netflix, Google, LinkedIn, Zillow and Amazon, that have used big data to drive profits. Baesens et al. (2016), in analyzing the various areas where big data could be used, offer a variety of innovative big data applications, including: Online-to-Offline Commerce; Networks of Smart Vehicles; and Proactive Customer Care. Alharthi et al. (2017) present several newer examples of companies (e.g., Etihad Airways, Walt Disney, United Parcel Service, Dublin City Council and the Daimler Group) who have had success with their big data projects. Some have gone so far as to proclaim that 'big data has become a strategic economic resource, similar in significance and liquidity to currency and gold' (Johnson, 2012).

While there are clearly instances of positive results, one has to ask: does the presence of such large quantities of data really lead to better understanding? As many commentators have claimed, the answer is at best equivocal, at worst, 'no'. Grover et al. (2020) write:

> The ready access to big data and powerful analysis methods may also encourage researchers to rely on size as a justification for the novelty of datasets as well as drawing on the power of computationally-intensive methods to impress the reader. If this is, indeed, a strong tendency in BDR [big data research], it may come at the cost of neglecting deeper intellectual engagement with substantive research questions that provide disciplinary value through their long-term relevance to the corpus of cumulative IS knowledge.

Nor does the availability of large data sets necessarily solve the problem that managers can make better decisions with more data. Fifty plus years ago, Ackoff argued that one of the great management myths was that managers needed more information. In fact, he claimed that managers suffered 'more from an over-abundance of irrelevant information than from a lack of relevant information' (Ackoff, 1967: B147). For those who might claim that Ackoff was correct and that with the application of big data analytics 'irrelevant' data would now become 'relevant' data, we would argue 'how could this be proved?' 'How can one be sure that through the application of big data analytics, irrelevant data either gets discarded or turns into relevant data?' 'And who determines what is relevant and irrelevant, for whom, and during what time period?' This is an issue discussed at length in Matthew Jones's insightful essay 'What we talk about when we talk about (big) data'. Jones (2019) makes a distinction between what he terms 'data in principle', which are what is actually recorded, versus 'data in practice', which is how they are used. He argues that only the latter are valuable, and they typically comprise 'only a small and not necessarily representative subset of the former'. A study undertaken by Veritas in 2016 noted that 85 per cent of data collected is irrelevant to business and is costing companies $3.3 trillion. The report claimed that it is the 'dark and redundant, obsolete and trivial (ROT) data' that has created this massive drain on resources (Veritas, 2016). Similar concerns are raised by Constantiou and Kallinikos (2015), who question whether those advocating big data analytics appreciate the semiotics which lie behind the notion of 'data'. They are especially concerned with alternative conceptions of 'meaning compatibility'. Questions associated with what relevant data is and how one can be sure the data is 'valid' is a subject to which we believe too little attention has been given. As Grover et al. (2020) worry: 'future generations of IS scholars may unintentionally inherit a brave new world of research where big data, computationally-intensive analysis techniques, and evidence triangulation will reign over theory, disciplinary relevance, and the importance of having a cumulative tradition'.

4.3 Big Data and Correlations

Not everyone is enamoured with big data. Some have argued that big data and associated data analytic techniques lead to lots and lots of correlations, but no theory. They argue that theory is needed to explain what data analytics discovers. Without an underlying theory, all one has are correlations. What lies beneath the correlations? Just because two things are correlated does not mean we understand anything. We might be able to predict behaviour, but understand nothing about why. This is the point made in Lee and Sobol (2012, emphasis in the original), where they state: 'Data . . . reveals *what* people do, but not *why* they do it'. Smith (2020), in his paper 'Data mining fool's gold', argues that correlations may be spurious or misleading, involve dubious data or come from data not representative of the population. He writes: 'Social media data are currently fashionable because they provide vast amounts of data, but their usefulness is questionable. Are the people who use social media representative of the population? Are the messages they send representative of their feelings? Are they even people?'

Others, such as Anderson (2008), proclaim that theory is no longer needed. The only thing that matters is being able to predict behaviour. As long as big data analytics can successfully predict behaviour, theory is irrelevant. He writes: 'Out with every theory of human behavior, from linguistics to sociology. Forget taxonomy, ontology, and psychology. Who knows why people do what they do? The point is they do it, and we can track and measure it with unprecedented fidelity.' Anderson concludes that: 'Correlation supersedes causation, and science can advance even without coherent models, unified theories, or really any mechanistic explanation at all. There's no reason to cling to our old ways.' Anderson's pronouncement caused quite a backlash from the scientific community, an example of which was Pigliucci (2009) claiming that what 'is perfectly clear is that he [Anderson] doesn't understand much about either science or the scientific method'.

Nevertheless, the big data bandwagon rolls on. Siegel (2013), for example, noted – with regard to predictive analytics – that: 'We usually don't know about causation, and we often don't necessarily care . . . the objective is more to predict than it is to understand the world . . . It just needs to work; prediction trumps explanation.' According to

Kitchin (2014), the proponents of big data analytics embrace four basic pillars, each of which he argues is fallacious. These pillars are: (1) Big Data can capture a whole domain and provide full resolution; (2) there is no need for a priori theory, models or hypotheses; (3) through the application of agnostic data analytics the data can speak for themselves free of human bias or framing, and any patterns and relationships within big data are inherently meaningful and truthful; and (4) meaning transcends context or domain-specific knowledge, thus can be interpreted by anyone who can decode a statistic or data visualization. With regard to providing full resolution, Kitchin, quoting Ribes and Jackson (2013), notes that 'data are not simply natural and essential elements that are abstracted from the world in neutral and objective ways and can be accepted at face value; data are created within a complex assemblage that actively shapes its constitution'. Next, he argues that big data does not arise from nowhere. For Kitchin, 'systems are designed to capture certain kinds of data and the analytics and algorithms used are based on scientific reasoning and have been refined through scientific testing. As such, an inductive strategy of identifying patterns within data does not occur in a scientific vacuum.' Third, just as data are not generated free from theory, neither can they simply speak for themselves free of human bias or framing. Lastly, he argues that 'whilst data can be interpreted free of context and domain-specific expertise, such an epistemological interpretation is likely to be anaemic or unhelpful as it lacks embedding in wider debates and knowledge'.

In the end however, he concludes:

> At present, whilst it is clear that Big Data is a disruptive innovation, presenting the possibility of a new approach to science, the form of this approach is not set, with two potential paths proposed that have divergent epistemologies – empiricism, wherein the data can speak for themselves free of theory, and data-driven science that radically modifies the existing scientific method by blending aspects of abduction, induction and deduction. Given the weaknesses in the empiricist arguments it seems likely that the data-driven approach will eventually win out and over time,

as Big Data becomes more common and new data analytics are advanced, will present a strong challenge to the established knowledge-driven scientific method. To accompany such a transformation the philosophical underpinnings of data-driven science, with respect to its epistemological tenets, principles and methodology, need to be worked through and debated to provide a robust theoretical framework for the new paradigm.

An analogy here might be helpful. In medicine, doctors prescribe drugs which have proven successful in dealing with specific ailments. If using drug X helps the patient deal with illness Z, it is prescribed. Why drug X works, however, is not always known. Consider the case of a patient suffering from 'pouchitis' which is an inflammation in the lining of a pouch created during surgery as a replacement for a removed colon. Gastroenterologists don't know what the cause of pouchitis is, but they treat it with the drug ciprofloxacin – a very powerful fluoroquinolone antibiotic that fights bacteria in the body. Exactly why an antibacterial treatment works on an inflammation is unclear. And that is where biomedical research comes in. By understanding chemical compounds, their molecular structures and their impact on human cells, pharmacology develops a 'theory' of why a particular drug works. Without such a pharmacological 'theory', one does not know why a drug works, or why it works in some patients but not others, or for how long, or what the correct dosage should be and so on. For patients who hear the phrase 'we think the drug works in the following way, but don't understand the mechanisms why', this is not likely to instil a sense of comfort in the drug. But the drug is prescribed because the data suggest that it 'works'. We feel the same way about big data. Pronouncements about such and such correlations are hardly reassuring that the researchers can explain why the observed human behaviour is the way it is.

More recently, one can start to see some researchers changing their belief that 'big data obviates the need for theory' to a more nuanced view where theory and big data need not be incompatible. Maass et al. (2018), for example, suggest that the two could be combined to yield better results. Simsek et al. (2019) similarly see value in some possible combined approach. They write:

> Our message is one of optimism tempered with realism. We believe that innovative research approaches concurrently leveraging the power of big data and the plurality of theoretical and empirical approaches can complement to advance both management research and big data practices. But, even as the need and opportunities for such innovations are manifold, they remain complex, challenging, and perhaps risky pursuits for individual researchers.

Johnson et al. (2019), noting the potential of big data, propose a research approach which leverages big data in building and testing theory. They believe that big data can be beneficial in the pursuit of theory-informed research. After considering the role of big data to theory, Abbasi et al. (2016) offer a view which sees possible synergy:

> ... big data has potentially important implications for theory. From an information value chain perspective, big data sources and associated IT artifacts have distinct implications for both knowledge acquisition and for decisions and actions (and related outcomes), which include system usage, performance, and satisfaction. The key nuances of big data artifacts stem from the four V characteristics. On one hand, these characteristics may simply inform well established IS theories by playing the role of antecedent constructs or of moderator/mediator variables. On the other hand, these characteristics can introduce complexity and risk in IT artifacts increasingly relying on big data, thereby opening up exciting new possibilities for utilization of theories that have seen relatively limited usage in IS.

They conclude by noting: 'one cannot understate the role of "theory" in big data research, we do need to acknowledge that theory has different forms in different traditions of research, and, thus, as research community, we need to be open to different types of abstractions offered as theoretical contributions'.

Notwithstanding these proposals for marrying big data with more traditional research approaches, Fricke (2015) is not buying it. He succinctly asserts that: 'data-driven science, the "fourth paradigm," is a chimera. Science needs problems, thoughts, theories, and designed experiments. If anything, science needs more theories and less data.' Pigliucci (2009) agrees. He contends: 'science advances only if it can provide explanations, failing which, it becomes an activity more akin to stamp collecting. Now, there is an area where petabytes of information can be used for their own sake. But please don't call it science.'

4.4 Big Data and Understanding

Bloom (1956) argues that 'understanding is the ability to marshal skills and facts wisely and appropriately, through effective application, analysis, synthesis, and evaluation. Doing something correctly is not, by itself, evidence of understanding.' It might have simply been the product of a set of codified rules appropriately applied. 'To understand is not only to have done something correctly but to be able to explain why a particular skill, approach, body of knowledge, etc. is – or is not – appropriate in a particular situation.'

John Dewey (1933) summarized the idea of understanding most clearly in *How We Think*. Understanding is the result of facts acquiring meaning for the individual. He writes: 'To grasp the meaning of a thing, an event, or a situation is to see it in its relations to other things: to see how it operates or functions, what consequences follow from it, what causes it, what uses it can be put to. This is in contrast to a thing without meaning to us, whose relations are not grasped' (1933: 137).

Wittgenstein would agree. In Wittgenstein's (1953) seminal book *Philosophical Investigations*, he argued that to have an understanding is not to have in mind a picture or an image, rather, it is to be able to do things with regard to the phenomenon – to perform it, to comment on it, to answer questions about it. For Sandelands (1990), explanation can be imparted, but understanding can only be developed. With reference to Ryle (1949), Sandelands notes it makes sense to ask, 'at what moment something was explained, but not to ask at what moment it is understood'.

Big data is like Dewey's 'a thing without meaning', or Wittgenstein's 'picture theory of meaning', or Sandeland's 'knowledge that explains things'.

One can perform all sorts of analysis using the data, but how is this transformed into understanding? As Smith (2020) describes, 'correlations do not equal understanding'.

With big data, machine learning and AI, a machine might be able to correctly solve a given problem, but does the machine 'understand' why? This sounds remarkably similar to the Turing test which Alan Turing proposed in 1950. He said in order for a computer to pass the Turing test, it would have to produce intelligent behaviour which was indistinguishable from that of a human. In other words, a human would not be able to tell if what was producing this intelligent behaviour was a computer or a human. While machines that make decisions mimicking human decision-making using the most sophisticated technology are now widely used, these machines do not 'understand' their decisions nor the implications of their actions. To be blunt, machines are not humans. They may exhibit behaviour which imitates that of a human, but imitate is not the same as actually 'being'. Such a dialogue is not new as the philosophical discussions about AI and human beings have been debated for well over half a century. We do not wish to enter this debate other than to acknowledge that a key point is that big data/machine learning/AI does not produce understanding. And it is 'understanding' that is what is important. We contend that without understanding, the knowledge produced by big data can lead to practice that is highly flawed and potentially dangerous.

An interesting twist to the 'understanding' dilemma associated with big data is to consider the reverse side where the human can no longer 'understand' the analysis or output of big data. Ekbia et al. (2015) note that big data poses a number of challenges to human beings:

> ... in terms of their cognitive capacities and limitations. On one hand, with improved storage and processing technologies, we become aware of how Big Data can help address problems on a macro-scale. On the other hand, even with theories of how a system or a phenomenon works, its interactions are so complex and massive that human brains simply cannot comprehend them.

This is a point also noted by Weinberger (2012) in his book *Too Big to Know*.

Fundamentally, our position is that without understanding, one may possess some type of knowledge, but not have ability to put this into practice or in the Wittgensteinian sense 'to perform it, to comment on it'. Consider the case of tennis. One can read any number of books on how to hit a forehand, but it is not until one actually starts to hit forehands that one 'understands' how to hit a forehand. One can read all the literature one wants on how Raphael Nadal imparts an incredible amount of spin on his forehand, but if you're not a tennis player, do you really 'understand' what this means or what kind of forehand this is? Non-tennis players can watch Nadal's forehand and think 'what's so special about that shot?' That is where understanding (or lack thereof) comes into play. For the non-tennis player, perhaps the best that can be hoped for is some appreciation for what goes into hitting a Nadal forehand, but not true understanding. And that is the point: through the surrogate of big data analytics, one can argue that our knowledge about such matters is 'better' (whatever that means), but is it? One succumbs to the illusion that more data, more sophisticated data analysis leads to 'better [fill in the blank]'. Often, it isn't the preponderance of data that leads to insight, but rather a specific case that resonates and is meaningful to the recipient. Yet, big data has the potential to drive out the insights that can be gained from unique circumstances, from analyzing specific human activities.

This is a theme taken up by Tricia Wang (2016) in her call for the use of 'thick data', which emerged out of her work with Nokia. She defines 'thick data' as 'precious data from humans that cannot be quantified'. For Wang, an ethnographer, *thick data* is detailed human behavioural data and is formed using ethnographic research methods to observe and analyze human emotions, actions, and perceptions. The stories and lives of prospective consumers of a company's product/services are critical to understanding whether these individuals will become customers or not. Such information cannot be gathered and analyzed by machines simply through the click of a button. It is achieved through constant research and by understanding *why* something is happening, not just *what* happened. She believes that organizations need to combine thick data with big data to be successful. She contrasts Nokia as an example of what happens when only big data is used for decision-making with Netflix, which used both to become one of the most successful companies on Earth. She also offered the example of NSA's Skynet, which used mobile device data to target suspected terrorists. Without thick data to supplement the big data gathered, Skynet likely was responsible for the killing of over 2,400 Pakistani, Yemeni and Somali individuals, the vast majority of whom were not terrorists (Naughton, 2016). This is what can happen when only big data are used to make decisions. Wang's plea for the use of thick data to complement big data is similar to Lindstrom's call for the importance of using 'small data' in any major organizational decision. Lindstrom's (2016) book, *Small Data: The Tiny Clues that Uncover Huge Trends*, is based on his time at LEGO, where he noted that the company had shunned detailed behavioural research with LEGO users in favour of large data sets. This led to several bad decisions, which almost led to the company's demise. Fortunately, Lindstrom convinced management that they needed to go back and study actual use behaviour. These small data sets showed where big data had led to numerous erroneous perceptions about LEGO's products and what needed to be changed, which they ultimately did.

Clearly, big data alone will not yield insight, nor understanding. Even the practitioner community worries about the lack of 'insight' which comes from big data. Dykes (2016), writing in *Forbes* magazine, maintains that what is missing from much of big data is 'actionable insights' – that is, what to do with the products of big data analysis. For Dykes, it is the missing actionable insights; for us, it is the missing understanding.

To drive home what our concerns are with the adoption of big data, and what it can mean for an organization, we offer a case study of big data adoption and use. In presenting the case, and then reflecting on what can be learned from it, we hope to shed light on the often-overlooked aspects of the application of big data.

4.5 Case Introduction: A Big Data Solution to a Public Policy Problem – Rising Pedestrian Deaths from Vehicle Crashes

From 2013 to 2018, pedestrian fatalities for motor vehicle crashes in the United States were on the rise. In 2018, 6,482 pedestrians were killed, signifying a 3.4 per cent increase from the prior year, and the largest number of pedestrian fatalities since 1990 (NHTSA, 2019). Key players in efforts to reduce pedestrian fatalities include the National Highway Traffic Safety Administration (NHTSA) and the US Department of Transportation Federal Highway Administration (FHWA), who maintain a myriad of funding opportunities for state, metropolitan and local governments who wish to improve pedestrian safety (US DOT, 2018). A ubiquitous (and reasonable) requirement to receive these federal funds for highway safety projects is to prove projects will have quantifiable impacts in reducing pedestrian fatalities or injuries. What has become the generally accepted means of proof is referred to as Data-Driven Safety Analysis (DDSA).

4.5.1 Highway Safety Methodology: Data-Driven Safety Analysis

Traditionally, state and local transportation agencies relied on 'hot spot' methods to identify roadway segments and intersections which may benefit from engineering or other types of countermeasures. These methodologies use crash history information, including crash location and severity, to plot crashes. Clusters of crashes are then identified and subsequently used to prioritize implementation of countermeasures. A weakness of traditional highway safety methods is that severe crashes are widely dispersed in most roadway networks, so the number of severe crashes for an individual roadway segment or intersection is usually low and fluctuates over time. However, the most problematic weakness of traditional highway safety methods is that they do not consider roadway segments or intersections on which no crashes occurred in the past. Data-driven safety analysis differs from traditional 'hot spot' safety analysis in that its methods use crash, roadway, traffic and other 'big data' information to create predictive models which identify risk factors. The risk factors can subsequently be used to screen an entire roadway network to identify segments and intersections which can benefit from the introduction of engineering countermeasures. The segments are then ranked in terms of propensity for crashes to occur (US FHWA, 2020a).

In general terms, data-driven safety analysis consists of two parts:

1. *Predictive analysis*, in which risk factors thought to be relevant to the propensity for a selected crash type (e.g., roadway departure crashes) on a selected roadway type (e.g., rural two-lane highways) are fitted with a predictive model to estimate the number of crashes. The most basic model for vehicle-only crashes includes the variables 'roadway segment length' and 'average daily vehicle traffic'. Additional factors (e.g., number of lanes, speed limit, curve radius, etc.) are added when modelling specific roadway types. In the case of pedestrian crashes, it is also necessary to add a variable containing information about pedestrian traffic on a roadway. Ideally, pedestrian count data would be collected, but in practice, surrogates for pedestrian counts such as population density are generally used.

2. *Systemic analysis*, in which the expected value of crashes is calculated for all roadway segments in a network which match the roadway type modelled. The expected values are used to rank the roadways to identify which segments have the highest propensity for the crash type modelled. This data is subsequently used to guide the selection of roadway segments on which countermeasures will be installed, thus reducing the potential for future crashes.

The benefits of data-driven safety analysis include informed decision-making, targeted investment and improved safety (US FHWA, 2020b). To execute this type of analysis on a statewide network of roadways, data including average daily traffic count, segment length, functional class (i.e., roadway type) and additional risk factors being considered must be available for the entire statewide

roadway network. Specific regulations regarding the basic data elements were updated in 2015 as part of the Fixing America's Surface Transportation Act (FAST Act) (US FHWA, 2016). The FHWA also established and maintains a Roadway Safety Data Program 'to advance State and local safety data systems and safety data analysis and evaluation capabilities'. However, due to the cost and complexity involved in collecting and maintaining roadway data at a statewide level, it has been challenging for most states to establish and maintain the data needed to perform quality analyses on statewide networks.

When executed properly, the data-driven safety analysis methodology is well-suited for identifying roadway segments and associated risk factors so that engineering countermeasures can be put in place to reduce the number of persons killed and injured on roadways. The methodology also provides the quantitative justification needed for federal funding of roadway safety improvements. It was for this reason that an individual state-level Department of Transportation (DOT) in the United States commissioned a state-wide analysis of pedestrian crashes and associated risk factors. We'll give this DOT the pseudonym 'Alpha' to preserve its anonymity.

4.5.2 The Project

Alpha experienced a rise in pedestrian crashes very similar to the national statistics described in the case introduction. Alpha wanted to provide data which would satisfy NHTSA and FHWA requirements for obtaining federal funds for projects related to improving pedestrian safety. This data would assist Alpha, metropolitan planning organizations (MPOs) and local governments within the state. Alpha's staff responsible for managing the project was comprised of mostly engineers who managed various projects related to highway safety. The staff had a very good reputation within the state and previously received praise from the FHWA and NHTSA for various projects and initiatives.

For the pedestrian study, Alpha contracted the work to an organization ('Consulting, Inc.') with experience in crash and roadway data analysis. The primary goal at the beginning of the study was to provide evidence of roadway-based risk factors (e.g., number of lanes, shoulder width, median type, etc.) associated with pedestrian fatalities and injuries in motor vehicle crashes. The scope of the study was state-wide and included all roadway types, with the exclusion of controlled access roadways such as interstates. Data for the study were obtained from crash reports and narratives completed by law enforcement and other investigating officers, roadway data maintained by Alpha, socioeconomic information from the US Census Bureau such as population density, and place information from the US Geological Survey providing locations of hospitals, schools, parks and other locations where pedestrians are typically present. Data preparation and initial analysis was complex, and required dozens of individual processes to inspect, clean, aggregate and join the data. It was in this phase of the project that Consulting, Inc. noticed problems with the data which would require the project goals to be reframed. More specifically, there were problems with the 'big data' on which the project relied.

4.5.3 Faulty Assumptions

A faulty assumption about information contained in the project data was made by Alpha, as well as Consulting, Inc. This assumption was the major contributor to delays which plagued the project. Both sides assumed that information contained in roadway data maintained by Alpha would be sufficient to conduct a data-driven safety analysis on the entire statewide roadway network. The assumption was far from the truth. Although Alpha maintained a Geographic Information System (GIS) database containing many potentially useful fields, a large percentage of roadways were missing information for most fields, including critical fields such as average daily vehicle traffic and roadway segment length. In addition to this, an up-to-date roadway segment identifier did not exist for a large portion of roadway segments in the statewide network. Because of these problems with the data, it was impossible to create a statistical model containing any roadway-based risk factors.

Once project goals and methodology were reformulated, the study resulted in quantitative data sufficient for use in assisting stakeholders with data requirements for federally funded projects. After numerous meetings discussing the actual state of the data, it was decided to create a predictive model solely based on surrogates for pedestrian traffic using a deprecated segment identifier. Expected values calculated using this model were subsequently used to rank roadway segments in terms of propensity for pedestrian crashes based solely on pedestrian exposure along each segment. The high level of commitment by Alpha's staff and Consulting, Inc. was key to this partial success. However, the study did not provide the depth of knowledge hoped for in terms of roadway-based risk factors related to pedestrian crashes. Project delays caused by the need to reformulate project goals and methodology also increased costs and reduced potential benefits. Pedestrian crash trends change over time, along with the usefulness of the associated crash data.

4.5.4 Analysis

Assumptions about what data is readily available and the quality of that data, in combination with misunderstandings about what big data statistical analysis and machine-learning methods can provide, largely led to the issues described in this case study. In this case, Big Data was also Bad Data in several important aspects. In addition to this, two other pitfalls described by Gary Smith and Jay Cordes in their book, *The 9 Pitfalls of Data Science*, may also have been involved – 'Worshiping Math' and 'Worshiping Computers' (Smith and Cordes, 2019).

According to Smith and Cordes (2019), 'Worshiping Math' occurs when stakeholders are so impressed or intimidated by statistical formulas and machine-learning algorithms commonly used in big data that they trust the maths more than expert domain knowledge, wisdom and common sense. In this case, the data-driven highway safety analysis methods are relatively new and there are still many competent highway engineers who are intimidated by the statistical components and language contained in them. This leads to a dynamic in which the engineers trust the produced analyses instead of properly questioning those who performed the analyses and what the analyses actually mean.

Along with 'Worshiping Math', 'Worshiping Computers' is a pitfall of big data in which stakeholders follow the mistaken assumption that computers are omniscient, incorrectly crediting the machines with common sense and wisdom (Smith and Cordes, 2019). In this case, Alpha's misconception was that big data software would automatically provide superior levels of information, especially given the perceived large quantity of data available. The reality of the case is that while a subset of the data may have been sufficient for some type of 'small data' project, no software or computation power can overcome such significant problems with the data as were present.

No party discussed in this case study – including federal agencies, state agencies and contractors – started off with the intention to derail such a potentially useful project or provide questionable results based on bad data. Alpha consisted of numerous engineers and professionals with years of experience in highway safety. The staff at Consulting, Inc. had years of experience collecting and managing data in the highway safety domain as well. So, what may have led such competent individuals down a path fraught with error? Technology lifecycle models developed by Gartner (2020) and others provide us with a useful framework for discussion of some possibilities. In the early stages of these models, new technology receives significant exposure marked by stories of success and failure. This is typically a period of fanfare for a technology, where publicity and hype overshadow proven viability.

Two technology items are relevant to our case discussion:

1. *Data Literacy* – the ability of an individual or organization to understand, communicate information and make decisions based on data.
2. *Big Data Analytics for Social Impact* – the use of statistics, machine learning or other analytics techniques in efforts to improve society.

Both items are included in the initial stage of Gartner's 2019 Hype Cycle™, with both still listed as 'On the Rise' in the 2020 hype cycle description (Kronz et al., 2020). This stage is marked by ever-inflating expectations without proven results. The state of data literacy in this case is very similar – assumptions about the state of the project data were inflated. In addition to this, although staff at Alpha and Consulting, Inc. were able to adequately describe the application and resulting value of a successful project, they did not have an adequate understanding of the analytic methods and data sources required to successfully complete the project. The current state of understanding around data for good also contributed to inflated expectations about available data. Such assumptions are easy to make – accurate representations of the number of lanes and speed limits of most US roadways can be displayed by the navigation software on smart phones or in vehicles. It would seem reasonable that a state DOT such as Alpha would have complete information on these two items. However, in Alpha's case, data for speed limits and number of lanes was missing in a substantial percentage of roadway records. Although it may seem that Alpha's staff should have been aware of this, siloed infrastructure within the organization may have amplified this misunderstanding.

Fortunately, the core issues of the case were partially resolved through high levels of time, effort, commitment and dedication to the project by Alpha and Consulting, Inc. Idealistic expectations were at the root of these issues, and three pitfalls around big data – 'Using Bad Data', 'Worshiping Math' and 'Worshiping Computers' – magnified the problems encountered in the case. Varying levels of data literacy among project team members contributed to the issues as well. Unrealistic expectations about the similarity between commercial roadway data and government roadway data were also a factor. As with any major shift in technology, Big Data presents unique challenges which must be addressed for it to be used ethically and effectively. If the challenges discussed in this case are not recognized and addressed, the possibility remains high that individuals or entities will be tempted to perform analyses which are misleading or use data that might be of dubious validity in order to fulfil federal funding requirements.

More generally, as the Alpha case shows, the underlying belief in the value and importance of using big data can lead to unreal expectations which simply cannot be fulfilled. The danger then is that the inability to deliver the expected benefits can lead to questionable practices and routines which hide the true problems in the analyses performed, leading to misleading or, worse, fallacious results. As Schrage (2014) writes: 'While the computational resources and techniques for prediction may be novel and astonishingly powerful, many of the human problems and organizational pathologies appear depressingly familiar. The prediction imperative frequently narrows focus rather than broadens perception. "Predicting the future" can – in the spirit of Dan Ariely's Predictably Irrational – unfortunately bring out the worst cognitive impulses in otherwise smart people.'

4.6 Implications of Big Data

As is common with most new technologies, there is considerable discussion about the new technology's implications, but these discussions are largely optimistic portrayals of how the new technology will create business value, lead to increased productivity, better jobs, greater job satisfaction and new skills and, overall, produce a 'better society'. The proponents of big data are no exception with their myriad reasons why big data will lead to exciting new possibilities and there are even 'cases' to support their claims (cf. LaValle et al., 2011; McAfee and Brynjolfsson, 2012; Alharthi et al., 2017). The inference is that other organizations need to follow the path of these 'leading-edge organizations' so they too can obtain the benefits. There is much less literature which questions the veracity of these claims. One exception is the study done by Lazer et al. (2014), who examined the infamous 'Google Flu' fiasco where Google Flu Trends (GFT) data was erroneously used to predict an outbreak of influenza in 2013 which never occurred. Lazer et al. postulated that the primary problem was 'big data hubris'. They write:

'Big data hubris' is the often implicit assumption that big data are a substitute for, rather than a

supplement to, traditional data collection and analysis. We have asserted that there are enormous scientific possibilities in big data. However, quantity of data does not mean that one can ignore foundational issues of measurement, construct validity and reliability, and dependencies among data. The core challenge is that most big data that have received popular attention are not the output of instruments designed to produce valid and reliable data amenable for scientific analysis.

Nokia's erroneous use of big data led them to believe that smartphones were a fad and to the shockingly bad decision to continue to build traditional mobile phones. The consequences of that disastrous decision are still being felt today at Nokia (Wang, 2016). A similarly poor use of big data at LEGO led to the company erroneously believing that the traditional LEGO bricks were too small and needed to be made much larger in size. This turned out to be totally fallacious and caused the company significant financial loss (Lindstrom, 2016). Other examples of failed big data uses include: the City of Boston deciding where there were potholes to repair based on biased social media data; an Analytics company who in tracking unemployment erroneously predicted a large swing in unemployment based on individuals increasingly searching 'jobs', only to discover it occurred just after the death of Steve Jobs, which led to the uptick in search on the term (Gent, 2016); companies such as Woolworths, Starbucks and American Airlines changing their loyalty programmes based on big data then finding substantial backlash because the data used did not reflect actual consumer sentiments (Feldman, 2016); the widespread criticism of Nordstrom for surreptitiously culling shopping information from the phones of customers who connected to their stores' free WiFi (Cohen, 2013); and the UK government's embarrassing failed system Gov.uk Verify (Evenstad, 2018). Yampolskiy (2017) offers a list of twelve recent examples of where algorithms developed from machine learning and big data proved disastrously wrong – a very recent example of which was the United Kingdom's Ofqual (Office of Qualifications and Examinations Regulation) application of an algorithm (generated from big data) to assign A-level grades to students who had their exams cancelled due to the pandemic. Unfortunately, the data used generated 'statistical models which reflected racial, gender and class inequalities and replicated them as data patterns while simultaneously endowing these patterns with an air of certainty, neutrality and objectivity', causing the generated A-level grades to be highly suspect. Eventually, this fiasco forced the UK government to drop these grades, although the resultant awkwardness still lingers (Zimmermann, 2020). Indeed, even Facebook had to embarrassingly admit that it enabled advertisers to target users with offensive terms like 'Jew hater', which Roose (2017) wittily termed 'Facebook's Frankenstein Moment'.

As the Alpha case study shows, there is an increasing expectation that organizations are expected to base their decisions on 'big data' with the concomitant use of big data analytic techniques. This has become not only the norm, but a requirement. The concern is that these large data sets provide lots of data, but do they lead to 'understanding'? Or more worryingly, that this big data requirement leads to labelling certain data as 'appropriate' and including them in the data set when they are not. Bad data are bad data irrespective of whether they are part of the 'big data' set or not. The concern is that the push for big data drives out more nuanced and thoughtful views of whether the data are really meaningful or not. Organizations embrace the façade of rigour and data-driven processes and in so doing perform analyses or use data that might be of dubious validity so as to comply with the pronouncements of consulting companies and shareholders who see the use of big data as necessary for successful decision-making. Such unintended consequences are real and are the product of the desire to be seen as using the latest, greatest technology. Hirschheim (1985) wrote about this in the mid-1980s in the context of office automation, but if one simply replaces 'office automation' with 'big data', the same arguments would hold. Then, of course, there are issues surrounding privacy and ethics in the use of big data. Simsek et al. (2019) note:

> We would be remiss not to touch upon the ethical and privacy issues surrounding big data. It has by

now become clear that the generation and storage of big data sets involve more challenges than usually anticipated, as shown for instance with the recent scandals such as Cambridge Analytica. To begin with, the availability of data is not a guarantee that their use would be ethical or even legal. In addition, there are issues and contradictory demands of transparency and protection of individuals' identities and personal knowledge.

Indeed, this is a theme taken up by Wigan and Clarke (2013), who argue that big data is ostensibly anathema to individual privacy.

We would like to offer another not-so-obvious example of how big data and associated technology can lead to social dysfunction. This was brilliantly displayed in the 'Nosedive' episode of the show 'Black Mirror'. Black Mirror is a Netflix sci-fi series which explores the underbelly of modern society, focusing particularly on the unanticipated consequences of new technologies. One episode titled Nosedive explores the consequences of a society using social media data to influence every individual's socio-economic standing (Mamo, 2018). In this episode, society has adopted new technology involving eye implants and mobile devices which allow everyone to share their daily activities. Each activity and interaction with others is rated on a scale of one to five stars, which is immediately transmitted and used to calculate a cumulative standing which then influences one's status in society. The episode follows what happens to the protagonist – Lacie Pound – as she goes through a series of disastrous interactions pushing down her cumulative score and consequent socio-economic status. The denouement leads Lacie to finally shed the iron-cage of social media ratings. The show offers an insightful look into the seductive power of technology, the big data that is generated by it and how this could lead to a dysfunctional future given individuals' obsession with image. For those who believe the show is far-fetched, one need only look at the Peeple mobile phone app and China's development of a national reputation system – 'Social Credit System'. Nosedive offers a compelling argument for the need to consider the consequences of adopting any new technology, especially a technology that is so pervasive that it affects everyone.

This is a point powerfully argued by Zuboff (2019, emphases in the original) in her notion of 'surveillance capitalism'. She writes:

> Surveillance capitalism unilaterally claims human experience as free raw material for translation into behavioral data. Although some of these data are applied to service improvement, the rest are declared as a proprietary *behavioral surplus*, fed into advanced manufacturing processes known as 'machine intelligence', and fabricated into *prediction products* that anticipate what you will do now, soon, and later. Finally, these prediction products are traded in a new kind of marketplace that I call *behavioral futures markets*. Surveillance capitalists have grown immensely wealthy from these trading operations, for many companies are willing to lay bets on our future behaviour.

4.7 Conclusions

While it is clear that big data has captured the imagination of companies, government and society, it is less clear whether this will lead to a 'better' environment (whatever that means and however that is measured) and for whom. As the Nosedive episode has exposed, the capturing of big data and its use can have significant deleterious consequences. And society, for the most part, has been remarkably unmoved by these possible harmful consequences probably because of their collective obliviousness to them. As Naughton (2019) writes: 'First of all there was the arrogant appropriation of users' behavioural data – viewed as a free resource, there for the taking. Then the use of patented methods to extract or infer data even when users had explicitly denied permission, followed by the use of technologies that were opaque by design and fostered user ignorance.'

Interestingly, according to Lepore (2020), this could likely have all been predicted. In her recent book *If Then: How the Simulmatics Corporation Invented the Future*, Lepore traces the history of Simulmatics Corporation. The company was launched in 1959 during the Cold War, mined data, targeted voters, manipulated consumers, destabilized politics and distorted knowledge – decades before Facebook, Twitter, Google and Cambridge

Analytica. They built what they termed the 'People Machine', which aimed to model people's behaviours in a variety of realms from buying products, to voting, to counterinsurgency, to predicting where and when urban riots would occur. As Lepore (2020) writes:

> Simulmatics is a relic of its time ... [it] was a small, struggling company. It was said to be the 'A-bomb of the social sciences.' But, like a long-buried mine, it took decades to detonate. The People Machine was hobbled by its time, by the technological limitations of the nineteen-sixties. Data were scarce. Models were weak. Computers were slow. ... Simulmatics failed. And yet it had built a very early version of the machine in which humanity would find itself trapped in the early twenty-first century, a machine that applies the science of psychological warfare to the affairs of ordinary life, a machine that manipulates opinion, exploits attention, commodifies information, divides voters, atomizes communities, alienates individuals, and undermines democracy. Facebook, Palantir, Cambridge Analytica, Amazon, the Internet Research Agency, Google: these are, every one, the children of Simulmatics.

She continues: 'By the time of the 2016 election, the mission of Simulmatics had become the mission of nearly every corporation. Collect data. Write code: IF/THEN/ELSE. Detect patterns. Predict behavior. Direct action. Encourage consumption. Influence elections.'

While one might take issue with the prominent role Lepore ascribes to Simulmatics' impact on today's big tech companies' use of big data to predict and shape human behaviour, her historical take on the subject should not be ignored. Indeed, as Mnookin (2020) writes: 'That Lepore overstates Simulmatics' role in this tale does not make her ultimate conclusions any less true, or any less terrifying.' As if to drive home this point, Lynn (2020) offers specific details on how companies such as Google, Amazon and Facebook have taken this to heart and now essentially 'control our lives'. But it might have been different. Mnookin highlights the missed opportunity to legislate some form of government policy on big data early on when it put into law the Privacy Act of 1974, which codified the fair information practices that governed the collection, maintenance, use and dissemination of information about individuals. The law was enacted because the government recognized that the aggregation of this data, 'while essential to the efficient operations of the government, has greatly magnified the harm to individual privacy that can occur'. Yet, they failed to offer any legislation to protect that same data from private corporations.

For those less concerned about potential dysfunctional societal implications and more concerned with business implications, this too has been equivocal. As Harford (2014) notes: 'Big data has arrived, but big insights have not. The challenge now is to solve new problems and gain new answers – without making the same old statistical mistakes on a grander scale than ever.' In other words, we may have developed a new sophisticated approach to making decisions (i.e., based on big data), but this does not yield insight or understanding. And without understanding, practice fails because decisions based on big data alone will continue to be problematic and often erroneous. What may be even worse is that, according to Wigan and Clarke (2013), this leads to an environment where it is often the individual who bears the consequences of an organization's erroneous big data decision-making. *Caveat emptor!*

References

Abbasi, A., Sarker, S. and Chiang, R. (2016). Big data research in information systems: Toward an inclusive research agenda. *Journal of the Association for Information Systems*, 17(2), i–xxxii.

Ackoff, R. (1967). Management misinformation systems. *Management Science*, 14(4), B147–B156.

Alharthi, A., Krotov, V. and Bowman, M. (2017). Addressing barriers to big data. *Business Horizons*, 60(3), 285–292.

Anderson, C. (2008). The end of theory: The data deluge makes the scientific method obsolete. *Wired*.

Baesens, B., Bapna, R., Marsden, J., Vanthienen, J. and Zhao, J. L. (2016). Transformational issues of big data and analytics in networked business. *MIS Quarterly*, 40(4), 807–818.

Bell, G., Hey, T. and Szalay, A. (2009). Beyond the data deluge. *Science*, 323(5919), 1297–1298.

Bloom, B. (ed.) (1956). *Taxonomy of Educational Objectives: The Classification of Educational Goals*. New York, NY: David McKay & Co.

Cohen, P. (2013). How Nordstrom uses WiFi to spy on shoppers. *Forbes*.

Constantiou, I. and Kallinikos, J. (2015). New games, new rules: Big data and the changing context of strategy. *Journal of Information Technology*, 30(1), 44–57.

Davenport, T. (2014). *Big Data @ Work: Dispelling the Myths, Uncovering the Opportunities*. Boston, MA: Harvard Business Review Press.

Dewey, J. (1933). *How We Think*. Buffalo, NY: Prometheus Books.

Dykes, B. (2016). Actionable insights: The missing link between data and business value. *Forbes*.

Ekbia, H., Mattioll, M., Kouper, I., Arave, G., Ghazinejad, A., Bowman, T. et al. (2015). Big data, bigger dilemmas: A critical review. *Journal of the Association for Information Science and Technology*, 66(8), 1523–1545.

Evenstad, L. (2018). The troublesome saga of Gov.uk Verify. *ComputerWeekly*, www.computerweekly.com/news/252450423/Govuk-Verify-a-troublesome-saga.

Feldman, D. (2016). When big data goes bad … *CustomerThink*, https://customerthink.com/when-big-data-goes-bad/.

Fricke, M. (2015). Big data and its epistemology. *Journal of the Association for Information Science and Technology*, 66(4), 651–661.

Galliers, R. D., Newell, S., Shanks, G. and Topi, H. (2017). Datification and its human, organizational and societal effects: The strategic opportunities and challenges of algorithmic decision-making. *Journal of Strategic Information Systems*, 26(3), 185–190.

Gandomi, A. and Haider, M. (2015). Beyond the hype: Big data concepts, methods and analytics. *International Journal of Information Management*, 35(2), 137–144.

Gartner. (2020). Gartner hype cycle. www.gartner.com/en/research/methodologies/gartner-hype-cycle.

Gent, E. (2016). Beware of the gaps in big data. *Engineering & Technology*, https://eandt.theiet.org/content/articles/2016/09/beware-of-the-gaps-in-big-data/.

Goes, P. B. (2014). Editor's comments: Big data and IS research. *MIS Quarterly*, 38(3), iii–viii.

Grover, V., Lindberg, A., Benbasat, I. and Lyytinen, K. (2020). The perils and promises of big data research in information systems. *Journal of the Association for Information Systems*, 21(2), 268–291.

Harford, T. (2014). Big data: Are we making a big mistake? *Financial Times Magazine*, www.ft.com/content/21a6e7d8-b479-11e3-a09a-00144feabdc0#axzz2yQ2QQfQX.

Hirschheim, R. (2020). The attack on understanding: How big data and theory have led us astray – a comment on Gary Smith's Data Mining Fool's Gold. *Journal of Information Technology*, 36(2), 176–183.

Hirschheim, R. (1985). *Office Automation: A Social and Organizational Perspective*. Chichester, UK: Wiley.

Johnson, J. (2012). Big data + big analytics = big opportunity. *Financial Executive*, 28(6), 50–53.

Johnson, S., Gray, P. and Sarker, S. (2019). Revisiting IS research practice in the era of big data. *Information & Organization*, 29(1), 41–56.

Jones, M. (2019). What we talk about when we talk about (big) data. *Journal of Strategic Information Systems*, 28(1), 3–16.

Kitchin, R. (2014). Big data, new epistemologies and paradigm shifts. *Big Data & Society*, 1(1), 1–12.

Kronz, A., Hare, J. and Krensky, P. (2020). Hype cycle for analytics and business intelligence. Gartner, www.gartner.com/doc/3988448.

LaValle, S., Lesser, E., Shockley, R., Hopkins, M. and Kruschwitz, N. (2011). Big data, analytics, and the path from insights to value. *MIT Sloan Management Review*, 52(2), 21–31.

Lazer, D., Kennedy, R., King, G. and Vespignani, A. (2014). The parable of Google Flu: Traps in big data analysis. *Science*, 343(6176), 1203–1205.

Lee, L. and Sobol, D. (2012). What data can't tell you about customers. *Harvard Business Review*, https://hbr.org/2012/08/what-data-cant-tell-you-about.

Lepore, J. (2020). *If Then: How the Simulmatics Corporation Invented the Future*. New York, NY: Liveright.

Lindstrom, M. (2016). *Small Data: The Tiny Clues that Uncover Huge Trends*. New York, NY: St Martin's Press.

Lynn, B. (2020). The big tech extortion racket. *Harper's Magazine*, https://harpers.org/archive/2020/09/the-big-tech-extortion-racket/.

Maass, W., Parsons, J., Purao, S., Storey, V. and Woo, C. (2018). Data-driven meets theory-driven research in the era of big data: Opportunities and challenges for information systems research. *Journal of the Association for Information Systems*, 19(12), 1253–1273.

Mamo, H. (2018). Taking a social media 'nosedive' and underrating common relationships in Black Mirror. https://medium.com/@heranmamo/taking-a-social-media-nosedive-and-under rating-common-relationships-in-black-mirror-9be23b3a5575.

Marr, B. (2016). *Big Data in Practice: How 45 Successful Companies Used Big Data Analytics to Deliver Extraordinary Results*. Chichester, UK: Wiley.

McAfee, A. and Brynjolfsson, E. (2012). Big data: The management revolution. *Harvard Business Review*, 90(10), 1–9.

Mnookin, S. (2020). The bumbling 1960s data scientists who anticipated Facebook and Google. *The New York Times*, www.nytimes.com/2020/09/15/books/review/if-then-jill-lepore.html.

National Highway Traffic Safety Administration (NHTSA). (2019). 2018 fatal motor vehicle crashes: Overview. https://crashstats.nhtsa.dot.gov/Api/Public/ViewPublication/812826.

Naughton, J. (2019). 'The goal is to automate us': Welcome to the world of surveillance capital. *The Guardian*.

Naughton, J. (2016). Death by drone strike, dished out by algorithm. *The Guardian*.

Pigliucci, M. (2009). The end of theory in science? *EMBO Reports*, 10(6), 534.

Ribes, D. and Jackson, S. (2013). Data bite man: The work of sustaining long-term study. In L. Gitelman (ed.), *'Raw Data' Is an Oxymoron*. Cambridge, MA: MIT Press, pp. 147–166.

Roose, K. (2017). Facebook's Frankenstein moment. *The New York Times*.

Ryle, G. (1949). *The Concept of Mind*. Chicago, IL: University of Chicago Press.

Sandelands, L. (1990). What is so practical about theory? Lewin revisited. *Journal for the Theory of Social Behavior*, 20(3), 235–262.

Schrage, M. (2014). Learn from your analytics failures. *Harvard Business Review*.

Siegel, E. (2013). *Predictive Analytics: The Power to Predict Who Will Click, Buy, Lie or Die*. Hoboken, NJ: Wiley.

Simsek, Z., Vaara. E., Paruchuri, S., Nadkarni, S. and Shaw, J. (2019). New ways of seeing big data. *Academy of Management Journal*, 62(4), 971–978.

Smith, G. (2020). Data mining fool's gold. *Journal of Information Technology*, 35(3), 182–194.

Smith, G. and Cordes, J. (2019). *The 9 Pitfalls of Data Science*. Oxford, UK: Oxford University Press.

Stephens-Davidowitz, S. (2017). *Everybody Lies: Big Data, New Data, and What the Internet Can Tell Us about Who We Really Are*. New York, NY: Dey Street Books, HarperCollins.

US Department of Transportation (US DOT). (2018). U.S. Department of Transportation Transit, Highway, and Safety Funds. www.fhwa.dot .gov/environment/bicycle_pedestrian/funding/ funding_opportunities.cfm.

US Department of Transportation Federal Highway Administration (FHWA). (2020a). Fact sheet – data-driven safety analysis. https://safety.fhwa .dot.gov/rsdp/factsheet/datadriven_safety_ analysis.pdf.

US Department of Transportation Federal Highway Administration (FHWA). (2020b). Roadway Safety Data Program – data-driven safety analysis (DDSA). https://safety.fhwa.dot.gov/rsdp/ ddsa.aspx.

US Department of Transportation Federal Highway Administration (FHWA). (2016). Guidance on state safety data systems. https://safety.fhwa .dot.gov/legislationandpolicy/fast/docs/ssds_ guidance.pdf.

Veritas. (2016). Veritas global databerg report finds 85% of stored data is either dark or redundant, obsolete, or trivial (ROT). www.veritas.com/ news-releases/2016-03-15-veritas-global-data berg-report-finds-85-percent-of-stored-data.

Walker, R. (2015). *From Big Data to Big Profits: Success with Data and Analytics*. New York, NY: Oxford University Press.

Wang, T. (2016). Why big data needs thick data. *Ethnography Matters*, https://medium.com/eth nography-matters/why-big-data-needs-thick-data-b4b3e75e3d7.

Weinberger, D. (2012). *Too Big to Know: Rethinking Knowledge Now that the Facts Aren't the Facts, Experts Are Everywhere, and the Smartest Person in the Room Is the Room*. New York, NY: Basic Books.

Wigan, M. and Clarke, R. (2013). Big data's big unintended consequences. *IEEE Computer*, 46(6), 46–53.

Wittgenstein, L. (1953). *Philosophical Investigations*. New York, NY: Macmillan.

Yampolskiy, R. (2017). What will happen when your company's algorithms go wrong? *Harvard Business Review*.

Zimmermann, A. (2020). The A-level results injustice shows why algorithms are never neutral. *The New Statesman*.

Zuboff, S. (2019). *The Age of Surveillance Capitalism: The Fight for a Human Future at the New Frontier of Power*. New York, NY: Public Affairs.

Power, Knowledge and Digitalization

A Qualitative Research Agenda

BOYKA SIMEONOVA and ROBERT D. GALLIERS

5.1 Introduction

Knowledge-sharing processes are recognized as important for innovation and competitive advantage and have been a subject of investigation within the fields of management, organization studies and information systems for two decades (e.g., Alavi and Leidner, 2001; Wang and Noe, 2010). While knowledge-sharing processes are of significant importance to organizations, they remain a challenge. We postulate that these processes are dependent on power dynamics. Further, knowledge sharing and the associated power dynamics are changing with the increased digitalization and learning algorithms (Faraj et al., 2018). The over-reliance on algorithms and trace data might obstruct knowledge and understanding of the outputs of these algorithms and big data (Ekbia et al., 2015; Faraj et al., 2018) and changing the role of expertise and knowing, and the future of work. Hence, it is important to question: What will get lost with too much data, automation, datafication and algorithmification? What is unique about human knowing which cannot be replaced or replicated by intelligent machines? What are the impacts of intelligent machines on organizational learning, knowing and power? How might power dynamics influence digitalization and knowledge sharing and vice versa?

Digitalization and big data may change the future of work and also the future of research, as empiricism and new approaches to data analysis emerge (Kitchin, 2014). However, trace data is not generated for the specific research and research questions (Howison et al., 2011) and over-reliance on trace data might obstruct understanding of phenomena and behaviour (Lee and Sobol, 2012).

Thus, scholars emphasize that science needs theory and explanations, not data (Fricke, 2015; Hirschheim, 2021), particularly for studying complex social phenomena and hidden factors, where it is important to understand behaviours, actions, processes and the effects of power which are not directly observable (Blackler, 2011; Leong et al., 2019). Hence, theorizing is particularly relevant to understand power, knowledge and digitalization to comprehend how power dynamics and mechanisms are enabled, what behaviours they enact, how these change knowledge-sharing processes and how digitalization and the use of technology are reinforcing or redistributing these, which is an example of the qualitative theorization provided in this chapter.

The knowledge-sharing literature gives predominance to knowledge as a static entity, which can be possessed and relatively easily shared (Marshall and Rollinson, 2004; Pozzebon and Pinsonneault, 2012) This perspective is often described in terms of 'knowledge as possession' (Cook and Brown, 1999). Similar 'power as possession' views predominate (Marshall and Rollinson, 2004), particularly those that connote power's unidimensional, episodic, functionalist and negative properties (Cendon and Jarvenpaa, 2001; Jasperson et al., 2002; Dhillon et al., 2011; Fleming and Spicer, 2014). In light of this, Marshall and Rollinson (2004) call for research that moves away from this static, controlling treatment of power and knowledge, towards a focus on more dynamic, constructive and practice-based perspectives and theories.

In line with this reasoning, the dominance of a particular epistemology such as that of possession may limit understanding and hence others (e.g.,

Pozzebon and Pinsonneault, 2012) recognize a need to incorporate different epistemologies in their theorizations. Treating power and knowledge as possession leads to analyses that are described as 'poorly placed to understand their dynamic, relational and processual character' (Marshall and Rollinson, 2004: 75).

Different forms of power are shown to exhibit different effects on knowledge-sharing processes (Pozzebon and Pinsonneault, 2012; Simeonova, 2018; Simeonova et al., 2018a, 2018b, 2020). However, their granular manifestations and effects on knowledge sharing remain limited and only partially understood. This is heightened with the effects of technology advancements, such as social media, learning algorithms, intelligent machine, and automation more generally (Leonardi, 2014, 2015, 2017; Faraj et al., 2018; Raisch and Krakowski, 2020; Simeonova et al., 2020), where the importance of knowledge and power is emphasized, redefined or reinforced.

Hence, the first aim of this chapter is to understand the multidimensional effects of the different forms of power on knowledge sharing, explicating their manifestations. The second aim is to integrate technology and theorize power, knowledge and digitalization and their dynamics in the age of digitalization.

To provide a multidimensional understanding and theorization of knowledge, power and digitalization, we utilize the following perspectives: epistemologies of knowledge and power as practice and possession (Pozzebon and Pinsonneault, 2012); personal and collective power (Blackler, 2011); episodic/power as possession and systemic/power as practice (Lawrence et al., 2012; Simeonova et al., 2020); as well as incorporating the role of information technology and its advancement (Simeonova et al., 2020). The resulting framework attempts to theorize the different forms of power, the role of technology and knowledge and their dynamics. The theorized framework includes the following quadrants: power as *possession*, based on the episodic and personal view of knowledge and power; power as *asymmetries*, based on the episodic and collective view of power and knowledge; power as *empowerment*, based on the systemic and personal view of power and

knowledge; and power as *practice*, based on the systemic and collective perspectives of knowledge and power. Within these quadrants, through digitalization, technology has either a restrictive and controlling role or a facilitative and coordinative role which redefines or reinforces power dynamics and their effects on knowledge processes, learning, knowing and innovation.

5.2 Perspectives on Knowledge and Power

5.2.1 Effects of Episodic and Systemic Power

Knowledge-sharing theories have epistemological assumptions about knowledge. As a consequence, the associated view on knowledge-sharing processes may vary depending on which epistemological perspective is followed. Cook and Brown (1999) argue that there are two main epistemological perspectives of knowledge: the epistemology of possession; and the epistemology of practice. From the epistemology of possession perspective, knowledge sharing is viewed as the process of transferring knowledge as a commodity from one place, person, unit or organization to another (Liyanage et al., 2009; Foss et al., 2010). The possession perspective is attributed with the following assumptions: knowledge exists; knowledge is accessible; knowledge is complete; and knowledge can get easily located and shared. Similar assumptions have been outlined in rational systems theories, which assume that people are equally willing to share knowledge and that their contributions are given an equal hearing (Bunderson and Reagans, 2011).

Knowledge from this possession view is depicted as 'stock of knowledge that can be captured, codified, processed, stored, distributed; possession of stocks of knowledge legitimates certain roles' (Pozzebon and Pinsonneault, 2012: 39). Thus, power from the possession view is considered as a 'resource that is possessed, a capacity, a property; something that is instantiated through certain control of access to resources' (Pozzebon and Pinsonneault, 2012: 39). The possession/

episodic view of power also involves, inter alia: authority; status; hierarchy; self-interest; exploitation; negative emotions; power asymmetries; monitoring; surveillance; discipline; compliance; and resistance (Cendon and Jarvenpaa, 2001; Bunderson and Reagans, 2011; Koch et al., 2012; Lawrence et al., 2012; Raman and Bharadwaj, 2012; Simeonova, 2018; Simeonova et al., 2020).

In light of the above, from the possession/episodic perspective, power is asymmetrically distributed within organizations and is considered as a personal resource used for self-interest (Kärreman, 2010; Lawrence et al., 2012). Thus, possession/episodic power is linked to power *over* traits described as hierarchy, control, coercion, authority and self-interest (Clegg, 1989; Clegg et al., 2006; Göhler, 2009; Simeonova, 2015, 2018). The knowledge as power perspective argues that, through sharing, people lose their power and advantage in their organization (Willem et al., 2006; Yang and Maxwell, 2011).

From the perspective of the epistemology of practice, however, it is argued that knowledge cannot (easily) get transferred 'as-is' from one organization or person to another (Orlikowski, 2002; Szulanski et al., 2004). From this perspective, the term 'knowing' has been used, since it emphasizes its emergent nature: arising through people's interactions where knowledge and action are constituted in practice (Blackler, 1995; Tsoukas, 1996; Orlikowski, 2002; Gherardi, 2010). Thus, the main foundations of this perspective are participating, collective action and interactions (Hicks et al., 2009). As such, knowledge sharing is not about the existing, readily accessible knowledge and its application, but rather about interactions and collective action. Thus, it is argued that knowing 'is an ongoing social accomplishment, constituted and reconstituted in everyday practice' (Orlikowski, 2002: 252).

Practice can also be viewed from the perspective of knowledge and power and has been defined as 'the interface between power and knowledge' (Messner et al., 2008: 71). Further, power effects are enacted through practices: 'people know what they are doing, they know why they are doing it, but they do not know what doing it does' (Townley, 1993: 235), which is an issue

heightened through the increased digitalization and utilization of technology and data. Thus, it is important to account for power when exploring knowledge processes and digitalization.

Pozzebon and Pinsonneault (2012: 39) describe knowledge as 'invested in practice; part of action' and explain power and politics as exercised 'through maneuvers, subtle tactics, techniques, activities; part of action'. Power as practice from a systemic perspective also includes (Cendon and Jarvenpaa 2001; Busquets, 2010; Bunderson and Reagans, 2011; Chuang et al., 2016; Simeonova et al., 2018a, 2018b, 2020):

- organizational culture;
- empowerment;
- collective orientation; social power;
- network; trust; social capital;
- common goals; communities of practice;
- exploration; innovation;
- transparency; autonomy;
- decision-making.

In contrast to the power as possession perspective, power from a systemic practice perspective is regarded as a potentially productive force, socially constructed through practices and interactions (Foucault, 1977; Foucault, 1980; Kärreman, 2010; Lawrence et al., 2012). Given the socially constituted, relational view, power is enacted through practices and interactions and hence is exercised through different mechanisms of social relations, micro-strategies and manoeuvres (Foucault, 1980). From this power *to* perspective, power is viewed as concerned with practice and empowerment (Göhler, 2009; Lawrence et al., 2012).

Blackler (2011) illustrates how power dynamics are incorporated into a theory of collective development. Blackler (2011: 729) notes the predominant view of power as coercion, force, manipulation and authority, and outlines it as limiting in understanding the effects of power as an everyday notion that people use in different ways: 'Rather than asking "what is power?" organisation scholars began to realise that it is more helpful to enquire "what kinds of behavior, and outcomes does the notion of power sensitise to?"'. Blackler (2011) goes on to emphasize the need to understand the influence of people and the exercise of power in

Table 5.1 A power framework

Power	Description
Personal and overt power	Reward, coercive and legitimate power Expertise Trust in a person; their valued information and their links with powerful others
Collective and overt power	The success of a unit in dealing with uncertainty; its control of resources and network centrality and its work
Personal and unobtrusive power	Critical consciousness Ability to construct principled choices
Collective and unobtrusive power	Control of agendas Use of taken-for-granted assumptions, rules, routines An organization's culture, its signs, symbols and basic assumptions

Source: Adapted from Blackler (2011).

practice: what power does and how is it distributed. Blackler (2011) outlines a framework that differentiates between personal, collective, overt and unobtrusive power, indicated in Table 5.1.

However, whether overt or unobtrusive, accounts of power and its episodic and systemic manifestations are often lacking. Hence, we postulate examining manifestations of power from the episodic/possession perspective and the systemic/practice perspective to account for different power dynamics and for different levels: personal and collective (Blackler, 2011; Lawrence et al., 2012; Pozzebon and Pinsonneault, 2012; Simeonova et al., 2020). A summary of the effects of power in knowledge sharing in light of the above conceptualization is outlined in Tables 5.2, 5.3 and 5.4, which are adapted and extended from Simeonova et al. (2018a, 2018b) and Simeonova et al. (2020). Table 5.2 outlines the effect of episodic power and its various manifestations.

The effects of episodic power and its manifestations have been demonstrated in Table 5.2, and it is clear that such assumptions and manifestations dominate the existing literature. Systemic power and its manifestations have not been extensively researched, as presented in Table 5.3.

Table 5.3 illustrates the relative lack of research on systemic power and its manifestations. The situation is similar with studies accounting for both episodic and systemic power and their dynamics. The effects of both episodic and systemic power are outlined in Table 5.4.

5.2.2 Power-Knowledge Sharing Framework

Based on the effects of episodic and systemic power, as outlined in Tables 5.2, 5.3 and 5.4, we develop a holistic framework on power and knowledge sharing. The framework builds on the above and on the following work and assumptions: differentiating between knowledge and power as possession and knowledge and power as practice (Pozzebon and Pinsonneault, 2012); personal and collective power (Blackler, 2011); episodic/power as possession and systemic/power as practice (Simeonova et al., 2020); episodic and systemic power (Lawrence et al., 2012). The framework is outlined at Figure 5.1.

The summary provided in Tables 5.2, 5.3 and 5.4, and in Figure 5.1, demonstrates that episodic and systemic power have numerous manifestations and links with knowledge. In addition, however, Marshall and Rollinson (2004) have argued that the omission of power can limit the understanding of knowledge processes – even more so in the age of digitalization, particularly as the role of IS is increasingly prevalent (Raisch and Krakowski, 2020). IS power manifestations, such as rules, norms, monitoring, surveillance, discipline and compliance (Raisch and Krakowski, 2020; Simeonova et al., 2020), might redistribute or reinforce power dynamics, which consequently might enhance or obstruct knowledge-sharing processes. It is important to examine how the human-

Table 5.2 Effects of episodic power

Forms of power	Perceived effects of power	Example references
Episodic: hierarchical, authoritative, legitimate power	Negative effect as people at higher hierarchical levels have access to more resources and can act as they deem appropriate.	Galinsky et al. (2008) Simeonova (2018)
	Management ban the use of Web 2.0 technologies for communication and knowledge sharing.	
	The self-interest of authoritative higher-power people dominates those of lower power as well as the organizational interests.	Brooks (1994) Gray (2001) Guinote (2007) Raman and Bharadwaj (2012)
	Power and status provide fewer constraints to higher-power actors and obstruct reflection in teams.	
	Use of knowledge management systems to increase managers' control and reduce employees' power.	
Episodic: knowledge as power	Perception that when sharing knowledge power or competitive advantage gets lost.	Lawrence et al. (2005) Haas (2006) Willem et al. (2006) Wang and Noe (2010) Yang and Maxwell (2011)
	Possession of unique information impedes knowledge sharing or leads to selective sharing.	
	Knowledge lost when using technology to share information.	
Episodic: equal consideration	Limited opportunity for people from lower levels to voice opinions; lack of consideration of ideas from the lower levels.	Lawrence et al. (2005) Galinsky et al. (2006) Smith et al. (2008) Bunderson and Reagans (2011) Heizmann (2011)
	Limited and reduced capacity to achieve goals for lower-power actors.	
	Obstruct consideration of ideas, experimentation, learning and sharing.	
Episodic: resource dependence	Organizations depending on key employees.	Inkpen and Tsang (2005) Muthusamy and White (2005) Galinsky et al. (2008) Barrett and Oborn (2010)
	Dependence between organizational branches; between alliance members; between subsidiaries in different countries.	
	Others treated in instrumental ways.	
Episodic: resistance	Information systems as power instruments in eliciting clashes with existing power structures, leading to resistance.	Markus (1983) Doolin (2004) Hussain and Cornelius (2009)
Episodic: procedural	Procedures, governing rules, prescribed norms of behaviour.	Wilkesmann et al. (2009)
Episodic: emotion	Contributions of others ignored; emotions not taken into consideration; experience of negative emotions.	Kumar et al. (2007) van Kleef et al. (2008) Koch et al. (2012)
	Not sharing knowledge and lessons learnt as it can generate negative emotions.	
Episodic: self-interest	Gain power over others to gain access to different resources.	Constantinides and Barrett (2006) Azad and Faraj (2011)
	Reinforce interests using power and politics. Power as a manifestation of strategy and interests through IS.	
Episodic: social discrimination	Social and status characteristics obstruct knowledge-sharing processes.	Bunderson (2003)
Episodic: power asymmetries	Power asymmetries, imbalances between vendor and client.	Ravishankar et al. (2013) Ravishankar (2015)
Episodic: control, surveillance	Enhance knowledge sharing using information systems and datafication to increase control and surveillance.	Hayes and Walsham (2001) Howcroft and Wilson (2003) Elmes et al. (2005) Lightfoot and Wisniewski (2014) Faraj et al. (2018) Raisch and Krakowski (2020)
	Obstruct learning and interpretation through automation, datafication, algorithmification, learning algorithms.	
	Information asymmetries: restricting access to information, filtering information.	
	Automation.	

Table 5.3 Effects of systemic power

Forms of power	Perceived effects of power	Example references
Systemic: goals, social aspects, collective orientation, social power	Positive effects on knowledge sharing include: shared goals, alignment with organizational goals, transparency, communities of practice, social capital. Collective orientation mitigates the effects of power and status differences which obstruct learning and knowledge sharing. Socialized use of power thus ameliorating negative effects.	Azad and Faraj (2011) Bunderson and Reagans (2011) Raman and Bharadwaj (2012) Contu (2013)
Systemic: empowerment	Remove resource constraints, participate in decision-making, reduce administrative obstacles. Communities, storytelling, sensemaking, sensegiving. IS to neutralize power asymmetries through exchange of ideas. Access to information considered to enable empowerment.	Howcroft and Wilson (2003) Huzzard (2004) Elmes et al. (2005) Brown et al. (2009) Barrett et al. (2016) Chuang et al. (2016) Leong et al. (2019)
Systemic: organizational culture	Organizational culture, 'unobtrusive' norms and ways of representing and working.	Blackler (2011)
Systemic: transparency, communication	Technology provides the opportunity to enable multiple voices without privileging individual opinions. Social media creates awareness of expertise, and facilitates locating of expertise, knowledge. Provide transparency and facilitate communication and interaction between hierarchical levels. Knowledge-management systems to facilitate knowledge-management processes. Augmentation.	Alavi and Leidner (2001) McAfee (2006) Leonardi et al. (2013) Leonardi (2014, 2015, 2017) Raisch and Krakowski (2020)

machine interactions influence power dynamics and knowledge, particularly as algorithms may constrain learning and enhance control and surveillance 'characterizing IT as a form of omnipresent architecture of control' (Raisch and Krakowski, 2020: 29).

5.3 Power and Knowledge in the Age of Digitalization

While the effects of AI remain somewhat unclear, increasing digitalization could lead to a radical transformation of work and society (Brynjolfsson and McAfee, 2014; Faraj et al., 2018). Important aspects of this radical transformation, brought about by AI, intelligent agents and other forms of digitalization, include issues concerning power dynamics. Bailey and Barley (2020: 2) note that:

... to the degree that the exercise of power in industry and on Wall Street gravitates toward

automating work, then current writers are mistaken in attributing loss of jobs solely to the technology itself. Moreover, if we recognize that power plays a crucial role in shaping the social outcomes of intelligent technologies, then it leaves open the possibility that a different zeitgeist might lead decision-makers to design and implement intelligent technologies in ways that augment work rather than replace workers.

In the age of digitalization, knowledge processes take on particular importance, given the danger of them getting lost in the algorithmic automation of work and decision-making (Brynjolfsson and McAfee, 2014; Davenport and Kirby, 2016; Aversa et al., 2018; Leidner et al., 2018; Faraj et al., 2018; Lindebaum et al., 2020; Raisch and Krakowski, 2020). An over-reliance on algorithms, intelligent technologies and big data might hamper learning and create technostress and IT use concerns, which posit challenges to knowledge work, learning, emotions, employment, organizational

Table 5.4 Effects of both episodic and systemic power

Forms of power	Perceived effects of power	Example references
Episodic: emotion Episodic and systemic: emotion	Ignoring contributions of others and not taking their emotions into consideration; experience of negative emotions. Emotions differ between levels when using organizational social networking sites. These are positive for new hires, negative for middle managers and non-users, positive and negative for executive managers.	Koch et al. (2012)
Episodic: network Systemic: network	Controlling resources, centralized decision-making, controlling strategic assets. Building structural holes building trust, actors' autonomy and self-control and the capacity of the network to recombine resources, co-creation. Reduce structural power deficit (i.e., authority, resources). Learning through a network: evening out power imbalances.	Busquets (2010) Ngwenyama and Nielsen (2014) Moe et al. (2017)
Episodic: structural Systemic: structural	Power and information technology governance: power of executive management to control strategy. Inter-organizational structural power: source of influence of powerful organizations over the less powerful, dependence. Cooperative power, focus on the community interests, empowerment.	Cendon and Jarvenpaa (2001) Bradley et al. (2012)
Episodic: behavioural Systemic: behavioural	Negative behavioural tactics: coercion, manipulation, resistance, self-interest. Positive behavioural tactics: obtaining external resources, creating alliances, helping build an infrastructure.	Cendon and Jarvenpaa (2001)
Episodic and systemic: multilevel, multi-stakeholder, network and context	Tools: surveillance, monitoring, control, resistance (episodic power); transparency, autonomy, multiple voices (systemic power). Rules: procedures, rules and norms (episodic power); organizational culture (episodic/systemic power). Community: trust, social capital, networks (systemic power). Division of labour: hierarchy, control, coercion (episodic power); empowerment (systemic power). Subject: employees, managers, executives, organization.	Simeonova et al. (2018a, 2018b)
Episodic: power as possession, power as control Systemic: power as practice, power as facilitation	Power as possession: hierarchical, authoritative, legitimate, knowledge, resource access, self-interest. Power as control: rules, norms, monitoring, surveillance, discipline, compliance, digitalization. Power as practice: shared goals/interests, communities of practice, social capital, trust, collaboration, network, empowerment, knowing. Power as facilitation: transparency, autonomy, multi-vocality, empowerment, discourse, decision-making, organizational culture.	Simeonova et al. (2020)

learning and professional identity (Blackler and McDonald, 2000; Acquisti et al., 2015; Faraj et al., 2018; Wagg et al., 2019; Bailey and Barley, 2020; Leidner and Tona, 2020; Tarafdar et al., 2020; Vaast and Pinsonneault, 2021). Bailey and Barley (2020) argue that the design and implementation of technologies are inscribed with political interests and agendas and, thus, are ignoring that the importance of power is a major issue. Power issues are also inscribed in the use of technologies and their strategic goal (Elmes et al., 2005).

	Personal	Collective
Episodic	**POWER AS POSSESSION** Control of resources, decision-making Coercive, legitimate Links to powerful actors Certain individuals more powerful than others Knowledge as power Hierarchical, authoritative, status Self-interest Fewer constraints for higher power individuals Obstruct reflection	**POWER AS ASYMMETRIES** Certain organizations/networks/departments more powerful than others Conflict Resource dependence Network centrality Unequal consideration, identity Social discrimination Ignoring contributions and emotions Information asymmetries Procedure
Systemic	**POWER AS EMPOWERMENT** Manoeuvres, tactics Emotions consideration Remove resource constraints Participate in decision-making Reduced administrative obstacles Sensemaking/sensegiving Identity, storytelling, reflection Autonomy Empowerment, knowing	**POWER AS PRACTICE** Organizational culture Collective goals, collective orientation Learning through network, communities of practice Recombine resources Eliminate power asymmetries Transparency, multivocality Cooperation, collaboration Trust Social capital

Figure 5.1 Power-knowledge sharing framework

Additionally, Simeonova et al. (2020: 232) note that: 'Digitalization and big data in organizations and society is pervasive, and accounting for the power dynamics are one (neglected) dimension in the evaluation of these technologies.' The important role of power in knowledge sharing and the role of technology is emphasized – hence, links between these elements are needed.

With regard to power, the extant research appears to revert to the commonly accepted aspects of power, as noted earlier in this chapter (i.e., manipulation, coercion, hierarchy, status in terms of power as possession manifestations). This has the potentially inadvertent result that, in the Knowledge and the Digital Economy, the impact of an increase in automation and digitalization and what this means for knowledge workers and professional identity, and emotions, remains unclear (e.g., Beaudry and Pinsonneault,

2005, 2010; Koch et al., 2012; Stein et al., 2015, 2019; Leidner et al., 2018; Tarafdar et al., 2020). The link between power, knowledge and digital remains side-lined. This is particularly the case for knowledge-sharing theories that emphasize the importance of knowledge processes, but lack an account for socially complex inquiries (Burton-Jones et al., 2017).

A crucial issue is the inscription of 'knowledge' in technologies and intelligent machines, particularly with regard to tacit knowledge (Forsythe, 1993). These systems have assumptions about knowledge and work, and these assumptions and their effects are unclear. Forsythe (1993: 462) explains that:

Expert systems are constructed through a process known as 'knowledge engineering' by practitioners in AI, some of whom identify themselves as knowledge engineers. Each expert system is intended to automate decision-making processes normally undertaken by a human expert by capturing and coding in machine-readable form the background knowledge and rules of thumb (heuristics) used by the expert to make decisions in a particular subject area (domain). This information is encoded in the system's knowledge base, which is then manipulated by the system's inference engine to reach conclusions relating to the tasks.

Forsythe (1993: 463) continues:

Expert systems contain stored information (referred to as knowledge) plus encoded procedures for manipulating that knowledge. One problem with such systems is that they are both narrow and brittle. That is, although they may function satisfactorily within narrow limits – a specific application, problem area, or domain – they tend to fail rapidly and completely when these vary from those limits or when challenged with situations that the system builders did not anticipate. This is referred to as the tendency of such systems to 'fall off the knowledge cliff'. Various knowledge-related problems can befall systems . . .

particularly with regard to tacit knowledge.

In this regard, Raisch and Krakowski (2020: 10) explain that: 'most managerial tasks are more complex, and the rules and models are therefore not fully known or readily available. In such cases, rule-based automation is impossible.' Raisch and Krakowski (2020) continue to explain that managers could utilize an augmentation approach to additionally explore the problem; however, the augmentation process cannot get delegated to the IT departments as the tacit knowledge of experts cannot be easily codified. Hence augmentation, augmented learning, is explained as a co-evolutionary process where machines learn from humans and humans learn from machines (Amershi et al., 2014; Brynjolfsson and Mitchell, 2017).

Raisch and Krakowski (2020: 2) distinguish between automation and augmentation: 'Whereas automation implies that machines take over a human task, augmentation means that humans collaborate closely with machines to perform a task.' Examples of automation and augmentation utilizing AI include:

- AI-based decision-making at Netflix (Westcott Grant, 2018);
- autonomous vehicles (Wakabayashi, 2018);
- augmenting and extending human capabilities at Deutsche Telekom (Deutsche Telekom, 2018); and
- augmented intelligence at IBM (La Roche, 2017).

However, the prevalence of algorithms and algorithmification and consequent negative effects are explained where human knowledge is reduced to operating algorithms which will hamper learning, contributions, experience and expertise – even in highly knowledge-intensive sectors (Faraj et al., 2018). It is also noted that automation, datafication, digitalization and algorithmification can increase the digital divide and social discrimination (Kaufman, 2006a, 2006b; Trauth, 2017; Faraj et al., 2018; Trauth et al., 2018; Díaz Andrade and Techatassanasoontorn, 2021).

It would seem that issues associated with power and knowledge are even more pertinent with the development of intelligent machines, where human agency is reduced, technology dominates decision-making and humans are replaced with machine agency (Demetis and Lee, 2018; Bailey and Barley, 2020; Raisch and Krakowski, 2020; Schuetz and Venkatesh, 2020). Questions arise related to human–computer interactions, decision-making, surveillance, ethics, substitution of humans, and positive and negative outcomes of technology (Schuetz and Venkatesh, 2020).

The link between IS, strategy and different forms of power has also been theorized in Simeonova et al. (2020: 232) as power as control and power as facilitation, and it is explained that: 'The role of IS predominantly depends on the role of actors and the strategy utilizing its facilitative or restrictive characteristics. However, implementation and use of IS could also challenge the status quo, current practices and redistributions of power.' The use of IS could enable empowerment and coordination, and has positive effects for individuals, organizations and society, described as digitally-led emancipation (Faraj et al., 2018; Simeonova et al., 2018a, 2018b, 2020; Chapter 6). However, IS considered from the power as control perspective can have negative effects such as coercion, oppression, discrimination and manipulation, and can be described as digitally-led exploitation (Faraj et al., 2018; Simeonova et al., 2018a, 2018b, 2020; Leong et al., 2019; Chapter 6). For example, the use of Decision Support Systems and 'big data' has limited the power of the actors in strategic decision-making (Aversa et al., 2018). The example demonstrates how Alonso lost the 2010 Grand Prix Championship because the algorithm provided a poor decision, and the Chief Race Strategist did not have the power to participate in the decision-making to change the decision of the algorithm (Aversa et al., 2018).

In sum, IS has the capacity to facilitate and restrict, and lead to emancipation and/or exploitation; however, in a context where knowledge is increasingly limited the effects of technology, datafication and algorithmification could be even more detrimental. People with valuable knowledge will not share, others will not learn, technologies will substitute tasks and work, humans and decision-making. The powerful will increase their power (e.g., Amazon, Google) because of their technology lead and exploitation practices. Ensuring the links between knowledge, knowing, learning, power, technology and strategy is very important for the current digital era.

The role of IS and digitalization is included in the power-knowledge sharing framework to evaluate its manifestations and effects (see Figure 5.2).

Through the integration of digitalization into the power-knowledge research, the following observations and avenues for further research are outlined. From the perspective of *power and digitalization as possession*, episodic power at a personal level is exercised, where IS is utilized to advance the powerful, through rules, surveillance, control and automation. Such utilization of IS and intelligent technologies will ultimately obstruct learning, knowledge-sharing processes, particularly tacit knowledge sharing and the consideration of opinions of others. The increased automation and digitalization will lead to a reduced understanding of how and why the algorithms have attained a particular solution and to the potential replacement of humans with machines. Hence, digitalization

reinforces the individual power over others. From the perspective of *power and digitalization as asymmetries*, IS increases power asymmetries between people and communities, and also between people and technology. IS as asymmetries provides unequal access to information, discrimination and enforcing algorithmic decision-making. Algorithmic decision-making and information asymmetries increase the power asymmetries which lead to unequal access to resources, unequal opinion consideration and contribution, expertise and knowledge. Hence, digitalization enforces algorithmification and information asymmetries. From the *power and digitalization as empowerment* perspective, IS is utilized to help provide autonomy, access to resources, participation in decision-making and a platform to voice opinions, and to challenge power structures. The emphasis is on the utilization of technology to achieve empowerment and enhance learning. Hence, digitalization is utilized to facilitate empowerment. From the *power and digitalization as practice* perspective, the collective aspect is emphasized with the utilization of technology to help build trust, social capital, increase transparency, multi-vocality and awareness of the collective knowledge and expertise. The utilization of IS helps with coordination, collaboration, and learning in communities and groups, which help to reduce power asymmetries. Hence, digitalization enhances collaboration and cooperation.

In light of the above framework and theorization, the power-knowledge-digitalization qualitative research agenda is outlined in Table 5.5.

We suggest that qualitative research methods can help to provide valuable insights from the utilization of the dynamic multilevel multidimensional power-knowledge-digitalization framework and the outlined research questions and agenda. Qualitative research could be utilized to investigate complex and multilevel social phenomena (Burton-Jones et al., 2017) and context (Pettigrew, 2012), and untangle multidimensional power dynamics, their effect on knowledge sharing and how these are changing with the increased digitalization. Particularly useful would be the utilization of an interpretive case studies approach to explore phenomena which are not directly

	Personal	Collective
Episodic	**POWER AS POSSESSION** Control resources, decision-making Individual power over others Knowledge as power: hierarchical, authoritative, status Self-interest Reflection obstructed **IS: POWER AS POSSESSION** IS enforces rules, surveillance, control, automation Digitalization enforces individual power over others	**POWER AS ASYMMETRIES** Organizational power over others (network, department) Resource dependence Unequal consideration of ideas and contributions Discrimination **IS: POWER AS ASYMMETRIES** IS enables monitoring and enforces norms, information asymmetries Digitalization enforces algorithmification and datafication
Systemic	**POWER AS EMPOWERMENT** Remove resource constraints Participate in decision-making Autonomy Reflection Sensemaking, sensegiving **IS: POWER AS EMPOWERMENT** IS enhances autonomy, learning Digitalization utilized to facilitate empowerment	**POWER AS PRACTICE** Organizational culture and trust Social capital Cooperation, collaboration Network learning, communities of practice **IS: POWER AS PRACTICE** IS facilitates transparency, multivocality Digitalization enhances collaboration and cooperation

Figure 5.2 Power-knowledge-digitalization framework

observable (e.g., Koch et al., 2012; Leonardi, 2013; Leong et al., 2015, 2019). Interpretive case studies guidelines are provided (Klein and Myers, 1999; Walsham, 1995, 2006), and their utilization in IS discussed (see Chapter 10).

5.4 Conclusion

This chapter provides the following contributions. First, we provide a granular understanding of the different power dimensions and their manifestations and effects on knowledge sharing, which in itself is a contribution in that understanding has been limited. Second, we develop a power-knowledge sharing framework to assist in theorizing power in

the context of knowledge sharing. We have incorporated digitalization and the roles of technology, and outlined power and digitalization as possession, asymmetries, empowerment and practice to develop a power-knowledge-digitalization framework. We provided avenues for future research in the digital era pertinent to digitalization, knowledge and power dynamics, and emphasized the importance of qualitative methods to understand complex social phenomena.

It is hoped that this power-knowledge-digitalization framework may provide a platform for this important work and qualitative research to commence around the research agenda and questions outlined. The value of qualitative research for answering these questions and conducting such

Table 5.5 Qualitative research questions and agenda

Power as possession	Power as asymmetries
1. How does power and digitalization as possession change the control and redistribution of resources, knowledge sharing and decision-making?	1. How does power and digitalization as asymmetries reduce or reinforce conflict, resource dependence and discrimination?
2. What is the role of power as possession in human–machine interactions and knowledge-sharing processes?	2. What is the role of power as asymmetries in human–machine interactions and knowledge-sharing processes?
3. How does power and digitalization as possession change the future of work, knowledge work, professional identity and emotions?	3. How does power and digitalization as asymmetries change the future of work, knowledge work, professional identity and emotions?
4. How might digitalization help to reduce or reinforce power as possession?	4. How might digitalization help to reduce or reinforce power as asymmetries?
Power as empowerment	**Power as practice**
1. How does power and digitalization as empowerment enhance participation in decision-making and access to resources?	1. How does power and digitalization as practice enhance trust between humans, and between humans and machines?
2. What is the role of power as empowerment in human–machine interactions and knowledge-sharing processes?	2. What is the role of power as practice in human–machine interactions and knowledge-sharing processes?
3. How does power and digitalization as empowerment change the future of work, knowledge work, professional identity and emotions?	3. How does power and digitalization as practice change the future of work, knowledge work, professional identity and emotions?
4. How do increased automation and intelligent machines enhance or obstruct empowerment?	4. How do increased automation and intelligent machines change the social links and power asymmetries?

research is paramount, as currently the fields and theories of Information Systems and Knowledge Management lack power frameworks, and links between knowledge, power and digitalization. We reinforce the value of qualitative research in the digital era as these complex phenomena require new theories, insights and understanding. The need for theorization in the current digital era is emphasized, as science needs theory and explanations, not simply data (Fricke, 2015; Hirschheim, 2021).

References

Acquisti, A., Brandimarte, L. and Loewenstein, G. (2015). Privacy and human behavior in the age of information. *Science*, 348(6221), 509–514.

Alavi, M. and Leidner, D. E. (2001). Knowledge management and knowledge management systems: Conceptual foundations and research issues. *MIS Quarterly*, 25(1), 107–136.

Amershi, S., Cakmak, M., Knox, W. and Kulesza, T. (2014). Power to the people: The role of humans in interactive machine learning. *AI Magazine*, 35(4), 105–120.

Aversa, P., Cabantous, L. and Haefliger, S. (2018). When decision support systems fail: Insights for strategic information systems from Formula 1. *Journal of Strategic Information Systems*, 27(3), 221–236.

Azad, B. and Faraj, S. (2011). Social power and information technology implementation: A contentious framing lens. *Information Systems Journal*, 21(1), 33–61.

Bailey, D. E. and Barley, S. R. (2020). Beyond design and use: How scholars should study intelligent technologies. *Information and Organization*, 30(2), 100–286.

Barrett, M. and Oborn, E. (2010). Boundary object use in cross-cultural software development teams. *Human Relations*, 63(8), 1199–1221.

Barrett, M., Oborn, E. and Orlikowski, W. (2016). Creating value in online communities: The sociomaterial configuring of strategy, platform, and stakeholders. *Information Systems Research*, 27(4), 706–723.

Beaudry, A. and Pinsonneault, A. (2010). The other side of acceptance: Studying the direct and indirect effects of emotions on information technology use. *MIS Quarterly*, 34(4), 689–710.

Beaudry, A. and Pinsonneault, A. (2005). Understanding user responses to information technology: A coping model of user adaptation. *MIS Quarterly*, 29(3), 493–524.

Blackler, F. (2011). Power, politics, and intervention theory: Lessons from organisation studies. *Theory and Psychology*, 21(5), 724–734.

Blackler, F. (1995). Knowledge, knowledge work and organisations: An overview and interpretation. *Organisation Studies*, 16(6), 1021–1046.

Blackler, F. and McDonald, S. (2000). Power, mastery and organisational learning. *Journal of Management Studies*, 37(6), 833–852.

Bradley, R. V., Byrd, T. A., Pridmore, J. L., Thrasher, E., Pratt, R. M. and Mbarika, V. W. (2012). An empirical examination of antecedents and consequences of IT governance in hospitals. *Journal of Information Technology*, 27(2), 156–177.

Brooks, A. K. (1994). Power and the production of knowledge: Collective team learning in work organisations. *Human Resource Development Quarterly*, 5(3), 213–235.

Brown, A., Gabriel, Y. G. and Gherardi, S. (2009). Storytelling and change: An unfolding story introduction. *Organisation*, 16(3), 324–334.

Brynjolfsson, E. and McAfee, A. (2014). *The Second Machine Age: Work, Progress, and Prosperity in a Time of Brilliant Technologies*. New York, NY: W. W. Norton.

Brynjolfsson, E. and Mitchell, T. (2017). What can machine learning do? Workforce implications. *Science*, 358(6370), 1530–1534.

Bunderson, J. (2003). Recognising and utilising expertise in work groups: A status characteristics perspective. *Administrative Science Quarterly*, 48(4), 557–591.

Bunderson, J. and Reagans, R. E. (2011). Power, status, and learning in organisations. *Organisation Science*, 22(5), 1182–1194.

Burton-Jones, A., Recker, J., Indulska, M., Green, C. P. and Weber, R. (2017). Assessing representation theory with a framework for pursuing success and failure. *MIS Quarterly*, 41(4), 1307–1334.

Busquets, J. (2010). Orchestrating smart business network dynamics for innovation. *European Journal of Information Systems*, 19(4), 481–493.

Cendon, V. and Jarvenpaa, S. (2001). The development and exercise of power by leaders of support units in implementing information technology-based services. *Journal of Strategic Information Systems*, 10(2), 121–158.

Chuang, C. H., Jackson, E. and Jiang, Y. (2016). Can knowledge-intensive teamwork be managed? Examining the roles of HRM systems, leadership, and tacit knowledge. *Journal of Management*, 42(2), 524–554.

Clegg, S. R. (1989). *Frameworks of Power*. London: Sage.

Clegg, S. R., Courpasson, D. and Phillips, N. (2006). *Power and Organisations*. London: Sage.

Constantinides, P. and Barrett, M. (2006). Large-scale ICT innovation, power, and organisational change: The case of a regional health information network. *Journal of Applied Behavioral Science*, 42(1), 78–90.

Contu, A. (2013). On boundaries and difference: Communities of practice and power relations in creative work. *Management Learning*, 45(3), 289–316.

Cook, D. and Brown, S. (1999). Bridging epistemologies: The generative dance between organisational knowledge and organisational knowing. *Organisation Science*, 10(4), 381–400.

Davenport, T. H. and Kirby, J. (2016). *Only Humans Need Apply: Winners and Losers in the Age of Smart Machines*. New York, NY: HarperCollins.

Demetis, D. and Lee, A. S. (2018). When humans using the IT artifact becomes IT using the human artifact. *Journal of the Association for Information Systems*, 19(10), 929–952.

Deutsche Telekom. (2018). Deutsche Telekom's guide for artificial intelligence. Digital Responsibility | Deutsche Telekom.

Dhillon, G., Caldeira, M. and Wenger, M. (2011). Intentionality and power interplay in IS implementation: The case of an asset management firm. *Journal of Strategic Information Systems*, 20(4), 438–448.

Díaz Andrade, A. and Techatassanasoontorn, A. A. (2021). Digital enforcement: Rethinking the pursuit of a digitally-enabled society. *Information Systems Journal*, 31(1), 185–197.

Doolin, B. (2004). Power and resistance in the implementation of a medical management information system. *Information Systems Journal*, 14(4), 343–362.

Ekbia, H., Mattioll, M., Kouper, I., Arave, G., Ghazinejad, A., Bowman, T. et al. (2015). Big data, bigger dilemmas: A critical review. *Journal of the Association for Information Science and Technology*, 66(8), 1523–1545.

Elmes, M., Strong, D. and Volkoff, O. (2005). Panoptic empowerment and reflective conformity in enterprise systems-enabled organizations. *Information and Organization*, 15(1), 1–35.

Faraj, S., Pachidi, S. and Sayegh, K. (2018). Working and organizing in the age of the learning algorithm. *Information and Organization*, 28(1), 62–70.

Fleming, P. and Spicer, A. (2014). Power in management and organisation science. *Academy of Management Annals*, 8(1), 237–298.

Forsythe, D. E. (1993). The construction of work in artificial intelligence. *Science, Technology, & Human Values*, 18(4), 460–480.

Foss, N., Husted, K. and Michailova, S. (2010). Governing knowledge sharing in organisations: Levels of analysis, governance mechanisms, and research directions. *Journal of Management Studies*, 48(5), 455–485.

Foucault, M. (1980). *Power/Knowledge: Selected Interviews and Other Writings, 1972–1977*. New York, NY: Pantheon.

Foucault, M. (1977). *Discipline and Punish*. Harmondsworth, UK: Penguin.

Fricke, M. (2015). Big data and its epistemology. *Journal of the Association for Information Science and Technology*, 66(4), 651–661.

Galinsky, A., Magee, J. C., Gruenfeld, D. H., Whitson, J. A. and Liljenquist, K. A. (2008). Power reduces the press of the situation: Implications for creativity, conformity, and dissonance. *Journal of Personality and Social Psychology*, 95(6), 1450–1466.

Galinsky, A., Magee, J. C., Inesi, M. K. and Gruenfeld, D. (2006). Power and perspectives not taken. *Psychological Science*, 17(12), 1068–1074.

Gherardi, S. (2010). Telemedicine: A practice-based approach to technology. *Human Relations*, 63(4), 501–524.

Göhler, G. (2009). 'Power to' and 'power over'. In S. R. Clegg, and M. Haugaard (eds), *The Sage Handbook of Power*. London: Sage, pp. 27–39.

Gray, P.H. (2001). The impact of knowledge repositories on power and control in the workplace. *Information Technology and People*, 14(4), 368–385.

Guinote, A. (2007). Power and goal pursuit. *Personality and Social Psychology Bulletin*, 33(8), 1076–1087.

Haas, M. (2006). Knowledge gathering, team capabilities, and project performance in challenging work environments. *Management Science*, 52(8), 1170–1185.

Hayes, N. and Walsham, G. (2001). Participation in groupware-mediated communities of practice: a socio-political analysis of knowledge working. *Information and Organization*, 11(4), 263–288.

Heizmann, H. (2011). Knowledge sharing in a dispersed network of HR practice: Zooming in on power/knowledge struggles. *Management Learning*, 42(4), 378–393.

Hicks, J., Nair, P. and Wilderom, C. P. (2009). What if we shifted the basis of consulting from knowledge to knowing? *Management Learning*, 40(3), 289–310.

Hirschheim, R. (2021). The attack on understanding: How big data and theory have led us astray – a comment on Gary Smith's Data Mining. *Journal of Information Technology*, 36(2), 176–183.

Howcroft, D. and Wilson, M. (2003). Paradoxes of participatory practices: The Janus role of the systems developer. *Information and Organization*, 13(1), 1–24.

Howison, J., Wiggins, A. and Crowston, K. (2011). Validity issues in the use of social network analysis with digital trace data. *Journal of the Association for Information Systems*, 12(12), 767–787.

Hussain, Z. I. and Cornelius, N. (2009). The use of domination and legitimation in information systems implementation. *Information Systems Journal*, 19(2), 197–224.

Huzzard, T. (2004). Communities of domination? Reconceptualising organisational learning and power. *Journal of Workplace Learning*, 16(6), 350–361.

Inkpen, A. C. and Tsang, E. W. (2005). Social capital, networks, and knowledge transfer. *Academy of Management Review*, 30(1), 146–165.

Jasperson, J. S., Carte, T. A., Saunders, C. S., Butler, B. C., Croes, H. J. and Zheng, W. (2002). Review: power and information technology research: A metatriangulation review. *MIS Quarterly*, 26(4), 397–459.

Kärreman, D. (2010). The power of knowledge: Learning from 'learning by knowledge-intensive firm'. *Journal of Management Studies*, 46(7), 1405–1416.

Kaufman, R. (2006a). Interdisciplinary perspectives on the 'digital divide' Part I: Economic perspectives. *Journal of the Association for Information Systems*.

Kaufman, R. (2006b). Interdisciplinary perspectives on the 'digital divide' Part II: Sociological perspectives. *Journal of the Association for Information Systems.*

Kitchin, R. (2014). Big Data, new epistemologies and paradigm shifts. *Big Data & Society*, 1(1), 1–12.

Klein, H. K. and Myers, M. D. (1999). A set of principles for conducting and evaluating interpretive field studies in information systems. *MIS Quarterly*, 23(1), 67–93.

Koch, H., Gonzalez, E. and Leidner, D. E. (2012). Bridging the work/social divide: The emotional response to organizational social networking sites. *European Journal of Information Systems*, 21(6), 689–706.

Kumar, M., Jha, V. and Vaidya, D. (2007). Empirical investigation of impact of organizational culture, prosocial behavior and organizational trust on sharing mistakes in knowledge management systems. PACIS Proceedings.

La Roche, J. (2017). IBM's Rometty: The skills gap for tech jobs is 'the essence of divide'. Yahoo! Finance, https://finance.yahoo.com/news/ibms-rometty-skills-gap-tech-jobs-essence-divide.html.

Lawrence, T., Malhotra, N. and Morris, T. (2012). Episodic and systemic power in the transformation of service firms. *Journal of Management Studies*, 49(1), 102–143.

Lawrence, T., Mauws, M. K., Dyck, B. and Kleysen, R. (2005). The politics of organisational learning: Integrating power into the 4I framework. *Academy of Management Review*, 30(1), 180–191.

Lee, L. and Sobol, D. (2012). What data can't tell you about customers. *Harvard Business Review.*

Leidner, D. E., Gonzalez, E. and Koch, H. (2018). An affordance perspective of enterprise social media and organizational socialization. *Journal of Strategic Information Systems*, 27(2), 117–138.

Leidner, D. E. and Tona, O. (2020). The CARE theory of dignity amid personal data digitalization. *MIS Quarterly*, 45(1), 343–370.

Leonardi, P. (2017). The social media revolution: Sharing and learning in the age of leaky knowledge. *Information and Organization*, 27(1), 46–59.

Leonardi, P. (2015). Ambient awareness and knowledge acquisition: Using social media to learn 'who knows what' and 'who knows who'. *MIS Quarterly*, 39(4), 746–762.

Leonardi, P. (2014). Social media, knowledge sharing, and innovation: Toward a theory of communication visibility. *Information Systems Research*, 25(4), 786–816.

Leonardi, P. (2013). When does technology use enable network change in organizations? A comparative study of feature use and shared affordance. *MIS Quarterly*, 37(3), 749–775.

Leonardi, P., Huysman, M. and Steinfield, C. G. (2013). Enterprise social media: Definition, history, and prospects for the study of social technologies in organisations. *Journal of Computer-Mediated Communication*, 19(1), 1–19.

Leong, C., Pan, S., Bahri, S. and Fauzi, A. (2019). Social media empowerment in social movements: Power activation and power accrual in digital activism. *European Journal of Information Systems*, 28(2), 173–204.

Leong, C., Pan, S., Ractham, C. P. and Kaewkitipong, L. (2015). ICT-enabled community empowerment in crisis response: Social media in Thailand flooding 2011. *Journal of the Association for Information Systems*, 16(3), 50–60.

Lightfoot, G. and Wisniewski, T. P. (2014). Information asymmetry and power in a surveillance society. *Information and Organization*, 24(4), 214–235.

Lindebaum, D., Vesa, M. and den Hond, F. (2020). Insights from 'the machine stops' to better understand rational assumptions in algorithmic decision making and its implications for organizations. *Academy of Management Review*, 45(1), 246–263.

Liyanage, C., Elhag, T., Ballal, T. and Li, Q. (2009). Knowledge communication and translation – a knowledge transfer model. *Journal of Knowledge Management*, 13(3), 118–131.

Markus, M. L. (1983). Power, politics, and MIS implementation. *Communications of the ACM*, 26(6), 430–444.

Marshall, N. and Rollinson, J. (2004). Maybe Bacon had a point: The politics of interpretation in Collective Sensemaking. *British Journal of Management*, 15(S1), 71–86.

McAfee, A. P. (2006). Enterprise 2.0: The dawn of emergent collaboration. *MIT Sloan Management Review*, 46(3), 21–28.

Messner, M., Clegg, S. and Kornberger, M. (2008). Critical practices in organisations. *Journal of Management Inquiry*, 17(2), 68–82.

Moe, C. E., Newman, M. and Sein, M. K. (2017). The public procurement of information systems: Dialectics in requirements specification. *European Journal of Information Systems*, 26(2), 143–163.

Muthusamy, S. and White, M. (2005). Learning and knowledge transfer in strategic alliances: A social exchange view. *Organisation Studies*, 26(3), 415–441.

Ngwenyama, O. and Nielsen, P. A. (2014). Using organisational influence processes to overcome IS implementation barriers: Lessons from a longitudinal case study of SPI implementation. *European Journal of Information Systems*, 23(2), 205–222.

Orlikowski, W. J. (2002). Knowing in practice: Enacting a collective capability in distributed organising. *Organisation Science*, 13(3), 249–273.

Pettigrew, A. (2012). Context and action in the transformation of the firm: A reprise. *Journal of Management Studies*, 49(7), 1304–1328.

Pozzebon, M. and Pinsonneault, A. (2012). The dynamics of client–consultant relationships: Exploring the interplay of power and knowledge. *Journal of Information Technology*, 27(1), 35–56.

Raisch, S. and Krakowski, S. (2020). Artificial intelligence and management: The automation-augmentation paradox. *Academy of Management Review*, 46(1), 192–210.

Raman, R. and Bharadwaj, A. (2012). Power differentials and performative deviation paths in practice transfer: The case of evidence-based medicine. *Organisation Science*, 23(6), 1593–1621.

Ravishankar, M. N. (2015). The realignment of offshoring frame disputes (OFD): An ethnographic 'cultural' analysis. *European Journal of Information Systems*, 24(3), 234–246.

Ravishankar, M. N., Pan, S. and Myers, M. (2013). Information technology offshoring in India: A postcolonial perspective. *European Journal of Information Systems*, 22(4), 387–402.

Schuetz, S. and Venkatesh, V. (2020). The rise of human machines: How cognitive computing systems challenge assumptions of user-system interaction. *Journal of the Association for Information Systems*, 21(2), 460–482.

Simeonova, B. (2018). Transactive memory systems and Web 2.0 in knowledge sharing: A conceptual model based on activity theory and critical realism. *Information Systems Journal*, 28(4), 592–611.

Simeonova, B. (2015). Power and knowledge within activity theory: Applying activity theory to knowledge sharing. Conference: European Group for Organizational Studies, Athens, Greece.

Simeonova, B., Galliers, R. D. and Karanasios, S. (2020). Strategic information systems and organisational power dynamics. In R. D. Galliers, D. E. Leidner and B. Simeonova (eds), *Strategic Information Management: Theory and Practice*, 5th edition. London and New York, NY: Routledge, pp. 221–238.

Simeonova, B., Karanasios, S., Galliers, R. D., Kelly, P. R. and Mishra, J. (2018a). Where is power in information systems research? Towards a framework. International Conference on Information Systems, San Francisco, CA.

Simeonova, B., Karanasios, S., Galliers, R. D., Kelly, P. R. and Mishra, J. (2018b). New ways of organising in collaborative knowledge sharing: Examining the effects of power. Conference: European Group for Organizational Studies, Tallinn, Estonia.

Smith, P. K., Jostmann, N. B., Galinsky, A. D. and Van Dijk, W. W. (2008). Lacking power impairs executive functions. *Psychological Science*, 19(5), 441–448.

Stein, M. K., Newell, S., Wagner, E. and Galliers, R. D. (2015). Coping with information technology: Mixed emotions, vacillation, and nonconforming use patterns. *MIS Quarterly*, 39(2), 367–392.

Stein, M. K., Wagner, E., Tierney, P., Newell, S. and Galliers, R. D. (2019). Datafication and the pursuit of meaningfulness in work. *Journal of Management Studies*, 56(3), 685–718.

Szulanski, G., Cappetta, R. and Jensen, R. C. (2004). When and how trustworthiness matters: Knowledge transfer and the moderating effect of causal ambiguity. *Organisation Science*, 15(5), 600–613.

Tarafdar, M., Maier, C., Laumer, S. and Weitzel, T. (2020). Explaining the link between technostress and technology addiction for social networking sites: A study of distraction as a coping behavior. *Information Systems Journal*, 30(1), 96–124.

Townley, B. (1993). Performance appraisal and the emergence of management. *Journal of Management Studies*, 30(2), 221–238.

Trauth, E. (2017). A research agenda for social inclusion in information systems. *The Data Base for Advances in Information Systems*, 48(2), 9–20.

Trauth, E., Joshi, K. D. and Yarger, L. K. (2018). Social inclusion in the information systems. *Information Systems Journal*, 28(6), 989–994.

Tsoukas, H. (1996). The firm as a distributed knowledge system: A constructionist approach. *Strategic Management Journal*, 17, 11–25.

Vaast, E. and Pinsonneault, A. (2021). When digital technologies enable and threaten occupational identity: The delicate balancing act of data scientists. *MIS Quarterly*, 45(3), 1087–1112.

Van Kleef, G. A., Oveis, C., Van Der Löwe, I., LuoKogan, A., Goetz, J. and Keltner, D. (2008). Power, distress, and compassion: Turning a blind eye to the suffering of others. *Psychological Science*, 19(12), 1315–1322.

Wagg, S., Simeonova, B. and Cooke, L. (2019). An activity theory perspective on digital inclusion. Conference proceedings: European Group for Organizational Studies, Edinburgh, UK.

Wakabayashi, D. (2018). Uber's self-driving trucks hit the highway, but not local roads. *The New York Times*, www.nytimes.com/2018/03/06/technology/uber-self-driving-trucks.html.

Walsham, G. (2006). Doing interpretive research. *European Journal of Information Systems*, 15(3), 320–330.

Walsham, G. (1995). Interpretive case studies in IS research: Nature and method. *European Journal of Information Systems*, 4(2), 74–81.

Wang, S. and Noe, R. A. (2010). Knowledge sharing: A review and directions for future research. *Human Resource Management Review*, 20(2), 115–131.

Westcott Grant, K. (2018). Netflix's data-driven strategy strengthens claim for 'best original content' in 2018. *Forbes*, www.forbes.com/sites/kristinwestcottgrant/2018/05/28/netflixs-data-driven-strategy-strengthens-lead-for-best-original-content-in-2018/?sh=13dcaa863a94.

Wilkesmann, U., Wilkesmann, M. and Virgillito, A. (2009). The absence of cooperation is not necessarily defection: Structural and motivational constraints of knowledge transfer in a social dilemma situation. *Organization Studies*, 30(10), 1141–1164.

Willem, A., Buelens, M. and Scarbrough, H. (2006). The role of inter-unit coordination mechanisms in knowledge sharing: A case study of a British MNC. *Journal of Information Science*, 32(6), 539–561.

Yang, T. and Maxwell, T. (2011). Information-sharing in public organisations: A literature review of interpersonal, intra-organisational and inter-organisational success factors. *Government Information Quarterly*, 28(2), 164–175.

Information Technology and Power

BOYKA SIMEONOVA and M. N. RAVISHANKAR

6.1 Introduction

In the past few decades, information technologies (IT) have exponentially developed, which has been described as the digital revolution. The development of these technologies has achieved new advancements, with intelligent machines, learning algorithms, artificial intelligence, social media, expert systems and decision support systems (Demetis and Lee, 2018; Faraj et al., 2018; Lyytinen et al., 2020; Schuetz and Venkatesh, 2020). These new technological advancements have created positive developmental opportunities and positive outcomes; however, they have also led to negative outcomes, and have created limitations to development. Often, positive outcomes of IT are cited along with negative outcomes: empowerment-control (Howcroft and Wilson, 2003; Elmes et al., 2005), coordination-control (Faraj et al., 2018), augmentation-automation (Raisch and Krakowski, 2020), inclusion-exclusion (Trauth, 2017), positive and negative emotions (Koch et al., 2012), and emancipatory and hegemonic effects (Miranda et al., 2016).

The thesis in this chapter is that IT has the capacity to lead to positive and negative outcomes; however, the enactment of underpinning mechanisms of power will influence whether the outcomes shift towards digitally-led emancipation or towards digitally-led exploitation.

Information technologies have significant positive outcomes and are increasingly utilized to tackle grand challenges: poverty alleviation (Li et al., 2019); health management (Sahay et al., 2017); environmental sustainability (Tim et al., 2018); crisis management (Leong et al., 2015); collective action (Wasko et al., 2004; Bennett and Segerberg, 2012; Sæbø et al., 2020; Chen et al., 2020), and development and empowerment (Chipidza and Leidner, 2019; Cui et al., 2019; Leong et al.,

2019; Simeonova et al., 2020). At organizational and individual levels, technology is used to facilitate knowledge creation and sharing, innovation and entrepreneurship, and build communities and identities, facilitate work, enable remote working, provide access to information, and help decision-making and strategizing (Wasko et al., 2004; Eseryel, 2014; Simeonova, 2018; Raman and Grover, 2020; Simeonova et al., 2020). Where IT has positive outcomes for society, organizations and individuals, we cluster these sets of positive outcomes as digitally-led emancipation.

The negative IT outcomes observed include: control and domination (Hussain and Cornelius, 2009; Hong et al., 2016); big data and datafication (Martin, 2015; Aversa et al., 2018); obstruction of learning and knowledge sharing, conflict and hierarchical structure (Argyris and Ransbotham, 2016); intelligent machines, learning algorithms (Lyytinen et al., 2020; Schuetz and Venkatesh, 2020); and development failure (Chipidza and Leidner, 2019). Where IT has negative outcomes for society, organizations and individuals, we cluster these sets of negative outcomes as digitally-led exploitation.

However, what has the digital revolution enacted (positive or negative outcomes) and how are these outcomes enacted? Why are the outcomes of IT utilization different? Why is IT which is implemented to achieve development often a failure (Chipidza and Leidner, 2019)? Are these effects short term or are they sustained? How could these outcomes change, for example, from negative to positive? What are the mechanisms which determine the outcomes of IT?

We postulate that the answer is in the underpinning power mechanisms and their fault lines. Consider the following example of the utilization of social media, Twitter, where an Indian sought help from a high-ranking official to return to India as other options were not available (such as an Indian consulate abroad). The high-ranking official acted on the request, helped to resolve the issue and the individual returned to India. Hence, the utilization of Twitter is an example of the enactment of episodic power leading to digitally-led emancipation. The effect is positive: the high-ranking official helped the individual. Hence, while IT has the capacity to lead to digitally-led emancipation or digitally-led exploitation, these depend on the underpinning power mechanisms and their fault lines. The fault lines of power are evident in that while the use of IT helped the individual in need on the occasion described, organized systems and relevant institutions to help people in need do not exist, hence a fault line of power exists.

We need to unpack the IT outcomes – that is, digitally-led emancipation and digitally-led exploitation and the underpinning mechanisms of power that contribute to these, along with the fault lines of power. Hence, we provide a conceptual framework that explains the underpinning mechanisms of episodic and systemic power that contribute to digitally-led emancipation and digitally-led exploitation. We outline two clusters of mechanisms following Lawrence et al. (2001): episodic power mechanisms, which are discrete episodes not rooted in systems and routines; and systemic power mechanisms, which are established in systems and routines.

We outline IT and emancipation (i.e., digitally-led emancipation) and IT and exploitation (i.e., digitally-led exploitation). We then focus on the role of episodic and systemic power mechanisms. We outline the types of power mechanism and their fault lines: episodic power and digitally-led emancipation; episodic power and digitally-led exploitation; systemic power and digitally-led emancipation; and systemic power and digitally-led exploitation. The obvious examples include systemic power mechanisms leading to digitally-led emancipation and digitally led exploitation, and episodic power mechanisms leading to digitally-led exploitation. The less obvious and theoretically interesting aspect is the enactment of episodic power mechanisms leading to digitally-led emancipation, as illustrated in the Twitter example. This chapter will theorize

the power mechanisms and their fault lines, and unpack how these are enacted.

We aim to contribute to the understanding of the links between power and IT in the following ways: we differentiate between positive and negative outcomes of IT (i.e., digitally-led emancipation and digitally-led exploitation); and we outline a new theorization of power mechanisms framework to explicate the enactments and outcomes of IT and their effects on individuals, organizations and society.

6.2 IT and Associated Outcomes

6.2.1 IT and Positive Outcomes, Digitally-Led Emancipation

The positive outcomes of IT are evident in the following areas where these span different levels: individual, organizational and societal.

A cluster of research has outlined positive IT outcomes when dealing with grand challenges: digital transformation and competitive advantage, social entrepreneurship, financial, social, digital inclusion, health management, crisis management, poverty alleviation, development and environmental sustainability (e.g., Mervyn et al., 2014; Sandeep and Ravishankar, 2016, 2018; Barrett et al., 2016; Currie and Lagoarde-Segot, 2016, 2017; Díaz Andrade and Doolin, 2016, 2019; Feller et al., 2017; Sahay et al., 2017; Tim et al., 2018; Vaast et al., 2017; Lagoarde-Segot and Currie, 2018; Joia and Santos, 2019; Li et al., 2019; Chipidza and Leidner, 2019; Díaz Andrade and Techatassanasoontorn, 2021).

Other positive IT outcomes are explicated through enabling the participation of people in government activities and collective action (Wasko et al., 2004; Bennett and Segerberg, 2012; Linders, 2012; Vaast and Levina, 2015; George and Leidner, 2019; Leong et al., 2019; Sæbø et al., 2020; Chen et al., 2020); empowerment (Simeonova et al., 2018a, 2018b; Cui et al., 2019; Leong et al., 2019; Ortiz et al., 2019; Chen et al., 2020; Simeonova et al., 2020); knowledge processes and organizational learning, and decision-making (Wasko et al., 2004; Majchrzak et al., 2013; Treem and Leonardi, 2013; Eseryel, 2014; Leonardi, 2014, 2015; Argyris and Ransbotham, 2016; Koch et al., 2012; Leidner et al., 2018; Simeonova, 2018; Raman and Grover, 2020).

A cluster of studies investigates collective action and the role of technology, which has been explained as connective action and digital activism (Bennett and Segerberg, 2012; George and Leidner, 2019). This cluster of studies provides examples of the effects of online platforms in enabling people to self-organize and voice their opinions – for example, the Arab Spring, the Spanish Los Indignados, Occupy Wall Street, the Umbrella Revolution in Hong Kong, Malaysia's environmental movement and Italy's Movimento Cinque Stelle (e.g., Rane and Salem, 2012; Anduiza et al., 2013; Leong et al., 2019; Sæbø et al., 2020). For example, Sæbø et al. (2020) explore the use of social media for collective action of the Italian political movement Movimento Cinque Stelle. The movement is a political organization with Grillo, a former comedian, as leader. The social media platform for the political movement has been launched as a forum for consultation about politics, promoting discussions, events and decision-making. Through the popularity and the collective action facilitated via the online platform, the movement has been voted the second largest party in Italy, obtaining 25 per cent of the votes in 2013. Social media supports the effective collective action through (re)creating frames, communicational ambidexterity, managing resilience and championing participation (Sæbø et al., 2020).

Another example of the positive effects of social media in collective action, connective action and digital activism is provided by the role of empowerment in Leong et al. (2019). The positive IT utilization outcomes include: providing a platform for people to voice opinions, managing the organization and redistribution of resources, empowerment, grassroots self-organization and participation. The study investigates a Malaysian environmental movement and outlines a framework for social media empowerment in social movements. Empowerment is explained as a mechanism through which communities gain command

of their activities. The lack of empowerment is explained as the inability to participate, influence and control. The inability to participate is described in situations when the community does not participate in agenda-setting or decision-making, as the participation is restricted to those in power, which is evident in the inability to voice opinions through a formal system. The inability to influence is evident in the ability of those in power to subordinate, suppress and exploit people. The inability to control is denoted when the community has limited access to resources to make decisions or to organize people, which is evident when the 'community remains oppressed and limited by the unequal distribution of its members' resources, and its members do not have the ability to take responsibility or ownership to guide and direct a solution' (Leong et al., 2019: 176). Their findings demonstrate that the Malaysian environmental movement is an exemplary case where community empowerment has been attained through the use of social media, and the government has acted on the requests of the community. The social movement protested against the construction of a power plant considered not to be environmentally sustainable. Social media has enabled Malaysians to share information and opinions, and organize campaigns and events in a grassroots manner, which has sustained the movement. The effects of the social movement are evident not only in the organization and in providing people with a platform to voice their opinions, but in the increased public awareness of environmental issues and the creation of a government agency to investigate the plans for the power plant.

The effects of collective action might differ depending on participation, agency, capacities and alignment with cause (Cardoso et al., 2019; George and Leidner, 2019). Additionally, the collective action and empowerment aspects might not be linked to political movements and activism. In an example of crisis management community self-organization, Leong et al. (2015) examine how social media empowers communities in crisis management. The research investigates the role of social media to empower the community in the Thailand flooding in 2011. The perspective followed that 'the empowerment roles of social media are enacted only when the actualization of power takes place' (Leong et al., 2015: 180). Hence, the study considers empowerment as a mechanism in which communities gain command of their activities – namely, empowerment as a process. From a process perspective, empowerment has structural, psychological and resource dimensions. The findings demonstrate that social media enables communities to attain collective participation through securing structural, psychological and resource empowerment. The structural empowerment is demonstrated by the increasing links and community participation, reducing the distance and alienation in the community. Resource empowerment is evident in the channelling of information onto the social media, thus reducing dependencies on the formal agencies, which increases the value of the platform and gains even greater participation, and also the facilitation of the capitalization and cultivation of local resources and their transformation into collective resources. The psychological empowerment role is outlined in voice expression, emotional resilience and sharing among community members (Leong et al., 2015).

6.2.2 IT and Negative Outcomes, Digitally-Led Exploitation

The negative effects of IT include: replacement of humans with metahumans and intelligent machines (Schuetz and Venkatesh, 2020; Lyytinen et al., 2020); automation, datafication and algorithmification (Raisch and Krakowski, 2020; Martin, 2015; Faraj et al., 2018); domination, control, emotion suppression and coercion (Hussain and Cornelius, 2009; Hong et al., 2016; Zheng and Yu, 2016); monitoring and surveillance (Howcroft and Wilson, 2003; Elmes et al., 2005; Iannacci and Hatzaras, 2012; Koch et al., 2012; Bernardi, 2017; Bernardi et al., 2017, 2019; Sahay et al., 2017); conflict and learning obstruction (Argyris and Ransbotham, 2016); and information asymmetries (Lightfoot and Wisniewski, 2014; Ghobadi and Clegg, 2015).

For example, in the context of online activism, Ghobadi and Clegg (2015) have examined the utilization of social media from activists against the regime in Iran. The regime suppressed the digital activism activities through constant surveillance, internet filtering and increased digital divide, which led to the decline of the digital activism. The case demonstrates that the powerful institution and regime retained their power and suppressed the digital activism activities against them through the means of control, information asymmetries, filtering information and the Internet, and surveillance and monitoring. Hence, Ghobadi and Clegg (2015) argue that the effects of IT might not be entirely predictable or planned. IT provides greater access to information; however, information can be inaccurate, filtered and controlled, and access to information can be unequal (Lightfoot and Wisniewski, 2014; Ghobadi and Clegg, 2015).

Lightfoot and Wisniewski (2014) explain that current technologies allow for data creation, information asymmetries and surveillance at an unprecedented scale. They outline the negative effects of information asymmetries in that information access and content are controlled, knowledge production is hindered, and surveillance and informational imbalances within societies are increased, which 'determines the possession of power'. In the surveillance society, people do not know what data is collected and how it is used, and also do not know when and why they are monitored (Lightfoot and Wisniewski, 2014; Kelly and Noonan, 2017). Furthermore, people accept the power asymmetries on the basis that what is provided is beneficial to them, without comprehending the negatives. However, surveillance is perceived as harmful as it hampers creativity, knowledge production and learning. It also restrains intellectual activities and restricts human rights and professional identity (Richards, 2013; Lightfoot and Wisniewski, 2014; Ghobadi and Clegg, 2015; Argyris and Ransbotham, 2016; Leidner and Tona, 2020; Vaast and Pinsonneault, 2021). Hence, Lightfoot and Wisniewski (2014) conclude that power arises from the organization of information.

Other negative IT effects include datafication, automation and algorithmification where these substitute humans with intelligent machines. The increased   datafication,   automation   and algorithmification leads to the hampering of learning, knowing, knowledge production and knowledge processes (Raisch and Krakowski, 2020), and to the incapacity to understand how machines and algorithms arrive at decisions (Ekbia et al., 2015; Faraj et al., 2018), which is also an issue with regard to the role of those developing the algorithms (Howcroft and Wilson, 2003). Other negative effects of algorithms are in the area of algorithmic decision-making (Elmer et al., 2015; Aversa et al., 2018). As a consequence of the predominant algorithmic decision-making utilization, context gets lost and experience gets ignored, hence leading to poor decision-making. However, people are subjected to following the algorithmic decisions which are on the path of replacing human decision-making and expertise (Aversa et al., 2018; Demetis and Lee, 2018; Faraj et al., 2018; Raisch and Krakowski, 2020).

In conclusion, the positive outcomes and digitally-led emancipation from IT utilization are evident; however, IT could also lead to negative outcomes and digitally-led exploitation. For example, the utilization of online platforms for collective action and its effects differs where the government stops the Internet and the communication, and monitors the activities of the activists (e.g., Ghobadi and Clegg, 2015), as opposed to enabling communication and consideration to the issues outlined (e.g., Leong et al., 2015). While social media has been the IT utilized in these examples, the outcomes of this utilization are different, leading to either digitally-led emancipation or digitally-led exploitation. Hence, it is not the technology which determines the outcomes – it is the utilization and enactment of the technology. We postulate that underpinning power mechanisms and fault lines are operating, which is why the outcomes of IT utilization are not consistent.

6.3 Power Mechanisms

The literature has recognized that IT can have both positive and negative effects, and the important role of power, as Young (2018: 341) has described:

Early research assumed ICT to be emancipatory e.g., Kanungo, 2004). IS scholars argued 'emancipatory knowledge will be acquired by developing countries through an adequate use of the technology' (Davis and Fonseca, 2006: 275–276). Such studies provided the foundation for the more nuanced view that is emerging. Research examining the emancipatory functions of media found that, paradoxically, ICTs are in some ways emancipatory, in others, hegemonic (Miranda et al., 2016). Emancipatory functions of ICT include truth exposure, democratization, community enhancement, inclusion, creative expression, economic facilities, political liberties, and facilitation of social change (Díaz Andrade and Urquhart, 2012; Miranda et al., 2016). Dysfunctions of ICT include perpetuating the interests of power elites through shaping of public consciousness, cultivation of ambivalence in the oppressed, proliferating displays of paternalism toward and devoicing of oppressed groups, and enforcement of oppressive systems (Lin et al., 2015; Miranda et al., 2016).

With regard to power, Giddens (1981: 357) affirms that it is 'the capacity to achieve outcomes' and explains: 'Whether or not these [outcomes] are connected to purely sectional interests is not germane to its definition. Power is not, as such, an obstacle to freedom or emancipation but is their very medium – although it would be foolish, of course, to ignore its constraining properties.' However, the role of power, in the existing IS literature, is predominantly linked to the hegemonic effects, not the emancipatory ones. Power is predominantly considered as negative, as opposed to a mechanism that can enact both digitally-led emancipation and digitally-led exploitation as outcomes of IT. Hence, power is predominantly considered from a power-as-possession perspective. However, power as possession is a unidimensional perspective on power, and different multidimensional perspectives on power exist (Lawrence et al., 2001, 2012; Pozzebon and Pinsonneault, 2012; Simeonova et al., 2018a, 2018b, 2020; Chapter 5).

For example, power from an individual perspective has been described as power as possession and also power as empowerment; from a collective perspective, it has been described as power as asymmetries and power as practice (Chapter 5). Within these power dynamics, information systems have a facilitative, coordinative or restrictive control role (Simeonova et al., 2020).

Hence, we theorize that power is a dynamic force which shifts the outcomes of IT towards either digitally-led emancipation or digitally-led exploitation, for which we utilize the episodic/systemic power perspective. To help understand these power dynamics, we utilize the episodic/systemic power conceptualization (Lawrence et al., 2001), where power is considered the underpinning mechanism affecting the outcomes of IT.

In their seminal article, Lawrence et al. (2001) outline power as a mechanism for achieving institutionalization. Following the episodic and systemic power conceptualization, they outline distinct power mechanisms – influence, force, discipline and domination – and examine their effects on the development and maintenance of institutions. The premise for the episodic and systemic modes of power is that power could be linked to actors and also to organized systems. Hence, Lawrence et al. (2001: 629) define episodic power: 'Episodic power refers to relatively discrete, strategic acts of mobilization initiated by self-interested actors.' Episodic modes of power have low stability with regard to institutionalization as these require constant activation of episodes to achieve continuity and sustainment of practices and institutions. However, the institutionalization is rapid, as it does not depend on continuous negotiations with the actors. On the contrary, the systemic modes of power achieve institutionalization at a slow pace, as these require continuous negotiations with the actors involved. However, systemic power leads to high stability of institutionalization, as it is integrated in routines and systems, and does not require constant activation. Hence, systemic power is explained as 'work[ing] through the routine, ongoing practices of organization' (Lawrence et al. [2001: 629]). In sum, episodic power operates through episodes of strategic action and requires continuous enforcement, while systemic power is integrated in systems of organized routine practices and does not require continuous enforcement.

Hence, we postulate the following:

1. IT has the capacity to lead to positive and negative outcomes, which are described as digitally-led emancipation and digitally-led exploitation.
2. The outcomes of IT are enacted through the exercise of power mechanisms.
3. The power mechanisms are not just linked to the negative effects of IT, hence following the distinction between episodic and systemic modes of power.
4. Theorization of power mechanisms, their enactment and fault lines in shifting IT outcomes towards digitally-led emancipation or towards digitally-led exploitation.

We utilize the episodic and systemic modes of power to understand how these power mechanisms enact the outcomes of IT. We outline the framework of power mechanisms and IT in Figure 6.1.

The obvious examples include systemic power mechanisms leading to digitally-led emancipation and digitally-led exploitation, and episodic power mechanisms leading to digitally-led

	Digitally-led emancipation	Digitally-led exploitation
Episodic	Collective action Participation	Manipulation Information asymmetries
Systemic	Empowerment Inclusion	Surveillance/monitoring Automation/algorithmification

Figure 6.1 Power mechanisms and IT

exploitation. The less obvious and theoretically interesting aspect is the enactment of episodic power mechanisms leading to digitally-led emancipation. We unpack these and particularly the episodic digitally-led emancipation power mechanisms.

The following mechanisms are theorized as mechanisms of episodic power contributing to digitally-led emancipation: *collective action* and *participation*. For example, Leong et al. (2019) demonstrate collective action and organization described as connective action and digital activism through social media in protesting against the development of a power plant which is not environmentally sustainable. The movement has managed to persuade the government to halt the project and to create an additional agency to evaluate the project and its environmental sustainability. The collective action, organization, participation and co-production utilized through the use of IT have led to providing the people with a voice for the emancipation of society, which in the described instance has been heard and acted upon. However, the example is an enactment of episodic power and realization of digitally-led empowerment as an instance, not as a systemic practice.

Other examples of participation and co-production are evident in the use of social media to request help. Approaching high-ranking officials directly on social media could occasionally trigger a lethargic bureaucracy to take action and get things done through exercising episodic power. However, it is an episode of power fault line as individuals in need should have established channels to get help and not have to utilize social media to approach high-ranking officials and request help. Such practices demonstrate the episodic power fault lines: it is not the remit of high-ranking officials; people might not have access to IT or the courage to approach high-ranking officials and ask for help via social media; such help should be available as an organized system from the relevant organization.

Next, the following mechanisms are theorized as mechanisms of episodic power contributing to digitally-led exploitation: *manipulation* and *information asymmetries*. For example, Cambridge

Analytica, which ran the American presidential digital campaign, have utilized a manipulation power mechanism. The manipulation of voters through social media is an example of an episode contributing to digitally-led exploitation, where people have been provided with filtered information to influence their votes. IT was utilized for covert and tailored practices to exploit people and their opinions, which resulted in the manipulation of the vote.

For example, control and information asymmetries are exhibited in the reaction of the Iranian government towards the digital activism activities (Ghobadi and Clegg, 2015). The efforts of the activists were controlled: the Internet and the information available were filtered to reduce the activities of the movement, which ultimately led to its decline. In addition, the increased instances of the datafication of individuals and society have increased digitally-led exploitation (Leidner and Tona, 2020).

At the other end of the continuum, the following mechanisms are theorized as mechanisms of systemic power contributing to digitally-led emancipation: *empowerment* and *inclusion*. Examples of opinions being considered, and people and communities being empowered, are evident in the utilization of IT for crisis management (Leong et al., 2015), promoting awareness and social cultural identity (Young, 2018) and social entrepreneurship (Sandeep and Ravishankar, 2016, 2018). Access to resources and participation in decision-making, empowerment, community empowerment, knowledge production and social entrepreneurship are examples of systems enabling digitally-led emancipation.

Another systemic power mechanism for digitally-led emancipation includes inclusion – for example, the provision of financial services in the Amazon river basin (Joia and dos Santos, 2019). It is an example of a government initiative to provide access to financial services in remote areas and islands in Brazil. A bank branch was installed via IT on a boat, Agência Barco, providing financial inclusion to remote areas. The initiative follows an organized system to achieve digitally-led emancipation through empowerment and inclusion. However, the lack of financial education and IT skills have proven to be obstacles to its success. Issues of social, digital and financial inclusion and skills are prominent in the current digital society (Díaz Andrade and Doolin, 2016, 2019). It is recognized that individuals, groups and communities are systematically excluded from access to opportunities and resources to IT (Trauth, 2017; Trauth et al., 2018; Díaz Andrade and Techatassanasoontorn, 2021). Hence, the systemic practices contributing to digitallyled emancipation could transform into systemic practices contributing to digitally-led exploitation, when people are coerced into the utilization of digital technologies at the workplace and for public services.

Lastly, the following mechanisms are theorized as mechanisms of systemic power and digitally-led exploitation: *surveillance/monitoring* and *automation/algorithmification*. Systemic practices of surveillance and monitoring leading to digitally-led exploitation are outlined in monitoring systems, performance measurement systems, automation and algorithmification of individuals. Surveillance and monitoring have transpired as systemic practices in organizations and society. This may or may not be covert; however, people might not be aware of when and why they are monitored (Workman, 2009; Iannacci and Hatzaras, 2012; Lightfoot and Wisniewski, 2014; Ghobadi and Clegg; 2015). These systemic practices contribute to digitally-led exploitation and negative outcomes of IT.

Automation and algorithmification are systemic power mechanisms contributing to digitally-led exploitation through hampering learning, experience and decision-making, and through replacing humans. The automation and algorithmification from organizations such as Amazon and Google have been utilized to collect and exploit data, eliminate competition and force organizations to follow their algorithms, which are against human rights (Naidoo, 2019).

Negative effects of algorithmic decision-making are outlined in an example of the Grand Prix in 2010 (Aversa et al., 2018), which Alonso lost because of the algorithmic pit decision. As a consequence of the decision, Alonso could not regain the lead in the championship. The result of the algorithmic decision-making was the loss of the championship and the Chief Race Strategist, even though he was instructed to follow the decision of the system. In that regard, the utilization of automation and algorithmification has been realized as digitally-led exploitation, where the Chief Race Strategist had no influence over the decisions. Such routinized and systemic practices explicated as digitally-led exploitation are increasingly the new norm of working. The increased algorithmification, automation and utilization of learning algorithms and algorithmic decision-making might obstruct knowledge production, innovation, exploration and learning (Demetis and Lee, 2018; Raisch and Krakowski, 2020; Simeonova et al., 2020; Chapter 5). And such routinized systemic organization can be easily attained with sustained negative effects, particularly as little regulation currently exists (Gozman et al., 2020).

In sum, IT has the capacity to lead to emancipation and exploitation depending on the enactment of power mechanisms. The enactment of episodic and systemic power mechanisms can contribute to digitally-led emancipation and digitally-led exploitation. The fault lines of power with regard to digitally-led emancipation demonstrate that emancipation attainment is quite difficult and not guaranteed, with short-term and not sustained positive effects. These can transform from emancipation to exploitation. The fault lines of power with regard to digitally-led exploitation demonstrate that exploitation attainment is not difficult, with sustained negative effects. And episodic-exploitation practices can transform into systemic-exploitation practices.

6.4 Conclusion

In this chapter, we have aimed to unpack the underpinning power mechanisms, and their fault lines and contribution to IT utilization outcomes – digitally-led emancipation and digitally-led exploitation.

The chapter developed a power mechanisms and IT framework to outline the episodic and systemic power mechanisms which lead to the digitally-led emancipation and digitally-led exploitation IT outcomes. The framework demonstrates the effects of the fault lines of power mechanisms and how these transition, for example, from episodic to systemic practices.

While episodic-exploitation practices might swiftly transform into systemic-exploitation practices, the fault lines of power in emancipation demonstrate that such transformation with regard to emancipation is difficult and not guaranteed. This demonstrates the dynamics of the power mechanisms and the realization of digitally-led emancipation and digitally-led exploitation.

In the current surveillance society, the systemic power practices contributing to digitally-led exploitation seem to be the most prevailing. Interestingly, and in contrast to the theories expounded by Lawrence et al. (2001), the systematization of episodes of digitally-led exploitation is rapid, particularly as the utilization of IT precedes regulation. In contrast, episodic practices contributing to digitally-led emancipation do not transform at a rapid pace (or these never transform) into systems contributing to digitally-led emancipation. A unique understanding provided in this theorization and chapter is that episodic power mechanisms have the capacity to lead to the realization of digitally-led emancipation. However, the transformation of these episodes into a system of practices is particularly challenging. The framework demonstrates that power mechanisms are dynamic and their enactment might shift IT outcomes towards both digitally-led emancipation and digitally-led exploitation.

These interesting findings outline other relevant questions: Are the episodic-emancipation practices reinforcing existing power structures, as opposed to increasing empowerment and emancipation? Can regulation challenge established systems contributing to exploitation? Are such practices an indication of how agile institutions are in monitoring and controlling these power mechanisms and IT? How can institutions sustain systemic-emancipation practices? These important questions are in need of exploration and qualitative research, particularly with regard to theory building, rich understanding of IT outcomes and power mechanisms.

References

Anduiza, E., Cristancho, C. G. and Sabucedo, J. M. (2013). Mobilization through online social networks: The political protest of the indignados in Spain. *Information, Communication & Society*, 17(6), 750–764.

Argyris, Y. A. and Ransbotham, S. (2016). Knowledge entrepreneurship: Institutionalising wiki-based knowledge-management processes in competitive and hierarchical organisations. *Journal of Information Technology*, 31(2), 226–239.

Aversa, P., Cabantous, L. and Haefliger, S. (2018). When decision support systems fail: Insights for strategic information systems from Formula 1. *Journal of Strategic Information Systems*, 27(3), 221–236.

Barrett, M., Davidson, E., Prabhu, J. and Vargo, S. L. (2016). Service innovation in the digital age: Key contributions and future directions. *MIS Quarterly*, 39(1), 135–154.

Bennett, W. L. and Segerberg, A. (2012). The logic of connective action. *Information, Communication & Society*, 15(5), 739–768.

Bernardi, R. (2017). Health information systems and accountability in Kenya: A structuration theory perspective. *Journal of the Association for Information Systems*, 18(12), 931–958.

Bernardi, R., Constantinides, P. and Nandhakumar, J. (2017). Challenging dominant frames in policies for IS innovation in healthcare through rhetorical strategies. *Journal of the Association for Information Systems*, 18(2), 81–112.

Bernardi, R., Sarker, S. and Sahay, S. (2019). The role of affordances in the deinstitutionalization of a dysfunctional health management information system in Kenya: An identity work perspective. *MIS Quarterly*, 43(5), 1178–1200.

Cardoso, A., Boudreau, M. C. and Carvalho, J. Á. (2019). Organizing collective action: Does information and communication technology matter? *Information and Organization*, 29(3), Article 100256.

Chen, J. V., Hiele, T. M., Kryszak, A. and Ross, W. H. (2020). Predicting intention to participate in socially responsible collective action in social networking website groups. *Journal of the Association for Information Systems*, 21(2), 341–365.

Chipidza, W. and Leidner, D. E. (2019). A review of the ICT-enabled development literature:

Towards a power parity theory of ICT4D. *Journal of Strategic Information Systems*, 28(2), 145–174.

Cui, M., Pan, S. L. and Cui, L. C. (2019). Developing community capability for e-commerce development in rural China: A resource orchestration perspective. *Information Systems Journal*, 29(4), 953–988.

Currie, W. and Lagoarde-Segot, T. (2017). Financialization and information technology: Themes, issues and critical debates – part I, pp. 1–6.

Currie, W. and Lagoarde-Segot, T. (2016). Financialization and information technology. *Journal of Information Technology*, 32(3), 211–216.

Davis, C. and Fonseca, F. (2006). Considerations from the development of a local spatial data infrastructure. *Information Technology for Development*, 12(4), 273–290.

Demetis, D. and Lee, A. S. (2018). When humans using the IT artifact becomes IT using the human artifact. *Journal of the Association for Information Systems*, 19(10), 5.

Díaz Andrade, A. and Doolin, B. (2019). Temporal enactment of resettled refugees' ICT-mediated information practices. *Information Systems Journal*, 29(1), 145–174.

Díaz Andrade, A. and Doolin, B. (2016). Information and communication technology and the social inclusion of refugees. *MIS Quarterly*, 40(2), 405–416.

Díaz Andrade, A. and Techatassanasoontorn, A. A. (2021). Digital enforcement: Rethinking the pursuit of a digitally-enabled society. *Information Systems Journal*, 31(1), 185–197.

Díaz Andrade, A. and Urquhart, C. G. (2012). Unveiling the modernity bias: A critical examination of the politics of ICT4D. *Information Technology for Development*, 18(4), 281–292.

Ekbia, H., Mattioll, M., Kouper, I., Arave, G., Ghazinejad, A., Bowman, T. et al. (2015). Big data, bigger dilemmas: A critical review. *Journal of the Association for Information Science and Technology*, 66(8), 1523–1545.

Elmer, G., Langlois, G. and Redden, J. P. (2015). *Compromised Data: From Social Media to Big Data*. New York, NY: Bloomsbury.

Elmes, M., Strong, D. and Volkoff, O. (2005). Panoptic empowerment and reflective conformity in enterprise systems-enabled organizations. *Information and Organization*, 15(1), 1–35.

Eseryel, U. Y. (2014). IT-enabled knowledge creation for open innovation. *Journal of the Association for Information Systems*, 15(11), 805–834.

Faraj, S., Pachidi, S. and Sayegh, K. (2018). Working and organizing in the age of the learning algorithm. *Information and Organization*, 28(1), 62–70.

Feller, J., Gleasure, R. C. and Treacy, S. (2017). Information sharing and user behavior in internet-enabled peer-to-peer lending systems: An empirical study. *Journal of Information Technology*, 32(2), 127–146.

George, J. J. and Leidner, D. E. (2019). From clicktivism to hacktivism: Understanding digital activism. *Information and Organization*, 29(3), 1–45.

Ghobadi, S. and Clegg, S. (2015). 'These days will never be forgotten . . .': A critical mass approach to online activism. *Information and Organization*, 25(1), 52–71.

Giddens, A. (1981). *The Constitution of Society*. Cambridge, UK: Polity Press.

Gozman, D., Butler, T. and Lyytinen, K. (2020). Regulation in the age of digitalization. *Journal of Information Technology*, 1–5.

Hong, Y., Huang, N., Burtch, G. and Li, C. (2016). Culture, conformity and emotional suppression in online reviews. *Journal of the Association for Information Systems*, 16(11), 736–758.

Howcroft, D. and Wilson, M. (2003). Paradoxes of participatory practices: The Janus role of the systems developer. *Information and Organization*, 13(1), 1–24.

Hussain, Z. I. and Cornelius, N. (2009). The use of domination and legitimation in information systems implementation. *Information Systems Journal*, 19(2), 197–224.

Iannacci, F. and Hatzaras, K. (2012). Unpacking ostensive and performative aspects of organisational routines in the context of monitoring systems: A critical realist approach. *Information and Organization*, 22(1), 1–22.

Joia, L. A. and dos Santos, R. P. (2019). ICT-equipped bank boat and the financial inclusion of the riverine population of Marajó Island in the Brazilian Amazon. *Information Systems Journal*, 29(4), 856–886.

Kanungo, S. (2004). On the emancipatory role of rural information systems. *Information Technology & People*, 17(4), 405–422.

Kelly, S. and Noonan, C. (2017). The doing of datafication (and what this doing does): Practices of edification and the enactment of new forms of sociality in the Indian public health service. *Journal of the Association for Information Systems*, 18(12), 872–899.

Koch, H., Gonzalez, E. and Leidner, D. E. (2012). Bridging the work/social divide: The emotional response to organizational social networking sites. *European Journal of Information Systems*, 21(6), 689–717.

Lagoarde-Segot, T. and Currie, W. (2018). Financialization and information technology: A multi-paradigmatic view of IT and finance – part II. *Journal of Information Technology*, 33(1), 1–8.

Lawrence, T., Malhotra, N. and Morris, T. (2012). Episodic and systemic power in the transformation of professional service firms. *Journal of Management Studies*, 49(1), 102–143.

Lawrence, T., Winn, M. I. and Jennings, P. (2001). The temporal dynamics of institutionalization. *Academy of Management Review*, 26(4), 624–644.

Leidner, D. E., Gonzalez, E. and Koch, H. (2018). An affordance perspective of enterprise social media and organizational socialization. *Journal of Strategic Information Systems*, 27(2), 117–138.

Leidner, D. E. and Tona, O. (2020). The CARE theory of dignity amid personal data digitalization. *MIS Quarterly*, 45(1), 345–360.

Leonardi, P. (2015). Ambient awareness and knowledge acquisition: Using social media to learn 'who knows what' and 'who knows whom'. *MIS Quarterly*, 39(4), 746–762.

Leonardi, P. (2014). Social media, knowledge sharing, and innovation: Toward a theory of communication visibility. *Information Systems Research*, 25(4), 786–816.

Leonardi, P., Leong, C., Pan, S., Bahri, S. and Fauzi, A. (2019). Social media empowerment in social movements: Power activation and power accrual in digital activism. *European Journal of Information Systems*, 28(2), 173–204.

Leong, C., Pan, S., Ractham, P. and Kaewkitipong, L. (2015). ICT-enabled community empowerment in crisis response: Social media in Thailand flooding 2011. *Journal of the Association for Information Systems*, 16(3), 174–212.

Li, L., Du, K., Zhang, W. and Mao, J. Y. (2019). Poverty alleviation through government-led e-commerce development in rural China: An activity theory perspective. *Information Systems Journal*, 29(4), 914–952.

Lightfoot, G. and Wisniewski, P. (2014). Information asymmetry and power in a surveillance society. *Information and Organization*, 24(4), 214–235.

Lin, C. I., Kuo, Y. and Myers, M. D. (2015). Extending ICT4D studies: The value of critical research. *MIS Quarterly*, 39(3), 687–712.

Linders, D. (2012). From e-government to we-government: Defining a typology for citizen coproduction in the age of social media. *Government Information Quarterly*, 29(4), 446–454.

Lyytinen, K., Nickerson, J. and King, J. L. (2020). Metahuman systems = humans + machines that learn. *Journal of Information Technology*, 36(4), 426–445.

Majchrzak, A., Faraj, S., Kane, G. C. and Azad, B. (2013). The contradictory influence of social media affordances on online communal knowledge sharing. *Journal of Computer-Mediated Communication*, 19(1), 38–55.

Martin, K. E. (2015). Ethical issues in the big data industry. *MIS Quarterly Executive*, 14(2), 67–85.

Mervyn, K., Simon, A. and Allen, D. (2014). Digital inclusion and social inclusion: A tale of two cities. *Information, Communication & Society*, 17(9), 1086–1100.

Miranda, M., Young, A. and Yetgin, E. (2016). Are social media emancipatory or hegemonic? Societal effects of mass media digitization in the case of the SOPA discourse. *MIS Quarterly*, 40(2), 303–329.

Naidoo, K. (2019). Surveillance giants. Amnesty International.

Pozzebon, M. and Pinsonneault, A. (2012). The dynamics of client-consultant power and knowledge. *Journal of Information Technology*, 27(1), 35–56.

Raisch, S. and Krakowski, S. (2020). Artificial intelligence and management: The automation-augmentation paradox. *Academy of Management Review*, 46(1), 192–210.

Raman, R. and Grover, V. (2020). Studying the multilevel impact of cohesion versus structural holes in knowledge networks on adaptation to IT-enabled patient-care practices. *Information Systems Journal*, 30(1), 6–48.

Rane, H. and Salem, S. (2012). Social media, social movements and the diffusion of ideas in the Arab uprisings. *Journal of International Communication*, 18(1), 97–111.

Richards, N. G. (2013). The dangers of surveillance. *Harvard Law Review*, 126(7), 1934–1965.

Sæbø, Ø., Federici, T. and Braccini, A. (2020). Combining social media affordances for organising collective action. *Information Systems Journal*, 30(4), 689–722.

Sahay, S., Sein, K. and Urquhart, C. (2017). Flipping the context: ICT4D, the next grand challenge for IS research and practice. *Journal of the Association for Information Systems*, 18(12), 835–850.

Sandeep, M. and Ravishankar, M. N. (2018). Sociocultural transitions and developmental impacts in the digital economy of impact sourcing. *Information Systems Journal*, 28(3), 563–586.

Sandeep, M. and Ravishankar, M. N. (2016). Impact sourcing ventures and local communities: A frame alignment perspective. *Information Systems Journal*, 26(2), 127–155.

Schuetz, S. and Venkatesh, V. (2020). The Rise of Human Machines: How Cognitive Computing Systems Challenge Assumptions of User-System Interaction. *Journal of the Association for Information Systems*, 21(2), 460–482.

Simeonova, B. (2018). Transactive memory systems and Web 2.0 in knowledge sharing: A conceptual model based on activity theory and critical realism. *Information Systems Journal*, 28(4), 592–611.

Simeonova, B., Galliers, R. D. and Karanasios, S. (2020). Strategic information systems and organisational power dynamics. In R. D. Galliers, D. E. Leidner and B. Simeonova (eds), *Strategic Information Management: Theory and Practice*, 5th edition. London and New York, NY: Routledge, pp. 221–238.

Simeonova, B., Karanasios, S., Galliers, R. D., Kelly, P. R. and Mishra, J. (2018a). Where is power in information systems research? Towards a framework. International Conference on Information Systems, San Francisco, CA.

Simeonova, B., Karanasios, S., Galliers, R. D., Kelly, P. R. and Mishra, J. (2018b). New ways of organising in collaborative knowledge sharing: Examining the effects of power. European Group for Organizational Studies, Tallinn, Estonia.

Tim, Y., Pan, S., Bahri, S. and Fauzi, A. (2018). Digitally enabled affordances for community-driven environmental movement in rural Malaysia. *Information Systems Journal*, 28(1), 48–75.

Trauth, E. (2017). A research agenda for social inclusion in information systems. *Data Base for Advances in Information Systems*, 48(2), 9–20.

Trauth, E., Joshi, K. and Yarger, K. (2018). ISJ editorial. *Information Systems Journal*, 28(6), 989–995.

Treem, J. W. and Leonardi, P. (2013). Social media use in organizations: Exploring the affordances of visibility, editability, persistence, and association. *The International Communication Association*, 36(1), 143–189.

Vaast, E. and Levina, N. (2015). Speaking as one, but not speaking up: Dealing with new moral taint in an occupational online community. *Information and Organization*, 25(2), 73–98.

Vaast, E. and Pinsonneault, A. (2021). When digital technologies enable and threaten occupational identity: The delicate balancing act of data scientists. *MIS Quarterly*, 45(3), 1087–1112.

Vaast, E., Safadi, H., Lapointe, L. and Negoita, B. (2017). Social media affordances for connective action – an examination of microblogging use during the Gulf of Mexico oil spill. *MIS Quarterly*, 41(4), 1178–1206.

Wasko, M., Faraj, S. and Teigland, R. (2004). Collective action and knowledge contribution in electronic networks of practice. *Journal of the Association for Information Systems*, 5(11–12), 493–513.

Workman, M. (2009). A field study of corporate employee monitoring: Attitudes, absenteeism, and the moderating influences of procedural justice perceptions. *Information and Organization*, 19(4), 218–232.

Young, G. (2018). Using ICT for social good: Cultural identity restoration through emancipatory pedagogy. *Information Systems Journal*, 28(2), 340–358.

Zheng, Y. and Yu, A. (2016). Affordances of social media in collective action: The case of free lunch in China. *Information Systems Journal*, 26(3), 289–313.

PART II

Methodological Considerations

Human Values in a Digital-First World: The Implications for Qualitative Research

HAMEED CHUGHTAI and MICHAEL D. MYERS

7.1 Introduction

How should human values be integrated into the studies of digital qualitative research, particularly in relation to the field of Information Systems (IS)? This question is becoming increasingly important as human values are always inscribed into our apps and devices (whether intentionally or unintentionally). Values are also inscribed into our research methods. This chapter discusses the implications for qualitative researchers of human values in a digital-first world.

Human values relate to one's predispositions of 'what is ethically good in life' that she or he strives to achieve in the world (Chughtai, 2020: 28). These include ethical, moral, cultural, political, aesthetic and social values, to name a few. Values are attached to things, technologies and places, as well as held by people.

A designer's ethical values may be intentionally or unintentionally inscribed into the finished artifact. A fascinating example is found in the work of Danish computer scientist Bjarne Stroustrup – the creator of the C++ programming language. Stroustrup (1994) says that many features of modern C++ relate to his core ethical values, deeply rooted in an existential worldview (p. 23):

> I find Kierkegaard's almost fanatical concern for the individual and keen psychological insights much more appealing than the grandiose schemes and concern for humanity in the abstract of Hegel or Marx. Respect for groups that doesn't include respect for individuals of those groups isn't respect at all. Many C++ design decisions have their roots in my dislike for forcing people to do things in some particular way.

Yet, when we use technology – from a programming language in complex tasks to a mobile phone in everyday conversations – we tend not to think about its underlying value structures. We do not always think, at least intentionally, about questions such as 'what are the core values of a designer (or a design team) and how does the designed technology relate to my values?' Why? It is because, when we use technology, we expect it to deliver the service or do the task as required. We also expect it to be *good* and do not expect that it will harm us in any way. These are obvious but critical observations and they need careful attention.

The person using a technology holds individual values. One may care more about a particular value, say digital privacy, and less about other values, such as safety. While the ethical and moral values attached to a technological artifact have attracted some attention (e.g., Friedman, 1997; Floridi, 2010; Friedman and Hendry, 2019), less is known about the implications of values held by people (human values) in researching our increasingly digital society.

In a digital society – or a *digital-first* world – digital technologies are simply taken for granted and almost all our human experiences become computer-mediated (Baskerville et al., 2020). Our research also becomes a computed human experience. This means that almost everything we do in our personal and professional lives is digitally mediated. For those of us who are qualitative researchers, the apps we use, the data we gather, our analysis of that data and the write-up of our qualitative research project – all of these activities are digitally mediated.

One implication of a digital-first world is that, if our digital technologies are created before a physical version, as opposed to technology representing physical reality, then the values inscribed into these technologies have the potential to shape our own values (Baskerville et al., 2020; Chughtai, 2020). As we rely on digital technologies more and more to conduct our essential everyday activities, including our own research activities, these technologies can promote some values and demote others.

Hence, the purpose of this chapter is to open up a discussion about human values in a digital-first world. We want to focus in particular on the implications for qualitative researchers. We begin our argumentation with the position that digital technologies impact human values in a digital society (and vice versa). We provide basic definitions of key concepts. This is then followed by a brief discussion of the current thinking and trends concerning human values. We conclude with some implications and suggestions for integrating human values into qualitative research and IS research more generally.

7.2 Human Values and (Digital) Qualitative Research

Qualitative researchers have long argued for the design and implementation of systems and technological artifacts to be conducted in an ethical manner (Friedman, 1997; Brey, 2000, 2018). In addition to improving organizational values (those that belong to the core value of a business or organization), it is suggested that researchers and practitioners should be sensitive to the social and cultural values of people who will be using the technologies. But how do researchers and designers go about supporting and upholding human values in practice? One problem is that the discussion surrounding values expects the reader to know *what a value is*. The distinction between values, norms, beliefs and morality is also often blurred, which can lead to ambiguity and thus undermine or downplay any discussion of values.

Human values can be understood at two levels: values attached to things (including artifacts, tools and technology, as well as places); and values held by people. According to Baier (1971), the value of a thing can be defined in terms of its power to benefit a person in some way. The values held by people can be interpreted in terms of their predispositions to use certain things to achieve certain ends. Borgmann (1984) uses this distinction to make a case for the promotion of human values in a good life. More recently, Chughtai (2020) also uses this distinction to explore human values in the context of digital work.

In human values scholarship, we observe a distinction between *intrinsic* and *instrumental* values (see Korsgaard, 1983; Rössler, 2018). A person or a thing is intrinsically valuable if it is valuable on its own. For example, the intrinsic value of an artwork can be stated in terms of its power to critique society or convey a message. On the other hand, instrumental values are found in those things that can be used as a means to obtain a valuable end. That is to say, an instrumentally valuable thing is not valuable on its own, but can be used to deliver some other value. For example, a computer programming language has no value by itself, but it can be used to create valuable software products and services. A thing or person can also be both instrumentally and intrinsically valuable, just as an activity can be intrinsically or instrumentally valuable. For example, someone might love their job for its own sake (e.g., an artist) because, to them at least, it is intrinsically valuable. They might not earn much money from their work as an artist. Another person, however, might hate their job, but they do it because it provides an income and hence it is instrumentally valuable.

Based on the above, our focal point is intrinsic human values that are held by people and can act as a moral compass for them. Brey (2018: 41, emphasis in the original) offers a working definition: '[Human] *Values* are ideals that people strive to realize in the real world. For example, if someone embraces freedom as a value, he or she will strive to act to promote conditions in the world that support or uphold people's freedoms.' Indeed, it is not possible to have a value be fully and permanently actualized. One always strives towards achieving that value to some degree. In their pursuit, people take actions that they believe are worthy and can help them realize their values. This process of evaluation of values is often referred to as 'valuation' (Brey, 2010: 46). Therefore, the concept of human values can also be understood as a sense of worth or what is *good* in life. A recurring theme in the human values literature is the promotion of a *good society* and how technology can bring goodness (Winner, 1983; Heikkerö, 2005; Fällman, 2010; Cath et al., 2018). Examples of human values that can promote good life include, but are not limited to, justice, fairness, equality and freedom, as well as those related to aesthetics, beauty and stability.

Next, we discuss three important areas of research where human values are used to advance methods and theories related to digital technologies. We will then provide some examples of how human values are informing contemporary qualitative research.

7.2.1 Value-Sensitive Design

The most recognizable application of values in digital research is value-sensitive design or VSD (see Friedman, 1997; Friedman and Hendry, 2019). This approach requires the designers of technology to consider values in favour of goodness so that the technology will benefit all and not just the key stakeholders. It is a radical approach that requires designers to entrench ethics into the built solutions with the aim that it will promote certain values. Ethical considerations drive the design process. Consider a mobile phone application (an app) that provides navigation services, such as Google Maps. A VSD approach would mean that the design should seek consent before using location data and inform the person of how the data will be used. It will also ensure that the data is not used in any other way that is not disclosed to the person. The value of privacy, for example, is promoted by paying attention to the design of the software so it does not contain harmful processes such as spyware, surveillance or data-mining without consent. We can then say that a technology can contribute towards human values as well as inflict disvalue (by working against the values). Researchers have contributed to the inclusion of values in design with approaches such as *reflective design* (Sengers et al., 2005). Other examples can be found in the emerging subarea of Systems for Human Benefit or S4HB, which is considered an extension to VSD (for an example of S4HB, see Hendry et al., 2017; and Venable et al., 2011).

7.2.2 Disclosive Computer Ethics

While Friedman says that it is the designers' responsibility to identify and uphold the appropriate values in designing new technologies, Brey (2000) wonders if this is possible without disrupting and changing the established digital practices in organizations where design is often 'morally opaque' (p. 11). In order to focus on the otherwise opaque digital practices, a disclosive computer ethics approach has been suggested. According to Brey (2010), 'the aim of disclosive ethics is to identify such morally opaque practices, describe and analyze them, so as to bring them into view, and to identify and reflect on any problematic moral features in them' (p. 51).

Many computer-related design practices often claim to have an attached moral value, but it is unclear how the values are upheld in design and practice. Without making the values visible, it is possible that an otherwise non-controversial design can do more harm than good. The case of the Facebook-Cambridge Analytica scandal related to illegal data mining is one such example. The scandal saw approximately 50 million Facebook profiles harvested by a firm called Cambridge Analytica. The data was used to profile US citizens. The firm was also associated with Donald Trump's election team, as well as the UK Brexit campaign. Amnesty International has referred to such practices as a threat to core human values and has questioned the business models of large IT organizations where surveillance of citizens and data harvesting are increasingly becoming a norm (see Amnesty International, 2019).

The disclosive computer ethics position holds that we cannot ignore contemporary digital practices just because there is no controversy related to them (for an excellent discussion of recent examples related to surveillance and human values, see Zuboff [2019]). Rather, values should be embedded in the design approach as a core principle. The task of disclosive computer ethics (as opposed to normative ethics) is to identify the human values and reveal the moral aspects of decision-making that are otherwise hidden in the practices and processes. The disclosive computer ethics approach aims to make the invisible visible and ready for inquiry.

7.2.3 Ethical Information Systems

Most qualitative researchers of digital technologies explore issues that occur in the context of business. Hence it is not a surprise that the question of ethics in the IS field remains business oriented (Mingers and Walsham, 2010; Walsham, 2012). Traditionally, ethical values are restricted to a discussion of effectiveness and increasing the efficacy of digital solutions that will meet the expectations of stakeholders (Chatterjee et al., 2009). However, this narrow focus has started to change. It has been argued that research should not be done solely for the benefit of a concerned business or organizations (e.g., Constantinides et al., 2012; Majchrzak et al., 2016), but also for the general good of the general public (Myers and Venable, 2014). The latter requires including and promoting human values through development of ethical information systems.

But ethics are not objective. Hence there is no such thing as (or even the possibility of) *the* ethical information system(s). Qualitative researchers are beginning to pay attention to other worldviews (e.g., Indigenous Peoples' cultures, LGBTQ+ populations, refugees and other marginalized groups in society) to include human values that are closer to the participants' (Ortiz et al., 2019; Chughtai et al., 2020) but that might be far from researchers' perspectives (Clarke and Davison, 2020). These are important steps to set the orientation of the field to diverse ethics-based perspectives.

In her study of the Klamath – an Indigenous group – Young (2018) explains how Indigenous cultural values shape digital technologies and vice versa. She found that digital technologies (in her case, technologies related to digital social media) can be used as instruments to uphold ethical values. Her study shows that, by embracing human values, marginalized groups can use digital technology to preserve Indigenous values through knowledge sharing and awareness, as well as through influencing the dominant political discourse. In this way, digital technologies can have some emancipatory power. Other related examples are documented and discussed by Ortiz and colleagues (2019), Chughtai and colleagues (2020) and Myers and colleagues (2020).

More recently, the pandemic associated with the coronavirus (COVID-19) has seen a rise in contact-tracing apps, which has alerted IS scholars to the challenges of reconciling human values which might sometimes be in conflict – for example, privacy and freedom. Rowe (2020) notes the value dilemma that the COVID-19 pandemic has revealed: 'we generally value privacy, but when we have an opportunity we are ready to trade it for something else' (p. 2). Gasser, Ienca, Scheibner, Sleigh and Vayena (2020) discuss this value dilemma and say that a conflict can arise between different values held by practitioners, researchers, policymakers and citizens. Gasser and colleagues provide a tentative set of principles based on 'beneficence, justice, non-maleficence, privacy, solidarity, and autonomy' to address value dilemmas concerning the use of digital technologies against the COVID-19 pandemic. These are important steps; but it remains to be seen how these principles will be used and refined (Sakurai and Chughtai, 2020).

7.3 The Role of Human Values in a Digital-First World

Today, research is increasingly being conducted in a *digital-first* world. A digital-first world is one where digital technologies are simply taken for granted and their primacy is evident. It refers to a digital society where, as Baskerville et al. (2020) describe, 'we see the world through computed reality' (p. 514). Most qualitative researchers use digital tools to conduct research even if their main context of research is not directly related to digital technologies. When we use these technologies, our experience of the world is shaped by them (see Figure 7.1).

At the core of Figure 7.1 is the argument for a digital-first world, which holds that there is an ontological reversal in progress. Baskerville et al. (2020) argue that, 'with digitization, digital objects are not simply a representation of the physical activities by firms and users; rather, digital objects are created first and these objects prompt physical activities and production of physical objects'

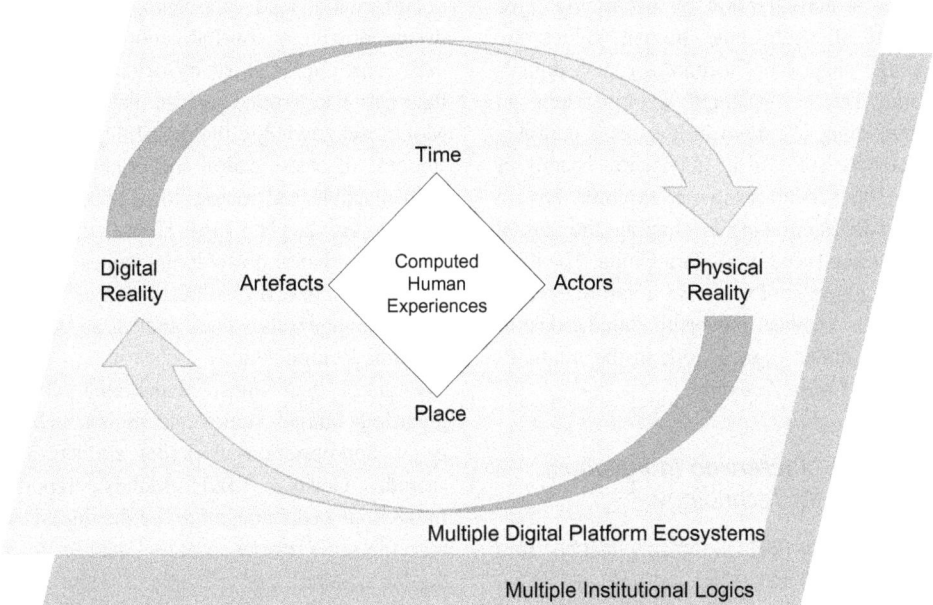

Figure 7.1 The framework of computed human experiences
Source: As described by Baskerville et al. (2020).

(p. 513). They suggest that the ontological reversal is creating human experiences that are a result of some sort of computation (e.g., a digital map connected to a GPS shapes the experience of the person using the maps). They call this phenomenon 'computed human experiences', which lie at the intersection of 'physical and digital reality' (p. 514). These experiences are 'curated by digital platform ecosystems [and] are shaped by multiple institutional logics' (p. 516).

Here, the relationship between the computed human experience (at the centre) and the institutional logics (at the margin) is significant for the study of human values. Haveman and Gualtieri (2017) define institutional logics as '*systems of cultural elements (values, beliefs, and normative expectations) by which people, groups, and organizations make sense of and evaluate their everyday activities, and organize those activities in time and space*' (emphasis in the original). We can say that Baskerville and colleagues' computed human experience thesis holds that experiences are shaped by values. What about values shaping our computed experiences? Take, for example, the ordinary case of

building one's family tree. Digital technologies such as the website *Ancestry* have large data sets (some of which are publicly available in some countries) that can build a comprehensive picture – a digital representation of a social concept. The experience is computed and the resulting digital picture shapes the viewer's idea of his or her family. Small digital details like boundary markers can have significant effects on how one understands where one's family begins and ends (Pálsson, 2007: 77). Based on the family codes and background, one might begin to understand oneself differently. A mundane computed experience can have a significant effect on someone's understanding of their place in the world (in this case, their wider family).

In his seminal anthropological inquiry of digital technologies' impact on society, Srinivasan (2017) reminds us that, to deconstruct technology, we must understand our human values that influence the design and development of technology. Our values make us what we are: human. But how can researchers go about interpreting those 'computed human experiences' by taking into account the values held by a person?

We offer a starting point by discussing three examples to illustrate how human values are shaping, and shaped by, technology in a digital-first world. The first example explores how an Indigenous value (*Kastom*) influences a complex digital database solution in the Pacific islands of Vanuatu. The second example explores how a cultural value (*Qinghuai*) is shaping the digital entrepreneurship scene in modern China. The third and final example explores how a spiritual value (*Duhkha*) can provide powerful foundations to understand complex digital work in the multicultural context of New Zealand.

7.3.1 Kastom – *Preserving Indigenous Values with Technology*

Geismar and Mohns (2011) offer rich insights from their study at the Vanuatu Kaljoral Senta (VKS). VKS refers to the Vanuatu Cultural Centre and National Museum of the Pacific island of Vanuatu. They wonder how digital technologies interact with Indigenous values in the projects of VKS that document and organize local knowledge and artifacts. To that end, they focus on the Vanuatu concept of *kastom*, which, although a pidgin word for custom, is quite different from Western historiography (see also Answer the Call of Vanuatu, n.d.). The notion of *kastom* is a way of life that comprises norms, culture, economy, art, and myths and magic. It explains how, in their everyday practices, Ni-Vanuatu – Melanesian people who are native to the islands of Vanuatu – engage with kastom in various forms such as kastom houses (sites to store artifacts and perform rituals), kastom tabu (objects and symbols related to Indigenous power structures) and kastom stories (narratives including myths and legends).

The study reported by Geismar and Mohns begins with an aim to understand how digital technologies interact with Indigenous values. Geismar and Mohns are aware of the socio-cultural complexities associated with the large relational database management systems (RDBMS) used to store culturally sensitive data. For example, an organization like a museum may decide to document and catalogue certain Indigenous information using RDBMS. But the database used for the documentation and cataloguing might have been designed with a non-Indigenous/Western worldview, and implemented by developers who bring their own background and familiarity. Geismar and Mohns acknowledge the possibility of an opaque 'process of classification and organization' that is both invisible and remote to the people (Geismar and Mohns, 2011: S136). Hence, the underlying question is that of postcolonial values: can colonial instruments like digital technologies be used to uphold Indigenous values and, in so doing, work towards decolonization?

Perhaps their most remarkable observation regarding human values and digital technologies is the appropriation of digital artifacts as being sacred. Geismar and Mohns report that Indigenous people began to see the digital artifacts with the same reverence as they had for their non-digital artifacts. For example, a Tabu Room for kastom was created as a repository for artifacts and documentation that hold some value for the Indigenous people (Ni-Vanuatu). More than a digital representation of reality, the digital material associated with the Tabu Room was subject to the same restrictions as the local kastom. In a sense, the digitized artifacts were seen primarily as kastom (as opposed to a copy or reproduction of the culture). Similarly, access and power structures were also reinforced. The otherwise computed human experience constituted 'a new genre of material culture' and created a possibility of preserving and improving Indigenous values (Geismar and Mohns, 2011: S136).

Based on the above, it can be argued that by contextualizing human values, it is possible to pave the path towards decolonization in theory and in practice. The issues and challenges related to human values can also be positively addressed by appropriately positioning the digital technologies. Next, we discuss a case of building digital solutions using spiritual values to promote social development.

7.3.2 Qinghuai – *Using Technology to Uphold Spiritual Values*

It has been argued that a critical aspect of digitalization research in the Chinese context is the use of traditional values such as *Guanxi* (a concept that explains the constitution of (in)formal ties in a social context). Qualitative researchers have found the notion of Guanxi helpful to explain the modes and structure of knowledge sharing using social ties and influences in a digital context (Huang et al., 2011).

Xiao, Tan, Leong and Tan (2021) point out that the pervasive nature of digital technology – what we would call a digital-first world – is disrupting the traditional environment and its associated values. In some cases, human values are embraced in a pursuit to do good in the digital world. Xiao and colleagues offer the concept of *Qinghuai*[1] to understand how internal processes of digital entrepreneurship are enacted in practice in a Chinese context. *Qinghuai* relates to one's spiritual values and is defined as 'a way of life that is associated with following one's heart (as opposed to perfect rationality)' and 'a moral commitment toward a spiritual ideal (e.g., contributing to society, conducting oneself in a righteous manner, etc.), as opposed to the pursuit of material or economic gains' (p. 8). More than a social form of entrepreneurship, Qinghuai is argued as something or someone in possession of a particular virtue. It is, therefore, a human value perspective oriented towards spirituality.

In their study of Qinghuai in three digital organizations, where digital technologies are pervasive, Xiao and colleagues offer examples showing how practices are informed by one's values. They observe that, in the digital work practices, many participants sacrificed their personal time and resources because 'they saw [it] as having an important societal purpose' and that 'they believed that they were chasing a spiritual goal and that "it was the right thing to do"' (p. 777). Xiao and colleagues argued that upholding the core value of Qinghuai was instrumental in actualizing the success of the three digital entrepreneurship start-ups they studied. They see this approach as contributing towards developing *responsible*

information systems (see Pan and Zhang, 2020; cf. Xiao et al., 2021: 780).

An important lesson here is that, in a *digital-first* world, human values are instrumental in enacting digital practices. As we saw in the previous example of the Vanuatu Cultural Centre, spiritual and moral values might be deeply rooted in people's everyday lives and thus less affected by the changes in the external environment. The example of Qinghuai shows that while one is immersed in digital technologies, at work and in everyday affairs, a *good* digital-first environment should enhance and uphold human values. This point is further cemented in our final example, which is discussed next.

7.3.3 Duhkha – *Overcoming Suffering Using Digital Technology*

Chughtai (2020) examines human values in his ethnography of digital work in an IT organization. The study documents and identifies human values in work practices and shows how IT professionals' work is influenced by their values. The broader ethnographic context of the study was New Zealand, where a rich mix of cultural values and access to digital technology is a given (at least in that part of the country where the research was conducted). The site of the study was a digital services organization, and the participants were the new generation of IT professionals who grew up in a digital-first world where technology is taken for granted. While the study documents different people's perspectives, a powerful example of human values at work is seen in the case of a digital worker called Sid, whose work practices were informed by his Buddhist values.

Sid's work ethics were informed by the spiritual value of *Duhkha* or suffering. In the Buddhist worldview, Duhkha or Dukkha is 'the true nature of all existence'.[2] Duhkha is a complex existential concept, which is often understood as sorrow, suffering or pain. But, at its core, it 'reflects a

---

[1] Xiao and colleagues provide the following useful etymological clarification (p. 776): 'Qing can be translated as "love" or "affection", while Huai can be translated as "bosom" or "mind". Together, the literal translation of Qinghuai is "the feelings and emotions that an individual possesses."'

[2] For an extended definition, see the entry for Duhkha in *Encyclopaedia Britannica*, www.britannica.com/topic/dukkha.

fundamental vulnerability to suffering and pain that can ultimately lead to world-weariness, the feeling that life is not worth living because there is no way to find meaning in it' (Ricard, 2014: 17). Overcoming Duhkha is a way of life and being in the world. It is possible that physical suffering or moral pain can lead to Duhkha; it can also be triggered by things over which we may or may not have any power. Examples include physical injury, disability (acquired, inflicted or by birth), war, disasters and losing a loved one. As a Buddhist, one must strive to overcome suffering and take action to minimize factors that could lead to suffering (for a detailed discussion of the concept, see Watts, 1985: 46ff; Ricard, 2014).

While Sid was embedded in a digital-first world, he saw technology as a way to uphold his spiritual values. As an IT engineer, he took decisions that would minimize disruption and proactively worked against potential error scenarios. The *good* use of digital technology, for him, was to '*bring out* true happiness' (Chughtai, 2020: 47, emphasis in the original). It is a powerful example of spiritual values informing digital work practices. While an engineer aims to minimize error in design, she or he may not see it as an existential issue or a cause of world-weariness. When one takes a value position, however, it orientates one's thinking and practices towards ethical and moral ideals.

The three examples discussed above (*Kastom*, *Qinghuai* and *Duhkha*) illustrate how values can influence people's use of digital technology in a digital-first world. This suggests that qualitative researchers must engage with human values in their research and go beyond topics associated with the mere use, adoption or acceptance of technology in a business context. The taken-for-granted assumptions regarding the complex relationship between human values and digital technology must be examined, critiqued and improved in order to make the world more inclusive and better for all.

7.4 Including Human Values in Digital Qualitative Research

Our values are moral compasses. In most cases, human values are deeply rooted in some form of

spirituality or religious belief, but also secular thoughts. The diversity of values adds the richness of meaning and experiences. In this chapter, we have tried to redirect the reader's gaze to the plurality of values and we hope that scholars and students of digital technology will examine, describe and integrate those values in the research (Escobar, 2018). We hope that qualitative researchers (as well as any other researchers interested in qualitative topics) will pay more attention to the changing nature of digital technology so that we will improve the human condition – not make it worse.

Our values are continually interacting with new and exciting digital technologies. With the emergence of a digital-first world, these experiences are becoming complex and computed; human values shape these experiences. There are some important implications and misconceptions for research on human values in a digital society, which we clarify and summarize next.

7.4.1 Begin with Values, End with Values

Human values have been marginalized in the studies of digital technologies in information systems research and qualitative research more generally. In a recent exhaustive review, Clarke and Davison (2020) warn that the status quo of information systems scholarship is 'generally unenthusiastic about, unwelcoming, and even hostile to research that does not privilege the business perspective' (p. 490). While design researchers have acknowledged the significance of human values for some time (Sellen et al., 2009), there is an implicit misconception among management researchers that only designers of technology should study values and others should focus on business and management concerns. Perhaps that is why most technology management studies use the term *value* as in (1) contributing benefit of some sort or (2) preference for a product or service (e.g., consumer value, organizational value or some other form of material benefit). It is a dangerous trend that disvalues human values. There is an immediate need to adjust our orientation in qualitative research related to digital phenomena. We recommend that qualitative researchers should explicitly disclose their values, acknowledge and address values of the participants and sites, and use these values as a guiding principle to understand and interpret their findings. Values should also be the end goal. A qualitative study should aim to improve the human condition.

7.4.2 From Values in Design to Values in Practices

We encourage designers to go beyond thinking about values only when they are designing systems. Instead of embedding value in a particular phase of design (e.g., prototype), values should be embedded in the research through and through. Researchers should examine how values embedded in artifacts relate to the values held by people, and how people interact with the technological artifacts in practice, before unthinkingly embedding a value-related concept in the design. Hence, it must be acknowledged that a digital technology's design is informed by values (including those related to researchers or designers) and efforts should be made so those values are made explicit when they are realized in practice.

As we learn from the study conducted by Geismar and Mohns (2011), different people use technologies in different ways; their values inform their ways of engagement. Another lesson learned from their study is this: The designers might have thought of human values in a particular way, but there are always unintended consequences, and people may use or even see the technological artifact radically differently from what was envisaged by the designers. Therefore, embedding values in design is not enough; the design of a particular digital technology might need to be improved continuously by learning from practices and how practices evolve in space (lived places) and time. Therefore, embedding values is not an immutable goal; instead, it is a moving target.

7.4.3 How Are Human Values Shaping and Shaped by Digital Society?

A new basic question has emerged: How are values influencing our digital society, and vice versa? In the broader context of qualitative research in a digital-first world, many questions arise as to how values will be influenced by digital technology and, in turn, how human values will influence the shaping of our digital society. For example, the rise of digital navigation systems on personal devices (e.g., Google Maps) is changing the perception of lived spaces. Digital mapping, therefore, is not just a digital enterprise, but it is also far-reaching and can change people's understanding of community and spatial awareness, more generally (for an example related to Indigenous people and digital mapping, see Chughtai et al., 2020). Hence, we call for more research on the complex relationship between values and technology at a socio-cultural level.

7.4.4 Plural Values, Plural Technologies, Plural Experiences, Plural Worlds

Are human values objective? Of course not. Different societies cherish diverse values and interpret values differently. Certain groups within a society may take a different position according to their perspective. Escobar (2018) has been arguing for embracing a plural view of lifeworlds. We add to his call and ask the question: What happens when plural values meet plural technologies in complex lifeworlds? It is perhaps the most challenging methodological problem for qualitative researchers working in marginalized contexts such as those related to the Global South and Indigenous worlds. It is tricky for three reasons:

1. Qualitative researchers often take a single theoretical/methodological perspective to conduct their study. This choice is often made for the sake of simplicity, but is riddled with ethical problems. A single perspective on human values can illuminate some values, but hide others. It also forces the researcher to assume that a single view of human values can reveal the whole picture.

2. If the methodological choice is grounded in an epistemology that is foreign to the participants' lifeworlds, then it can create problems of colonization or further marginalizing the marginalized (Chughtai et al., 2020: 300).

3. Researchers also hold specific values, which should be disclosed and acknowledged in the study.

Without addressing each of the three issues, a qualitative study of values and technology will be incomplete and partial, and may have problems of authenticity. Different technologies are developed with different values and used by people holding diverse values. In order to embrace and appreciate the plurality of experiences related to technology, or the plural computed humane experiences, it is essential to take a pluralistic approach.

7.4.5 Examine and Describe Computed Human Experiences

A computation requires appropriate interpretation to make sense of it. Similarly, we see the rise of *computed* human experiences, which we believe is the beginning of a much larger change in how we see and experience the world around us. For example, if a person's sense of justice is based on their computed human experience (e.g., background profiling using available data sets), then it is possible that they may see it as something *normal*. What is seen as normal, however, might undermine fundamental human rights.

To move forward, we must carefully interpret the new forms of experiences, including those related to human bodies, gender and politics (Chughtai, 2021; McKenna and Chughtai, 2020). Two important questions for qualitative researchers to ask are: How do people interpret their computer-mediated experiences? And how do we as researchers make sense of these experiences? We suggest studying computed experiences by taking a value position that explicitly recognizes what values are promoted and demoted by the experience. The task of qualitative researchers is to examine, describe, critique and improve our computer-mediated experiences.

7.4.6 Are We Heading towards a World with Computed Human Values?

We suggest that qualitative researchers should think about a problem that might occur in the not too distant future. Consider the following: there is a possibility of the emergence of computed human values, which might be directly or indirectly related to computed human experiences. Since one's values are firmly rooted in one's everyday experiences, it can be argued that the emergent values might have an aspect of computation as well in a digital-first world. Computed human values could be those future values that are rooted in continuous and emergent computed human experiences.

We are not there yet, but we can learn essential lessons from the ubiquity of the Internet. In some countries, such as Finland, access to the Internet is a legal right for every citizen. In other words, the social structure and functioning of society (in the Finnish example) relies on digital technology, which in turn contributes towards computed human experiences. Like Finland, most of the youth of the modern world has not seen a world without the Internet (even if access is not guaranteed as a basic human right).

Another example is related to the increasing use of Blockchain technologies. Researchers have begun to show how Blockchain-based solutions can affect human values in terms of a sense of belonging, equity, ethics of hierarchy and power structures (Kewell et al., 2017; Tang et al., 2019). When Blockchain technology becomes commonplace, the new generation will have a very different experience of the world and, in so doing, a different value set.

A change to human values is always slow, gradual and invisible. Hence, while we are beginning to see new computed human experiences, the full implications of this new digital first world are yet to emerge. Today, there are no examples of computed human values, but this does not mean that we will never see them. As qualitative researchers, we should be ready to address the complex moral and ethical problems related to them.

7.5 Conclusions

We conclude this chapter with an invitation to be sensitive to the diversity of values in society. By integrating a diversity of human values in qualitative studies, concrete steps can be taken towards interdisciplinarity in research. An interdisciplinary approach favours the plurality of values and asks the researchers to be sensitive to the values of their participants. By drawing on diverse values, researchers will be able to develop new and otherwise unfamiliar narratives of working with and living alongside technological changes such as those related to computed human experiences and values.

References

Amnesty International. (2019). Facebook and Google's pervasive surveillance poses an unprecedented danger to human rights, www.amnesty.org/en/latest/news/2019/11/google-facebook-surveillance-privacy/.

Answer the Call of Vanuatu. (n.d.). What is Kastom, www.vanuatu.travel/en/local-knowledge/local-knowledge-what-is-kastom.

Baier, K. (1971). What is value? An analysis of the concept. In K. Baier and N. Rescher (eds), *Values and the Future: The Impact of Technological Change on American Values*. New York, NY: Free Press, pp. 33–67.

Baskerville, R. L., Myers, M. D. and Yoo, Y. (2020). Digital first: The ontological reversal and new challenges for information systems research. *MIS Quarterly*, 44(2), 509–523.

Borgmann, A. (1984). *Technology and the Character of Contemporary Life: A Philosophical Inquiry*. Chicago, IL: University of Chicago Press.

Brey, P. (2018). The strategic role of technology in a good society. *Technology in Society*, 52(C), 39–45.

Brey, P. (2010). Values in technology and disclosive computer ethics. In L. Floridi (ed.), *The Cambridge Handbook of Information and Computer Ethics*. Cambridge: Cambridge University Press, Vol. 4, pp. 41–58.

Brey, P. (2000). Disclosive computer ethics. *Computers and Society*, 30(4), 10–16.

Cath, C., Wachter, S., Mittelstadt, B., Taddeo, M. and Floridi, L. (2018). Artificial intelligence and the 'good society': The US, EU, and UK approach. *Science and Engineering Ethics*, 24(2), 505–528.

Chatterjee, S., Sarker, S. and Fuller, M. (2009). Ethical information systems development:

A Baumanian postmodernist perspective. *Journal of the Association for Information Systems*, 10(11), 787–815.

Chughtai, H. (2021). Taking the human body seriously. *European Journal of Information Systems*, 30(1), 46–68.

Chughtai, H. (2020). Human values and digital work: An ethnographic study of device paradigm. *Journal of Contemporary Ethnography*, 49(1), 27–57.

Chughtai, H., Myers, M. D., Young, A. G., Borsa, T., Cardo, V. M., Demirkol, Ö. et al. (2020). Demarginalizing interdisciplinarity in IS research: Interdisciplinary research in marginalization. *Communications of the Association for Information Systems*, 46(1), 296–315.

Clarke, R. and Davison, R. M. (2020). Through whose eyes? The critical concept of researcher perspective. *Journal of the Association for Information Systems*, 21(2), 483–501.

Constantinides, P., Chiasson, M. W. and Introna, L. D. (2012). The ends of information systems research: A pragmatic framework. *MIS Quarterly*, 36(1), 1–19.

Escobar, A. (2018). *Designs for the Pluriverse: Radical Interdependence, Autonomy, and the Making of Worlds*. Durham, NC: Duke University Press.

Fällman, D. (2010). A different way of seeing: Albert Borgmann's philosophy of technology and human–computer interaction. *AI & Society*, 25(1), 53–60.

Floridi, L. (ed.) (2010). *The Cambridge Handbook of Information and Computer Ethics*. Cambridge: Cambridge University Press.

Friedman, B. (ed.) (1997). *Human Values and the Design of Computer Technology*. Cambridge: Cambridge University Press.

Friedman, B. and Hendry, D. G. (2019). *Value Sensitive Design: Shaping Technology with Moral Imagination*. Cambridge, MA: MIT Press.

Gasser, U., Ienca, M., Scheibner, J., Sleigh, J. and Vayena, E. (2020). Digital tools against COVID-19: Taxonomy, ethical challenges, and navigation aid. *Lancet Digital Health*, 2(8), e425–e434.

Geismar, H. and Mohns, W. (2011). Social relationships and digital relationships: Rethinking the database at the Vanuatu Cultural Centre. *Journal of the Royal Anthropological Institute*, 17(S1), S133–S155.

Haveman, H. A. and Gualtieri, G. (2017). Institutional logics. In *Oxford Research*

Encyclopedia of Business and Management, https://oxfordre.com/business/view/10.1093/acrefore/9780190224851.001.0001/acrefore-9780190224851-e-137.

Heikkerö, T. (2005). The good life in a technological world: Focal things and practices in the West and in Japan. *Technology in Society*, 27(2), 251–259.

Hendry, D. G., Woelfer, J. P. and Duong, T. (2017). U-District Job Co-op: Constructing a future vision for homeless young people and employment. *Information Technology & People*, 30(3), 602–628.

Huang, Q., Davison, R. M. and Gu, J. (2011). The impact of trust, guanxi orientation and face on the intention of Chinese employees and managers to engage in peer-to-peer tacit and explicit knowledge sharing. *Information Systems Journal*, 21(6), 557–577.

Kewell, B., Adams, R. and Parry, G. (2017). Blockchain for good? *Strategic Change*, 26(5), 429–437.

Korsgaard, C. M. (1983). Two distinctions in goodness. *Philosophical Review*, 92(2), 169–195.

Majchrzak, A., Markus, M. L. and Wareham, J. (2016). Designing for digital transformation: Lessons for information systems research from the study of ICT and societal challenges. *MIS Quarterly*, 40(2), 267–277.

McKenna, B. and Chughtai, H. (2020). Resistance and sexuality in virtual worlds: An LGBT perspective. *Computers in Human Behavior*, 105, 106–199.

Mingers, J. and Walsham, G. (2010). Toward ethical information systems: The contribution of discourse ethics. *MIS Quarterly*, 34(4), 833–854.

Myers, M. D., Chughtai, H., Davidson, E. J., Tsibolane, P. and Young, A. G. (2020). Studying the other or becoming the other: Engaging with indigenous peoples in IS research. *Communications of the Association for Information Systems*, 47(1), 382–396.

Myers, M. D. and Venable, J. R. (2014). A set of ethical principles for design science research in information systems. *Information & Management*, 51(6), 801–809.

Ortiz, J. C. A., Young, A. G., Myers, M. D., Bedeley, R. T., Carbaugh, D., Chughtai, H. et al. (2019). Giving voice to the voiceless: The use of digital technologies by marginalized groups. *Communications of the Association for Information Systems*, 45(1), 21–38.

Pálsson, G. (2007). *Anthropology and the New Genetics*. Cambridge: Cambridge University Press.

Pan, S. L. and Zhang, S. (2020). From fighting COVID-19 pandemic to tackling sustainable development goals: An opportunity for responsible information systems research. *International Journal of Information Management*, 55, 1–6.

Ricard, M. (2014). A Buddhist view of happiness. *Journal of Law and Religion*, 29(1), 14–29.

Rössler, B. (2018). *The Value of Privacy*. London: Wiley.

Rowe, F. (2020). Contact tracing apps and values dilemmas: A privacy paradox in a neo-liberal world. *International Journal of Information Management*, 55, 1–5.

Sakurai, M. and Chughtai, H. (2020). Resilience against crises: COVID-19 and lessons from natural disasters. *European Journal of Information Systems*, 20(5), 585–594.

Sellen, A., Rogers, Y., Harper, R. and Rodden, T. (2009). Reflecting human values in the digital age. *Communications of the ACM*, 52(3), 58–66.

Sengers, P., Boehner, K., David, S. and Kaye, J. J. (2005). Reflective design. Paper presented at the 4th Decennial Conference on Critical Computing: Between Sense and Sensibility. Aarhus, Denmark.

Srinivasan, R. (2017). *Whose Global Village? Rethinking How Technology Shapes Our World*. New York, NY: New York University Press.

Stroustrup, B. (1994). *The Design and Evolution of C++*. New York, NY: Addison-Wesley.

Tang, Y., Xiong, J., Becerril-Arreola, R. and Iyer, L. (2019). Ethics of blockchain: A framework of technology, applications, impacts, and research directions. *Information Technology & People*, 33(2), 602–632.

Venable, J. R., Pries-Heje, J., Bunker, D. and Russo, N. L. (2011). Design and diffusion of systems for human benefit: Toward more humanistic realisation of information systems in society. *Information Technology & People*, 24(3), 208–216.

Walsham, G. (2012). Are we making a better world with ICTs? Reflections on a future agenda for the IS field. *Journal of Information Technology*, 27(2), 87–93.

Watts, A. (1985). *The Way of Zen*. New York, NY: Random House.

Winner, L. (1983). Technē and politeia: The technical constitution of society. In P. T. Durbin and F.

Rapp (eds), *Philosophy and Technology*. Dordrecht, the Netherlands: Springer, pp. 97–111.

Xiao, X., Tan, B., Leong, C. and Tan, F. T. C. (2021). Powered by 'Qinghuai': The melding of traditional values and digital entrepreneurship in contemporary China. *Information Systems Journal*, 31(6), 769–802.

Young, A. G. (2018). Using ICT for social good: Cultural identity restoration through emancipatory pedagogy. *Information Systems Journal*, 28(2), 340–358.

Zuboff, S. (2019). *The Age of Surveillance Capitalism: The Fight for a Human Future at the New Frontier of Power*. New York, NY: Public Affairs.

One Picture to Study One Thousand Words

Visualization for Qualitative Research in the Age of Digitalization

HANI SAFADI, MARIE-CLAUDE BOUDREAU and SAMER FARAJ*

8.1 Introduction

Today's world is characterized by an ever-increasing influx of data generated at an unparalleled scale and speed. Trace data resulting from the digitalization of social and organizational lives provide new opportunities for researchers in the social sciences, management and humanities (Latour, 2010; George et al., 2016; Rai, 2016). By applying computational techniques from statistics, machine learning and pattern recognition to data that is large in scale, rich in details and expanding over time, it is possible to understand patterns of individual and group behaviour that were once beyond the reach of the scientific method (Lazer et al., 2009; Watts, 2013; Agarwal and Dhar, 2014; DiMaggio, 2015; Abbasi et al., 2016; Berente et al., 2019; Johnson et al., 2019).

While the availability of trace data and the advancement of computational methods to analyze it allow researchers to test new hypotheses and validate theories, the exploration and inductive understanding of social phenomena are more challenging and require new tools and apparatus (Gaskin et al., 2014; Pentland et al., 2020). This is particularly more prevalent when questions are not well defined and data are unstructured, making quantification and computing less amenable. Researchers trained in the qualitative tradition are familiar with the difficulties, challenges and efforts involved in gaining a deep understanding of qualitative data (Finlay, 2002; Bansal et al., 2018). These challenges are only exacerbated when analyzing trace data in digitalized contexts, such as in social media and virtual worlds (Schultze, 2012; McKenna et al., 2017).

Advances in scientific knowledge are often the synergistic outcomes of advances in methods and theories (e.g., Van de Ven and Poole, 1990). For instance, a survey of prior Nobel awards in physics, chemistry and medicine shows that many winners were recognized for advancing scientific tools and apparatus, which in turn inspired advances in theoretical knowledge (Greenwald, 2012).

Advancing methods and tools is nothing novel to the qualitative research community that pioneered multiple methods (including, among others, grounded theory, case studies and process theorization) to legitimize qualitative research in the social sciences (Glaser and Strauss, 1967; Eisenhardt, 1989; Lee, 1989; Langley, 1999). Qualitative researchers in the information systems research community also pioneered advances in qualitative methods, including mixed-methods, processes research and computational theory development

* Hani Safadi would like to acknowledge support from the University of Georgia Terry-Sanford research award and funding from the Institute of Museum and Library Services (IMLS) National Digital Platform initiative (Grant LG7217007817). He would like to acknowledge his collaborators on the IMLS grant, professors Nicholas Berente, Richard Watson and Usha Rodrigues. He would like to acknowledge professors Emmanuelle Vaast and Aron Lindberg for providing feedback on an earlier draft of this chapter.

(Venkatesh et al., 2013; Gaskin et al., 2014; Berente et al., 2019; Pentland et al., 2020).

In this chapter, we argue for further advancing qualitative research methods by creating tools to investigate digital traces of digital phenomena. We specifically focus on large-scale textual data sets and show how interactive visualization can be used to augment qualitative researchers' capabilities to theorize from trace data. We ground our approach on prior work in sensemaking, visual analytics and interactive visualization (Russell et al., 1993; Munzner, 2014), and show how tasks enabled by visualization systems can be synergistically integrated with the qualitative research process. Finally, we apply these principles with several open-source text mining and interactive visualization systems.

We hope that this chapter stimulates further interest and provides specific guidelines for developing and expanding the repertoire of open-source systems for qualitative research.

8.2 Qualitative Research Methods in the Age of Digitalization

We use the term digitalization to refer to the increased prevalence of information and communication technology as a medium for social activities and interactions. Digitalization is pervasive in both the personal and the professional lives of many people worldwide. Digital technology is unique in that it leaves a digital exhaust of trace data as a by-product of online interactions and activities (Neef, 2014). While acknowledging the privacy concerns of making social activities largely transparent (Zuboff, 2015; Stohl et al., 2016), trace data of digitalized contexts offer a unique opportunity for researchers to study and understand social phenomena at an increasing scale and scope (Latour, 2010; Berente et al., 2019).

Researchers using qualitative research methods face two special challenges when examining trace data. First, the scale of the data challenges the capacity of researchers to systematically, comprehensively and rigorously analyze all data (Gioia et al., 2013). Second, because digital trace data is typically left data, researchers are distant from the focal phenomenon, which challenges their ability for iterative and reflexive sensemaking (Walsh, 1995; Finlay 2002) and the degree to which they can bring their background knowledge and personal experience to the process of knowledge creation (Polanyi, 1962; Cook and Brown, 1999; Tsoukas, 2009). These two challenges are interdependent. For instance, the grounded theory methodology suggests that researchers build an incremental understanding of data to generate theory and augment their data until they reach theoretical saturation (Glaser and Strauss, 1967; Walsh et al., 2015).

Recently, there have been multiple attempts to bridge the gap between qualitative and quantitative research. These approaches fall within the broad category of mixed-methods and aim to provide guidelines and best practices for integrating quantitative and qualitative methods for studying quantitative and qualitative data (Venkatesh et al., 2013; Zachariadis et al., 2013; Berente et al., 2019; Lindberg, 2020). Mixed-methods have been successfully applied in studying multiple digital phenomena, including online communities (Levina and Vaast, 2015), digital platforms (Hukal et al., 2020) and social media (Vaast et al., 2017). However, whereas mixed-methods bridge the gap by substituting qualitative inquiry for quantitative inquiry, they do not expand the scope for qualitative methods to study digital trace data.

Focusing on this goal, we maintain that new apparatuses are needed to study digital phenomena (Østerlund et al., 2020). As an illustration of such an apparatus, consider ThreadNet – an open-source tool for contextualizing events using networks and visualizations (Pentland, 2016). While digital traces provide rich and fine-grained data about processes, contextual information is often missing. By enriching it with context, ThreadNet makes process trace data more informative for systematic inquiry about the dynamics of processual phenomena (Pentland et al., 2020).

Within the overall objective of creating tools for advancing qualitative research methods, we focus on tools that facilitate the study of a large set of textual documents from trace data. Notwithstanding the importance of different kinds of trace data and different techniques for analyzing it (Berente et al., 2019), researchers' understanding of data underlying the phenomenon is the cornerstone of qualitative research (Bansal et al., 2018) and is most challenging when data is large and distant from the researcher. Information systems for improving sensemaking can bridge this gap between digital trace data and qualitative researchers. We outline below the principles of designing such systems and the predominant role of interactive visualization in enabling sensemaking tasks.

8.3 Interactive Visualization for Improving Human Sensemaking

Humans are *informavores*; they survive in their environment by constantly ingesting and organizing information in a two-process loop (Miller, 1984). The first process is *information foraging*, which refers to information seeking, gathering and consumption. The second process, *sensemaking*, refers to representing information in mental schemas to develop insights through the manipulation of these schemas and the creation of knowledge or direct action based on the insight (Russell et al., 1993; Pirolli and Card, 2005). A better understanding of information foraging and sensemaking allows people, when possible, to modify their strategies or the structure of the environment to maximize their rate of gaining valuable information (Pirolli and Card, 1999).

Information foraging extends to many situations in which people seek to understand issues and events that are novel, ambiguous or confusing, or in some other way violate prior expectations (Maitlis and Christianson, 2014). This is particularly true for researchers when novel observations yield surprising results and call for reconsidering existing models and theories (Richardson and Kramer, 2006). The need for sensemaking arises when people experience a cognitive gap resulting from novel observations (Dervin, 2003). Sensemaking involves fitting new data into existing mental models and adjusting mental models around data (Klein et al., 2006a; Klein et al., 2006b).

Effective analytical reasoning requires a mix of information foraging and sensemaking

(Shrinivasan and van Wijk, 2008). For example, qualitative researchers working with text documents need to connect threads of evidence to create concepts and categories for understanding the body of texts (Langley, 1999; Gioia et al., 2013). Researchers can do this manually for a small number of documents, but as the volume grows and the corresponding number of concepts and categories within the documents grows larger, foraging and sensemaking processes become difficult for manual analysis (Stasko et al., 2008). In the past three decades, computer and information systems have been designed to improve and support information foraging and sensemaking.

8.3.1 Improving Information Foraging

Information foraging involves collecting and organizing external information. For example, qualitative researchers working with text documents need to connect evidence to form hypotheses and theories of potential interest. This work involves reading and organizing text and identifying concepts and entities in addition to their relationships (e.g., spatial, temporal, causal). The constructed mental models allow for further development of hypotheses in the sensemaking process. The foraging process relies on human memory to process information and represent schemas as internal mental models. Limits of internal cognition and memory limit the scaling of this process of a large amount of data (Neisser, 1976).

To overcome the limits of internal cognition and memory, *external representations* of information provide a shareable object of thought and change the cost structure of the inferential landscape (Kirsh, 2009). External representations swap cognition with perception by invoking the human visual system to perform a significant amount of visual information processing in parallel with cognition at the preconscious level (Munzner, 2014: ch. 6). External representations can be used to substitute and to complement internal representations in improving cognitive tasks (Hegarty, 2004; Liu et al., 2008). Herbert Simon argued that mathematics can be viewed as changes in representation that make explicit what was previously implicit: 'Solving a problem simply means representing it so as to make the solution transparent' (Simon, 1996: 132).

Visual external representation is often used because of the superiority of human vision and visual perception of all other senses (Anderson et al., 2005). While humans possessed an advanced visual sensory system and perception, developing language, particularly reading and writing, came much later. External representations seek to shift the burden between cognition and perception by visualizing textual and numerical data (Munzner, 2014). Larkin and Simon (1987) provide several examples of problems that are very hard to solve without relying on external visual representations.

Visual representations are used for the construction of arguments and the exploratory investigation and evaluation of alternative hypotheses (Shrinivasan and van Wijk, 2008). Alternative data representations are visually presented to analysts to support analytical reasoning (Endert et al., 2014). Early visual analytics systems focused on transforming data to produce multiple representations that evoke different situated cognitive strategies and lead to more efficient and effective reasoning (Liu et al., 2008). Visual external representation also offers several benefits, such as organizing data by spatial location to speed up search and recognition and bundling similar information for a specific problem-solving inference (Munzner, 2014).

Creating visual representations is our first guiding principle for empowering qualitative researchers to investigate trace data of digital phenomena.

8.3.2 Improving Sensemaking

The sensemaking process relies on the schema produced in the information-foraging process to make decisions and reach insights. External representation helps to alleviate the cognitive overload of short-term memory by engaging the visual perception system to ingest a large volume of information. However, human attention also has severe limits. Conscious search for items is an operation that grows more difficult as the number of items increases (Shirley et al., 2015: ch. 20). Performance in search tasks degrades quickly with far worse results after several hours than in the first few minutes (Ware, 2012). Systems designed for improving sensemaking should enable its users' focus on making judgements while automating the routine tasks. This principle is referred to as Human-In-The-Loop (Schirner et al., 2013).

The Human-In-The-Loop principle stresses the importance of interactivity between the system and its users and augmenting their cognitive capability rather than replacing it (Endert et al., 2014). Textual data sets are hard to represent and visualize in a single static view. By responding to user input and changing the view on demand, the system overcomes the limitations of a static visual encoding and enables the user to comprehend the high-level patterns, but also sensemake based on the details (Munzner, 2014: 244). Interactive visualization is different from but complementary to static visualization typically used in reporting research results. Whereas static visualization enables researchers to communicate their understanding of the data ex-post, interactive visualization enables researchers to gain such understanding.

Interactivity is the second guiding principle for empowering qualitative researchers to investigate trace data of digital phenomena.

8.3.3 Zooming in and out from Data to Representation and Back

One key task in analyzing textual data involves synthesizing concepts and ontologies from the text (Gotz et al., 2006; Wright et al., 2006). Discovering concepts, exploring their relationships and eliciting evidence from documents is one step towards gaining a comprehensive understanding of the target phenomenon. However, developing a personal understanding of this text requires a deep and reflexive interaction through it (Finlay 2002; Charmaz, 2006: ch. 8) where researchers reflect on their past experiences as well as experiences of the 'generalized other' people represented in the data. New knowledge is created when researchers explicate their background knowledge and distance themselves from their old understanding of the phenomenon (Tsoukas, 2009).

Zooming in and out is used as a metaphor when investigating digitalized phenomena. This metaphor can further guide creating research apparatus. For example, through computational apparatus, complex digital trace data can be examined across multiple spatial and temporal cross-sections via computational methods (Latour, 2010; Gaskin et al., 2014). In qualitative research, zooming in and out enables forming understanding at multiple levels of abstractions (Gioia et al., 2013), as well as connecting the dots between these levels across contexts (Nicolini, 2009).

Visual analytics systems embrace the continuous exploration of the data (Chau et al., 2011). These systems can facilitate zooming in and out of the data by presenting both the original text and its summary representation (Shrinivasan and van Wijk, 2008). Beyond presenting the original data and its visual summary, systems can provide summaries at different levels of granularity with linkages between these levels (Stasko et al., 2008; Brehmer et al., 2014).

Providing multiple representations of trace data at different levels of granularity along with their associations is the third guiding principle for empowering qualitative researchers to investigate trace data of digital phenomena.

In sum, visualization, interactivity and multiple representations are the three guiding principles for designing visualization systems for qualitative research of trace data. Surprisingly, qualitative and even quantitative research in social science rarely uses interactive visualization during the research phase. Systems are developed in other disciplines to combine the best of computation and human perception for analyzing textual documents. Building on the three principles, we show how visualization can be used in tandem with qualitative theorizing from data.

8.4 Interactive Visualization for Qualitative Research

We now show how interactive visualization can be used to improve the process of qualitative research. We focus on grounded theory methodology (GTM) as a class of methods to build a theory based on the systematic analysis of qualitative data (Charmaz, 2006; Suddaby, 2006; Morse et al., 2009; Urquhart, 2013; Walsh et al., 2015). As

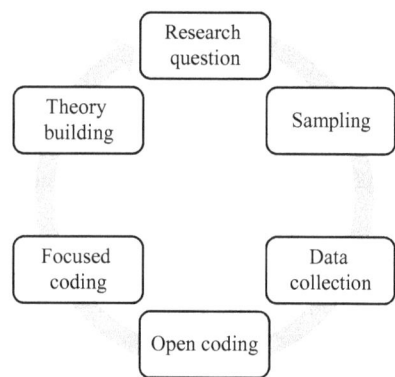

Figure 8.1 The process of grounded theory methodology

outlined by Tweed and Charmaz (2011), this particular focus enables us to be specific about the different stages in the research process (Figure 8.1). Notwithstanding this focus, the association between the research stages and the roles of interactive visualization to improve them is general and should apply to different traditions in qualitative research (Bansal et al., 2018).

8.4.1 Grounded Theory Methods Research Process and Challenges of Trace

Figure 8.1 illustrates the process of GTM. Briefly stated, the process begins from an initial research interest followed by theoretical sampling to collect data suitable to answer the question. This data is analyzed incrementally with open coding to identify concepts and categories. More data is added incrementally to expand and add nuances to identified themes until reaching saturation. Next, selective and focused coding is applied to identify several types of relationships among identified concepts. At this stage, defined concepts and relationships are constantly compared to different interpretations of data. These interpretations are finally woven into an emergent theory, and a chain of evidence is created to transparently show how this emergent theory came about (Glaser and Strauss, 1967; Charmaz, 2006; Walsh et al., 2015). Within this process, four activities are challenging with trace data: theoretical sampling, coding, constant comparison and the creation of a chain of evidence.

8.4.1.1 Theoretical Sampling

Theoretical sampling strategies are important in grounded methods because they allow researchers to get into the data and provide a significant direction for theorizing (Thomas and James, 2006; Urquhart et al., 2010). With trace data, this important aspect of grounded theorizing is transformed into creating questions for the systematic yet relevant extraction of meaning for the analysis and theory building (Pan and Tan, 2011). First, instead of limited access to in-depth data such as interviews and observations, researchers have quasi-unlimited access to distant data. Sampling becomes an issue of reducing the large data set and selecting parts that can lead to interesting insights. Second, the collected data lack context. Although the data are large, they are fragmented and may not necessarily result in a cohesive understanding of the phenomenon under consideration. The search for leads in the data and reconstructing context involves a huge cognitive overload. As a result, researchers risk gravitating towards specific understandings of multifaceted phenomena rather than considering all potential interpretations offered by data (Levina and Vaast, 2015). Theoretical sampling in this context thus challenges the 'relatedness' validity criterion, that is, the extracting of a meaningful sample from a large data set.

8.4.1.2 Coding

Within GTM, the coding process involves two approaches: substantive coding (which typically includes open and selective coding); and theoretical coding. Whereas substantive coding refers to the conceptualization of empirical data (and often is taken directly from the language of the data, via in vivo codes), theoretical coding involves advanced abstractions to provide a framework for enhancing the explanatory power of the emerging grounded theory. As with other concepts in GTM, theoretical codes must show 'earned relevance'; that is, they must not be preconceived or forced into the analysis. Still, it is easy to fall into the trap of conceptualizing concepts that are known from the start. To address this challenge, researchers can use predefined high-level sociological constructs known as 'coding families' (Glaser, 1978).

Even with these suggestions, theoretical coding remains a source of struggle among grounded theorists (Glaser, 2005, 2013). This challenge is only exacerbated by the volume and variety of trace data. There is much more data to code and more concepts to explore. Relying on pre-existing codes can be enticing given the large number of documents that researchers need to sift through. Glaser (2013) warned that researchers should apply as many theoretical codes from as many sources as possible. They should also refrain from the temptation of over-relying on one's 'pet' codes, that is, those associated with theories researchers happen to be familiar with. In other words, researchers, as they proceed to theoretical coding, should refrain from trying to 'fit the data' into preconceived conceptualization. On the other hand, the families of codes suggested by Glaser (1978) and Strauss and Corbin (1998) may already be too limiting. Thus, 'appositeness', which is a validity criterion referring to the suitability or fitting of the data to the context, is challenged in the context of large textual trace data sets.

8.4.1.3 Constant Comparison

Constant comparison is an analysis technique frequently used within GTM (Urquhart et al., 2010). The premise behind this technique is that by comparing and contrasting many similar and dissimilar data units, a researcher is more likely to generate dense categories and properties about the phenomenon under study. For example, a researcher might want to compare all social media users with a certain property value with all other users with different property values and analyze what other properties emerge as salient differences. She or he may also use a 'flip-flop' technique (Strauss and Corbin, 1998), which involves turning a concept upside down and looking for extreme cases. Another approach to constant comparison is to conduct 'far-out' comparisons, where a researcher compares and contrasts a contextualized data set with another data set associated with a different context to potentially uncover new properties that might not have been obvious to the researcher from the onset.

Whereas constant comparison is a powerful approach to increasing one's theoretical sensitivity

(Glaser, 2005, 2013), it becomes a challenge when applied to trace data. For example, researching social media impact, a researcher has an immense population to leverage. Even a small slice of such a potential data set will be quite significant in volume (Vaast et al., 2017). The researcher is also constrained by whatever the data reveal. For example, the data may be about a single platform or one group of users (Levina and Arriaga, 2014), making comparisons with other platforms or groups of users impossible. Constant comparison can benefit from integrating and relating data sets from different sources, although this is not practically feasible given the lack of standardization of data formats. 'Comprehensiveness', therefore, is at stake when proceeding to the constant comparison approach in the context of trace data of digital phenomena.

8.4.1.4 Chain of Evidence

One of the strengths of the grounded theory method is its ability to provide a chain of evidence (Charmaz, 2006). Indeed, given the detailed approach and guidance provided by the method, grounded theorists should be in a position of strength to explain their coding process, how categories (and their properties) emerge, how relationships between categories were established and how categories were combined to form larger concepts. By doing this, they avoid charges often directed to qualitative researchers – namely, that they are selective about the data they use to back up their theory (Urquhart, 2013). Whereas such a chain of evidence always adds to trustworthiness, it can, in some epistemological traditions such as positivism or critical realism (Zachariadis et al., 2013), also be used in verification, wherein other researchers can independently verify the findings by reproducing the grounded theorist's analysis.

Verification and more generally the quality, reproducibility and accountability of qualitative research have been the subject of much attention in the literature (Seale, 1999), not only for grounded theorists, but also for all qualitative researchers. Although the chain of evidence can be used to support trustworthiness or encourage verification, it is rarely detailed in journal-length publications, primarily due to space limitation. Grounded theorists, indeed, often have to choose between explaining their theory or the chain of evidence leading to it (Urquhart, 2013). If they do expose their chain of evidence, it is often in a highly summarized format, where a subset of raw data is shown to support codes that are then combined into categories. Often missing are the details of how the researcher revealed categories (e.g., by comparing slices of a data set via the constant comparative technique, discussed earlier), how properties emerge as particularly relevant or irrelevant, and which alternative open coding families were considered, and the insight they provided. Dealing with trace data compounds this challenge, as publication space limitations in addition to the expansiveness of analyzed data impose a trade-off in writing and reporting findings. On the downside, not being as transparent and comprehensive regarding the chain of evidence calls into question the trustworthiness of the research findings.

Table 8.1 summarizes the key challenges posed by trace data to grounded theorists. The availability of trace data combined with the advances of computational techniques has led to increased interest in computational methods to analyze the data and

Table 8.1 Key challenges to grounded theorists relying on textual trace data

Challenged validity criteria	Challenged research activities	Description of the challenge
Relatedness	Theoretical sampling	Extracting a meaningful sample for a large data set
Appositeness	Theoretical coding	Coding a large number of documents without being limited to a preexisting set of codes
Comprehensiveness	Constant comparison	Comparing and contrasting data and codes across different dimensions
Trustworthiness	Chain of evidence	Summarizing and presenting results

mixed-methods for combining quantitative and qualitative inquiries. Not addressing these challenges compels researchers to favour quantitative methods over qualitative ones. Fortunately, computational techniques can be used for enriching qualitative research, as we describe below.

8.4.2 Interactive Visualization Tasks

We outlined the three guidelines for designing interactive visualization systems to support qualitative research. We now expand on how such a system can meet the challenges of researching trace data. We rely on the taxonomy of tasks enabled by a visualization system illustrated in Figure 8.2, adapted from Munzner (2014: 47). In the discussion below, we use the term 'the system' to briefly refer to the interactive visualization system designed to enable these tasks.

8.4.2.1 Analyze

The system's most common task is to allow the user to understand existing data presented visually to generate new knowledge. This new knowledge can be a new hypothesis, but also a validation or disconfirmation of an existing one. The system can also allow the user to annotate existing data and visualizations to record this new knowledge (Munzner, 2014: ch. 3).

In GTM, researchers usually go through several rounds of coding (typically, open, axial and theoretical). Open coding is a key analytical task in GTM in which researchers make sense of data and their experiences, and reflect on meanings and actions. These meanings entail labelling bits of data according to what they indicate for conceptual development (Charmaz, 2006: ch. 5). Presenting high-level summaries of text can help in this step. In axial coding, initial codes are sorted, compared and synthesized. Multiple visualizations can support different coding tasks (i.e., open, axial). Here, the system can automate the process of creating an initial set of codes, a process that is often extremely tedious and time-consuming, and allow the search for further refinement of codes, as well as annotating the data with these codes. The system can accelerate the open and axial coding so that researchers can focus on theoretical coding.

8.4.2.2 Search

Another common task enabled by the system is searching for information of interest. This task is very important in the context of trace data. The search task can be just a simple lookup if users already know what they are looking for, locate if the data is known but their location is unknown, or browse if the location is known. Finally, if neither data nor their location is known, the system can nonetheless support exploration tasks (Munzner, 2014: ch. 3).

In the context of GTM, searching can be useful in the sampling phase. Traditionally, GTM researchers collect rich data from primary sources. However, with trace data, it becomes important to effectively search for these sources in the heap of available documents. Second, within identified documents, a search is needed to locate interesting excerpts. This is necessary for long documents and can substitute the intensive interviewing techniques employed with primary sources. Searching can be based on codes identified previously, or using semantic criteria to group documents similar to others that the researchers deem interesting.

In addition to identifying documents of interest, the system can link and integrate the documents to reconstruct context. By connecting and linking fragmented unstructured textual data, the system helps researchers deal with establishing the boundaries of their investigations. Hence, link by link, researchers can discover new texts of potential relevance. Connecting documents can be automated by identifying common concepts and arranging them over time. Finally, researchers can define texts of primary importance to them to aid the system in reorganizing the searched collection.

8.4.2.3 Query

Once the target data and location are known, users can query it to identify, compare and summarize. The progression of these three activities corresponds to an increase in the inclusivity of identified data: one, some or all. Identify refers to a single target, compare refers to multiple targets and summarize refers to the full set of possible targets (Munzner, 2014: ch. 3).

➔ Analyze

➔ Consume

➔ *Discover*   ➔ *Present*   ➔ *Enjoy*

➔ Produce

➔ *Annotate*   ➔ *Record*   ➔ *Derive*

➔ Search

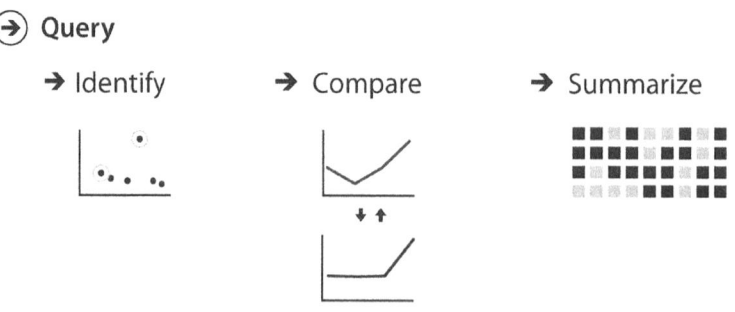

	Target known	Target unknown
Location known	Lookup	Browse
Location unknown	Locate	Explore

➔ Query

➔ Identify   ➔ Compare   ➔ Summarize

Figure 8.2 Tasks enabled by visualization
Source: Adapted from Munzner (2014: 47).

These tasks can be used to support theoretical sampling, selective and axial coding, and theory building. Theoretical sampling requires adding further selective data to refine and fill major codes. This can be supported by identifying documents to match existing codes. Coding can be facilitated with direct querying to summarize uncoded documents. This task can be extended to include relationships among codes. Theory-building can benefit from querying for comparison and

Table 8.2 How proposed system implementation responds to challenges of using GTM with big data

Challenged validity criteria	Challenged research activities	Interactive visualization
Relatedness	Theoretical sampling	• Creating a high-level presentation of text • Creating an initial set of concepts and providing leads for related documents
Appositeness	Theoretical coding	• Automating the creation of open codes • Experimenting with pre-existing codes • Freeing researchers' time to focus on theoretical coding
Comprehensiveness	Constant comparison	• Integrating and relating data sets • Searching and contrasting many similar and dissimilar data units
Trustworthiness	Chain of evidence	• Sharing access to data visualization with the research audience (transparency) • Promoting the reproducibility of findings

summaries (e.g., constant comparison). The system can also locate similar and contrasting documents based on a search criterion or starting from an initial set of documents.

Finally, the system can provide shareable visualizations that can be used to promote the transparency and reproducibility of findings. Transparency can be promoted by providing the audience of the research with access to the same interactive visualization that the researcher has. This is especially relevant when trace data is public and ethical and legal issues of sharing access are addressed appropriately. By providing links to the data and a chain of evidence, the reproducibility of the research is improved. Visualization as well as underlying data can serve as an open repository of knowledge that other researchers can use to build cumulative knowledge of the target digitalized phenomenon.

Table 8.2 summarizes how interactive visualization tasks can address the challenging research activities and validity criteria associated with qualitative research of trace data.

8.5 System Evaluation and Demonstration

We now demonstrate how visualization tasks can be implemented with open-source systems. For this discussion to generalize to other systems, we first explicate our criteria for selecting these systems, as well as the general criteria for evaluating any visualization system.

8.5.1 Selection Criteria

Text visualization is a vast area of study and there are many open-source text visualization systems (Kucher and Kerren, 2015, 2019).[1] The systems we chose are useful for social sciences and management because they have been developed with research applications in mind. In selecting the three systems, we first excluded proprietary text mining and visualization systems such as Leximancer (McKenna et al., 2017) and MineMyText (Müller et al., 2016). We focus mainly on open-source software not only because of its low cost, but also because openness, transparency and extensibility are the core ethea of science that need to be promoted in the digital era.

8.5.2 Evaluation Criteria

8.5.2.1 Algorithms

All visualization systems rely on data processing algorithms for accessing and manipulating the underlying data sets. Visualization algorithms are beyond the scope of this chapter, but they are, nonetheless, an important criterion when evaluating a visualization system (Munzner, 2014). Also,

[1] See https://textvis.lnu.se.

of particular interest to visualizing trace data are algorithms used to process text. The algorithms fall under the broad umbrella of natural language processing (NLP). Here, again, NLP is a large and fast-evolving field (Eisenstein, 2019). We outline four mainstream classes of NLP algorithms used in contemporary text visualization systems, including the three systems we review.

First, to provide access to large text, text visualization systems use *information retrieval* algorithms to index the text and provide fast search capabilities (Manning et al., 2008). The information retrieval algorithms can also provide a semantic layer from grouping excerpts that are related together (Landauer et al., 2013). For example, because the two words 'horse' and 'rider' come together in many documents, they have short semantic distance, suggesting that the term 'horse rider' is a standalone entity or concept (Cilibrasi and Vitanyi, 2007).

Second, the main challenge with textual data sets is to lend the data amenable to quantification and computation. Given the focus on identifying concepts and themes that map to theoretical codes and extracting relationships to formulate hypotheses, *named entity recognition* (NER) being used for extracting higher-level representations (e.g., concepts and entities) from text is one central task in NLP (Satoshi Sekine and Nobata, 2002). NER algorithms typically focus on categories such as locations, names, organizations, dates and money (Klein et al., 2003). NER systems are built with supervised training using labelled data. State-of-the-art NER systems are very precise, reaching almost human-level capabilities (Collobert et al., 2000).

Third, although precise and standardized, NER does not work well for concepts that do not fit within its predefined categories. Very often, concepts are not predefined, but are rather emergent from data. *Topic modelling* is one unsupervised approach that aims to help text analytics by identifying latent topics based on co-occurring words (Chuang et al., 2012). The emergent nature of topics makes them useful for exploring trends in large textual documents such as science publications (Blei and Lafferty, 2007). Topic models relying on word co-occurrence in documents have

been extended to model authorship (Rosen-Zvi et al., 2010), time (Dou et al., 2012) and relationships among topics (Blei and Lafferty, 2007). Topic modelling has recently reached wide adoption in the social sciences (DiMaggio et al., 2013; Hannigan et al., 2019).

Fourth, more recently, textual analysis using *deep neural networks* (DNN) became a mainstream approach, with many promising results. DNNs benefit from large data sets, making them a natural choice for analyzing big unstructured data. DNNs can outperform prior NLP techniques (Collobert et al., 2000; Collobert and Weston, 2008). DNNs are capable of extracting a higher representation from raw data (LeCun et al., 2015). Such representation includes meaning and semantics when data are text (Bengio et al., 2013). Word representation using DNNs is used to extract sentiments (Socher et al., 2013), syntax (Turian et al., 2010; Mikolov et al., 2013) and even semantics from the raw unprocessed text (Kumar et al., 2015; Xiong et al., 2016).

8.5.2.2 Visual Encoding and Interaction Idioms

Research in information visualization shows that different types of visual channels vary in their effectiveness in human perception. As a result, specific visual channels are recommended for presenting different types of data. For example, categorical data are best represented with shapes and colours. Ordinal data are best visualized with size or position on a scale. Relational data are best represented with networks, proximity and containment areas (Munzner, 2014). Compared to these data types, there is less research on visual idioms for text (Stasko et al., 2008). A small amount of text can be presented in verbatim or tabular views. However, this is not feasible for a large amount of text because reading and understanding text is a cognitively taxing process.

Modern text-encoding idioms emphasize the importance of words, concepts and topics. For example, a word cloud provides a high-level summary of text by highlighting the most frequent words (Heimerl et al., 2014). Another powerful external representation for text is a network representation (Singhal, 2012). This representation assumes that if concepts and relationships from the text are known, they can be visualized with a graph. This visualization summarizes the text and allows for comprehending its scope and meaning without reading it. These concepts and relationships can be manually labelled, such as in GTM open and axial coding.

Visualization systems supporting multiple representations provide multiple views of the data to support the tasks of analyzing, searching and querying. The views should be linked to allow the user to comprehend the data at different granularities and minimize complexity when necessary. One common configuration includes views of data, knowledge and navigation (Shrinivasan and van Wijk, 2008). The navigation view allows for searching and filtering with automatic summarization and a high-level presentation of the data set. The knowledge view allows for the selection of, exploration and zooming in and out to specific documents and excerpts. Finally, the data view provides the original textual data, as well as the context in which it occurs.

8.5.3 Open-Source Systems for Interactive Visualization of Text

8.5.3.1 Topic Modelling and Topic Visualization

First, we focus on topic modelling, which is a technique gaining wide adoption in social science and management (DiMaggio et al., 2013; Grimmer and Stewart, 2013; Hannigan et al., 2019; Safadi et al., 2020; Schmiedel et al., 2019). Topic modelling uses the latent Dirichlet allocation (LDA) algorithm (Blei et al., 2003) to categorize the content of many text documents into a set of substantively important coding categories or topics. As an algorithmic approach that requires a minimum of human intervention, the method is more inductive than traditional approaches to text analysis in the social and human sciences (Mohr and Bogdanov, 2013). Many open-source packages for topic modelling and visualization are readily available, such as MALLET (McCallum, 2002), Gensim (Rehurek and Sojka, 2010), Termite (Chuang et al., 2012) and LDAVis (Sievert and Shirley, 2014).

As an example of using topic modelling, consider a researcher examining the mailing list of an open-source community (Safadi, 2015: ch. 6). Topic modelling can be used to uncover common frequent words and their associations with the mainlining list posts. Figure 8.3 shows such topics using the Termite visualization package. The researcher can use this visualization to understand the themes in the mainlining list, give these topics theoretical labels and discard noisy ones. For example, the induced topics can be grouped to topics about technical tasks (e.g., programming), support tasks (e.g., installation), and community communication (e.g., organizing meetings).

8.5.3.2 ODIN: Interactive Exploration of Concepts and Associations

The first author of this chapter, along with collaborators at the University of Georgia, was awarded a planning grant from the Institute of Museum and Library Services to develop the Open Data Innovation (ODIN) platform for the goal of making open government data repositories useable by processing and visualizing text data for human sensemaking.[2] Making complex interrelated information not just available, but truly accessible, is critical for an informed society. Beyond open government data, ODIN can process any textual data sets and integrate and link various data types, which makes it a useful tool for qualitative researchers (Safadi and Boudreau, 2017).

Figure 8.4 shows an interactive session in ODIN in which a researcher explores a large data set composed of thousands of tweets about data science from 2010 to 2016 (Vaast et al., 2015). ODIN offers three integrated views: navigation (left), knowledge (centre) and data (left). The navigation view allows researchers to explore data by creating concepts based on search queries. These concepts are then extracted from the text and visualized in the knowledge view as a network in which nodes are entities and linkages correspond to source text entity associations. Interacting with the knowledge view brings the source data into the data view. In this example, the researcher wants to look up

---

[2] See https://hanisaf.github.io/odin-front.

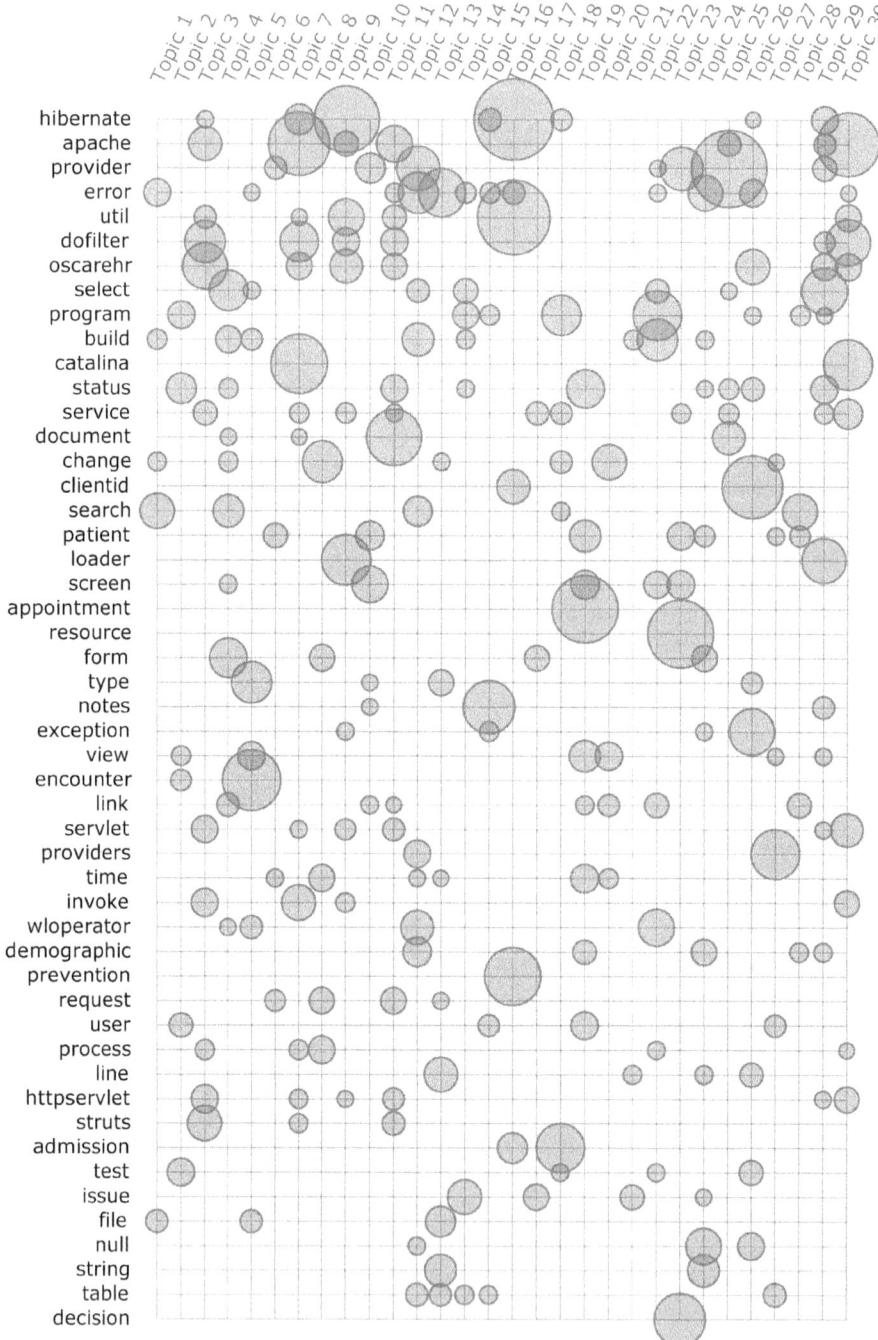

Figure 8.3 Topics extracted from the content of an open-source project's mailing list

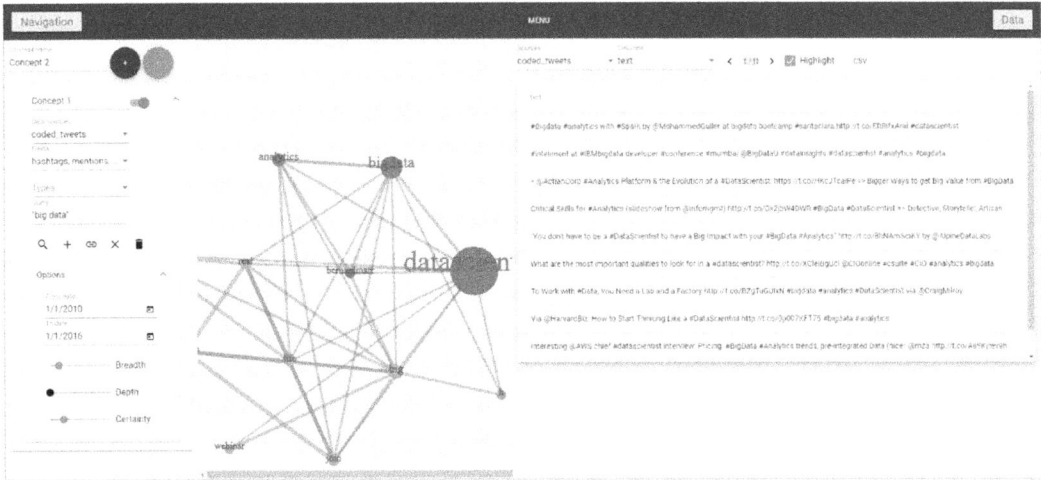

Figure 8.4 ODIN system in action with a large data set of tweets

tweets related to 'big data' and visualize the hashtags and mentions in the tweets. The knowledge view shows a strong association between big data and analytics. The researcher clicks on the link and the tweets are shown in the data view. The researcher can further tune the query, explore the knowledge view by zooming in and out on concepts and relationships, and consult the documents for evidence, annotation and coding.

The ODIN system also allows the researcher to analyze annotated data. For example, having coded the data with codes indicating the pragmatics of the tweets and the groups of their tweeters, the researcher can now probe into the association between these two code categories for constant comparison (Figure 8.5). ODIN reveals commonalities and differences in the pragmatics among groups. For example, students are particularly associated with socializing and discussing skills. Furthermore, ODIN can repeat this analysis over time to uncover temporal patterns. Finally, researchers can save and share their ODIN sessions with others for collaboration and presentation.

Under the hood, ODIN uses multiple technologies and algorithms. It relies on open-source libraries for text indexing and processing. It uses information retrieval and named entity recognition for uncovering concepts from the text. It relies on latent semantic analysis and similarity distance to establish associations among these entities. The

chosen technologies and algorithms scale for millions of documents and thereby provide efficient and real-time capabilities for analyzing, searching and querying digital trace data.

8.5.3.3 Overview: Document Mining and Visualization

Overview is an open-source document mining and visualization system that offers multiple text-processing tools and a wide range of visualization and annotation capabilities (Brehmer et al., 2014).[3] Overview is also extensible and enables users to develop their custom visualizations. A unique feature of Overview is processing scanned documents with optical character recognition (OCR), making it a useful tool for researching archived data. Overview supports multiple use cases such as hypothesis generation, hypothesis verification, searching, locating, identifying and summarization.

Figure 8.6 shows Overview being used to research 625 White House email messages in scanned PDF formats concerning drilling in the Gulf of Mexico before the 2010 BP oil spill (Brehmer et al., 2014). The researcher can probe the documents, as well as create multiple visualizations such as the shown word cloud. It is also possible to tag and organize the documents into categories.

---

[3] See www.overviewdocs.com.

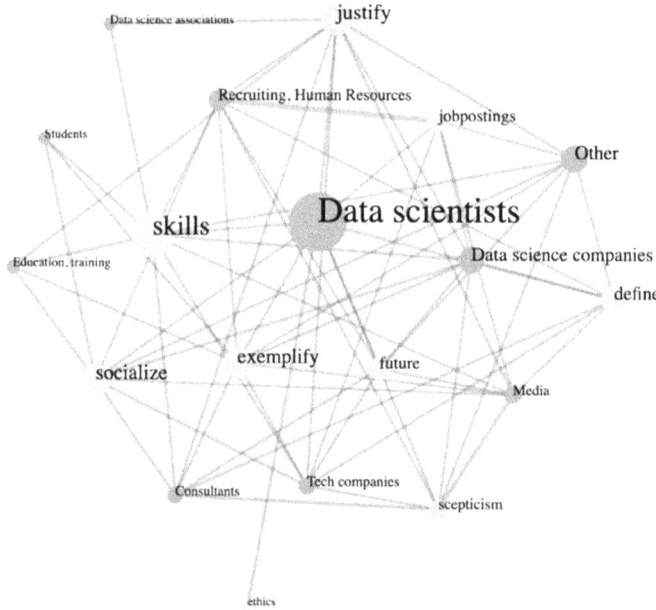

Figure 8.5 The association among member groups and practices

Figure 8.6 Using Overview to research a collection of scanned documents

8.6 Conclusion

Social and organizational lives are being digitized, leaving traces that can be used to understand their dynamics and complex nature. Often a roadblock for research, access to data is no longer an issue. On the other hand, researchers have access to multiple new distant contexts in which they analyze more data than was traditionally done before (Levina and Vaast, 2015; Abbasi et al., 2016;

Berente et al., 2019; Johnson et al., 2019). This new brave digital world creates opportunities and challenges for researchers trained in the qualitative research tradition.

In this chapter, we called for expanding the role of visualization to help qualitative researchers in researching digital trace data. Rooted on human information foraging and sensemaking processes, we proposed a paradigm for the continuous interaction between an interactive visualization system capable of extracting and visualizing patterns from textual data, and a researcher whose expertise and interpretive skills are essential for theorizing. We specifically showed how visualization tasks can be used to meet challenges in theoretical sampling, coding, constant comparison and building a chain of evidence. Finally, we provided a set of criteria to evaluate visualization systems, as well as demonstrated three available open-source systems.

Advances in science require advances in methods and tools (Greenwald, 2012). Although a readily 'off-the-shelf' system is not yet available, we believe that the qualitative research community is not far from achieving this important goal. We hope that this chapter will stimulate further interest within the qualitative research community to come together and invest further effort in creating tools for researching trace data of digitalized phenomena.

Beyond qualitative research methods, our approach builds on the long-standing discipline of cybernetics (Fararo and McClelland, 2006) and underscores the importance of incorporating human deep understanding and sensemaking in data analytics tasks. In the current rush to artificial intelligence, machine learning and cognitive computing, we argue that human judgement is still supreme for ambiguous and challenging tasks (Hindman, 2015). Systems designed to leverage large data should provide ample opportunities for human judgement and follow guidelines and design patterns to support this core idea.

References

Abbasi, A., Sarker, S. and Chiang, R. (2016). Big data research in information systems: Toward an inclusive research agenda. *Journal of the Association for Information Systems*, 17(2), i–xxxii.

Agarwal, R. and Dhar, V. (2014). Editorial – big data, data science, and analytics: The opportunity and challenge for IS research. *Information Systems Research*, 25(3), 443–448.

Anderson, C. H., Van Essen, D. C. and Olshausen, B. A. (2005). Directed visual attention and the dynamic control of information flow. In L. Itti, G. Rees and J. Tsotsos (eds), *Neurobiology of Attention*. London, Burlington, MA and San Diego, CA: Elsevier, pp. 11–17.

Bansal, P. T., Smith, W. K. and Vaara, E. (2018). From the editors: New ways of seeing through qualitative research. *Academy of Management Journal*, 61(4), 1189–1195.

Bengio, Y., Courville, A. and Vincent, P. (2013). Representation learning: A review and new perspectives. *IEEE Transactions on Pattern Analysis and Machine Intelligence*, 35(8), 1798–1828.

Berente, N., Seidel, S. and Safadi, H. (2019). Research commentary – data-driven computationally intensive theory development. *Information Systems Research*, 30(1), 50–64.

Blei, D. M. and Lafferty, J. D. (2007). A correlated topic model of science. *Annals of Applied Statistics*, 1(1), 17–35.

Blei, D. M., Ng, A. Y. and Jordan, M. I. (2003). Latent dirichlet allocation. *Journal of Machine Learning Research*, 3, 993–1022.

Brehmer, M., Ingram, S., Stray, J. and Munzner, T. (2014). Overview: The design, adoption, and analysis of a visual document mining tool for investigative journalists. *IEEE Transactions on Visualization and Computer Graphics*, 20(12), 2271–2280.

Charmaz, K. (2006). *Constructing Grounded Theory: A Practical Guide through Qualitative Analysis*. London: Sage, Vol. 10.

Chau, D. H., Kittur, A., Hong, J. I. and Faloutsos, C. (2011). Apolo: Making sense of large network data by combining rich user interaction and machine learning. In *Proceedings of the 2011 Annual Conference on Human Factors in Computing Systems*. New York, NY: ACM Press, Vol. 46, pp. 167–176.

Chuang, J., Manning, C. D. and Heer, J. (2012). Termite: Visualization techniques for assessing textual topic models. In *Proceedings of the International Working Conference on Advanced Visual Interfaces*. New York, NY: ACM Press, pp. 74–77.

Cilibrasi, R. L. and Vitanyi, P. M. B. (2007). The google similarity distance. *IEEE Transactions on Knowledge and Data Engineering*, 19(3), 370–383.

Collobert, R. and Weston, J. (2008). A unified architecture for natural language processing. Proceedings of the International Conference on Machine Learning, Helsinki, Finland.

Collobert, R., Weston, J., Bottou, L., Karlen, M., Kavukcuoglu, K. and Kuksa, P. (2000). Natural language processing (almost) from scratch. *Journal of Machine Learning Research*, 1, 1–48.

Cook, S. D. N. and Brown, J. S. (1999). Bridging epistemologies: The generative dance between organizational knowledge and organizational knowing. *Organization Science*, 10(4), 381–400.

Dervin, B., Foreman-Wernet, L. and Lauterbach, E. (eds) (2003). *Sense-Making Methodology Reader: Selected Writings of Brenda Dervin*. Cresskill, NJ: Hampton Press.

DiMaggio, P. (2015). Adapting computational text analysis to social science (and vice versa). *Big Data & Society*, 2(2), 1–5.

DiMaggio, P., Nag, M. and Blei, D. (2013). Exploiting affinities between topic modeling and the sociological perspective on culture: Application to newspaper coverage of U.S. government arts funding. *Poetics*, 41(6), 570–606.

Dou, W., Wang, X., Skau, D., Ribarsky, W. and Zhou, M. X. (2012). LeadLine: Interactive visual analysis of text data through event identification and exploration. Proceedings of the IEEE Conference on Visual Analytics Science and Technology 2012, Seattle, WA.

Eisenhardt, K. M. (1989). Building theories from case study research. *Academy of Management Review*, 14(4), 532–550.

Eisenstein, J. (2019). *Introduction to Natural Language Processing*. Cambridge, MA: MIT Press.

Endert, A., Hossain, M. S., Ramakrishnan, N., North, C., Fiaux, P. and Andrews, C. (2014). The human is the loop: New directions for visual analytics. *Journal of Intelligent Information Systems*, 43(3), 411–435.

Fararo, T. J. and McClelland, K. A. (2006). Introduction: Control systems thinking in sociological theory. In K. A. McClelland and T. J. Fararo (eds), *Purpose, Meaning, and Action: Control Systems Theories in Sociology*. New York, NY: Palgrave Macmillan, pp. 1–27.

Finlay, L. (2002). 'Outing' the researcher: The provenance, process, and practice of reflexivity. *Qualitative Health Research*, 12(4), 531–545.

Gaskin, J., Berente, N., Lyytinen, K. and Yoo, Y. (2014). Toward generalizable sociomaterial inquiry: A computational approach for 'zooming in & out' of sociomaterial routines. *MIS Quarterly*, 38(3), 849–871.

George, G., Osinga, E. C., Lavie, D. and Scott, B. A. (2016). Big data and data science methods for management research. *Academy of Management Journal*, 59(5), 1493–1507.

Gioia, D. A., Corley, K. G. and Hamilton, A. L. (2013). Seeking qualitative rigor in inductive research: Notes on the Gioia methodology. *Organizational Research Methods*, 16(1), 15–31.

Glaser, B. G. (2013). *No Preconceptions: The Grounded Theory Dictum*. Mill Valley, CA: Sociology Press.

Glaser, B. G. (2005). *The Grounded Theory Perspective III: Theoretical Coding*. Mill Valley, CA: Sociology Press.

Glaser, B. G. (1978). *Theoretical Sensitivity: Advances in the Methodology of Grounded Theory*. Mill Valley, CA: Sociology Press.

Glaser, B. G. and Strauss, A. L. (1967). *The Discovery of Grounded Theory: Strategies for Qualitative Research*. New York, NY: Aldine de Gruyter.

Gotz, D., Zhou, M. X. and Aggarwal, V. (2006). Interactive visual synthesis of analytic knowledge. Proceedings of the IEEE Symposium on Visual Analytics Science and Technology 2006, Baltimore, MD.

Greenwald, A. G. (2012). There is nothing so theoretical as a good method. *Perspectives on Psychological Science*, 7(2), 99–108.

Grimmer, J. and Stewart, B. M. (2013). Text as data: The promise and pitfalls of automatic content analysis methods for political texts. *Political Analysis*, 21(3), 267–297.

Hannigan, T., Haans, R. F. J., Vakili, K., Tchalian, H., Glaser, V. L. et al. (2019). Topic modeling in management research: Rendering new theory from textual data. *Academy of Management Annals*, 13(2), 586–632.

Hegarty, M. (2004). Diagrams in the mind and in the world: Relations between internal and external visualizations. In A. F. Blackwell, K. Marriott and A. Shimojima (eds), *Diagrammatic Representation and Inference: Third International Conference, Diagrams 2004, Cambridge, UK. Proceedings*. Berlin and Heidelberg, Germany: Springer, pp. 1–13.

Heimerl, F., Lohmann, S., Lange, S. and Ertl, T. (2014). Word cloud explorer: Text analytics based on word clouds. Hawaii International Conference on System Sciences, Waikoloa, HI.

Hindman, M. (2015). Building better models: Prediction, replication, and machine learning in the social sciences. *Annals of the American Academy of Political and Social Science*, 659(1), 48–62.

Hukal, P., Henfridsson, O., Shaikh, M. and Parker, G. (2020). Platform signaling for generating platform content. *MIS Quarterly: Management Information Systems*, 44(3), 1177–1206.

Johnson, S. L., Gray, P. and Sarker, S. (2019). Revisiting IS research practice in the era of big data. *Information and Organization*, 29(1), 41–56.

Kirsh, D. (2009). Interaction, external representation and sense making. In N. A. Taatgen and H. van Rijn (eds), *Proceedings of the 31st Annual Conference of the Cognitive Science Society*. Austin, TX: Cognitive Science Society, pp. 1103–1108.

Klein, D., Smarr, J., Nguyen, H. and Manning, C. D. (2003). Named entity recognition with character-level models. Proceedings of the Conference on Natural Language Learning at HLT-NAACL 2003, Edmonton, Canada, Vol. 4, pp. 180–183.

Klein, G., Moon, B. and Hoffman, R. R. (2006a). Making sense of sensemaking 1: Alternative perspectives. *IEEE Intelligent Systems*, 21(4), 70–73.

Klein, G., Moon, B. and Hoffman, R. R. (2006b). Making sense of sensemaking 2: A macrocognitive model. *IEEE Intelligent Systems*, 21(5), 88–92.

Kucher, K. and Kerren, A. (2019). Text visualization revisited: The state of the field in 2019. In J. Madeiras Pereira and R. G. Raidou (eds), *EuroVis 2019 – Posters*. The Eurographics Association, pp. 29–31.

Kucher, K. and Kerren, A. (2015). Text visualization techniques: Taxonomy, visual survey, and community insights. 2015 IEEE Pacific Visualization Symposium (pacificVis), Hangzhou, China.

Kumar, A., Irsoy, O., Su, J., Iyyer, M., Bradbury, J. et al. (2015). Ask me anything: Dynamic memory networks for natural language processing. *ArXiv*, pp. 1–10, http://arxiv.org/abs/1506.07285.

Landauer, T. K., McNamara, D. S., Dennis, S. and Kintsch, W. (2013). *Handbook of Latent Semantic Analysis*. London: Psychology Press.

Langley, A. (1999). Strategies for theorizing from process data. *Academy of Management Review*, 24(4), 691–710.

Larkin, J. and Simon, H. (1987). Why a diagram is (sometimes) worth ten thousand words. *Cognitive Science*, 11(1), 65–100.

Latour, B. (2010). Tarde's idea of quantification. In M. Candea (ed.), *The Social after Gabriel Tarde: Debates and Assessments*. New York, NY: Routledge, pp. 145–162.

Lazer, D., Pentland, A. S., Adamic, L., Aral, S., Barabasi, A.-L., Brewer, D. et al. (2009). Life in the network: The coming age of computational social science. *Science*, 323(5915), 721–723.

LeCun, Y., Bengio, Y. and Hinton, G. (2015). Deep learning. *Nature*, 521(7553), 436–444.

Lee, A. S. (1989). A scientific methodology for MIS case studies. *MIS Quarterly*, 13(1), 33–50.

Levina, N. and Arriaga, M. (2014). Distinction and status production on user-generated content platforms: Using Bourdieu's theory of cultural production to understand social dynamics in online fields. *Information Systems Research*, 25(3), 468–488.

Levina, N. and Vaast, E. (2015). Leveraging archival data from online communities for grounded process theorizing. In K. D. Elsbach and R. M. Kramer (eds), *Handbook of Qualitative Organizational Research: Innovative Pathways and Methods*. Abingdon, UK and New York, NY: Routledge, pp. 215–224.

Lindberg, A. (2020). Developing theory through integrating human and machine pattern recognition. *Journal of the Association for Information Systems*, 21(1), 90–116.

Liu, Z., Nersessian, N. and Stasko, J. (2008). Distributed cognition as a theoretical framework for information visualization. *IEEE Transactions on Visualization and Computer Graphics*, 14(6), 1173–1180.

Maitlis, S. and Christianson, M. (2014). Sensemaking in organizations: Taking stock and moving forward. *Academy of Management Annals*, 8(1), 57–125.

Manning, C. D., Schütze, H. and Raghavan, P. (2008). *Introduction to Information Retrieval*. Cambridge: Cambridge University Press.

McCallum, A. K. (2002). Mallet: A machine learning for language toolkit, http://mallet.cs.umass.edu.

McKenna, B., Myers, M. D. and Newman, M. (2017). Social media in qualitative research: Challenges and recommendations. *Information and Organization*, 27(2), 87–99.

Mikolov, T., Yih, W. and Zweig, G. (2013). Linguistic regularities in continuous space word representations. Proceedings of NAACL-HLT, Atlanta, GA.

Miller, G. A. (1984). Informavores. In F. Machlup and U. Mansfield (eds), *The Study of Information: Interdisciplinary Messages*. New York, NY: Wiley-Interscience, pp. 111–113.

Mohr, J. W. and Bogdanov, P. (2013). Introduction – topic models: What they are and why they matter. *Poetics*, 41(6), 545–569.

Morse, J. M., Stern, P. N., Corbin, J. M., Charmaz, K. C., Bowers, B. and Clarke, A. E. (2009). *Developing Grounded Theory: The Second Generation*, Vol. 5: *Developing Qualitative Inquiry*. Walnut Creek, CA: Left Coast Press.

Müller, O., Debortoli, S., Junglas, I. and vom Brocke, J. (2016). Using text analytics to derive customer service management benefits from unstructured data. *MIS Quarterly Executive*, 15(4), 243–258.

Munzner, T. (2014). *Visualization Analysis and Design*. Boca Raton, FL: CRC Press.

Neef, D. (2014). *Digital Exhaust: What Everyone Should Know about Big Data, Digitization and Digitally Driven Innovation*. Upper Saddle River, NJ: Pearson Education.

Neisser, U. (1976). *Cognition and Reality: Principles and Implications of Cognitive Psychology*. San Francisco, CA: W. H. Freeman/Times Books/ Henry Holt & Co.

Nicolini, D. (2009). Zooming in and out: Studying practices by switching theoretical lenses and trailing connections. *Organization Studies*, 30(12), 1391–1418.

Østerlund, C., Crowston, K. and Jackson, C. (2020). Building an apparatus: Refractive, reflective, and diffractive readings of trace data. *Journal of the Association for Information Systems*, 21(1), 1–22.

Pan, S. L. and Tan, B. (2011). Demystifying case research: A structured-pragmatic-situational (SPS) approach to conducting case studies. *Information and Organization*, 21(3), 161–176.

Pentland, B., Recker, J., Wolf, J. and Wyner, G. M. (2020). Bringing context inside process research with digital trace data. *Journal of the Association for Information Systems*, 21(5), 1214–1236.

Pentland, B. T. (2016). ThreadNet: Tracing and visualizing associations between actions. IFIP Working Group 8.2, Dublin, Ireland.

Pirolli, P. and Card, S. (2005). The sensemaking process and leverage points for analyst technology as identified through cognitive task analysis. Proceedings of International Conference on Intelligence Analysis, McLean, VA.

Pirolli, P. and Card, S. (1999). Information foraging. *Psychological Review*, 106(4), 643–675.

Polanyi, M. (1962). Tacit knowing: Its bearing on some problems of philosophy. *Reviews of Modern Physics*, 34(4), 601–616.

Rai, A. (2016). Synergies between big data and theory. *MIS Quarterly*, 40(2), iii–ix.

Rehurek, R. and Sojka, P. (2010). Software framework for topic modelling with large corpora. Proceedings of LREC 2010 Workshop on New Challenges for NLP Frameworks, Valletta, Malta.

Richardson, R. and Kramer, E. H. (2006). Abduction as the type of inference that characterizes the development of a grounded theory. *Qualitative Research*, 6(4), 497–513.

Rosen-Zvi, M., Chemudugunta, C., Griffiths, T., Smyth, P. and Steyvers, M. (2010). Learning author-topic models from text corpora. *ACM Transactions on Information Systems (TOIS)*, 28(1), 1–38.

Russell, D. M., Stefik, M. J., Pirolli, P. and Card, S. K. (1993). The cost structure of sensemaking. Proceedings of the SIGCHI Conference on Human Factors in Computing Systems (CHI'93), Amsterdam, the Netherlands.

Safadi, H. (2015). Knowledge creation in health IT online communities. Thesis, McGill University Libraries, https://escholarship.mcgill.ca/concern/ theses/ng451m74d.

Safadi, H. and Boudreau, M.-C. (2017). Design of an interactive visual system to support grounded process theorizing from qualitative data. *Academy of Management Proceedings*, 2017, 11597.

Safadi, H., Johnson, S. L. and Faraj, S. (2020). Who contributes knowledge? Core-periphery tension in online innovation communities. *Organization Science*, 32(3), 752–775.

Satoshi Sekine, K. S. and Nobata, C. (2002). Extended named entity hierarchy. Third International Conference on Language Resources and Evaluation (LREC 2002), Las Palmas, Spain.

Schirner, G., Erdogmus, D., Chowdhury, K. and Padir, T. (2013). The future of human-in-the-loop cyber-physical systems. *Computer*, 46(1), 36–45.

Schmiedel, T., Müller, O. and vom Brocke, J. (2019). Topic modeling as a strategy of inquiry in organizational research: A tutorial with an application example on organizational culture. *Organizational Research Methods*, 22(4), 941–968.

Schultze, U. (2012). Performing embodied identity in virtual worlds. *European Journal of Information Systems*, 23(1), 84–95.

Seale, C. (1999). Quality in qualitative research. *Qualitative Inquiry*, 5(4), 465–478.

Shirley, P., Ashikhmin, M. and Marschner, S. (2015). *Fundamentals of Computer Graphics*. Boca Raton, FL: CRC Press.

Shrinivasan, Y. B. and van Wijk, J. J. (2008). Supporting the analytical reasoning process in information visualization. Proceedings of the Annual CHI Conference on Human Factors in Computing Systems, Florence, Italy.

Sievert, C. and Shirley, K. (2014). LDAvis: A method for visualizing and interpreting topics. Proceedings of the Workshop on Interactive Language Learning, Visualization, and Interfaces, Baltimore, MD.

Simon, H. A. (1996). *The Sciences of the Artificial*. Cambridge, MA: MIT Press.

Singhal, A. (2012). Introducing the knowledge graph: Things, not strings. https://blog.google/products/search/introducing-knowledge-graph-things-not/.

Socher, R., Perelygin, A., Wu, J. Y., Chuang, J., Manning, C. D., Ng, A. and Potts, C. (2013). Recursive deep models for semantic compositionality over a sentiment treebank. Proceedings of the Conference on Empirical Methods in Natural Language Processing, Seattle, WA.

Stasko, J., Görg, C. and Spence, R. (2008). Jigsaw: Supporting investigative analysis through interactive visualization. *Information Visualization*, 7(2), 118–132.

Stohl, C., Stohl, M. and Leonardi, P. M. (2016). Managing opacity: Information visibility and the paradox of transparency in the digital age. *International Journal of Communication*, 10(1), 123–137.

Strauss, A. L. and Corbin, J. M. (1998). *Basics of Qualitative Research: Techniques and Procedures for Developing Grounded Theory*. Thousand Oaks, CA: Sage, Vol. 2.

Suddaby, R. (2006). From the editors: What grounded theory is not. *Academy of Management Journal*, 49(4), 633–642.

Thomas, G. and James, D. (2006). Reinventing grounded theory: Some questions about theory, ground and discovery. *British Educational Research Journal*, 32(6), 767–795.

Tsoukas, H. (2009). A dialogical approach to the creation of new knowledge in organizations. *Organization Science*, 20(6), 941–957.

Turian, J., Ratinov, L., Bengio, Y. and Turian, J. (2010). Word representations: A simple and general method for semi-supervised learning. Proceedings of the 48th Annual Meeting of the Association for Computational Linguistics, Uppsala, Sweden.

Tweed, A. and Charmaz, K. (2011). Grounded theory methods for mental health practitioners. In D. Harper and A. R. Thompson (eds), *Qualitative Research Methods in Mental Health and Psychotherapy: A Guide for Students and Practitioners*. Chichester, UK: John Wiley, pp. 131–146.

Urquhart, C. (2013). *Grounded Theory for Qualitative Research: A Practical Guide*. London and Los Angeles, CA: Sage.

Urquhart, C., Lehmann, H. and Myers, M. D. (2010). Putting the 'theory' back into grounded theory: Guidelines for grounded theory studies in information systems. *Information Systems Journal*, 20(4), 357–381.

Vaast, E., Safadi, H. and Cohen, L. (2015). The distributed construction of an occupational community with social media. International Conference of Information Systems, Fort Worth, TX.

Vaast, E., Safadi, H., Lapointe, L. and Negoita, B. (2017). Social media affordances for connective action: An examination of microblogging use during the Gulf of Mexico oil spill. *MIS Quarterly*, 41(4), 1179–1205.

Van de Ven, A. and Poole, M. (1990). Methods for studying innovation development in the Minnesota innovation research program. *Organization Science*, 1(3), 313–335.

Venkatesh, V., Brown, S. A. and Bala, H. (2013). Bridging the qualitative-quantitative divide: Guidelines for conducting mixed methods research in information systems. *MIS Quarterly*, 37(1), 21–54.

Walsh, I., Holton, J. A., Bailyn, L., Fernandez, W., Levina, N. and Glaser, B. (2015). What grounded theory is ... a critically reflective conversation among scholars. *Organizational Research Methods*, 18(4), 1–19.

Walsh, R. A. (1995). The approach of the human science researcher: Implications for the practice of qualitative research. *Humanistic Psychologist*, 23(3), 333–344.

Ware, C. (2012). *Information Visualization: Perception for Design*. Waltham, MA: Elsevier.

Watts, D. J. (2013). Computational social science: Exciting progress and future directions. *Bridge on Frontiers of Engineering*, 43(4), 5–10.

Wright, W., Schroh, D., Proulx, P., Skaburskis, A. and Cort, B. (2006). The Sandbox for analysis: Concepts and methods. Proceedings of the SIGCHI Conference on Human Factors in Computing Systems, Montreal, Quebec, Canada.

Xiong, C., Merity, S. and Socher, R. (2016). Dynamic memory networks for visual and textual question answering. Proceedings of the International Conference on Machine Learning, New York, NY.

Zachariadis, M., Scott, S. and Barrett, M. (2013). Methodological implications of critical realism for mixed-methods research. *Management Information Systems Quarterly*, 37(3), 855–879.

Zuboff, S. (2015). Big other: Surveillance capitalism and the prospects of an information civilization. *Journal of Information Technology*, 30(1), 75–89.

Demystifying the Digital

A Case for Hybrid Ethnography in IS

NICOLA ENS, MARI-KLARA STEIN
and TINA BLEGIND JENSEN

9.1 Introduction

There was a distinct point when embedded text message bubbles began appearing in film scenes, showing what otherwise would be a silent conversation between actors. What once felt strange, or like a quirky little touch, has largely become a normalized part of cinematic experience, necessary to the storytelling of our modern digital lives. Such is the reality we find ourselves in today, where digital technologies mediate social interaction in multiple overlapping and partial ways, within and outside organizations. For instance, the modern office uses collaborative software tools, like Microsoft Teams, to share documents, engage in 'watercooler' chatter and collaborate on multi-actor projects. With an increase in non-co-located practices, the reliance on easily accessible and highly effective technologies to facilitate collaboration and communication has only increased (Eckhardt et al., 2019). Similarly, digital labour platforms are increasingly pervasive work providers, with social media becoming online meeting spaces for workers to share best practices and organize around issues of labour rights (Möhlmann and Zalmanson, 2018). Even within our homes, Siri and Alexa facilitate mundane tasks like grocery shopping and appliance maintenance. To understand the digitally mediated worlds we inhabit, embedded research designs which draw on multiple sources of digital and non-digital data present great opportunity (Hine, 2017). Drawing on the data created in our online interactions represents a novel addition to sources like interviews and observations, introducing greater understanding of technologies as part of the social systems in which they are found (Hedman et al., 2013). A key question for IS scholars, who largely study phenomena at the intersection of technology, people and organization, is how our research designs can capture the ongoing sociotechnical entanglements that occur in hybrid online and offline spaces.

In this chapter, we unfold one possible methodology that could help IS researchers conduct such studies, that of hybrid ethnography. By 'hybrid', we refer to studies with fieldsites that transcend online and offline spaces, with qualitative digital and non-digital data.[1] By 'ethnography', we refer to an overall approach to immersive participatory fieldwork, seeking to understand ways of being in the world (Van Maanen, 2011). With that come certain conventions, such as 'the ethnographer participating, overtly or covertly, in people's daily lives for an extended period of time, watching what happens, listening to what is said and/or asking questions through informal and formal interviews, collecting documents and artefacts' (Atkinson and Hammersley, 2007: 3). Ethnographic study is a less prescriptive method and more guiding principles; including qualitative study through participant observation and time spent immersed in the field as core tenants (O'Reilly, 2012). We suggest that hybrid ethnography can take various configurations, with the primary contention being that the sociotechnical study of digital technologies is an ideal environment for such a method.

The approach taken in this chapter is not a radical departure from what has come before.

---

[1] We refer to online and offline spaces as a matter of practicality, while noting that this distinction is artificial in nature. That is to say we do not suggest that there is strict separation between online/offline worlds or selves and in fact they are blended.

Much is written about the use of digital data in qualitative field study, under various terms such as virtual ethnography (Hine, 2000; Pink et al., 2016), virtual worlds (Schultze, 2010; Boellstorff et al., 2012), digital sociology (Marres, 2017), netnography (Kozinets, 2015) and digital anthropology (Coleman, 2010). Even sources for traditional IS methods have suggested the inclusion of digital data (e.g., Oates, 2006). There are, of course, differences across such approaches with emphasis put on different techniques, the subtleties of which would require an entire chapter in and of itself. However, overall, there is an agreement of the 'internet as a messy fieldwork environment that crosses online and offline worlds, and is connected and constituted through the ethnographer's narrative' (Postill and Pink, 2012: 126). Much of this work already acknowledges the benefit in hybridity, and we do not claim otherwise. In fact, the term hybrid ethnography has been used previously to describe fieldsites that span across online and offline spaces (Przybylski, 2020). We purposefully select the term for use in this chapter to put forth hybrid ethnography as a vital way to conduct qualitative IS studies. Wading through these previous literatures, and their various conventions and discussions, this chapter brings various strands of conversation together to help IS researchers engage in hybrid ethnography in its various configurations.

The type of hybrid ethnography we suggest is appropriate when an online site is the explicit focus of the study, such as the case with studies of online communities, where non-digital data is collected to explain the online dynamics. However, we also suggest that hybrid ethnography is appropriate in studies of offline research objects, for example, studying the work practices of a group and including the online sites in the study. This focus means that in hybrid ethnography, all field studies will entail a number of different spaces online and offline, and digital and non-digital data sources, creating a number of challenges the researcher must balance. Table 9.1 provides examples of various configurations of hybridity in IS through previously conducted research. It should be noted that not all of these studies are labelled as hybrid, or even as ethnographies; however, all illustrate various

elements of the configurations of hybridity, based on which we list three overall challenges.

Ethnography is an art best learned by doing (O'Reilly, 2012), a sentiment we take to heart. Bearing this in mind, we provide a guide for researchers performing their fieldwork, supporting reflexive decision-making in the hybrid ethnographic process. Practically, this chapter takes departure in the first author's experience in a hybrid ethnographic study of platform-mediated work practices. In particular, the research has followed sellers who use the US-based app Poshmark to sell new and used clothing as a source of income. The study has been in progress for over two years, with data collection beginning in 2018. The study is hybrid, having been collected in multiple online spaces, with digital data from social media platforms, press releases, the digital platform itself and historic data from the Internet archive, as well as offline spaces, with non-digital data including the sellers' annual three-day conference Poshfest 2019, a local event with sellers, as well as through interviews.

The chapter is broken down into three themes. These are chosen explicitly from the first author's experience, representing challenges that have been encountered during the study, which we feel all researchers conducting hybrid ethnography will engage with in some capacity (see Table 9.1). These are: (1) navigating unbounded fieldsites; (2) managing technological opacity; and (3) working with diverse data. Each of these issues overlaps, and the challenges can manifest in unique combinations. For instance, while the aforementioned study of Tripadvisor represents relative uniformity of data, the technology behind it is highly opaque (Scott and Orlikowski, 2012). In a similar vein, while studying a surgical robot is highly visible, the data generated in such a study, images and drawings is highly diverse (Sergeeva et al., 2020). Each theme provides an introduction by way of background literature, combined with an in-depth example from the first author's own fieldwork, and as such is written in the first person. Speaking broadly to the three largest research challenges, the chapter does not touch on the equally important ethical issues associated with digital data collection. This decision is made as ethical issues

Table 9.1 Sample configurations of hybrid ethnography

Configurations of hybridity	Sample studies	Challenges in hybrid ethnography
Fieldsite as relatively bounded	Schultze's (2000) study on knowledge work practices illustrates hybrid ethnography within a bounded site. The study was conducted within a single company, focused on one knowledge management software. Data were collected through participant observation and interviews, diverse electronic documents, including internal messages and PowerPoints, as well as generic sales material about the tool itself.	Questions of inclusion and exclusion – navigating unbounded fieldsites
Fieldsite as highly unbounded	Coleman's (2014) work on the 'anonymous' movement represents a study with a highly unbounded fieldsite. Coleman traced the movement of anonymous members through online channels, including 4chan and IRC chat. She also identified participants and conducted interviews, both online and in person. At each turn, decisions had to be made as to what to include, exclude and which paths to follow, with no clear criteria of what was within the site.	
Technology as relatively transparent	Sergeeva et al.'s (2020) study of coordination in robotic surgery illustrates a visible, physical technology. The authors observed a Da Vinci endoscopic surgical robot being used in twenty-three diverse surgeries, hand-drawing pictures of movement, taking photographs and writing notes, visibly tracing what it was doing through their observations.	The observability of technology – managing technological opacity
Technology as highly opaque	Rosenblat's (2018) study of Uber illustrates the complexities that arise when studying Uber's proprietary and thus highly opaque algorithms. By drawing on the drivers' intimate knowledge of the ways in which algorithms appear to control their work, the author constructs an in-depth understanding of how the technology functions.	
Data sources as relatively uniform	Scott and Orlikowski's (2012) study of Tripadvisor represents data sources that are relatively uniform, despite being embedded in a complex site. Here, the authors build on user-generated reviews and online documents which are used in combination with data collected from hoteliers in one region.	The uniformity of data – working with diverse data sources
Data sources as highly diverse	Erickson's (2010) study of microblogging practices of distributed communities represents a high diversity of data sources, drawing on geolocation data, screen shots of images and time/date stamps, as well as in-depth ethnographic interviews conducted both in-person and via video-conferencing software.	

are highly contextual, and the assumption is made that these are best navigated in conjunction with the local ethics boards and within the relevant legal conventions.[2] Building on lessons learned through this study, the purpose of the chapter is to guide IS researchers in their pursuit of hybrid ethnographic studies.

[2] The Association of Internet Researchers (AOIR) facilitates an Ethics Working Committee, composed of ethicists and researchers. They have produced several guides that can guide hybrid research designs.

9.2 Navigating Unbounded Fieldsites

This section discusses one of the primary issues in hybrid ethnography – defining the fieldsite. Defining any fieldsite, hybrid or not, is an active pursuit, brought into being through the ethnographer's engagement, surrounding the critical decisions of inclusion and exclusion (Atkinson, 2015). Early work within the ethnographic tradition had a certain degree of boundedness, stemming from the researcher's engagement in geographically removed cultures. Here we can think of scholars such as Malinowski (1922), who lived disconnected from home in enclosed fieldsites. A general shift towards interconnected and global societies, as well as the pervasiveness of mass media, has brought increasing attention to the issue, spurring new conceptions of how to actively define a fieldsite (Hine, 2017). Particularly for IS scholars, who are studying the interplay between people, technology and organization, defining boundaries has become a cornerstone issue (Markham and Baym, 2009). This section discusses how the hybrid ethnographer can navigate unbounded fieldsites in their research.

Already from the early noughts, ethnographers had begun to consider online spaces as important fieldsites. Hine's (2000) early work, for instance, mapped the current terrain pointing to two primary approaches: the Internet as culture, and the Internet as cultural artifact. The 'Internet as culture' approach started in computer-mediated communication and studied online communities or virtual worlds as sites of culture (see, for instance: Baym's (2000) exploration of a soap opera discussion group or Boellstorff's (2008) deep dive into Second Life). The second approach, largely stemming from science and technology studies, examines the Internet as a product of culture, produced within specific contexts by specific people (for instance, Hafner and Lyon's (1998) history of the Internet). Much of the early work reflects a spatial notion of *being online*, and thus is focused on how to relate online fieldsites to their offline corollaries, encouraging researchers to think about the similarities and differences between our online and offline selves (Oates, 2006). Similarly, Schultze (2010) focused on embodiment in these new spaces, and how avatars created new experiential forms. Other foci of these early guidelines include mitigating the challenges of online fieldsites, offering caution that online ethnography will always be partial in nature and not methodologically pure (Hine, 2000).

Since these early studies, the fluidity of technology use has shifted the focus from linking online and offline to the navigation of embedded online/offline worlds (Hine, 2017). Thus, to a large degree, there is consensus that to pursue digitally mediated phenomena requires some form of multi-sitedness, following activity across spaces, where the challenges relate to

the complexity of this arrangement (Boellstorff et al., 2012). Seaver (2017) suggests 'scavenger methods' as one solution, advocating that one follows breadcrumbs whenever possible. In this sense, the scavenger researcher mimics the partiality of knowing experienced by their interlocutors, 'figuring out their world by piecing together heterogeneous clues' (p. 6). Similarly, Hine (2017) reminds us that it is the researcher's theoretical curiosity that brings the fieldsite into being, offering advice to think through interlocutors' experiences when making choices related to the inclusion of spaces within the same study.

Because the nature of hybrid fieldsites varies so drastically, some authors suggest we need entirely new ways to think through site construction. For example, Burrell (2009) advocates viewing fieldsites as networks, shifting from spaces of dwelling to a mapping of the social phenomena under study. When taking a network standpoint, the researcher should think critically about the points they can enter the network, guided by what access each position affords access to. Furthermore, the researcher should think through the multiple networks in a site, be they social or technical, focusing on interconnections. Burrell (2009) also reminds us of one important aspect of site definition, knowing when and where to stop. Here, the advice is practically oriented. Stop when you run out of time – bearing in mind, of course, the usual attention to theoretical saturation. Another approach to fieldsite definition is offered by Postill and Pink (2012), who suggest that sociality is the key criterion, crisscrossing platforms, search engines and hyperlinks, as well as offline spaces. Focusing on routines, mobilities and socialities of interlocutors should allow the researcher to traverse online and offline interconnections fluidly.

As illustrated by the above, the way we have defined ethnographic sites has shifted with the increasing embeddedness of digital technology in our daily lives. Early studies of bounded virtual worlds and online communities paved the path to hybrid designs, spanning online and offline spaces. While some advice is offered in how to address the complex issue of site definition, a great degree is left in the hands of the hybrid ethnographer to navigate their unbounded fieldsite within each individual study.

Illustrative example

My study of Poshmark began haphazardly, as many ethnographic pursuits do, stumbling across something which piques interest, leading to an eventual deep dive and immersion in the fieldsite. I was a brand-new PhD fellow, writing about twenty-first-century digital work practices, and stumbled across the profile of a seller on Instagram. Following the hashtags (#momboss #poshboss #reseller #posher), I was cast into a fascinating social world of female home-based entrepreneurship. Uncovered were hundreds of sellers, primarily women, who scoured thrift stores in rural America to source merchandise for their online platform stores. Initially, the interest was on the pervasiveness of the phenomenon, and the strong identification these sellers had with the Poshmark App. For better or for worse, at this point I had not read a great deal about digital methods and was relatively open and forced to rely on my instinct as an ethnographer, learned in diverse environments ranging from a tech start-up, community spaces and asylum centres. To keep track of the sellers, an Instagram account was created, and I began chatting casually to sellers through comments and the messaging function. I also followed the links many sellers had to their YouTube channel and watched informational videos about how to shop, photograph and list merchandise, often where sellers showed how quickly and efficiently they could perform these tasks.

After several months of engagement in this fieldsite, it became clear that, besides the Poshmark selling platform, Instagram and YouTube were used promotionally to display the aesthetically pleasing aspects of selling, while obscuring the informal sides of sellers' work. At this point, insecurities arose over the reach of my scientific claims – for example, as a study on Instagram and YouTube, it might be more suited to focus solely on influencer dynamics rather than a study of work. Simultaneously, because the fieldsite did not have a natural boundary, I had large questions of 'what counted' as being within those bounds. While the starting point was Poshmark, many sellers used several platforms in conjunction, and questions of exclusion were raised if a seller used Etsy and eBay as well. Driven by my own curiosity, I did not dwell on these questions and instead continued my study by following links from Instagram, or what was said in conversations with sellers, treating Poshmark as an entry point rather than a final destination. I also expanded my site to include Facebook, driven by intuition that reselling groups must exist. Many of the first groups I found were for eBay sellers; however, these served as an important entry point to other related groups, including those specifically for Poshmark. To find groups, I used both the recommender algorithm on Facebook, while following breadcrumbs to niche groups when they were mentioned in conversation. For instance, I repeatedly heard about a group who ran large-scale A-B testing and tracked it down through conversations across several groups. Similarly, when a dispute resulted in bullying, I found a group who was explicitly drama-free, removing people if the conversation moved in that direction. Facebook has become an important source for understanding the day-to-day work happening around Poshmark, not visible on media like Instagram. I also frequently use Google to search information about features, tactics and the like, and find myself on Reddit forums, private blogs and the company's own website. It was through my participation in all of these sites on a continual basis that I learned about the company's annual conference Poshfest, and was able to travel to Phoenix to engage in proximal data collection. Visiting with hundreds of people, including representatives from Poshmark itself, was a great opportunity to speak with people more candidly in a face-to-face form.

The unbounded fieldsite of this ethnography spans the Poshmark platform, Facebook, Reddit, YouTube, Instagram, websites, blogs, a three-day conference and a smaller one-day event for sellers. Through all of these sites, I periodically conduct ad hoc interviews with participants when I have further questions. Within these confines, I have observed thousands of interlocutors, some over several years, others for a brief instant. I no longer question my ethnographic authority on the site, despite not being able to name every participant or having a firm understanding of where the boundaries of the study are. I have long accepted the condition that it is simply not possible to draw links across all of my fieldnotes in a person-centric manner. In fact, precisely because I did not question the boundaries, I have followed activities more or less freely and built the rich understanding of the site I have today.

This process of unravelling has been far from perfect, and at points I ended up down rabbit holes that were purely guided by the nature of digital platforms, as attention sucks rather than my research focus. For instance, when drama would break out within the community, I would often follow the gossip obsessively, spending hours typing fieldnotes that said more about a niche personal gripe than the fieldsite overall. In terms of knowing when to stop collecting data, I generally follow a thread until nothing is novel. Having just crossed the two-year mark of data collection, I am not as heavily immersed in the site as I once was. Instead, I passively browse sites and collect data sporadically when something significant changes in the space – for example, a new feature is launched, or there is sudden controversy surrounding a decision. However, it is not that the activities in the fieldsite stop, or that I can fully walk away from it, because unlike a spatially removed site it is always close at hand, right in one of the convenient apps on my smartphone. Instead, the discipline rests with me to explore when I have questions and to disengage when the time is appropriate – a boundary I continually manage.

As highlighted, moving to hybrid ethnography challenges researchers to navigate unbounded fieldsites. Here, the hybrid ethnographer must weigh each decision of inclusion and exclusion, balancing cautions of over-collection against curiosity and discovery. The process inevitably involves some wrong turns; however, it offers potential for rich data through complex site construction.

9.3 Managing Technological Opacity

The issue of technological opacity within ethnography is one largely born with the inclusion of digital data into ethnographic studies. By technological opacity, we mean the ability of the researcher to understand the role technology plays in the fieldsite (Hultin, 2019). This issue is of core relevance to hybrid ethnographers, where movement is fluid between online and offline spaces and data is collected in digital and non-digital data forms. Technological opacity has many causes, stemming from the anonymity of the Internet (Hine, 2000) to the corporate interests that structure the algorithms and behaviours on it (Kozinets, 2015). Being a hybrid ethnographer means actively working with the opacity of technology to account for the role it plays in the sites. This section discusses how the hybrid ethnographer can manage technological opacity in their research.

When digital data is collected for research, the object of study becomes an entanglement of the social and digital, rendering the question of whether we research society or the technology itself complex (Marres, 2017). The data collected from digital media sites has features both of human behaviour *and* of the digital devices in which they are expressed. Thus, when collecting data from social media, the researcher must be aware of this manifold influence. One of the core reasons that such opacity is rendered is due to the algorithms that dominate many of the social spaces online. To this end, Burrell (2016) outlines the ways in which algorithms can be opaque. Algorithms are opaque as they are generally purposefully kept a secret by the companies that create them, and even when access is offered, researchers generally lack the technical literacy to understand them. Finally, regardless of our technical literacy, algorithms are adaptive, evolving over time, and in constant interaction with multiple other algorithms, creating opacity (O'Neil, 2016).

In these conditions, work on the ethnographic study of algorithms is particularly helpful to understand how we could mitigate some of the issues. For instance, Seaver (2017) argues that as opposed to a technologically founded definition of algorithms, we need to understand them as fundamentally cultural. The focus is shifted to making algorithms visible 'not as stable objects interacted with from many perspectives, but as the manifold consequences of a variety of human practices' (p. 4). Key to the approach is a multi-faceted view of technology through the eyes of interlocutors, through off-the-record chats with developers where possible, and by seeing through official press releases and publications. Christin (2020) follows a similar approach, reminding us that the study of algorithms is inherently black-boxed, involving partiality of knowledge. Her solution is precisely through

ethnographic study, suggesting that working from *within* we can begin to open this black box. She suggests strategies of refraction, studying the difference when an algorithm is introduced; comparison, moving across sites to see algorithmic impacts in different contexts; and finally triangulation, drawing on multiple sources of data. These approaches make space for onto-logical multiplicity, allowing the technologies in focus to exist in different forms depending on where one stands (Mol, 2002).

Illustrative example

During my study of Poshmark, I became specifically interested in the sharing algorithm, which is the backbone of sociality on the platform and how goods circulate. Because of the centrality of this function, it was difficult to continue without in-depth knowledge of it. For weeks, I obsessed over how to gain proprietary knowledge about the sharing algorithm, knowing full-well the company would not be willing to give access to it. I did a complete deep dive, scouring the terms of service agreement, listening to podcasts and searching through the Internet archive, as well as reading historic posts on Facebook to create a timeline of the Poshmark app development. However, I became frustrated, feeling that, no matter how much I learned my knowledge of the algorithm was partial in nature. Given the partiality of my knowledge, at points I questioned whether I could write about the sharing feature at all, as I could not describe it in detail. As IS scholars, we pride ourselves on our focus on the IT artifact and thus it felt even more crucial that I be able to account for the specific shaping this feature was having.

At one point, I reflected on when I had been here before. Admittedly, in other ethnographic work, there had been moments where I was trying to retrospectively construct how an event had played out and could not seem to grasp it in full. For instance, while doing fieldwork in a tech start-up, I had been told no fewer than three different accounts of the founding story of the company. In that context, I had been perfectly comfortable still reporting on the company, recognizing that these accounts were all simultaneously valid. In other words, while in other contexts I recognized the lack of singular truth so commonly associated with constructivist research, when it came to the study here, I had conflated issues of hard-wired code and sociotechnical phenomena. Because I was studying a technological feature, it seemed like there was some objective truth to be gained. By accepting that what I was studying manifested in my fieldsite, I was able to instead focus my attention to the more pertinent issues – not what the sharing algorithm technically did, but how the algorithm was *experienced* in the web of messy work structures my interlocutors existed in. Through engaging with interlocutors, I realized that the algorithm had changed not only because of changes to the underlying code, but also because of the platform's scaling and growth. I was then able to use press releases and news stories as historical sources to create a holistic timeline of the feature's development. I used my time at the annual conference Poshfest to deepen my understanding of the sharing algorithm, attending a workshop related specifically to the algorithms, and asking representatives from the company more pointed questions about its development. I also collected stories from long-term sellers of their personal experience of the algorithm's change over time. It was through these processes that I uncovered many of the unintentional algorithmic changes – for instance, when a regular update to the Poshmark app had removed a beloved short-cut that many sellers had become accustomed to. Instead of uncovering the 'truth' of the sharing algorithm, I built a plausible story of the social understanding of it in my ethnographic site – a story that was historically situated and woven through several different iterations, which reflected the experience of my interlocutors.

This small example repeated itself many times over in my ethnographic study. Because I study activities across different platforms, the algorithms involved are endless. If I were to account for everything technological that influences the activity in the space, I would need to write an entire book before I could even begin to describe the analysis at hand. Thus, studying technology diligently for me is about following when technology matters, when it creates changes and discussion or when it is a focal point of activity. In this sense, interlocutors can tell you in different ways why technology is a concern and exactly what it is doing for them, which can be enriched by drawing on multiple sources.

In sum, the opacity of technology is an issue born with the inclusion of digital data into ethnographic studies. Precisely because technology plays such a large role in these spaces, it becomes an important factor to account for. However, many aspects of modern technology are highly opaque, creating challenges for the hybrid ethnographer when accounting for the role of technology.

9.4 Working with Diverse Data

Hybrid ethnography increases the sorts of data collected, including digital web-native content which has hyperlinks, and is to some degree ephemeral, alongside non-digital data such as interviews and fieldnotes. Web-native content, navigated via hyperlinks or hashtags, can be difficult to capture in text-based fieldnotes. Simultaneously, data collection often links multiple offline and online spaces which the researcher must draw together to construct coherence – for example, when a conversation extends across several sites. This section discusses how the hybrid ethnographer can work with diversity of data in their research.

One way in which data in hybrid ethnography is more diverse surrounds the changing role of the researcher in data generation. In a traditional ethnographic study, the researcher distils the fieldsite into their own fieldnotes (Emerson et al., 2011). However, when collecting digital data, there are multiple content creators (Vaast and Urquhart, 2018). This is a conceptual shift for ethnographers, who begin including multi-vocality in their fieldnotes (Przybylski, 2020). Hybrid ethnographers must also manage the changing linguistic convention of digital data, including acronyms, emojis and hashtags. These changes to communication are not only visual conventions, but also impact the structural ways in which communication happens in such environments (Vaast and Urquhart, 2018). For instance, hashtags are an integral part of navigating online spaces, serving as vital links between content. Being an ethnographer in online spaces often means using these same hashtags, becoming a part of the web of communication with others (Postill and Pink, 2012).

Because of the specific structure of the Internet, some authors advocate abandoning traditional methods in favour of putting the Internet at the fore of their research design. One voice in this space is Rogers (2009, 2015), who, under the rubric of 'digital methods', advises researchers to take natively digital elements as their starting point. He suggests a number of these, including the link, the website, the search engine, the spheres, the webs, post-demographics and networked content. For each of these starting points, Rogers provides a specific approach. For instance, starting with the link, the researcher should investigate how an actor is defined through the type of hyperlinks given and received. While each of the starting points vary in method, all indicate a shift from user-centric modes of data collection to larger-scale network mapping, which is then used to zoom in on relevant areas of analysis through either qualitative or quantitative means. Rogers's approach has been favoured within digital sociology (Marres, 2017) and is the backbone of the long-standing Digital Methods Initiative.

Beyond different linguistic conventions, and changing structural elements, digital data can also be ephemeral, changing or disappearing entirely in a dynamic fashion (Hine, 2015). Because of this property, hybrid ethnographers have a tendency to over-collect data to mitigate the risk of missing

Hybrid ethnography creates data that take widely different forms and can include everything from traditional interviews, to a static social media post, to an in-depth description of a feature crossing several sites, sometimes over several years. The hybrid ethnographer must navigate these messy worlds in pursuit of understanding. As with traditional ethnographic study, data will always exist in 'headnotes', the notes in the mind and memory of the researcher (Ottenberg, 2019). Ethnography is, after all, about immersion and experience, and in its hybrid sense, the goal is the same – it is only the means that differ.

9.5 Takeaways

Based on the above, we can derive a number of takeaways for researchers wishing to do hybrid ethnography in diverse IS studies. Each of these is outlined below and summarized in Table 9.2.

From the perspective of *navigating unbounded fieldsites*, there are three takeaways related to: immersion in the fieldsite; understanding hybrid worlds; and guiding the fieldsite construction with reflexivity. First, we recommend that hybrid ethnographic researchers immerse themselves in the fieldsite, following the spaces where their interlocutors engage, and exploring openly when activity moves across diverse spaces. Rather than dwelling on questions of inclusion and exclusion, it is often beneficial, particularly in the initial phase of research, to take this open strategy. This allows the hybrid ethnographer to explore unconventional paths. For instance, while constructing the Poshmark fieldsite, whether to exclude eBay sellers presented a dilemma; however, by including

them, other relevant Facebook groups were discovered. Second, there is great potential in using interlocutors' descriptions to create a fluid picture of hybrid worlds – for example, transcending the online and offline spaces. Much of the digital content collected in the study of Poshmark is highly descriptive, giving great insight not only into the digitally mediated aspects of sellers' work, but also into their holistic lifeworld. While the study could reflect on a more bounded digital phenomenon, such as the influencer dynamics, it does not need to, as using hybrid methods allows for collection beyond a single social media site. Finally, we urge hybrid ethnographers to guide their fieldsite construction with reflexivity. While this sounds like simple advice, in practice it is much more difficult when there is 'always one more link to click'. As shown in the example above, it is all too tempting to get carried away in novel gossip, swayed more by curiosity than one's research phenomenon. Practically speaking, time provides one cure: as events become less novel, there is a natural focus and bounding. However, in the initial phases of fieldsite construction, when analyses remain relatively open and discoveries plentiful, ethnographers should continually question and describe the pathways they traverse to guide their site construction.

In relation to *managing technological opacity*, the advice offered relates to understanding technology through the experience of interlocutors, seeking plausible understandings and constructing multidimensional views of technology via multiple sources. The first piece of advice pertains to using the experience of interlocutors as the entry point into technology in the space. For example, understanding the sharing algorithm in Poshmark from a

Table 9.2 Takeaways for hybrid ethnographers

Navigating unbounded fieldsites	Get immersed into the fieldsite following engagements and activities	Create an understanding of hybrid worlds via interlocutors' descriptions	Guide the fieldsite construction with reflexivity
Managing technological opacity	Understand technology through the experience of interlocutors	Seek plausible understandings rather than objective technical description	Draw on multiple sources to construct a multidimensional view of technology
Working with hybrid data	Form holistic understanding from fragments	Work on different temporal planes	Learn the languages of each space

purely technical perspective was less illuminating than viewing it through the sellers' accounts of how it impacts their daily work. This entry point to technology allowed for a rich understanding of the algorithm to be constructed. Second, we remind researchers to seek plausible understandings of technologies, rather than objective technical descriptions. For hybrid ethnographers, trying to understand the proprietary algorithms of platforms can be a particularly messy task, and notions of objective truth are fallacious, leading only to frustration. In these cases, studying technology as plausible and tentative will help ethnographers build on their working knowledge and continue despite opacity. Finally, we point to the importance of drawing on multiple sources to construct a multidimensional view of technology. While this advice might seem counter-intuitive to understanding technology through the experience of interlocutors, that is not the case. For example, while the sellers' experience of the sharing algorithm revealed its relationship to scaling and growth, historical data helped construct a longitudinal account of these changes. Similarly, company data, such as terms of service and company communication, revealed strategic changes over time. This is to say that to understand technology from an ethnographic standpoint is to draw on multiple, multifaceted sources.

In terms of *working with hybrid data*, the takeaways centre on forming holistic understanding from fragmented data, working on different temporal planes and learning the languages of each space. With our suggestion, to seek holistic understanding from fragmented data, we do not imply that an objective 'view from nowhere' exists. Rather, we highlight how in hybrid ethnography high degrees of fragmentation exist, which can be partially mitigated through a patchworked form of understanding. To achieve this, the researcher should ask questions across the data. For instance, during the study of Poshmark, sellers were often asked to reflect back on various periods of time. Their answers were then used to search historically for posts about that period or look for official company information in the form of press releases. This form of piecing it together helps the hybrid ethnographer construct rich fieldnotes. Second, we suggest that researchers work on different temporal

planes, collecting data across different time horizons. This is indeed one of the core benefits of introducing hybridity to ethnographic studies, as the ethnographer through the use of digital data can often travel back in time to different periods to ask questions. These trips back in time can be used as small jogs to interlocutors' memory, or as standalone. In the study of Poshmark, while initially the research period was set by the ethnographic time spent in the field, expanding the time horizons allowed the inclusions of several important events outside of the initial scope. Finally, we highlight that researchers must learn the language of each space they include in their hybrid design. Different sites will often illuminate different aspects of their site. For example, while Poshmark sellers use YouTube to show their work process, it is often a highly polished version of this, aimed at generating views rather than showing reality. On Facebook, sellers would frequently remark that they could not keep up with the speeds claimed in these YouTube videos. Learning to decode these spaces is vital to putting data together, realizing what each will contribute to the study. Table 9.2 provides an overview of these takeaways.

9.6 Conclusions

This chapter has drawn on experiences in one hybrid ethnographic study to provide IS researchers with a toolbox of how they could conduct research of this nature. We conclude with a few general remarks for researchers who wish to engage in such a pursuit.

While we have discussed the challenge of navigating unbounded fieldsites, and in particular discussed the reflexivity required to restrain data collection, we wish to further restate the importance of discipline to shut off, tune out and finally leave the field completely. While these have always been issues within ethnography, the natural distance of the fieldsite, as well as agreements around access, often dictate these decisions. These elements are generally not present when the fieldsite is partially one click away on a mobile phone (Burrell, 2009). Personal limitations of when to engage in data collection have to be developed on the fly, notifications turned off or separate devices used to demarcate personal communication from the field. These issues, however, often continue to challenge the researcher, when there are endless potential data sources 'out there' (Coleman, 2014). In terms of leaving the field completely, decisions are equally difficult. While conventions such as theoretical saturation still apply, if we accept that we are no longer claiming to study a bounded cultural-whole, then the question of capturing completeness is no longer problematic, and instead the researcher stops when they must, when time is up (Hine, 2000). In this instance, the ethnographer is in the uncomfortable position of walking away, like they would with a physical site, closing with it the digital possibilities, despite them always being somewhat digitally accessible.

Working with hybrid data, in which the aim is to form a holistic understanding from fragments, and where you work on different temporal planes, is no easy feat. Therefore, we remind researchers wishing to pursue these approaches of the importance of structuring their data appropriately. Reflexivity of our own practice as researchers becomes critical in these cases, where standing back to ensure that we are structuring data collection according to experiences we seek to capture is paramount (Hine, 2017). Practising reflexivity can help limit both the size and focus of data sets in hybrid ethnography. This practice can be extended by using in-depth memo writing to have conversations with ourselves, to extrapolate our headnotes and to link discussions across multiple fieldnotes. To that end, confessional writing, like the accounts in the illustrative examples above, allows researchers to step outside their own head and reflect on their engagement in these spaces (Schultze, 2000). Similarly, when managing the challenges related to technological opacity, as outlined in this chapter, it is important for IS researchers to reflect on their accounts of the sociotechnical environment they are engaged with, inviting its materiality into interviews and descriptions of practices (see Hultin, 2019). Incorporating these less conventional accounts into traditional publishing can be challenging and we may need new presentational modalities

to incorporate this type of writing, along with the multi-modal hyperlinked data that hybrid ethnography incorporates (Avital et al., 2017).

This chapter resituates a traditional ethnographic approach to hybrid *qualitative* data. This was an intentional choice, positioned to highlight the continued importance of such classic approaches to complement the manifold quantitative approaches that have arisen over the past years, rooted in large scraped data sets (Howison et al., 2011; Gaskin et al., 2014). That being said, there is no reason that precludes the inclusion of quantitative techniques in a hybrid ethnographic approach. In particular, these techniques provide ample opportunity for how data is collected (as highlighted by Andersen and Hukal in Chapter 16). Other examples include Erickson (2019), who argues that a mixed methodological approach drawing on trace data and traditional field methods is beneficial for revealing 'important new patterns for understanding humans' relationship(s) with technology' (p. 301). In a similar line of argument, scholars have suggested 'diffractive' readings of trace data, which incorporate multiple levels of analysis, supplemented with participant observation and interviews (Østerlund et al., 2020). In a different vein, Venturini's (2010) 'controversy mapping' cuts through the distinction between qualitative and quantitative methods, using large data sets to create network maps of online debate, which are then used to guide zoomed-in qualitative analysis. Similarly, Safadi et al. (Chapter 8) argue that large-scale textual data sets can be used to create interactive visualizations which enable qualitative theorization. These approaches could be used to supplement the approaches outlined in this chapter. Thus, we suggest there is an open field for IS researchers to explore their own diverse configurations of hybrid ethnography, practising scavenger methods (Seaver, 2017) to create innovative research designs – the only limitation being that we should not place too much faith in uncontextualized data and outsource our conclusions blindly to algorithmic means of collection. Driven by creativity and curiosity, we hope to see the incorporation of hybrid ethnography in greater degrees in the IS field in the future.

References

Atkinson, P. (2015). *For Ethnography*. London: Sage.

Atkinson, P. and Hammersley, M. (2007). *Ethnography: Principles in Practice*. New York, NY: Routledge.

Avital, M., Mathiassen, L. and Schultze, U. (2017). Alternative genres in information systems research. *European Journal of Information Systems*, 26(3), 240–247.

Baym, N. K. (2000). *Tune in, Log on: Soaps, Fandom, and Online Community*. Thousand Oaks, CA: Sage.

Boellstorff, T. (2008). *Coming of Age in Second Life: An Anthropologist Explores the Virtually Human*. Princeton, NJ: Princeton University Press.

Boellstorff, T., Nardi, B., Pearce, C. and Taylor, T. L. (2012). *Ethnography and Virtual Worlds: A Handbook of Method*. Princeton, NJ: Princeton University Press.

Burrell, J. (2016). How the machine 'thinks': Understanding opacity in machine learning algorithms. *Big Data and Society*, 3(1), 1–12.

Burrell, J. (2009). The field site as a network: A strategy for locating ethnographic research. *Field Methods*, 21(2), 181–199.

Christin, A. (2020). The ethnographer and the algorithm: Beyond the black box. *Theory and Society*, 49(5–6), 897–918.

Coleman, E. G. (2010). Ethnographic approaches to digital media. *Annual Review of Anthropology*, 39(1), 487–505.

Coleman, G. (2014). *Hacker, Hoaxer, Whistleblower, Spy: The Many Faces of Anonymous*. London: Verso Books.

Eckhardt, A., Endter, F., Giordano, A. and Somers, P. (2019). Three stages to a virtual workforce. *MIS Quarterly Executive*, 18(1), 19–35.

Emerson, R. M., Fretz, R. I. and Shaw, L. L. (2011). *Writing Ethnographic Fieldnotes*. Chicago, IL: University of Chicago Press.

Erickson, I. (2019). Working, being, and researching in place: A mixed methodological approach for understanding digital experiences. In R. Mir and S. Jain (eds), *The Routledge Companion to Qualitative Research in Organization Studies*. New York, NY: Routledge, pp. 291–305.

Erickson, I. (2010). Geography and community: New forms of interaction among people and places. *American Behavioral Scientist*, 53(8), 1194–1207.

Gaskin, J., Berente, N., Lyytinen, K. and Yoo, Y. (2014). Toward generalizable sociomaterial inquiry: A computational approach for zooming in and out of sociomaterial routines. *MIS Quarterly*, 38(3), 849–872.

Hafner, K. and Lyon, M. (1998). *Where Wizards Stay up Late: The Origins of the Internet*. New York, NY: Simon & Schuster.

Hedman, J., Srinivasan, N. and Lindgren, R. (2013). Digital traces of information systems: Sociomateriality made researchable. International Conference on Information Systems, Milan, Italy.

Hine, C. (2017). From the virtual to the embedded, embodied, everyday internet. In L. Hjorth, H. Horst, A. Galloway and G. Bell (eds), *The Routledge Companion to Digital Ethnography*. Abingdon, UK and New York, NY: Routledge, pp. 21–29.

Hine, C. (2015). *Ethnography for the Internet: Embedded, Embodied and Everyday*. Milton Park, UK: Bloomsbury Academic.

Hine, C. (2000). *Virtual Ethnography*. Thousand Oaks, CA: Sage.

Howison, J., Wiggins, A. and Crowston, K. (2011). Validity issues in the use of social network analysis with digital trace data. *Journal of the Association for Information Systems*, 12(12), 767–797.

Hultin, L. (2019). On becoming a sociomaterial researcher: Exploring epistemological practices grounded in a relational, performative ontology. *Information and Organization*, 29(2), 91–104.

Kozinets, R. (2015). *Netnography: Redefined*. Thousand Oaks, CA: Sage.

Malinowski, B. (1922). *Argonauts of the Western Pacific: An Account of Native Enterprise and Adventure in the Archipelagoes of Melanesian New Guinea*. London: Routledge.

Markham, A. and Baym, N. (2009). *Internet Inquiry: Conversations about Method*. London: Sage.

Marres, N. (2017). *Digital Sociology*. Cambridge, UK: Polity Press.

Mol, A. (2002). *The Body Multiple: Ontology in Medical Practice*. Durham, NC: Duke University Press.

Möhlmann, M. and Zalmanson, L. (2018). Hands on the wheel: Navigating algorithmic management and Uber drivers. International Conference on Information Systems, Seoul, South Korea.

Oates, B. J. (2006). *Researching Information Systems and Computing*. Thousand Oaks, CA: Sage.

O'Neil, C. (2016). *Weapons of Math Destruction: How Big Data Increases Inequality and*

Threatens Democracy. Portland, OR: Broadway Books.

O'Reilly, K. (2012). *Ethnographic Methods*. New York, NY: Routledge.

Østerlund, C., Crowston, K. and Jackson, C. (2020). Building an apparatus: Refractive, reflective, and diffractive readings of trace data. *Journal of the Association for Information Systems*, 21(1), 1–22.

Ottenberg, S. (2019). Thirty years of fieldnotes: Changing relationships to the text. In R. Sanjek (ed.), *Fieldnotes*. Ithaca, NY: Cornell University Press, pp. 139–160.

Pink, S., Horst, H., Postill, J., Hjorth, L., Lewis, T. and Tacchi, J. (2016). *Digital Ethnography: Principles and Practice*. London: Sage.

Postill, J. and Pink, S. (2012). Social media ethnography: The digital researcher in a messy web. *Media International Australia*, 145(1), 123–134.

Przybylski, L. (2020). *Hybrid Ethnography: Online, Offline, and in between*. London: Sage.

Rogers, R. (2015). *Digital Methods*. Cambridge, MA: MIT Press.

Rogers, R. (2009). *The End of the Virtual: Digital Methods*. Amsterdam, the Netherlands: Amsterdam University Press.

Rosenblat, A. (2018). *Uberland: How Algorithms Are Rewriting the Rules of Work*. Berkeley, CA: University of California Press.

Schultze, U. (2010). Embodiment and presence in virtual worlds: A review. *Journal of Information Technology*, 25(4), 434–449.

Schultze, U. (2000). A confessional account of an ethnography about knowledge work. *MIS Quarterly: Management Information Systems*, 24(1), 3–40.

Scott, S. V. and Orlikowski, W. J. (2012). Reconfiguring relations of accountability: Materialization of social media in the travel sector. *Accounting, Organizations and Society*, 37(1), 26–40.

Seaver, N. (2017). Algorithms as culture: Some tactics for the ethnography of algorithmic systems. *Big Data and Society*, 4(2), 1–12.

Sergeeva, A. V., Faraj, S. and Huysman, M. (2020). Losing touch: An embodiment perspective on coordination in robotic surgery. *Organization Science*, 31(5), 1248–1271.

Vaast, E. and Urquhart, C. (2018). Building grounded theory with social media data. In R. Mir and S. Jain (eds), *The Routledge Companion to Qualitative Research in Organization Studies*. New York, NY: Routledge, pp. 408–421.

Van Maanen, J. (2011). *Tales of the Field: On Writing Ethnography*, 2nd edition. Chicago, IL: Chicago University Press.

Venturini, T. (2010). Diving in magma: How to explore controversies with actor-network theory. *Public Understanding of Science*, 19(3), 258–273.

Case Study Research Revisited

BOYKA SIMEONOVA and GUY FITZGERALD

10.1 Introduction

The rationale for this chapter was to revisit the role and the use of case studies in information systems research, both in the past and for the future. Case studies as a research method originally had a bit of a chequered past, with positivist/quantitative research methods dominating in the early days of the discipline. However, it was argued that case studies always had an important role and emerged as more prominent in the 1990s and beyond. They never replaced positivist/quantitative methods, but seemed to establish themselves as a legitimate approach, with a greater degree of acceptance, in the discipline. The importance of case studies is discussed, from the various early classic cases through to more recent modern cases and their contribution. The importance of case studies supporting the strengths of positivist/quantitative research is highlighted and it is called for better recognition of the potential of mixed-method and multi-method research. The chapter presents a further debate about what might happen to case study research in the future, particularly in the digital era and with the emergence of new forms of digital research data. The chapter recognizes the value of case studies and it is argued that they still have much to offer. The chapter also highlights the differences in perspectives, perceptions and understanding of case study concepts, including definitions. This lack of agreement and disparity, even among advocates of case study research, highlights the need for a discussion of some issues, uses, roles and the future of case studies, which is the aim of this 'case study research revisited'.

10.2 History of the Case Study

Interestingly, there does not seem to be a definitive history of the case study as a form of academic research method. Perhaps this is because, according to Flyvbjerg (2011), the case study 'has been around as long as recorded history', which would seem difficult to document. This introduction to the history of the case study is not going to be definitive either, partly because it would be a huge project and would likely be quite controversial. Further, it is not the real purpose of this chapter. However, it is worth rehearsing some of the elements to inform the later discussions. Gerring (2006) says that the 'case study method has a long and largely neglected history' and that it starts with Frederic Le Play (1806–1882) in France, although whether these early cases would be recognized as case studies today is debatable because they included 'a substantial proportion of quantitative analysis', which may have been an early attempt at mixed-method research! Tellis (1997) also indicates that the earliest use of the case was from Europe, and predominantly from France. In relation to the disciplines using case study research, Harrison et al. (2017) suggest that it had its roots in anthropology, history, psychology and sociology 'when lengthy, detailed ethnographic studies of individuals and cultures were conducted'. There then seems to be a bit of a gap until the early twentieth century in the United States, where the University of Chicago was influential in the use of the case method in sociology through investigating people in their natural settings with the objective of gaining insights into experiences and 'how individuals constructed their worlds' (Harrison et al., 2017). These case studies were relatively well known and influential and the approach of the 'Chicago School' was to gain some considerable reputation. However, there were of course critics, and there was a resultant 'rebellion against Chicago' and its methods in favour of more scientific and quantitative methods (Lengermann,

1978). Perhaps this was the first instance of academic 'method wars'.

This rebellion has been described as 'undeniably won' by the positivists and led to the decline of the Chicago School and indeed the case study approach in general. Tellis (1997) states that it 'resulted in the denigration of case study as a methodology' and the advance of quantitatively based studies. It is argued that this situation continued throughout the 1940s and indeed through to the 1960s and 1970s, and that during this period quantitative empirical results were considered to be much more rigorous and the 'standard' of evidence (Harrison et al., 2017).

In the mid- to late 1960s, what has been termed the 'second generation' of case study began to emerge (Johansson, 2003). According to Tellis (1997), some researchers were concerned with the predominance and limitations of quantitative methods and were considerate to other approaches. In particular, Glaser and Strauss (1967) were experimenting with qualitative field study methods, not dissimilar to those of the Chicago School, in combination with quantitative analysis, which is known as Grounded Theory. This, according to Harrison et al. (2017), led to a renewed interest and revival in the case study method. In the early 1960s, Glaser and Strauss studied interactions between medical staff and patients (Glaser and Strauss, 1965) and during this study encountered what they described as an 'overemphasis' on the need to verify theory to the detriment of generating theory. They thought it should at least receive equal treatment and that there was a lack of social theory deriving from empirical research (Glaser and Strauss, 1967). If they could resolve these conundrums, they believed it would be 'more successful than theories logically deduced from a priori assumptions' (Glaser and Strauss, 1967). As a result, they outlined what Kenny and Fourie (2014) term 'a pioneering methodology', which filled the 'embarrassing gap between theory and empirical research' (Glaser and Strauss, 1967). Yin also described a process for case study research where formal theories guide the research and are tested as part of the outcome, highlighting, according to Harrison et al. (2017), 'his realist approach to qualitative case

study research'. Thus, Glaser and Strauss and Yin helped revive the use of case studies and 'accelerated the renewed use of the methodology' (Tellis, 1997). They not only helped revive it, but they also structured and formalized it in their various ways, and by providing guides and methodological rigour they helped others to adopt the method more easily.

The following period (from the 1970s) provided 'numerous examples of applications of the case study method' (Tellis, 1997), with the earliest examples in the fields of law and medicine, as well as sociology, but followed by many other fields (e.g., anthropology and education). Although it seems this revival was relatively slow, as Strauss observed, it took around two decades for Grounded Theory to be accepted as legitimate by other sociology contemporaries (Strauss and Corbin, 1994). Even so, quantitative research was still the dominant method. However, the case study method, if not an equal of quantitative methods, was at least a recognized method that could get published in journals in the relevant fields.

As indicated above, education was one of the domains in which some advocated case study research, and influential in this context were Stake (1995, 2006) and Merriam (1998, 2009). Harrison et al. (2017) say that Stake 'used a constructivist orientation to case study. This placed more emphasis on inductive exploration, discovery, and holistic analysis that was presented in thick descriptions of the case.' Stake was advocating interpretive, qualitative methods that were less quantitative and positivistic than those of Glaser and Strauss or Yin. Stake explains that his view of case studies is drawn from 'naturalistic, holistic, ethnographic, phenomenological, and biographic research methods', and continues: 'The qualitative researcher emphasizes episodes of nuance, the sequentiality of happenings in context, the wholeness of the individual', with a further 'emphasis on interpretation' (Stake, 1995). Indeed, his 1995 book was titled *The Art of Case Research*, which epitomizes his approach. As mentioned earlier, Stake was influential in advocating and popularizing this kind of case study research approach in contrast to the more positivistic approach of others, such as Yin.

Case-based research gained popularity and acceptance in various social science disciplines and also in information systems (IS), relatively early in the discipline. The IS discipline is usually stated as having its origin around the mid-1960s (Davis, 2000). (It was also known as MIS – Management Information Systems, particularly in the United States.) Indeed, Tellis (1997) highlights its use outside sociology, specifically in education and MIS. Benbasat et al. (1987) suggest that descriptive case studies were first used in the context of end-user computing research, citing the work of Rockart and Flannery (1983). However, Bryant et al. (2013) suggest that one of the first case studies was that of Mann and Williams (1960), who examined the dynamics of organizational change associated with the implementation of electronic data processing equipment. They also suggest that 'in these early days the preferred format within academic IS appears to have been case studies usually centring on ground-breaking and innovative IS implementation and use' (Bryant et al., 2013).

Hirschheim and Klein (2012) in their 'Glorious and not-so-short history of the information systems field' divide IS history into the following eras. The first era is from the start of IS in the mid-1960s to the mid-1970s. In this first era, they argue 'there was no real discussion of research methodology ... but Schools of Thought'. These Schools of Thought provided an important foundation for the discipline and involved systems theory, systems thinking, systems dynamics, sociotechnical systems, etc. Yet, despite these predominantly systems-based and social Schools of Thought, the main research activity of the period was quantitative and positivistic, and this persevered into the second era (the mid-1970s to the mid-1980s). However, during this second era, the issue of research methodology was more prominent and a number of different research approaches began to emerge to counter the still prevailing quantitative approaches. One example was the case study work by Kling in 1974 in researching the use of IT in providing social welfare in public agencies (Kling, 2004). Kling 'was a key founder of social analyses of computing. He was a leader among that most rare of species: the

sociologically acute computer scientist' (Wellman and Starr, 2004). There were also others pushing more qualitative research approaches in IS and adopting case study methods, and over the next decade or so a frame of work emerged.

Hence, the third era (the mid-1980s to the mid-to late 1990s) have seen an increase in examples of IS research adopting a range of qualitative methods, including case studies.

In 1987, Benbasat was able to argue that 'the case study research method is particularly well-suited to IS research, since the object of our discipline is the study of information systems in organizations, and interest has shifted to organizational rather than technical issues' (Benbasat, 1987). By 1989, Allen Lee identified that 'there is a strong case-study tradition in the academic field of management information systems' (Lee, 1989), with all his supporting examples, except one, being published in the 1980s. In 1991, research by Orlikowski and Baroudi (1991) identified that the case study was the most common qualitative method used in information systems. This has been frequently cited in many subsequent papers, although the wording adopted was not in fact in the original paper.

Hirschheim and Klein's (2012) final identified era was the late 1990s to around 2010. In this era, it is argued that things changed and that 'tremendous progress in terms of the field's acceptance of interpretive research methods' (Chen and Hirschheim, 2004) was achieved. A huge range of interpretive approaches were to be seen, including critical research, structuration theory and actor network theory. In terms of interpretive approaches, the case study was probably the most common of the interpretive methods and a proliferation was to be observed, especially in the early part of this era. As an indication of the acceptance of interpretive and case-based research, some of the previously highly positivistic journals began to be more accepting of a range of approaches with, for example, *Management Information Systems Quarterly* journal appointing more pluralistic editors (including, in 1999, Allen Lee, who was very strongly associated with the case study method, as Editor-in-Chief). There is a journal specifically dedicated to case-based research: the *Journal of Information Technology Cases & Applications*, launched in 1999.

As we have seen, Hirschheim and Klein's final era finished in around 2010, but another decade has passed since then. So, what has happened since – from around 2010 to 2020 (i.e., the current era)?

This chapter aims to examine the use of case studies in recent years (i.e., the current era), which is characterized by increased digitalization and the availability of large sets of data, known as trace data. First, however, we provide some definitions and concepts describing the case study research method.

10.3 Some Definitions

To start, what do we mean by a research method? It has been defined as 'the logical procedure employed by a science, i.e. the set of specific practices it uses to render the development of its demonstrations and theories clear, understandable and irrefutable' (Aktouf, 1987, quoted in Gagnon, 2010). A somewhat similar and perhaps more amenable definition is that of Mingers (2003), who suggests it is 'well defined sequences of operations that if carried out proficiently yield predictable results'. However, definitions and terminology are vague among many authors and terms are used interchangeably (e.g., research methods, research techniques and research strategies).

As a way of organizing thoughts in this context, we utilize the hierarchy suggested by Cecez-Kecmanovic (2011), which, among other benefits, provides a graphical representation of a complex situation (Figure 10.1). The hierarchy starts with the meta-theoretical assumptions. These are essentially the philosophical assumptions for the overall strategy of conducting research and the overall arguments for knowledge construction and justification, including theories and theorizing. They include ontology and epistemology assumptions

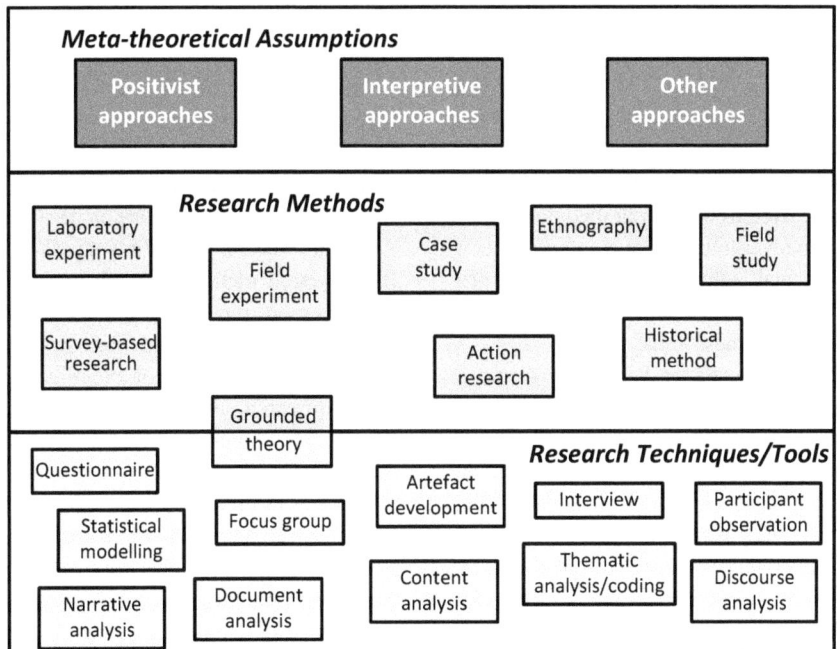

Figure 10.1 The IS research methodological landscape
Source: Cecez-Kecmanovic (2011).

and determine the research approaches or paradigms. The two most common approaches are interpretivist and positivist. There are, of course, others, such as critical realism, sociomateriality, etc. The point about this layer is that it is often simply implied and not discussed in much detail in research studies. The next layer contains the research methods which usually relate to particular research approaches/meta-theoretical assumptions. Unfortunately, these particular links are not illustrated in the diagram, but it is well known, for example, that interpretive approaches might utilize case studies, action research, ethnography, etc. Some can be used by more than one research approach – an example is the case study, which can be used by both interpretive and positivist researchers. The next layer is the techniques and tools for data collection and analysis which can be considered by the researcher to implement their research. These are aligned with the adopted research method and, often, the meta-theoretical assumptions. As an example, 'researchers adopting an interpretivist approach and a case study method may use questionnaires, focus groups, interviews and participant observation as data collection techniques and thematic analysis and coding as data analysis techniques' (Ezzy, 2002). Note that Cecez-Kecmanovic (2011) indicates that Grounded Theory can be both a method and a technique, and hence it is on the boundary. It is certainly considered as a research method by most authors as it involves interpretive assumptions concerning how social reality is constructed and provides a well-defined set of procedures to be followed to achieve these ends.

Having this landscape or framework helps in understanding the concepts under discussion. In relation to the case study research method, it emerges that quite a few authors fail to define the term, assuming that their readers will know what constitutes case study research. Others simply state something quite vague – for example, 'it is a research strategy for understanding a situation'. Still other authors list previous case study authors and/or examples as illustrations of what they mean. Swanborn (2010) states that 'case study methodology constitutes a difficult and confusing field because many research traditions use the same

expression, "case study" and a world of difference exists, for instance, between case studies in traditional anthropology and, say, Yin's work, which focuses on changes in organisations'.

We focus on the case study in the information systems and management context. In this domain, where the case study is defined, the most commonly used definition is that provided by Yin. For Yin, a case study is an empirical method that 'investigates a contemporary phenomenon (the "case") . . . within its real-world context, especially when the boundaries between phenomenon and context may not be clearly evident' (Yin, 2018). The importance of richness of study into the phenomenon is usually a common feature, as is the importance of the context in which the phenomenon occurs. The second part of Yin's definition suggests that there are many variables and complexities in the phenomenon that are difficult to isolate from those in the context, and indeed a case study will probably not isolate all of them. According to Aczel (2016), Yin's definition 'shows the importance of a case study as a research design. It represents in foreground the qualitative orientation and the great importance of a methodological and conceptual pluralism.'

Another aspect of Yin's definition is the apparent equivalence of 'case study' and 'phenomenon'. Yet, elsewhere, Yin explains the subject of the case study being the phenomenon (Yin, 2018). For Yin, the phenomenon is the question or situation which is sought to investigate. Yin suggests that the relevant research method might be a survey or poll. Whereas other types of questions, 'how' or 'why' 'are more explanatory and likely to lead to the use of a case study, history, or experiment as the preferred research method'. Yin explains, 'it is because such questions deal with the tracing of operational processes over time, rather than mere frequencies or incidence' (Yin, 2018). The fact that case study research primarily focuses on answering how- and why-type questions means that it is therefore essentially of an exploratory, descriptive or explanatory nature (Yin, 2018).

The phenomenon is the focus of the study/the question/the thing sought to investigate. The context relates to the external elements or data of the case study. For example, the group which has been identified to interview are the actors or participants in the case, who are an important part of understanding the phenomenon. Those outside of that group are the context. Equally, the context could be about the issues of the case: perhaps if the phenomenon is about how and why something has happened, the researcher might explore the way in which some services have been provided. Which services they focus on are part of the case, but those services they do not focus on are outside the case and are thus context. These decisions are about 'bounding' the case. Yin specifies that, in case study research, these decisions are blurred and thus difficult to decide upon. As a result, the boundaries may have to be changed as the case develops and evolves. This is considered as a strength of case studies and 'can lead to an entirely new understanding of a case – an understanding that was not necessarily appreciated at the outset of the case study' (Yin, 2018).

It has already been seen that Cecez-Kecmanovic (2011) indicates that the case study method can be interpretive or positivist. For Yin, the case study is argued to be positivistic – that is, it is an analytic approach which must be conducted according to rigorous processes and only by following rigorous processes can it lead to generalization. Furthermore, according to Tumele (2015), the researcher acts as a commentator rather than as an interpreter. However, Yin does not expressly define his meta-theoretical assumptions – it is others who interpret this (Yazan, 2015). Crotty (1998), for example, says that Yin demonstrates positivist leanings by the fundamental notions of objectivity, validity and generalizability. Further, anyone who explains the 'yielding established facts' is, for Crotty, a positivist. Yazan (2015) adds that Yin's research design conditions – construct validity, internal validity, external validity and reliability – are indicative of positivism. However, Yin's positivism should not necessarily be equated with a quantitative approach. In fact, Yin does not distinguish between the two (quantitative and qualitative), or rather suggests that both types of data are relevant. For example, Yin explains that, in relation to analysis: 'Case studies typically combine data collection techniques such as interviews, observation, questionnaires, and document and text analysis. Both qualitative data collection and analysis methods (which are concerned with words and meanings) and quantitative methods (concerned with numbers and measurement) may be used' (Yin, 1994).

Other authors have a different view. Stake, for example, is at the other end of the spectrum and is a proponent of interpretive case studies. Stake (1995) clearly states the interpretive epistemological stance and argues that knowledge is constructed rather than discovered. For Stake, case study researchers are interpreters and gatherers of interpretations, and he explains the following levels of interpretation. The first is the researcher interpreting the findings from the case. The second is the participants in the case who are themselves interpreting their understanding and activities in the case, typically when they are interviewed. The third level is that of the reader of a case study, who also interprets the findings according to the presentation and their own understanding, knowledge, values, etc. As a result, there are, Stake argues, multiple relevant perspectives, 'but there is no way to establish, beyond contention, the best view' (Stake, 1995).

In the IS domain, Klein and Myers (1999) are the dominant interpretive case study reference (6,000+ citations, according to Google Scholar). Klein and Myers outline a set of principles for conducting and evaluating such research that is designed to help 'IS researchers to understand human thought and action in social and organizational contexts; it has the potential to produce rich insights into information systems phenomena including the management of information systems and information systems development'. The principles identified by Klein and Myers (1999) are as follows. The first is the Hermeneutic Circle: 'This principle suggests that all human understanding is achieved by iterating between considering the meaning of parts and the whole that they form.' Second, is the Principle of Contextualization: this '[r]equires critical reflection of the social and historical background of the research setting, so that the intended audience can see how the current situation under investigation emerged'. Third is the Principle of Interaction Between Researchers and their Subjects: this '[r]equires critical reflection on how the research materials (or "data") were socially constructed through the interaction between the researchers and participants'. Fourth is the Principle of Abstraction and Generalization: this '[r]equires relating the idiographic details revealed by the data interpretation through the application of principles one and two to theoretical, general concepts that describe the nature of human understanding and social action'. Fifth is the Principle of Dialogical Reasoning 'to possible contradictions between the theoretical preconceptions guiding the research design and actual findings'. Sixth is the Principle of Multiple Interpretations of the 'possible differences in interpretations among the participants'. Finally, the Principle of Suspicion 'to possible "biases" and systematic "distortions" in the narratives collected from the participants'. These principles were an attempt to improve the rigour of interpretive research in IS and counter the assumption that positivist criteria and principles of case study research, as recommended by Yin, were also relevant and appropriate for interpretive case study research, and especially should not be used as evaluative criteria by reviewers and editors.

Understanding context is a key task of interpretive methods, which are 'aimed at producing an understanding of the context of the information system, and the process whereby the information system influences and is influenced by the context' (Walsham, 1993). In addition, '[i]nterpretivists argue that organizations are not static ... As a consequence, interpretive research seeks to understand a moving target' (Klein and Myers, 1999). They are, of course, not the only authors to emphasize the importance of context in case studies and IS. Pettigrew (1987) explained context in relation to the 'what', 'why' and 'how' of case study research: 'The "what" of change is encapsulated under the label content, much of the "why" of change is derived from an analysis of inner and outer context, and the "how" of change can be understood from an analysis of process' (Pettigrew, 1987). Avgerou (2001) outlined some principles for contextualization in IS: 'technology innovation should be considered in relation to socio-organizational change; analysis should consider not only the local organizational, but also the national and international context; analysis should consider both the technical/rational decisions and actions involved in the innovation process and the cultural, social and cognitive forces of such a process'.

Abstraction and generalization have been a contentious issue and a criticism levied at case study research. However, the criticism is typically about empirical generalization and statistical significance. For case studies research, it is more about theoretical generalization which is based on the validity of the argument. As Walsham states, it is about 'the plausibility and cogency of the logical reasoning used in describing the results from the cases, and in drawing conclusions from them' (Walsham, 1993). Lee and Baskerville (2003, 2012) explain different types of generalization. They explain that '[g]eneralizability is a major concern to those who do, and use, research. Statistical, sampling-based generalizability is well known, but methodologists have long been aware of conceptions of generalizability beyond the statistical' (2003). They outline a framework that organizes generalizability into the following types: generalizing from data to description – 'generalizing data to a measurement, observation, or other description'; generalizing from description to theory – 'generalizing measurement, observation or other description to a theory'; generalizing from theory to description – 'generalizing a theory, confirmed in one setting, to descriptions of other settings'; and generalizing from concepts to theory – 'generalizing a variable, construct, or other concept to a theory'. This is a useful categorization which at the least indicates that there are types of generalization beyond statistical, but also helps to identify the type of generalization relevant to specific research approaches/methods. Lee and Baskerville (2003) advocate for the correct generalizability categorization of case studies research – that is, from description to theory.

Tsang (2014) also argues that 'case studies have merits over quantitative methods in terms of theoretical generalization, identifying disconfirming cases and providing useful information for assessing the empirical generalizability of results'. Additionally, advocating for the generalizability of interpretive cases studies research, Walsham (1995) outlined four types of generalizations: the development of concepts; the generation of theory; the drawing of specific implications; and the contribution of rich insight. The role of theory is the key point, and it is explained that interpretive researchers are interested in 'using theory more as a "sensitizing device" to view the world in a certain way. Interpretive researchers in information systems tend not to generalize to philosophically abstract categories but to social theories such as structuration theory or actor network theory' (Klein and Myers, 1999). Eisenhardt also emphasized the aspect of building theory from case studies; however, in a positivist approach it is about hypotheses development (Eisenhardt, 1989). Walsham (1995) highlights the key role of theory and in IS case studies it can be utilized as follows: as an initial guide to design and data collection; as part of an iterative process of data collection and analysis; or as a final product of the research.

The differing epistemological and meta-theoretical perspectives are highlighted by Sarker et al. (2018b) in their study of qualitative publications in IS journals between 2001 and 2017. In relation to qualitative case study approaches, they identified what they termed 'genres', or types, as being: positivist case study; interpretive case study; exploratory case study; and ethnographic case study.

The first genre identified is the positivist case study, characterized as having a realist, data-centric focus, with data as facts or shared reality. Theory is generalizable and can be validated or falsified. Analysis is typically deductive, but can also be inductive. Sarker et al. (2018b) found that for the positivist case 'Yin (1994) is the dominant methodological reference, followed by Miles and Huberman (1994), Eisenhardt (1989), and Benbasat et al. (1987)'. The second case genre is the interpretive case study. Analysis is largely inductive, with theory used as 'a lens or scaffolding' to frame the research or as an outcome. Data is typically socially constructed and findings are interpreted as 'novel insights' or 'plausible reinterpretation of phenomena'. Klein and Myers (1999) is the dominant reference, with a broad range of other references (Sarker et al., 2018b). The third

identified case genre is the exploratory case study. This is a bit of a mishmash according to Sarker et al. (2018b), and is typically about 'exploring' a phenomenon that is not well understood. Such exploratory cases 'often end with insights, lessons, or a preliminary framework'. They tend to adopt a realist view of data and, although they are not strongly data-centric, they also tend to exhibit induction rather than deduction. Yin also appears to be the dominant reference, with Eisenhardt (1989) and Dubé and Paré (2003). The fourth genre identified is the ethnographic case study. Ethnography is distinguished by the primary source of evidence being the researcher participating in the activities of the social group of the case study, usually over a significant period. The data of the case is that of observation and perceptions of the researcher as a participant in the case in some way. As Myers (1999) states:

> In a case study, the primary source of data is interviews, supplemented by documentary evidence such as annual reports, minutes of meetings and so forth. In an ethnography, these data sources are supplemented by data collected through participant observation. Ethnographies usually require the researcher to spend a long period of time in the 'field' and emphasize detailed, observational evidence [Yin, 1994].

The identification of these genres is useful not just as a categorization, but also because different genres require different methods and details, as well as different evaluations. Interestingly, Sarker et al. (2018a) found in their study that quite a few qualitative papers (38 per cent) had no identifiable genre. How many of these were case studies was not mentioned, but the one example they used as an illustration was a case study that demonstrated what they term 'inconsistency and confusion' in its methodological and epistemological identity and, in particular, a mixing of positivist and interpretive ideas and methods and references.

We argue that authors should be explicit with regard to their epistemological stance. We also emphasize the need for the use of appropriate references for the relevant genre and would additionally suggest the use of a broader range of references (above and beyond Yin) from the disciplines relating to case study understanding and adoption that have much to offer the IS research community. In some disciplines, the case study is and has been the dominant research method – for example, anthropology, comparative political science and sociology (Campbell, 1975). In relation to references, there is very little use of, for example, Stake as an interpretive reference despite the fact that he is regarded, outside of the IS discipline, as a leading expert in the genre.

10.3.1 Multiple Case Studies

Many definitions of case study include the notion that it is singular. Merriam (1998), for example, says that a case is 'a single entity, a unit around which there are boundaries'. A case can be, and has been described as, a person, a programme, a group, a policy, a department, an organization, an event, a social unit, a process, etc. Thus, it seems it can be almost anything. In the IS literature, the case or phenomenon of interest is usually the organization, or sub-set of the organization – for example, but not limited to, a department or a function.

Sometimes, a study can be of multiple cases, or multiple instances of the phenomenon within a case (Cavaye, 1996). Multiple case studies are where a phenomenon is studied in more than one different case, which could be multiple organizations, events or social groups. In the IS context, these are relatively rare, although they exist – a reason being that they are difficult to conduct and resource-consuming, and perhaps provide less richness.

10.3.1.1 Case Study Benefits

There are several advantages in using case studies. First, a case study involves the examination of data conducted within the context of its use (Yin, 1994) – that is, within the situation in which the activity takes place. A case study might be interested, for example, in the process by which a subject comprehends an authentic text. To explore the strategies used by the reader, the researcher must observe the subject within their environment, such as reading in the classroom or reading for leisure.

This contrasts with other methods (e.g., experiments) which actively isolate a phenomenon from its context to focus on a limited variable (Zainal, 2007). Second, a case study explores or describes data in a real-life situation, with the complexity and richness inherent in such environments (this is different from the context benefit, although they are sometimes conflated). Third, a case study enables the rich studying and understanding of a phenomenon. Fourth, a case study is very flexible in terms of the types of research questions that can be answered; as already noted, they are particularly suitable for how- and why-type questions. Fifth, a case study can employ a huge variety of data collection and data analysis techniques, including both qualitative and quantitative techniques. Finally, a case study can be generalizable.

Case studies in IS have particular benefits, according to Dubé and Paré (2003), who identify five in particular. The first is their ability to focus on the organization level rather than the specifics of, for example, a particular technology. This aligns well with the reduced emphasis on technology in IS (or a more computer science focus) towards one based more on people and the organizational context in which a technology exists, where most of the more intractable issues exist (Benbasat et al., 1987). Second, case studies are important in understanding the rapid technological change via cases of real-life experiences. Third, they are relevant for investigating holistic issues, particularly those involving technology, people and organizations and their interactions. Fourth, they 'open the way to new ideas and new lines of reasoning and pinpoint the opportunities, challenges and issues facing IT specialists and managers' (Dubé and Paré, 2003). Finally, they are relevant for hypothesis generation and testing.

10.3.2 Criticisms of Case Study

Although having many benefits, case studies have been criticized as having many weaknesses over the years. Indeed, they have been called illegitimate by some and have been deemed as 'nothing more than story-telling' (Diefenbach, 2009). A common criticism is that they are not representative. This means that a single (or even multiple) case study cannot be said to be representative of the phenomenon being studied, as it is a one-off. As such, they cannot be said to be representative of the population in a statistical method. This is undeniably true and admitted by case study proponents (e.g., Cavaye, 1996). Nevertheless, it is argued that they can still be representative of several instances of that type of case with those particular characteristics, although it cannot be proved that it is representative of all of the population. So, it is a more limited form of representation than that of statistical significance. The reader has to be convinced that the case is more than just one instance and that it outlines the experiences and understanding of a situation. For others, it is not about representativeness; it is more about a case being 'a slice from the life world' (Denzin, 1983) and this slice is what gives it its power: it is what Yin (2009) terms 'direct evidence'. However, as outlined earlier, case studies can achieve generalization particularly from description to theory (Lee and Baskerville, 2003, 2012).

Another criticism of case studies is that of bias, and this is usually about the bias of the researcher, although it can also be about other things, including the bias of the methods employed in measurement, sampling and analysis. Yin provides advice about avoiding bias, including techniques such as multiple researchers, triangulation, saturation and coding. Indeed, the positivist case study researcher is exhorted to be neutral, or at least to be a neutral observer and advocate for the repeatability of the conclusions (Darke et al., 1998). The interpretivist researchers emphasize the accurate collection of data and weighing of evidence, etc., but they acknowledge the concept of interpretation, which is somewhat biased by the researchers' values and previous experiences (refer to the earlier discussion of Stake's views on interpretive case studies).

A second form of bias is that of the case study participant, usually the interviewee. They may well be biased in their understanding and interpretation of the situation, either knowingly or not. For the interpretive researcher, this does not matter as this is their perception at the point of the data collection, and thus part of their construction of reality, whereas for the positivist they might try to find an explanation or a 'truth' in the situation. In the IS

literature, the case study is often at the organization or department level and it has been suggested that managers (or indeed anyone) may paint themselves in a particular favourable light for the benefit of the case study and perhaps their subsequent careers. (Miles, 1978) explained about aggrandizement, as well as protection responses, in case study research which could lead to unreliable and invalid conclusions. He also stated that the process requires a great deal of skill and time that most researchers do not have (Miles, 1978). In relation to case studies involving successful (or not) implementations of technology, it is often the 'winners' or survivors who most heavily influence the evidence. In the London Ambulance Case Study (Fitzgerald and Russo, 2005), the main participants were the people remaining in the organization after the failure followed by the success. It was difficult to find people who were not there (under the cloud of the failure) and perhaps their story was not fully heard, particularly the Chief Executive who had been forced to resign, although many were still there and were interviewed.

Last bias arises from the effects the researcher has on the participants and the case in general by the presence of the researcher, which might influence the study as a result. This effect may lead to the participants seeking to provide the researcher with what they think is required. 'The researcher is influencing what is happening just by the sharing of concepts and interpretations with personnel at the site' (Walsham, 1995), and it is suggested that this is inevitable to some extent, but the researcher should be aware and do their best to mitigate any such bias. Action research is a form of this, as the researchers are also a participant, and often an interventionist, in the research process (Baskerville, 1999).

10.3.3 Classic Case Studies

In the past, case studies, with their benefits and weaknesses, have been an important part of progress in the IS discipline (as has been seen in the discussion of IS history earlier) and there have been a number of what might be termed 'classic case studies'. One is highlighted, although it is just one of quite a few that could have been provided. The classic case is an IS implementation study by

Markus (1981). It examined the use of a 'production planning and profit analysis system' in two manufacturing plants. In one division it was a failure and in another it was a success. 'It was readily accepted in one plant and staunchly resisted in the other, in spite of repeated managerial interventions' (Markus, 1981). Markus initially attributed this to a lack of participation in the systems design in the failure division, which was a common explanatory theory. However, it was discovered that both divisions had had the opportunities to participate, but the failure division had not considered these. Yet, the analysis of the case through a political and 'power dissonance' perspective revealed a more likely explanation for the failure. The introduction of the system created changes to the power structures to the detriment of those involved, which led to resistance and failure of the system. These related to the following aspects: 'changing patterns of access to and control over information, by altering formal authority for performance evaluation and responsibility for action initiation, and by symbolizing values and images at odds with those accepted in the organizational culture' (Markus, 1981).

The case study was highly regarded. It questioned some previously accepted explanations for implementation failures – not just participation, but also support from executive management. It introduced power and politics as somewhat new perspectives (at least in IS) of analysis and explanation. According to Benbasat and colleagues, Marcus was interested in answering the 'why' question: 'Why was the system used in one plant and not in another? The fact that both units were within a single company increased the internal validity of the case. A large number of possible causes for the acceptance in one plant and not in the other could be eliminated since the sites shared the same organizational setting and company history' (Benbasat et al., 1987). Thus, Markus added to the domain knowledge of IS implementation for both theory and practice. In terms of a case study, the research spanned a period of six years and was described in some detail. The case study method was acceptable, even in IS in this early period, and demonstrated that it could provide a major contribution to the domain.

10.3.4 Recent Case Studies

Having described a classic case and the contribution to the discipline, we next outline some more recent examples.

The first case is that of Chanias et al. (2019), who utilized a case study for theory building by examining the formulation and implementation of a digital transformation at a pre-digital organization. The case study was of a leading European financial services provider (AssetCo) at the start of a digital transformation process. As a successful leader on the market, AssetCo was not under particular pressure to digitalize; however, a new CEO decided to implement a digital transformation strategy (DTS) that has led to AssetCo being seen as an innovator and has increased the organization's reputation. However, as AssetCo lacked digital innovation skills, the process was challenging.

The authors describe their case as an interpretive case study following the principles of Klein and Myers (1999). They followed a hermeneutic orientation (Cohen et al., 2000), a non-linear approach (Walsham, 1995), a narrative analysis (Myers, 2013), a thematic analysis and a context-process-content framework (Pettigrew, 1987, 2012). The case highlighted the DTS as dynamic with emergent strategies and a constant need to align and realign activities. The case study approach captured the digital transformation as a 'moving target' with episodes of digital strategy and aligning. These episodes are depicted as recurring. The digital transformation theorization from the case study demonstrated that when pre-digital organizations implement digital transformation strategy, 'the structural properties of the organization are not stable, but continually in a state of flux'. Such theorization is argued to be potentially valuable to other organizations going through a digital transformation, and particularly for pre-digital organizations.

In another recent case study of Blockchain implementation, Du et al. (2019) focus on the effective implementation of Blockchain and the affordance-actualization theory, and explain the rationale for the case study method research: the study is exploratory in need of rich qualitative data; and there is a need to study actions to understand affordances and their actualization. Primary data collected included observations of the system in use at AirSouth Group (Klein and Myers, 1999) and Eisenhardt was referenced to explain that interviews were conducted to attain 'theoretical saturation, where new information started to repeat existing findings (Eisenhardt, 1989)'. The data was analyzed following coding guides from Klein and Myers (1999) and Pan and Tan (2011), and with similarities to axial coding from Strauss and Corbin (1998).

The case study is the AirSouth Group, a Chinese conglomerate founded in 2000, in the aviation, tourism, logistics, financial services, real estate and other industries. The organization managed over 400 subsidiaries served by over 15,000 suppliers and was in need of digitalizing its procurement division to manage payments. The organization collaborated with ChainSolution (a Blockchain specialist) and two Blockchain systems were developed: a Blockchain-enabled wallet system which allowed subsidiaries and suppliers to settle payment; and a Blockchain system which allowed the automation of transactions. This led to the further development of a Blockchain-enabled financing system for loans from financial institutions. The authors explain that the 'case is valuable in that it provides researchers access to a FinTech phenomenon that was previously difficult to investigate. First, the user organisation effectively implemented blockchain when few had done so. Second, the case provides access to both the user organisation and the technology provider, granting a dual perspective on blockchain implementation.' The utilization of the case study method has allowed for the extension of the affordance-actualization theory and for the identification of organizational context as an important element in affordance actualization. The elements include: a subculture that supports collaboration; the corporate strategy and digitalization; and a culture that supports intrapreneurship. An important contribution from the case and the findings is offering insights into how Blockchain can be implemented within an organization, particularities around Blockchain specific success factors, the important role of culture to support collaboration and the successful Blockchain implementation.

10.3.5 Digital Trace Data

Hopefully, these last two recent case study examples, both from 2019, indicate the continuing power of the case study method in the information systems domain. We next provide two recent examples of case studies which utilize a relatively new kind of data: digital trace data. Digital trace data has been defined as 'records of activity (trace data) undertaken through an online information system (thus, digital). A trace is a mark of a sign of passage; it is recorded evidence that something has occurred in the past' (Howison et al., 2011). For trace data, the system is the data collection tool. The availability of trace data in large volumes provided by the increased digitalization of various aspects of social and economic activity has led to the emergence of new forms of data-driven research (Kitchin, 2014). Research based on large digital trace data sets has also been termed 'big data research' (Grover et al., 2020), and typically uses computationally intensive analytical methods. For the researcher, this is a new resource that is proving difficult to ignore, particularly as the data are often publicly available and relatively easy to access.

The first example of a case with trace data is that of Leong et al. (2019), who study social media use in digital activism in the context of an environmental movement in Malaysia. The particular movement was created to protest against the development of a new power plant and to increase awareness around the environmental issues involved. The utilization of social media helped to disseminate information, empower the community and get their opinion across to the government. The government considered the concerns of the community, halted the development of the new power plant and created an agency to investigate its environmental sustainability. Data were collected from semi-structured interviews, focus groups and digital content from social media, with the objective of explaining how social media can empower people and as a result a theory of social media community empowerment based on the participation of grassroots actors was developed. Additionally, the case enabled the examination of some often hidden factors and effects – for example, power and empowerment (Leong et al., 2019).

The next example of an IS case study employing trace data is that of Andersen and Bogusz (2019). The authors suggest that bitcoin Blockchain is probably the first case of an autonomous way of organization, with its properties of distribution of control, manipulation and the autonomous generation of the source code, hence it is an appropriate case to study organization. The authors explain the study as a longitudinal multi-method study (Venkatesh et al., 2013). These innovative applications are still emergent and therefore difficult to study, which is why they utilized trace data. The authors scraped community interactions from a forum, collecting 314,551 interactions between 2010 and 2016. The authors explain that: 'Overall, our methods were grounded in inductive reasoning and rested on the use of two sources of data: digital trace data from the Bitcoin online community and extensive documentation. These data both imbue our computational findings with context (Gaskin et al., 2014) and ensure the veracity of our findings' (Andersen and Bogusz, 2019).

The authors explain that: 'The data was analysed using the computational natural language processing technique Latent Dirichlet Allocation (LDA). LDA reveals patterns in a set of data by extracting unobserved groupings (latent themes) based on semantic similarities between different parts of the data. These groupings were then used manually to identify the topic of each "conversation"' (Andersen and Bogusz, 2019), which enabled the identification of the forks. A Blockchain fork is essentially a change or update in the software, like a new version, often taking a different direction from the original. The authors were able to examine not only when and how these occurred to support new objectives, but also when new ideas were incorporated into the existing infrastructure. The identification of these patterns of organization was argued to be valuable for future designers of Blockchain infrastructures.

Although the Bitcoin Blockchain study of Andersen and Bogusz (2019) is described as a case study, it is perhaps of a somewhat different kind from the Leong et al. (2019) example, or the more traditional form where the predominant data collection technique is via interview, where the participants are selected by the researcher(s) as relevant to the study of the phenomenon. In most case studies, the data collected are primary data – that is, the researcher(s) collected the data themselves from source for the purposes of the study. Clearly, this is not the case with trace data. Additionally, one of the main advantages of the case study method is deemed to be the capturing and explanation of context and contextualization of the phenomenon. The question for case studies utilizing digital trace data is whether the context of that digital conversation can also get captured. It is not completely clear how context was captured through the algorithmic analysis; however, the authors explained that the analysis produced 'semantic clusters determined by co-occurrence of terms' which were consequently coded to identify the topic of the conversations which allowed an understanding of the context (Andersen and Bogusz, 2019). Thus, they seem to have identified the context of the identified forks from the conversations which were compared to 'analytical memos based on additional data' and their knowledge of the community (Andersen and Bogusz, 2019). Thus, case studies and other qualitative research approaches using trace data can, it seems, extract contextual information. Pentland et al. (2020) also argue that context information can be included from trace data which could provide 'qualitative inquiry of the context of digital trace data' (Pentland, et al. 2020). Context is necessary for case study research and, as Avgerou (2019) explains, 'context matters'. However, it is not such an easy task to extract context from trace data and it is much simpler to apply computation analytics to the trace data and ignore context.

Context is not easily captured through trace data because trace data is collected as a result of an event or activity occurring which predominantly does not provide the context for that event. Trace data are simply collected as a by-product of an event or activity. Howison et al. (2011) term this 'found' data and send a strong note of caution regarding its nature and validity in IS research. There are other issues. One of them, according to Hanseth and Lyytinen (2010), is that 'it is impossible to untangle the data from the technical nature of the information infrastructures capturing the traces' and researchers are required to prepare trace data before they can use it in their studies. Grover et al. (2020) suggest that trace data research has promise, but identify a number of 'conjectures' that suggest that IS research should be quite wary about its growth and the way in which it is used. A further issue is the lack of methodological guidance, with several quite different approaches adopted by researchers. Despite these concerns, trace data studies have been growing rapidly in the IS domain; for example, Grover et al. (2020) report that 16 per cent of papers from 2016 to 2018 in the main IS journals were of this type.

10.4 Mixed-Method Research Involving Case Studies

Having discussed some criticisms of case studies and provided some illustrations of case studies, both classic and contemporary, we next outline and discuss ways of tackling some of these criticisms and issues.

One of the main criticisms, particularly from quantitative researchers, is the case study's lack of representativeness (i.e., its lack of statistical rigour) and it being only one (or a few) instance(s) of a phenomenon. From a statistical perspective, there is little counter argument to this; it is usually not statistically significant. Of course, this does not mean that it does not represent something of interest, rather that it cannot be proved as statistically significant. One way that these criticisms can be tackled, or ameliorated at least, is to perhaps mix methods. The qualitative researcher, although often aware of the limitations of quantitative methods, should not reject their strengths. Qualitative researchers' view of quantitative limitations is based on two issues, according to Kaplan and Duchon (1988): either they portray users as passive in relation to technology; or they view organizations as acting rationally. Despite these concerns, there are many ways that methods can be usefully combined to produce effective information systems research. Indeed, mixed-method research across many disciplines has been recommended – for example, history and philosophy of science (Steel et al., 2017), and accounting

(Modell, 2005). However, in information systems there are, it seems, relatively few examples (Gable, 1994; Venkatesh et al., 2013) and this is described by Mingers (2003) as 'a paucity'. The term 'mixed method' means the combination of different research methods in the same study or of the same phenomenon. However, in IS, the term 'multi-method' is also very commonly used to mean the same thing and has led to misunderstanding and confusion (Peng et al., 2011). According to Peng et al. (2011), they are not the same. Multi-method means the use of multiple methods taken from a single approach – that is, they could be both qualitative or quantitative, but not both. Mixed method is the term for using methods from different approaches.

According to Mingers (2003), the most common form of mixed method is the combination of survey and case study. The reason for this is probably that quantitative survey-based research can be very powerful, particularly in the early exploration of a phenomenon, and that combined with a case study it can create an effective triangulation, without too many incommensurate paradigms and assumptions.

As an example, Gable (1994) studied IS consultant success factors using a combination of survey and case study. Gable used the term 'multi-method' to describe the approach. (However, following the earlier definitions, this was 'mixed-method' research because it used methods from two different approaches.) This serves to emphasize the point about confusion of terms. We will use the term 'mixed method' for Gable's research. Gable started with a single pilot case study, followed by a multiple case study of five firms, followed by a survey. The pilot case was to establish context and identify problems and issues. The multiple cross-cases were analyzed for performance across five variables derived originally from the literature. This enabled the construction of a new conceptual model for success, which was then designed, with hypotheses, and operationalized for the survey, conducted with many organizations. The statistical links observed from the results, except for one, were as hypothesized. The cases were used to help explain and understand the one lack of correlation. Gable concluded that the mixed-method study provided the following: the ability to interpret the survey findings as a result of rich detail from the cases; a means of triangulation; a source for pilot testing the survey instrument; a contextual relevance for the variables selected; and an aid to identify an ex-poste model (Gable, 1994). In this example, Gable used the case studies prior to the survey to help understand the context and construct the model, with the main objective being the construction and validation of a model. The benefits of the mixed-method approach are very likely to have led to better research outcomes than if Gable had just undertaken the survey without the cases, as the cases provided the rich understanding gained of the context and the practicalities of interacting with consultants in differing circumstances. Unfortunately, many quantitative survey papers exist with clearly little rich understanding of the context, limited explanations provided for the findings, and inadequate or inappropriate samples. A study by Pinsonneault and Kraemer (1993) indicated that survey research in information systems 'is often misapplied and is plagued by five important weaknesses': poor sampling; low response rates; weak linkages between units of analysis and respondents; over-reliance on cross-sectional surveys; and single methods. Although the Pinsonneault and Kraemer study was a while ago, our opinion is that, despite some excellent exceptions, there is still plenty of room for improvement.

Another example of quantitative and qualitative mixed-method research is provided by Peng and Nunes (2009). This was a study of post-implementation Enterprise Resource Planning (ERP) adoption in China. This was early in the Chinese experience of ERP and most of the studies were based in the West. A survey of state-owned Chinese enterprises in a particular sector and province was undertaken using a deductive quantitative questionnaire to establish several issues, including whether the Western-based theories were applicable in this context. The survey revealed a set of ERP risks with significant correlations between those risks. However, 'it was also identified that the results related to certain risk items were very different from original expectation. Consequently, the researchers decided to seek further explanation and verification of these

questionnaire findings through the follow-up case study'. The case enabled a better understanding of the complex risk networks and the people factors associated with them. 'The integrated findings of the study suggest that it is in organization processes and human-oriented aspects that the more dangerous and difficult-to-manage risks can be found in these companies' (Peng and Nunes, 2009). Thus, the survey established the ten risks and the statistical validity, whereas the case study element of the research enabled the understanding of the complexity and the people elements of the risk leading to an identification of the main risks that were the most critical and difficult to resolve.

It is thus argued that mixed-method research can be very positive and that the combination leads to better, and more valid, outcomes than just one method on its own. The most common form of mixed-method research in information systems appears to be the combination of qualitative and quantitative, with either way around being appropriate, depending on the situation and objectives.

A relatively new form of mixed- and multi-method research in IS could be the mixing of digital trace data research with other forms, such as the case study, to consider their different strengths and weaknesses. Grover et al. (2020), for example, suggest that mixing digital trace data (or BDR as they term it) and theory-based approaches might be appropriate. The key aspect of this is 'the importance of injecting human creativity into the BDR process' (Grover et al., 2020). They quote Vaast et al. (2017) as an example where cluster analysis was used to identify groups of Twitter users, whose tweets could then be examined qualitatively to understand how various groups differed in their social media communications.

Venkatesh et al. (2013) summarize mixed-method research as follows: complementarity (gaining additional insights); completeness (obtain comprehensiveness); developmental (one method provides inferences/questions to be tested in the next); expansion (explain/expand further); confirmation (confirm from one with the other); compensation (gaps/weaknesses with another method); and diversity (obtain divergent findings). 'Developmental' and 'Completeness' are the two most common purposes in IS, according to Venkatesh et al. (2013).

10.5 Conclusion

This chapter has sought to revisit case study research in information systems. To this end, we began by providing a somewhat general history of the case study and then more specifically in information systems. The 'revisit' next outlined some of the issues, problems and understanding of case study research that have hindered its progress – starting with the problem of defining what a case study is and the fact that there are so many different definitions. This inevitably causes problems and is recommended to align to one agreeable definition, but this seems unlikely given the range of different definitions with their emphasis on different elements and aspects of a case study. At the very least, it would be useful for authors to expound on their research method and what they mean, but as we have seen, quite a few researchers fail to do even this. Further, and perhaps more importantly, authors should recognize that case studies can be both interpretive and positivist, and thus the researcher's epistemological stance needs to be stated and discussed. It is even the case that some qualitative researchers adopt definitions and discussions of their method using Yin as their primary reference, seemingly failing to acknowledge Yin's work as positivist. In this context, we identify a need for a framework for considering and aligning research methods and recommend the methodological landscape of Cecez-Kecmanovic (2011) as useful in this respect.

We also highlighted case study issues relating to context, phenomena and rich understanding. These are, of course, strengths of the case study approach rather than hindrances, so it is recommended that they (and other strengths of the method) be directly explained by authors. The important issue of the potential generalization of research based on a case study is also discussed. Generalization is an issue often used to undermine the case study method and it is important for authors to understand this and the forms of generalization that can be legitimately achieved, as discussed in the chapter.

Unfortunately, critics sometimes adopt a purely statistical perspective of generalization that should not be applied to interpretive case studies. Authors need to outline a strong case for any generalizations based on the literature that exists in support of case study generalization and the particular methods and genres employed. It is hoped that this chapter will be of beneficial guidance in this respect.

The next part of the 'revisit' was to present an example of a classic case study from the late 1980s, by Markus (1981). This was provided to illustrate the success of an early case study and its contribution that helped change attitudes to case studies in IS.

Next, we highlighted two recent IS cases (both published in 2019) that hopefully indicate that the case study continues to provide worthwhile contributions to IS. One is about digital transformation in an organization that is very topical; however, the benefit of this case is the discovery that the transformation was not linear, but involved a series of transformations and iterations. The case approach highlighted the non-linear element and the struggle involved in the process, counterpointing the more usual start and end comparison of a transformation. The second case is highlighted partly because of its Blockchain innovation and new technology focus, but mainly due to the important role of the cultural context that was revealed, which probably would not have been discovered with any other method.

Finally, we presented two recent IS cases which utilized trace data (published in 2019 and 2020). The use of trace data is increasingly popular for various research methods; it is available in large volumes and is collected as a result of a digital event. Most examples of IS trace-data-based research are positivist/quantitative (e.g., Faraj and Johnson [2011]), but the two examples presented above are case studies. However, these are quite different in their utilization of trace data. Leong et al. (2019) have utilized trace data in addition to primary data (i.e., interviews and focus groups). Andersen and Bogusz (2019) have utilized trace data in addition to secondary data (i.e., documentation). For some, this may not be what they consider to be a case study, as it lacks any direct interviews with participants, which is 'the cornerstone of a case study'. However, as discussed above, the definition of a case study is often vague and Yin's definition, utilized by many IS authors, does not specifically include the technique of primary interviews. Other forms of data collection are acceptable as long as the study is rich and the context is of primacy. In contrast, Leong et al.'s (2019) utilization of trace data in addition to primary data has enabled the understanding of context and actor interactions, which are the essence of the case studies research method. The case study method enabled the examination of hidden factors and effects (i.e., power and empowerment), which, as explained earlier, would not have been achieved with another method.

The two papers are highlighted as important examples of perhaps one direction in which case study research is going with the availability of large volumes of trace data. In this chapter, we have suggested caution and identified some of the limitations of trace data of which researchers need to be aware when conducting their research. Researchers are encouraged to consider mixed methods and multi-methods to benefit from the advantages of the traditional case study method and the utilization of trace data.

In conclusion, we hope to have demonstrated the value and benefits of the case studies research method and advocate that case studies as a method have much to offer to the IS discipline, as they enable the understanding of not just traditional phenomena, but also new and complex phenomena, such as Blockchain, enabling rich and contextual explanations and theorizations.

References

Aczel, P. (2016). Case study method. *International Journal of Sales, Retailing and Marketing*, 4(9), 15–22.

Andersen, J. V. and Bogusz, C. I. (2019). Self-organizing in blockchain infrastructures: Generativity through shifting objectives and forking. *Journal of the Association for Information Systems*, 20(9), 1242–1275.

Avgerou, C. (2019). Contextual explanation: Alternative approaches and persistent challenges. *MIS Quarterly*, 43(3), 977–1006.

Avgerou, C. (2001). The significance of context in information systems and organizational change. *Information Systems Journal*, 11(1), 43–63.

Baskerville, R. (1999). Investigating information systems with action research. *Communications of the Association for Information Systems*, 2(19), 1–32.

Benbasat, I., Goldstein, D. and Mead, M. (1987). The case research strategy in studies of information systems. *MIS Quarterly*, 11(3), 368–386.

Bryant, A., Black, A., Land, F. and Porra, J. (2013). Information systems history: What is history? What is IS history? What IS history? ... and why even bother with history? *Journal of Information Technology*, 28(1), 1–17.

Campbell, D. T. (1975). The case study. *Comparative Political Studies*, 8(2), 178–193.

Cavaye, A. L. (1996). Case study research: A multi-faceted research approach for IS. *Information Systems Journal*, 6(3), 227–242.

Cecez-Kecmanovic, D. (2011). On methods, methodologies and how they matter. European Conference on Information Systems, Helsinki, Finland.

Chanias, S., Myers, M. D. and Hess, T. (2019). Digital transformation strategy making in pre-digital organizations: The case of a financial services provider. *Journal of Strategic Information Systems*, 28(1), 17–33.

Chen, W. and Hirschheim, R. (2004). A paradigmatic and methodological examination of information systems research from 1991 to 2001. *Information Systems Journal*, 14(3), 197–235.

Cohen, M., Kahn, D. and Steeves, R. (2000). How to analyze the data. In M. Cohen, D. Kahn and R. Steeves (eds), *Hermeneutic Phenomenological Research: A Practical Guide for Researchers*. Thousand Oaks, CA: Sage, pp. 71–85.

Crotty, M. (1998). *The Foundations of Social Research: Meaning and Perspective in the Research Process*. London: Sage.

Darke, P., Shanks, G. and Broadbent, M. (1998). Successfully completing case study research: Combining rigour, relevance and pragmatism. *Information Systems Journal*, 8(4), 273–289.

Davis, G. (2000). Information systems conceptual foundations: Looking backward and forward. In R. Baskerville, J. Stage and J. DeGross (eds), *Organizational and Social Perspectives on Information Technology*. Boston, MA: Kluwer, pp. 61–82.

Denzin, N. K. (1983). Interpretive interactionism. In G. Morgan (ed.), *Beyond Method: Strategies for Social Research*. Beverly Hills, CA: Sage, pp. 129–146.

Diefenbach, T. (2009). Are case studies more than sophisticated storytelling?: Methodological problems of qualitative empirical research mainly based on semi-structured interviews. *Quality & Quantity*, 43(6), 875–894.

Du, W. D., Pan, S. L., Leidner, D. E. and Ying, W. (2019). Affordances, experimentation and actualization of FinTech: A blockchain implementation study. *Journal of Strategic Information Systems*, 28(1), 50–65.

Dubé, L. and Paré, G. (2003). Rigor in information systems positivist case research: Current practices, trends, and recommendations. *MIS Quarterly*, 27(4), 597–636.

Eisenhardt, K. (1989). Building theories from case study research. *Academy of Management Review*, 14(4), 532–550.

Ezzy, D. (2002). *Qualitative Analysis: Practice and Innovation*. Crows Nest, NSW: Allen & Unwin.

Faraj, S. and Johnson, L. (2011). Network exchange patterns in online communities. *Organization Science*, 22(6), 1464–1480.

Fitzgerald, G. and Russo, N. (2005). The turnaround of the London ambulance service computer-aided despatch system. *European Journal of Information Systems*, 14(3), 244–257.

Flyvbjerg, B. (2011). Case study. In N. K. Denzin and Y. S. Lincoln (eds), *The Sage Handbook of Qualitative Research*. Thousand Oaks, CA: Sage, pp. 301–316.

Gable, G. G. (1994). Integrating case study and survey research methods: An example in information systems. *European Journal of Information Systems*, 3(2), 112–126.

Gagnon, Y. (2010). *The Case Study as Research Method: A Practical Handbook*. Quebec: Presses de l'Université du Québec.

Gaskin, J., Berente, N., Lyttinen, K. and Yoo, Y. (2014). Towards generalizable sociomaterial inquiry: A computational approach for zooming in and out of sociomaterial routines. *MIS Quarterly*, 38(3), 850–871.

Gerring, J. (2006). *Case Study Research: Principles and Practices*. New York, NY: Cambridge University Press.

Glaser, B. and Strauss, A. (1967). *The Discovery of Grounded Theory: Strategies for Qualitative Research*. Chicago, IL: Aldine.

Glaser, B. and Strauss, A. (1965). Temporal aspects as a non-scheduled status passage. *American Journal of Sociology*, 71(1), 48–59.

Grover, V., Lindberg, A., Benbasat, I. and Lyytinen, K. (2020). The perils and promises of big data research in information systems. *Journal of the Association for Information Systems*, 21(2), 268–293.

Hanseth, O. and Lyytinen, K. (2010). Design theory for dynamic complexity in information infrastructures: The case of building internet. *Journal of Information Technology*, 25(1), 1–18.

Harrison, H., Birks, M., Franklin, R. and Mills, J. (2017). Case study research: Foundations and methodological orientations. *Forum Qualitative Sozialforschung/Forum: Qualitative Social Research*, 18(1), 1–17.

Hirschheim, R. and Klein, H. K. (2012). A glorious and not-so-short history of the information systems field. *Journal of the Association for Information Systems*, 13(4), 188–235.

Howison, J., Wiggins, A. and Crowston, K. (2011). Validity issues in the use of social network analysis with digital trace data. *Journal of the Association for Information Systems*, 12(12), 767–787.

Johansson, R. (2003). Case study methodology. A keynote speech at the International Conference 'Methodologies in Research' organized by the Royal Institute of Technology in cooperation with the International Association of People–Environment Studies, Stockholm, Sweden.

Kaplan, B. and Duchon, D. (1988). Combining qualitative and quantitative methods in information systems research: A case study. *MIS Quarterly*, 12(4), 571–586.

Kenny, M. and Fourie, R. (2014). Tracing the history of grounded theory methodology: From formation to fragmentation. *Qualitative Report*, 19(52), 1–9.

Kitchin, R. (2014). Big data, new epistemologies and paradigm shifts. *Big Data Society*, 1(1), 1–12.

Klein, H. and Myers, M. D. (1999). A set of principles for conducting and evaluating interpretive field studies in information systems. *MIS Quarterly*, 23(1), 67–93.

Kling, J. L. (2004). Rob Kling and the Irvine School. *Information Society: An International Journal*, 20(2), 97–99.

Lee, A. S. (1989). A scientific methodology for MIS case studies. *MIS Quarterly*, 13(1), 33–50.

Lee, A. S. and Baskerville, R. (2012). Conceptualizing generalizability: New contributions and a reply. *MIS Quarterly*, 36(3), 749–761.

Lee, A. S. and Baskerville, R. (2003). Generalizing generalizability in information systems research. *Information Systems Research*, 14(3), 221–243.

Lengermann, P. (1978). The founding of the American Sociological Review: The anatomy of a rebellion. *American Sociological Review*, 44(2), 185–198.

Leong, C., Pan, S., Bahri, S. and Fauzi, A. (2019). Social media empowerment in social movements: Power activation and power accrual in digital activism. *European Journal of Information Systems*, 28(2), 173–204.

Mann, F. C. and Williams, L. K. (1960). Observations on the dynamics of a change to electronic data-processing equipment. *Administrative Science Quarterly*, 5(2), 216–256.

Markus, M. L. (1981). Implementation politics: Top management support and user involvement. *Systems, Objectives, Solutions*, 1(4), 203–215.

Merriam, S. (2009). *Qualitative Research: A Guide to Design and Implementation*. San Francisco, CA: Jossey-Bass.

Merriam, S. (1998). *Qualitative Research and Case Study Applications in Education*. San Francisco, CA: Jossey-Bass.

Miles, M. (1978). Qualitative data as an attractive nuisance: The problem of analysis. *Administrative Science Quarterly*, 24(4), 590–601.

Miles, M. and Huberman, A. (1994). *Qualitative Data Analysis: An Expanded Sourcebook*. Thousand Oaks, CA: Sage.

Mingers, J. (2003). The paucity of multimethod research: A review of the information systems literature. *Information Systems Journal*, 13(3), 234–249.

Modell, S. (2005). Triangulation between case study and survey methods in management accounting research: An assessment of validity implications. *Management Accounting Research*, 16(2), 231–254.

Myers, M. D. (2013). *Qualitative Research in Business and Management*, 2nd edition. Thousand Oaks, CA: Sage.

Myers, M. D. (1999). Investigating information systems with ethnographic research. *Communications of the Association for Information Systems*, 2(23), 1–19.

Orlikowski, W. J. and Baroudi, J. J. (1991). Studying information technology in organizations: Research approaches and assumptions. *Information Systems Research*, 2(1), 1–28.

Pan, S. L. and Tan, B. (2011). Demystifying case research: A structured–pragmatic–situational (SPS) approach to conducting case studies. *Information and Organization*, 21(3), 161–176.

Peng, G. C. and Nunes, M. (2009). Identification and assessment of risks associated with ERP post-implementation in China. *Journal of Enterprise Information Management*, 22(5), 587–614.

Peng, G. C., Nunes, M. and Annansingh, F. (2011). Investigating information systems with mixed-methods research. Proceedings of the International Workshop on Information Systems Research Trends, Approaches and Methodologies, Rome, Italy.

Pentland, T., Recker, J., Wolf, J. R. and Wyner, G. (2020). Bringing context inside process research with digital trace data. *Journal of the Association for Information Systems*, 21(5), 1214–1236.

Pettigrew, A. M. (2012). Context and action in the transformation of the firm: A reprise. *Journal of Management Studies*, 49(7), 1304–1328.

Pettigrew, A. M. (1987). Context and action in the transformation of the firm. *Journal of Management Studies*, 24(6), 649–670.

Pinsonneault, A. and Kraemer, K. (1993). Survey research methodology in management information systems: An assessment. *Journal of Management Information Systems*, 10(2), 75–105.

Rockart, J. and Flannery, L. (1983). The management of end-user computing. *Communications of the ACM*, 26(10), 776–785.

Sarker, S., Xiao, X., Beaulieu, T. and Lee, A. S. (2018a). Learning from first-generation qualitative approaches in the IS discipline: An evolutionary view and some implications for authors and evaluators (part 1/2). *Journal of the Association for Information Systems*, 19(8), 752–774.

Sarker, S., Xiao, X., Beaulieu, T. and Lee, A. S. (2018b). Learning from first-generation qualitative approaches in the IS discipline: An evolutionary view and some implications for authors and evaluators (part 2/2). *Journal of the Association for Information Systems*, 19(9), 909–923.

Stake, R. E. (2006). *Multiple Case Study Analysis*. New York, NY: Guilford.

Stake, R. E. (1995). *The Art of Case Study Research*. Thousand Oaks, CA: Sage.

Steel, D., Gonnerman, C. and O'Rourke, M. (2017). Scientists' attitudes on science and values: Case studies and survey methods in philosophy of science. *Studies in History and Philosophy of Science*, 63(2017), 22–30.

Strauss, A. and Corbin, J. (1998). *Basics of Qualitative Research: Grounded Theory Procedures and Techniques*. Thousand Oaks, CA: Sage.

Strauss, A. and Corbin, J. (1994). Grounded theory methodology: An overview. In N. K. Denzin and Y. S. Lincoln (eds), *Handbook of Qualitative Research*. Thousand Oaks, CA: Sage, pp. 273–285.

Swanborn, P. G. (2010). *Case Study Research, What, Why and How?* London: Sage.

Tellis, W. (1997). The Qualitative Report, https://nsuworks.nova.edu/tqr/vol3/iss2/4/.

Tsang, E. W. (2014). Case studies and generalization in information systems research: A critical realist perspective. *Journal of Strategic Information Systems*, 23(2), 174–186.

Tumele, S. (2015). Case study research. *International Journal of Sales, Retailing & Marketing*, 4(9), 68–78.

Vaast, E., Safadi, H., Lapointe, L. and Negoita, B. (2017). Social media affordances for connective action: An examination of microblogging use during the Gulf of Mexico oil spill. *MIS Quarterly*, 41(4), 1178–1205.

Venkatesh, V., Brown, A. and Bala, H. (2013). Bridging the qualitative-quantitative divide: Guide for conducting mixed methods research in information systems. *MIS Quarterly*, 37(1), 855–878.

Walsham, G. (1995). Interpretive case studies in IS research: Nature and method. *European Journal of Information Systems*, 4(2), 74–81.

Walsham, G. (1993). *Interpreting Information Systems in Organizations*. Hoboken, NJ: Wiley.

Wellman, B. and Starr, R. H. (2004). Sociological Rob: How Rob Kling brought computing and sociology. *Information Society: An International Journal*, 20(2), 91–95.

Yazan, B. (2015). Three approaches to case study methods in education: Yin, Merriam, and Stake. *Qualitative Report*, 20(2), 134–152.

Yin, R. K. (2018). *Case Study Research and Applications*, 6th edition. Thousand Oaks, CA: Sage.

Yin, R. K. (2009). How to do better case studies. In L. Bickman and D. Rog (eds), *The SAGE Handbook of Applied Social Research Methods*. Thousand Oaks, CA: Sage, pp. 256–280.

Yin, R. K. (1994). *Case Study Research, Design and Methods*. Thousand Oaks, CA: Sage.

Zainal, Z. (2007). Case study as a research method. *Jurnal Kemanusiaan*, 5(1), 1–6.

Social Media Qualitative Research Vignettes

ALEX WILSON, JOSH MORTON and
BOYKA SIMEONOVA

11.1 Introduction

Social media provides researchers with novel approaches to conducting qualitative digital research. Particularly within the Information Systems (IS) discipline, there is novelty because social media is a tool for collecting data and an important phenomenon to be researched. Indeed, it can potentially perform different roles in the same study. However, as McKenna et al. (2017: 87) note, qualitative studies using social media data are limited compared to the substantial volume of quantitative research being conducted using social media: 'There is literally a flood of qualitative data pouring into the Internet every day ... all of which can be downloaded, interpreted, and analyzed by the qualitative researcher. At the moment quantitative colleagues are utilizing this flood of data ... By contrast, qualitative studies in IS using social media data are few and far between.' Indeed, this is developed in Lee and Sarker's Chapter 2: 'the ubiquitous digitization of phenomena is different from the ubiquitous appearance of data'. As such, there is much needed for qualitative researchers to do in terms of interpretation of data, as well as the research skills needed for developing appropriate research designs and methods. McKenna et al. (2017) also recognize that qualitative methodologies for research using social media have not yet been established, which creates a significant barrier to using social media in qualitative research. Hence, a reflection on the characteristics of social media and the design of qualitative research at different levels of analysis is needed.

The aim of this chapter is twofold. First, we consider the question of 'how' social media is used for qualitative research, detailing prominent tools and methods, and some of the pertinent opportunities and challenges they provide to researchers. Second, we consider a question of 'what' social media helps qualitative researchers to understand and we highlight examples to demonstrate the opportunities (and challenges) of working at different levels of analysis. Levels range from supra-organizations through to those at organizational and work-practice levels. We have written up these examples as vignettes to provide a systematic description of concrete situations (Schoenberg and Ravdal, 2000; Baptista et al., 2017) where social media research has been conducted using different levels of analysis. We start by outlining the social media phenomenon and then establish definitions for social media. We then consider the challenges in qualitative social media research before examining the (often overlooked) issue of level of analysis in qualitative social media research.

11.2 The Social Media Phenomenon

The social media phenomenon is defined by its dramatic development, where developments have helped set the everyday linkages between people through various platforms (Treem and Leonardi, 2013). Social media increasingly serve as tools which facilitate intra- and inter-organizational activities connecting digitally peers, customers, suppliers and organizations. This includes, but is not limited to, cooperative product and service development (Piller et al., 2011; Bogers et al., 2018; Newell et al., 2020), open forms of collaboration and organizing (Baptista et al., 2017; Hutter et al., 2017), and socially complex crowd activities (Majchrzak et al., 2009; Majchrzak and Malhotra,

2020). Social media is also a platform which provides knowledge from stakeholders (von Krogh, 2012), such as governments, social groups, and organizations and their leaders, and the development of new workspaces (Baptista et al., 2020). For many institutions, organizations and their stakeholders, there is recognition that they must be well prepared for the challenges and opportunities brought about by social media (Kaplan and Haenlein, 2011).

Social media provides a new opportunity for researchers to collect data. As a method of data collection, social media provides qualitative researchers with the means to examine phenomena in novel approaches and to gain new understanding from those who use social media to create content on and across various platforms (Arriagada and Ibanez, 2020), heralding a range of possibilities for data collection through digital methods. Digital methods are increasingly important for qualitative research because they unlock an abundance of new methods for researchers to use and these have been brought to the fore by the arrival of contemporary communication technologies (Whiting and Pritchard, 2020). Considering the abundance of qualitative data created every day through a range of social media platforms, including Twitter, Facebook and LinkedIn, and on blogs, wikis and digital content sites, all of which can be downloaded, interpreted and analyzed by the qualitative researcher, the possibilities and opportunities for qualitative researchers are plentiful. For qualitative researchers considering the utilization of social media methods, it is pertinent to establish how to approach research design for using social media data and what it is that qualitative data drawn from social media helps researchers to understand.

11.2.1 Defining Social Media

The emergence of new media, and social media specifically, is a recent phenomenon and ever-changing as new platforms rise change in popularity and in their use in society and organizations (Plesner and Gulbrandsen, 2015). Social media was popularized with the development of the Internet in the early to mid-2000s and accessible to consumers – that is, creating a Network Society, a society whose social structure consists of networks powered by micro-electronics-based information and communication technologies (Castells, 2009, 2013), which indicates a shift from traditional communication and media theories (e.g., McLuhan, 1962; McQuail, 1983). The origins of social media can be traced to the emergence of the first services for online communities in the mid-1990s (e.g., Sixdegrees.com) and these in essence simply attempted to map a set of links between people (Kirkpatrick, 2010). This started a trend on social media platforms where users can generate profiles and are the creators of social media content.

Through the early to mid-2000s, a range of social networking sites triggered a surge in social networking; examples include LinkedIn, Facebook and Twitter. Social networking platforms started to compete to dominate the social media environment, each trying to capture the largest base of users and the unprecedented volume of information they create (Kirkpatrick, 2010). The term 'social media' emerged from the surge in social networking, and web-based applications which include collaborative content generation and knowledge co-production platforms by dispersed users, social tagging and news, platforms for professionals and careers, media content creation sites and virtual worlds, where the collective intelligence of the crowd is leveraged to produce knowledge, data and content (Surowiecki, 2004; Majchrzak and Malhotra, 2020). Social media exists in the 'information society' and creates a rich source of data for researchers to examine – particularly data for research on media and communication (e.g., Plesner and Gulbrandsen, 2015), computing and IS (Huang et al., 2013), marketing (Kaplan and Haenlein, 2011), innovation (Roberts and Pillar, 2016), and leadership and work (Morton et al., 2020).

Various types of social media have been researched from a range of perspectives and across numerous disciplines, thus generating different definitions of social media (Ngai et al., 2015). Following these developments, Kaplan and Haenlein (2010) attempted to categorize social media platforms into the following types (see Table 11.1).

Table 11.1 Types of social media and examples

Type of social media	Example social media platform
collaborative projects	Wikipedia
blogs and microblogs	Twitter
social news networking sites	Digg
content communities	YouTube
social networking platforms	Facebook
virtual game-worlds	World of Warcraft
virtual social worlds	SecondLife

Social media therefore require careful consideration by researchers so as not to conflate them as a meta-construct (comprising technologies, platforms, users, the content produced and how it is used) with social media as a platform or technology. A main concern for any researcher working with social media must be to clearly define the type of social media that features in their research.

A viable approach is therefore to define the term social media by pointing towards the aforementioned types of platforms (Table 11.1) that people recognize as social media (Majchrzak et al., 2009; Treem and Leonardi, 2013). Alternative definitions and theorization of social media can be sought from a referential approach which focuses on what social media technologies enable their users to perform or not. However, it has been argued that studies focusing on the features of specific social media technologies and platforms in this way provide limited understanding of why *use* of a technology produced specific effects. Thus, studies of this type provide cues about a specific type of social media and use these to guide the understanding of technologies in a particular social or organizational context, but they do not develop theory about the consequences of social media use for organizing (Treem and Leonardi, 2013). This limitation considered, studies have focused on an affordances approach to explain if and how uses of social media differ from existing forms of computer-mediated communication. It has been argued that social media afford behaviours that were

unattainable before these new and powerful technologies emerged. These specific affordances, visibility, persistence, editability and association, can influence and alter knowledge sharing and power processes in institutions and organizations (Treem and Leonardi, 2013).

Another clear divide in social media definitions is those which are more targeted at organizational settings, commonly referred to as enterprise social media (Kane, 2015). Leonardi and colleagues define enterprise social media as web-based platforms that provide workers with the opportunity to: '(1) communicate messages with specific co-workers or broadcast messages to everyone in the organization; (2) explicitly indicate or implicitly indicate particular co-workers as communication; (3) post, edit, and sort text and files linked to themselves or others; (4) view the messages, connections, text, and files communicated' (Leonardi et al., 2013: 2). In summary, social media has two main elements. First is the use of platforms and tools for organizational communication with external entities, and this includes customers, vendors, clients, groups and the public in general. Second is how organizations have increasingly used social media for communication.

Clearly, the various definitions which derive from uses of social media have implications for qualitative research. Social media also provides researchers with novel tools for data collection and an area of research which is of importance to various fields. The opportunities and challenges require reconsideration in terms of research design. It has also been stressed that the mass utilization of networked computing since the mid-1990s has seen the development of new cultural formations that are novel due to their online context, and so consequently require new research methodologies (e.g., Kozinets, 2002; Kozinets et al., 2014).

11.3 Challenges in Qualitative Social Media Research

Elaborating on the outline of the social media phenomenon in qualitative research, in this section we summarize some of the challenges that confront the researcher in their research design. With careful consideration these are manageable, yet these challenges specific to social media require consideration in qualitative research design. Elaborating on the work of McKenna et al. (2017), the chapter outlines these challenges in terms of social media data, the operationalization of qualitative research and quality concerns.

11.3.1 Social Media Data

Two main challenges emerge about social media data: its volume; and data as digital texts. As indicated in this chapter, the volume of social media data available is substantial, referred to collectively as 'big data'. For McKenna et al. (2017), there were around 500 million tweets per day on Twitter; using the same source, there are currently around 740 million tweets per day on the platform (Internet Live Stats, 2021). 'Big data' is the essence of social media. Because of the volume of data, McKenna et al. (2017) prescribe electronic data management tools to store, categorize and manage the social media data collected. However, they also emphasize that the researcher must have a strategy for cleaning or filtering data to arrive at the richness associated with rigorous qualitative research. Lee and Sarker (in Chapter 2) and Vaast and Urquhart (2017) also argue for careful consideration for the interpretation of social media data. Thus, computational filtering and/or mining (McKenna et al., 2017), theoretical sampling using data slicing (Vaast and Urquhart, 2017), and careful distinction between 'digital traces' and data (Lee and Sarker, in Chapter 2) are all viable approaches to tackle this challenge.

Second, data has changed as social media users produce a huge range of digital texts that researchers may study. Vaast and Urquhart (2017) describe the characteristics and provide examples of digital texts (see Table 11.2).

Consequently, social media provides the researcher with a new range of digital texts which constitute information as users interpret these. We would add to the pressing need to theorize the social media environment in which texts are produced (McKenna et al., 2017; Vaast and Urquhart, 2017) that the intertextuality (Fairclough, 1992) of digital texts is considered by qualitative

Table 11.2 Illustrative characteristics of digital texts with examples

Illustrative characteristics of digital texts	
Characteristic	**Example**
Held in digital format	Emails, chat threads
Contained on a website	Web content
Co-produced by more than one individual	Web forums, wikis
Ephemeral	Comments on a link, and news
Entrench other discourses	Link within a webpage, linking digital text
Contains images	Avatar, web content
Contains video	YouTube clips
Lack of context	Microblog posts (e.g., 'tweets' of 140 or fewer characters)
Linguistic innovations	Acronyms

researchers. That is, digital texts rarely stand alone and the production of one text readily creates the production or co-production of new texts through the affordances in the use of social media (Treem and Leonardi, 2013). The volume and veracity of social media data have implications for the operationalization of research.

11.3.2 Operationalization of Research: Lack of Visual Cues and New Behaviours

There are also practical considerations when working with social media to collect data and hence how the researcher operationalizes their research should be a relevant component of their research design. For example, despite the unprecedented volume of data available, the types of social media data available to researchers can also be constraining as visual and/or non-verbal cues are often lost (McKenna et al., 2017) that would otherwise be provided in other methods of data collection, such as interviews, focus groups and direct observation. Vaast and Urquhart (2017) suggest that e-interviews can help qualitative researchers restore the non-verbal cues (e.g., expressions, mannerisms, etc.) observable in interviews. Many of the digital texts produced are visual (e.g., videos, images, avatars), but may only partially resolve this constraint. For example, a YouTube video may well contain visual cues, yet it also may comprise several revisions, or production notes may be available. Thus, social media researchers must acclimatize to interpreting these visual cues, and recognize that visual cues may be another layer of intertextuality.

Social media has also enabled new behaviours to emerge. As McKenna et al. (2017) outlined, 'flaming' (Papacharissi, 2002) and 'whispering' (Garcia et al., 2009) are behaviours not normally visible, for example, when the researcher conducts the data collection. Lurking or whispering[1] are behaviours afforded by social media, but are difficult or impossible to observe as social media behaviours. Additionally, malicious behaviours, such as 'trolling' (trolls aim to upset as many people as possible, using any tools at their disposal, [Phillips, 2015]) or actors who disseminate misinformation (Shin et al., 2018), require researchers to analyze reflexively the data they collect and interpret such behaviours. Indeed, this is a specific strength of qualitative research. While the quantification of textual social media data might yield impressive volumes of data, these new (and potentially harmful) behaviours could get easily omitted. Finally, social media researchers should not presume that the digital texts available to them were produced by an actor. The recent increase in social media 'bots' (Assenmacher et al., 2020) means that digital texts are being produced (or manipulated) by these bots.

11.3.3 Quality Concerns: Digital Inclusion, Origins of Data and Authenticity

Finally, there are also concerns about the quality of social media data that flow from the digital divide, the origins of data and its authenticity (McKenna et al., 2017). Quality in qualitative research should be

the main reason explained for a well-articulated and robust research design and the criteria outlined by Lincoln (1995) remain an important source for researchers. We highlight these quality concerns in accordance with social media research because they may serve to transgress one or more of the quality criteria in qualitative research if not considered by the researcher.

While McKenna et al. (2017) use the term 'digital divide', the term 'digital inclusion' is more appropriate to capture what Lincoln (1995: 282) discusses as the quality criterion of 'voice': 'Attention to voice – to who speaks, for whom, to whom, for what effectively creates praxis, even when no praxis was intended'. This is especially important as certain groups such as the young and the educated (Ameripour et al., 2010; McKenna et al., 2017) are more prominent on social media than others. However, the notion of inclusion (and voice) has certain assumptions about social media, such as 'the Chinese do not have/use social media'. While China may block or limit some Western social media, it is certainly not bereft of social media – Weibo, WeChat, QQ, TikTok, Renren and YouKu are a few major examples (which should perhaps urgently be added to Kaplan and Haenlein's (2010) very influential, but Westernized, classification of social media). The role of the researcher is to locate the voice and silence in their research (Lincoln, 1995).

A further quality issue emerges from the type of user- (not the research-) generated data. The origins of social media data require careful consideration in conducting social media research. The strengths of social media data in its abundance also generate potential weaknesses: as Lee and Sarker (in Chapter 2) discuss with big data, social media researchers must consider the volume and veracity of data. That is, the data are no longer *generated* (e.g., by arranging an interview) nor *guided* (e.g., by asking specific questions and providing verbal prompts) by the researcher. In consequence, social media data may not answer the precise research questions posed by the researcher and the data may also be untrustworthy or inauthentic (McKenna et al., 2017), particularly when considered alongside some of the new behaviours observable on social media. Developing the discussion about the

---

[1] Lurking is where participants in social media use passive behaviours: they listen to, observe and perhaps record the 'conversations', but do not interact with the contributors to the social media to any great extent. How does one study such passive behaviour if it is not visible or obvious? (See McKenna et al., 2017.)

authenticity of social media data, McKenna et al. (2017) also indicate that users may be anonymous or someone else using a pseudonym and that the possibility of anonymity provides some social media users with the scope to behave without integrity. Any of these aspects of social media data therefore raises questions about the authenticity, or trustworthiness, of that data.

Social media researchers therefore have a rich source of data available to them. The previous sections have also outlined some issues for researchers to consider as they craft their programmes of research. While we agree with McKenna et al. (2017) that software-based solutions to help researchers with storing, organizing and filtering data reduce the volume (quantity) and noise (irrelevance), we also recommend methodological developments as a potential way to conduct qualitative research. The use of ethnographic approaches is discussed next.

11.4 Ethnography/Netnography as a Qualitative Research Method

There are some researchers who consider ethnographies of online environments and social media to be a distinctive methodological approach, while it could also be argued that online ethnographic methods enable reflection on fundamental assumptions.

A plethora of terms have emerged in the literature to describe ethnographies which incorporate exploration of social media, including digital ethnography (Pink et al., 2015), connective ethnography (Dirksen et al., 2010), network ethnography (Berthod et al., 2016) and cyber-ethnography (Ward, 1999), among others. Netnography is another ethnographical approach which guides the understanding and interpretation of online interactions between societies and organizational stakeholders where there are norms, rules, common values, distinct identities, and language and conversational conventions (Hine, 2000; Feher, 2019). The researcher needs to interpret these complex environments (Kozinets, 2002), as opposed to developing measures or causation. The term 'netnography' has gained usage as an expression

referring to online or internet ethnography, particularly in inter-organizational and consumer contexts (Beckmann and Langer, 2005; Kozinets, 2019), and is an exemplar method for this type of research.

Netnography provides several opportunities for qualitative research. It provides a remote, unobtrusive means of collecting rich data at (and perhaps across) national and societal levels of analysis and within or between organizations. It is also naturalistic and therefore provides qualitative scholars with access to ever-evolving materials and cues. These user-generated materials document everyday experiences, providing background into the symbolism of communities (Kozinets, 2002). Social media can be used to connect the user-generated materials to outputs in longitudinal studies of organizational and social change (Morton et al., 2020). Online ethnographies help the study of social media situations, such as a political or national event or crisis in society (Ahmed, 2019).

Tools available for analyzing data in qualitative social media research are varied, with a range of options for the synthesis and reduction of data. For example, content analysis can be used for the systematic labelling of social media content, including text, audio and visual communication. Various thematic analysis approaches can be utilized to provide a rigorous process through which patterns are located within data through data familiarization, coding, and developing and revising themes. Social network analysis can be used as a method to map and understand links and communication between entities, organizations and individuals. Although often associated with quantitative approaches, semantic analysis may also provide opportunities for qualitative scholars to examine the language used and the link between occurrences of words and phrases in societal and organizational interactions (Ahmed, 2019).

11.5 Qualitative Social Media Research: Different Levels of Analysis

In this section, different levels of analysis for qualitative social media research are considered: the supra-organizational level; the organizational level; and the work-practice level. These levels convey what qualitative researchers can gain cues from using social media, with several illustrative example vignettes for each level.

11.5.1 Supra-Organizational Level

The supra-organizational level is broad in that it captures extensive institutional issues concerning government and societies. This is the most comprehensive of the levels, and here social media can be studied as the structures and mechanisms of social order and cooperation governing behaviours between groups – for example, the co-action and interactions between national institutions and government and its citizens, such as through transparency of communications and participation in national-level conversations (e.g., on policy and strategy). Existing work at this level has examined the citizen co-production enabled through social media which empowers participation in national and governmental activities (Bonson et al., 2012). Hence, social media is an enabler and a tool for change, not reduced to a source for data collection. Linders (2012) outlines the different initiatives and categories of coproduction that exist: 'citizen-to-government' – designed for people to provide their opinions to the government; 'government-to-citizen' – designed to inform people and consider behaviour when developing policies; and 'citizen-to-citizen' – organization when communities govern their actions with little interference from the government (Linders, 2012). Therefore, social media is an example of the source for change

empowering people to participate in the government through citizen co-production (Linders, 2012; Mergel and Bretschneider, 2013).

In the context of societal concerns, social media provides opportunities and new ways of organizing, and for collective action among, for example, professional societies, activist groups and communities. The utilization of social media at the societal level can be demonstrated through, for example, the literature on collective action (Han et al., 2020; Majchrzak and Malhotra, 2020). Collective action and openness (e.g., Amrollahi and Rowlands, 2017; Schlagwein et al., 2017) through the utilization of social media (e.g., Twitter, Wikis) have demonstrated certain affordances, for example, societal challenges (e.g., the Gulf of Mexico oil crisis; Vaast et al., 2017), knowledge empowerment (Dobusch and Kapeller, 2017) and advocacy (Morton et al., 2020). Different types of users or roles and how they participate in collective action have been emphasized: advocates, supporters and amplifiers (Vaast et al., 2017). This shows how social media data collection can be utilized in the form of collecting posts (e.g., Tweets) as researchers have increasingly utilized the social media data as sources of data for their investigations (e.g., Chau and Xu, 2012; Baptista et al., 2017). The importance of data-driven inductive research in enriching the theoretical range has recently been highlighted (Galliers, 2011). Social media and other forms of trace data have necessitated original modes of inquiries. The IS discipline has promoted such novel methodologies, where the role of social media is a tool and a source for data collection.

Vignette 1 – UK government accounts utilization

This first vignette demonstrates how government departments in the United Kingdom utilize social media for interaction with stakeholders and the public. In the United Kingdom, the most important social-media metrics for government departments include how much the public utilizes and interacts with its posts – for example, sharing or commenting on content created by various governmental social media accounts. The government also outlines the importance of platform-specific metrics, such as, for example, reach of hashtags (Twitter), video views and subscribers (YouTube), and blog subscribers (blog platforms). On this basis, departments such as the Ministry of Defence (MoD) and the Foreign, Commonwealth & Development Office have emerged as leaders in social media use and popularity on global platforms such as Facebook – the most popular platform in the United Kingdom, where at the end of 2020 they had over 444,000 and 358,000 followers respectively. Government departments also identify which platforms to use in targeting audiences and how to capture public needs. For example, platforms such as Twitter and Instagram are most popular among millennials (Grigg, 2019). Carl Newns, Director of Defence Communication for the MoD, stated that the department uses social media to stream events (e.g., the D-Day 75th anniversary commemorations). However, interactions on UK government and political party accounts have not been without controversy. In the run-up to the 2019 UK General Election, existing government and Conservative Party accounts were rebranded to mimic official fact-checking services and were accused of misleading the public.

Lastly, at the supra-organizational level, cases also exist which have, for example, built on the core institutional concept of legitimation to illuminate how new forms of this notion emerge in line with advances in social media. Works have studied social media-driven legitimation processes and what is outlined as a 'networked strategy' for managing legitimacy (Castelló et al., 2016). The networked strategy is characterized by construction of 'cultural rules'. Further, works have studied the discursive practices which are prominent on social media and how these convey legitimacy (Glozer et al., 2019). This includes communicative practices linked to specific organizational activities, such as their corporate social responsibility and sustainability (Morton, 2020). While the use of social media has been an area of research in legitimacy, the area also outlines a gap in which a focus on bots could further advance how legitimation might be occurring in contemporary organizational contexts and be relevant to qualitative inquiry.

11.5.2 Organizational Level

At the organizational level, which is focused on the inter- and intra-organizational activities across various sectors, industries and regions, the emphasis has been on enterprise social media. It has been highlighted that enterprise social media can increase the individual meta-knowledge, which is the knowledge of 'who knows what' and 'who knows whom', in organizations and in the work of their stakeholders (Leonardi, 2017).

Vignette 2 - Managing legitimacy via social media platforms at Pret a Manger

This vignette briefly illustrates how Pret a Manger, and their CEO, have used social media platforms, including blogging channels and Twitter, to interact with stakeholders and to collect opinions regarding sustainability issues, such as the usage of single-use cups, and have synthesized these towards legitimation for the organization.

For example: 'How do we help more customers to bring reusable coffee cups to @Pret? We're considering to increase the discount for bringing your own cup from 25p to 50p. The filter coffee would cost just 49p!' (Pret a Manger CEO Twitter account.)

Such interactions demonstrate the isolated use of social media for a communication with important stakeholders (particularly its direct customers) to gain understanding of stakeholder opinions and to respond to them directly as a means of managing legitimacy around environmental issues. Such strategic responses and the use of contemporary technologies in enhancing communication around legitimacy are more prominent as organizations utilize such platforms for more communication with stakeholders and customers.

Some studies have investigated the practices of organizations to understand more about how they are using social media for effective communications and for external networking and collaboration (Majchrzak et al., 2009). There have been various studies which have conducted field experiments in large organizations focusing on social media as the context, the phenomenon and the tool. Thus, when studying organizations, social media is a tool for communicating and gaining meta-knowledge and is not reduced to a source of data collection. There is a paucity, however, in how social media technologies can help individuals to identify who knows what and who knows whom at work, which might subsequently lead to organizational processes such as knowledge transfer (von Krogh, 2012). The team level of analysis is concerned with groups and communities within organizations and institutions, and that exist in society. There has also been focus at this level on the virtual spaces enabled by social media through which the work of teams and communities is constructed (Koles and Nagy, 2013), providing rich cues for qualitative research.

Vignette 3 – Product development

This vignette provides a brief example of a social media exchange between two companies, BrewDog and Aldi, which emerged when shoppers drew similarities between Aldi's 'Anti-Establishment' own-brand beer and BrewDog's flagship Punk IPA. This resulted in social media accounts, specifically on Twitter, associated with BrewDog and Aldi having communication which resulted in the development of a new product for the former. BrewDog CEO James Watt suggested it would create 'YALDI IPA' in a mocking social media post. In return, the main Twitter account for Aldi replied with a suggestion that the product be changed to ALD IPA, and this began to be sold on the BrewDog online store and at Aldi stores. BrewDog and Aldi also announced that for every case sold they would each plant one tree.

11.5.3 Work Practice Level

Lastly, the work-practice level is focused on the work of social media in practice, such as with teams and individuals in organizations. Organizations invest (increasingly) in social media and its use; however, the opinions on their effect diverge. For example, while many organizations invest in social media, some have also restricted their use (Koch et al., 2012). This sets the focus on the social media use in practice and among teams and individuals.

In a specific example, Koch et al. (2012) investigate the implementation of a social media programme to help new hires' acclimatization and examine the associated experiences when using the social media. In terms of the empirical work and use of social media as a method, Koch et al. (2012) have utilized a case studies research method with rich and longitudinal data collected: interviews, observations and focus groups. Hence, social media is utilized as a tool to help acclimatization at the organization, and not as a source of data. The experiences of the social media utilization differed. The new hires had experience as the use of social media helped with their acclimatization and development. The middle managers exhibited a negative experience as their power and status were avoided by the employees and the new hires. The executives exhibited positive and negative experiences regarding the tool utilization, as it is not used for work tasks. At this level, social media can also focus on the role of leaders and their use of social media.

For example, research has demonstrated the social media use in strategy processes and practice (Baptista et al., 2017). Studies can be designed to explain the variations, mechanisms and consequences of social media use among managers and leaders in this regard, including longitudinal perspectives of their use.

Vignette 4 – Leadership and social media use

This final vignette is an example for the work-practice level through the use of social media by Kevin Roberts, the former Saatchi & Saatchi CEO who now works as an independent consultant. Since 2007, Roberts has maintained a blog containing various digital content containing reflective, professional accounts of leadership, marketing and strategy. This integrates other types of media, such as links to online video platforms (e.g., YouTube). Such social media provides an account of leadership change, and the blog in this instance outlines issues ranging from reflections on the early days of social media such as Facebook, to the financial crisis of 2008, to the current situation.

11.6 Conclusions and Recommendations for Future Research

In conclusion, we outline the following broad recommendations for qualitative social media research.

First, we argue that there is much potential to studying social media at the levels outlined in this chapter. In reflecting on how social media is used for qualitative digital research, studies can seek to understand how researchers choose different platforms and how these 'change in popularity' (indeed, not only as a research tool, but also in terms of use within organizations and institutions). We argue that the researcher must consider the type of social media data, the operationalization of their research and new quality concerns when working with social media data. Further, understanding the role of different stakeholders and creators on distinct platforms will be important to such research choices, and how they utilize features and create content which affords particular impacts for research and for research contexts. These are important areas which would enhance the understanding at, and even across, super-organizational, organizational and work-practice levels.

Second, we emphasize the need for researchers to consider the levels of analysis emphasized in this chapter in order to understand what social media help researchers to understand. For instance, longitudinal research can be valuable in understanding the work of social media in practice and then attempting to link this to broader phenomena, including but not limited to strategic aspects, institutional change and national initiatives. It is also possible to consider micro-level instances of social media usage, such as leadership trends and the digital work of organizations or institutions and their actors, which would also outline the potential negative effects (the 'dark side') of social media.

References

Ahmed, W. (2019). Using Twitter as a data source: An overview of social media research tools. *LSE Impact Blog*, https://blogs.lse.ac.uk/impactofso cialsciences/2019/06/18/using-twitter-as-a-data-source-an-overview-of-social-media-research-tools-2019/.

Ameripour, A., Nicholson, B. and Newman, M. (2010). Conviviality of internet social networks: An exploratory study of Internet campaigns in Iran. *Journal of Information Technology*, 25(2), 244–257.

Amrollahi, A. and Rowlands, B. (2017). Collaborative open strategic planning: A method and case study. *Information Technology & People*, 30(4), 832–852.

Arriagada, A. and Ibanez, F. (2020). Content creators and platform evolution in the social media ecology. *Social Media + Society*, 6(3), 1–12.

Assenmacher, D., Clever, L., Frischlich, L., Quandt, T. D., Trautmann, H. and Grimme, C. G. (2020). Demystifying social bots: On the intelligence of automated social media actors. *Social Media+ Society*, 6(3), 1–16.

Baptista, J., Stein, M. K., Klein, S., Watson-Manheim, M. and Lee, J. (2020). Digital work and organisational transformation: Emergent digital work configurations in modern organisations. *Journal of Strategic Information Systems*, 29(2), 6–16.

Baptista, J., Wilson, A. D., Galliers, R. D. and Bynghall, S. (2017). Social media and the emergence of reflexiveness as a new capability for open strategy. *Long Range Planning*, 50(3), 322–336.

Beckmann, C. and Langer, R. O. (2005). Netnographie. In R. Buber (ed.), *Qualitative Marktforschung Konzepte – Methoden – Analysen*. Wiesbaden, Germany: Gabler, pp. 216–226.

Berthod, O. P., Grothe-Hammer, M. and Sydow, J. (2016). Network ethnography: A mixed-method approach for the study of practices in interorganizational settings. *Organizational Research Methods*, 20(2), 299–323.

Bogers, M., Chesbrough, H. and Moedas, C. G. (2018). Open innovation: Research, practices, and policies. *California Management Review*, 60(2), 5–16.

Bonson, E., Torres, L., Royo, S. and Flores, F. (2012). Local E-Government 2.0: Social media and corporate transparency in municipalities. *Government Information Quarterly*, 29(2), 123–132.

Castelló, I. O., Etter, M. and Årup Nielsen, F. (2016). Strategies of legitimacy through social media: The networked strategy. *Journal of Management Studies*, 53(3), 402–426.

Castells, M. (2013). *Communication Power*. Oxford: Oxford University Press.

Castells, M. (2009). *The Rise of the Network Society.* Hokoken, NJ: Wiley-Blackwell.

Chau, M. and Xu, J. (2012). Business intelligence in blogs: Understanding consumer interactions and communities. *MIS Quarterly*, 36(4), 1189–1216.

Dirksen, V., Huizing, A. and Smit, B. (2010). 'Piling on layers of understanding': The use of connective ethnography for the study of (online) work practices. *New Media & Society*, 35(1), 33–44.

Dobusch, L. and Kapeller, J. (2017). Open strategy-making with crowds and communities: Comparing Wikimedia and Creative Commons. *Long Range Planning*, 51(4), 561–578.

Fairclough, N. (1992). Intertextuality in critical discourse analysis. *Linguistics and Education*, 4(3–4), 268–293.

Feher, K. (2019). Digital identity and the online: Footprint strategies – an exploratory and comparative research study. *Journal of Information Science*, 46(2), 192–205.

Galliers, R. D. (2011). Further developments in information systems strategising: Unpacking the concept. In R. D. Galliers and W. L. Currie (eds), *The Oxford Handbook of Management Information Systems: Critical Perspectives and New Directions.* Oxford: Oxford University Press, pp. 329–345.

Garcia, A. C., Standlee, A. I., Bechkoff, J. and Cui, Y. C. (2009). Ethnographic approaches to the internet and computer-mediated communication. *Journal of Contemporary Ethnography*, 38(1), 56–86.

Glozer, S., Caruana, R. and Hibbert, S. A. (2019). The never-ending story: Discursive legitimation in social media dialogue. *Organization Studies*, 40(5), 625–650.

Grigg, I. (2019). Which government departments are the best at using social media? *PR Week.*

Han, Y., Ozturk, P. and Nickersen, J. (2020). Leveraging the wisdom of the crowd to address societal challenges: Revisiting the knowledge reuse for innovation process through analytics. *Journal of the Association for Information Systems*, 21(5), 1126–1156.

Hine, C. P. (2000). *Virtual Ethnography.* London: Sage.

Huang, J., Baptista, J. and Galliers, R. D. (2013). Reconceptualizing rhetorical practices in organizations: The impact of social media on internal communications. *Information & Management*, 50(2–3), 112–124.

Hutter, K., Nketia, B. A. and Fuller, J. (2017). Falling short with participation – different effects of ideation, commenting, and evaluating behavior on open strategizing. *Long Range Planning*, 50(3), 355–370.

Internet Live Stats. (2021). Twitter usage statistics, retrieved from www.internetlivestats.com/twitter-statistics/.

Kane, G. C. (2015). Enterprise social media: Current capabilities and future possibilities. *MIS Quarterly Executive*, 14(1), 1–16.

Kaplan, A. M. and Haenlein, M. (2011). How to waltz the social media/viral marketing dance. *Business Horizons*, 54(1), 253–263.

Kaplan, A. M. and Haenlein, M. (2010). Users of the world, unite! The challenges and opportunities of social media. *Business Horizons*, 53(1), 59–68.

Kirkpatrick, D. (2010). *The Facebook Effect.* New York, NY: Simon & Schuster.

Koch, H., Gonzalez, E. and Leidner, D. E. (2012). Bridging the work/social divide: The emotional response to organizational social networking sites. *European Journal of Information Systems*, 21(6), 689–706.

Koles, B. and Nagy, P. (2013). Virtual worlds as digital workplaces: Conceptualizing the affordances of virtual worlds to expand the social and professional spheres in organizations. *Organizational Psychology Review*, 4(2), 175–195.

Kozinets, R. V. (2019). *Netnography: The Essential Guide to Qualitative Social Media Research.* London: Sage.

Kozinets, R. V. (2002). The field behind the screen: Using netnography for marketing research in online communities. *Journal of Marketing Research*, 39(1), 61–72.

Kozinets, R. V., Dolbec, C. P. and Earley, A. (2014). Netnographic analysis: Understanding culture through social media data. In U. Flick (ed.), *Sage Handbook of Qualitative Data Analysis.* London: Sage, pp. 262–276.

Leonardi, P. M. (2017). Ambient awareness and knowledge acquisition: Using social media to learn 'who knows what' and 'who knows whom'. *MIS Quarterly*, 39(4), 746–762.

Leonardi, P. M., Huysman, M. and Steinfield, C. (2013). Enterprise social media: Definition, history, and prospects for the study of social technologies in organizations. *Journal of Computer-Mediated Communication*, 19(1), 1–19.

Lincoln, Y. S. (1995). Emerging criteria for quality in qualitative and interpretive research. *Qualitative Inquiry*, 1(3), 275–289.

Linders, D. (2012). From e-government to we-government: Defining a typology for citizen coproduction in the age of social media. *Government Information Quarterly*, 29(4), 446–454.

Majchrzak, A., Cherbakov, L. and Ives, B. (2009). Harnessing the power of the crowds with corporate social networking tools: How IBM does it. *MISQ Executive*, 8(2), 103–108.

Majchrzak, A. and Malhotra, A. (2020). *Unleashing the Crowd: Collaborative Solutions to Wicked Business and Societal Problems*. London: Palgrave Macmillan.

McKenna, B., Myers, M. D. and Newman, M. (2017). Social media in qualitative research: Challenges and recommendations. *Information & Organization*, 27(2), 87–99.

McLuhan, M. (1962). *The Gutenberg Galaxy*. Toronto: University of Toronto Press.

McQuail, D. (1983). *Mass Communication Theory*. London: Sage.

Mergel, I. and Bretchneider, S. I. (2013). A three-stage adoption process for social media use in government. *Public Administration Review*, 73(3), 390–400.

Morton, J. (2020). Hybrid legitimation strategies for managing the same legitimacy gap in the coffee industry. *Academy of Management Proceedings*.

Morton, J., Wilson, A. D. and Cooke, L. (2020). The digital work of strategists: Using open strategy for organizational transformation. *Journal of Strategic Information Systems*, 29(2), 1–17.

Newell, S., Morton, J., Marabelli, M. and Galliers, R. D. (2020). *Managing Digital Innovation*. London: Red Globe Press.

Ngai, E. W. T., Tao, S. S. C. and Moon, K. K. L. (2015). Social media research: Theories, constructs, and conceptual frameworks. *International Journal of Information Management*, 35(1), 33–44.

Papacharissi, Z. (2002). The virtual sphere: The internet as the public sphere. *New Media & Society*, 4(1), 5–23.

Phillips, W. (2015). *This Is Why We Can't Have Nice Things*. Cambridge, MA: MIT Press.

Piller, F., Vossen, A. and Ihl, C. G. (2011). From social media to social product development: The impact of social media on co-creation of innovation. *De Unternehmung*, 66(1), 7–27.

Pink, S., Horst, H., Postill, J., Hjorth, L., Lewis, T. and Tacchi, J. (2015). *Digital Ethnography: Principles and Practice*. London: Sage.

Plesner, U. P. and Gulbrandsen, I. T. (2015). Strategy and new media: A research agenda. *Strategic Organization*, 13(2), 153–162.

Roberts, D. and Pillar, F. (2016). Finding the role for social media in innovation. *MIT Sloan Management Review*, 57(3), 41–46.

Schlagwein, D., Conboy, K., Feller, J., Leimeister, J. M. and Morgan, L. (2017). 'Openness' with and without information technology: A framework and a brief history. *Journal of Information Technology*, 32(1), 297–305.

Schoenberg, N. E. and Ravdal, E. H. (2000). Using vignettes in awareness and attitudinal research. *International Journal of Social Research Methodology*, 3(1), 63–74.

Shin, J., Jian, L., Driscoll, K. P. and Bar, F. (2018). The diffusion of misinformation on social media: Temporal pattern, message, and source. *Computers in Behavior*, 83, 278–287.

Surowiecki, J. E. (2004). *The Wisdom of Crowds: Why the Many Are Smarter than the Few*. London and New York, NY: Anchor.

Treem, J. W. and Leonardi, P. M. (2013). Social media use in organizations: Exploring the affordances of visibility, editability, persistence, and association. *The International Communication Association*, 36(1), 145–189.

Vaast, E., Safadi, H., Lapointe, L. and Negoita, B. (2017). Social media affordances for connective action: An examination of microblogging use during the Gulf of Mexico oil spill. *MIS Quarterly*, 41(4), 1178–1205.

Vaast, E. and Urquhart, C. (2017). Building grounded theory with social media data. In R. Mir and S. Jain (eds), *The Routledge Companion to Qualitative Research in Organization Studies*. Abingdon, UK and New York, NY: Routledge, pp. 406–421.

von Krogh, G. (2012). How does social software change knowledge management? Toward a strategic research agenda. *Journal of Strategic Information Systems*, 21(2), 154–164.

Ward, K. J. (1999). Cyber-ethnography and the emergence of the virtually new community. *Journal of Information Technology*, 14(1), 95–105.

Whiting, R. and Pritchard, K. (2020). *Collecting Qualitative Data Using Digital Methods*. London: Sage.

Co-Inquiring in a Digital Age

Enhancing the Practice of Strategy Work in Government Organizations through Action Research

JOE MCDONAGH, DAVID COGHLAN
and PAUL COUGHLAN

12.1 Introduction

Good strategy work in all its forms seeks to harness the transformational effect of digital technologies in terms of their influence on individuals and groups and the related social and organizational systems in which they are embedded. In government organizations, digital transformation is not confined to the realms of information and communications technology (ICT) strategy at either organizational or whole-of-government levels. Neither is it confined to the realms of the ICT community within or across government organizations. Rather, digital transformation as a key strategic theme is a major preoccupation for all senior managers and it forms a defining element of strategy work at all levels, including corporate, business and functional.

Digital transformation is also a major strategic theme for researchers from many diverse disciplinary backgrounds. Reflecting on the increasingly pervasive influence of digital technologies, the emergence of big data and data analytics invites researchers to explore new questions, extending the reach of model-based research. Often, the questions are formulated independently of practice and, yet, look to identify causal relationships among variables in a specific domain. The associated idealized problems are explored through models which are partial and include perspectives related only to the analytical method or technique. The guiding assumption is that missing perspectives, such as the impact of human action or interaction

on the performance of a process, do not impact the effectiveness of the model-based solutions. A partial model of an idealized problem may provide valuable insights within a limited domain, but cannot be characterized as explanatory, or even descriptive, of practice. So, it is left to other researchers or the practitioner to identify and include these missing perspectives in the frame and to explore their impact through different means, all based on prior knowledge or active exploration of practice. It is here that the opportunity arises for researchers from different philosophical perspectives to collaborate in knowledge production towards improving research quality.

These two sets of challenges arise in different but related contexts: practice and research. The availability of new forms of data and of data manipulation capabilities has the potential to enhance the quality of the interaction between and integration of research and practice. However, over-reliance on data manipulation brings risks which, if not recognized, may reduce the perceived space for developmental conversations and lead to inappropriate conclusions. We explore these challenges in the remainder of the chapter. We begin in the context of practice and look at strategy work and related digital challenges. We then make the case for engaged and enlightened inquiry before contrasting Mode 1 and Mode 2 knowledge production.

We proceed to sharpen our focus on the theory and practice of action research as a Mode 2 approach to knowledge production. Here, we pay particular attention to the action researcher. We subsequently turn to the practice context and explore both the case for and process of inquiring together into the practice of strategizing in a government organization. This is followed by our discussion which speaks to the practice of action research, enhancing the practice of strategy and the outcomes of co-inquiry. The chapter concludes by reaffirming the central role of action research in knowledge production and emphasizing how the practice of action research is itself being transformed by enabling digital technologies during the current COVID-19 pandemic. Our contention throughout is that good practice informs research and good research informs practice.

12.2 Strategy Work and the Digital Challenge

Harnessing the transformational potential of digital technologies looms large in a recent survey of key issues and trends in the management of ICT in government organizations (Kappelman et al., 2020). While matters relating to leadership, strategy and change are intertwined throughout the top issues confronting organizations at this time, competence in these three areas of professional management practice is deemed not only critical to success, but also most difficult to find in practice. Related deficits frequently loom large in the recurring narratives of failed strategic, organizational and technological change initiatives that mark the landscape of government organizations (Beer and Eisenstat, 2000; Crittenden and Crittenden, 2008; Davenport and Westerman, 2018; Carlton, 2019; Chanias et al., 2019; Correani et al., 2020).

Reflecting on the pervasive nature of digital transformation (Vial, 2019) and the related challenges embedded in strategy work in government organizations, consider the following for a moment in a European context. How might government harness the transformational potential of digital technologies in the following scenarios: shaping the future of work (anytime, anywhere) in government organizations, an ever-present challenge not least due to the current COVID-19 pandemic; extending and deepening a country's global

diplomatic footprint as reflected in the rapid expansion of its network of embassies and consulates in response to Brexit; and transforming corporate functions (e.g., finance, human resources, ICT) as part of the ongoing agenda for renewal and reform of government organizations. What policies and strategies are most relevant in these scenarios and how might they be adequately captured and expressed in system-wide and organizational statements of strategy? These are but a small sample of the grand digital challenges which are central to ongoing strategy work in government organizations at this time. And, of course, an ever-present challenge for all involved in work of this nature is to determine and exploit the enabling role that good research has to play.

In the realm of professional management practice, the discipline and practice of strategizing are uniquely positioned to attend to the challenge of digital transformation in government organizations. At its very heart, strategizing is about the astute allocation of scarce resources to priority goals, objectives, actions and outcomes. In the context of digital transformation, good strategizing determines these priority goals, objectives, actions and outcomes, along with related sequencing, timing and investment considerations. The quality of these strategic commitments is always a function of the quality of strategy practices and processes adopted by senior managers. Further, the adoption of exemplary strategy practices and processes leaves a defining imprint on a government organization's landscape. At a minimum, such strategy work:

- is routinely rooted and grounded in the human and organizational system in which this work is being progressed, while simultaneously attending to a range of human and organizational factors that will, in due time, mark the difference between success and failure;
- forms an integral part of on-the-job leadership development with a view to fostering the strategy and change capabilities (including digital leadership and digital transformation) of all senior managers (Yammarino et al., 2012);
- promotes an increasingly cohesive and unified way of being for senior managers where high

degrees of transparency, openness, trust and mutual support are the norm in organizational life;

- cultivates a commitment to co-creating and co-owning a family of strategies (e.g., corporate, business, functional) that are coherent and aligned, and set a clear strategic development path for the years ahead;
- promotes seamless integration of strategy work in all its forms (development, implementation and review) and aligns such work with career development goals and objectives of all involved;
- blends multiple forms and modes of inquiry with a view to enriching strategy work and enhancing its overall quality;
- nurtures respect for and assimilation of distinct forms of knowledge which are routinely distributed across and embedded in diverse communities of scholars and professional managers (Van de Ven and Johnson, 2006; Wimelius et al., 2020); and
- encourages the exploitation of large-scale data sets to support evidence-based decision-making by senior managers (Loshin, 2013; Rosseau, 2018).

12.3 Engaged and Enlightened Inquiry

While exemplary strategy work has the potential to foster a unified approach to development and change in government organizations, the work itself is characterized by a continuous process which requires: accommodating the interests and needs of a diverse array of individuals and groups; capturing distinct forms of wisdom, knowledge, skill and expertise that are widely distributed across academic and professional communities; blending diverse forms and modes of inquiry that are both fit-for-purpose and aligned with the appropriate phase of strategy work; and linking various forms of strategy practice that fully harness the developmental nature and potential of this work.

By way of giving purpose and direction to the agenda for digital transformation, strategy work benefits immensely from engaged and enlightened forms of inquiry that draw on the rich wisdom,

knowledge, skill and expertise of individuals and groups within and across organizations. As individuals and groups inquire together, distinct forms of knowing (e.g., see Heron and Reason's (1997) classification of presentational, propositional, experiential and practical knowing) enrich and enlighten strategy work. Of particular relevance is practical knowing differentiated for each specific situation. Immersed in the flow of collaborative inquiry, all involved recognize its transformative effect in the here and now and its potential to renew and reform the human activity system(s) being inquired into.

Infusing the flow of collaborative inquiry with a well-crafted scholarly dimension enhances the quality of strategy work and contributes directly to all involved through on-the-job leadership development (Yammarino et al., 2012). It has the potential to inspire and enthuse individuals and groups as they see their own development as a cornerstone on which good strategy work is founded. Of course, determining the precise nature and boundaries of this scholarly dimension is itself a collaborative endeavour to which participating individuals and groups contribute.

When considering the adoption of engaged and enlightened forms of inquiry that are enriched by high-quality scholarly work, it is important to recognize that strategy work unfolds to a discernible pattern in government organizations. That pattern suggests a series of phases through which work progresses, with each phase encapsulating specific developmental challenges and supporting strategy practices. Matching modes and forms of inquiry with the developmental challenges in each unfolding phase is essential.

12.4 Mode 1 and Mode 2 Knowledge Production

At its core, research is about knowledge production. People produce knowledge through engaging in the operations of human knowing: the empirical level of experiencing and questioning, the intellectual level of understanding, the rational level of reflection, marshalling evidence and judging, and, when action is intended, the responsible level of decision-making and taking action (Lonergan, 1992; Cronin, 2017). The history of science and social science demonstrates that knowledge is produced through different ways of applying the operations of experience, understanding and judgement. Methods that produce deductive explanation, interpretivist understanding and action are grounded in different assumptions about each of these operations and how they combine to produce different forms of knowledge. As Coghlan, Shani and Hay (2019) explore, these differences may be understood in terms of a differentiation of consciousness, whereby different forms of knowing are appreciated and held together through a process of interiority – that is, a focus on how people know, rather than on what they know. Albeit within a strand of inquiry that is termed qualitative, the chapters in this handbook illustrate the variety of assumptions and methods through which knowledge is produced.

Gibbons et al. (1994), Gibbons et al. (2011) and Nowotny et al. (2001, 2003) categorize forms of knowledge production in terms of what they term Mode 1 and Mode 2 knowledge production. They describe Mode 1 research as characterized by the explanatory knowledge that is generated in the context of an academic discipline. It is research that arises from an academic agenda and that agenda usually takes place within a singular discipline and is accountable to that discipline. In this respect and as Gibbons et al. (1994) comment, Mode 1 expresses what people usually mean by the term 'science'. By this is meant that the aim of the research is to produce universal knowledge and build and test theory within a disciplinary field by drawing causal inferences from the data to test hypotheses. The type of knowledge acquired is universal knowledge in that the data are context free and validated by logic, measurement and consistency of prediction and control. The role of the researcher is that of an observer and the relationship to the setting is detached and neutral.

In contrast, Gibbons and colleagues (1994) present Mode 2 as the 'new' knowledge production and describe it as an emerging paradigm that is increasingly pervasive alongside the incumbent Mode 1. There are five main characteristics of Mode 2 knowledge production that distinguish it

from Mode 1. First, Mode 2 knowledge is generated in the *context of application*. Mode 1 knowledge can also result in practical application, but is separated from the actual knowledge production in time and space. In Mode 2, there is no such division between knowledge production and application. Second, Mode 2 knowledge production is *transdisciplinary*, mobilizing a range of theoretical perspectives and practical methodologies to address issues. Transdisciplinarity goes beyond interdisciplinarity in that the interaction of scientific disciplines is much more dynamic and results cannot be reduced easily to disciplinary parts. In addition, research results diffuse to practitioners during the process of knowledge production itself rather than afterwards. Third, Mode 2 knowledge production is *reflexive*, through a sensitivity to the process of the research itself and to, for example, the dynamics of transdisciplinarity. Compared to Mode 1, Mode 2 knowledge is a dialogic process and incorporates multiple views. The Mode 2 researcher is explicitly sensitive to broad social consequences. Fourth, Mode 2 knowledge production is a *heterogeneous* process with *organizational diversity* in that who is involved and how changes as the project proceeds. Fifth and similar to Mode 1, Mode 2 knowledge production requires *quality control*, but it takes on a different form. The traditional discipline-based peer review systems of Mode 1 are supplemented by additional criteria along various combinations of economic, political, social and cultural criteria. It becomes more difficult to determine 'good science' because knowledge is evaluated against quality criteria extending beyond the judgement of academic peers and is not conducted using the traditional scientific method. In sum, the Mode 2 knowledge producer combines theoretical knowledge with applied, practical knowledge to address particular scientific and organizational issues. In contrast to Mode 1 knowledge producers, who seek to find generalizable laws across contexts taking a disengaged, scientific approach, Mode 2 knowledge producers are closely tied to applied contexts and work to achieve concrete results by creating actionable knowledge that can advance organizational causes.

There have been several reflections on the application of the Mode 1 and Mode 2 construct to management and organizational research (e.g., Swan et al., 2010; Bresnen and Burrell, 2012; Guerci et al., 2019). Coghlan, Shani and Dahm (2020) explore how interiority enables such researchers to hold both Mode 1 and Mode 2 in terms of differentiated consciousness rather than polarizing them. Thus, for example, researchers can use Mode 1 method and tools within a Mode 2 paradigm. A survey of information from data analytics may provide valuable information that feeds into discussion to assess a situation and to plan shared action. MacLean, McIntosh and Grant (2002) in their broad review of Mode 2 argue that the social sciences have an established tradition of Mode 2 research, particularly in research conducted through action research. Accordingly, we advance the theory and practice of action research as a Mode 2 approach to knowledge production and now introduce action research.

12.5 Action Research

Action research is essentially an interventionist form of research where action researchers are taking action in the present tense to co-generate practical knowledge in collaboration with those who are affected by the action. It does not distinguish between theory and practice, rigour and relevance, research and action. It is grounded in the 'action turn', that the purpose of research is to create practical knowledge and needs to demonstrate quality dimensions of being rigorous, relevant and reflective. It has long adopted an integrative approach to research as incorporating three inquiries and voices: the first-person voice of individuals inquiring into their own thinking and learning in-action; the second-person inquiry into the collaborative engagements between the actors as co-researchers to achieve goals and to deliver actionable knowledge; and the third-person contribution to knowledge for dissemination to a wider audience.

In the context of management and organization studies, action research has been traditionally defined as an approach to research which is based on a collaborative problem-solving relationship between researchers and clients which aims at both

addressing an issue and generating new knowledge. A definition provided by Coghlan and Shani (2018: 3) captures the main themes of action research:

> Action research may be defined as an emergent inquiry process in which applied behavioural science knowledge is integrated with existing organisational knowledge and applied to address real organisational issues. It is simultaneously concerned with bringing about change in organisations, in developing self-help competencies in organisational members and in adding to scientific knowledge. Finally, it is an evolving process that is undertaken in a spirit of collaboration and co-inquiry.

This definition captures the critical themes that constitute action research: that as an *emergent inquiry process* it engages in an unfolding story, where data shift as a consequence of intervention and where it is not possible to predict or to control what takes place. It focuses on *real organizational issues*, rather than issues created particularly for the purposes of research. It operates in the people-in-systems domain and *applied behavioural science knowledge* is both engaged in and drawn upon. Action research's distinctive characteristic is that it addresses the twin tasks of bringing about *change in organizations* and in generating robust, actionable *knowledge*, in an evolving process that is undertaken in a spirit of *collaboration and co-inquiry*, whereby research is constructed *with* people, rather than *on* or *for* them.

From a comprehensive framework of the action research process, articulated originally by Shani and Pasmore (1985), four factors act as a foundation.

- *Context*: Socio-economic factors in the global and local economies and societies provide the wide context in which action research takes place. Organizational characteristics, such as resources, history, formal and informal organizations and the degrees of congruence between them affect the readiness and capability for participating in action research. The external and internal contexts ground the rationale and purpose of the action research project and its outcomes address some issue in that context.

- *Quality of relationships*: The quality of relationship between members of the system and researchers is central to action research. In this relationship the participants engage as partners in co-inquiry and in shared planning, enacting and evaluating action strategies. Each brings its own perspective and competence to the project and both contributions are valued.
- *Quality of the action research process itself*: The quality of the action research process is grounded in the dual focus of addressing the chosen organizational action and in the development of knowledge. This dual focus is enacted through engaging explicitly in cycles of planning, taking action and evaluating the action and attending to these cycles in the present tense so that the dual focus of the project unfolds over time.
- *Outcomes*: The dual outcomes of action research are some level of sustainability (human, social, economic, ecological) and the development of self-help and competencies out of the action and the creation of actionable theory through the action and inquiry.

The complexity of the context in most efforts has a significant impact on how the action research project is framed, the relationships that are established and nurtured, the inquiry and action mechanisms that develop, the quality of the inquiry and discovery process within and across levels of the system, the shared insights generated and the change actions taken. The dynamic nature of the collaboration during an action research project suggests the need to develop an understanding and appreciation about the essence of practical knowing, particularly as it unfolds during the processes of inquiry and action.

12.6 Foundations of Action Research

Action research has many origins and roots, notably in the social psychology of Kurt Lewin and in various schools of liberation thought (Greenwood and Levin, 2007; Bradbury, 2015). While the organization development (OD) tradition of organizational change which grew out of the

work of Lewin, the sociotechnical work of the Tavistock Institute in the United Kingdom and the workplace democracy work in Scandinavia are the major roots in the field of organizational and management studies (Pasmore, 2001; Bradbury et al., 2008), there are significant roots of action research existing in education and community development. The consciousness-raising work of Freire and the Marxist-based liberation movements, feminist approaches to research, the return to epistemological notions of praxis and the hermeneutic school of philosophy associated with the work of Habermas are important strands and expressions of action research which did not grow out of the post-Lewin tradition in organizations.

In a summary of Lewin's concept of action research, Argyris, Putnam and Smith (1985) note that action research involves change experiments on real problems in social systems by focusing on a particular problem and seeking to provide assistance to a client system. Like social management more generally, it involves iterative cycles of identifying a problem, planning, acting and evaluating. The intended change in an action research project typically involves re-education – that is, that the change intended by change agents is typically at the level of norms and values expressed in action. Action research challenges the status quo from a participative perspective, which is congruent with the requirements of effective re-education. It aims to contribute simultaneously to basic knowledge in social science and to social action in everyday life. Accordingly, high standards for developing theory and empirically testing propositions organized by theory are not to be sacrificed nor the relation to practice to be lost.

12.7 The Philosophies of Action Research

There is a great deal written about ontology, epistemology and methodology underpinning action research (Susman and Evered, 1978; Baburoglu and Ravn, 1992; Greenwood and Levin, 2007; Coghlan, 2011; Bradbury, 2015). Debates about objectivist and subjectivist ontologies and epistemologies, critical realism and the role of construction create a sense of acute eclecticism and sometimes bewilderment. What is important to grasp at the outset is that because of its focus on both action and research, beyond the creation of theory only, action research does not fit into the quantitative-qualitative polarization that is common in categorizing research approaches. It is a science of action, following the action turn to replace the linguistic turn of postmodernism (Coghlan et al., 2019).

Susman and Evered (1978: 601) make the case that action research 'constitutes a kind of science with a different epistemology that produces a different kind of knowledge, a knowledge that is contingent on the particular situation and which develops the capacity of members of organizations to solve their own problems'. In using the term 'scientific', they argue, there is a need to move away from adopting frameworks from natural sciences in order to engage with the world of practice. They emphasize that the conditions from which people try to learn in everyday life are better explored through a range of philosophical viewpoints: Aristotelian praxis, hermeneutics, existentialism, pragmatism, process philosophies and phenomenology. They propose that action research provides a corrective to the deficiencies of positivist science by being future-oriented, collaborative, agnostic and situational, implying system development and so generating theory grounded in action. In these terms, it accords with Gibbons et al.'s (1994) notion of Mode 2 knowledge production introduced above.

Coghlan (2016) explores how action research operates in the realm of practical knowing or knowledge produced in the context of application in Mode 2 terms. He frames it in terms of four characteristics: (1) knowing in this mode is concerned with the everyday concerns of human living; (2) much of knowing in this mode is socially constructed and reconstructed continuously; (3) attention to the uniqueness of each situation is essential; and (4) practical knowing and action is driven by values and is fundamentally ethical in that in practical action judgements about what is the appropriate or best thing to do are made. Within a framework of an extended epistemology practical knowing integrates experiential, presentational and propositional forms of knowing

in the acts of practical engagement (Heron and Reason, 1997).

Attention to the uniqueness of each situation demands that inquiry takes place in the present tense. Much of what is referred to as qualitative research is focused on the past. Action research builds on the past and takes place in the present, with a view to shaping the future. Accordingly, engagement in the cycles of action and reflection performs both a practical and philosophical function in its attentiveness and reflexivity as to what is going on at any given moment and how that attentiveness yields purposeful action. Accordingly, abductive reasoning plays a central role as provisional understanding is generated and develops throughout the process (Coghlan and Shani, 2020). In the realm of practical knowing, each situation is unique as no two situations are identical. What works in one setting or worked at an earlier time may not work now. Remembering what worked before is an insight into situations which are similar but not identical. What took place on a previous occasion is irretrievable and obsolete and accordingly needs to be revisited and modified in the light of the present unique situation. If the uniqueness of the present situation is ignored, then there is a serious threat to learning and changing. Common statements such as 'we have always done it this way' or 'we have done this before so we know how to do it now' need to be challenged. The relationships between the action researcher and organizational members are developed and nurtured in the present. This is achieved through the qualities of listening, trust building, mutual respect and co-inquiry. Therefore, practical knowing needs to be differentiated for each specific situation and action researchers need to be attentive in the present tense and engage in listening, questioning and testing assumptions as the project unfolds. In the action research literature, this process is typically expressed in terms of cycles of action and reflection.

In working within the realm of practical knowing where knowing is always incomplete and where reflexive attentiveness to unfolding contextual dynamics is central to both understanding and action, action research's emphasis on cycles of action and reflection is paramount. In its original Lewinian and simplest form, the action research cycle comprises a pre-step and three core activities: planning action, taking action and fact-finding. The pre-step involves naming the general objective. Planning comprises having an overall plan and a decision regarding what the first step to take is. Action involves taking that first step, and fact-finding involves evaluating the first step, seeing what was learned and creating the basis for correcting the next step. So, there is a continuing 'spiral of steps, each of which is composed of a circle of planning, action and fact-finding about the result of the action' (Lewin, 1997: 146).

12.8 Quality in Action Research

As with all approaches to rigorous inquiry, the action research paradigm requires its own quality criteria. The argument is that action research should *not* be judged by the criteria of positivist science, but rather within the criteria of its own terms and show itself to be rigorous, reflective and relevant (Pasmore et al., 2008). Eden and Huxham (1996) provide an extensive list of the fifteen characteristics of good action research. The foundational characteristics reflect the intentionality of the researcher to change an organization, that the project has some implications beyond those involved directly in it, and that the project has an explicit aim to elaborate or develop theory, as well as be useful to the organization. Theory must inform the design and development of the actions. Eden and Huxham place great emphasis on the enactment of the action research cycles, in which systematic method and orderliness is required in reflecting on the outcomes of each cycle and the design of the subsequent cycles. Accordingly, rigour in action research typically refers to how data are generated, gathered, explored and evaluated, and how events are questioned and interpreted through multiple action research cycles.

Returning to Coghlan and Shani's (2018) definition of action research above, good action research may be judged in terms of the four factors from that definition: how the context is assessed; the quality of collaborative relationships between researchers and members of the system; the quality of the action research process itself as cycles of action and reflection are enacted and that the dual outcomes reflect some level of sustainability (human, social, economic and ecological); and the development of self-help and competencies out of the action and the creation of new knowledge from the inquiry. While an action research intervention may not be replicable as the exigencies of a particular situation may not be repeated, the learning needs to be transferable and the process may be transportable to other situations.

Reason (2006) addresses the issue of quality and argues that action research is characteristically full of choices. An important element of choice and transparency is how organizational politics are managed and how the embedded routines, both enabling and defensive, are explored (Argyris, 2010; Schein and Schein, 2017). A frequent challenge is to establish a shared mode of collaborative inquiry and to get out of an established pattern of meeting that is grounded in turf protection, political manoeuvring and defensive routines. As action research is conducted in the present tense, attentiveness to these choices and their consequences, and being transparent about them are significant for considering the quality of action research. Reason argues that action researchers need to be aware of the choices they face and make them clear and transparent to themselves and to those with whom they are engaging in inquiry and to those to whom they show their research in writing or presentations. The explicit attention to these questions and to the issues of rigour, relevance, reflexivity and quality of collaborative inquiry take action research beyond the anecdotal narration of events, to rigorous and critical questioning of experience leading to actionable knowledge for both scholarly and practitioner communities.

A critical element is the process of inquiring into what experiences the participants have of the system, into how they have understood their experience and into how they have made judgements (Coghlan, 2009). At the heart of such collaborative inquiry is the articulation by the participants of how they have come to interpret events and make value judgements, how they have weighed options in making concrete choices and how they have decided what action to take. Such inquiry helps to build trust and a mode of dialogue so as to address the difficult issues and choices facing the group (Shani and Coghlan, 2021).

12.9 The Action Researcher

Action research is fundamentally a process of systemic change whereby a system engages in a change in the present tense, thereby generating the practical knowledge in the context of the application of change. The cycle of action and reflection is enacted around a framework: understanding the need for change, framing the change, undertaking the change and sustaining the change (Pasmore, 2011). Those engaging in the action research attend to how the questions about these elements are posed and answered and how they may support or threaten the success of interventions and so generate reflection on creating more positive outcomes from change endeavours.

The theory and practice of action research creates a profile and challenges for those conducting action research. The profile of the action researcher is one who can learn-in-action and can work collaboratively with others in the context of the uncertainty of the unfolding story of the project and the expectations of scholarship. Accordingly, the challenges for researchers are to be knowledgeable in the organizational disciplines of, for example, organization dynamics, strategy, change and teamworking, and to be skilled in collaborative work and in making intervention.

Further, the action researcher needs to be competent and confident engaging in a living inquiry through first-, second- and third-person practice.

- *First-person practice* refers to the personal and professional learning of action researchers as they engage in the challenging work of an action research project. Action researchers need to learn that their active presence in the project is itself an intervention and how they themselves are instruments in the generation of data. Accordingly, a high level of self-awareness is required of them. As they attend to the data of sense (what they are seeing, hearing, etc.) and are interacting with

other participants in the project, they need to attend to the data of their consciousness (how they are thinking, interpreting, what they are feeling, etc.). Holding both data of sense and data of consciousness is called interiority (Coghlan et al., 2019). From the cognitional operations of experience, understanding and judgement, a general empirical method which is simply the enactment of operations of human knowing may be derived (Coghlan, 2010; Coghlan et al., 2019). This method is grounded in being attentive to data of sense and of consciousness, exploring intelligently what the data might mean and coming to judgement as to the best or most probable explanation for the data.

- *Second-person practice* addresses action researchers' engagement in collaborative work in co-inquiry and shared action with others on issues of mutual concern, through face-to-face dialogue, conversation, joint decision-making and shared action (Shani and Coghlan, 2021). The general empirical method – be attentive to experience, be intelligent in envisaging possible explanations of the experience, be reasonable in preferring as probable or certain the explanations that provide the best account for the experience and be responsible for one's actions – underpins the collaborative inquiry orientation of action research as it seeks to generate the practical knowledge of addressing the core issues and of contributing to knowledge. In the second-person exchanges, the action researcher and organizational members engage in honest conversations in interpreting events and the variety of actions that envisage ends, select means, evaluate outcomes and capture learning. The conversations focus on strategies and actions, how participants figure out what they mean, how they are understood, what is considered to be of value and what might need to be done, and what happens when change is attempted and what might be learned. The co-inquiry process engages participants in discussing the multiple meanings that exist in a collective venture and seeks to enable participants to express the meanings they hold, listen to, understand and appreciate the meanings other participants hold, and to create new meaning in response to external and internal opportunities and threats. In this context, action researchers employ a variety of engagement skills. Schein (2013) describes several types of inquiry. *Exploratory inquiry* is where experience is elicited by generating accounts of what has taken and is taking place in the organization. *Diagnostic inquiry* is where understanding is elicited by exploring how the experience is understood and what causal interpretations are being made. *Confrontational inquiry* is where the conversation moves to a more explicit sharing of different ideas generated by new perspectives. Schein argues that if sufficient time is not devoted to exploratory and diagnostic inquiry, confrontational inquiry closes down the conversation and traps the action researcher into prescribing solutions and creating dependence. Schein's intervention types of helpful conversation provide a useful typology of second-person skills for the action researchers. As well as being skilled in the use of each intervention, knowing which one to use in what circumstances is an exercise in interiority.

- *Third-person practice* is an impersonal practice and is actualized through disseminating the action research's contribution to an audience beyond those directly involved, such as through dissemination by reporting and publishing. Action research intentionally merges theory with practice on the grounds that actionable knowledge can result from the interplay of knowledge with action. It demands an explicit concern with theory that is generated from the conceptualization of the particular experience in ways that are intended to be meaningful to others.

Having advanced the theory and practice of action research as a Mode 2 approach to knowledge production, we now return to the practice and setting of strategy work and the digital challenge where, we contend, this approach is particularly relevant.

12.10 The Case for Co-inquiry

Administrative innovations in the form of *organizational review programmes* and *organizational capability reviews* have been implemented in Western European government organizations over the last fifteen years (Ahern, 2007; Murray, 2007; O'Riordan, 2011; Department of Public Expenditure and Reform, 2012). Future-oriented reviews of this nature identify the transformational shifts that government organizations must undergo in order to deliver on their vision, mission and mandate for the years ahead. These reviews regularly involve engaging with a series of capability-building measures in order to ensure that government organizations are fit-for-purpose. They make a significant contribution to the strategic direction and development of such organizations.

A recurring theme that permeates reviews of this nature is the need to build executive leadership capabilities in the areas of strategy and change, including digital transformation in all its forms. For example, this need is expressed strongly in the context of good governance in government organizations and also features prominently in the most recent strategy for development and innovation in an Ireland context (Department of Public Expenditure and Reform, 2016, 2017). It is recognized that many government organizations struggle with capability gaps in these areas and the challenge of digital technologies and digital transformation makes the need for action more pressing than ever before.

There is strong evidence from reviews of this nature that senior managers in government organizations find it difficult to harness the developmental and transformational nature of strategy work in all its forms. They struggle with the challenge of aligning a family of strategies and effectively exploiting the transformational potential of digital technologies in renewing and reforming the work of organizations. More generally, strategy work is fragmented and piecemeal and the challenge of digital technologies and digital transformation is perceived as the work of the ICT community and not that of senior managers. Harnessing the integrative and transformational potential of modern digital technologies requires much of senior managers, especially with regard to the practice of strategy work.

In 2012 to 2013, acting as a researcher, one of the authors inquired with a range of senior managers, drawn from Western European government organizations. The focus was the enduring lacuna in strategy work in government organizations. There emerged agreement on the need for fresh thinking and a new approach to strategizing that would harness its developmental and transformational potential. There was also agreement on the need to engage all senior managers in the work of strategizing, the need to seamlessly integrate the agenda for digital transformation in this work, and the need to start small and to subsequently scale-up based on the adoption of innovative strategy practices as and where appropriate.

What commenced quietly as a series of informal conversations in 2012 to 2013 has evolved into a stream of collaborative research whose purpose is to both inform and transform the practice of strategy work in government organizations. Incorporating a wide range of strategy work in twelve such organizations, this stream of collaborative inquiry has surfaced novel insights and perspectives for scholars and professional managers alike.

12.11 The Practice of Co-Inquiry

To illuminate the practice of co-inquiry in shaping the agenda for development and change in these organizations, one particular case is selected and presented here due to its exemplary nature and its unforeseen and unintended consequences for this collaborative research programme. The case relates to the evolution and development of a government organization and its senior management network (SMN) between the period 2013 and 2018. The organization's role and remit was significantly expanded during this period as it assumed the functions of a separate organization which was being wound down as part of a Western European government's drive to cull and merge government organizations.

Having addressed the theme of leading transformational change within and across government organizations at a meeting of government executives hosted by a leading European university in May 2013, the researcher subsequently responded positively to an initial request from the Director General (DG) of the case organization to engage in

conversation about the planned expansion of the organization and a subsequent request to collaborate as part of this critical organizational change programme.

At the outset of the change programme, these were two separate organizations with diverse histories, cultures, organizational strategies and senior management styles (among an array of other diverse characteristics). Of all the possible approaches to development and change, the DG and researcher together favoured an approach that would allow senior managers from both organizations to co-create and co-own the future together. The commitment to co-creation and co-ownership were deemed essential to harnessing the deep wisdom, knowledge, skill and expertise of senior managers from both organizations.

As part of the preferred approach to development and change, the DG and researcher nurtured a style that was emergent, inclusive, emancipatory, participatory and highly democratic. They also favoured having senior managers work in partnership on joint diagnosis, joint action planning, joint intervention and joint evaluation. An additional requirement was that the approach should promote on-the-job leadership development and should be linked to the career development goals and objectives of all involved.

As part of this commitment to co-creating the future, eighteen senior managers commenced meeting in the autumn of 2013 and over the next year made significant progress in determining how best to work together and what to do together. Together, they explored the histories, cultures, management styles and management practices of both organizations. Together, they engaged in diagnosing the strengths and weaknesses of two separate senior management teams and the merits of referring to the new collective senior management entity as a group, a team or a network. Together, they explored what kind of organizational work might best fit with the need for on-the-job leadership development, while also contributing to a unified and cohesive group of senior managers. Diagnosis and action planning were always the product of these joint or collective activities and were always based on cherished democratic processes.

The fruits of working in partnership throughout this first year were very significant. Together, the eighteen senior managers opted for the organic development and growth of a new SMN where managers individually and collectively played a central role in shaping the future of an expanded organization. The SMN agreed that strategy work was its number one priority and here it decided to co-create its own approach to strategy work from the ground up. It took a deep dive into the past experience and practice of strategy work in both organizations and took stock of what might constitute exemplary strategy work at some point in the future. Based on these assessments, the SMN opted to devise an approach to strategy work that met the particular needs of an expanding organization. Such an approach had to be deployable not only in shaping a new corporate strategy, but also in framing supporting human resource development (HRD) and ICT strategies, among others.

Having eighteen senior managers involved in shaping the form and function of a new SMN involved multiple cycles of joint diagnosis, joint action planning, joint intervention and joint evaluation. Learning in action was a central part of this development journey which was enriched enormously by the presence of senior managers from two very different organizational backgrounds. The iterative, adaptive, democratic and emancipatory nature of this development path added immensely to all senior managers.

With regard to the work that the SMN engaged in, it was agreed from the outset that it had to be of a cross-organizational nature and that it had to contribute to a holistic understanding of the organization and the environment it operated in. So, rather than opting for a textbook or cookie-cutter approach to strategy work, the SMN opted for a values-led approach that evolved in the form of five distinct phases which were progressed over a fifteen-month period. Strategy work in each phase incorporated both socially focused and technically focused activities. The purpose of the former was to strengthen the capability of individuals and groups to engage productively in strategy work, while the purpose of the latter was to produce excellent strategy artifacts in the form of frameworks and supporting action plans in the first

instance. The phases and related activities were all determined together by senior managers working in unison.

The SMN and strategy work have continued to evolve since 2013 and the organization is now viewed as a role model of strategizing for others to follow. The principles and practices underpinning the success of the SMN have influenced the formation of similar networks in other organizations. This was never the intention at the outset. Further, strategy work has extended beyond development to include a full cycle of implementation and review. It has also extended beyond corporate strategy to include HRD and ICT strategies and the related exploitation of modern digital technologies. While not foreseen initially, success here has significantly shaped the expectations of strategy work in the roll-out of organizational capability reviews.

The SMN through its strategy work has spearheaded a radical transformation of the ICT landscape across the organization. It has redefined its own role vis-à-vis ICT, created a new ICT directorate, transitioned disparate ICT units into this new cohesive and strategically focused directorate, transitioned to a new ICT leadership team and instituted new ICT governance arrangements. Many of these radical organizational shifts were deemed essential to laying a firm foundation for the more effective exploitation of digital technologies into the future. For the most part, this programme of ICT-related change was characterized by processes that were emergent, emancipatory, inclusive, participatory and highly democratic.

12.12 Discussion

Through the lens of Mode 2 knowledge production conducted in the context of application, this discussion focuses on two points for reflection: the case described above as an instance of the theory and practice of action research in action; and the practical knowledge extrapolated from the case as a contribution to how the practice of strategy for digital transformation may be enhanced. These two third-person contributions emerge from the second-person collaborative work of the participants, supported by the first-person learning of the action researcher. We structure the discussion as four related reflections: reflecting on the case; the practice of action research; enhancing the practice of strategy; and expanding the outcomes of co-inquiry.

12.12.1 Reflecting on the Case

What commenced as an informal conversation between a practitioner and a researcher in the summer of 2013 has evolved into an exemplary case of how to successfully interconnect strategic, organizational and technological change in a government organization context. But what exactly was the role of the researcher in this case? How did the researcher secure such access and what exactly was the researcher doing between 2013 and 2018?

On reflection, the researcher secured access on the basis of both his teaching and research capabilities. These capabilities focused on development and change in government organizations and the researcher's willingness to engage, enable and empower senior managers to embrace joint diagnosis, joint action planning, joint intervention and joint evaluation in their own organizational setting. While the researcher consciously and openly infused all development processes with a wide range of supporting scholarly insights, materials and activities, at no point did the researcher decide for others what they had to decide for themselves. Through exploratory, diagnostic and confrontational interventions, the researcher actively helped the SMN to make sense of its rich meanderings by promoting rigour and discipline when dealing with a wide array of often-conflicting qualitative data sets.

12.12.2 The Practice of Action Research

What might we learn about action research from the above case? Reflecting on the case, it can be seen how the core elements of action research as introduced above are present. The overall setting and initiative was grounded in and driven by the *context* of the imperatives for transformational change from government policy. In this context, the relevant government organizations reviewed

their experiences and capabilities and identified the changes they needed to make, particularly in the area of digital technologies, to deliver their vision, mission and respective mandates. What is also evident is how the senior managers and the action researcher created a collaborative environment together in which they explored sensitive and critical issues in a genuine partnership as a second-person process. The success of any such partnership is predicated on an environment of trust and mutual respect for participants' experience and perspectives and the *quality of relationships* and conversation that foster honest dialogue and respectful listening (Shani and Coghlan, 2021). That the participants were senior managers who had both the responsibility and the mandate to lead change was a central element of the initiatives. The study of their organizations and the conversations from those studies led to engagement in *continuous cycles of planning action, taking action and reviewing actions*. In terms of the dual *outcomes*, change resulted and continues in these organizations and robust practical knowledge has been generated both in the field of digital transformation in government organizations and the role action research plays in generating such knowledge (the subject of this chapter). An associated element of the learning from the case is how the action researcher played an interventionist role in both the action and the knowledge-creation activities.

12.12.3 Enhancing the Practice of Strategy

Clearly, the case introduced above illustrates the development and enhancement of strategy work in a government context. However, moving beyond the specific case and reflecting on the broader stream of inquiry as it has unfolded since 2012 to 2013 and the related range of strategy work across twelve organizations, what can one say about the process of inquiring together as reflected in this work? What are the distinctive features of such inquiry and how did they manifest themselves in the range of initiatives and organizations involved in this research endeavour? An insight into the process reveals how co-inquiry has a transformative effect on both the practice of strategizing and the wider body of knowledge within the strategy and related disciplines. Seven striking characteristics emerge.

First, organizations participating in this research programme accept that the fragmented nature of strategy work is a direct reflection of how individuals and groups behave in practice. The root of the issue is primarily behavioural in nature and its consequences manifest themselves in a range of disjointed or fragmented initiatives. To achieve purposeful integration (including the integration of strategy and digital technologies), there is a need to engage a wide range of individuals and groups in co-creating and co-owning both the strategy process itself and related outputs and outcomes which emerge over time.

Second, co-creating and co-owning the strategy process provides individuals and groups with a wide range of opportunities to inquire together into what constitutes exemplary strategy work and to determine together how best to transform strategy practices at individual, group and organizational levels. Insights from such co-working regularly contribute to a much deeper development and change agenda for all involved.

Third, the process of inquiring together involves a continuous cycle of joint diagnosis, joint action planning, joint-intervention, and joint evaluation and reflection. It is informed and enriched by the appropriate use of scholarly insights and perspectives; the diverse sets of wisdom, knowledge, skill and expertise of individuals and groups involved; and the use of appropriate internal and external data sets to support an evidence-based approach to joint diagnosis and related action planning.

Fourth, taking affirmative action manifests itself in the form of a stream of focused interventions at individual, group and organization levels. For example, at individual level the emphasis is often on empowering senior managers to shape the direction and development of their careers through focused mentoring (which involves multiple cycles of diagnosis, action planning, intervention and evaluation). At group level, the emphasis is regularly on building the collective capability of senior managers to shape and give effect to robust strategy processes, which also involves multiple cycles of development and change. At organization level, the emphasis is often on issues of adaptation and

integration and the related creation of a supporting family of strategies. Irrespective of the level involved, the emphasis is always on intervention and learning real-time in the process.

Fifth, co-inquiry harnesses the power of peers in terms of peer networking, peer mentoring, peer learning, peer evaluation and review, and peer support. Indeed, in almost all the participating organizations, the joining together of co-inquiry with the power of peers provides a very strong basis on which to progress an explicit agenda for on-the-job leadership development.

Sixth, the process of co-inquiry and engaging in work that is rigorous, relevant and reflective allows professional managers to find and express their voice in the co-production of knowledge which is not the sole preserve of scholars. From this research programme, there is strong evidence that senior managers are committed to creating new knowledge in the belief that it has potential way beyond the confines of their own particular setting.

Finally, the process of co-inquiry provides scholars with a stream of opportunities to support their own development and growth. For legitimacy, scholars need a rich understanding of the context within which development is taking place along with the interrelated roles of strategy, change and digital technology in that regard. Scholars also need a deep awareness of and sensitivity towards the dynamics of change at individual, group, organization and system-wide levels. Scholars who adopt a Mode 2/action research approach will invariably know the significance of nurturing enduring relationships; the importance of promoting a values-based approach to development and change; the need to be wise stewards of all that is entrusted to them; the value of exercising servant-based co-leadership where the health and well-being of others and the organizations they work in are always priority; and the value of remaining hidden in plain sight while they quietly instruct, teach, counsel and watch over others as part of the research endeavour.

12.12.4 Expanding on the Outcomes of Co-Inquiry

The outcomes of co-inquiry over a sustained period of time have a deeply transformational effect at multiple levels. Such co-inquiry has a transformational impact on individuals in terms of how they see themselves, how they see themselves in relation to others and how they see themselves in relation to the organization they work in. Such inquiry also has the capacity to transform intra- and inter-group functioning, while also transforming strategy practices at intra- and inter-organizational levels. Well-architected co-inquiry leaves an enduring imprint across an organization's landscape, especially when integrated with the pursuit of exemplary strategy work. A critical element of action research in the definition provided above is how it develops self-help competencies in the participants. In other words, participants in an action research initiative learn the twin skills of enacting cycles of action and reflection on critical issues and of dialogic conversation. An enduring outcome of action research is how it provides a platform for exploring and exploiting continuous change. Pasmore's (2015) model of leading complex continuous change as cycles of discovering, deciding, doing and discerning is enhanced by the experience of learning by participants in action research.

One of the significant fruits of the collaborative research programme described is to be found in the manner in which it has shaped and contributed to the current approach to *organizational capability reviews* being implemented in government organizations. Many of the features of exemplary strategy work (development, implementation and review) as evidenced in and emerging from this Mode 2/action research programme have been used as the benchmark against which to measure government organizations undergoing review. These features have also informed a series of system-wide action learning initiatives where the emphasis has been on groups of government organizations working in unison to transform their respective strategy practices. In sum, the Mode 2 approach is contagious as it creates a culture of shared experimentation and reflection, and contributes to processes of organizational learning.

The research programme also reveals the consequences of starting with a strong commitment to inquiring together and subsequently rowing back on this approach due to an inability or unwillingness to deal with thorny and difficult inter- and intra-group issues at senior management levels. The process of rowing back always seems to inflict a wound on the soul of an organization, resulting in strategy work, its processes and outcomes, and the individuals and groups involved being impoverished.

12.13 Conclusion

Data are fundamental to research-based claims. Good practice would suggest that these claims are based on well-articulated interpretations of the data. However, the availability of databases and associated digital analytical techniques may lull researchers into a false sense of trust in the scope and apparent comprehensiveness of such data. The result may be a rush to conclusion without the need for developmental conversations or reflection. Yet, strategy development is an area of practice where different individuals may interpret the same data very differently. As such, there is value in co-inquiry, not just by researchers, but also with collaboration between researchers and practitioners. In this chapter, we have illustrated the nature and value of such co-inquiry. We have located our thinking in the context of strategizing in government organizations and built our argument around the particular value of action research and Mode 2 knowledge production.

We contend that the digital challenge in practice and research can and, indeed, should be overcome by attention to the philosophy underpinning the research and the process supporting the practice. In complex processes, there is and must be room for interpretation – not just of the research outcome, but also during the process of knowledge production. In that sense, strategizing is a lived experience for those involved. This perspective might seem not to fit with those who embrace the promise of the scope of digital data and the array of analytical tools available. However, the strategizing case presented shows how the investment in time, thought, questioning, relating and silence is essential to producing good practice and quality research in a data-rich context. Here, that quality fits with that context and is rigorous, reflective, relevant and responsible. That latter dimension of quality recognizes that co-inquiry which 'levels the playing field' demonstrates respect among the researchers and practitioners, accommodates different perspectives and, ethically, does not exploit any stakeholder for personal gain. It is also clear that such co-inquiry places particular demands on the researcher and the practitioner – in every sense, they are in the process together.

Consistent with Gable's (2020) call for researchers to engage in longitudinal thematic research programmes that incorporate Mode 2 forms of co-inquiry, the thematic research programme introduced in this chapter continues apace even throughout this global pandemic. This is a time of opportunity laden with the potential to transform many of our practices. This is true also of the practice of action research. Modern digital technologies are transforming the very nature of strategy work itself and increasingly facilitating emergent, emancipatory, inclusive, participatory and highly democratic strategy practices and processes. Action research is without doubt a critical enabler in the renewal and reform of such practices and processes and is supported by the ever-increasing array of digital technologies that facilitate working in unison while working apart.

References

Ahern, B. (2007). Stepping up to the mark: The Taoiseach's organisational review programme for departments & offices. *LINK*, Issue No. 49.

Argyris, C. (2010). *Management Traps*. New York, NY: Oxford University Press.

Argyris, C., Putnam, R. and Smith, D. (1985). *Action Science*. San Francisco, CA: Jossey-Bass.

Baburoglu, O. and Ravn, I. (1992). Normative action research. *Organization Studies*, 13(1), 19–34.

Beer, M. and Eisenstat, R. A. (2000). The silent killer of strategy implementation and learning. *MIT Sloan Management Review*, 41(4), 29–40.

Bradbury, H. (2015). *The Sage Handbook of Action Research*, 3rd edition. London: Sage.

Bradbury, H., Mirvis, P., Neilsen, E. and Pasmore, W. A. (2008). Action research at work: Creating the future following the path from Lewin. In P. Reason and H. Bradbury (eds), *The Sage Handbook of Action Research*, 2nd edition. London: Sage, pp. 77–92.

Bresnen, M. and Burrell, G. (2012). Journals à la mode? Twenty years of living alongside mode 2 and the new production of knowledge. *Organization*, 20(1), 25–37.

Carlton, D. (2019). Situational incompetence: The failure of governance in the management of large-scale IT projects. *Journal of Modern Project Management*, 7(2), 68–69.

Chanias, S., Myers, M. D. and Hess, T. (2019). Digital transformation strategy-making in pre-digital organizations: The case of a financial services provider. *Journal of Strategic Information Systems*, 28(1), 17–33.

Coghlan, D. (2016). Retrieving the philosophy of practical knowing for action research. *International Journal of Action Research*, 1(12), 84–107.

Coghlan, D. (2011). Action research: Exploring perspectives on a philosophy of practical knowing. *Academy of Management Annals*, 5(1), 53–87.

Coghlan, D. (2010). Seeking common ground in the diversity and diffusion of action and collaborative management research methodologies: The value of a general empirical method. In W. A. Pasmore, A. B. (Rami) Shani and R. W. Woodman (eds), *Research in Organizational Change and Development*. Bingley, UK: Emerald, Vol. 18, pp. 149–181.

Coghlan, D. (2009). Toward a philosophy of clinical inquiry/research. *Journal of Applied Behavioral Science*, 45(1), 106–121.

Coghlan, D. and Shani, A. B. (Rami). (2021). Abductive reasoning as the integrating mechanism between first- second- and third-person practice in action research. *Systemic Practice & Action Research*, 34(4), 463–474.

Coghlan, D. and Shani, A. B. (Rami). (2018). *Action Research for Business and Management Students*. London: Sage.

Coghlan, D., Shani, A. B. (Rami) and Dahm, P. C. (2020). Knowledge production in organization development: An interiority-based perspective. *Journal of Change Management*, 20(1), 81–98.

Coghlan, D., Shani, A. B. (Rami) and Hay, G. W. (2019). Toward a social science philosophy of organization development and change. In D. A. Noumair and A. B. (Rami) Shani (eds), *Research in Organizational Change and Development*. Bingley, UK: Emerald, Vol. 27, pp. 1–29.

Correani, A., De Massis, A., Frattini, F., Petruzzelli, A. M. and Natalicchio, A. (2020). Implementing a digital strategy: Learning from the experience of three digital transformation projects. *California Management Review*, 62(4), 37–56.

Crittenden, V. L. and Crittenden, W. F. (2008). Building a capable organization: The eight evers of strategy implementation. *Business Horizons*, 51(4), 301–309.

Cronin, B. (2017). *Phenomenology of Human Understanding*. Eugene, OR: Pickwick Publications.

Davenport, T. and Westerman, G. (2018). Why so many high-profile digital transformations fail. *Harvard Business Review*, https://hbr.org/2018/03/why-so-many-high-profile-digital-transform ations-fail.

Department of Public Expenditure and Reform. (2017). Our public service 2020: Development and innovation. Dublin, Ireland, www.ops.gov .ie/app/uploads/2019/08/Our-Public-Service-2020-WEB.pdf.

Department of Public Expenditure and Reform. (2016). Code of Practice for the Governance of State Bodies. Dublin, Ireland, www.per.gov.ie/en/revised-code-of-practice-for-the-governance-of-state-bodies/.

Department of Public Expenditure and Reform. (2012). *Organisational Review Programme: Progress Report on Implementation*. Dublin, Ireland: Government Publications Sales Office.

Eden, C. and Huxham, C. (1996). Researching organizations using action research. *British Journal of Management*, 7(1), 75–86.

Gable, G. G. (2020). Viewpoint: Information systems research strategy. *Journal of Strategic Information Systems*, 29(2), 1–19.

Gibbons, M., Limoges, C., Nowotny, H., Schartzman, S., Scott, P. and Trow, M. (1994). *The New Production of Knowledge*. London: Sage.

Gibbons, M., Limoges, C. and Scott, P. (2011). Revisiting mode 2 at Noors Slott. *Prometheus*, 29(4), 361–372.

Greenwood, D. and Levin, M. (2007). *Introduction to Action Research*, 2nd edition. Thousand Oaks, CA: Sage.

Guerci, M., Radaelli, G. and Shani, A. B. (Rami). (2019). Conducting mode 2 research in HRM: A phase-based framework. *Human Resource Management*, 58(1), 5–20.

Heron, J. and Reason, P. (1997). A participatory inquiry paradigm. *Qualitative Inquiry*, 3(3), 274–294.

Kappelman, L., Johnson, V. L., Mclean, E., Torres, R., Snyder, M., Kim, K. et al. (2020). The 2019 SIM IT issues and trends study. *MIS Quarterly Executive*, 19(1), 69–104.

Lewin, K. (1997). Action research and minority problems. In *Resolving Social Conflicts*. Washington, DC: American Psychological Association, pp. 143–154 (original publication, 1946).

Lonergan, B. J. (1992). *The Collected Works of Bernard Lonergan*, Vol. 3: *Insight: An Essay in Human Understanding*, F. Crowe and R. Doran (eds). Toronto: University of Toronto Press.

Loshin, D. (2013). *Big Data Analytics: From Strategic Planning to Enterprise Integration with Tools, Techniques, NoSQL, and Graphs*. San Diego, CA: Elsevier.

MacLean, D., McIntosh, R. and Grant, S. (2002). Mode 2 management research. *British Journal of Management*, 13(2), 189–207.

Murray, J. A. (2007). Organisational capacity reviews: Building capacity. Paper presented at IPA National Conference, Delivering for the Citizen: Transforming Government Performance, pp. 1–24.

Nowotny, H., Scott, P. and Gibbons, M. (2003). 'Mode 2' revisited: The new production of knowledge. *Minerva*, 41(3), 179–194.

Nowotny, H., Scott, P. and Gibbons, M. (2001). *Re-thinking Science: Knowledge and the Public in an Age of Uncertainty*. Cambridge, UK: Polity Press.

O'Riordan, J. (2011). Organisational capacity in the Irish Civil Service: An examination of the Organisation Review Programme. Research paper number 3, State of the public service series. Institute of Public Administration, Dublin.

Pasmore, B. (2015). *Leading Continuous Change: Navigating Churn in the Real World*. Oakland, CA: Berrett-Kohler.

Pasmore, W. A. (2011). Tipping the balance: Overcoming persistent problems in organizational change. In A. B. (Rami) Shani, R. W. Woodman and W. A. Pasmore (eds), *Research in Organizational Change and Development*. Bingley, UK: Emerald, Vol. 19, pp. 259–292.

Pasmore, W. A. (2001). Action research in the workplace: The socio-technical perspective. In P. Reason and H. Bradbury (eds), *Handbook of Action Research*. London: Sage, pp. 38–47.

Pasmore, W. A., Woodman, R. and Simmons, A. L. (2008). Toward a more rigorous, reflective, and relevant science of collaborative management research. In A. B. (Rami) Shani, S. A. Mohrman, W. A. Pasmore, B. Stymne and N. Adler (eds), *Handbook of Collaborative Management Research*. Thousand Oaks, CA: Sage, pp. 259–292.

Reason, P. (2006). Choice and quality in action research practice. *Journal of Management Inquiry*, 15(2), 187–203.

Rosseau, D. M. (2018). Making evidence-based organisational decisions in an uncertain world. *Organisational Dynamics*, 47(3), 135–146.

Schein, E. H. (2013). *Humble Inquiry: The Art of Asking Instead of Telling*. Oakland, CA: Berrett-Kohler.

Schein, E. H. and Schein, P. A. (2017). *Organizational Culture and Leadership*, 5th edition. San Francisco, CA: Jossey-Bass.

Shani, A. B. (Rami) and Coghlan, D. (2021). *Collaborative Inquiry for Organization Development and Change*. Cheltenham, UK: Edward Elgar.

Shani, A. B. (Rami) and Pasmore, W. A. (1985). Organization inquiry: Towards a new model of the action research process. In D. D. Warrick (ed.), *Contemporary Organization Development: Current Thinking and Applications*. Glenview, IL: Scott Foresman & Co., pp. 438–448. [Reproduced in D. Coghlan and A. B. (Rami) Shani (eds). (2010). *Fundamentals of Organization Development*. London: Sage, Vol. 1, pp. 249–260.]

Susman, G. I. and Evered, R. D. (1978). An assessment of the scientific merits of action research. *Administrative Science Quarterly*, 23(4), 582–601.

Swan, J., Bresnen, M., Robertson, M., Newell, S. and Dopson, S. (2010). When policy meets practice: Colliding logics and the challenges of 'mode 2' initiatives in the translation of academic knowledge. *Organization Studies*, 31(9–10), 1311–1340.

Van de Ven, A. H. and Johnson, P. E. (2006). Knowledge for theory and practice. *Academy of Management Review*, 31(4), 802–821.

Vial, G. (2019). Understanding digital transformation: A review and a research agenda. *Journal of Strategic Information Systems*, 28(2), 118–144.

Wimelius, H., Mathiassen, L., Holmstrom, J. and Keil, M. (2020). A paradoxical perspective on technology renewal in digital transformation. *Information Systems Journal*, 31(1), 198–225.

Yammarino, F. J., Salas, E., Serban, A., Shirreffs, K. and Shuffler, M. (2012). Collectivist leadership approaches: Putting the 'we' in leadership science and practice. *Industrial & Organisational Psychology*, 5(4), 382–402.

PART III

Illustrative Examples and Emergent Issues

Observing Artifacts

How Drawing Distinctions Creates Agency and Identity

SVEN-VOLKER REHM, LAKSHMI GOEL and
IRIS JUNGLAS

Ut deus sit naturae artifex, homo artificiorum deus – just as God is the artifex of nature, so is man the God of artifices. Giambattista Vico (1668–1744), De Antiquissima Italorum Sapientia, Ch. VII.3

Heinz: The software engineers, they say, we construct the program, we play god with respect to the program design.

Ernst: And programs are without doubt artifacts. And our entire rational knowledge is an artifact as well – that was the revolutionary insight of Vico. . . .

Heinz: Tell me, what was misunderstood there? Cited from: Heinz von Foerster and Ernst von Glasersfeld (2010: 124) and translated by the authors.

13.1 Introduction

The conceptualization of IT artifacts as an object of study has garnered a long-standing discourse in the Information Systems (IS) field – one that has been progressively informed by varying philosophical, epistemological and ontological stances (March and Smith, 1995; Orlikowski and Iacono, 2001; Weber, 2003; Akhlaghpour et al., 2013; Carlile et al., 2013; Cecez-Kecmanovic et al., 2014, 2020). We are recently witnessing a new chapter in this discourse with regard to the nature, quality and extent of our relationship with information technology (Yoo, 2010; Baskerville et al., 2020). Considering our persistent embeddedness into digital information infrastructures that have become ever-more complex, distributed and pervasive, we, as researchers, are prompted to rethink

our conception of an IT artifact, and how we approach our object of study.

Looking back in time, we see that the IT artifact has traditionally been viewed as somewhat static in that it is created, implemented and then appropriated if, and only if, users decide to do so (e.g., Dennis et al., 2008). In order to describe it, we have often used 'artifact-centric' descriptions. For instance, we have used conceptions of functionality and affordances (Akhlaghpour et al., 2013) to grasp and express its existence.

More recently, however, ubiquitous technologies, such as embedded systems, or mobile, wearable and smart devices, have fundamentally changed the nature of the interplay between us and technology. They have altered meanings and patterns of social interactions (Yoo, 2010: 216) across all aspects of life, including the emergence of new routines, unbeknown emotional responses, the formation of attachments, new forms of appropriations and uses, and new forms of knowledge exchanges. The distributed and ubiquitous nature of these technologies insistently calls into question how we can define the boundaries of the 'artifact' we observe.

Simultaneously, the very same technologies have also reached new levels of adaptivity. Today, application software and systems are designed such that their action potential offered to us can adapt in-use. As Kallinikos et al. (2013) remark, 'digital artifacts are intentionally incomplete and perpetually in the making', which 'is both an opportunity and a problem' (Kallinikos et al. (2013); citing Garud et al., 2008; Zittrain, 2008). We can observe the effects of such adaptivity in various contexts. In additive manufacturing, for instance, user communities continuously enhance the usage potential of 3D-printing devices by sharing their newest developments. Scholars have called this 'an ontological reversal' in that 'digital objects are created first and these objects prompt physical activities and production of physical objects' (Baskerville et al., 2020; referencing Baudrillard, 2006).[1] Another example are platform-based software development environments that allow a community of users to build and reconfigure apps and extend core functionalities. Empowered by the capability to modify *their* artifacts in-use, users may not just appropriate a system to their purpose, but also become co-creators who profoundly alter the action potential of the 'artifact' offered to others.

As a result of these developments, our aspiration to study our relationship with IS has to go beyond the artifact-centric view, because the artifact is either difficult to grasp in its entirety, or the artifact has altered its action potential, and hence its 'identity', since we last looked at it, or both. The 'artifact' eludes our access – and so do the effects that we seemingly see emerging from technology use. For example, we might identify an agency being exerted when observing a temporally emergent constitutive entanglement, perhaps during the use of a certain type of application system at some point in time (the time of its observation). But how is this agency significant when the relations of the corresponding entanglement change? And who or what created this agency in the first place? It seems little space is left for the *ceteris paribus* assumption to govern rigorous and testable investigations.

This elusiveness proves problematic for the observance of technology, which is arguably imperative for conducting any form of empirical research in our field. Where do we stand on this issue? In the IS field, there are predominantly two ontological perspectives for studying our relationship with IS: a substantialist and a relational ontology (Cecez-Kecmanovic et al., 2014). Each of these involves certain assumptions about the

concepts required to observe and describe our relationship with technology. The substantialist ontology, for example, assumes that 'human beings and things – the social and the material – exist as separate and self-contained entities that interact and affect each other' (Cecez-Kecmanovic et al., 2014: 809). In contrast, the relational ontology assumes that the social and the material are inseparably intertwined (Orlikowski and Scott, 2008) and only brought into being as entities, human beings and things through our experience of their collective performativity (i.e., their 'relations').[2]

Both ontologies are important in their own right as they create separate avenues for discourse and insights. Despite their seemingly divergent assumptions, the two views have something in common:[3] both ontologies, however contradictory, rest on *observations* of our experiences with technology. What would happen to these ontologies if the *things* (i.e., artifacts, agencies and the like) we assume to observe are no longer observable? Arguably, the technological developments of recent times have led us to that point already.

While there have been suggestions for the improvement of methodology, it is still a challenge to 'think differently about emerging and increasingly intertwined social and technological phenomena and explore bold visions and methodological innovations' (see, e.g., Cecez-Kecmanovic et al., 2020: 253, and the Special Issue of the *Journal of the Association for Information Systems*, Vol. 21, issue 1, 2020).

---

[1]   The assumed traditional ontology is that digital objects are the outcome of physical activity, not vice versa.

[2]   In the given reference, there is no definition of the 'relational ontology' without recurrence to 'relations', so we try to re-formulate briefly the underpinnings of the sociomaterial perspective as it has been proliferated in many IS publications. We acknowledge that this does not represent some points of the base assumptions that were made, for instance, by Orlikowski and Scott (2008), their predecessors and the ensuing discourse.

[3]   We believe that each of the discourses following the respective ontology has provided for substantial and insightful research in our field of study. There are, of course, many other ontologies that refer to the study of information, technology, communication and human relations within and beyond the IS discipline, with their respective discourses.

Because of the elusive nature of the IT artifact that we have briefly sketched above, we believe that it is worthwhile to reconceptualize *how we draw distinctions* around our relationship with technology. Our intention with this chapter is to suggest a perspective that helps IS researchers to reflect on their observations and communications, so as to explicate and verbalize our relationship with technology. We do so by drawing on a formalism that allows us to create structures between observations, the *Laws of Form* by George Spencer-Brown (1969).

In the following, we first provide a backdrop on how sociomateriality research in IS has approached the challenge to observe artifacts. We then leave the realm of IS literature to discuss how observing and objects relate to each other using a moderate constructivist stance. We formalize these considerations with the help of the Laws of Form notation. Thereafter, we provide some examples for how to notate concepts used in the IS literature. We finish with some methodological comments on how qualitative empirical research might further address arising challenges.

13.2 Challenges in Observing IT Artifacts

One of the most fundamental objectives in the IS field is to explain how information and technology can be used to construct, maintain and change social organizations. As researchers, we appreciate the IS field because of its diversity and openness. Unlike many other disciplines, we draw on a plethora of other disciplines to advance our own. We can cut across geographies and age groups, delve deeply into technical details or focus on the behavioural side of things, disentangle muddles of communicational traces or study user requirements, develop theories or algorithms. All of those are viable pursuits, and because of it, we have learned that for the sake of scientific discourse, we have to break the resulting gamut of worldviews down into viable ontologies that allow us to pursue research and discourse on *our* topics.

One domain of such ontologies refers to technology use in organizations. For students and

researchers in the field of communication, technology and organizing, a characteristic and recurring notion is our relationship with IS. This relationship is exemplified by the complex and dynamic interrelations and phenomena that appear between human actors, such as software engineers and users, their actions and practices, and technologies, usually manifested as material objects such as IT artifacts in their respective organizational context. Overall, we focus on these intricate, and at times surprising or alarming, interrelations and phenomena – not least because they form the basis for our contributions to practice *and* scholarly discourse in other domains.

For example, widely adopted in the discipline is the belief that the social and the material are profoundly related, so that 'it makes little sense to talk about one without talking about the other' (Leonardi, 2013: 60). At the same time, concerns exist about the potential loss of the IT artifact as a symbol for technology because it 'disappears' and gets subsumed into a social and material entanglement (see, e.g., Baskerville, 2012). One reason for this concern might be that it is particularly *the technology*, as the material that we can design to our intentions (i.e., more easily than the 'social'), and this concern is ever-more pronounced with progressively malleable technology as we have outlined before. More so, scholars have acknowledged that the design of material objects can induce certain social behaviours (Niedderer, 2007; Curtis et al., 2017: 564). Prior to the inception of the term 'sociomateriality', the motivation for research on this notion was formulated as follows:

> ... we must theorize about the meanings, capabilities, and uses of IT artifacts, their multiple, emergent, and dynamic properties, as well as the *recursive transformations occurring in the various social worlds in which they are embedded*. We believe that the lack of theories about IT artifacts, the ways in which they emerge and evolve over time, and how they become interdependent with socio-economic contexts and practices, are key unresolved issues for our field and ones that will become even more problematic in these dynamic and innovative times. (Orlikowski and Iacono, 2001: 133, emphasis added)

This motivation is closely linked with the notion of observing IT artifacts, or technology in general; a notion that goes back to the earliest ideas and conceptualizations about the relation between humans and the world. Several aspects play into this: We, as observers, observe something, an artifact, its use, or a phenomenon in its social context as a result of social construction or natural (e.g., physical-chemical) effects; we ourselves are bound to our social context; we use different means for our observations (e.g., technical instruments) and we engage in discussions that fuel discourse about our measurements and interpretations. Moreover, we draw conclusions about why and how observed behaviours occur and changes happen, whether we have invented, imagined or discovered them, and if all of these were existing beforehand or generated by us.

Consequently, the discourse on sociomateriality subsumes multiple stances, constructs, research methods and types of contributions, and ways in which interdependencies and relationships or, respectively, the entanglements of the social and material, can be researched, observed and described. Different ontological positions have emerged to address and argue this issue, in particular agential and critical realism (see, e.g., Barad, 2003; Leonardi, 2013; Mutch, 2013; Scott and Orlikowski, 2013; Cecez-Kecmanovic et al., 2014). We will not reproduce this discussion here, but want to point to three exemplary considerations that specifically engage with the challenge of observing IT artifacts in-use.[4] We will later formalize how these considerations generate different forms of observations.

Many IS scholars have taken recourse to Barad (1996; 1998; 2003; 2007), who formulates an (agential realist) ontological position for how we observe the world while using technology artifacts. Barad focused on the observation of physical phenomena and the social construction of scientific knowledge (Barad, 1996: 162). She describes the use of an *apparatus* by an observer for observation that performs an 'agential cut' between the world and what we can observe (2003: 815). She argues that 'phenomena are the ontological inseparability of agentially intra-acting "components." That is, phenomena are ontologically primitive relations – relations without preexisting relata' (2003: 815). In her view, the observation carries an agency in the agential cut that 'enacts a local resolution within the phenomenon of the inherent ontological indeterminacy' (2003: 815). In other words, the agential cut 'makes all entities what they are in a particular situation' (Cecez-Kecmanovic et al., 2014: 811), because objects do not own any characteristics apart from what is being inscribed upon them through the measurement apparatus.[5]

For observing IT artifacts, researchers of sociomateriality have concluded that '[it] is through intra-action that material-discursive practices reconfigure relations and thus delineate entities and enact their particular properties' (Cecez-Kecmanovic et al., 2014: 811). The artifact is thus observed *as* (or: in form of) a specific entity *because our observing* one relationship (out of indeterminate potential relations) exerts a performativity in a given situation (the effect); and, consequently, we can ascribe to the effect an identity – namely, 'the artifact' with boundaries and locally determined properties (Cecez-Kecmanovic et al., 2014: 811). One such property could also be *agency* that is attributed to an artifact (Leonardi, 2013: 62).

A formulation in line with Barad's considerations is that of Orlikowski and Scott's (2008), who argue that the social and the material are 'inherently inseparable' (2008: 456). In their view, humans, organizations and technology 'are assumed to exist only through their temporally emergent constitutive entanglement' (2008: 457), which means that social and material action alike

---

[4] We are thankful to Paul Leonardi for his summary of philosophical foundations of sociomateriality (Leonardi, 2013). While we acknowledge that the field has advanced in terms of philosophy and theory, we want to make our readers aware of this account. Also, we refer to it in order to formulate some sample statements for our discussion that are approachable by those who are well immersed in sociomateriality, as well as by those who are not.

[5] Barad (2003: 815) provides an example involving the measurement of diffraction of light waves. See also the adoption of this motive by Østerlund et al. (2020).

constitute organization. They are concerned with the scholarly *practice* of sociomateriality and emphasize the notion of performativity – that is, 'how relations and boundaries between humans and technologies are not pre-given or fixed, but enacted in practice' (2008: 462). This practice lens consequently intends to 'analyze the flow of situated action' (2008: 462). While organizations at large persist as 'recurrently enacted and patterned set of relations, reproduced over time and space' (2008: 462), this lens observes how people actively configure 'situated work performances' by fusing multiple meanings and materialities (2008: 460).

In his formulation of imbrication, Leonardi (2011) provides yet another suggestion for observability of artifacts while they undergo progressive changes. His view tentatively follows a substantialist ontology in assuming that self-contained entities exist on which we act from the outside. Further, there are distinct human and material agencies, which 'are effective in producing outcomes only when they are mutually interlocking' (Cecez-Kecmanovic et al., 2014: 813). This is because 'people decide how they will respond to a technology' (Leonardi, 2011: 151). A technology is flexible 'not necessarily … because of any inherent properties of the artifact. Rather, it is flexible because it is embedded in a context where people can have it modified to fit their needs in relatively short order' (2011: 148). Leonardi empirically observes these decisions and modification processes through which human and material agencies are repeatedly imbricated to produce changes in routines and technologies. Some figurations of agencies appear as routines, others as technologies. In other words, both '[routines] and technologies are constituted by different imbrications of the same basic agencies' (2011: 154). When new figurations are enacted, for instance, because of shifting goals that cannot be achieved due to technological constraints, reconfigurations of the technology's materiality or of the organizational communication patterns (routines) are provoked (2011: 154, 155–163).

These are just three, but sufficiently diverse, considerations on observing IT artifacts in-use. They make it unequivocally clear that there are good reasons to abandon the classical, objectified (reified)

conception of the 'IT artifact' and to extend our uses and notions of its identity. Each perspective offers a distinct notion of identity for the 'artifact'. Following Barad (2003), the artifact is created by its enactment (i.e., the apparatus enforces agential cuts while observing performativity) and obtains an identity characterized by locally determined properties. In the case of Orlikowski and Scott (2008), we observe the flow of a situated practice that at some point enacts an idea and identity of the artifact as a fusion of agencies, meanings and materialities. And in the case of Leonardi (2011), we directly observe how agencies re-figurate technological materialities (or routines), which allows the creation of an artifact's identity by specifying the technical properties of technology.

The commonality among the three perspectives is that each makes a point of *observing the object without objectifying the object*. What is being observed, and how, and what is becoming the 'artifact', differs in each case. How are these notions of artifacts, given their ontological disparity, different from one another? How are their apparatuses and insights commensurate? Of particular concern for answering such questions is, we believe, to discern what is observable, and what is not. In other words, at what points do we draw distinctions in our observing? To approach this question, we will in the following section introduce a formalism to express related considerations from prior research.

13.3 Observing without Object

13.3.1 Observing and Observability

Our knowledge and understanding of the world differs significantly, with varying backgrounds, life experiences, expertise levels, contextual conditions and so on that we build upon when we observe the world around us or when we participate in conversations.[6] We use our own words to

---

[6] These considerations are based, to some extent, on the works of Ranulph Glanville, who worked on the conditions of the possibility for observation, communication, language, and the emergence of knowledge and learning (see, e.g., Glanville, 2001).

describe what we observe (e.g., an object), and we each experience at least slight differences in what we actually observe. How do we then know that we speak of the same thing as a referent?

One way to address this issue is by using an objective description. However, objectivity of our knowledge about the world requires the dismantling of the account of an observation from the properties of the observer and from the observation process itself. As has been argued earlier, nothing of the observation will then remain – independent of whether people, plants, animals or sensors have carried out the observation (Glanville, 1978; Foerster, 2003: 288). If instead we take a subjective stance, we are required, as part of our research practice, to measure results against certain recognized methods and conventions of research. In addition, we also have to acknowledge the role of the researcher and her apparatuses as part of the research process (as mentioned earlier; see, e.g., Barad, 2003: 188).

The subjectivity poses a paradox if we want to express *how good* our conventions actually are. After all, expressing how good our conventions are defines how good the results will be.[7] This issue is even more pronounced in the context of IT artifacts that are increasingly complex as we cannot be sure that the 'object' we have taken for granted in previous research is still of the principle kind that we have originally conceived. In fact, we now know that we cannot perceive – or observe – it in its *actual* form. This raises fundamental questions for empirical research: How can we formally treat our observations in a way that allows us to (1) understand the world in our own ways, with our own meanings – yet, (2) treat the world and our conversations *as if* our understandings were about the same thing and of the same kind? How can a formal system allow us to do that?

Of course, there is a long-standing debate about objectivity and truth (see, e.g., Mingers and

Standing, 2020), along with various contemporary philosophical positions that have arisen from these fundamental considerations. Given our pragmatic quest to observe the IT artifact, we neither want to resort to solipsism as an epistemological position,[8] nor engage with these justified positions in this article. Instead, we focus on how we, as qualitative researchers, can construct a system of observations that lets us collaboratively construe observations.

We start this exercise from a moderately constructivist position. Thus, the ensuing question is about the formal description of the differences and congruencies that appear in our conversations (Baecker, 2017) – for example, the differences and congruencies in the context of IT artifacts that are 'lost' in entanglements. We often do *not see* that there are commonalities, congruencies or consistencies in two individual observations, which might lead to endless negotiations about the meaning of observations (von Foerster, 2003: 211). In our daily experience, however, it is not too much of a problem to identify something (rather: some *thing*) as an object of reference, but we might find it challenging to describe it as if we were to share the same observations (or understanding) about it.

Thus, the formalization of observing cannot start from the object to be observed because we cannot define it unanimously or bijectively; we can solely start from an awareness about the act, or process of *observing*. More specifically, the starting condition for observing that needs to be fulfilled before we can discuss some *thing* is that we can distinguish between us as observers and everything else as that which we observe. In other words, we must be able to *observe ourselves*. When we observe ourselves, we are observable, and we are being observed (by us).[9] Accordingly, the *observability of an object*

---

[7] In addition, as some readers will have experienced in writing or receiving reviews for qualitative research, at times the account given might be warranted strict and rigorous application of conventions (e.g., for interpretation), but the account given or the outcome presented cannot really be comprehended (retrospectively rationalized) by the reader.

[8] For an elegant argument about why solipsism, or the idea that only one's own mind is sure to exist, is to be rejected in awareness of a community, and its ethical implications, see von Foerster (2003: 226).

[9] We do not further discuss this triadic, cyclic and self-referential definition of observing. An extensive discussion about it was conducted in the discourse on second-order cybernetics, notably by authors such as Bateson (1979), Maturana and Varela (1980), Glanville (2001), von Glasersfeld (2002), von

lies in its observing – its 'being observed'. And, our observing exerts the agency that brings the object and its identity into being.[10]

Thus, *observability* is not a characteristic of the object, but an agency exerted by the act, or process of observing. This, in turn, allows for a definition of what an object is. As we will show later, in observing, we define and delimit the object through our accounts and in our own ways by associating certain qualities with 'our' objects (von Foerster, 2003: 309). These qualities, however, are *attributes* – not (objective) properties of the object as we observe it, or an object that is 'out there' (Glanville, 2001; see also Luhmann, 1987: 657). In that sense, the result of our observation says more about our observing than about the object that has been observed. *Observing* thus can be conceptualized as an act in which we distinguish something (perhaps the 'object') from something else, and in which we explicitly specify this difference through an indication. By identifying (naming) and notating this indication, we create the basis for communicating about our observations, and for communication in general (of both: signals as well as abstract ideas; see Shannon, 1948; Shannon and Weaver, 1949).

Following these arguments, it is the *agency of observing* that allows us to form knowledge about the world in general, and the objects we want to

discuss. How this agency unfolds needs further attention particularly because the objects (e.g., IT artifacts) we consider in our research today have become more complex and thus more difficult to observe, as we have argued in a previous section.[11] The discussion can be furthered along two possible avenues.

One avenue is to ask what exactly is happening when we observe with regard to our cognitive understanding. Responses to this question have been presented across various disciplines, including neurosciences (McCulloch and Pitts, 1943; Northoff, 2011, 2018) and biology (Maturana and Varela, 1980). We do not want to pursue this path here. As an alternative avenue, we can focus on the formalization of the act of observing. By doing so, we can potentially arrive at a proposition about the quality of observations that enables comparability – that is, how well our and others' observations (or our account thereof) are congruent and linkable, and therefore warrant authority for the depiction of objects. Particularly disciplines such as mathematics (e.g., Peirce, 1933; Spencer-Brown, 1969), cybernetics (Shannon and Weaver, 1949; von Foerster, 1969), communication and psychotherapy (Pask, 1970; Watzlawick et al., 1974), as well as sociology (Luhmann, 1987; Baecker, 1993, 2006) have followed this path.[12] In fact, in one of the seminal works in this discourse, the mathematician George Spencer-Brown has proposed an elegant formalization of the act of observing in his book *Laws of Form*, which we introduce in the following sections.

13.3.2 Formalizing Observing: The Laws of Form

The Laws of Form, drawn from the works of George Spencer-Brown (1969), provide a system

---

Foerster (2003) and von Foerster and von Glasersfeld (2010). For an approachable source to the neuroscientific aspects of this fundamental ability for brain-self and brain-object differentiation, see Northoff (2011: 8).

[10] By 'being', we mean that the object, as we observe it, is enacted in our account of our observation. By account of our observation, we mean the way we rationalize or explicate our observing to ourselves and to others; this can follow different modes of communication as, for instance, in language, or as different types of measurements (which are also descriptions of observations; see Glanville, 1978; Maturana and Varela. 1980: 39). Ultimately, we want to share our observations with others who are also observers of themselves and us: 'Anything said is said by an observer. In his discourse the observer speaks to another observer, who could be himself; whatever applies to the one applies to the other as well' (Maturana and Varela, 1980: 8).

[11] I.e., recognizing and describing objects (what we colloquially call 'observability') becomes more difficult. However, as observability is a function of observing, this calls for increased *capabilities* to observe.

[12] These two avenues arise from the distinction between cognitive awareness processes and explicit (social) communication, which can be considered as reflective awareness and acting (see Luhmann, 1987: 560).

of notations and rules that he calls 'the primary algebra'. The system – while not being without criticism – has found application in a diversity of fields, including mathematics, sociology, psychology (e.g., family therapy) and others. In its conception, it rests on the tradition of symbolic logic as represented by scholars such as Boole, Lewis Caroll (Charles Dodgson), Cantor, Frege, Charles Sanders Peirce, Russell, Whitehead, Hilbert, Ludwig Wittgenstein, Kurt Gödel and many more (Kauffman, 2017). In appearance (i.e., in its notation and basic assumptions), it is close to the mathematics of C. S. Peirce (Kauffman, 2001).

Central to the thesis of the Laws of Form is the concept of distinction. This focus on distinctions, rather than a set of axioms as in other mathematical systems, entails a fundamental unlearning and reconsideration in that the observer does *not* look for objects, matter, substance or content, but for distinctions (Luhmann, 1998: 60; cited in Lau, 2005: 11; Kauffman, 2017). A distinction is realized by making a 'mark', which divides a marked state and an unmarked state. The instruction to draw a distinction as a starting point is the basis for all further calculus to be developed.

13.3.3 The Laws of Form Notation

This section provides a brief introduction to the notation of the Laws of Form. We encourage our interested readers to consult other papers that primarily focus on explaining the development of the notation with regard to how it is used today (e.g., Baecker, 2006; or the Special Issue of *Cybernetics and Human Knowing,* Vol. 24, 2017). Scholars have admitted that it is not an easy undertaking to accustom oneself to and immerse oneself in the kind of thinking the Laws of Form imply, as it spans contexts of mathematics, logics, technology and East Asian philosophy (Schönwälder-Kuntze et al., 2009: 23). For the mathematically inclined reader, it therefore makes sense to read at least the main chapters of Spencer-Brown's book to conceive and retrace his calculus. In the next paragraphs, we follow the guidelines by Baecker (2006) and Kauffman (2017) for presenting the basic ideas and elaborate on them further with examples.

The Laws of Form entail a combinatorial mathematical system: the *calculus of indications*. The notation is of extraordinary simplicity because it uses a single sign, ⌐, called 'the *mark*', which, after its operation, is termed 'the *cross*'. The mark helps us formally indicate a *distinction* we draw by accomplishing three things: (1) marking the inside (i.e., what is included); (2) marking the outside (i.e., the context in which our distinction exists); and (3) arranging a boundary with separate sides (i.e., a marked and an unmarked side) and where the boundary needs to be crossed in order to reach the other side. Drawing a distinction creates a *form*, as illustrated in Figure 13.1.

The distinction, as a separation of the two sides (states), is, in fact, an operation. However, it hides the observer who draws the distinction as well as the operation of drawing the distinction itself (Baecker, 2006: 124). The form contains the *space*, or *context*, in which the distinction is being drawn. This makes the definition of the form self-referential in the sense that no additional boundary conditions are required for its definition. In other words, the form (that indicates a distinction drawn by an observer) is being observed by another observer. The latter observer thus needs to focus on the form *as well as* on the act of observing by reflecting on how variances in observing allow one to arrive at the presented form. As Spencer-Brown experimentally proves in his calculus, 'the first distinction, the mark, and the observer are … in the form, identical' (Spencer-Brown, 1969: 63).

The possibility of reflecting about both sides of the form is termed *re-entry*. It entails re-entering the distinction into the distinction. As Figure 13.2 shows, this is indicated by a second outside mark

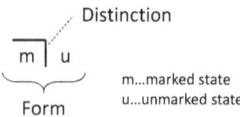

Figure 13.1 The form

Figure 13.2 Re-entry

that adds a little 'hook' on the lower-left side of the form. This ensures two operations, by crossing the first (or original) distinction, and by marking the first distinction by another one that is deferred (or shifted). Both operations express that distinctions occur in two conditions: in one it is used as-is, and in the other it is reflected on. In fact, every time an observer reconsiders an existing distinction, the distinction turns from a mark into a *cross* (Baecker, 2006: 124).

While Spencer-Brown details how calculations using the form can be performed, in this chapter, we will omit this account and focus solely on the notation. For our understanding of drawing distinctions, the method of depicting indications with the help of marked states (indications) and unmarked states (context) is primarily relevant. The form allows us to put our observations (i.e., indications of operations) into context, as shown in Figure 13.3. As mentioned before, the context is not fixed, but reflexive, and might invoke further contexts with additional reflections or observations (Figure 13.4).

The possibility for re-entry has implications for the logics of observing. Re-entry is a time-consuming act for an observer, in which an indication is reconsidered/re-enacted (by re-entering the distinction into the distinction). As Figure 13.5 shows, an observed – or identified, indicated – *a* is thus identifiable (left side of the equation) only in the course of a reiteration of its distinction*s* (plural! right side of the equation). This illustrates that the 'a' for which we assume an identity in fact

form = operation | context

Figure 13.3 Exemplification for form and states

form = operation | context | context'

Figure 13.4 Exemplification for form and states with two contexts

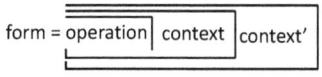

Figure 13.5 Identity as a result of oscillation in the form of notation

oscillates between repeated, and varying, observations. As von Foerster (1969: 11) notes, this oscillation *generates* time.

Dealing with observed variables or structures as referents used in the form, such as 'a', this way avoids antinomies as we have them in Aristotelian logic. In Spencer-Brown's logic, an *a* is an *a* (identity) only when it is distinct from something else (indication) which it is not – but the existence of the other (context) is an existential prerequisite for *a*'s existence. We need to carefully note that the *distinction* does not just represent that *a* has been existing (i.e., before), but that it *causes a's existence* in the first place (i.e., by drawing the distinction).

At this point, we are able to conceptualize what an 'object' is. 'Object' is a term to describe a certain self-referential concept residing in the circular, recursive operations of indication represented by the form – mark, cross and re-entry – which constitute self-referentiality (Glanville, 1990; Baecker, 2015). In this circular 'process of becoming', the object distinguishes itself (is self-distinguishing, and self-distinguished): 'Through this [process of circularity], certain established abilities (properties) of Objects may be subsumed in this discussion, and therefore not elaborated. Of these, the possibility of interrelationship and computation are the most important, for they explain [/]allow the apparent nesting of Objects and hence distinctions drawn' (Glanville, 1990: 3). For qualitative research, this implies that we create 'meaning' not by identifying an object and its characteristics for some purpose, but by *assigning and reproducing meaning in the distinctions* that we draw. 'The purpose of a distinction is to [draw] itself' (Glanville, 1990: 6). Put differently, and as we will argue later, only by inciting this process of becoming – by communicating and discussing it with others – are we able to generate meaning.

13.3.4 Consequences for the Role of Researchers as Observers

The considerations in the prior sections make lucid that we can understand the Laws of Form as *instructions* for us researchers as observers. The instruction to 'Construct[]: Draw a distinction'

(Spencer-Brown, 1969: 3) is a prompt to enact (or re-enact) a creative act of indication (von Foerster, 1969: 9). Hence, as a result, the agency of observing emerges through which we can 'construct' identity from oscillation.

The prompting character of the *Laws* denotes the starting point for the dialogue about observations. In fact, Spencer-Brown emphasizes the *motivation* of observers. As researchers, we typically have already recognized differences, conflicts, deviating values, etc., or have been made aware of those by others (other observers) (Baecker, 1993: 12). Spencer-Brown writes: 'There can be no distinction without motive, and there can be no motive unless contents are seen to differ in value. If a content is of value, a name can be taken to indicate this value. Thus the calling of the name can be identified with the value of the content' (Spencer-Brown, 1969: 1). The observer, or several observers, take recourse on these motives in their conversation in order to draw (further) distinctions. Within the formal system of the Laws of Form, this recourse by drawing distinctions generates a *universe of discourse* in which the observers can further account for their *observations* as well as for their *observing*.[13] Other distinctions that might arise from other motives may generate different universes of discourse, or, if you wish, ontological positions.

When observers can account for their observing, this means that the act, or operation of drawing distinctions in and by itself, can be discussed.[14] This is of importance because we can now create two referents, one represented in the distinction that is being observed (as an 'observed distinction'), and

one in the distinction as it is just being indicated (an 'observing distinction', or just 'indication').

This has implications for qualitative research, particularly on the role and discussion of the researcher as observer. First, the fact that we cannot make an indication without drawing a distinction may lead to some confusion for our research process, because 'all distinctions, thought and language are seen to be aspects of each other, all aspects of the form of distinction. We know that language, our language, describes itself and can comment on itself' (Kauffman, 2017: 7; see also von Foerster's 2003: 96, remarks on dialogics). Thus, any conversation about observations is also a dialogue about the observers themselves.

Second, we need to start with pre-existing motives and distinctions before we can argue about *our distinctions*. At the same time, if we want to contribute to an existing discourse, we will need to re-enact the relevant distinctions that have been made prior to our observations or rationalizations. Only through such formal use of distinctions can our account of observations be linked with the preceding or ensuing account of others. Re-entry thus fuels a self-referential dialogue as a continuous process of reproducing existing acts and simultaneously constituting novel yet connectable acts. As Luhmann (1987) elaborates in his discussion of this 'double contingency', this process involves the autopoietic reproduction of internal distinctions, as well as the reproduction of the possibility for reproduction (Luhmann, 1987: 258, 293, 657). In other words, our observing is in fact a selection process that happens between observers. Each oscillation reproduces the (possibility for) differences included in distinctions and thus implies that with each iteration, other possibilities are selected and different actions and futures become possible.

Our relationship to the objects we consider is thus self-referential (Luhmann, 1987: 656). This means that we can only pursue empirical research by 'inciting the self-referentiality of the object and leveraging its inherent dynamics' (Luhmann, 1987: 657, translated).[15] For qualitative research, this

---

[13] Spencer-Brown more radically says that, in fact, a *universe* is being created in the physical sense, not just a 'universe of discourse' as we interpret the Laws of Form here in our context.

[14] There is much more to say about the implications of indications on our identity as observers. As Baecker (2015) has argued with recurrence on Heidegger, observers can be seen as 'be-ings', understood as 'an inclusive concept comprehending female, male, transgender, and gender-neutral versions' (Baecker, 2015: 55). This obvious link to feminism and gender studies is not by chance (e.g., Barad's claim to 'intra-act responsibly', 1996: 188–189) – yet so far not sufficiently addressed in IS literature.

[15] A better translation might be 'eigen movement' instead of dynamics. How this incitement is to be

means that with a progressing system of distinctions based on our observing (e.g., when triangulating interpretations of data between researchers), we do not necessarily improve our representation of reality, or the 'object' that we consider, but simply render our interaction with our 'objects' more transparent, refining our distinctions (Luhmann, 1987: 657). This leads to an emergent reality that does not rely on the characteristics of the object itself.

13.4   Implications for Qualitative Empirical Research in Information Systems

13.4.1 Examples from IS Research

We use the three perspectives on IT artifacts in-use as described by Barad (2003), Orlikowski and Scott (2008) and Leonardi (2011) earlier for an exercise to prepare three forms (Figure 13.6). For each form, we suggestively add the notation 'artifact' on the left side of the equation and qualify its use later.

As is evident at first glance, all forms are of the same *structure*. In each case, there are two oscillating indications, which again oscillate; the outer ones provide the *context* for the inner indication to occur. The *content* of the forms, however, differs significantly, depending on whether operations, instruments, (substantialist) properties or (relational) principles are specified. The left side of the equation – what we suggestively call 'artifacts' – reveals the different views the authors have taken with their observations (in brackets).

For instance, in equation (2), we interpret Orlikowski and Scott (2008: 460), who provide an

example of sociomateriality in office work. At an engineer's workplace, we see the mixture and assembly of objects arranged all along her previous project work, which overall form a *sociomaterial assemblage*. In the *flow of situated action*, everyday practice reconfigures observable 'situated work performances' out of a myriad of options to entangle agencies (for reasons invisible to the ignorant observer, but embodied by the engineer). The 'artifact' that this performative observation identifies exists temporally as *constitution by situated practice*, which oscillates within the space of potential *entangled agencies*. Both of them result from the recursive reiterations between the *flow of situated action* within the *sociomaterial assemblage*.

We leave it up to our readers as an exercise to reiterate the short descriptions from the previous section to rationalize the three forms we created. Very probably, readers will find alternative formulations of the forms when consulting the referenced authors on their works. In this sense, it is a literal *exercise* to rethink and reiterate the distinctions we have drawn in order to exercise the re-entry for these forms. However, the comparable syntax of the equations allows us to see how the content differs, for instance, in terms of predefined substance (material agency) versus assumed operations (flow of situated action) versus triggered phenomena (agential intra-action). All forms (1) to (3) would require further elaboration in order to explicitly notate how the form can be amended by *where and when* (i.e., spatially and temporally) distinctions happen, and by the *how* (e.g., whether the apparatus for observing is relevant to a given ontology, or not). This is important because it allows us to discuss in what way the intended outcomes (left sides of equation) *can* or *should be* measured. For instance, can or should it be measured as a flow (sequence), or as a constitution (combination), or as a practice? Or something else?

We want to note that the above examples are the result of *our* interpretation of accounts that the original authors formulated in the referenced papers. That said, we do not claim that our notation of forms mirrors correctly what the original authors had in mind. This is, in fact, part of the game. Our understanding, the authors' understanding and the readers' understanding are different (even if a

accomplished is an open question to the practice of empirical investigation. This conclusion, as Luhmann (1987: 657) remarks, holds if the *self-referential constitution of objects* is to be researched. All other classical ways of measurement and classification remain valid. In this case, self-referentiality is abstracted from, and substituted by, the analytic frame for measuring. For instance, 'one can still count motorbikes on the Isle of Man' (1987: 658).

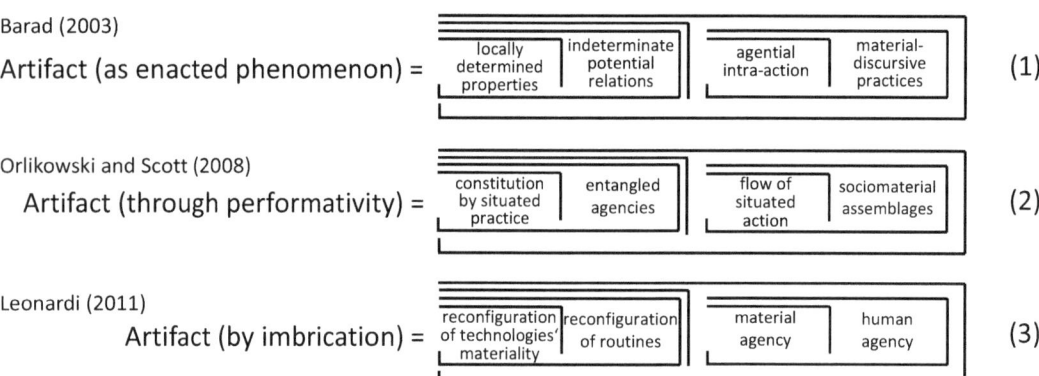

Barad (2003)

Artifact (as enacted phenomenon) = [locally determined properties | indeterminate potential relations] [agential intra-action | material-discursive practices] (1)

Orlikowski and Scott (2008)

Artifact (through performativity) = [constitution by situated practice | entangled agencies] [flow of situated action | sociomaterial assemblages] (2)

Leonardi (2011)

Artifact (by imbrication) = [reconfiguration of technologies' materiality | reconfiguration of routines] [material agency | human agency] (3)

Figure 13.6 Exemplary forms resulting from an interpretation of IS research accounts

reader is one of the original authors, and even if a reader is one of us, the authors of this chapter). What matters is not so much the content of the presented forms – this is secondary. It is the form of the form that matters here.

What we hope our examples showcase are the differences and similarities, or congruencies, that appear in the forms – as 'difference of identity and difference' (Luhmann, 1987: 27). The forms are just temporary reference points of a discussion. In this vein, the *form calculus* is an envelope that conditions degrees of freedom for further deliberations, because each form not only 'defines', but also carries, pointers to elements of uncertainty (Baecker, 2013: 149). If we do not accept these uncertainties, we need to tackle them with further scrutiny.

13.4.2 Methodological Implications

Our brief and admittedly abridged account of current challenges in researching technology use in organizations, and more generally our relationship with information systems, is meant to illustrate the zeitgeist that has brought forth a diverse set of ontological positions for thinking about such issues. We showcased this aspect by using the example of sociomateriality in IS. While the various and currently existing ontological positions each have their own value, they seem, and probably are for the time being, inherently disjoint, and at times incommensurable. We believe, however, that all of them have a common denominator in that they rest their ontologies on *observations* – and the preceding and

ensuing *distinctions* that they require. In this chapter, we have briefly outlined the Laws of Form as a formalism to capture this aspect of distinction as a common denominator.

As a field, we are fortunate to have this diversity of ontological positions, because it allows us to take different viewpoints on complex phenomena that concern us, to pursue diverse purposes and to target novel contributions. More so, as we see technology's complexity increase, spreading and multiplying in our environments, our set of qualitative empirical methodologies needs to become more diverse. More specifically, the requisite variety of our capabilities needs to align with that of what we study.[16] We therefore suggest rethinking the foundations and means we use to draw distinctions in qualitative empirical research of information systems. Particularly, when we acknowledge – and accept – that 'our things' (i.e., our objects and artifacts) become ever-more complex, evading and going beyond our existing capacity to observe, we should not (only) ask, 'what is this thing?' or 'what does it do?', but rather: 'why does "it" show?' And 'when does "it" become?' (see also Ashby, 1956: 1). We need to be careful as to the unlearning of prior conceptualizations that *drawing distinctions* according to Spencer-Brown's calculus affords. The most prominent idea might be to fundamentally abandon the concept of 'identity', for

---

[16] Congruent with the Conant-Ashby theorem (Ashby, 1956: 124; Conant and Ashby, 1970).

example, the definition of an object in space and time, in favour of the concept of distinction.[17]

We next discuss how two concepts of the Laws of Form might apply to qualitative empirical research in IS. Be cautioned that this account is incomplete for two reasons. First, we have far from portrayed all of the concepts and conclusions that are generally linked with, or drawn from, the Laws of Form. Second, much more discussion is required on the side of qualitative methods to apprehend the impact of this kind of thinking on our accustomed conventions for doing research.

13.4.2.1 Observing with Distinctions: Conditioned Co-Production

The conceptualization of our objects of study (e.g., artifacts) can be informed by the idea of *conditioned co-production*. Conditioned co-production implies that objects do not originate in isolation, but appear from making distinctions, which begets a triadic structure. In the foreword of his book in the 1994 edition, Spencer-Brown writes: 'Any indication implies duality, we cannot produce a thing without coproducing what it is not, and every duality implies triplicity: what a thing is, what it isn't, and the boundary between them.' In this way, the triadic structure becomes a vehicle to describe that the observed 'reality', or the possibility of existence, is always inseparably linked with the approach or the way to observe some thing. Indicating – a time-consuming operation – enables drawing and adapting (crossing) distinctions, thus providing the precondition for the possibility of observation (Luhmann, 1993: 198).

The triadic structure becomes the starting point of considerations. The notion of 'distinctness' replaces what we know as 'separateness' – that is,

a function of previous concept definitions and properties of an object that define its identity. As a result of this way of thinking, several well-accepted concepts appear as problematic, because they are based on the idea of separability. Among them are: objects (isolated elements); predicates (properties of objects); and references and relations between objects (defined relationships between isolated objects/properties) (Schönwälder-Kuntze et al., 2009: 43).

Distinctions are the predecessors of relations, and thus also become predecessors to any relational or substantialist ontology. Being aware of conditioned co-production, we can no longer study single units of analysis independently from the triad, as all elements of the triad exist simultaneously and without ordering. This primacy of distinctions also holds true for our arguments about where and when agency and causality are to be attributed. Conditioned co-production, understood as obligation and necessity to draw distinctions, should not, however, be interpreted as a constraint, but as an opportunity to divide and detail every distinction further. In fact, such treatment can increase, or decrease, the complexity of considerations (forms). In other words, we need to repeatedly justify our leanings towards ontologically separating or entangling, terms that both need to become expressions for *relations of distinctness* (not separateness).

13.4.2.2 Reasoning with Distinctions: Injunction

Using the idea of distinction to formalize our observations requires an approach to reasoning, different from the classical search for identity. Spencer-Brown elaborates on these considerations by arguing that 'the primary form of mathematical communication is not description, but injunction' (Spencer-Brown, 1969: 64). For him, the formal notation is not descriptive, but must be understood as a 'set of commands' (1969: 64). This conception is different from other notions, such as Wittgenstein's famous proposition: 'whereof one cannot speak thereof one must be silent' (from Wittgenstein's Tractatus, Spencer-Brown, 1969: 64; see also Wittgenstein, 1963: 115). As

---

[17] There is more to be said about the *unlearning process* with regard to the role of language as primacy in our capacity for observing as has been laid out in the works of B. L. Whorf and his theory of linguistic relativity (see Whorf, 1940). Whorf argues that our shared cultural context implies language patterns that define how our minds' linguistic systems condition selection processes – that is, determining how we observe and what categories and types we *are able to* isolate or identify.

Spencer-Brown argues, this proposition is true for *descriptions*, but not for *instructions*. He gives the analogy of a music composer, who does not *describe* her composition in terms of her feelings when listening to it, but notates it as a form of instructions so others can reproduce the musical piece (Spencer-Brown, 1969: 64).

The *procedural character of drawing distinctions* generates a creative momentum in the Laws of Form. There 'are' no objects or artifacts; rather, we continuously carry out indication processes or actions that generate or sustain *states* that we can observe – states that can change or dissolve. This shifts our attention as researchers towards the everyday indicative actions of individuals, or the implicit or explicit routines and protocols in organizations that govern indication processes (Schönwälder-Kuntze et al., 2009: 290).

It also carries implications for the process of arriving at insights and the cognitive faculty (*Erkenntnisvermögen*) of qualitative research. Drawing distinctions allows us to carry out reductionist processes while simultaneously generating new insights. Spencer-Brown has characterized this approach to arrive at findings as *injunctive*, in contrast to deductive or inductive approaches. Injunctive approaches create insight through *re-enacting the generative differentiation or deconstruction processes*, in contrast to reaffirming identities between predefined objects. As Goffman has expressed in his account about the organization of individual experience, 'what is sovereign is relationship, not substance' (Goffman, 1974: 560–561). Hazelrigg (1992: 255) explains: 'This means that "thingness" is an effect, not a self-identical entity bearing intrinsic properties. Neither object nor "subject", neither [observer] nor interpretation's object, is first of all a substantial entity of independent integrity, which, having been so constituted already, *then enters into* relationships. Rather, each is a fluid nexus of relations' (emphasis in the original). Making an indication creates a distinction, and each distinction hints at (and is an indication towards) itself. This way *distinctions create relations* which we subsequently use to capture and link phenomena in our observations (which can be elements carrying an identity, or performances and agencies ascribed to

entanglements, etc.); they thus precede both substantialist and relational ontologies. Due to different levels of analysis and complexity of differentiations, the resulting processes fan out and permit multifaceted views, allowing the creation of very different 'worlds', or spheres of analysis (Schönwälder-Kuntze et al., 2009: 32).

Following these arguments, injunction provides an opportunity to rethink and reframe causality across ontologies as well, because *cause* need not be *assigned* to objects and their relationships (e.g., agencies), but attributed to the agency of observing oscillating distinctions. We can thus avoid the 'illusion of understanding' (Sloman and Lagnado, 2015) and the paradoxical notions of our generally spatio-temporal and narrative sensemaking of causality (Sloman and Lagnado, 2015: 241). This has implications for how we deal with causality in theorizing (Mingers and Standing, 2017; Markus and Rowe, 2018). Injunction enables the co-enactment of a theorizing process and acts as a means to define *how to produce* distinctions. In that sense, injunction represents a predecessor to abductive research (Peirce, 1933; Behfar and Okhuysen, 2018) as it *precedes* the separation of objective and subjective reality. It emphasizes the agency our observing entails, and creates the boundary conditions that subsequently – in abductive research – allow us to speculate about plausible explanations for these observations. Hence, it becomes a denominator for any interpretive stance.

As part of this process, we also encounter oscillations – that is, repeatedly performed distinctions (re-entries), which allow us to grasp the change process with regard to perceived conditions, states, appropriated values and assumed perspectives over time (Schönwälder-Kuntze et al., 2009: 182). The concept of re-entry creates a dynamic conception of observing, enabling an observer to formally observe how previous values, intentions, opinions, etc. shift *within one form* over time. The form provides for a 'fluid nexus of relations' (Hazelrigg, 1992: 255) – that is, the space within which values change. For example, changes in the materiality and performativity of entanglements are possible and performed. Through oscillations, Spencer-Brown offers an instrument to observe patterns as effects of re-entries of distinctions in themselves, and thus extends Wittgenstein's Tractatus programme (Fuchs and Hoegl, 2015: 190). This may allow us to observe and formalize untapped phenomena in the dynamics of material-discursive practices – for instance, self-reference, recursion, self-similarity, feedback, circularity, imaginary states and paradoxical states (Schönwälder-Kuntze et al., 2009: 191, 292).

13.5 Provisional Summary and Outlook

We end our chapter with a short summary and some conjectures and suggestions for future engagement with the Laws of Form in the IS field.

As technologies become increasingly complex, malleable and continuously co-created by users and software engineers, they test the limits of our observability. This raises major concerns for conducting empiric research that relies on observations like qualitative approaches do. To address this issue, and to provide a basis for communication and comparison of observations, we suggest abandoning the traditional concept of identity in lieu of the concept of distinctions. We provide a short description of how this can be achieved through the Laws of Form notation and describe the associated underlying assumptions to reframe our empiric inquiries.

A reconsideration of our role as observers might hold some surprises for agential or critical realists, as well as other positions. While we have not dwelled on this issue here, it is not by chance that the ideas of the Laws of Form have been taken up by fields such as gender and diversity studies, or psychotherapy, long ago. We might rethink our role as designers and users of technology in similar ways (i.e., in a more emancipated and self-reflective perspective), as has been successfully done in the mentioned fields of research. This inherently links with our capacity to tackle complexity and responds to the notion of conflict-through-design interventions (Baecker, 2013: 276). Our conceptualization of objects of research might also undergo some changes. Where we have been using concepts, such as routines or agencies, tied to things or behaviours, we might be able to disentangle these further and arrive at conceptions

of our relationships with technology that better mirror emergent, evolving or transformative processes.

Overall, the basic tenets of the Laws of Form might be a helpful addition to our repertoire of qualitative empirical research in IS. Particularly, questions about what 'IT artifacts' mean to us – from a sociomaterial or other point of view – may become even more surprising and self-revealing in the future. The promise is that more is to be learned about us researchers and our relationship with technology.

References

Akhlaghpour, S., Wu, J., Lapointe, L. and Pinsonneault, A. (2013). The ongoing quest for the IT artifact: Looking back, moving forward. *Journal of Information Technology*, 28(2), 150–166.

Ashby, W. R. (1956). *An Introduction to Cybernetics*, 1976 edition. London and New York, NY: Methuen, distributed by Harper & Row.

Baecker, D. (2017). A calculus of negation in communication. *Cybernetics and Human Knowing*, 24(3–4), 17–27.

Baecker, D. (2015). The be-ing of objects. *Cybernetics and Human Knowing*, 22(2–3), 49–58.

Baecker, D. (2013). *Form und Formen der Kommunikation*, Suhrkamp-Taschenbücher Wissenschaft, 3rd edition. Frankfurt am Main, Germany: Suhrkamp, Vol. 1828.

Baecker, D. (2006). The form of the firm. *Organization*, 13(1), 109–142.

Baecker, D. (1993). Im Tunnel. In D. Baecker (ed.), *Kalkül der Form, Suhrkamp Taschenbuch Wissenschaft*. Frankfurt am Main, Germany: Suhrkamp, pp. 12–37.

Barad, K. (2007). *Meeting the Universe Halfway: Quantum Physics and the Entanglement of Matter and Meaning*. Durham, NC: Duke University Press.

Barad, K. (2003). Posthumanist performativity: Toward an understanding of how matter comes to matter. *Signs*, 28(3), 801–831.

Barad, K. (1998). Getting real: Technoscientific practices and the materialization of reality. *Differences*, 10(2), 88–128.

Barad, K. (1996). Meeting the universe halfway: Realism and social constructivism without contradiction. In L. H. Nelson and J. Nelson (eds), *Feminism, Science, and the Philosophy of Science.* Dordrecht, the Netherlands: Springer, Vol. 256, pp. 161–194.

Baskerville, R. (2012). Reviving the IT in the IS. *European Journal of Information Systems*, 21(6), 587–591.

Baskerville, R. L., Myers, M. D. and Yoo, Y. (2020). Digital first: The ontological reversal and new challenges for IS research. *MIS Quarterly*, 44(2), 509–523.

Bateson, G. (1979). *Mind and Nature: A Necessary Unity*, 2002 edition. Cresskill, NJ: Hampton Press.

Baudrillard, J. (2006). *The System of Objects.* London: Verso.

Behfar, K. and Okhuysen, G. A. (2018). Perspective – discovery within validation logic: Deliberately surfacing, complementing, and substituting abductive reasoning in hypothetico-deductive inquiry. *Organization Science*, 29(2), 323–340.

Carlile, P. R., Nicolini, D., Langley, A. and Tsoukas, H. (eds). (2013). *How Matter Matters: Objects, Artifacts, and Materiality in Organization Studies.* Oxford: Oxford University Press, Vol. 3.

Cecez-Kecmanovic, D., Davison, M., Fernandez, W., Finnegan, P., Pan, L. and Sarker, S. (2020). Advancing qualitative IS research methodologies: Expanding horizons and seeking new paths. *Journal of the Association for Information Systems*, 21(1), 246–263.

Cecez-Kecmanovic, D., Galliers, R. D., Henfridsson, O., Newell, S. and Vidgen, R. (2014). The sociomateriality of information systems: Current status, future directions. *MIS Quarterly*, 38(3), 809–830.

Conant, R. C. and Ashby, W. R. (1970). Every good regulator of a system must be a model of that system. *International Journal of Systems Science*, 1(2), 89–97.

Curtis, A. M., Dennis, A. R. and McNamara, K. O. (2017). From monologue to dialogue: Performative objects to promote collective mindfulness in computer-mediated team discussions. *MIS Quarterly*, 41(2), 559–581.

Dennis, A. R., Fuller, R. M. and Valacich, J. S. (2008). Media, tasks, and communication processes: A theory of media synchronicity. *MIS Quarterly*, 32(3), 575–600.

Fuchs, P. and Hoegl, F. (2015). Die Schrift der Form. In B. Pörksen (ed.), *Schlüsselwerke des Konstruktivismus.* Wiesbaden, Germany: VS Verlag für Sozialwissenschaften, pp. 165–196.

Garud, R., Jain, S. and Tuertscher, P. (2008). Incomplete by design and designing for incompleteness. *Organization Studies*, 29(3), 351–371.

Glanville, R. (2001). An observing science. *Foundations of Science*, 6(1–3), 45–75.

Glanville, R. (1990). The self and the other: The purpose of distinction. In R. Trappl (ed.), *Cybernetics and Systems '90: Proceedings of the Tenth European Meeting on Cybernetics and Systems Research, Held at the University of Vienna, Austria.* Singapore: World Scientific, pp. 349–356.

Glanville, R. (1978). The nature of fundamentals, applied to the fundamentals of nature. In G. J. Klir (ed.), *Applied General Systems Research. Recent Developments and Trends*, NATO Conference Series. Boston, MA: Springer, Vol. 5, pp. 401–409.

Goffman, E. (1974). *Frame Analysis: An Essay on the Organization of Experience.* New York, NY: Harper & Row.

Hazelrigg, L. (1992). Reading Goffman's framing as provocation of a discipline. *Human Studies*, 15(2–3), 239–264.

Kallinikos, J., Aaltonen, A. and Marton, A. (2013). The ambivalent ontology of digital artifacts. *MIS Quarterly*, 37(2), 357–370.

Kauffman, L. H. (2017). Foreword: Laws of form. *Cybernetics & Human Knowing*, 24(3–4), 5–15.

Kauffman, L. H. (2001). The mathematics of Charles Sanders Peirce. *Cybernetics & Human Knowing*, 8(1–2), 79–110.

Lau, F. (2005). *Die Form der Paradoxie: Eine Einführung in die Mathematik und Philosophie der 'Laws of Form' von George Spencer Brown*, 5th edition. Heidelberg, Germany: Carl-Auer-Verlag.

Leonardi, P. M. (2013). Theoretical foundations for the study of sociomateriality. *Information and Organization*, 23(2), 59–76.

Leonardi, P. M. (2011). When flexible routines meet flexible technologies: Affordance, constraint, and the imbrication of human and material agencies. *MIS Quarterly*, 35(1), 147–167.

Luhmann, N. (1998). *Die Gesellschaft der Gesellschaft.* Suhrkamp-Taschenbuch Wissenschaft. Frankfurt am Main, Germany: Suhrkamp.

Luhmann, N. (1993). Die Paradoxie der Form. In D. Baecker (ed.), *Kalkül der Form.* Suhrkamp-Taschenbuch Wissenschaft. Frankfurt am Main, Germany: Suhrkamp, Vol. 1068, pp. 197–212.

Luhmann, N. (1987). *Soziale Systeme: Grundriss einer allgemeinen Theorie*, 1st edition. Frankfurt am Main, Germany: Suhrkamp.

March, S. T. and Smith, G. F. (1995). Design and natural science research on information technology. *Decision Support Systems*, 15(4), 251–266.

Markus, M. L. and Rowe, F. (2018). Is IT changing the world? Conceptions of causality for information systems theorizing. *MIS Quarterly*, 42(4), 1–26.

Maturana, H. R. and Varela, F. J. (1980). *Autopoiesis and Cognition: The Realization of the Living*. Dordrecht, the Netherlands: Reidel.

McCulloch, W. S. and Pitts, W. (1943). A logical calculus of the ideas immanent in nervous activity. *Bulletin of Mathematical Biophysics*, 5(4), 115–133.

Mingers, J. and Standing, C. (2020). A framework for validating information systems research based on a pluralist account of truth and correctness. *Journal of the Association for Information Systems*, 21(1), 117–151.

Mingers, J. and Standing, C. (2017). Why things happen – developing the critical realist view of causal mechanisms. *Information and Organization*, 27(3), 171–189.

Mutch, A. (2013). Sociomateriality – taking the wrong turning? *Information and Organization*, 23(1), 28–40.

Niedderer, K. (2007). Designing mindful interaction: The category of performative object. *Design Issues*, 23(1), 3–17.

Northoff, G. (2018). *The Spontaneous Brain. From the Mind-Body to the World-Brain Problem*. London and Cambridge, MA: MIT Press.

Northoff, G. (2011). *Neuropsychoanalysis in Practice: Brain, Self, and Objects*. Oxford: Oxford University Press.

Orlikowski, W. J. and Iacono, C. S. (2001). Research commentary: Desperately seeking the 'IT' in IT research – a call to theorizing the IT artifact. *Information Systems Research*, 12(2), 121–134.

Orlikowski, W. J. and Scott, S. V. (2008). Sociomateriality: Challenging the separation of technology, work and organization. *Academy of Management Annals*, 2(1), 433–474.

Østerlund, C., Crowston, K. and Jackson, C. (2020). Building an apparatus: Refractive, reflective, and diffractive readings of trace data. *Journal of the Association for Information Systems*, 20(1), 1–22.

Pask, G. (1970). The meaning of cybernetics in the behavioural sciences. (The cybernetics of behaviour and cognition; extending the meaning of 'goal'). In J. Rose (ed.), *Progress of Cybernetics*, Vol. 1: *Main Papers, The Meaning of Cybernetics, Neuro- and Biocybernetics*. London: Gordon & Breach, Science Publishers, pp. 15–44.

Peirce, C. S. (1933). *Collected Papers* (Charles Hartshorne and Paul Weiss, eds). Cambridge, MA: Belknap Press of Harvard University Press.

Schönwälder-Kuntze, T., Wille, K. and Hölscher, T. (2009). *George Spencer Brown: Eine Einführung in die 'Laws of Form': [Lehrbuch]*, 2nd edition. Wiesbaden, Germany: VS, Verlag für Sozialwiss.

Scott, S. V. and Orlikowski, W. J. (2013). Sociomateriality – taking the wrong turning? A response to Mutch. *Information and Organization*, 23(2), 77–80.

Shannon, C. E. (1948). A mathematical theory of communication. *Bell System Technical Journal*, 27(3), 379–423.

Shannon, C. E. and Weaver, W. (1949). *The Mathematical Theory of Communication*, 1963 edition. Urbana, IL: University of Illinois Press.

Sloman, S. A. and Lagnado, D. (2015). Causality in thought. *Annual Review of Psychology*, 66, 223–247.

Spencer-Brown, G. (1969). *Laws of Form*. London: Allen & Unwin.

von Foerster, H. (1969). Laws of form. Whole Earth Catalog, spring: 14. Cited from: Die Gesetze der Form. In D. Baecker (ed.), *Kalkül der Form, Suhrkamp Taschenbuch Wissenschaft*. Frankfurt am Main, Germany: Suhrkamp, Vol. 1068, pp. 9–11.

von Foerster, H. (2003). *Understanding Understanding: Essays on Cybernetics and Cognition*. New York, NY: Springer.

von Foerster, H. and von Glasersfeld, E. (2010). *Wie wir uns erfinden: Eine Autobiographie des radikalen Konstruktivismus*, 4th edition. Heidelberg, Germany: Carl-Auer-Systeme.

von Glasersfeld, E. (2002). Cybernetics and the theory of knowledge. *UNESCO Encyclopedia*. Section on System Science and Cybernetics, p. 255.

Watzlawick, P., Weakland, J. H. and Fisch, R. (1974). *Change: Principles of Problem Formation and Problem Resolution*, reprint 2011. London and New York, NY: W. W. Norton.

Weber, R. (2003). Still desperately seeking the IT artifact. *MIS Quarterly*, 27(2), 183–194.

Whorf, B. L. (1940). Science and linguistics. *Technology Review*, 42(6), 229–231, 247–248.

Wittgenstein, L. (1963). *Logisch-philosophische Abhandlung: Tractatus logico-philosophicus*, 36th edition. Frankfurt am Main, Germany: Suhrkamp, Vol. 12.

Yoo, Y. (2010). Computing in everyday life: A call for research on experiential computing. *MIS Quarterly*, 34(2), 213–231.

Zittrain, J. (2008). *The Future of the Internet and How to Stop it*. New Haven, CT: Yale University Press.

Algorithms as Co-Researchers

Exploring Meaning and Bias in Qualitative Research

WENDY ARIANNE GÜNTHER, MARK THOMPSON, MAYUR P. JOSHI and STAVROS POLYKARPOU

14.1 Introduction

Augmenting traditional qualitative methods with advanced algorithmic tools – a phenomenon we refer to as algorithmic qualitative research – raises important epistemological and methodological questions for researchers. As a revealing example, Jones (2016) offers an arresting vignette that encapsulates some of the challenges for qualitative researchers who use computational analysis in their work. It is of a 1949 meeting between Father Roberto Busa (a Jesuit priest) and Thomas J. Watson (CEO of IBM) in the IBM HQ office. In the meeting, Busa secured Watson's support for building a comprehensive index of some 11 million medieval Latin words in the works of St Thomas Aquinas and related authors. This was not to be just any index. All the words were to be 'lemmatized' – that is, arranged in alphabetical order and grouped according to their various multiple forms, along with their verbal context and original location. This created almost limitless ways for subsequent researchers to interpret the totality of these works (see Manovich, 2011). The successful endeavour that followed is credited by many as the birth of humanities computing.

Jones's story juxtaposes a priest-academic qualitative researcher with IBM, an organization with iconic space-related, political, commercial, military and industrial reach that perhaps best symbolizes the scientist approach dominant during the early Cold War. In doing so, Jones has opened a revealing window into some inherent tensions in the use of computer-based data analysis for building qualitative understanding. Far from an uncomplicated hitching of IBM's computational might to augment or expedite a qualitative investigation,

Jones has shown how Busa's creation of his index was a delicate and unfolding sociotechnical accomplishment (see Ribes and Jackson, 2013) that used technological affordances (Zammuto et al., 2007) and cultural practices to *ultimately shape the data and the meanings* that ensued so that data and meaning became inseparable: 'The "founding moment" of digital humanities ... was the creation of a radically transformed, reordered, disassembled, and reassembled version of one of the world's most influential philosophies' (Ramsay, 2011, in Jones, 2016: 147).

In the late 1950s, Busa conducted a later project in partnership with IBM: a computerized analysis of the fragmented Dead Sea Scrolls. This involved 'experiment[ing] with a form of literary data processing, an open-ended, step-wise (algorithmic), and iterative process of dissolving and reconstituting the texts as linguistic data in forms that could be rearranged and analyzed in any number of ways' (Jones, 2016: 144), in which '"filling in the gaps" as in a "crossword puzzle", but also potentially filling holes in the story of how the text got fragmented, was an added result of the process' (2016: 147). Jones described this process as exposing new dimensions in the composition of the strata of the cultural record itself.

As well as their foundational interest for the field, these two vignettes can perhaps be helpful for qualitative researchers as they formulate strategies for evaluating the use of algorithms in their own work. Both examples root the subsequent use of a growing array of digital analytical tools within the foundational acknowledgement that qualitative researchers' reflexive relationship with the process of selecting, forming, processing and interpreting data is necessarily synthetic, or even creative. This is because these activities inflect, and are in turn inflected by, the data themselves. This conflation challenges the traditional distinction (Weber, 2003) between analysis based on *verstehen* (interpretive, participatory and centring on meaning) and *erklären* (objective explanation; Tully, 1994). This distinction is often encouraged, and underscored, by an empiricist view of 'big data' as revealing inherent truth (Kitchin, 2014). Therefore, we argue that qualitative researchers could benefit from close attention to the way in which meaning emerges through a reflexive dance between researcher(s) and algorithm(s).

Recognition that this fundamental epistemological relativity dates from the start of the digital humanities (and is therefore nothing new) challenges the idea that, even using less sophisticated computing technologies, data can ever be separated objectively from the researcher or from the research process. In turn, this acknowledgement reveals the lie in the view that algorithms offer a helpful rigour and objectivity to an otherwise unstructured discipline (e.g., Ramsay, 2011). As we argue, in the age of 'big data', 'data science' and 'artificial intelligence', this aspiration towards – and often belief in – objectivity is more illusion than reality; there is a danger that both researchers and consumers may attribute data with an objectivity which it does not possess, with illusory consequences for both parties.

In a helpful development of this 'inseparability position', Jones (2019: 6, no relation) has offered a summary of common empiricist assumptions about data and 'big data' and outlined challenges to each of these assumptions. Common assumptions about data are, first, that data are 'referential' in that they reflect some phenomenon, entity or object that exists independently in the 'real' world; second, that data are 'natural' in that they exist out in the world, waiting to be collected and analyzed; third, that data are 'foundational' in that they 'are the base on which our understanding of the world is built'; fourth, that data are 'objective' in that they represent raw facts without being infused with bias; and, fifth, that data are 'equal' in the most literal sense (i.e., that 'all data are equivalent' and similar in terms of quality). In turn, assumptions about 'big data' are that they are: first,

'revolutionary', in that they will transform the way we think about and understand the world; second, 'voluminous', in that they are being generated and collected in large volumes and at high speeds; third, 'universal', in that anything can be datafied and captured in data; and, fourth, 'exhaustive', in that 'n = all' (Jones, 2019: 6).

Jones's detailed challenging of these assumptions, and underscoring of the 'complexity, consequentiality and constructed character of data' (2019: 14), offers a firm basis for building on Jones's (2016) interest in how algorithmic research can expand the spectrum of interpretation and theory-building within the humanities (Manovich, 2011) without succumbing to what would be, in this context, a naïve empiricism. This empiricism is something that Father Busa tried to avoid via careful reflection when dealing with IBM back in a markedly empiricist Cold War America. Although Jones's (2019) focus was data itself, not algorithmic qualitative research, our perspective resonates strongly with his (and Busa's) challenging of the empiricist assumptions that often surround both of these.

Building on Jones's (2019) work, we investigate the inseparability of algorithms and the researchers who apply those algorithms in qualitative research. Our arguments are indebted to Heidegger's (1977) phenomenological view of technology – which invites a critique of claims to any separability of user from algorithm – as well as recent accounts that treat algorithms as actants (Glaser et al., 2021). By joining the recent discourses in sociology and computer science (e.g., Pääkkönen and Ylikoski, 2021), we extend this logic of epistemological relativity – hitherto applied in the context of studies *of* technologies – to the phenomenon of studies *with* technologies, where researchers employ algorithmic tools in undertaking their qualitative research. We illustrate that algorithms require researchers' active involvement in several decisions which are consequential to – and potentially a consequence of – the outcome researchers obtain at each stage of research, in the manner of a 'reflexive dance' between the researcher and their algorithmic co-researcher.

In the remainder of the chapter, we first highlight the relational interactions that occur during algorithmic qualitative research. Such interactions can involve algorithm(s) and researchers, as well as software tools and hardware. All of these interactions open spaces for additional dimensions of qualitative understanding (Jones's [2016] additional dimensions in the strata of the cultural record). Next, we articulate and explore some of the associated checks and balances that qualitative researchers can employ to help themselves engage actively, and reflexively, in the relational interactions between various parties. To corroborate our argument, we use the example of topic modelling – a popular machine-learning technique that qualitative (as well as quantitative) researchers are increasingly using to analyze textual data (Hannigan et al., 2019) – to demonstrate how researchers can work with algorithms to transparently acknowledge and expose their interactions and the associated considerations that they are necessarily introducing into their research. Conversely, we illustrate that the effect of glossing over, or neglecting, such transparency can be a methodological opaqueness surrounding these constitutively relational interactions. It can also lead to an associated bias, in the form of *unacknowledged* introduction of perspectives into the data. In sum, we offer suggestions for using algorithms to create transparency and meaning – rather than opacity and bias – in algorithmic qualitative research practices.

14.2 When Tools Become Models: Checks and Balances in the Creation of Meaning

Our practice-based appraisal of the use of algorithms for qualitative ends reflects our concern about: (1) the implications of the introduction of technology for qualitative researchers as a more central and agential element of their research; and (2) the unfolding interrelationship between the algorithm(s) and the researcher(s). Our perspective is indebted to Heidegger's notion of modern technology as *Gestell* (enframing or 'black-boxing'). *Gestell* is the way in which technological devices are inscribed with and hide the multiplicity of dependencies and relations that are needed for

them to work in one way and not another. The result is that the user becomes disengaged from what these technologies are actually doing. In order to increase our awareness and understanding of these dependencies and relations, Heidegger (1977) has argued that the 'solution' is to strive for a 'free' relationship with technology – in other words, a relationship that stresses focal, engaged practices rather than disengaged, 'enframed' consumption.

Heidegger's phenomenological view of technology invites a critique of claims to any separability of the researcher from the algorithm and resonates with Latour's (1990) famous dictum that 'technology is society made durable'. Both of these views invite an acknowledgement of the *embodied* and *unfolding* nature of a *relationship* between researchers and technology, in which disembodied things have no meaning aside from people's always already directed experience: 'What we "first" hear is never noises or complexes of sounds, but the creaking wagon, the motorcycle … It requires a very artificial and complicated frame of mind to "hear" a "pure noise"' (Heidegger, 1962: 207). This is an example that Introna and Ilharco (2011) liken to the difference between hearing music and hearing disconnected, meaningless noise (it would not be possible for a listener who had grown up listening to Mozart's music to hear solely in terms of the latter). The allegory here is the inability of any qualitative researcher to claim any objective or detached relationship to the data or algorithm.

14.2.1 Acknowledging the Inseparability of Algorithms from Researchers in Practice

Following a critique by Dreyfus (1993) that was itself inspired by Heidegger, the field of artificial intelligence (AI) underwent something of a pivot away from representationalist aims based on objective detachment towards notions of embodiment and possibility. This reorientation contains a recognition of the open-ended, iterative nature of our relationship with things 'as possibilities for'. Suchman (1987) has described this approach when contrasting the representationalist notion of future 'plans' with the unfolding reality of 'situated actions'. For qualitative researchers seeking to work effectively with algorithms, the 'embodied turn' towards technology and meaning implies a strongly iterative, as well as provisional, reflexive and self-aware approach to the *directedness* of the unfolding interface between technology and qualitative researchers: 'The transparent interface is one that allows both fluid interaction and active manipulation. It is neither intuitive nor invisible; it exists but is not entirely conspicuous. The user is aware of it and manipulates it to learn from it, acts through it to accomplish goals, creatively misuses it when necessary, and copes with its flaws' (Wendt, 2013).

14.2.2 Neither Visible nor Invisible: Transparent

In modern situations, this interface can be between multiple researchers working in interdisciplinary teams on the one hand, and multiple machines on the other. For example, Mackenzie (2017) has identified the hundreds of thousands of cores involved in Google Compute. In addition, Suchman (2006) has considered 'privileged machines' that assign subject-positions to dispersed participants. Recalling Heidegger (1977), there is surely a danger that the directedness of the interface under such dispersed conditions is never interrogated reflexively and therefore actualized. In this way, the nature of the interface is not transparent but opaque to the researcher, who is thus excluded from the *verstehen* – the understanding, or meaning – that they seek, and whose relationship to the interface becomes accordingly uninformed: the relationship becomes one of enframed and disconnected consumption, with potentially dangerous consequences (see also Newell and Marabelli, 2015). An opaque interface between researcher and algorithm is a particular danger when other members of a dispersed team – coders or data scientists – subscribe to a mindset and research approach based on *erklären*. This is because, as Winner points out, a mindset approach can become inscribed into the technology, which can become 'so thoroughly biased in a particular direction that it regularly produces results heralded as wonderful breakthroughs by some social interests and crushing setbacks by others' (Winner, 1999: 25–26).

Far from an objective empirical exercise, algorithmic qualitative research is better conceptualized as a reflexive dance between researchers, a phenomenon (however defined), algorithms, software tools and hardware. This dance opens opportunities at every turn for the creative introduction of meaning *and* bias. Drawing on Heidegger's ideas, the pursuit of transparency about the nature of interfaces and *practices* between various actors in the research process becomes a matter of pressing, if under-recognized, concern for the field of algorithmic qualitative research.

Adhering to this view, our use of the term 'bias' does not refer to any intentional or unintentional influence by researchers that potentially distorts the results of a study. Instead, it refers to negligence by researchers in not acknowledging and not consciously reflecting on their selection of one version of reality over alternative plausible realities. In other words – recognizing the inseparability of qualitative researchers from the reality they create – bias is not a distortion of the truth, but a non-recognition and/or failure by researchers to explain the reason(s) for the path they choose. Transparency and reflexivity are two key principles that qualitative researchers can adopt in order to minimize such bias (Galdas, 2017).

We suggest that acknowledging a 'reflexive dance of meaning and bias' between researchers and their algorithmic co-researchers can encourage greater transparency and mindfulness in three different places where meaning is necessarily generated during the practice of algorithmic qualitative research. First, the specific algorithm that researchers choose to adopt directs attention to certain *algorithm-derived* meanings. This is at the expense of other potential meanings. The adoption of certain patterns means many potentially interesting yet more nuanced patterns or outliers may be overlooked (George et al., 2014). Second, scholars have highlighted that contrary to humans, algorithms and 'AI systems are not able to understand the situations humans experience' (Dwivedi et al., 2021: 6). Therefore, the researcher plays a pivotal role in feeding data into the algorithm, making sense of different configurations and resulting patterns, and proactively validating models and their underlying assumptions to determine if they reflect an 'acceptable' take on reality. We label this second type of intervention *interpretation-derived* meaning. Third, and contrary to popular belief, algorithms do not always simply converge on just one objective truth. Due to an algorithm's sensitivity to input data, parameter configurations and even inherent degrees of randomness, those who rely on algorithms to analyze data are likely to find themselves exploring multiple realities. By favouring one model over another, researchers may be ignoring other potentially relevant perspectives. We term this third type of intervention *selection-derived* meaning. Due to these challenges, researchers may in practice continuously find themselves trying to choose between many different meanings.

The implication, following Heidegger, is that as qualitative researchers using algorithms, we should strive to achieve transparency about the nature of the inscribed meanings of the various tools that we use in our research. We should also examine how these meanings shape our research practices. Winograd and Flores (1986) have summarized Heidegger's hammer and nail example: 'To the person doing the hammering, the hammer as such does not exist. It is a part of the background of readiness-to-hand that is taken for granted without explicit recognition or identification as an object. It is part of the hammerer's world, but is not present any more than are the tendons of the hammerer's arm' (Winograd and Flores, 1986: 36). It is only in moments of 'breakdown' (for example), when the hammer breaks or misses the nail, that its properties become transparent to the hammerer. One potentially helpful framework within which to encourage such a transparency is Rockwell and Sinclair's (2016) 'agile hermeneutics'. This is an approach to algorithmic research firmly rooted in the acknowledgement that: 'Research in humanities computing begins then, in the breakdown, when tools become models. It proceeds in an iterative cycle of constructing, testing, analyzing, and reconstructing these models in order to discover how the thing imitated may better be known. By definition a model cannot be true' (McCarty, 2003: 1232).

Central to this approach is the firm acknowledgement that algorithms break text apart and re-synthesize, becoming surrogates of the text (not the

text itself) as they demarcate, digitize, encode and interpret it. This process has been called a 'remixing of meaning' (Barthes, 1972: 216, in Rockwell and Sinclair, 2016). If methodological transparency is key to understanding how different types of meanings become infused in the process of algorithmic qualitative research, this transparency surely starts with conscious mindfulness by the researcher towards: (1) the range of practices in the reflexive dance between researchers, the phenomenon and algorithms; (2) the iterative development of, layering of and interaction between actors, tools and models; (3) the synthesis of new representations; and (4) the comparisons and dialogues that emerge through, and between, all these practices. To corroborate our case with a popular illustrative example, we consider the range of practices and decisions involved when applying 'topic modelling'.

14.2.3 An Illustrative Case of Topic Modelling

Qualitative (and quantitative) researchers are increasingly relying on topic-modelling algorithms to help them analyze large collections of documents and identify latent dimensions or 'topics' along which those documents can be described (Hannigan et al., 2019). Topic models are 'models for uncovering the underlying semantic structure of a document collection' (Blei and Lafferty, 2009: 71). Although topic-modelling algorithms are starting to attract interest for their ability to 'automate text analysis' and thereby 'mitigate the cost of manual categorization' (Bao and Datta, 2014: 1373), only a few of the studies that rely on these techniques are actually transparent about the intensive practices, critical choices, opportunities for meaning-creation, and risks of introducing and reinforcing bias at each of the research stages (Günther and Joshi, 2020).

Most qualitative research includes the three stages of research design, data collection and data analysis (Shadish et al., 2002; Dubé and Paré, 2003), during which researchers typically try to facilitate transparency and create meaning while minimizing opacity and bias. In the case of techniques like topic modelling, two additional research stages may be added (although we note that all phases are constitutive of one another and part of the overall research process). The first is *data preparation* (Schmiedel et al., 2019). Although not recognized as a distinct phase in extant literature on traditional qualitative research methods, researchers are typically required to undertake a range of different pre-processing steps before data can effectively be used as input to any algorithm (see Hickman et al., 2022 for various pre-processing steps in text mining). Moreover, the output of running such an algorithm on the (pre-) processed data is generally a *model* that needs to be validated and interpreted (Hannigan et al., 2019; Schmiedel et al., 2019) in terms of whether it accurately represents (and predicts) the phenomenon of interest. Thus, *model validation and interpretation* can be considered a final and additional research stage that conceptually comes after the data-analysis phase.

Applying topic modelling in qualitative research involves a range of different practices and choices in each of the stages of research design, data collection, data preparation, data analysis, and model validation and interpretation. In the next few paragraphs, we summarize these practices and choices and explain how they present opportunities for creating transparent meaning and introducing and reinforcing bias. By doing so, we hope to illustrate

that applications of machine learning and sophisticated algorithms in qualitative research are not straightforward. Rather, knowledge emerges through the reflexive dance between researchers, algorithms, tools and the phenomenon itself; a recursive balancing act between creating meaning and unpacking bias must be achieved at each stage. A summary of this account is presented in Figure 14.1.

14.2.3.1 Research Design

Applying algorithmic intelligence in research involves a hierarchy of decisions at the *research design stage*. Each of these decisions presents opportunities for transparent meaning creation, as well as opacity and bias. First, relying on algorithms to achieve a given research objective is itself a conscious choice that is very likely to be informed by a theoretical model of the problem or cultural phenomenon. The assumption must be that the phenomenon of interest can accurately be captured through data (e.g., textual data) and that any pattern in those data as captured by algorithms also represents a meaningful pattern occurring in 'the real world' (Jones, 2019). Then there are many different algorithms from which researchers can choose, each bearing its own underlying

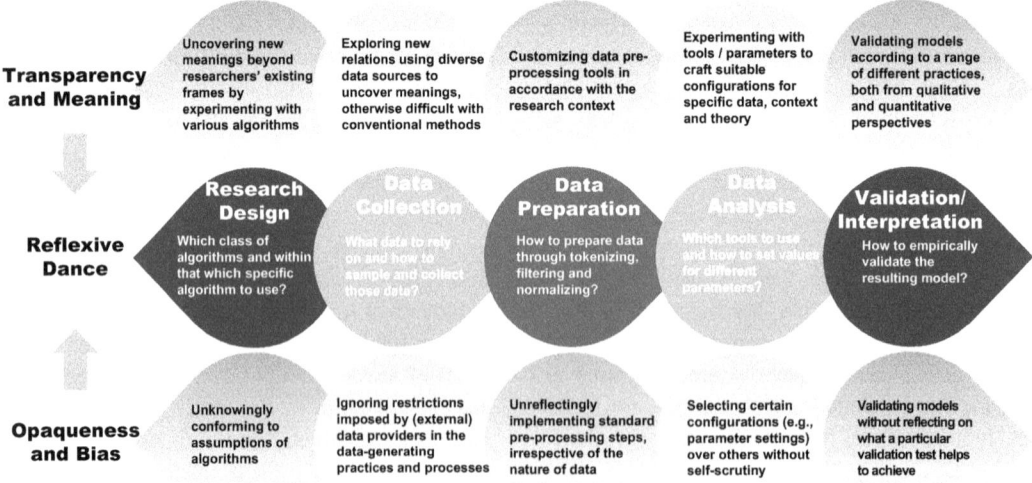

Figure 14.1 A reflexive dance of meaning and bias across the stages of algorithmic qualitative research

assumptions. For example, researchers may rely on supervised or unsupervised learning approaches, and may choose between applying topic modelling or other text-mining algorithms. While supervised approaches often start from a theoretical framework and are designed to automatically code data in line with existing theories, unsupervised approaches are intended to uncover meanings that go beyond existing theories, based on a process of exploration (Brynjolfsson and McAfee, 2017). Once a researcher has decided to rely on unsupervised topic modelling techniques to analyze documents (for example), there are still many different algorithms that (s)he could consider as candidates to perform the actual analyses, such as Latent Semantic Analysis (LSA), Latent Dirichlet Allocation (LDA), Nonnegative Matrix Factorization (NMF) and Structural Topic Models (STM). Each of these algorithms has its own limitations, strengths and presumptions (see, e.g., Berry et al., 2007; Sidorova et al., 2008; Chang et al., 2009; Blei, 2012; Evangelopoulos et al., 2012; Roberts et al., 2013; Belford et al., 2018).

Explaining – or glossing over – choices made in the research design phase can also present opportunities for introducing transparency – or opaqueness – to the research. On the one hand, researchers can use algorithms to complement traditional approaches and gain new insights that reach beyond pre-existing frames of reference by analyzing large quantities of data from many different sources (Hannigan et al., 2019; Schmiedel et al., 2019). In doing so, they can exploit the opportunity to choose from a range of different algorithms to transparently identify, explain and compare different meanings in their specific research context. For instance, researchers can experiment with several supervised and unsupervised learning algorithms to identify various patterns that might be helpful in identifying different meanings, if they are cognizant about the underlying assumptions of those algorithms.

On the other hand, if left uninterrogated and unexplained, the choices made in the research design phase are also opportunities for opaqueness and bias. This is because assumptions embedded within the algorithms can be unknowingly incorporated into the research. For example,

the Bag-of-words assumption that applies to many topic-modelling algorithms suggests that the order of words in a text does not matter (Blei, 2012). Therefore, some researchers may anticipate and affirm that the effect of the order of the words in their documents is negligible and will not affect their research outcomes and conclusions. Others may consider this assumption problematic and put efforts into finding or developing alternative algorithms (e.g., Bao and Datta, 2014[1]). By adopting certain algorithms, researchers already make inferences about their data and favour certain meanings over others. This becomes a problem when the researcher is not aware of the assumptions associated with the adopted algorithm(s) or how specific choices in the research design may affect the results. Thus, it is extremely important that researchers unpack *how* algorithms create meaning, how the underlying assumptions do or do not align with the specific research context, and what types of algorithm-derived meaning will be favoured over others.

14.2.3.2 Data Collection

Relying on algorithmic intelligence requires researchers to make a range of idiosyncratic decisions in the *data collection stage* that are consequential for the inferences drawn from the analysis. The choice of data source and sampling strategy is one crucial decision that may affect how the phenomenon is represented and understood.

Researchers may benefit from the increased access to user-generated data that are continuously being created beyond the boundaries of academia, such as on social media platforms and forums. Scholars have increasingly highlighted the opportunities of such 'big data' for research and how various data sources may, if analyzed well, help in the creation of meaning. For example, George and colleagues have highlighted how unstructured textual data, such as articles, blogs and emails, may

[1] Please note that some of the examples used in the chapter are from the articles which are more quantitatively oriented. We have used such examples of practices from quantitatively oriented articles when they are equally applicable to qualitatively oriented studies.

have embedded in them information on relationships that 'are typically unavailable in firm-level datasets that allow representative statistical inference' (George et al., 2014: 325). Similarly, Goes has suggested that the '[b]arriers between online and offline representations of human behavior are disappearing fast' and that access to data from many different sources has significant implications for researchers in a range of different disciplines (Goes, 2014: vii).

Despite the potential benefits of relying on big data in research, the processes of creating and collecting the data also present many opportunities for reinforcing opaqueness and bias. Specifically, it may be unclear how data 'came to be' and to what extent they may (or may not) reflect a 'particular way of understanding the world' (see Jones, 2019: 6). Jones reinforces Kitchin (2014) by warning us that data are always 'a sample of the reality' they describe and that the assumption of 'n = all' does not always hold in practice (2019: 13). This has significant implications in the context of academic research, where it is extremely important to gain access to a representative sample (Abbasi et al., 2016). External data providers often offer only limited access to researchers. As a result, researchers may be analyzing a sample of data whose selection criteria have been decided by the external data providers and inscribed in the biographies of their algorithmic tools, which sometimes remain hidden from the researchers (Madsen, 2015). For instance, Bapna et al. (2019) have performed topic modelling on Facebook posts and illustrated the potential limitations of relying on platform-enabled application programming interfaces (APIs): 'For some firms, we were not able to gather posts all the way back to the date the firm joined Facebook, possibly because of restricted access settings by some firms, or limits set by Facebook on historic data' (2019: 435). Similarly, researchers who rely on web crawlers may face limitations and risk inconsistencies in the data due to restrictions imposed by the websites and platforms.

Researchers thus face a responsibility to adopt a somewhat critical stance to ensure that their sample is representative of the phenomenon under study, especially when data originate from external data sources and it is not clear how these data came to

be. In some cases, researchers may have to intervene and go out of their way to identify different perspectives of the same phenomenon (e.g., Lash and Zhao, 2016; Samtani et al., 2017) by combining a range of data-collection approaches to create a more holistic picture (e.g., by collecting data through APIs as well as web crawlers) or triangulating and comparing data about the same phenomenon from multiple sources (e.g., analyzing data from Facebook and Twitter, as opposed to only using one platform).

14.2.3.3 Data Preparation

Given the unstructured nature of most (textual) data sources, one of the most critical steps in applying algorithmic intelligence is *preparing the data* and organizing them – with the help of a host of *facilitating algorithms* – into a format that the *main algorithm* can read (Schmiedel et al., 2019). In the case of topic modelling, researchers typically engage in practices of *tokenizing, filtering* and *normalizing* terms using various algorithmic tools to prepare the data (Evangelopoulos et al., 2012; Hannigan et al., 2019; Schmiedel et al., 2019). First, most topic models require a 'document term matrix' as input data, which specifies how many times a specific word or term occurs in a specific document. A researcher applying topic modelling thus needs to decide on what actually counts as a 'term' during a process of *tokenizing*. Second, researchers applying topic modelling may decide that not all terms are equally relevant or meaningful and subsequently remove certain terms through a process of *filtering*. For example, terms such as 'the' and 'be' are frequently occurring words that often carry little actual meaning (also known as 'stop words'), and thus researchers tend to remove them (Hannigan et al., 2019). While filtering, some researchers specifically exclude additional stop words that are not included in default stop word lists but still represent 'noise' (e.g., Dong et al., 2018), demote common and high-frequency words because they are unlikely to carry any distinct meaning (e.g., Evangelopoulos, 2016), and remove extremely rare and infrequent phrases because they may be considered insignificant (e.g., Chen et al., 2019). Finally, researchers may put effort into *normalizing* terms by ensuring that similar words 'do not appear separately in the per topic word distributions' (Schmiedel et al., 2019: 949). Common forms of normalization include stemming, or 'stripping off any affixes' of words while keeping the stem, and lemmatization, which (as opposed to stemming) always normalizes words to a *valid* base form (Bird et al., 2009: 107). Some additional strategies that researchers might adopt to prepare data include converting terms into lowercase, standardizing abbreviations and their full counterparts (e.g., BI and 'Business Intelligence') and combining frequently occurring combinations of words or *n-grams* that reflect a distinct concept (e.g., 'machine learning' and 'return on investment'; Bird et al., 2009; Hannigan et al., 2019; Schmiedel et al., 2019).

Researchers have many opportunities both to create transparent meaning and to introduce opaqueness and bias while engaging in tokenizing, filtering and normalizing. On the one hand, researchers may consider decision points as opportunities to overcome some of the limitations associated with algorithm-derived meaning and to introduce a larger focus on interpretation-derived meaning. As such, the key questions underlying many of these practices are which data elements carry meaning and which data elements represent noise that might limit the interpretability and potentially even the validity of the algorithmic results. The answers to these questions depend on the (researchers' understanding of the) phenomenon, the researchers' mindset, the nature of the data, the type of algorithms used and the kinds of conclusions that will be drawn from the results. For example, researchers may filter terms because they want to limit any noise in the resulting topics or because they are concerned with improving the validity of the model and the interpretability of the results (e.g., Huang et al., 2018). Even in traditional qualitative research methods, researchers invariably engage in the processes of filtering and selecting relevant data, but many of those choices are made and revised subconsciously in an iterative manner. When engaging with algorithmic approaches, researchers are encouraged to make these decisions before running the algorithm, while still being mindful and constantly reflecting on the consequences of their decisions.

However, practices of tokenizing, filtering and normalizing may become problematic when researchers forego critical reflection on their implications. Any decision in the data preparation phase may potentially affect the results, especially in the case of topic modelling algorithms that are relatively sensitive to the nature of the data and the order in which data are fed into the algorithm (e.g., Agrawal et al., 2018). Thus, it is first extremely important that researchers are aware of how each of their choices might reflect their pre-existing assumptions; and, second, that researchers are also transparent about the steps they performed in the process of creating meaning and the assumptions underlying these steps. For example, if researchers filtered 'non-meaningful' stop words or noise, then they should clearly establish why they believe that the terms do not carry meaning within their specific research context and how, in their opinion, this has allowed the algorithm to reflect an acceptable take on reality.

Some researchers who adopt topic modelling may choose to deliberately forgo performing any pre-processing steps because they feel that they do not possess the necessary domain knowledge to make informed choices (e.g., Shi et al., 2017) or because they do not wish to introduce any bias (e.g., Lee et al., 2016). However, we contend that 'no intervention' does not imply 'no bias'. As argued previously, different meanings and opaque biases are often already embedded in data, and algorithms themselves can also add additional algorithm-induced meanings. Thus, researchers play a crucial role in identifying different assumptions within the data and algorithms and may be forced to closely engage with the domain and experiment with different pre-processing steps.

14.2.3.4 Data Analysis

Implementing an algorithm to conduct *data analysis* is not a straightforward task and, even after settling on a particular algorithm, researchers still need to make decisions about the tools and model parameters that may affect the results. First, researchers need to decide which tools (e.g., programming languages and packages) they are going to use; these tools may differ in their assumptions and underlying implementations (e.g., how the model is optimized after each iteration). Second, researchers need to decide how to set the *input parameters* that represent the primary constants and initialization settings of the algorithm. In the case of topic modelling, researchers need to decide on the *number of topics* as a crucial input parameter (Hannigan et al., 2019). Nonetheless, '[h]ow to determine the appropriate number of topics is an area of ongoing research and debate' (Giorgi and Weber, 2015: 350) because a 'number of topics too small might generate sets of words that are too general, and thus not useful; too many topics might, on the other hand, extract topics that are very specific to specific documents, and thus not useful to understand [ing] general trends' (Giorgi et al., 2019: 825).

In addition to generic input parameters, researchers also need to consider parameters that are specific to the chosen algorithm. For example, in the case of LDA, researchers must determine the values of hyperparameters that represent assumptions regarding how many topics are typically contained in one document and how many words are typically associated with one topic (Binkley et al., 2014). The choice of such parameters in topic modelling and similar machine-learning algorithms is crucial as the model outputs of these algorithms are very sensitive to different (and even similar) parameter configurations (Belford et al., 2018). Researchers will likely experiment with different configurations of parameters, with each run using a different configuration leading to a different model.

Accordingly, researchers who apply topic modelling and other sophisticated algorithms need to devise ways to appraise tools, choose values for their parameter settings and evaluate intermediate models based on a number of criteria. These choices and the associated criteria are likely to be informed by the researcher's theoretical framework, understanding of the phenomena under study, epistemological convictions and knowledge of the assumptions underlying the chosen algorithm. For example, while some researchers rely on computational measures (facilitating

algorithms), such as perplexity score to decide on the optimal configuration of parameters (e.g., the number of topics and hyperparameters), other researchers may choose to focus more on whether the resulting topics intuitively make sense to human observers (Hannigan et al., 2019). Interestingly, the model with the highest perplexity score is not always the most meaningful, semantically (as suggested by Chang et al., 2009). Some researchers continuously reflect on both algorithm-derived meanings and interpretation-derived meanings in the data analysis phase. These crucial decision points represent opportunities to explore different meanings, identify potential biases (by experimenting with different configurations of parameters and potentially uncovering new meanings), and validate the extent to which the model and its results are meaningful and make sense within the specific research context.

At the same time, the decision points in the data analysis phase are also opportunities for opaqueness and bias if researchers do not scrutinize the tools, configurations, criteria and process of experimentation that have led to the final outcome. For example, while different parameter configurations may lead to distinct models, researchers may unreflectively pick (default) configurations without considering the consequences for the model and research outcomes. Furthermore, researchers relying on quantitative measures such as perplexity score may unintentionally treat a model's predictive capability as potentially more important than its qualitative interpretability (Chang et al., 2009). While it is normal to make such assumptions as part of knowledge building, this becomes problematic when the researcher is unaware of or not *transparent* about the assumptions that have been made. By selecting certain tools, configurations and models over others, researchers inevitably introduce their own *selection-bias*, which warrants self-scrutiny.

The example of topic modelling suggests that the analysis phase is emblematic of the reflexive dance between the researchers, their understanding of the phenomenon and the algorithm, and that the resulting 'model' is merely a creative artifact that emerges as a result of this dance attempting to create meaning and unpack biases. In this phase, it is crucial that researchers understand and critically reflect on all types of meaning: how the algorithm introduces algorithm-derived meaning; how the researcher may be introducing interpretation-derived meaning; and how the selection process causes the researcher to select certain meanings over others.

14.2.3.5 Model Validation and Interpretation

As described at the beginning of this section, the research phase of *model validation and interpretation* is often not treated as a distinct research phase in the extant literature. However, we treat it as a distinct phase for the purposes of this chapter owing to its important role in helping researchers to reflect on the choices they make throughout a study and their necessary interaction with algorithms. Model validation gives researchers a chance to identify, acknowledge and reflect on potential biases they may have absorbed or ignored in earlier stages. In other words, it is an opportunity for researchers to empirically validate the choices they made in the preceding phases. Researchers can follow various strategies to validate their final topic models, including evaluation of the semantic quality of topic models, sensitivity analysis, comparison with other methods and comparison with external information. We briefly describe each of these strategies while simultaneously reflecting on how they present opportunities for transparency and meaning, as well as for opaqueness and bias.

First, researchers can validate the semantic quality of their topic models (Hannigan et al., 2019) by ascertaining the quality of topics and examining topic-document allocations. Scholars typically ascertain the quality of topics by qualitatively examining the top ten to thirty words associated with a topic to see if the topics make sense and assigning a label to them. For instance, Kaplan and Vakili (2015) follow this labelling approach to validate the usefulness of topics and to describe distinct concepts with the help of human experts. This practice also helps qualitative researchers assign interpretation-derived meaning to their algorithmic outputs and determine whether the topics that the dimensions signify make sense and are

relevant to answering the research question (Schmiedel et al., 2019).

A complementary approach to validating the semantic quality of topic models involves examining the *topic-document allocation*. Whereas evaluating topic quality demonstrates if the topics make sense on their own, validation of topic-document allocation is a means of ascertaining if the topics generated from the model actually represent the themes in the original documents from which the topics were initially generated (e.g., Bao and Datta, 2014). These practices are enacted by both quantitative and qualitative researchers to infuse, identify and evaluate interpretation-derived meaning. Paradoxically, this practice of validation could also become an occasion for introducing opaqueness and bias if, for example, researchers selectively analyze only a few documents to confirm their assumptions.

Moreover, researchers can validate their topic models by performing sensitivity analyses, which establish the sensitivity of the topic model output to choices made during data collection and analysis. Researchers may assess sensitivity to different parameter values such as the number of topics (e.g., Shi et al., 2016; Haans, 2019; Yue et al., 2019), sensitivity to the data themselves through different data samples (e.g., Gong et al., 2018; Geva et al., 2019), or even sensitivity to the chosen algorithm by comparing results with other competing algorithms (e.g., Bao and Datta, 2014; Larsen and Bong, 2016). Although the purpose of performing sensitivity tests is to ensure that the output produced by the topic model cannot be attributed to one specific choice only, qualitative researchers may also embrace model variety and explore a range of different meanings (Evangelopoulos et al., 2012), empirically validate algorithmic assumptions and ascertain whether the most stable model reflects an acceptable reality. While performing sensitivity analyses allows researchers greater confidence in interpreting the results and critically reflecting on their choices, they still must be clear about their intentions in performing sensitivity analyses and their criteria for evaluating the results.

Researchers can also validate their topic models by performing *empirical* comparisons through a range of other methods and measures. Such validation practices may require researchers to rely on computational measures to compare topic model outputs with other text-mining methods. For instance, Nielsen and Börjeson (2019) compared their topic model outcomes with outcomes from co-word mapping and co-citation analysis. Researchers can also compare their topic model outputs with other non-text-mining approaches (e.g., Shi et al., 2016; Croidieu and Kim, 2018). Again, these tests afford researchers a chance to revisit their choice of a specific class of algorithmic approaches (e.g., topic modelling). At the same time, researchers risk opaqueness and conformity to the unknown underlying assumptions of facilitating algorithms and validation methods.

Finally, one of the most important yet least common validation approaches is to compare the topic model output with external information. The underlying logic of this approach is that the topics should co-vary with some external information that describes similar trends and phenomena (e.g., Bao and Datta, 2014). Although this practice can be helpful to validate whether the algorithm-based representation is to some extent referential of the phenomenon as per complementary sources (Hannigan et al., 2019), researchers still must be conscious of their own mental models and how these influence their sampling criteria, as well as the meanings inscribed in complementary data. In general, while researchers should be encouraged to interpret and validate algorithmic representations and models, they should also be transparent about what they consider to be acceptable validation criteria and how this may lead them to favour one 'acceptable' reality over another.

14.3 Using Algorithms to Create Transparency and Meaning

Our conceptualization of algorithmic qualitative research as a reflexive dance has several implications for researchers aiming to make use of algorithms in qualitative research. We therefore propose several strategies that can help researchers in the creation of transparency and meaning and avoiding opacity and bias; these strategies are considered canonical in qualitative research, but are less so in algorithm-based research.

14.3.1 Engaging with the Domain

Through our illustrative case study of topic modelling, we demonstrated how qualitative researchers are continuously engaged in a reflexive dance with algorithms to create meaning. However, to engage in this process, researchers must have (or develop) an understanding of what can potentially be considered a 'meaningful' decision within the specific domain and phenomenon of interest. For example, in a scenario where researchers intend to perform topic modelling to identify latent topics in a collection of hospital reviews (Salge et al., 2022), researchers should be knowledgeable enough about the domain of healthcare and the context surrounding the reviews to be able to make inferences about which terms carry meaning or which configurations of parameters lead to meaningful topics. Building on Jones (2019), we argue that algorithmic models are *not* independent of the 'real world' and that researchers need to engage with the real world to consider what counts as 'meaningful' and to eventually develop algorithmic representations that reflect an acceptable take on reality. We therefore offer the following specific recommendations for engaging with the domain to create transparency and meaning in algorithmic qualitative research.

We encourage researchers to actively engage in an exploration phase to become familiar with existing theories, the specific domain context and the phenomenon of interest – as one might do in case studies (Yin, 1981; Eisenhardt, 1989) – while also remaining closely connected to the given domain in each subsequent research phase (Klein and Meyers, 1999). Such an exploration phase should include consideration of existing conceptualizations and theories that have traditionally been deployed to explain the phenomenon of interest. While some researchers have warned that the rise in data analytics may lead to the 'end of theory' (Anderson, 2008, in Abbasi et al., 2016), our illustration supports the view that existing ideas and theories are intrinsically intertwined with the data, algorithms and process of algorithmic qualitative research. As illustrated in Figure 14.1, even 'unsupervised' algorithmic approaches such as topic modelling still warrant a careful balancing act between introducing meaning and unpacking potential bias. As such, researchers must be aware of existing theories and critically reflect on how these may be infused into the data, algorithms and creative artifacts that they are relying on to interpret the phenomenon, but researchers must also remain open to unforeseen patterns (Hannigan et al., 2019).

Researchers should also take care to embed themselves into the social context that they are studying and familiarize themselves with the domain of interest (Barrett and Oborn, 2018; Avgerou, 2019), while also actively engaging with the data and algorithms. Referring to the previous example of applying topic modelling to hospital reviews, researchers may try to reach out to healthcare experts and doctors, and even to people who have posted reviews to become acquainted with potentially relevant concepts and the vocabulary used to describe certain practices or ideas. This engagement will enable the discovery of 'meaning' in the reflexive dance between the researcher and their algorithmic co-researchers. Failure to engage with the domain and with relevant stakeholders risks discarding certain topics and insights as meaningless that in practice may indeed be meaningful.

Another tactic that researchers might adopt to further engage with the domain is to include domain experts in *different phases* of the research. In the case of topic modelling, domain experts may be included in: (1) the research design phase to help researchers decide on which algorithmic assumptions might hold true in reality; (2) the data collection stage to gain insights into how the data came to be (Jones, 2019); (3) the data preparation phases to help researchers decide which data elements represent noise versus meaning; (4) the analysis phase to help researchers put choices and intermediary findings into context and to allow experimentation with different models (e.g., Evangelopoulos et al., 2012); and (5) the final validation phase to help validate the model and the researchers' take on reality (e.g., Kaplan and Vakili, 2015).

14.3.2 Considering a Multi-Disciplinary Approach

We have explored the importance of acknowledging researcher-infused meaning and of engaging with the domain. Given that researchers must still pay attention to algorithm-derived meanings that may be enforced by certain (facilitating) algorithms, we advocate a multi-disciplinary approach. Having conceptualized algorithms as 'co-researchers' in the practice of algorithmic qualitative research, we emphasize that reflecting on algorithm-derived meaning is important because infused meanings can be subtle and often opaque to the researchers adopting the algorithms.

One way to facilitate mindfulness of possible algorithm-derived meanings is by working in multi-disciplinary collaborative research projects. For example, when applying topic modelling, qualitative researchers can collaborate with computer scientists, statisticians and mathematicians who have specific expertise in algorithmic approaches. While qualitative researchers may be able to offer rigorous engagement with the domain, computer scientists, statisticians and mathematicians may be able to offer rigorous engagement with the algorithms and an understanding of the range of different algorithms (and their assumptions) from which the researchers can select. Notably, the goal of collaborating should not be to divide tasks or let technical experts alone complete the algorithmic analysis. While different researchers may each take the lead in their area of expertise, they should also closely collaborate in a process of co-creating knowledge (e.g., Tashakkori and Creswell, 2007; Barrett and Oborn, 2018). This implies that those researchers who are more focused on implementing algorithms will need to be familiar with the domain, and those who are focused on interpreting the qualitative value of models and the meaning of the results must have sufficient knowledge about the nature of the algorithm and its underlying assumptions.

14.3.3 Adopting Complementary Methods

To maintain control of the meaning being derived through algorithmic tools, researchers may consider complementing algorithmic approaches with insights gained via other qualitative research methods (e.g., Karanović et al., 2020; Salge et al., 2022).

Previously, we explained how reaching out to domain experts can help researchers to become engaged with the domain. To effectively capture relevant meanings expressed by domain experts, researchers may rely on semi-structured interviews and focus groups, which allow multiple perspectives to be captured (Patton, 2002; Tracy, 2013). Researchers can additionally adopt ethnographic methods to become fully immersed in the respective social (and online) contexts (Van Maanen, 2011; Jarzabkowski et al., 2014), as well as to critically reflect on the different types of meaning inscribed in the data and algorithms (Christin, 2020). These approaches enable researchers to gain insights that can help inform 'meaningful' decisions while also preventing opaqueness and bias.

Qualitative methods can benefit researchers in each of the research phases for applying algorithms to understand qualitative phenomena. For example, in the data collection phase, researchers should attempt to understand the contextual realities of those who have created the data and can do so by collecting and reviewing qualitative documentation or interviewing the individuals or organizations responsible for creating the data (Schultze and Avital, 2011; Karanović et al., 2020). More ambitious researchers may fully immerse themselves in the contextual reality from which the data arise (Van Maanen and De Rond, 2017). In the data preparation phase, researchers may first qualitatively code data elements to familiarize themselves with relevant and meaningful jargon and concepts, which will subsequently help them to discern meaningful data from noise. In the data analysis phase, researchers may rely on methods that combine qualitative (human) evaluation with algorithmic measures, while experimenting with different configurations to create a model that reflects an acceptable take on reality (see Chang et al., 2009). Similarly, researchers can combine algorithmic approaches with traditional qualitative methods such as historical case study methods (e.g., Giorgi et al., 2019), thereby adopting a concurrent triangulation strategy (Creswell, 2003).

Adopting complementary methods can be especially useful in the model validation and interpretation phase. For example, researchers may qualitatively and collaboratively code the top terms and documents associated with certain topics and consider intercoder reliability measures to identify different meanings and trigger discussions about emerging themes and patterns; they might also present the resulting themes, labels and patterns to an expert audience and organize focused sessions to determine if the results are representative of the phenomenon (e.g., Kaplan and Vakili, 2015; Hannigan et al., 2019). Additionally, one important opportunity for researchers to interpret and evaluate a model is to validate their model outputs by comparing them to external information or trends (Bao and Datta, 2014; Hannigan et al., 2019). In sum, in each of the research phases, researchers can adopt a range of qualitative and ethnographic methods to balance between transparently creating 'meaning' and preventing opaqueness and bias.

14.4 Conclusion

Qualitative researchers are increasingly employing machine-learning algorithms as an integral part of their methodology. Although the nature of the technologies employed in research has continuously evolved since Father Busa's collaboration with IBM in 1949, the vignette is still noteworthy today and is probably the first example of a qualitative researcher engaging deeply and reflexively with the inherent tension between the *materiality of data* (words and symbols in his case as well as ours) *manipulated by the computer*, and the possible *meanings of the data* that emerge as *interpreted by the researcher* when the data are radically transformed, reordered, disassembled and reassembled: 'Working on physical entities which the philologist uses and classifies, the computer has served above all to demarcate the borders between the graphic and the semantic' (Busa, 1990: 339).

Busa's comment shows a scrupulous separation of symbols and meaning (computers manipulate material symbols; humans attribute meanings to the patterns thus formed). However, there is a close interrelationship: as Jones (2016: 157) established, while borders between the graphic and the semantic – symbols and meaning – undoubtedly exist and should be recognized, Busa's practice was a dynamic and iterative partnership with the computer within a system of feedback and feedforward loops. Both the graphic and semantic emerge from this partnership having been reciprocally altered – a close intertwining that Busa recognized, harbouring no illusions of scientific objectivity.

Applying a Heideggerian framework to our acknowledgement of this reciprocal alteration between the graphic and semantic, we have focused here on the essential methodological challenge that arises in this recursive algorithm-researcher partnership, namely the need for mindful acknowledgement and exposure of the various points in the partnership at which one may have shaped the other. Accordingly, we have identified five phases of algorithmic qualitative research to discuss examples of how the creative meaning-making – of algorithm-derived meaning, interpretation-derived meaning and selection-derived meaning – inherent in each stage of the partnership can be made transparent to the reader using topic modelling. What's more, we have also highlighted the dangers of glossing over or disregarding such meaning-making, which results in problematic opacity and bias. That such bias is more likely to go unacknowledged within a research community that remains inclined to attribute algorithms with objectivity is concerning. We hope that our practice-based interrogation of qualitative researchers' use of algorithms may contribute towards challenging assumptions of algorithmic objectivity and provide reflexivity in critically interrogating algorithmic qualitative research practices.

References

Abbasi, A., Sarker, S. and Chiang, R. (2016). Big data research in information systems: Toward an inclusive research agenda. *Journal of the Association for Information Systems*, 17(2), i–xxxii.

Agrawal, A., Fu, W. and Menzies, T. (2018). What is wrong with topic modeling? And how to fix it using search-based software engineering. *Information and Software Technology*, 98, 74–88.

Anderson, C. (2008). The end of theory: The data deluge makes the scientific method obsolete. *Wired*, www.wired.com/2008/06/pb-theory/.

Avgerou, C. (2019). Contextual explanation: Alternative approaches and persistent challenges. *MIS Quarterly*, 43(3), 977–1006.

Bao, Y. and Datta, A. (2014). Simultaneously discovering and quantifying risk types from textual risk disclosures. *Management Science*, 60(6), 1371–1391.

Bapna, S., Benner, M. J. and Qiu, L. (2019). Nurturing online communities: An empirical investigation. *MIS Quarterly*, 43(2), 425–452.

Barthes, R. (1972). *The Structuralist Activity: Critical Essays*. Evanston, IL: Northwestern University Press.

Barrett, M. and Oborn, E. (2018). Bridging the research-practice divide: Harnessing expertise collaboration in making a wider set of contributions. *Information and Organization*, 28(1), 44–51.

Belford, M., Mac Namee, B. and Greene, D. (2018). Stability of topic modeling via matrix factorization. *Expert Systems with Applications*, 91, 159–169.

Berry, M. W., Browne, M., Langville, A. N., Pauca, B. P. and Plemmons, R. J. (2007). Algorithms and applications for approximate nonnegative matrix factorization. *Computational Statistics & Data Analytics*, 52(1), 155–173.

Binkley, D., Heinz, D., Lawrie, D. and Overfelt, J. (2014). Understanding LDA in source code analysis. Proceedings of the International Conference on Program Comprehension, Hyderabad, India.

Bird, S., Klein, E. and Loper, E. (2009). *Natural Language Processing with Python: Analyzing Text with the Natural Language Toolkit*. Sebastopol, CA: O'Reilly Media, Inc.

Blei, D. M. (2012). Probabilistic topic models. *Communications of the ACM*, 55(4), 77–84.

Blei, D. M. and Lafferty, J. D. (2009). Topic models. In A. N. Srivastava and M. Sahami (eds), *Text Mining: Classification, Clustering, and Applications*. London: Chapman & Hall, pp. 71–94.

Brynjolfsson, E. and McAfee, A. (2017). The business of artificial intelligence. *Harvard Business Review*, 7, 1–20.

Busa, R. (1990). Informatics and the new philology. *Computers and the Humanities*, 24(5–6), 339–343.

Chang, J., Gerrish, S., Wang, C., Boyd-Graber, J. L. and Blei, D. M. (2009). Reading tea leaves: How humans interpret topic models. *Advances in Neural Information Processing Systems*, 22, 288–296.

Chen, L., Baird, A. and Straub, D. W. (2019). An analysis of the evolving intellectual structure of health information systems research in the information systems discipline. *Journal of the Association for Information Systems*, 20(8), 1023–1074.

Christin, A. (2020). Algorithmic ethnography, during and after COVID-19. *Communication and the Public*, 5(3–4), 108–111.

Creswell, J. (2003). *Research Design: Qualitative, Quantitative, and Mixed Methods Approaches*, 2nd edition. Los Angeles, CA: Sage.

Croidieu, G. and Kim, P. H. (2018). Labor of love: Amateurs and lay-expertise legitimation in the early U.S. radio field. *Administrative Science Quarterly*, 63(1), 1–42.

Dong, W., Liao, S. and Zhang, Z. (2018). Leveraging financial social media data for corporate fraud detection. *Journal of Management Information Systems*, 35(2), 461–487.

Dreyfus, H. (1993). *What Computers Still Can't Do: A Critique of Artificial Reason*, 2nd edition. Cambridge, MA: MIT Press.

Dubé, L. and Paré, G. (2003). Rigor in information systems positivist case research: Current practices, trends, and recommendations. *MIS Quarterly*, 27(4), 597–636.

Dwivedi, Y. K., Hughes, L., Ismagilova, E., Aarts, G., Coombs, C., Crick, T. et al. (2021). Artificial intelligence (AI): Multidisciplinary perspectives on emerging challenges, opportunities, and agenda for research, practice and policy. *International Journal of Information Management*, 57, 1–47.

Eisenhardt, K. M. (1989). Building theories from case study research. *Academy of Management Review*, 14(4), 532–550.

Evangelopoulos, N. (2016). Thematic orientation of the ISJ within a semantic space of IS research. *Information Systems Journal*, 26(1), 39–46.

Evangelopoulos, N., Zhang, X. and Prybutok, V. R. (2012). Latent semantic analysis: five methodological recommendations. *European Journal of Information Systems*, 21(1), 70–86.

Galdas, P. (2017). Revisiting bias in qualitative research: Reflections on its relationship with funding and impact. *International Journal of Qualitative Methods*, 16(1), 1–2.

George, G., Haas, M. R. and Pentland, A. (2014). Big data and management. *Academy of Management Journal*, 57(2), 321–326.

Geva, H., Oestreicher-Singer, G. and Saar-Tsechansky, M. (2019). Using retweets when shaping our online persona: Topic modeling approach. *MIS Quarterly*, 43(2), 501–524.

Giorgi, S. and Weber, K. (2015). Marks of distinction: Framing and audience appreciation in the context of investment advice. *Administrative Science Quarterly*, 60(2), 333–367.

Giorgi, S., Maoret, M. and Zajac, E. J. (2019). On the relationship between firms and their legal environment: The role of cultural consonance. *Organization Science*, 30(4), 803–830.

Glaser, V. L., Pollock, N. and D'Adderio, L. (2021). The biography of an algorithm: Performing algorithmic technologies in organizations. *Organization Theory*, 2(2), 1–27.

Goes, P. B. (2014). Editor's comments: Big data and IS research. *MIS Quarterly*, 38(3), iii–viii.

Gong, J., Abhishek, V. and Li, B. (2018). Examining the impact of keyword ambiguity on search advertising performance: A topic model approach. *MIS Quarterly*, 42(3), 805–829.

Günther, W. and Joshi, M. (2020). Algorithmic intelligence in research: Prevalent topic modeling practices and implications for rigor in IS and management research. International Conference on Information Systems, virtual conference.

Haans, R. F. (2019). What's the value of being different when everyone is? The effects of distinctiveness on performance in homogeneous versus heterogeneous categories. *Strategic Management Journal*, 40(1), 3–27.

Hannigan, T., Haans, R. F., Vakili, K., Tchalian, H., Glaser, V., Wang, M. et al. (2019). Topic modeling in management research: Rendering new theory from textual data. *Academy of Management Annals*, 13(2), 586–632.

Heidegger, M. (1962). *Being and Time*. Oxford, UK and Cambridge, MA: Blackwell.

Heidegger, M. (1977). The question concerning technology. In D. F. Krell (ed.), *Basic Writings*. New York, NY: HarperCollins, pp. 213–238.

Hickman, L., Thapa, S., Tay, L., Cao, M. and Srinivasan, P. (2022). Text preprocessing for text mining in organizational research: Review and recommendations. *Organizational Research Methods*, 25(1), 114–146.

Huang, A. H., Lehavy, R., Zang, A. Y. and Zheng, R. (2018). Analyst information discovery and interpretation roles: A topic modeling approach. *Management Science*, 64(6), 2833–2855.

Introna, L. and Ilharco, F. (2011). Phenomenology, screens, and screenness: Returning to the world itself. In R. D. Galliers and W. Currie (eds), *The Oxford Handbook of Management Information Systems: Critical Perspectives and New Directions*. Oxford: Oxford University Press.

Jarzabkowski, P., Bednarek, R. and Lê, J. K. (2014). Producing persuasive findings: Demystifying ethnographic textwork in strategy and organization research, *Strategic Organization*, 12(4), 274–287.

Jones, M. (2019). What we talk about when we talk about (big) data. *Journal of Strategic Information Systems*, 28(1), 3–16.

Jones, S. (2016). *Roberto Busa, S. J., and the Emergence of Humanities Computing: The Priest and the Punched Cards*. London: Routledge.

Kaplan, S. and Vakili, K. (2015). The double-edged sword of recombination in breakthrough innovation. *Strategic Management Journal*, 36(10), 1435–1457.

Karanović, J., Berends, H. and Engel, Y. (2020). Regulated dependence: Platform workers' responses to new forms of organizing. *Journal of Management Studies*, 58(4), 1070–1106.

Kitchin, R. (2014). Big data, new epistemologies and paradigm shifts. *Big Data Society*, 1(1), 1–12.

Klein, H. K. and Myers, M. D. (1999). A set of principles for conducting and evaluating interpretive field studies in information systems. *MIS Quarterly*, 23(1), 67–93.

Larsen, K. R. and Bong, C. H. (2016). A tool for addressing construct identity in literature reviews and meta-analyses. *MIS Quarterly*, 40(3), 529–551.

Lash, M. T. and Zhao, K. (2016). Early predictions of movie success: The who, what, and when of profitability. *Journal of Management Information Systems*, 33(3), 874–903.

Latour, B. (1990). Technology is society made durable. *Sociological Review*, 38(Supp. 1), 103–131.

Lee, G. M., Qiu, L. and Whinston, A. B. (2016). A friend like me: Modeling network formation in a location-based social network. *Journal of Management Information Systems*, 33(4), 1008–1033.

Mackenzie, A. (2017). *Machine Learners: Archaeology of a Data Practice*. Cambridge, MA: MIT Press.

Madsen, A. K. (2015). Between technical features and analytic capabilities: Charting a relational affordance space for digital social analytics. *Big Data & Society*, 2(1), 1–15.

Manovich, L (2011). Trending: The promises and the challenges of big social data. Manovich, http://manovich.net/index.php/projects/trending-the-promises-and-the-challenges-of-big-social-data.

McCarty, W. (2003). Humanities computing, www.mccarty.org.uk/essays/McCarty,%20Humanities%20computing.pdf.

Newell, S. and Marabelli, M. (2015). Strategic opportunities (and challenges) of algorithmic decision-making: A call for action on the long-term societal effects of 'datification'. *Journal of Strategic Information Systems*, 24(1), 3–14.

Nielsen, M. W. and Börjeson, L. (2019). Gender diversity in the management field: Does it matter for research outcomes? *Research Policy*, 48(7), 1617–1632.

Pääkkönen, J. and Ylikoski, P. (2021). Humanistic interpretation and machine learning. *Synthese*, 199(1), 1461–1497.

Patton, M. Q. (2002). *Qualitative Research & Evaluation Methods*, 3rd edition. Thousand Oaks, CA: Sage.

Ramsay, S. (2011). *Reading Machines: Toward an Algorithmic criticism*. Champaign, IL: University of Illinois Press.

Ribes, D. and Jackson, S. J. (2013). Data bite man: The work of sustaining long-term study. In L. Gitelman (ed.), *'Raw Data' Is an Oxymoron*. Cambridge, MA: MIT Press, pp. 147–166.

Roberts, M. E., Stewart, B. M., Tingley, D. and Airoldi, E. M. (2013). The structural topic model and applied social science. Advances in Neural Information Processing Systems Workshop on Topic Models: Computation, Application, and Evaluation, Lake Tahoe, NV.

Rockwell, G. and Sinclair, S. (2016). *Computer-Assisted Interpretation in the Humanities*. Cambridge, MA: MIT Press.

Salge, T. O., Antons, D., Barrett, M., Kohli, R., Oborn, E. and Polykarpou, S. (2022). How IT investments help hospitals gain and sustain reputation in the media: The role of signaling and framing. *Information Systems Research*, 33(1), 110–130.

Samtani, S., Chinn, R., Chen, H. and Nunamaker Jr, J. F. (2017). Exploring emerging hacker assets and key hackers for proactive cyber threat intelligence. *Journal of Management Information Systems*, 34(4), 1023–1053.

Schmiedel, T., Müller, O. and vom Brocke, J. (2019). Topic modeling as a strategy of inquiry in organizational research: A tutorial with an application example on organizational culture. *Organizational Research Methods*, 22(4), 941–968.

Schultze, U. and Avital, M. (2011). Designing interviews to generate rich data for information systems research. *Information and Organization*, 21(1), 1–16.

Shadish, W. R., Cook, T. D. and Campbell, D. T. (2002). *Experimental and Quasi-Experimental Designs for Generalized Causal Inference*. Boston, MA: Houghton, Mifflin & Co., Vol. XXI.

Shi, Z., Lee, G. M. and Whinston, A. B. (2016). Toward a better measure of business proximity: Topic modeling for industry intelligence. *MIS Quarterly*, 40(4), 1035–1056.

Shi, D., Guan, J., Zurada, J. and Manikas, A. (2017). A data-mining approach to identification of risk factors in safety management systems. *Journal of Management Information Systems*, 34(4), 1054–1081.

Sidorova, A., Evangelopoulos, N., Valacich, J. S. and Ramakrishnan, T. (2008). Uncovering the intellectual core of the information systems discipline. *MIS Quarterly*, 32(3), 467–482.

Suchman, L. (2006). *Human-Machine Reconfigurations*. Cambridge: Cambridge University Press.

Suchman, L. (1987). *Plans and Situated Actions: The Problem of Human-Machine Communication (Learning in Doing: Social, Cognitive and Computational Perspectives)*. Cambridge: Cambridge University Press.

Tashakkori, A. and Creswell, J. W. (2007). Exploring the nature of research questions in mixed methods research. *Journal of Mixed Methods Research*, 1(3), 207–211.

Tracy, S. J. (2013). *Qualitative Research Methods: Collecting Evidence, Crafting Analysis, Communicating Impact*. Chichester, UK: Wiley-Blackwell.

Tully, J. (1994). *Philosophy in an Age of Pluralism*. Cambridge: Cambridge University Press.

Van Maanen, J. (2011). Ethnography as work: Some rules of engagement. *Journal of Management Studies*, 48(1), 218–234.

Van Maanen, J. and de Rond, M. (2017). The making of a classic ethnography: Notes on Alice Goffman's *On the Run*. *Academy of Management Review*, 42(2), 396–406.

Weber, M. (2003). *The Protestant Ethic and the Spirit of Capitalism*. New York, NY: Courier Dover.

Wendt, T. (2013). Designing for transparency and the myth of the modern interface. *Ux Magazine*, https://uxmag.com/articles/designing-for-transparency-and-the-myth-of-the-modern-interface.

Winner, M. (1999). Do artifacts have politics? In D. A. MacKenzie and J. Wajcman (eds), *The Social Shaping of Technology*, 2nd edition. London: Open University Press, pp. 28–40. (Originally printed in *Daedalus*, 109(1), winter 1980.)

Winograd, T. and Flores, F. (1986). *Understanding Computers and Cognition: A New Foundation for Design*. Norwood, NJ: Ablex.

Yin, R. K. (1981). The case study crisis: Some answers. *Administrative Science Quarterly*, 26(1), 58–65.

Yue, W. T., Wang, Q. H. and Hui, K. L. (2019). See no evil, hear no evil? Dissecting the impact of online hacker forums. *MIS Quarterly*, 43(1), 73–95.

Zammuto, R. F., Griffith, T. L., Majchrzak, A., Dougherty, D. J. and Faraj, S. (2007). Information technology and the changing fabric of organization. *Organization Science*, 18(5), 749–762.

Sensemaking about HRV Data of High-Performing Individuals

Crafting a Mixed Methods Study

STEFAN KLEIN, STEFAN SCHELLHAMMER and NATHALIE MITEV

15.1 Introduction: Combining Algorithmic Data Analysis and Qualitative Sensemaking

The context of this chapter is a study on patterns of sustainable high performance in digital work settings, asking: How well do high performers cope with occupational strain and how do they cope? (RQ 1 & 2) For this study,[*] we have designed and performed a multi-method research approach in order to validate, augment and complement quantitative physiological data with qualitative data. We have used qualitative methods to interpret and contextualize 24-hour Heart Rate Variability (HRV) measurements. More importantly, we have crafted our research as a dialogical, relational enterprise aiming at co-producing meaning and joint sensemaking with the study participants.

While the discourse about methodological rigour highlights the expectation to follow the procedures and conventions of the research community, we would like to emphasize the salience of *skilful crafting and performing* of research. Beyond answering the 'what' and 'why' of the methodological choices, we want to reflect in particular on the 'how', asking: How are qualitative methods crucial to validate and interpret quantitative data and why is the performing of research formative for the outcome? (RQ 3 & 4)

Our research addresses different *stakeholders* and thus serves multiple purposes: (1) the participants, for whom their HRV data became a prompt to reflect on their work practices; (2) their peers, who find themselves in similar situations and might benefit from the results; (3) IBM's management, who potentially become implicated by the results of our work; and (4) we as researchers and our academic community. We had already been working in the field of technostress and HRV measurements for years, when suddenly a unique opportunity to get access to a sample of high-performing knowledge workers presented itself. In order to actually get access to the workshop participants, we had to pitch in front of the responsible IBM managers, and had to convince the project owner and eventually the participants themselves, whose participation was strictly voluntary. The different stakeholders had different needs, expectations and incentives with regard to our involvement. In response, we created different narratives and produced different outcomes of our research.

Ngwenyama (2019) has articulated ten claims (C1–C10), which explicate basic 'investigative and communicative practices of science'. We refer to five of those claims as principles guiding our research (2019: 11–12):

C1. The question that the researcher proposes to investigate is relevant and persisting in the field of study. . . .

C3. The theoretical approach/perspective that the researcher has selected for the inquiry is appropriate for investigating the research question. . . .

* Disclaimer: We do not have financial interests in the project. We had a research contract and IBM reimbursed mainly expenses and equipment.

C5. The methodology that the researcher has selected is appropriate for investigating the research question given the theoretical approach and empirical situation.

C6. The empirical situation selected for the inquiry is appropriate for observing the phenomenon or phenomenal behavior that the researcher is investigating.

C7. The methodology has been applied in a systematic manner and carefully documented to allow for replication or corroboration by other researchers.

Specifically, we introduce our field of study conceptually and empirically (C1, C6) and we reflect on the theoretical underpinnings of coping as well as augmenting quantitative data (C3). We elaborate on our research approach and the underlying rationale (C5). The discussion reflects on the execution of the research (C7).

15.2 Conceptual Background

The conceptual background provides pointers to relevant literature on the transformation and demands of work (1), approaches to coping with these demands (2), and the methodological discourse about limitations of data, data analytics and approaches to complement data and sensemaking (3). The literatures we are drawing on come from different disciplines and fields of study: organization studies, medical sociology, sociology, psychology, computer science and information systems. They provide reference points for our research approach, exploration and sensemaking. In addition, we used them in our fieldwork as prompts for questions, conversations and sensemaking for the participants.

15.2.1 The Demands of High Performance Work: Interested Self-Endangerment

This section illustrates *the relevance and pertinence of our research questions 1 and 2 (C1)* against the backdrop of technology-induced transformation of work (Baptista et al., 2020), which has led to an intensification, fragmentation and

delimitation of work. IBM, like many corporations, has embraced a decentralized organizational model and has built a performance-based management culture around it (Perlow and Kelly, 2014). Employees have as much autonomy and freedom as the work environment allows for, but their performance is closely monitored and they have to meet well-defined but increasingly difficult to achieve targets, sometimes facing a shrinking workforce and a correspondingly increasing workload. The constellation of organizational framework, freedom to shape and organize one's work, and customer focus resembles that of self-employed individuals, but in a complex organizational environment. This setting, often reinforced by a distinct management style of indirectly asking for extraordinary performance (Isak, 2016) or a 'hidden curriculum' (Sostrin, 2016), puts individuals at risk of exhausting and harming themselves (Krause et al., 2014). Such flexible multi-project work environments require employees to take more control over structuring their work, the flow of tasks, the pace of their work and the use of tools (devices, apps, etc.), and to actively draw boundaries by taking time off, taking breaks, exercising or spending time with family and friends.

15.2.2 Ways of Coping

Our research is informed by three complementary lenses which provide us with *appropriate theoretical perspectives on coping – namely, research questions 1 and 2 (C3)*. We introduce each of them shortly in the following.

15.2.2.1 Salutogenesis

Salutogenesis is a well-established concept in healthcare. Instead of focusing on what makes people sick (pathogenesis), it aims to understand the mechanisms of successfully coping with stressors.

Salutogenesis has been coined by the medical sociologist Aaron Antonovsky in 1968:

> Antonovsky tried to find the solution to the salutogenic question why some people, regardless of major stressful situations and severe hardships, stay healthy, while others do not. How do people

manage their inability to control their life? ...
Sense of Coherence (SOC) refers to an enduring
attitude and measures how people view life and, in
stressful situations, identify and use their general
resistance resources to maintain and develop
their health. (Eriksson and Lindström, 2007: 938)

Sense of coherence is composed of three
dimensions:

(1) [*comprehensibility*] a global orientation that
    expresses the extent to which one has a perva-
    sive, enduring though dynamic feeling of con-
    fidence that the stimuli deriving from one's
    internal and external environments in the
    course of living are structured, predictable,
    and explicable;
(2) [*manageability*] the resources are available to
    one to meet the demands posed by these
    stimuli; and
(3) [*meaningfulness*] these demands are chal-
    lenges, worthy of investment and engagement.
    (Antonovsky, 1987: 19)

Antonovsky depicted the ease (H+)/dis-ease (H-)
continuum, whereby individuals are confronted
with stressors, which create tensions. These might
lead to a breakdown causing diseases or a coping
with the tensions, which increase health and well-
being (H+) (see Figure 15.1).

While a major stream in the IS literature looks at
how technology creates stress (technostress, e.g.,
Ayyagari et al., 2011), we take instead a salutogenetic perspective and look at examples of successful coping and aim to identify effective coping
mechanisms.

15.2.2.2 Mindfulness and Resonance

A backdrop for sustainable work is mindfulness, a
state of alertness, attentiveness and active awareness (Langer, 1989). It complements the cognitive
aspects of sensemaking by a more holistic, bodily
view of the individual. *Sensemaking* and *being
mindful* emphasize the mental and emotional side
of work and life: finding meaning in what we do
and how we live (sensemaking) and being attentive
to our body, emotions and indeed our environment
(mindfulness).

Mindfulness is often associated with (guided)
meditations and breathing exercises (see, e.g.,
www.freemindfulness.org/download). It is related
to the physiological condition of coherence,
increased entrainment and synchronization between
physiological systems, specifically cardiovascular
activity and breathing (McCraty, 2015: 24–28).

In the context of this study, we look at mindfulness first as a sense of self-awareness and an attentiveness to taking care of bodily needs. Second, we
see it as an opportunity to consciously and actively
take breaks and engage in little practices to calm
down or regain a sense of coherence.

Rosa and Wagner (2019) have developed a sociology of connection or connectedness to the world
based on the notion of resonance. They portray
resonance as a distinct, authentic mode of relating
to the world in all its facets: ourselves, others, the
way we live (i.e., concrete experiential spheres –
e.g., family and politics, work and sport, religion
and art). Resonance implies finding something out
there that moves or touches us and – in return – the

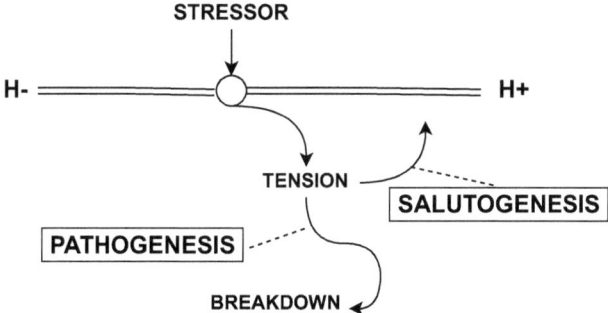

Figure 15.1 Antonovsky's own way of explaining the health continuum and the salutogenetic direction
Source: Lindström (2012).

sense of being able to reach the world out there, to leave a trace. We refer to resonance as a systematic, ongoing, dialogic mode of relating to oneself and the world, the opposite of alienation or a purely instrumental view of the world, a sensitivity and 'skilful attention to distinctions of worth in a domain' (Dreyfus and Kelly, 2011: 213).

15.2.2.3 Crafting Work and Detachment

Organizational scientists (Wrzesniewski and Dutton, 2001; Sturges, 2012) have emphasized the role of actively crafting work, which includes structuring tasks but also finding meaning in one's work and relating to others while at work: 'We propose that employees craft their jobs by changing cognitive, task, and/or relational boundaries to shape interactions and relationships with others at work. These altered task and relational configurations change the design and social environment of the job, which, in turn, alters work meanings and work identity' (Wrzesniewski and Dutton, 2001). Thus, *crafting work* and *engaging with others* refer to individual habits and routines at work as well as in our private lives, which relate to ways of taking or regaining control in practical matters.

While crafting, mindfulness and resonance look at how individuals find meaning in their work, and thereby achieve higher engagement in their work and better performance (Tims et al., 2013, 2015; Dan et al., 2020), detachment looks at strategies to disconnect from work, to re-establish boundaries that have become blurred in digital modes of organization in which employees can always be connected.

Psychological detachment is a well-researched recovery strategy. Relationships between detachment, job-related outcomes and psychological well-being have been empirically established (Sonnentag and Fritz, 2015; Wendsche and Lohmann-Haislah, 2017). Psychological detachment is defined as 'refraining from job-related activities and mentally disengaging from work during nonwork time' (Sonnentag and Fritz, 2015: 72). This definition emphasizes the importance of both the physical and the psychological facet of switching off.

15.2.3 On Method: Questioning and Augmenting Data and Analytics

The swift diffusion of algorithmically based decision-making has raised concerns about the validity and transparency of its results. For most users (and decision-makers), the inference mechanisms are black-boxed and incomprehensible, even when the algorithms were to be disclosed (Hahn et al., 2019), which they typically are not for commercial reasons. This has raised calls for fair, accountable and transparent algorithmic decision-making processes and underscored 'the criticality and urgency to engage multi-disciplinary teams of researchers, practitioners, policy makers and citizens to co-develop, deploy and evaluate in the real-world algorithmic decision-making processes designed to maximize fairness and transparency' (Lepri et al., 2018).

HRV analysis is the outcome of algorithmic processing of the data and relating them to existing data sets for reference and calibration. We took care to be transparent in our choice of equipment and software, but more importantly, we separate the reported results (Table 15.5) from their interpretation, for which we relied on the dialogue with the participants.

Recent literature reports on organizational approaches to improve and indeed control for the validity of algorithmic data. Grønsund and Aanestad (2020) have documented the emergence of new work configurations to augment algorithmic data and show how much the human needs to remain in the loop, while Waardenburg et al. (2018) report on the newly created role of data analysts to help the police force make sense of predictive policing data.

We have collaborated with an experienced HRV data analyst, who could not only read the data reports and make sense of them, but was also able to offer possible explanations of the data to the individual participants and support the process of sensemaking.

Kelly and Noonan (2017) have explored practices of datafication in the Indian Public Health Services. In what they call 'edifying practices of datafication', a dialogic engagement in 'conversation, mutual exploration and learning' (p. 12) is crucial for sensemaking of the data.

In a similar way, we have engaged our study participants in dialogues of sensemaking of their data, which involve validating, augmenting and contextualizing.

15.3 Research Approach

C5 The methodology that the researcher has selected is appropriate for investigating the research question given the theoretical approach and empirical situation. (Ngwenyama, 2019: 12)

The primary goal of our research is to identify how high performers cope with the daily demands of their jobs. In order to study both patterns and effects of work, we combined qualitative data collection (interviews and diaries) with quantitative collection of biometric data (24-hour ECG/HRV data). As self-reported stress in particular among male employees can be lower than physiologically measured stress, biometric data served both as a control, in particular as we captured data during sleep, and as a prompt to sensitize the participants in our study and discuss and contextualize findings. The former afforded us with rich insights into each individual's work situation. The diaries served our participants as a memory aid allowing them to relate their perception of the situation with the physiological measurements.

Our overall approach is to collect biometric data and to complement those with qualitative modes of data collection to gather a broader and more diverse set of information and – crucially – to actively involve the study participants in our research. The dialogue on their data, but also on their experience of work, their crafting of work and detachment strategies, is the core of our research approach.

In order to achieve this, we have designed and crafted a distinctive configuration of methods and ways to perform our research.

15.3.1 Case, Sample, Access

Our fieldwork is associated to our involvement with IBM's High Performer Program (HPP), which was designed to support and coach top-performing IBM employees in Europe, the Middle East and Africa. HPP was run by IBM Europe's Software Cross Unit Enablement team and IBM Smarter Workforce (Kenexa), while the Heart Rate Variability/sustainability module is integrated into HPP as part of the research collaboration between IBM and our university. We had the opportunity of participating in this programme and our study became integrated into the mandatory programme, but as a voluntary component to ensure participants were willing to share, and be open and reflexive. It had the advantage of providing access to a ready-made sample, an appropriate sample for a salutogenic study, which is crucial as high performers are usually too busy to be researched on stress. Our role in this programme was compatible with the aforementioned conceptual design.

IBM had invited the top 10 per cent performing individuals via their superiors/managers; their approach was based on recognition of their performance (an IBM metric) and their enrolment was voluntary. The resulting sample was homogeneous in terms of performance, and heterogeneous on all other accounts (gender, age, nationality, background, education, specialization, sales/pre-sales, etc.). Their sample consisted of individuals who are doing well and have achieved a high level of resilience, corresponding to our aim of understanding the effects of work in a technology-intensive environment from a salutogenic perspective, oriented towards understanding coping mechanisms to achieve well-being in 'survivors'.

Negotiating access required a balancing act between confidentiality of individual results, aggregated reports that might be useful for IBM and consent to publish results. We highlighted benefits for the stakeholder groups (high performers, IBM, university). We also referred to a record of previous studies at our university – one of them with IBM – on technology-induced stress in the workplace. IBM agreed for us to participate and we were introduced at the beginning of the workshops as independent researchers and thus different from the team of coaches recruited by IBM. We had to negotiate the amount of formal time available for us to 90 minutes during the workshops. The measurements were integrated into the workshops. IBM contributed financially to our technical data collection costs and travel expenses.

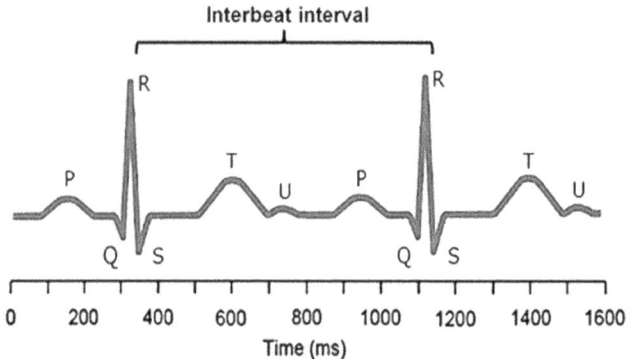

Figure 15.2 An ECG heart rate trace
Source: www.ncbi.nlm.nih.gov/pmc/articles/PMC5882295/figure/F1/.

15.3.2 HRV Data Collection and Algorithmic Analysis

As self-reported stress has limitations and can be unreliable (Cavanaugh et al., 2000; Masood et al., 2012), we used (quantitative) HRV measurements as a metric of strain or well-being.

HRV measures the variation of intervals between two heartbeats (RR interval variation, one metric found in ECGs). If we assume, for example, a pulse (heart rate) of sixty beats per minute, the intervals between individual beats can vary between 0.5 and 2 seconds. A higher variability is regarded as an indicator of a better health. The RR interval variation is influenced by the sympathetic and parasympathetic interactions in the autonomic nervous system (Berntson et al., 1997). HRV has been found to be a valid method to measure the autonomic effects of workplace, work environment, workloads and working time (Togo and Takahashi, 2009). While short-term measurements are widespread, 24-hour ECGs provide richer insights into an individual's condition, including recovery overnight. Such measurements generate in excess of 100,000 data points, if only the R-R intervals are considered.

The biosensor devices collect ECG data up to 1,000 Hz (we used 500 Hz) and movement data (3D acceleration). The collected data (about 100 MB per 24-hour measurement) are algorithmically analyzed using Cardiscope™ software, 'a holistic approach to analyse and interpret the human's autonomous and cardio-vascular functions. A long-term ECG provides just so much more information than only the occurrence of arrhythmias usually used for disease management. Specific heart rate patterns tell us about the major control loops, which keep us alive and in balance, or – even at an early stage – are indicators for a derailment' (http://cardiscope.com/cms/).[1] Cardiscope™ computes individual dashboards of physiological parameters, including strain, regeneration and quality of sleep.

At a high level, the outcomes of biosensor data collections are presented as statistical HRV parameters and enriched by possible explanations (see section 15.4.3). Yet, this outcome is the result of numerous choices we have made.

Table 15.1 provides a summary of key choices researchers have to make and the choices we made in order to highlight the many contingencies and choices which shape the data collection and analysis, yet often remain unreported.

Figure 15.3 illustrates one of Cardiscope™'s dashboards.

---

[1] Cardiscope has recently been acquired by Bittium (www.bittium.com/medical/bittium-cardiac-explorer). The Cardiscope website, which we quote, is no longer accessible; yet, a current description is available at www.smartmedical.co.uk/products/categories/autonomic-function-testing-hrv/analysis-software/cardiscope-analytics-real-time.

Table 15.1 Researchers' choices regarding data collection, analysis and presentation of results

Design choices	Explanation	Choices we made ...
Selection of biosensors	There is a growing market of consumer devices for HRV measurements (normal pulse metres are not sufficient). Yet, the measurement over an extended period of time can easily lead to erroneous measurements (artifacts).	As a result of several pre-studies and experimentation with different data collection formats, we chose Faros-180[2] sensors, a well-established FDA-approved device.
Period of data collection	Measurement periods vary from 1 minute to 24 hours (or more); for a discussion of different options, see: www.hrv4training .com/blog/hrv-measurements-duration.	We opted for 24-hour measurement (morning day 1 until morning day 2) in order to include quality of sleep. This choice was facilitated by the distinctive setting of a workshop and the willingness of the test persons for a more sensitive data collection. We asked participants to keep a diary. The two-day workshop provided a 'normalized' (i.e., comparable) setting for the participants, even though it was not a typical work day for them.
Choice of setting for data collection	The empirical environment is supposed to mirror the relevant setting for the purpose of the study. (C6)	We had originally opted for two measurements per individual (one in a realistic work scenario, the other off work) in order to be able to contrast and compare the readings. However, we did not find a sufficient number of individuals who would do the measurements off work. Therefore, we chose 24-hour measurement during the coaching workshop instead. This was not perfect as a work environment, yet reasonably close in terms of occupational demands, and it provided a 'normalized' and comparable day for all participants. The study participants all had a similar schedule for the 24 hours and it was easier for us to observe and document their schedule.
Software for data analysis and presentation of results	The amount of data requires algorithmic processing and analysis. Yet, the algorithmic development and data processing was out of scope for our own research and resources.	We opted for Cardiscope™ because it was well reviewed in our research community and recommended by our data analyst. In addition, we ran tests on our data set with other HRV software packages to check for basic validity.
Setting boundaries for data	HRV data are quite sensitive data. Their interpretation needs to consider gender and age of test persons.	Cardiscope™ has built a large database of HRV data in order to be able to control for age and gender.
Health data analyst	The person who does the analysis of the dashboard information.	We familiarized ourselves with HRV analysis, yet we included an experienced health data analyst, who has been doing HRV studies for years, in our team in order to ensure sufficient experience for the data analysis.

15.3.3 Qualitative Data Collection and Sensemaking

In order to become meaningful, HRV data have to be validated and contextualized. Therefore, we interviewed the participants for 10 minutes, with IBM authorization, during the IBM virtual preparation day prior to the workshops to collect basic

information about their professional situation. We asked specifically if the interviewees perceive their current pace of work as sustainable (*sensitizing*):

- Your background: Role and time at IBM?
- At the moment, do you think your work style is sustainable?
  In other words: Can you maintain your current pace of work for another 5 years?
- What is essential for you to deliver sustainable high performance?

---

[2] The current version of the sensor is called Bittium Faros™ (www.bittium.com/medical/bittium-faros).

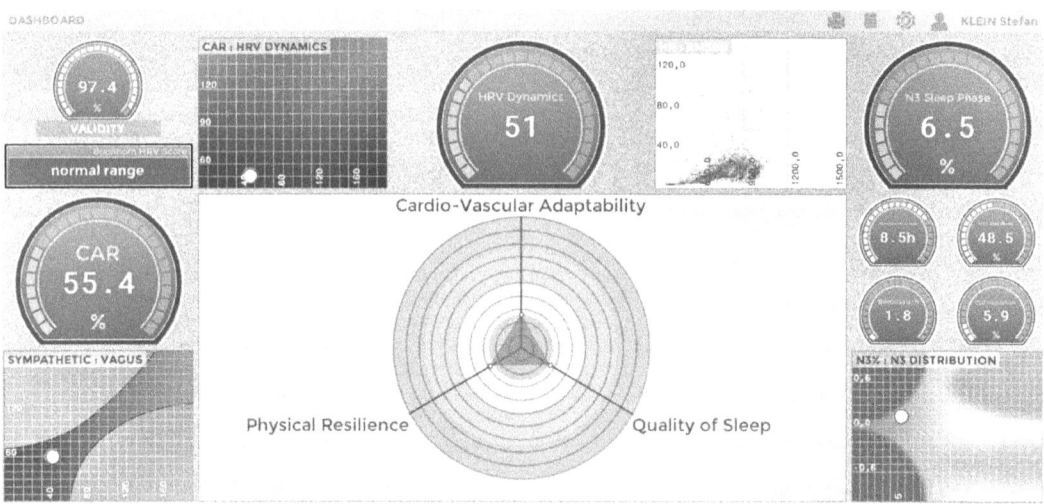

Figure 15.3 Cardiscope™ HRV dashboard 1

Source: http://cardiscope.com/cms/cardiscope-analytics/dashboard-details.html.

Given that most of the participants did not know one another, we saw focus groups as an opportunity to encourage the participants to share experiences and practices they had developed in order to provide mutual support and orientation (*sharing*). During the workshops, we therefore organized 60-minute focus group sessions with five to six participants in order to explore their sense of coherence:

- What is for you a perfect workday?
- In your work, what makes you happy, gives you a sense of profound satisfaction?
- Where do you find acknowledgement, appreciation and recognition of your efforts, your commitment, the work you do?
- What are good reasons for gratitude about your work setting?

We invited the participants to individual virtual feedback sessions, which took place several weeks after the workshop, as we needed time to process and analyze our data. The sessions included individual feedback and analysis of the HRV data and coaching, and lasted about an hour each. The sessions functioned as joint sensemaking of the HRV data by relating them to diary entries and interview data (*sensemaking* and orientation), as well as a reflection on their work practices and habits. The

individual interviews and debriefings aimed at sensitizing the participants to their situation, to make sense of the physiological findings and to orientate them towards more sustainable work practices. In this way, the HRV measurements have become prompts for an exploration of work and detachment practices, and the sense of coherence.

15.3.4 Configuring the Research

C7 The methodology has been applied in a systematic manner and carefully documented. (Ngwenyama, 2019: 12)

Table 15.2 gives an overview of the ways we have collected data and engaged with the participants across three different settings. For each step, we provided introductions about ourselves and the purpose of our research, as well as the role, rights and benefits for the participants.

The configuration of the seven steps is the result of earlier studies, extensive pretesting, reflections, discussions among the research team, improvisation and steep learning across three workshops.

During the first workshop, we had distributed the biosensors for the participants to take home and do two 24-hour measurements. However, only a few actually did the measurements and collecting the

Table 15.2 Main steps of engaging with participants and collecting data

Introduction	Data collection/purpose	Analysis
During the virtual days prior to the workshops: **Sensitizing**		
1. Introduction by IBM, explaining the background and purpose of our study	10-minute interview, key questions: Can you maintain your current pace of work for the next five years?	Coding of responses into three categories
During the three workshops: **Sharing**		
2. Introduction by IBM, explaining HRV, logistics of data collection, voluntariness/informed consent, confidentiality	24-hour HRV measurements (full day and night)	Cardiscope™ analytics, data analysis by HRV expert analyst, coding results into three categories
3. Introducing focus group themes	Focus group interviews, five to six participants, 60 minutes	In order to facilitate candid conversations, we only took a few notes after the interviews. They demonstrated how some of the participants were struggling to achieve a 'sense of coherence'.
4. Brief introduction about the dual purpose: demonstrating the effects of meditation through real-time display of HRV data, providing the participants with a break	Guided 5-minute breathing meditation	-
5. Signalling our availability for (informal) conversations, questions, etc., including with coaches	Participatory observation and informal conversations, building trust	Developing a better sense of the IBM culture (e.g., dinner speeches by vice presidents)
During the debriefings: **Sensemaking**		
6. Explaining the analysis approach and clarifying boundaries ('this is not a medical diagnosis')	Part 1: Confidential feedback on individual HRV results	No documentation; anonymized reflections on participants' responses
7. Setting the stage for the interview and joint reflection of the work situation	Part 2: Interview, reflection on work situation and coping strategies	Coding interviews with regard to detachment strategies and portfolios

devices became a major hassle. Our interpretation was that the participants were too busy during their work to even bother with the measurement, which – despite our instructions – proved to be too complicated to be administered without any support.

15.4 Findings

Although the main purpose of this chapter is to explore the combination of algorithmic data analysis and qualitative sensemaking, we provide a brief overview of the main findings of our study. While we cannot engage deeply with the data here, it serves as the empirical background of our overall argument.

15.4.1 Sample Structure

The sample of our research consisted of seventy-two participants in IBM's High Performer Program. Access to this programme was contingent on their past performance on the job and the explicit recommendation by their superiors. This group was split into three equally sized cohorts with whom we engaged separately over the course of one year.

Table 15.3 details the level of participation in our study.

After the initial interview, twenty participants chose not to continue with HRV measurements. Six of the remaining forty-nine participants experienced problems with the sensor hardware, which rendered the data inadequate. Thus, we collected usable HRV data from forty-three participants. Within this group, thirteen participants did not react to invitations for debriefing and/or did not submit the required consent forms or the measurement could not be properly used (e.g., consumption of alcohol, short measurement, etc.). As a result, we were able to solicit a complete data set for thirty participants across all cohorts.

The final sample consisted of six female and twenty-four male participants. The average age of these participants was 35, with the youngest being 25 and the eldest over 50.

15.4.2 Sensitizing: Qualitative Results (First 10-Minute Interview)

During the first virtual interview, we asked all participants: Can you maintain your current pace of work for another five years?

Table 15.3 Participation across the cohorts and the steps of our research

Participation	Cohort 1	Cohort 2	Cohort 3
Total	24	24	24
10-minute interviews	23	23	24
HRV measurements	07	18	18
Debriefing interviews	06	12	12
Complete data set	06	12	12

The question did not work out with one participant, but our analysis of the remaining sixty-eight revealed the following picture:

- 50 per cent responded with a clear, confident 'yes';
- 22 per cent gave a somewhat tentative 'yes': 'at the moment, as long as . . . is the case';
- 16 per cent said cautiously 'no': 'I can manage for now, but can't endure it for long'; and
- 12 per cent provided a clear 'no': 'my situation is definitely not sustainable'.

As shown in Table 15.4, the smaller sample of those who participated across all steps of our study mirrors this self-assessment.

Taken at face value, these self-assessments would suggest that the majority has found ways to cope with a taxing workload in a sustainable manner. But it would also suggest that a significant number of employees identified as most valuable to the company do not perceive their pace of work as sustainable. We interpret the relatively high number of negative answers as an indication that we may have succeeded in positioning ourselves as independent of their organizational context and trustworthy individuals.

15.4.3 Sharing: HRV

The algorithmic analysis of the collected HRV data provides a number of parameters that can serve as indicators for the lifestyle of our participants. We started with a four-tier categorization for our HRV data, which mirrored the coding we used for the initial question in our qualitative

Table 15.4 Comparison of (N = 68) [all interviews] vs. (N = 30) [interviews of individuals with HRV Data]

Answer	Number (N)	(%)	Number (N)	(%)
Confident 'Yes'	34	50%	13	43%
Ambiguous 'Yes'	15	22%	8	27%
Ambiguous 'No'	11	16%	6	20%
Confident 'No'	8	12%	3	10%
Sum	68		30	

Table 15.5 Categorization of HRV results

HRV parameters	High HRV	Medium HRV	Low HRV
Number (N)	17	9	4
(%)	57%	30%	13%
CAR	>100	60–100	<60
HRV Dynamics	>100	70–100	<70
N3 Sleep Phase	>12	5–10	0–5
CO_2 Regulation	0–5	6–20	>20
SDNN	>110	90–110	<90
pNN 50%	>10	6–10	<5
Min. heart rate	<40	40–49	>50
Avg. heart rate (day)	<70	70–90	>90
Avg. heart rate (night)	<65	65–75	>75

Note: NN: normal-to-normal; SDNN: standard deviation of all NN intervals; pNN50: NN50 count divided by the total number of all NN intervals (Malik et al., 1996).

interview. Yet, we eventually adopted a three-tier coding, which aims at increasing the confidence of our categorization in particular at the ends of the spectrum, as the four-tier categorization suggested a false sense of accuracy of our data and analytical apparatus. We struggled with labelling these categories appropriately and switched labels several times. In particular, we took issue with labelling someone 'exhausted' for several reasons. First, the categorization may be erroneous, the data is just one observation and despite our efforts to control the measurement, particular readings may have several causes unknown to us at that point. Second, particular labels may trigger strong emotional responses, which may foreclose further engagement with participants. And, third, on the level of the entire sample, these labels lose their grounding in the individual contexts and suggest a sense of uniformity that is unwarranted.

Table 15.5 provides an overview of the parameters we chose to include and the labels we finally settled for.

The HRV analysis suggests that 57 per cent of the participants can be qualified as resilient (i.e., they show a good balance of strain and regeneration). Yet, similar to the percentages in the self-assessment data, about 13 per cent (four participants) would identify as experiencing physiological stress, possibly exhaustion and a lack of regeneration.

Figure 15.4 illustrates how the HRV parameters are depicted in the dashboard.

15.4.4 Sensemaking: Validating and Contextualizing HRV Data

Combining the interview and physiological data allows for gauging the extent to which our participants' awareness of their sustainability is consistent with their physiological state. Three individuals with the best high HRV assessed their work pace as unsustainable. In contrast, of those four who showed clear signs of strain and exhaustion in the HRV data, only one acknowledged upfront in the first interview the difficulty of keeping up with the current pace. Table 15.6 puts the number of individuals categorized in a particular HRV category in relation to their answer during the interview.

The first virtual interview afforded us some insight into our sample and the individuals' perception of the sustainability of their current work situation. In line with the literature, we observed the contrast between an individual's self-perception and the measurements we took.

In our third phase, the feedback interview, we presented our participants with their HRV data and our analysis thereof. These interviews were conducted several weeks (up to three months) after the measurements took place. In order to contextualize the readings, we had asked them to keep a reflective diary and we had access to their tightly planned schedule during the workshop.

During the first 30 minutes of each interview, we walked them through a visualization of the data and explained the readings and how to interpret them. We therefore refrained from simply revealing how we categorized their HRV state; indeed, this categorization would be kept in the background although it would become clear over the course of the interview. Our participants were

Table 15.6 Matching HRV and self-assessment

| HRV state | 'Can you maintain your current pace of work for another five years?' Individuals who answered in the self-assessment with ... | | | | |
	Confident 'yes'	Ambiguous 'yes'	Ambiguous 'no'	Confident 'no'	Match HRV: self-assessment
High HRV	9	5	1	2	82%
Medium HRV	3	1	4	1	55%
Low HRV	1	2	1	0	25%

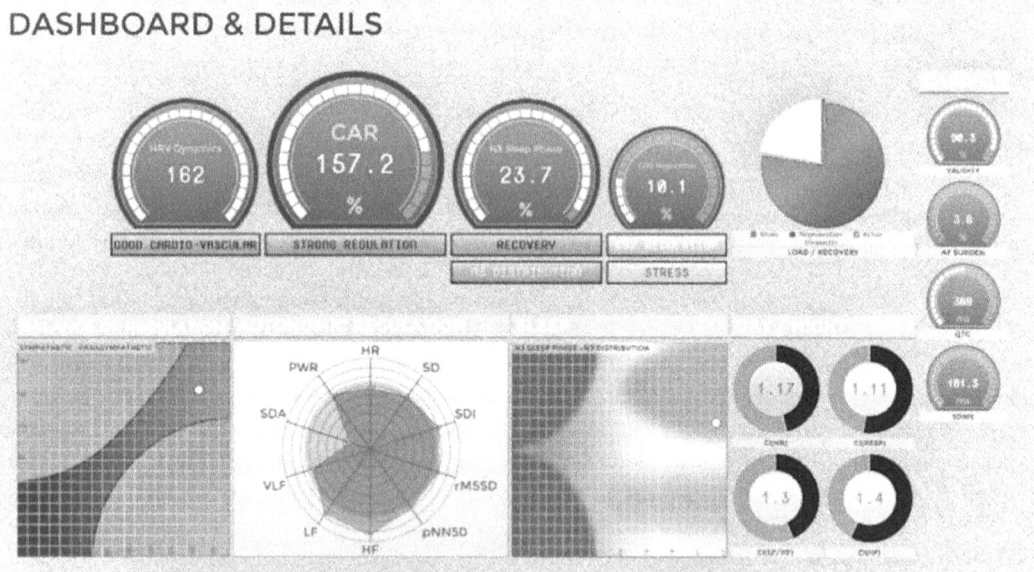

A simple visual interface allows you to extract the most important key findings of a recording, like a cardiac risk assessment, the appraisal of the heart fitness, the level of resilience and the balance between sympathetic and para-sympathetic regulations. Particular attention is paid to the influence and quality of sleep. The processes triggered by the autonomic system during the night/sleep reveal the exposure of the individual to conditions that cannot be consciously influenced.

Key HRV parameters are supported by a large database of more than ten thousand analysed 24 hour recordings of ECG and HRV.

Standard HRV parameters in conjunction with newly developed indices, customisable plots/trends and tables are available within the software for greater depth of analysis if required.

Figure 15.4 Cardiscope™ HRV dashboard 2

generally quite impressed by the level of insight the data showed. While the interview was framed as our intent to share the result of our work, we gained quite intimate insights into their work situation and their situation during that specific day of the measurement. Several participants mentioned that they would have kept an even more detailed diary, if they had known the level of detail at which HRV data operates. It became clear to us why we had to exercise caution in our interpretation of the data, since the consumption of alcohol or medication and illnesses such as a cold would impact the data. In one instance of low HRV, we cautiously advised them to consult a physician to follow up on the readings.

In the second half of the 60-minute debriefings, we conducted a semi-structured interview concerning their work environment and coping practices. We found that participants with high HRV consciously integrated regular breaks into their daily work, while those exhibiting a low HRV did not. While this finding in itself is not surprising, we gathered intriguing insights into the difficulty of setting boundaries for work. Some told us 'I have learned to politely and respectfully say "no" to my boss or my client, if I have to or in case their requests conflict with "private" appointments, such as sports or time off. I often come back to them later and explain myself.' This ability to say 'no' was portrayed as a hard-won achievement to retain or regain some control over the workday and a relentless onslaught of demands.

15.5 Discussion

> C7 The methodology has been applied in a systematic manner and carefully documented. (Ngwenyama, 2019: 12)

In this section, we want to augment 'systematically applying the methodology' by a reflection on the performative side of the research: how we engaged with the participants and how we managed to involve the participants in joint sensemaking and thereby as co-producers of meaning.

15.5.1 Skilful Execution and Orchestration of the Research: 'A Fool with a Method Is Still a Fool'

Research methods don't guarantee good research any more than recipes guarantee quality cooking. For us, every workshop posed a profound challenge of performing the research and at the same time assessing, reflecting, learning and exploring alternatives. For the first workshop, we had arrived later than the coaches and participants, which – as we found out – reinforced our outsider role and made it much harder to engage the participants.

During the other two workshops, we arrived on time and were introduced as a member of the team of coaches and facilitators, yet with our distinct university background.

Within the scope of the involvement we had negotiated with IBM, we orchestrated the complex research approach (see Table 15.2) with fine-tuned dynamics, which started with the brief (virtual) episode of introduction and sensitizing, followed by the on-site introductions, the HRV measurements, the formal and informal interviews and debriefing.

Our physical presence proved to be an important reassurance for the study participants, as we had follow-up questions and a few incidents of measurement problems. While the HRV measurements were going on, we engaged small groups of participants in the focus group interviews and learned about how they crafted their work and how to engage them in a reflection about their 'sense of coherence'. This revealed both structural similarities of their work, but also significant differences in how individuals coped with the demands of their work and what they experienced as pain points (e.g., lack of recognition, career uncertainty or the absence of an overall sense of expectations, i.e., 'when is enough enough?').

Being on site during the workshops provided the researchers with a plethora of contextual information, casual conversations and observations, which informed and created a reference point for the final part of the engagement with the participants: the debriefing interviews.

Our research practice involved going back and forth between extensive preparation (pre-studies, steep learning and constant reflection) and doing. For instance, thinking through what we could ask from the study participants as preparation and pre-test of our approach, how to answer our research questions and gain their reflections on their work situation and sense of coherence, how to use the 24-hour HRV measurements and how to debrief.

15.5.1.1 Engagement

The approach we had chosen put us on the line in multiple ways. We clearly established our role as researchers with a research agenda and bound by rules of good academic practice (informed consent, confidentiality, etc.). At the same time, we were introduced as part of the IBM team of consultants, so that our participation in the workshop was clarified and officially endorsed.

While we had already asked quite a personal (intimate) question during the initial virtual contact ('Do you think you can keep up your current pace of work for the next five years?'), we sensed that being on site during the entire workshop, which was a bit like an off-site boot camp, was essential to be recognized as group members, who were naturally involved in casual conversations over meals, during breaks, etc.

15.5.1.2 Problematizing the Quality of Data

Biosensor data are a well-established metric for well-being and occupational health (Togo and Takahashi, 2009), and are a key component of our study. Yet, there are three important factors influencing the interpretation of the data:

1. The data-based reports, which we analyzed, are contingent on the process of data collection and analysis. Therefore, we took great care in documenting our design and procedural choices.
2. HRV data are sensitive to numerous effects, such as infections, alcohol consumption, etc., which may not be visible during the data collection.
3. We involved an experienced health data analyst in order to tap into her rich experience for the analysis.

Our HRV measurements yielded diverse outcomes in the highly select group of high performers (among the top 10 per cent at IBM). In as much as the HRV readings are associated with work-related demands, the result suggests that some of the high performers pay a high personal price (including risking health and well-being) to achieve and maintain their performance.

The triangulation of HRV and interview data yielded the anticipated discrepancies between physiological data and self-assessment. Assuming again that the HRV readings indicated occupational strain, our findings suggest either a limited or biased self-awareness and a false and potentially

dangerous sense of confidence and security with regard to their well-being or an unwillingness to admit the experienced level of strain to oneself or to others.

15.5.1.3 Contextualizing HRV Data

We therefore embedded the interpretation of the HRV data into a rich collection of qualitative data to contextualize the data:

1. We tried to get a sense of the participants in our study and their self-assessment ('can you keep your pace . . .') during the initial interviews.
2. We made ourselves available for casual conversations and observed the coaching workshop as much as possible.
3. We engaged small groups of participants in focus group interviews about their work and their relation to peers, managers and clients, as well as work crafting.
4. The debriefing first elicited their individual reflection on their own situation. The second step of the debriefing was a dialogue about the individual's HRV data and their interpretation. The health data analyst introduced what she saw in the data in order to solicit feedback firstly in terms of elaborating about what was going on as a potential explanation and secondly to encourage the individual's engagement with their data as much as they were able to make sense and were willing to share what they thought.

The debriefing constituted an almost therapeutic engagement, although we were clear about the limits of our role with regard to medical diagnosis or advice.

In the end, a main role of the HRV data was to provide prompts for a dialogue about the working situation and sustainable performance. Yet, the HRV measurement fitted the professional profile of the IBMers, most of whom were intrigued to learn about their own HRV data and to do the measurement. We attribute this to an engineering or technology-orientated culture and the proliferation of devices and software for measuring fitness, cardiovascular performance and sleep, but also the setting of a secluded conference venue.

15.5.2 Co-Production of Meaning

In line with Kelly and Noonan's dialogic engagement with healthcare data in 'conversation, mutual exploration and learning' (2017: 12), we engaged the study participants during the debriefings in a dialogue and mutual exploration of the meaning of their HRV data. We recognized the participants' curiosity towards the data, like looking into a mirror, finding out something about themselves and looking for resonance of the data and their own experience. As the data (see Figure 15.5 for a sample HRV rhythmogram) provided a somewhat dark, blurred or murky mirror image, they provided a prompt and an invitation to the participants to sense their own body and to reflect on their daily routines and how they affect them.

The dialogue with the data analyst about what the data might or might not mean or reveal made them juxtapose the granular, minute-by-minute data accounts with their own recollections and engage in joint sensemaking. It also yielded a sense of regret that they had not kept a more detailed diary to assist the interpretation.

The conversation about the data analysis provided prompts for the subsequent reflection on:

- the work situation;
- the sense of coherence and crafting work;
- the coping/detachment strategies; and
- the balancing act of work/non-work in a highly competitive, high performance work culture and environment.

For the researcher, performing the research means to have 'skin in the game', being present as a person, engaging in the dialogue with the study participants beyond exploring a research question. We were very clear in our conversation with the participants that participation was strictly voluntary, that they owned their own data (and could ask us to delete them at any time) and that we relied on their collaboration to make sense of their data. Yielding control to the participants about what and how much they would share was a relief and protection against overstepping the line or intruding into sensitive information.

15.6 Conclusions

Beyond the well-recognized advantages of combining quantitative and qualitative data collection and research methods (Venkatesh et al., 2013), our research demonstrates the importance of qualitative research to engage with study participants, find out whether the data resonate with their own experience and perception, and to co-create meaning (joint sensemaking) of quantitative findings.

Metaphorically speaking, we have been moving from a set of recipes (methods), to configuring a kitchen (Weisberg et al., 2014; Charnas, 2016) with equipment (devices) and a dedicated team, doing several cooking sessions to improve the configuration and engaging with several groups of clients to include their feedback in the overall process of learning. As much as a good recipe alone does not guarantee a delicious meal, a method does not guarantee good research results (Cicourel, 1964).

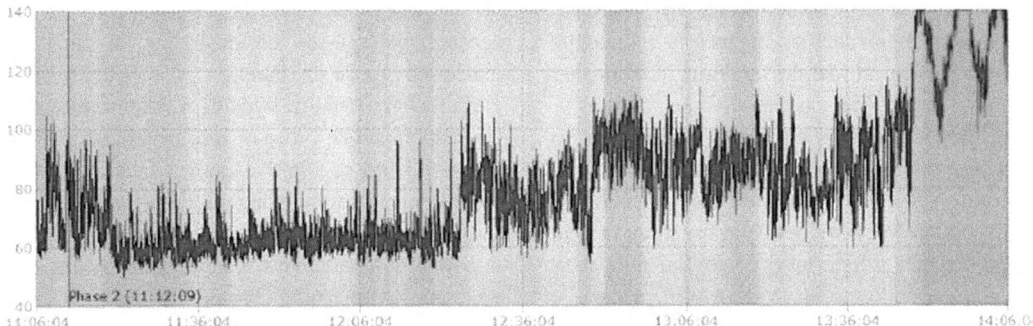

Figure 15.5 Sample of HRV rhythmogram

15.6.1 Don't Take Data at Face Value – Brain in the Game

HRV data are not 'given' as the Latin origin of 'data' suggests, but they are constructed in many ways. Therefore, the obvious purpose of a combined qualitative analysis (primarily individual and focus group interviews) is to validate and triangulate the findings, in particular to compare self-reported well-being (or stress) with the HRV data.

Capturing HRV data requires a plethora of highly specific technical, methodological and logistical choices, which have an immediate effect on the outcome. We spent a significant amount of time and effort to secure a reasonably good quality of data and to select established, well-tested analysis software, with a large data set in the background for calibration purposes.

In other words, HRV data are highly contingent on the participants, the process and devices of data collection and the algorithms of data processing.

'Brain in the game' suggests that this is a significant intellectual exercise, which requires attention to detail, background knowledge, skilful crafting and cooperation with experts.

15.6.2 Qualitative Approach as a Way of Engaging the Study Participants – Skin in the Game

More importantly, we were aiming to sensitize the participants to reflect on their work situation and practice (sense of coherence), which would not only provide an explanation for the physiological state, but at the same time – potentially – initiate a process of transformation.

Qualitative approaches by design are relational: the research establishes or engages in a dialogue with the participant and the emerging relationship will have an influence on the outcome.

We sought to actively engage the participants, to empathize with their situation and to build trust as a backdrop for an honest and open reflection of their situation. We have designed the study to give the participants a high level of control over their data and our ability to make sense of their data.

The researcher's role is a delicate balancing act between distance, as we are not therapists, and closeness, as we want to authentically engage with the participants.

15.6.3 Crafting and Performing Research

Our study is an example of careful orchestrating and configuring of the research process in order to validate, augment and complement our data.

We borrow and extend the notion of 'crafting research' used by Prasad (2017) as in the title for her book on qualitative research. Crafting includes configuring the different steps and components of the research, the equipment, the methods and the analysis approaches, as well as orchestrating the research – that is, planning and pre-testing, the logistics of fitting our data collection into the workshops – which provided the setting for our research. The goal of crafting our research is not just a methodology, but it is also part of a research practice, which is 'appropriate for investigating the research question given the theoretical approach and empirical situation' (Ngwenyama, 2019: 12). The other – only analytically separated – part of the research practice is the performing of research.

We use performing research in a broader sense than Ackroyd and O'Toole (2010), referring to the practice of doing research, reflecting the process of research: 'how researchers make decisions along the way that impact the research findings … behind-the-scenes … window into the real world practice of qualitative research, which at times is messy and unpredictable' (Hesse-Biber and Leavy, 2011). Pickering (1995) has articulated a performative view of research, which recognizes the agency of the researcher and the ongoing process of accommodating her understanding in light of material or social resistance.

It crucially requires building a relationship with the participants in order to gain insights into their life world and coping strategies, which are essential for our understanding of the results and as support for any prescriptive results, but more importantly to involve the participants in the co-production of meaning (Mason, 2015).

We proposed the continuation and extension of our study to IBM, specifically to do a workshop with the participants of our study focusing on crafting work, mindfulness and detachment and a second HRV measurement, and a workshop for managers to reflect on their own work, but also on their leadership role.

References

Ackroyd, J. and O'Toole, J. (2010). *Performing Research: Tensions, Triumphs and Trade-Offs of Ethnodrama*. Stoke-on-Trent, UK: Trentham.

Antonovsky, A. (1987). *Unraveling the Mystery of Health: How People Manage Stress and Stay Well*. San Francisco, CA: Jossey-Bass.

Ayyagari, R., Grover, V. and Purvis, R. (2011). Technostress: Technological antecedents and implications. *MIS Quarterly*, 35(4), 831–858.

Baptista, J., Stein, M.-K., Klein, S., Watson-Manheim, M. B. and Lee, J. (2020). Digital work and organisational transformation: Emergent digital/human work configurations in modern organisations. *Journal of Strategic Information Systems*, 29(2), article 101618.

Berntson, G. G., Bigger Jr, J. T., Eckberg, D. L., Grossman, P., Kaufmann, P. G., Malik, M. et al. (1997). Heart rate variability: Origins, methods and interpretive caveats (Committee Report). *Psychophysiology*, 34(6), 623–648.

Cavanaugh, M. A., Boswell, W. R., Roehling, M. V. and Boudreau, J. W. (2000). An empirical examination of self-reported work stress among U.S. managers. *Journal of Applied Psychology*, 85(1), 65–74.

Charnas, D. (2016). *Work Clean the Life-Changing Power of Mise-en-Place to Organize Your Life, Work and Mind*. New York, NY: Rodale Books.

Cicourel, A. V. (1964). *Method and Measurement in Sociology*. New York, NY: Free Press.

Dan, C.-I., Roşca, A. C. and Mateizer, A. (2020). Job crafting and performance in firefighters: The role of work meaning and work engagement. *Frontiers in Psychology*, 11, 894.

Dreyfus, H. and Kelly, S. D. (2011). *All Things Shining: Reading the Western Classics to Find Meaning in a Secular Age*. New York, NY: Free Press.

Eriksson, M. and Lindström, B. (2007). Antonovsky's sense of coherence scale and its relation with quality of life: A systematic review. *Journal of Epidemiology and Community Health*, 61(11), 938–944.

Grønsund, T. and Aanestad, M. (2020). Augmenting the algorithm: Emerging human-in-the-loop work configurations. *Journal of Strategic Information Systems*, 29(2), article 101614.

Hahn, T., Ebner-Priemer, U. and Meyer-Lindenberg, A. (2019). Transparent artificial intelligence – a conceptual framework for evaluating AI-based clinical decision support systems, https://ssrn.com/abstract=330312.

Hesse-Biber, S. N. and Leavy, P. (2011). *The Practice of Qualitative Research*, 2nd edition. Los Angeles, CA: Sage.

Isak, C. (2016). Motivated self-endangerment: How indirect management can hurt you. *Tech Acute*, http://techacute.com/motivated-self-endangerment/.

Kelly, S. and Noonan, C. (2017). The doing of datafication (and what this doing does): Practices of edification and the enactment of new forms of sociality in the Indian public health service. *Journal of AIS*, 18(12), 872–899.

Krause, A., Baeriswyl, S., Berset, M., Deci, N., Dettmers, J., Dorsemagen, C. et al. (2014). Selbstgefährdung als Indikator für Mängel bei der Gestaltung mobil-flexibler Arbeit: Zur Entwicklung eines Erhebungsinstruments. *Wirtschaftspsychologie*, 4, 49–59, www.psychologie-aktuell.com/index.php?id=184&tx_ttnews%5Btt_news%5D=3833&tx_ttnews%5BbackPid%5D=185&cHash=d51d629405#marker4.

Langer, E. J. (1989). *Mindfulness*. Reading, MA: Addison-Wesley.

Lepri, B., Oliver, N., Letouzé, E., Pentland, A. and Vinck, P. (2018). Fair, transparent, and accountable algorithmic decision-making processes. *Philosophy & Technology*, 31(4), 611–627.

Lindström, B. (2012). Salutogenesis – an introduction. Folkhälsan Research Center, Helsinki, www.centrelearoback.org/assets/PDF/04_activites/clr-GCPB121122-Lindstom_pub_introsaluto genesis.pdf.

Malik, M., Bigger, J. T., Camm, A. J., Kleiger, R. E., Malliani, A., Moss, A. J. and Schwartz, P. J. (1996). Heart rate variability: Standards of measurement, physiological interpretation, and clinical use. *European Heart Journal*, 17(3), 354–381.

Mason, K. (2015). Participatory action research: Coproduction. *Governance and Care: Geography Compass*, 9(9), 497–507.

Masood, K., Ahmed, B., Choi, J. and Gutierrez-Osuna, R. (2012). Consistency and validity of self-reporting scores in stress measurement surveys. Annual International Conference of the IEEE Engineering in Medicine and Biology Society, San Diego, CA.

McCraty, R. (2015). *Science of the Heart: Exploring the Role of the Heart in Human Performance*. Boulder Creek, CA: HeartMath Institute.

Ngwenyama, O. (2019). The ten basic claims of information systems research: An approach to interrogating validity claims in scientific argumentation, https://ssrn.com/abstract=3446798.

Perlow, L. A. and Kelly, E. L. (2014). Toward a model of work redesign for better work and better life. *Work and Occupations*, 41(1), 111–134.

Pickering, A. (1995). *The Mangle of Practice: Time, Agency, and Science*. Chicago, IL: University of Chicago Press.

Prasad, P. (2017). *Crafting Qualitative Research: Working in the Postpositivist Traditions*, 2nd edition. London and Armonk, NY: Routledge and M. E. Sharpe.

Rosa, H. and Wagner, J. C. (2019). *Resonance: A Sociology of Our Relationship to the World*, English edition. Cambridge, MA: Polity Press.

Sonnentag, S. and Fritz, C. (2015). Recovery from job stress: The stressor-detachment model as an integrative framework. *Journal of Organizational Behavior*, 36(Supp. 1), S72–S103.

Sostrin, J. (2016). The hidden curriculum of work. *Strategy + Business*, www.strategy-business.com/blog/The-Hidden-Curriculum-of-Work?gko=2121d&utm_source=itw&utm_medium=20160809B&utm_campaign=respB.

Sturges, J. (2012). Crafting a balance between work and home. *Human Relations*, 65(12), 1539–1559.

Tims, M., Bakker, A. B. and Derks, D. (2015). Job crafting and job performance: A longitudinal study. *European Journal of Work and Organizational Psychology*, 24(6), 914–928.

Tims, M., Bakker, A. B. and Derks, D. (2013). The impact of job crafting on job demands, job resources, and well-being. *Journal of Occupational Health Psychology*, 18(2), 230–240.

Togo, F. and Takahashi, M. (2009). Heart rate variability in occupational health – a systematic review. *Industrial Health*, 47(6), 589–602.

Venkatesh, V., Brown, S. A. and Bala, H. (2013). Bridging the qualitative-quantitative divide: Guidelines for conducting mixed methods research in information systems. *MIS Quarterly*, 37(1), 21–54.

Waardenburg, L., Sergeeva, A. and Huysman, M. (2018). Hotspots and blind spots. In U. Schultze, M. Aanestad, M. Mähring, C. Østerlund and K. Riemer (eds), *IFIP Advances in Information and Communication Technology. Living with Monsters? Social Implications of Algorithmic Phenomena, Hybrid Agency, and the Performativity of Technology*. Cham, Switzerland: Springer, pp. 96–109.

Weisberg, D. S., Hirsh-Pasek, K., Golinkoff, R. M. and McCandliss, B. D. (2014). Mise en place: Setting the stage for thought and action. *Trends in Cognitive Science*, 18(6), 276–278.

Wendsche, J. and Lohmann-Haislah, A. (2017). A meta-analysis on antecedents and outcomes of detachment from work. *Frontiers in Psychology*, https://doi.org/10.3389/fpsyg.2016.02072.

Wrzesniewski, A. and Dutton, J. E. (2001). Crafting a job: Revisioning employees as active crafters of their work. *Academy of Management Review*, 26(2), 179–201.

The Rich Facets of Digital Trace Data

CHAPTER 16

JONAS VALBJØRN ANDERSEN and PHILIPP HUKAL

16.1 Introduction

A growing share of social interactions takes place in digital environments where they continuously, simultaneously and unequivocally produce vast amounts of digitally encoded information: so-called digital trace data (Hedman et al., 2013; Berente et al., 2019; Lindberg, 2020; Østerlund et al., 2020). Computational research methods have made the use of such data increasingly popular to study a variety of social science phenomena (Lazer et al., 2009; Cioffi-Revilla, 2010; Alvarez, 2016). Often, digital trace data is heralded for its abundance, claiming that digital traces are valuable because of the large-scale patterns one can derive from them (Lazer and Radford, 2017). This view tends to overlook the richness of digital trace data captured by its unique characteristics. However, paying attention to the specific characteristics of digital trace data allows investigations of socio-technical interactions in unprecedented depth as well as breadth.

In this chapter, we demonstrate how IS researchers can leverage the richness captured in the digital traces of social interactions within digital environments. We do so by proposing an approach to qualitative computational analysis based on 'faceting' of digital trace data. To illustrate how the faceting approach can be applied to data analysis, we describe the construction of three 'facets' inherent to digital trace data. Specifically, we show how researchers can focus on social structures (relational facet), sequences (processual facet) and meaning (semantic facet). We explain how to construct and work with each facet as a combination of analytical activity carried out by the analyst (data unit separation, data discretization, category validation and conceptualization), as well as the analytical focus to which analytical activities are

directed: the analysis of relations, processes or semantics.

We demonstrate the depth contained in the traces of social interaction with digital technology which offers ways to leverage the richness of digital trace data in qualitative IS research. Recognizing these rich facets of digital trace data thus offers a methodological vocabulary for the generation of research questions that working with digital trace data is well suited to answer.

16.2 Digital Trace Data

The term 'digital trace data' refers to all forms of digitally encoded information stemming from human interaction with digital technology (Howison et al., 2011; Hedman et al., 2013; Lindberg, 2020; Østerlund et al., 2020; Pentland et al., 2020b). Digital trace data may include, but are not limited to, user logs from interaction with computing devices, source code data from version control systems such as GitHub or archival records from mailing lists, as well as posts from discussion boards. As footprints of social activity rendered by digital technology, digital traces are especially valuable to the analysis of interactions between social actors with a wide range of digital technology artifacts (Gaskin et al., 2014; Lazer and Radford, 2017); not unlike archaeologists, IS researchers can in this way turn to detectable residues of technology-enabled social life in complex interactions with artifacts surrounding our everyday activity (Yoo, 2010).

Digital trace data have proven invaluable to many pertinent information systems research topics. For instance, constructing interaction networks from source code has made structures in software applications accessible at a scale that, until recently, was unthinkable (Baldwin et al., 2014). Similarly, sequences of technical changes have been used to study interdependencies in hitherto latent development routines (Lindberg et al., 2013). Others also demonstrated the utility of trace data for the extraction of meaningful concepts from large bodies of user-generated text (Debortoli et al., 2016; Müller et al., 2016).

Collecting data of this kind often involves the use of dedicated computational tools capable of interacting with the system that generated the data in the first place. As such, the lion's share of empirical work in this space has involved collecting data represented in formats such as text, counts, logs, posts, likes, clicks or executable source code. Such data are often gathered using computational techniques including interacting with standardized interfaces and databases (e.g., via web application programming interfaces; APIs), custom data collection methods (e.g., scraping web data), or using vast public or proprietary repositories akin to archives (e.g., email lists or source code repositories). The outcome of such data collection regularly results in data sets in structured tabular (e.g., database tables, .sql or .csv) or hierarchical (e.g., JSON or XML) formats, either form necessitating further use of computational tools for data processing and analysis.

As the format of trace data might be more or less structured, operationalizing trace data is not straightforward. To support working inductively with digital trace data, analysts thus need a language to explain how and to what end digital trace data are being used in IS research. Several aspects set digital trace data apart from data that most social scientists are trained to handle competently, and analysts face three interrelated challenges: abundance, multimodality and dynamism of digital trace data.

Abundance refers to the sheer amount of data necessary to uncover deep insights from traces. The phenomena of interest to most IS scholars are often fully or in part situated within increasingly complex and multifaceted digital environments. Therefore, collecting raw digital trace data necessarily involves capturing as many details and different aspects of social and technical interactions in that environment as possible at as high

a resolution and level of richness as possible (Venturini, 2009). The richness of the initial raw data collection is important for conducting qualitative analysis to retain a maximum degree of freedom in defining and changing the scope and unit of analysis at a later stage. Therefore, it is important not to reduce the volume or nature of observations to be extracted from the digital traces.

In contrast to other research traditions, qualitative researchers often cast a wide net so that it is possible to extract several aspects at different levels of abstraction from the raw data. For qualitative researchers, in particular, trace data affords richness detail with fewer constraints as to what constitutes a data point, an observation or a unit of analysis. This retains the possibility to both focus on specific details and observe these at scale later on (Venturini and Latour, 2010; Venturini, 2012). Therefore, the data collection process must make as few assumptions about the resulting data points as possible to maintain the highest possible degree of information in the traces, even at the expense of complexity, dimensionality and variety in the data.

Multimodality refers to the many different aspects of social interaction that is retained in digital traces. Most empirical work draws on the integration of different kinds of data obtained from a variety of sources, all of which recognize different aspects of digital traces (Østerlund et al., 2020). For instance, most trace data were never generated for the purpose of social research. This introduces several issues that analysts need to reflect on (Howison et al., 2011; Lindberg, 2020; Østerlund et al., 2020). First and foremost, digital traces constitute a 'found' data source in the sense that they are not constructed with a data collection instrument such as a survey or an interview protocol. In contrast to carefully designed and established instruments such as questionnaire items in survey research, construct validity is imposed onto trace data. What traces represent and how well they capture a phenomenon has to be established empirically from the ground up (Howison et al., 2011; Salganik, 2017). As discussed in depth by others, this process requires extreme care during the operationalization (e.g., Howison et al., 2011), conceptualization (e.g., Østerlund et al., 2020) and inference (Lindberg, 2020).

Dynamism refers to a change in the systems that produced trace data records. As digital traces are produced and shaped by information systems, it is important to understand the inherent logic of the technological and organizational system in which they are produced and manipulated (Venturini et al., 2018; Østerlund et al., 2020). One such defining aspect of trace data sets is what has been referred to as 'drift' (Salganik, 2017; Pentland et al., 2020a). Drift introduces the potential for error as the underlying system producing and disseminating trace data is subject to change over time, yet such changes are often inscrutable to the analyst. For example, how a certain action, such as posting a message to an online discussion board, changes over the course of the trace record will have a significant impact on the validity of the resulting analysis (Howison et al., 2011; Salganik, 2017). While this ambivalence of digital artifacts is a matter of course for many IS theorists (Kallinikos et al., 2013; Kitchin, 2014; Faulkner and Runde, 2019), these threats are novel to most analysts and merit attention.

In combination, abundance, multimodality and dynamism of digital trace data require researchers to be explicit about what, how and why they have collected and manipulated trace data records in their work. By stating analytical activities and analytical focus as part of a computational qualitative research design, the researcher can begin to deliver on the promise of digital trace data to represent social phenomena in digital environments at both depth and breadth. In the next section, we present a framework that allows qualitative researchers to focus on specific facets of digital trace data while addressing the potential pitfalls associated with analyzing digital trace data while leveraging its immense richness.

16.3 Facets of Digital Trace Data

In what follows, we articulate an analytical framework for digital trace data that revolves around identifying and refining its different facets. Facets can be understood as the analyst's commitment to the how, what and why of working with trace data that are framing a respective analysis. We use the term 'facet' to describe working with digital trace data along two dimensions: the analytical activity performed by the analyst; and the analytical focus through which research is carried out. A facet is the result of specific *analytical activities* (A); a_1 unit separation, a_2 discretization, a_3 validation and a_4 conceptualization (specified in detail in section 16.3.1), as well as the *analytical focus* to which such activity is directed; for example, the analysis of relations R, processes P or semantics S (described in section 16.3.2). Facets are thus the result of a researcher performing analytical activities with a specific analytical focus in research designs drawing from digital trace data. A single facet is not paradigmatic for all computational work, but provides a vocabulary for defining and explicating the nature and role of digital trace data, as well as the analytical process conducted for a specific research project. We will describe how to construct facets in greater detail in the following sections.

16.3.1 Analytical Activities

Typically, conducting trace data analysis using computational techniques can be summarized by several activities (cf. Marsland, 2014): First, the data are operationalized through separation and initial data processing in such a way that is suitable for analysis. Second, each sample is further distinguished by its discrete elements, or variables, resulting in constructs that can be stored in a 'clean' or 'tidy' data set ready for analysis (cf. Wickham, 2014). Third, preliminary or exploratory analysis is conducted to validate preliminary operationalizations of constructs. Fourth, emergent patterns can be conceptualized in the form of, for example, relations, processes or meaning. While we describe these activities in a linear sequence, analysts will find themselves performing most if not all of them by iterating between the four activities. This also includes repeating activities in any order throughout, understanding the trace data and refining ideas for subsequent analysis work. Table 16.1 summarizes the activities that are detailed in the following subsection.

The first activity a_1 involves the *separation* of the data into ontological units. Units of data define

Table 16.1 Analytical activities in computational analysis of trace data

Analytical activity	Description	Computational implementation	Analytical outcome
a_1 Separation	Specific data units such as interactions between individuals, logged events or text documents are singled out and processed as the (tentative) unit of analysis.	Subsetting and 'data wrangling' (for instance, in Python or R, but also database query languages such as SQL).	A data set with clear units of analysis (e.g., time intervals, interactions or units of text). (Usually, this means well-defined rows in tabular format.)
a_2 Discretization	Identification of specific categories for each data unit (e.g., time stamp and author for forum posts or direction and strength for social interactions).	Data cleaning, for example, raw mark-up into discrete documents using regular expressions or time stamps into discrete events.	A tidy data set with a clear distinction between data units and discrete data points representing each unit (usually well-defined and tidy columns in tabular format).
a_3 Validation	Applying exploratory data analysis and visualization techniques to identify emergent patterns from the data.	Network graph models, sequence/process models, topic modelling.	Descriptive visualizations showing emergent patterns in the data. This can include, for example, visualizations of topic models, network diagrams or sequential patterns.
a_4 Conceptualization	Conceptualizing the entities of interest (relations, processes or semantics) in a way that prepares explanation of emergent patterns.	Various forms of data visualization. Descriptive statistics of the output of computational analysis (or subsets).	Typically reported as integration with and reference to existing theory, tables or graphical models.

what is observable in the analysis and will typically be represented by rows in a tabular data format. The raw data has such a form that it must be interpreted through a script or application in order to translate it into a readable format (i.e., in tabular or other structured formats). As trace data samples are usually multimodal, it is necessary to identify and define the data units that are relevant for each specific analysis. Normally, raw digital trace data does not exist in a concise format that is readily structured for analysis, and it often consists of data from various sources. This means that data must be cleaned and separated into units of interest for the analyst such as, for example, posts, transactions, tweets, updates, profiles and interactions. In performing this separation, it is important to make sure that important aspects are not arbitrarily short-circuited by leaving out salient data units such as, for example, hashtags or direct mentions in social media data.

The second activity a_2 refers to the *discretization* of data units into meaningful

fractions. This includes evaluating the compatibility of emerging data units by comparing them with already included data units in such a way as to maintain them all in the same setting, thus producing a hierarchy or relative positioning of each data unit. This is especially important in tracing the processes by which one emerging ontology redefines or displaces another, as is the case in digital innovation (Godoe, 2000; Svahn et al., 2009). In practical terms, this means that trace data units should in some way be turned into discrete data to describe the relative strength or position of each data unit. Having separated and discretized the digital trace data, one can now begin validation and construct operationalization.

The third activity a_3 describes the identification and *validation of patterns and categories* emerging from the data. At this point, it is useful to employ various data exploration and visualization techniques to support categorization through trace data (Rogers, 2009, 2013; Venturini and Latour, 2010). This can be achieved using traditional descriptive statistics or other descriptive techniques from Natural Language Processing (Landauer et al., 1998; Chang et al., 2013) and Social Network Analysis (Granovetter, 1973; Prell, 2012). In addition, many analysts focus on a range of different data visualizations around ideas of converging and diverging tendencies in (groups of) the data. The aim is to validate the discretization and generate patterns for further analysis.

The fourth and final activity a_4 involves the conceptualization of digital trace data. Concepts are generated iteratively through an abductive process in which the researcher oscillates between computational and human pattern recognition (Lindberg, 2020). First, an initial proposition or working hypothesis is generated by the researcher identifying preliminary concepts and potential relations in the digital trace data. This usually yields 'narrow concepts' referring to a conceptualization that is still very specific to the respective data set being analyzed (Urquhart et al., 2009). Second, narrow concepts are then abstracted, and their relations corroborated, leading to more and more refined ideas. Through iteration and abductive reasoning, such refined ideas pave the way to substantive theory and eventually even formal theoretical considerations that aid the generalization of insight beyond the research context (Zachariadis et al., 2013).

16.3.2 Analytical Focus

The focus of computational analysis is tied to the characteristics of digital trace data that we described above. As we have outlined, digital traces are especially valuable to the reconstruction of social interaction, as well as the investigation of artifact-level data in great detail (Lazer and Radford, 2017; Østerlund et al., 2020). Most digital trace data thereby allow the analyst to focus on rich qualitative differences by focusing on either of the aspects described below in the analysis of social interaction with digital technology.

First, a relational focus **R**. Digital traces provide rich and directly accessible accounts of the micro-events that make up the emergence and evolution of social structure (Howison et al., 2011). The most commonly applied methodology to study relations

among entities is graph theory-based (social) network analysis (Howison et al., 2011; Sinclair, 2016). Therein, entities of interest (e.g., actors) are examined towards the number and type of connections to other entities. Network graphs are subsequently summarized through quantification of metrics at different levels of abstraction (i.e., graph, sub-community or node). Often, the quantification is complemented by visualization or qualitative inquiry into the formation, strength and persistence of found relations between entities resulting in a given structure.

Second, a processual focus **P**. Digital traces often have a distinct temporal dimension. Digital trace data, therefore, offer a great deal of insight into the antecedents and consequences of social interaction by utilizing the availability of temporality contained in such traces (Østerlund et al., 2020). This has profound consequences for the way in which researchers can think about inference, evidence and explanation of processes of interaction with digital artifacts (Cloutier and Langley, 2020). Most trace data are time-stamped or allow for the imposition of a temporal ordering principle. Researchers interested in processual aspects of trace data can therefore reconstruct processes of sociotechnical interaction by employing a wide range of sequence analysis methodologies (Gaskin et al., 2014; Pentland et al., 2020b). In this way, the processual focus on digital trace data opens up computational analysis which 'involves considering phenomena dynamically – in terms of movement, activity, events, change and temporal evolution' (Langley, 2007: 271) at an unprecedented level of detail.

Third, a semantic focus **S**. Digital traces also contain manifestations of meaning in digital environments expressed in the shape of, for example, status updates, comments or emails. This analytical focus aims at discerning semantic patterns in text corpora or collections of documents. This allows researchers to study meaning or discourse among a great number of people at a resolution that is sensitive to individual-level effects. To that end, the analysis seeks to reveal patterns in a set of documents by computationally extracting unobserved groupings based on semantic similarities between different parts of the data (such as words, phrases, sentiments, etc.) from natural language represented in textual data (Debortoli et al., 2016). Popular analysis methods include, but are not limited to, techniques associated with Natural Language Processing (Landauer et al., 1998; Chang et al., 2013), topic modelling techniques such as Latent Semantic Analysis (LSA) (Deerwester et al., 1990; Landauer et al., 1998; Wild and Stahl, 2007) or Latent Dirichlet Allocation (Sievert and Shirley, 2014). The outcome of computational analysis with a semantic focus is often a specific discursive composition or map, either in terms of differences between distinct semantic groupings or by tracing specific semantic patterns over time.

In conclusion, digital trace data can be used as a raw material that can be refined through computational analysis. Directing a set of shared analytical activities to a specific analytical focus reveals different types of emergent patterns of relations, processes or meanings. In the following section, we will show how qualitative researchers can apply computational methods to reveal three specific facets relating to relations, processes and meaning.

16.4 Constructing Facets from Digital Trace Data

As a guide for many research designs that are conceivable using computational analysis, facets of digital traces are constructed by A – a set of specific analytical activities $(a_1...a_4)$ performed with raw trace data – guided by one specific analytical focus (*Relational*, *Processual* or *Semantic*). By using the word 'facet', we seek to capture the multiple ways in which analytical activity and analytical foci can be combined in a given study design. Facets thus offer a vocabulary to assess others' work while allowing one to structure one's own computational analysis. To that end, this section outlines two important aspects of working with facets of digital trace data: (1) how analysts can construct different facets from trace data; and (2) which potential research questions can be derived from these rich facets. The facets suggested in Table 16.2 are meant as an illustration of the general framework for qualitative computational analysis, and do not represent an exhaustive

Table 16.2 Characteristics of selected digital trace facets

	Relational facet	Processual facet	Semantic facet
Research focus	Connections between actors and/or artifacts	Sequences of events capturing the interaction between actors and/or artifacts	Semantic patterns of narrative, discourse or sentiment
General computational analysis approach	Network Analysis	Sequence Analysis	Text Analysis
Typical data set	List of entities (actors/artifacts) and connections between each possible pair of entities. Tabular or hierarchical format.	Event logs with, for example, time stamp, actor, activity type and metadata. Commonly in tabular format.	A collection of text documents in the form of, for example, emails, forum posts, articles, etc. Commonly in hierarchical form.
Illustrative analysis techniques	Social Network Analysis Relational Event Modelling	State/Event Sequences Time-to-event Analysis Optimal matching Markov chain modelling	Topic Modelling Sentiment Analysis
Illustrative reference	Granovetter (1973) Trier (2008) Borgatti et al. (2009)	Abbott and Hrycak (1990) Pentland et al. (2020b) Ritschard et al. (2008) Gaskin et al. (2014) Lindberg et al. (2013)	Müller et al. (2016) Johnson et al. (2015) Debortoli et al. (2016)

list of ways in which researchers can analyze digital traces.

16.4.1 Relational Facet

An important facet that can be derived from trace data is what we refer to as the 'relational facet'. The relational facet aims to analyze and conceptualize social relations from digital trace data. Relations can be studied in a variety of ways, but in the context of digital trace data, we have focused specifically on relational structures made up of a set of linkages between social or technological entities through network analysis as the most commonly applied computational technique to such analysis (Granovetter, 1973; Wasserman and Faust, 1994). The investigation of actor relations has long been a focal interest of social scientists, but with the advent and maturation of computational tools, the scale and speed with which relations among entities can be captured and analyzed have increased. Summarized under the label of 'social network analysis', a range of techniques enable the extraction of meaningful insight into the sociotechnical relations from digital trace data (Scott, 1994; Prell, 2012). Network analysis has increasingly been applied in the social sciences (Knoke and Yang, 2008; Cioffi-Revilla, 2014) and recently also in the context of qualitative analysis using digital trace data (Whelan et al., 2016).

In general, network analysis focuses on a set of relations, or linkages, between a population of entities. The entities being analyzed can represent individuals, teams, organizations, technologies or a mix of different entities. Irrespective of the nature of the entities one wishes to represent, network analysis literature most commonly refers to network entities as vertices or nodes. Nodes are connected via links that are most often referred to as edges. The entire set of edges between nodes is called a network graph. Network graphs can be represented in the form of an adjacency matrix or for larger graphs as a list of nodes and attributes, representing if and how edges between nodes exist (Cornwell, 2015a). Irrespective of the exact analysis, network representations seek to capture the structure of links among the population of nodes. The resulting network graph can then be used for

computational manipulation to examine the structural properties of a given network graph or to explore the role and position of individual nodes within the network. Network analysis produces both mathematical and visual output, both of which are interpretable for analysis. It is, however, important not to confuse the output of network analysis with analytical results as we know it from qualitative research as they are purely descriptive and do not involve conceptualization or interpretation. Thus, network analyses, in the form of a structured representation or network graph, provide access to the structural properties of the network, and can as such be used as input to build theory analogous to a set of descriptive codes (Urquhart et al., 2009; Miles et al., 2014). A network graph is not a theory in and of itself.

Subsequent analyses are at the analyst's discretion and can be applied to at least three levels of analysis: at the network level, sub-network level and individual level. In the language of network analysis, this is equivalent to analyzing an entire network, its sub-communities or its nodes. On the network level, points of interest for understanding the global structure of a given network typically include its density (i.e., the ratio of actual to the maximum possible connections in a graph) or its centralization (i.e., the empirical frequency distribution of the number of edges per node). On the sub-network level, groups of nodes are investigated to infer groupings and links between groups. Metrics of interest include clustering coefficients (the degree to which groups of nodes tend to cluster together) and modularity (i.e., how separated and distinct communities are in the network). Finally, on the individual level, specific nodes of the network are assessed towards their specific position within a network graph. Node-level metrics can, for example, include node centrality (i.e., number of links to a node, indicating, for example, its relative importance) or betweenness (i.e., the number of connections between other nodes that pass through a specific node, measuring the importance of a node's ability to connect to other portions of the graph).

Howison et al. (2011) discuss in some detail the validity issues that arise when applying network analysis to digital trace data. Here, we will focus

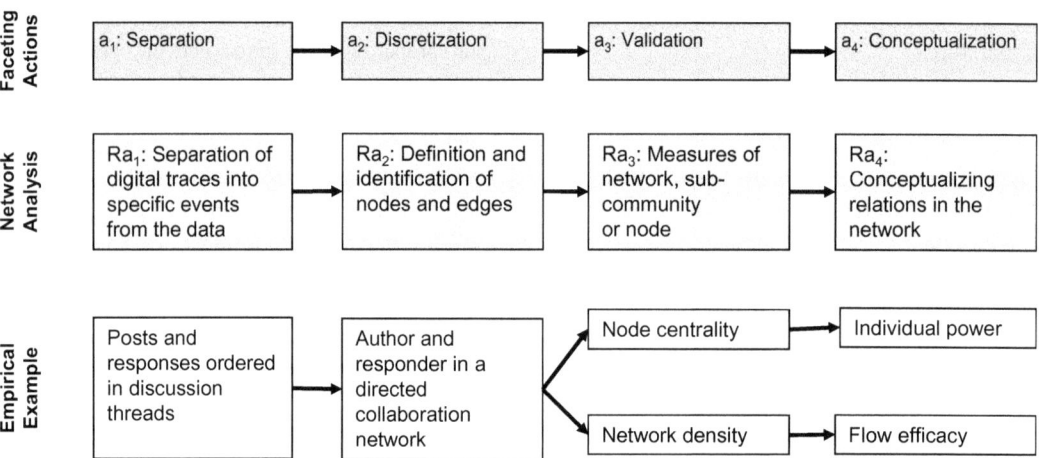

Figure 16.1 Steps in the creation of the relational facet of digital trace data
Source: Adapted from Howison et al. (2011).

on how to apply network analysis to conceptualize relational and social structures using digital trace data. To construct a relational facet from trace data, one must adapt the four analytical activities described above to network analysis as shown in Figure 16.1.

As mentioned above, a wide variety of nodes can be analyzed depending on the type of digital trace data that is collected. Most digital trace data represent records of relations of actors and artifacts in an information system. As such, they include a wide variety of different information that could potentially yield a structural representation of relations among actors and/or artifacts (i.e., a network). Consider an online forum displaying posts and comments, direct mentions of users and hyperlinks between posts. All these different elements can be arranged to yield various network structures between social actors and the artifacts of the discussion forum.

16.4.1.1 Ra₁: Separation

After collecting digital trace data with a relational focus, the next step is to identify a unit of analysis and separate the data into equivalent units. The data unit separation defines what kind of network is being analyzed (e.g., communication network, dissemination network, affiliation network, etc.). For example, the data unit for the aforementioned

online discussion forum allows us to define different entities and their relations. One could either: focus on users (nodes) and take their appearance in a discussion thread as indicators for a relation (edges); or view individual posts (nodes) as having a connection (edges) whenever they relate to the same topic under discussion anywhere on the forum. Unit separation thus refers to the way in which the entities that the researcher wishes to observe are defined through the traces at her disposal (see, e.g., Moretti, 2013).

When a data unit has been identified, the raw data can then be separated into a structured data table where each row represents the smallest data unit (e.g., a single user or comment). Specifically, the raw data should be separated into a tabular form with each row representing a connection and each column representing source node, target node, time stamp and affiliation. At this point, it might be useful to add columns referencing the hierarchical structure of the data, such as 'parent post' or similar, depending on the chosen scope. This structured format allows for further analysis of our analytical units by separating them into discrete units.

Already at this point, some initial decisions are made about the ontological hierarchy inherent in the data by foregrounding a specific separation of the digital traces into corresponding data units (Venturini et al., 2018). Data unit separation thus has direct consequences for the scope of analyses that can be employed at later stages in the process, as it would be impossible to choose a different scope of analysis such as individual posts or discussion threads without repeating this step.

16.4.1.2 Ra$_2$: Discretization

When the network scope has been defined and data units separated, the digital traces can then be divided into discrete relational units. As the smallest unit of analysis of a relation consists of two related individuals, the digital trace data should be represented in a format consisting of a source node, a target node and possibly some descriptive data points that relate to the quality of the relation. In terms of network analysis, this means representing the data as either an adjacency matrix (Moreno, 1934; Cioffi-Revilla, 2014) or as a node and an edge list, as that can be used by many software implementations such as Gephi (Bastian et al., 2009) and igraph (Csardi and Nepusz, 2006). Adjacency matrix representation of relational structures builds on matrix algebra and adopts its notation. As an example, we can consider a network with i nodes represented in an adjacency matrix M. Figure 16.2 shows an

adjacency matrix representation of a network consisting of a collection of N nodes ($n_1\ldots n_i$). Each of the edges is then represented by a numerical value denoting the strength, or weight, of the relation. For instance, the relation between nodes n_2 and n_3 has strength 2, while there is no link between nodes n_1 and n_3. Each cell in the adjacency matrix represents the existence of a relation, or edge, between any of the adjacent node pairs. The value in each cell can be used to denote either a categorical characteristic or continuous strength of each edge or can be represented in a binary way where edges are represented by 1 and the absence of an edge by 0.

While fairly intuitive, the adjacency matrix representation is quite limited in terms of qualitative detail richness of either nodes or edges. Therefore, and for grounds of computational efficiency, many statistical software packages such as those mentioned above operate with edge and node lists. An edge list has two basic columns for the source node and target node, representing a directed network graph. Also, it can contain a number of columns representing different strengths, labels and descriptive data about each edge. Furthermore, the analyst can compile a node list containing attributes, meta-data and descriptions for each node. Together, this representation

	n_1	n_2	n_3	n_4	n_5	n_6	n_7	n_8	$\ldots n_i$
n_1	0	1	0	0	0	0	0	3	
n_2	1	0	2	0	1	2	0	0	
n_3	0	2	0	0	0	0	1	0	
n_4	0	0	0	0	0	0	0	0	
n_5	0	1	0	0	0	1	0	0	
n_6	0	2	0	2	1	0	0	1	
n_7	0	0	0	0	0	0	0	0	
n_8	3	0	0	0	0	1	0	0	
$\ldots n_i$									

Figure 16.2 Section of adjacency matrix MN

allows for a richer interpretation of network structures as it allows the researcher to add each attribute data point as a layer in subsequent analysis and conceptualization.

16.4.1.3 Ra$_3$: Validation

In order to validate and interpret relevant categories from the digital trace data in the context of the relational facet, a graph visualization of the network should be generated. The illustration can add different qualitative as well as quantitative attributes by, for example, making node size dependent on the in-degree (i.e., the number of connections to each node from other nodes) and can determine node colour based on a categorical attribute, such as job role, gender or technology usage. The colour of edges or lines between nodes can equally be visualized depending on specific attributes associated with each relation. This method can be used to interpret the structure of the network as a whole (e.g., the efficacy of information flows through the network) or individual nodes (e.g., the individual power of a single node based on its relative position).

Once such patterns have been identified, they can then be validated through several metrics describing node position and network structure. For example, the relative importance of individual nodes can be validated through the degree centrality metric, which denotes the number of links connecting a specific node, and information flow efficacy can be validated using the network density metric, which denotes the number of actual links relative to the total number of possible links in the entire network.

Having extracted such patterns from the data and validated them through visualization and network metrics, a categorization of network nodes, sub-communities and structural properties of the entire network emerges. While this categorization relies on domain knowledge, the resulting categories and the boundaries between them emerge exclusively from the empirical analysis of the digital trace data. The patterns and categories resulting from grounded computational techniques are thus the basis for later conceptualization and theory building.

16.4.1.4 Ra$_4$: Conceptualization

Conceptualization in the relational facet involves building theory in which qualitative attributes of nodes and edges are analyzed in an ongoing process of assembling, reconfiguring and aligning research questions with outcomes of computational data analysis (Weltevrede, 2016). A conceptualization of relations through network analysis invokes several validity issues relating to the entire process from information systems in which digital traces are produced over the selection of the unit of analysis and discretization of the data to drawing inferences from network analyses. Consequently, the conceptualization of relational structures should consider: (1) boundary conditions and limitations due to the specific validity issues associated with network analysis (Howison et al., 2011); (2) an explication of the events that are aggregated to define relational entities (Trier, 2008); (3) the actors involved in the network and their connections (Knoke and Yang, 2008; Prell, 2012); and (4) the relational patterns that emerge as a result of the analysis (Cioffi-Revilla, 2014). For example, the conceptualization of the relative importance of an individual node in a network should take into account the system in which the digital trace data was produced, as well as any other validity issues associated with the mining, sampling, discretization and analysis of the data. Perhaps centrality indicates a person doing much of the work without having much power.

Finally, to interpret the node level and community or cluster-level analyses, the emergent relational structure in the entire network as a whole should be explicated to provide context. The importance of a node being very central is interpreted differently depending on whether the network as a whole is very dense and well connected, or if it is situated in an inherently sparse network of relations.

Summing up, computational implementation of network analysis provides researchers with a toolbox for analyzing and conceptualizing relations from digital trace data. However, analyzing relations is but one way in which digital traces can be faceted to generate insights about a digital environment.

16.4.2 Processual Facet

Another important facet of digital trace data relates to its processual nature. Often, digital traces tie in temporal elements as they capture sociotechnical interaction in relation to time. Consider a working day beginning in the morning of each weekday, followed by a commute, time spent at a place of work, another commute and ending with time at home. Such instances abound and illustrate that social interaction occurs in sequences that are of salience not because of an explicit time stamp, but because of the order in which they occur (Abbott, 1990; Cornwell, 2015a). Similar processes are often also captured in trace data which in turn lends such data to the investigation of processes.

A family of analysis techniques that is capable of dealing with such processual observations is sequence analysis (Abbott, 1990, 1995; Biemann and Datta, 2014). Sequence analysis techniques are well established in the social sciences (Heise, 1989; Abbott, 1995) in an attempt to complement variance-based analysis techniques. Sequence methods focus on diachronicity by exploring changes in a unit of analysis through time and space and provide a powerful toolbox for computational research designs. Despite variation in approaches, a relational facet of digital trace data can be constructed through the following analytical activities.

16.4.2.1 Pa₁: Separation

After collecting potential process trace data, the first step towards constructing a processual facet is the definition of the sequence of events as it pertains to the chosen unit of analysis. The identification and classification of the unit of analysis establish a typology of the object under study. Drawing from the disciplines informing sequence analysis in the social sciences, data unit separation is often metaphorically expressed as determining the 'DNA of a unit of analysis' (see, e.g., Gaskin et al., 2010). The result of a robust unit separation is thus a mutually exclusive and collectively exhaustive description of the invariant parts constituting the unit of analysis (Heise, 1991; Abbott, 1995). This is often followed by qualifying the variant attributes that capture the anticipated

variation across the population under study. Expressed in terms of 'category and instance' or 'component and permissible arrangement' (Gaskin et al., 2010), the general purpose of a typology is the creation of a vocabulary needed to classify the object under study. This definition guides the creation of the processual facet going forward. Consider, for instance, that one was interested in constructing sequences of students undergoing education. In this example, the unit of analysis would be the individual student (the invariant part), whereas the stages of each student's education – such as the academic degrees obtained over time – are the variant parts that differ across units of analysis, as well as over time.

16.4.2.2 Pa₂: Discretization

Constructing the processual facet involves the definition of discrete events. Records of events express an important expectation of the multimodality in the data needed to construct processes from digital trace data (Pentland et al., 2020b). Conceptually, sequences are finite sets of ordered elements such as occurrences, states or activities following some ordering principle (Biemann and Datta, 2014). Most commonly, event order is achieved by imposing temporal, spatial or logical hierarchy onto elements of the set (Abbott, 1990; Cornwell, 2015b). Trace data often contain explicit or implicit information on the temporality of social interaction. Explicit temporality of interaction in trace data refers to direct time stamps associated with observations. For instance, the metadata used to annotate digital traces regularly involves some form of a record of continuous calendar time as it relates to the logged interaction through the system in which it occurs. Digital traces as diverse as emails, forum posts and source code changes are therefore often time-stamped in a one-to-one relationship with a specific and detailed record of time per record of activity. In contrast, implicit temporality refers to the imposition or reconstruction of temporal order in a way that is meaningful to social actors.

This first step of discretization thus needs to provide the analyst interested in processual facets of trace data with an answer as to what constitutes the 'when' of the interaction. Sequence analysis allows categorical, discrete, continuous and even multidimensional data scales (Abbott, 1990; Biemann and Datta, 2014). Regardless of the cardinality of measurement, eligible events can include points in continuous linear calendar time or simplified temporally or spatially ordered items. In case the temporality is merely implied, event order can also be identified empirically (e.g., by observing the order in which social activity occurred, for instance, tasks in routine) or conceptually (e.g., by linking actual observations to abstract representations of the order of an archetypal process). The decision by the analyst as to what constitutes the timing of an event is important early on as it affects the process of data collection, manipulation and analysis going forward.

16.4.2.3 Pa₃: Validation

Records of activity complete sequence data sets by complementing the former elements, unit of analysis and records of events. As such, records of activity capture the variant attributes of the unit of analysis through the instances of the specified events and thus offer an opportunity for early validation of involved constructs. The processual facet requires mutually exclusive categories of

activity to differentiate the types of event that any unit of analysis could undergo (Gaskin et al., 2014). Sequences are generally differentiated between state and event sequences. State sequences explore the status of a unit of analysis at specific time points, whereas event sequences represent changes in states. While state sequences are suitable to investigate timing and duration of instances, event sequences allow detailed examination of transitions from one state to another and thus are well suited for investigations of shifts and changes in processes (Abbott, 1990). Either states or events are selected to form consecutive sets of unambiguously categorized and ordered instances in relation to the specified unit of analysis (Ritschard et al., 2008; Gaskin et al., 2014). These categories form the study's sequence alphabet (Abbott, 1990; Cornwell, 2015b), denoting the types of event that each unit of analysis could experience. Categories can be theoretically or empirically informed to distinguish types of events. Determined by the respective study design, an activity might, for example, denote different actors in a selected process stage, product attributes and their developments, or a job position held at a given point in time. In Figure 16.3, we visualize a generic sequence data set S. Therein,

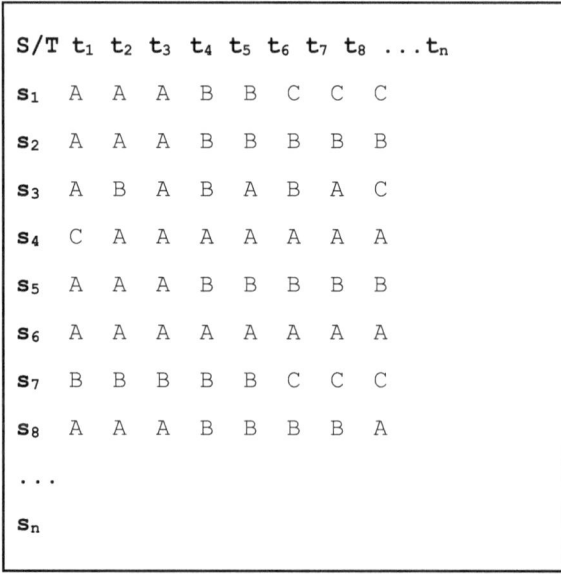

Figure 16.3 Generic categorical sequences

each cell represents one of three discrete activity types (A, B or C) recorded for each observation $(s_1...s_n)$ at each event time point $(t_1...t_n)$. Such sequence data can be generated from any trace data that allows the identification of units of analysis, records of events and a mutually exclusive categorical definition of activity.

16.4.2.4 Pa₄: Conceptualization

Steps $(Pa_1...Pa_3)$ yield the basis for computational research with the focus of analyzing processes using sequence analysis: (1) typology of the unit of analysis for which sequence data is collected, the actual sequence data consisting of (2) records of events and (3) records of activity (Abbott 1990, 1995; Heise, 1991; Ritschard et al., 2008; Gaskin et al., 2014). Once these elements are in place, the conceptualization step includes the designation of the processual change in the constituent parts of a unit of analysis over time. For instance, many different tasks can be performed on a sequence data set such as the generic illustration above. Consequently, the conceptualization of change can take various forms. Generally, sequence patterns are distinguished as either recurrent or non-recurrent depending on the uniqueness of events and applied sampling, as well as whether approaches focus on an entire sequence or sub-sequence as the main outcome of analysis (Abbott, 1990). Additionally, the identification of patterns in trace data can serve as an analytical focus in its own right or serve as a complementing part for further analysis (Heise, 1989; Abbott, 1990; Biemann and Datta, 2014). Therefore – and pending the quality and quantity of observations that are transformed into sequences – a wide variety of analyses can be performed on sequence data, with each deployed technique offering a different foundation for inference and theorization (Abbott, 1995, 1990; Biemann and Datta, 2014).

For qualitative IS researchers, using digital trace data to generate the processual facet offers a range of possibilities to investigate changes over time at a high level of detail. In particular, collating observations into sequences allows the exploration of processes through detailed stratification of the data

(Pentland et al., 2020b). What makes the processual facet 'rich' are the possibilities of including diverse contextual information. What has been called 'combinatoric explosion of fine-grained categories' (Pentland et al., 2020b) allows the analyst to discover and explain change trajectories by singling out observations or groups of observations. Emergent patterns within or across groups lend themselves to iteratively defining categories and informing theorizing by iterating between emergent ideas and established concepts (cf. Urquhart, 2001). Popular approaches to analyzing sequence data that help with finding, differentiating and validating patterns in data include, but are not limited to:

- *Pattern Analysis*: detection of repetitions within or across sequences.
- *Optimal matching*: measuring and comparing similarity and dissimilarity between sequences (wholly or in parts).
- *Cluster analysis*: resemblance-based analysis of groups of sequences on metrics at the discretion of the researcher.
- *Coalescent analysis*: associating changes within sequences to shared events at the beginning and/ or end of the sequence.
- *Transition analysis*: examining change between sequence-adjacent elements (e.g., Markovian analysis of transition points and their probabilities).

Figure 16.4 maps the steps involved in creating the processual facet from digital trace data using Lindberg et al. (2013) as an example, who in turn implemented sequence analysis as described by Gabadinho et al. (2011).

In summary, sequence analysis offers a toolbox to IS researchers to generate the 'processual facet' inherent in digital trace data. The processual facet can be generated on every level of abstraction, thus supporting diverse research interests in information systems studies (individual, team, organization, industry, etc.). Through sequence analysis, the processual facet is thus well suited to investigate trajectories of change through exploration of granular patterns, compositions and conditions of activity within and across sociotechnical systems.

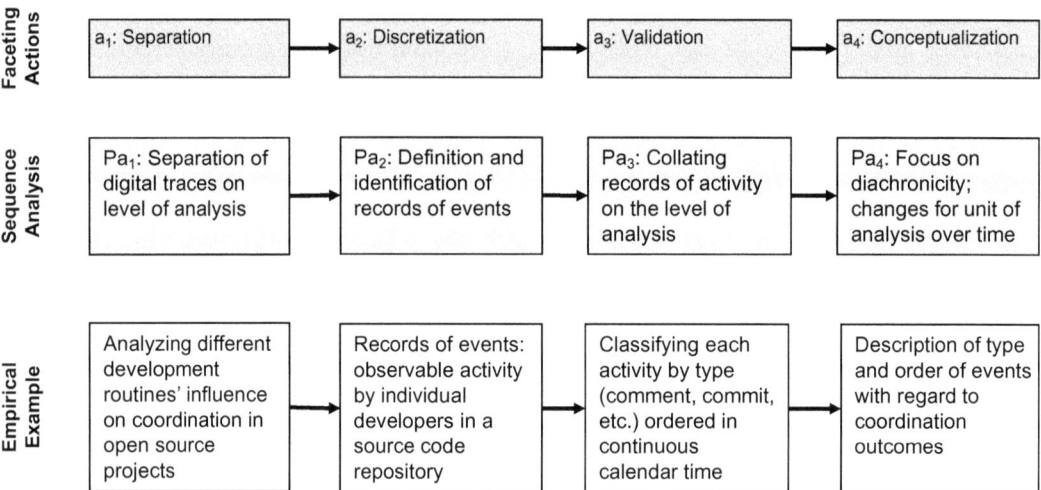

Figure 16.4 Steps in the creation of the processual facet of digital trace data
Source: Adapted from Lindberg et al. (2016).

16.4.3 Semantic Facet

Yet another important facet that can be derived from trace data is what we refer to as the 'semantic' facet. That is the investigation of discourse, sentiment or meaning from trace data summarized by the label 'Natural Language Processing'.

The semantic facet is aimed at conceptualizing patterns of meaning in a large body of text. Given the vast number of documents that are typically extracted from digital traces, the emerging semantic patterns are often not visible to the individual actor or analyst, as it would not be viable for an individual to read and process the sheer volume of text in a structured way (Debortoli et al., 2016). Therefore, semantic patterns are often referred to as 'latent' in the sense that they reveal emergent meanings at a high level of abstraction (i.e., across vast historical records, accounts in long event logs, entire authorships or distributed community discourse).

To construct a semantic facet, such latent patterns must be extracted from digital traces of natural language. This is most frequently achieved by applying topic modelling techniques (Steyvers and Griffiths, 2007; Blei, 2012). Topic modelling techniques are models that reveal patterns in a set of documents by extracting unobserved groupings (latent themes) based on semantic similarities

between different parts of the data. Topic models are generally divided into models that extract latent semantic patterns based on either term frequency such as latent derelict allocation (LDA) (Sievert and Shirley, 2014) or semantic closeness such as latent semantic analysis (LSA) (Landauer et al., 1998; Chang et al., 2013). In common for both types of topic model is that they reveal latent patterns that would not be accessible by other means than computational analysis techniques.

While most topic modelling originates in probabilistic statistics (Blei, 2012; Landauer et al., 2013), it is increasingly being applied in qualitative research designs as a means of providing descriptive and axial coding (Glaser and Strauss, 1967) of large collections of documents (see, e.g., Andersen and Ingram Bogusz, 2019), or as a part of an inductive computational research design (Cioffi-Revilla, 2014).

As illustrated in Figure 16.5, the construction of a semantic facet includes translating each faceting action into analytical steps aimed at conceptualizing latent patterns of meaning from digital trace data.

16.4.3.1 Sa₁: Unit Separation

In the first step in creating the semantic facet, textual content and relevant attributes should be

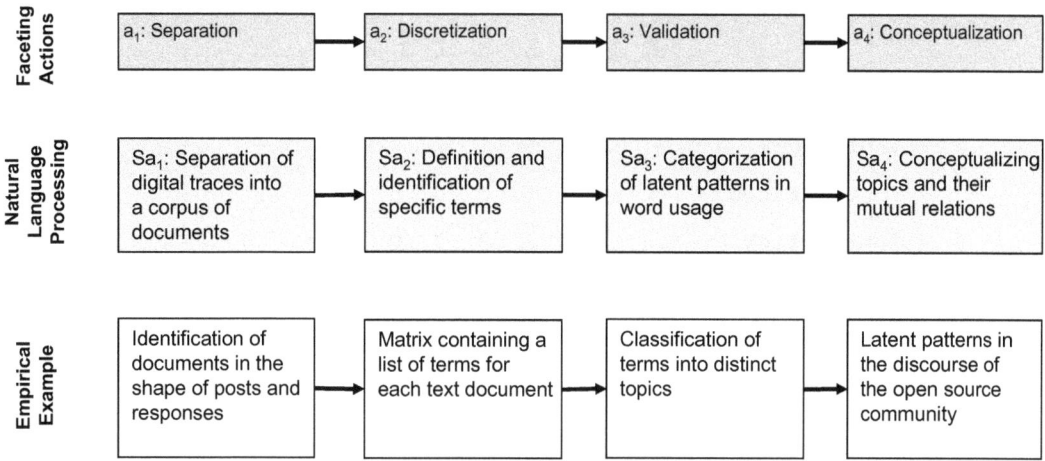

Figure 16.5 Steps in the creation of the semantic facet of digital trace data
Source: Adapted from Blei et al. (2003) and Debortoli et al. (2016).

extracted from the digital trace data and separated into a collection of distinct documents, often referred to as a 'corpus' (Blei et al., 2003), and a set of relevant attributes to be used for cross-sectional analysis. As digital trace data is found and, in that sense, secondary or tertiary data, they often contain a significant amount of noise in the form of, for example, duplicate entries, symbols that delineate the different elements, tabs and white spaces, as well as empty or non-language entries. For example, social media posts may contain duplicate records and automated records generated by bots, and information collected by web crawlers may include some of the mark-ups from the original website (Debortoli et al., 2016). Another challenge with separating digital traces into a corpus of distinct documents stems from the structure of digital traces collected from online sources such as social media or online discussion forums. In social media posts and online discussion boards, documents are not necessarily analogous, but are organized in a threaded structure, where the main post enlists several comments or responses (Choi et al., 2013). The researcher then has the option to focus on either each separate exchange or entire threads as the unit of analysis depending on whether the research question focuses on, for example, key opinion leaders or power relations or is directed at the general discourse. In case of the

latter, posts in the same threads should be combined into single documents, and attributes should be summarized or concatenated.

When the text has been cleaned and separated into distinct documents, attributes for cross-sectional analysis should be cleaned or, if necessary, calculated or constructed from existing attributes. To ensure transparency and reliability, exact procedural description for how attributes were cleaned or constructed should be provided (e.g., in the form of a coded script).

16.4.3.2 Sa$_2$: Discretization

Having identified a corpus of documents, discrete terms are identified for each document. In order to transform words in the corpus of text documents to discrete units of meaning, a number of procedures are followed to transform them into discrete semantic units by decreasing syntactic variation and to distinguish meaningful terms from noise.

As a first step, words are reduced to their stem so that variations of the same word (such as, for example, 'bank', 'banking' and 'banker') are reduced to their semantic stem (i.e., 'bank'). A further step to transform words into discrete semantic units is to transform all letters into lower case so capitalized and lower-case instances of the

	d_1	d_2	d_3	d_4	d_5	d_6	d_7	d_8	$...d_i$
t_1 post	1	0	0	0	0	0	0	3	
t_2 bank	0	1	0	0	1	2	0	0	
t_3 branch	0	2	0	0	0	0	0	0	
t_4 click	0	1	0	1	0	0	0	0	
t_5 communit	0	2	0	2	1	0	0	1	
t_6 custom	0	2	0	2	1	0	0	1	
t_7 transf	0	1	0	0	0	0	0	0	
$...t_j$									

Figure 16.6 Term-document matrix

same word are identical. To reduce noise and weed out common terms, words that are commonly used in any kind of document and that are therefore of little semantic value are excluded from the terms to be analyzed. Such a list of generally used terms is generally referred to as 'stopwords', and includes redundant words such as 'and', 'the', 'to', etc. (Landauer et al., 2013). After transforming words into discrete semantic units and removing noise, a distribution of terms $(t_1...t_j)$ over the document corpus $(d_1...d_i)$ is generated and represented as a term-document matrix as shown in Figure 16.6. For instance, we can see that the document d_1 contains a single occurrence of the term 'post' and that document d_2 contains two mentions of the term 'branch'.

Having transformed words into discrete semantic terms, each term is then weighed by how prominent and exclusive it is to a particular document. Topic models that are based on semantic closeness (such as, for example, LSA) rather than term frequency (like, for example, LDA) will apply an algorithm called term frequency-inverse document frequency, or TF-IDF (Salton et al., 1975) to this end, while term frequency-based models have built-in model parameters that can be set post hoc (such as, for example, the lambda parameter in an LDA model). When this is done, the model can be fitted to derive topics or categories from the text.

16.4.3.3 Sa₃: Validation

To categorize meaning within the semantic facet, words across the documents in the text corpus must be assigned to distinct topics. To this end, a topic model is fitted to detect patterns in the term-document matrix. Different topic models represent different approaches to clustering related words, but in its simplest form, words that appear often in the same document are seen as being semantically related. The result is a distribution of words and their frequencies clustered into several topics (Debortoli et al., 2016). However, this usually does not directly result in distinct categories of terms that are easily interpretable as meaningful topics. Often, this requires exploration of different settings of concentration parameters that determine how exclusive documents are towards associating with specific topics (a document-topic distribution usually denoted as the alpha distribution) and how exclusive topics are to words that also appear in other categories (a term-topic distribution also referred to as the beta distribution). Exploring the text in this way at different levels of magnification is often helpful in validating the meaningfulness of the emerging topics. This exploration and fine-tuning of the lens that is a topic model is not an exact science, but a research activity more akin to sensitivity and abstraction as known from, for example, grounded theory (Glaser, 1978; Urquhart et al., 2009).

16.4.3.4 Sa₄: Conceptualization

The activities in the semantic facet include separating the digital trace data into a corpus of text documents, identifying discrete terms in the corpus and validating that terms have been categorized into a meaningful set of topics (Steyvers and Griffiths, 2007; Blei, 2012; Debortoli et al., 2016). Having processed the digital trace data in this way, the researcher can now conceptualize patterns of meaning. Semantic patterns are typically conceptualized in one of three ways: understanding and interpretation of an individual topic; understanding and interpretation of the relationships between different topics; and understanding the different topics that are covered within a specific document or a set of documents. The meaning of each topic can be induced by examining the term-topic distribution – that is, the list of most prevalent words within each category. Having all versions of the raw digital trace data allows the researcher to qualitatively analyze the topics at different levels of abstraction, from examining prevalent terms as descriptive coding to zooming into specific documents to derive contextual meaning at high resolution (Rogers, 2013).

There are several ways of interpreting and understanding patterns in the relation between topics, ranging from applying principal component analysis and plotting inter-topic distance maps (Sievert and Shirley, 2014), to examining the prevalence of several topics over time (e.g., Andersen and Ingram Bogusz, 2019). Finally, semantic patterns can be conceptualized in the topics that are covered in an individual document or a set of related documents like, for example, documents by the same author, articles using the same keywords or documents written within a particular time frame.

As the outcomes of topic modelling and natural language processing techniques are generally descriptive, some kind of additional conceptualization is necessary in order to derive patterns of meaning from digital trace data. While most literature on topic modelling suggests either explanatory or predictive approaches to conceptualizing patterns of meaning from topic modelling (Debortoli et al., 2016), natural language processing is increasingly applied in inductive research designs

as a way of identifying concepts and their relations from textual data (Jockers, 2013; Rogers, 2013).

16.5 Utilizing the Rich Facets of Digital Trace Data

As we demonstrated above, researchers have the opportunity to gain deep insight into social interaction with digital technology using the rich facets inherent in digital trace data. We have identified at least three such facets focusing on (1) structures (relational facet), (2) sequences (processual facet) or (3) meaning (semantic facet). By explaining how researchers can generate these facets, we can also point to a range of research questions that can be addressed using computational analysis approaches to generate respective facets of digital trace data. We summarize the facets, relevant computational techniques for implementation and related research questions in Table 16.3.

16.6 Conclusions

Social phenomena occur in digital environments which requires the interaction with dedicated computational tools to observe them effectively. Such phenomena were long thought impenetrable for qualitative researchers due to the tradition of collecting and analyzing rich, small n data. In contrast, digital trace data were long thought beneficial for their abundant availability, implying that it is the scale of such data that is valuable.

To counter this misconception, in this chapter we have proposed and substantiated a way for IS researchers to leverage the richness captured in digital trace data. Specifically, we have shown that digital trace data can be faceted to reveal patterns relating to social structures (relational facet), sequences (processual facet) and meaning (semantic facet). The chapter provides an approach through which researchers can construct a rich facet from trace data by following a series of analytical activity steps (data unit separation, data discretization, category validation and conceptualization). Showcasing how researchers can work

Table 16.3 Unit of analysis and examples of relevant research questions for each facet

Faceting approach to digital trace data	Unit of analysis	Relevant computational techniques	Examples of related research questions
Relational facet	The structure of relations between a group of actors	Social Network Analysis Network visualization Explorative analysis of node attributes Graph Models/ Descriptions Degree Distributions	→ What are the power relations between actors in a group? → How does information diffuse through a communication network? → Why do nodes differ in their relative importance to a focal network? → How do groups carry out certain activities? → What kind of actors assume which roles in the network? → What is the role of groups of members in a network? → How and why does the structure of a network change over time?
Processual facet	The sequence (elements) of technology-mediated social activity	State/Event Sequence Analysis Relational Event Models Event Structure Models Survival Analysis Narrative Networks	→ What are the consequences of sequence X with attribute Y? → Why did a certain process outcome occur? → How and why does a unit of analysis change over time? → What contextual factors determine differences in change trajectories? → Why do certain process elements occur together (or not)? → Why do certain process elements occur early/late/never in a sequence?
Semantic facet	Patterns of meaning across a collection of documents	Natural language processing Topic modelling Distance maps Cross-sectional analysis	→ How is a particular topic discussed within a particular community? → What is the landscape of the discourse? → How does a discourse shift over time? → Who are the key influencers?

with different aspects of digital trace data reveals the richness inherent in such data. This is useful as it pays attention to the specific characteristics of digital trace data and enables a large number of investigations of sociotechnical interactions in unprecedented depth as well as breadth.

References

Abbott, A. (1995). Sequence analysis: New methods for old ideas. *Annual Review of Sociology*, 21(1), 93–113.

Abbott, A. (1990). A primer on sequence methods. *Organization Science*, 1(4), 375–392.

Abbott, A. and Hrycak, A. (1990). Measuring resemblance in sequence data: An optimal matching analysis of musicians' careers. *American Journal of Sociology*, 96(1), 144–185.

Alvarez, R. M. (2016). *Computational Social Science: Discovery and Prediction*. New York, NY: Cambridge University Press.

Andersen, J. V. and Ingram Bogusz, C. (2019). Self-organizing in blockchain infrastructures: Generativity through shifting objectives and forking. *Journal of the Association of Information Systems*, 20(9), 247–265.

Baldwin, C., MacCormack, A. and Rusnak, J. (2014). Hidden structure: Using network methods to map system architecture. *Research Policy*, 43(8), 1381–1397.

Bastian, M., Heymann, S. and Jacomy, M. (2009). Gephi: An open-source software for exploring and manipulating networks. Proceedings of the Third International Conference on Weblogs and Social Media, San Jose, CA.

Biemann, T. and Datta, D. K. (2014). Analyzing sequence data: Optimal matching in management research. *Organizational Research Methods*, 17(1), 51–76.

Blei, D. M. (2012). Probabilistic topic models. *Communications of the ACM*, 55(4), 77–84.

Blei, D. M., Ng, A. Y. and Jordan, M. I. (2003). Latent dirichlet allocation. *Journal of Machine Learning Research*, 3(1), 993–1022.

Borgatti, S. P., Mehra, A., Brass, D. J. and Labianca, G. (2009). Network analysis in the social sciences. *Science*, 323(5916), 892–895.

Chang, K., Yih, W. and Meek, C. (2013). Multi-relational latent semantic analysis. Conference on Empirical Methods in Natural Language Processing, Seattle, WA.

Choi, K. S., Im, I. and Yoo, Y. (2013). Liquid communication: An analysis of the impact of mobile micro-blogging on communication and decision-making. International Conference on Information Systems, Milan, Italy.

Cioffi-Revilla, C. (2014). *Introduction to Computational Social Science: Principles and Applications*. London: Springer.

Cioffi-Revilla, C. (2010). Computational social science. *Wiley Interdisciplinary Reviews: Computational Statistics*, 2(3), 259–271.

Cloutier, C. and Langley, A. (2020). What makes a process theoretical contribution? *Organization Theory*, 1(1), Article 2631787720902473.

Cornwell, B. (2015a). Network methods for sequence analysis. In *Social Sequence Analysis: Methods and Applications*. New York, NY: Cambridge University Press, pp. 155–251.

Cornwell, B. (2015b). Theoretical foundations of social sequence analysis. In *Social Sequence Analysis: Methods and Applications*. New York, NY: Cambridge University Press, pp. 21–56.

Csardi, G. and Nepusz, T. (2006). The igraph software package for complex network research. *InterJournal, Complex Systems*, 1965(5), 1–9.

Debortoli, S., Müller, O., Junglas, I. and vom Brocke, J. (2016). Text mining for information systems researchers: An annotated topic modeling tutorial. *Communications of the Association for Information Systems*, 39(1), 110–135.

Deerwester, S., Dumais, S. T. and Landauer, T. K. (1990). Indexing by latent semantic analysis. *Journal of the American Society for Information Science*, 41(6), 391-407.

Faulkner, P. and Runde, J. (2019). Theorizing the digital object. *MIS Quarterly*, 43(4), 1279–1302.

Gabadinho, A., Ritschard, G. and Studer, M. (2011). Analyzing and visualizing state sequences in R with TraMineR. *Journal of Statistical Software*, 40(4), 1–37.

Gaskin, J., Berente, N., Lyytinen, K. and Yoo, Y. (2014). Toward generalizable sociomaterial inquiry: A computational approach for zooming in and out of sociomaterial routines. *MIS Quarterly*, 38(3), 849–871.

Gaskin, J., Schutz, D., Thummadi, V., Weiss, A., Berente, N., Lyytinen, K. and Yoo, Y. (2010). Design DNA: A methodological artifact for sequencing of socio-technical design patterns. International Conference on Information Systems, St Louis, MO.

Glaser, B. G. (1978). *Theoretical Sensitivity: Advances in the Methodology of Grounded Theory*. Mill Valley, CA: Sociology Press.

Glaser, B. G. and Strauss, A. (1967). *The Discovery of Grounded Theory*. Chicago, IL: Aldine Publishing.

Godoe, H. (2000). Innovation regimes, R&D and radical innovations in telecommunications. *Research Policy*, 29(9), 1033–1046.

Granovetter, M. S. (1973). The strength of weak ties. *American Journal of Sociology*, 78(6), 1360–1380.

Hedman, J., Srinivasan, N. and Lindgren, R. (2013). Digital traces or information systems: Sociomateriality made researchable. International Conference on Information Systems: Reshaping Society through Information Systems Design, Milan, Italy.

Heise, D. R. (1991). Event structure analysis: A qualitative model of quantitative research. In N. Fielding and R. Lee (eds), *Using Computers in Qualitative Research*. Newbury Park, CA: Sage, pp. 1–22.

Heise, D. R. (1989). Modeling event structures. *Journal of Mathematical Sociology*, 14(2–3), 139–169.

Howison, J., Wiggins, A. and Crowston, K. (2011). Validity issues in the use of social network analysis with digital trace data. *Journal of the Association for Information Systems*, 12(12), 767–797.

Johnson, S. L., Safadi, H. and Faraj, S. (2015). The emergence of online community leadership. *Information Systems Research*, 26(1), 165–187.

Jockers, M. L. (2013). *Macroanalysis: Digital Methods and Literary History*. Urbana and Champaign, IL: University of Illinois Press.

Kallinikos, J., Aaltonen, A. and Marton, A. (2013). The ambivalent ontology of digital artifacts. *MIS Quarterly*, 37(2), 357–370.

Kitchin, R. (2014). The reframing of science, social science and humanities research. In *The Data Revolution: Big Data, Open Data, Data Infrastructures & Their Consequences*. London: Sage, pp. 128–149.

Knoke, D. and Yang, S. (2008). *Social Network Analysis: Mapping and Exploring the Network Society*. London: Sage.

Landauer, T. K., Foltz, P. W. P. and Laham, D. (1998). An introduction to latent semantic analysis. *Discourse Processes*, 25(2–3), 259–284.

Landauer, T. K., McNamara, D. S., Dennis, S. and Kintsch, W. (eds) (2013). *Handbook of Latent Semantic Analysis*. London and New York, NY: Psychology Press.

Langley, A. (2007). Process thinking in strategic organization. *Strategic Organization*, 5(3), 271–282.

Lazer, D., Pentland, A., Adamic, L., Aral, S., Barabási, A., Brewer, D. et al. (2009). Computational social science. *Science*, 323(5915), 721–723.

Lazer, D. and Radford, J. (2017). Data ex machina: Introduction to big data. *Annual Review of Sociology*, 43(1), 1–21.

Lindberg, A. (2020). Developing theory through integrating human & machine pattern recognition. *Journal of the Association for Information Systems*, 21(1), 90–116.

Lindberg, A., Berente, N., Gaskin, J. and Lyytinen, K. (2016). Coordinating interdependencies in online communities: A study of an open source software project. *Information Systems Research*, 27(4), 751–772.

Lindberg, A., Gaskin, J., Berente, N., Lyytinen, K. and Yoo, Y. (2013). Computational approaches for analyzing latent social structures in open source organizing. International Conference on Information Systems, Milan, Italy.

Marsland, S. (2014). *Machine Learning: An Algorithmic Perspective*. Boca Raton, FL: CRC Press.

Miles, M. B., Huberman, A. M. and Saldaña, J. (2014). *Qualitative Data Analysis: A Methods Sourcebook*, 3rd edition. Thousand Oaks, CA: Sage.

Moreno, J. L. (1934). *Who Shall Survive? A New Approach to the Problem of Human Interrelations*. Washington, DC: Nervous and Mental Disease Publishing Co.

Moretti, F. (2013). 'Operationalizing': or, the function of measurement in modern literary theory. *Journal of English Language and Literature*, 60(1), 3–19.

Müller, O., Junglas, I., vom Brocke, J. and Debortoli, S. (2016). Utilizing big data analytics for information systems research: Challenges, promises and guidelines. *European Journal of Information Systems*, 2(1), 289–302.

Østerlund, C., Crowston, K. and Jackson, C. (2020). Building an apparatus: Refractive, reflective & diffractive readings of trace data. *Journal of the Association for Information Systems*, 21(1), 1–43.

Pentland, B. T., Liu, P., Kremser, W. and Hærem, T. (2020a). The dynamics of drift in digitized processes. *MIS Quarterly: Management Information Systems*, 44(1), 19–47.

Pentland, B. T., Recker, J., Wolf, J. R. and Wyner, G. (2020b). Bringing context inside process research with digital trace data. *Journal of the Association for Information Systems*, 21(5), 1214–1236.

Prell, C. (2012). *Social Network Analysis: History, Theory & Method*. London, New Delhi, Singapore, Los Angeles, CA and Washington, DC: Sage.

Ritschard, G., Gabadinho, A., Muller, N. S. and Studer, M. (2008). Mining event histories: A social science perspective. *International Journal of Data Mining, Modelling and Management*, 1(1), 68–90.

Rogers, R. (2013). *Digital Methods*. Cambridge, MA: MIT Press.

Rogers, R. (2009). New media & digital culture. Text prepared for the inaugural speech, Chair, University of Amsterdam, May, pp. 1–25.

Salganik, M. (2017). *Bit by Bit: Social Research in the Digital Age*. Princeton, NJ: Princeton University Press.

Salton, G., Wong, A. and Yang, C. (1975). A vector space model for automatic indexing. *Communications of the ACM*, 18(11), 613–620.

Scott, J. (1994). Social network analysis. *Journal of the British Sociological Association*, 22(1), 109–127.

Sievert, C. and Shirley, K. (2014). LDAvis: A method for visualizing and interpreting topics. Proceedings of the Workshop on Interactive Language Learning, Visualization, and Interfaces, Baltimore, MD.

Sinclair, B. (2016). Network structure and social outcomes: Network analysis for social science. In M. R. Alvarez (ed.), *Computational Social Science: Discovery and Prediction*. New York, NY: Cambridge University Press, pp. 121–140.

Steyvers, M. and Griffiths, T. (2007). Probabilistic topic models. *Handbook of Latent Semantic Analysis*, 427(7), 424–440.

Svahn, F., Henfridsson, O. and Yoo, Y. (2009). Mangling the sociomateriality of technological regimes in digital innovation. International Conference Information Systems, Phoenix, AZ.

Trier, M. (2008). Research note – towards dynamic visualization for understanding evolution of digital communication networks. *Information Systems Research*, 19(3), 335–350.

Urquhart, C. (2001). An encounter with grounded theory: Tackling the practical and philosophical issues. In E. M. Trauth (ed.), *Qualitative Research in IS: Issues and Trends*. London and Hershey, PA: Idea Group Publishing, pp. 104–140.

Urquhart, C., Lehmann, H. and Myers, M. D. (2009). Putting the 'theory' back into grounded theory: Guidelines for grounded theory studies in information systems. *Information Systems Journal*, 20(4), 357–381.

Venturini, T. (2012). Building on faults: How to represent controversies with digital methods. *Public Understanding of Science*, 21(7), 796–812.

Venturini, T. (2009). Diving in magma: How to explore controversies with actor-network theory. *Public Understanding of Science*, 19(3), 258–273.

Venturini, T., Bounegru, L., Gray, J. and Rogers, R. (2018). A reality check(-list) for digital methods. *New Media & Society*, 22(2), 317–341.

Venturini, T. and Latour, B. (2010). The social fabric: Digital traces and quali-quantitative methods. Proceedings of Future En Seine, Paris, France.

Wasserman, S. and Faust, K. (1994). *Social Network Analysis: Methods and Applications*. Cambridge: Cambridge University Press.

Weltevrede, E. (2016). Repurposing digital methods: The research affordances of platforms and engines. PhD dissertation, University of Amsterdam.

Whelan, E., Teigland, R., Vaast, E. and Butler, B. (2016). Expanding the horizons of digital social networks: Mixing big trace datasets with qualitative approaches. *Information and Organization*, 26(1–2), 1–12.

Wickham, H. (2014). Tidy data. *Journal of Statistical Software*, 59(10), 1–23.

Wild, F. and Stahl, C. (2007). Investigating unstructured texts with latent semantic analysis. In R. Decker and H.-J. Lenz (eds), *Advances in Data Analysis*. Berlin and Heidelberg, Germany: Springer, pp. 383–390.

Yoo, Y., Henfridsson, O. and Lyytinen, K. (2010). The new organizing logic of digital innovation: An agenda for information systems research. *Information Systems Research*, 21(4), 724–735.

Zachariadis, M., Scott, S. and Barrett, M. (2013). Bridging the qualitative-quantitative divide: Guidelines for conducting mixed-method research in information systems. *MIS Quarterly*, 37(3), 855–879.

Balancing the Momentum of Datafication with Qualitative Researchers as Design Thinkers

GONGTAI WANG, ANDREW BURTON-JONES and
SAEED AKHLAGHPOUR*

17.1 Introduction

Almost everything nowadays can be recorded in digital data, from the individual to the organization, from the artificial to the natural, from the animate to the inanimate, and from the online to the offline. It could be said that we are in an age of *datafication* – the quantification, recording and analysis of phenomena, and ultimately the world and all human activity (Mayer-Schönberger and Cukier, 2013; Lomborg, 2020). The data being generated are predicted to grow to 175 Zettabytes by 2025, an amount almost impossible to fathom, let alone download and process (Reinsel et al., 2018). Given its richness, variety and growth, and the relentless digital transformation that flows with it, this emerging body of digital data is claimed as a new oil field. Some believe that buried in this field are treasures highly amenable to quantitative analysis. Entire fields are emerging from this belief, such as personalized medicine (Weiss et al., 2012), predictive maintenance (Carvalho et al., 2019) and precision farming (Liakos et al., 2018), to name a few.

While this vision might be seductive, the quantitative paradigm it relies on has limitations that are well known to qualitative researchers, in that it all too often underappreciates the social context surrounding data and analyses. Sometimes, consequences like data-driven discrimination go so far as to magnify the dark side of our society (Kim, 2016; Ledford, 2019), leading to adverse social

consequences (e.g., fear, anxiety, anger and shame imposed on welfare recipients by Australia's 'robo-debt' algorithmic debt recovery system), or the abandonment of high-profile projects (e.g., IBM's abandonment of facial recognition technology).

Given this risk, how should researchers respond to help our stakeholders proceed effectively? As the role of data scientists and engineering designers is already accepted, we take the space here to focus on qualitative research. As we will explain, qualitative researchers can help data scientists and engineering designers to maximize the benefits, and reduce the risks, of datafication.

Based on this view, we propose in this chapter how qualitative researchers can play an active role in datafication research and practice by weaving together ideas from the history of technology and design-thinking research. We suggest that datafication research needs constant reflection on the sociotechnical nature of datafication in terms of what, why and how data are collected, stored, analysed, and used. Specifically, building on 'technological momentum' (Hughes, 1969, 1994), we propose 'datafication momentum' as a concept referring to the tendency for datafication systems (defined as information systems (IS) that enable and constrain datafication) to receive more influence from social systems in their young stage and exert more influence on social systems in their mature stage. This concept highlights that datafication systems are never neutral, but are always subject to potential biases and constraints. If researchers and practitioners fail to observe this risk, they may let the biases and constraints of past social and technical forces sneak into datafication systems and become amplified.

* Acknowledgements: This research was supported by funds from the Australian Research Council, ARC LP170101154.

Our thesis is built on the idea of 'IS research as a design project' (Boland and Lyytinen, 2004) that calls for IS researchers to act as change agents. From this view, we call for qualitative researchers to engage in datafication research and practice with a 'qualitative researchers as design thinkers' mindset – a mindset that encourages them to actively engage in and think and act as a designer to shape datafication towards a more desirable future. To facilitate this thinking, we propose 'design forensics' as a research practice that qualitative researchers can perform.

17.2 Datafication Momentum

17.2.1 Technological Momentum

While it is widely agreed that technology is subject to social and technical forces, it is unsettled whether the technical shapes the social more, or vice versa. As a result, different variants of technical determinism and social constructivism co-exist in the literature. Researchers typically argue for a simultaneous mutual shaping of the technical and the social, perhaps because this is less controversial than clarifying which one comes first or is primary (Hughes, 1969, 1994).

Rejecting the division between technical determinism and social constructivism, Hughes (1969, 1994) proposes *technological momentum*, which Hughes and followers empirically observed across studies on the history of various technologies such as electric power systems (Heymann and Nielsen, 2013) and public transport systems (Davis, 1992). It refers to the tendency for social and technical forces to exert alternative effects as technological systems develop over time (see Figure 17.1).

Specifically, a technological system is more susceptible to social system influence in its younger stages, and then it starts to impose more deterministic influences on social systems as it matures (Hughes, 1969, 1994). It should be noted that this does not mean that once the technological system starts to exert influences the latter stage will never be changed. However, while the social system still affects the technological system over time, the technological system seeks the greatest level of persistence (see, for example, the fight between motor buses and street railways in Davis, 1992). This concept of technological momentum has important implications for understanding datafication.

17.2.2 Datafication: Moving away from a Naturalistic View

Underlying datafication is the metaphor that 'data is the new oil' (Van der Aalst, 2014). And, because such oil/data is valuable, researchers and practitioners are looking for ever-more data to mine: to capture more, extract more and know more. Like oil, the creation of data also tends to be attributed to the hand of nature. That is, like petroleum processing, this image of data processing typically assumes that data is just 'out there', ready to be acquired and mined, and does not concern itself with how and why the data is created in the first place or kept over time. Instead, most attention is paid to how to process data in terms of volume, variety and velocity (Sharda et al., 2016), with the assumption that an analysis of such data will lead to an understanding (through that data) of the social and material world. The basic assumption seems to be that as long as the processing is truthful to the data that it starts with, the outcome is

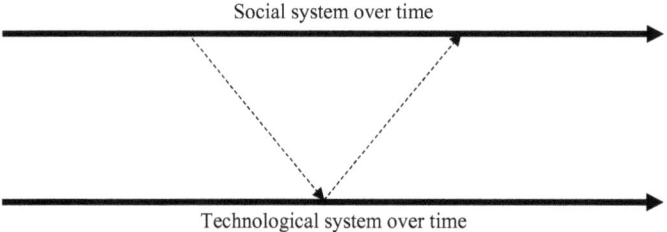

Figure 17.1 Technological momentum

truthful to the world. This *naturalistic view of datafication*, however, has been increasingly problematized (Kitchin, 2014; Mejias and Couldry, 2019).

A major limitation of this naturalistic view is that it does not account enough for how datafication systems are created and shaped. They are, of course, significantly shaped by social forces, and these forces can have long histories. Put simply, data is artificial rather than natural (Gitelman and Jackson, 2013; Kitchin, 2014; Mejias and Couldry, 2019), and it has been shaped since its creation. What devices offer entry to the digital world, who has access to the devices, what data can be generated, what data should be stored, how data is interpreted, etc. are all shaped by diverse values and aims of social actors. Even data that seek to record brute facts of natural objects are still framed by social processes (Monteiro and Parmiggiani, 2019). Even for data to be 'data', they have to be enacted as 'data' in datafication practices (Kelly and Noonan, 2017). Sometimes, social forces dissolve in the background and are hard to detect, but their effects can still be strong. As a result, even when datafication systems are intended to be neutral, they may still become racist and sexist (Chander, 2017; Hamilton, 2019; Lambrecht and Tucker, 2019) as biases in past and present social systems are inscribed in data and data structures as data collection, storage and processing procedures and devices are ultimately performed and developed by social actors. In turn, the inscribed biases in the earlier development of a datafication system can be stabilized and even amplified as the later use of the system exerts technical forces to shape the social system; for example, based on past data sets, an intelligent ad system might show high-income job vacancies to men more often than to women (see more examples in Cossins, 2018). Researchers need to be attentive to this 'social shaping' (Williams and Edge, 1996) aspect, as datafication is transforming the foundation of the decision-making in many settings of our lives and work such as recruitment, advertising adjudication and even war (Scharre, 2018).

In this chapter, we use the idea of technological momentum (Hughes, 1969, 1994) as a conceptual basis to reveal the often overlooked interactions of datafication systems and social contexts. We began by using this lens to review the academic and industry literature on datafication and its history. This led us to identify six forces driving datafication momentum, discussed next.

17.2.3 Forces Driving Datafication

Our review of forces driving datafication was designed to be indicative rather than exhaustive. That is, we sought to identify key points for discussion rather than provide an exhaustive analysis. We focused on two aspects: (1) what social forces shape datafication systems; and (2) what technical forces of datafication systems shape social systems. We saw forces as mechanisms (Tsoukas, 1989; Van de Ven, 1992) driving critical events (Langley et al., 2013) over the course of datafication since the 1940s (Press, 2013a, 2013b). Overall, our analysis revealed three social forces that shape datafication systems, and three technical forces of datafication systems that shape social systems (see Figure 17.2).

Our review highlighted three social forces, which we label as expertise, pragmatics and cognitive forces. First, *expertise force* refers to the

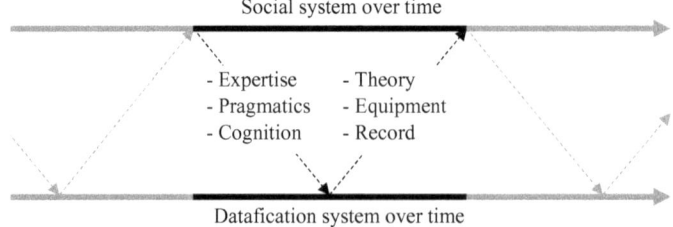

Figure 17.2 Forces driving datafication

higher influence of people with credible and authentic research and work experience, skills, knowledge and education backgrounds of collecting, storing, analyzing and interpreting data. As established in social studies (Foucault, 1977; Li and Sadler, 2011; Hauskeller, 2020), expertise brings power. In the history of datafication, we found that experts from two major reference disciplines of datafication (computer science and statistics) have been more privileged to define what and how data should be collected, stored, analyzed and interpreted (Merry, 2016).

Second, *pragmatics force* refers to the tendency that people, especially practitioners, make design decisions with an emphasis on practical efficiency and effectiveness. This practical emphasis may prioritize, for example, the costs of hardware, energy or time (Van der Aalst, 2014; Sharda et al., 2016). As a result, it is merely a small set of social and material entities from the boundless world that are datafied, and only a subset of this data is eventually deemed relevant and valuable for retaining and analyzing. The decisions that bind data sets are often driven by practical concerns due to limited resources (Sharda et al., 2016). Pragmatics force is particularly evident in the historical development of 'black box' artificial intelligence (AI) systems where, because of their performance in solving practical problems, researchers and practitioners widely created and accepted them despite their inability to understand why the systems arrive at specific decisions and what risks are involved (Agrawal et al., 2018; Haenlein and Kaplan, 2019).

Third, *cognitive force* refers to the fact that data and data structures that fit with established cognitive patterns are more likely to be accepted than those that do not. This force is particularly evident in data visualization. As human cognitive capabilities are limited, data and data structures are expected to be presented in the form that is easier to understand (Van der Aalst, 2014). Besides, human cognition tends to stick to previously used frames and people are reluctant to abandon them (Thompson and Schonthal, 2020). Although the presentation of data and data structures has been evolving, the evolvement shows a parallel trajectory to the analytical and theoretical development

and preferences of people in the corresponding era (Friendly, 2008).

Similarly, our review highlighted three technical forces, which we label as theory, equipment and record forces. First, *theory force* refers to the fact that theories from reference disciplines, such as statistics, computer science, politics and psychology, on which datafication systems are built, regulate subsequent datafication practices in terms of data collection, analysis and interpretation. It has long been argued that technological artifacts are theory-based (Mehlenbacher, 2010). The most established theories often decide how technological artifacts are designed, which then decide how they can be used. In other words, human behaviours are influenced by the theories inscribed in the artifacts and procedures they use (see examples in Thaler and Sunstein, 2009; Norman, 2013).

Second, *equipment force* refers to the impact of technological features and capabilities of devices-in-use on determining what data can be collected and how data can be stored and analyzed. The emergence of datafication is largely stimulated by the technical advances in sensor technology, computing power and storage capacity (Van der Aalst, 2014; Sharda et al., 2016). A lack of sufficiently advanced sensor technology, computing power or storage capacity limits the volume and variety of collectable and storable data. Thus, the data available for analysis is largely framed by the devices-in-use. Although the technological features and capabilities are constantly advancing, a portion of available data at any particular time is already constrained by the limitations of past technologies.

Third, *record force* refers to the role of data records stored in databases in enabling and constraining possible analyses and what insights can be extracted. The creation and measurement of categories depend on available data (Merry, 2016). Analyses extract insights from data records. However, if data is not collected in the first place, it is not possible to extract insights. For example, analyses on cross-device activities are not possible if corresponding logs are not taken about when, how and why people shift between devices (Churchill, 2017). In a similar vein, while data records are strongly framed by a particular data structure, the analysis is likely to be influenced by the corresponding structure as well; for example, as it is often said, a machine-learning model is only as good as its data (cf. Boyd et al., 2014).

Together, these social and technical forces suggest that various logics can be inscribed in datafication systems throughout their historical development; in turn, the logics once inscribed can become increasingly stable and exert a significant influence on subsequent social systems. In this regard, datafication is characterized by a similar feature of technical momentum, which therefore can be termed as *datafication momentum.*

Given such a conceptualization, one should not assume datafication systems are neutral and let datafication develop without reflection. What can be done is to strive for neutrality (although it is unlikely to be fully achievable) by helping designers and users of datafication systems to develop and maintain a reflective awareness of the inevitable logic inscriptions that may bias insights from the systems. We contend that IS researchers in particular should make their best efforts to maintain this reflective awareness and view every IS research as an opportunity to shape datafication systems towards a more desirable future state. In fact, we might now be at a critical juncture as datafication is starting to gain significant traction (Cao, 2017). However, once widely accepted political, economic and value norms around datafication are established, reshaping them will be much more difficult (cf. Hughes, 1994). In what follows, we explain how qualitative researchers specifically can contribute to this agenda by acting as design thinkers and helping data scientists and engineering designers maintain a reflective awareness.

17.3 Qualitative Researchers as Design Thinkers

17.3.1 Information Systems Research as a Design Project

Boland and Lyytinen (2004) propose a design view of IS research. Arguing against a traditional, passive research approach that focuses on developing conceptual and theoretical representations of the world, they urge IS researchers to actively help reshape the world by developing theories to guide IS design and inform IS designers. That is, IS researchers should not just report what is going on, but they should also take action to improve the human condition.

We draw on this view to call qualitative IS researchers to actively shape datafication projects towards more positive ends. When engaging in such work, we urge them to think beyond the immediate IS artifact not only for shaping the future it is going to create, but also for rethinking the past it will be built on. After all, the design springing to the future has to step on the present that is merely a surface of the past. As Boland and Lyytinen (2004: 57–60) point out:

> Our understanding of this world is echoed in our evolving concepts, terms, vocabularies, key words, models, and so forth that are used in these linguistic moves ... We utilize and quote earlier theories and artifacts that we have learned, built, and internalized as well as the words and concepts passed on by our ancestors; we use software packages and instruments (resources) that are critical in our data collection and analysis or design practice ... We also design indirectly by highlighting certain sociotechnical organization features and hiding others – by serving some goals and needs in organizations, but overlooking others ... We cannot and do not conduct our research without exercising values in selecting, operationalizing, and giving order to particular features of a socio-technical landscape, and valuing them in certain ways as effective, appropriate, or harmful, which we then encourage others to take seriously as being real components of their world.

In short, IS researchers should account for how IS artifacts have become what they look like today. By understanding the past, qualitative IS researchers can learn the key design decisions that shaped the existing IS artifacts now shaping our world. As design research suggests, 'designing against the status quo requires bringing deep understanding of underlying system dynamics, both present and historical' (Beckman, 2020: 154). Similarly, going beyond existing IS artifacts (Boland and Lyytinen, 2004) requires attending to and rethinking their past that has been shaping the present and may pave the ground for the future.

17.3.2 Qualitative Researchers as Design Thinkers

Motivated by Boland and Lyytinen's (2004) call to view IS research as a design project, we suggest that qualitative researchers fulfil this role by acting as design thinkers. In making this suggestion, we do not seek to imply that *only* qualitative researchers can take this role. We do not seek to enter into a banal contrast between quantitative vs. qualitative research, or positivism vs. interpretivism (Hassan and Mingers, 2018). Quantitative and qualitative research both have their strengths (Weber, 2004). However, while the strengths of quantitative research are well known in datafication initiatives, the above-mentioned 'social shaping' aspects have received insufficient attention. It is for this reason that we focus our discussion on qualitative research.

By suggesting that qualitative IS researchers act as design thinkers, we are calling them to think like a designer who not only observes but also proactively influences a datafication project. Despite the various understandings of the defining features of design thinkers (Owen, 2007; Viljoen and Van Zyl, 2009; Razzouk and Shute, 2012), the literature generally suggests that they should follow three principles:

- First, design thinkers should be *empathetic*. The ultimate goal of design should be 'to support and advance human dignity and human rights' (Buchanan, 2001: 37). Design thinkers should be able to attend to, absorb and digest the needs and wants of all stakeholders that may be affected by their design.
- Second, design thinkers should be *holistic*. As it often involves various areas and actors, design has to be a coherent whole to function effectively (Buchanan, 1992, 2015). This not only means making sure all design fragments are made coherent in terms of meanings and functions (Buchanan, 2015), but also requires an inclusive consideration of human beings and the environment (Viljoen and Van Zyl, 2009).

- Third, design thinkers should be *critical*. Fundamentally rethinking established design often enables designers to identify hidden needs that are not yet realized by users (Verganti, 2017). Good designs often emerge as designers proactively rethink their own work and strive to improve the quality of their ongoing designs (Schön, 1984; Beckman, 2020).

In their roles as design thinkers, we argue that qualitative researchers can apply these three principles to facilitate and drive datafication projects to shape a better future. They can also promote an understanding of the history of a given datafication system and highlight what this past implies in terms of future social consequences. Given the importance of understanding the past and its effects on the present and future, we describe a new practice in the next section that qualitative researchers-as-design-thinkers can enact: the practice of design forensics.

17.4 Design Forensics

17.4.1 Design Forensics as a Genre of Design Ethnography

An essential tool of qualitative researchers is ethnographic research. Ethnographic research seeks to gain an in-depth understanding of participants by observing and interacting with them in their native habitat. With such an approach, qualitative researchers not only analyze what participants say, but also seek to go deeper to understand what users do not say (Atkinson and Hammersley, 2007). Ethnographic research has long been used by qualitative researchers in IS research studying the design, adoption, adaptation and use of IS artifacts (Myers, 1997, 1999). Its advantage is to understand participants' behaviours beyond what they say they are doing, by seeing what they are actually doing through participatory observation. The basic idea is that people's values are reflected in their behaviours (Churchill, 2017). More recently, stepping further from traditional ethnographic research, design ethnography emerged as a research stream that argues for extending the role of IS researchers from observers and learners to creators and teachers (Baskerville and Myers, 2015). It bridges the gap between research and practice (Harvey and Myers, 1995) as IS researchers unveil new subtleties learned from the observed IS design that in turn feed new knowledge into further IS design (Hughes et al., 1994; Harvey and Myers, 1995).

Various guidelines have been proposed for conducting ethnographic research and design ethnography (Atkinson and Hammersley, 2007; Baskerville and Myers, 2015). However, the temporal scope is often bracketed from the entrance to the field onwards. Ethnographic research on IS design is often bounded by the timeline of a project and takes the project's commencement as its start. Likewise, it is also limited to the social scope of the project with a predefined organizational boundary. However, in light of datafication systems' potential social impacts due to past social shaping, a design ethnographer should also have an in-depth understanding of the design history of the datafication systems and have an inclusive consideration of all actors that are potentially affected by it. In the material below, we do not intend to replace existing ethnographic guidelines, as there are already many good ones available for traditional ethnographic research (Atkinson and Hammersley, 2007) and for design ethnography (Harvey and Myers, 1995; Myers, 1997; Baskerville and Myers, 2015). Rather, we seek to complement them.

In particular, we focus our proposal on *design forensics* as a genre of design ethnography. We propose this as a research practice where researchers conduct ethnographic research on datafication with a concern for understanding what the key design decisions were/are, and why and how they were/are made while designing a datafication system. Traditional design ethnography often focuses on understanding design goals, users' requirements or design activities (Baskerville and Myers, 2015). The more recent variants call for researchers' active engagement in shaping participants' conditions (Baskerville and Myers, 2015). Both streams are *prospective*. Design forensics adds to these an attention to the past and how it continues to the present and its implications for the future. In this sense, it is *retrospective*. Its

implication for a datafication project is to understand why a given datafication system is designed as it is. Design forensics may facilitate data scientists and engineering designers to reflect on their past design decisions as ethnographic research often reveals new understandings to participants as they interact with researchers (Hovorka and Germonprez, 2010; Baumer and Silberman, 2011). In addition to a reflection on the past, design forensics may also record the ongoing design decision-making that can be retrieved by future users and help them understand the limitation and advantage of the datafication system.

Like other genres of ethnography, design forensics aims to understand datafication system designers' and users' behaviours beyond what they say they are doing, by analyzing what they *do* (and have done). The overarching goal of design forensics is to understand the motivations, perceptions and interpretations of data scientists and engineering designers in their design and use of datafication systems that may have implications for the desirability of the future affected by the design and use of the systems. Next, we propose a set of more concrete principles for the conduct and evaluation of design forensics for achieving its overarching goal.

17.4.2 A Set of Principles for Design Forensics

The overarching problem that we seek to address is the insufficient attention to the social shaping of datafication. Analyses that start from digital data logs and activity traces without an attention to their past (e.g., why they were created and kept) are limited in uncovering biases and understanding their effects (Churchill, 2017). While advanced analytics technology allows rapid pattern identification, it is less likely to uncover the decisions that frame the collection, storage, analysis and interpretation of the data. The 'qualitative researchers as design thinkers' mindset can help counteract this effect of datafication momentum. As a *research practice* that applies a design-thinker's mindset, we believe design forensics can offer great help. With this in mind, we propose three principles for design forensics. These principles are inspired by the above three principles of thinking like a designer, and a feature of design ethnography that while studying participants, researchers also empower them to reflect on their conditions (Barab et al., 2004).

17.4.2.1 Design Principle 1: Empathetic Datafication

The first principle, *empathetic datafication*, calls for *achieving and maintaining an in-depth understanding of how design decisions considered the people that will be influenced by a datafication system*. As noted above, design thinkers should be empathetic: they should consider human dignity and human rights (Buchanan, 2001). The ultimate motivation of design is the improvement of human conditions (Boland et al., 2008). Therefore, the empathetic principle is often claimed as the most critical one for design thinkers. Applying this principle in the context of datafication research, qualitative researchers should understand if design decisions have considered the people that will be influenced by the design and use of a datafication system. As explained earlier when discussing the concept of datafication momentum, datafication not only solves functional problems. Datafication systems also have intended and unintended implications for human dignity and human rights. Ignoring this in the design and use of a datafication system may lead to adverse consequences. And, conversely, when this principle is applied as part of design forensics, it can empower and stimulate data scientists and engineering designers to become aware of this aspect of their design and future use of a datafication system.

17.4.2.2 Design Principle 2: Datafication Totality

The second principle, *datafication totality*, calls for *a comprehensive and holistic consideration of what sociomaterial factors shaped/shape the design decisions of a datafication system*. Design in general (Buchanan, 1992, 2015; Kimbell, 2012) and IS design in particular (Carlsson et al., 2011; Lee, 2016) involve many social and material factors. Datafication totality refers to how completely these factors and their interrelationships have been considered. This is important because,

as the common saying in data analytics goes, 'you can't act on the data you can't analyze, you can't analyze data you don't collect, and you can't collect what you don't measure' (Neyland, 2017). In short, failing to consider relevant elements exerts a force (Williams et al., 2018). Ultimately, datafication systems are representational systems that contain partial surrogates of the world. They do not include all social and material entities, or even all attributes of the entities included. Issues such as access to and availability of digital resources can cause datafication systems to under-represent or over-represent certain groups of social and material entities, creating biases. By following the datafication totality principle, a qualitative researcher-as-design-thinker would seek to understand if/how the design decisions considered all relevant sociomaterial factors and the effects of omissions. By enacting this principle of design forensics, qualitative researchers can help data scientists and engineering designers to be more complete and more considerate in their design and use of datafication systems.

17.4.2.3 Design Principle 3: Reflective Criticism

The third principle, *reflective criticism*, calls for *attention and critical evaluation of upstream design decisions of a datafication system*. Different from principle 2, which assesses what constitutes and shapes a datafication system, this principle considers whether attention has been paid to critically reflect on the system's past. Being critical is an essential attitude for designers as it helps them realize the limitation of existing designs and go beyond them (Verganti, 2017). Arguably, this type of critical attitude is a driving force of improvements in human society over time (Ingold, 2015). In a design context, this attitude can help drive innovations and likewise help uncover biases. A key idea underlying datafication momentum is that social forces affect design decisions and inscribe biases in datafication systems, which in turn may shape social systems in which they are used. Instead of assuming the design decisions are benign or neutral, datafication researchers should always be mindful of the inscribed design decision (e.g., who made these decisions, and how and why they were made). By being mindful in this way, qualitative researchers-as-design-thinkers can help data scientists and engineering designers to improve datafication systems and be alert to potential biases.

17.4.2.4 Summary of Design Principles

Together, these three principles in design forensics can help researchers reveal and highlight the design decisions inscribed in given datafication systems and how and why they have been shaped by what social and material factors. For example, while studying the design of an algorithm predicting the likelihood of a criminal reoffending, qualitative researchers should not only take the standpoint of the courts, but also empathize with the defendants and understand how various algorithm outputs may change their life (i.e., empathetic datafication). Meanwhile, they should also take into account the various social and technical factors that have been constituting and shaping the systems that collect, store and analyze the data about the defendants, such as their suburb socioeconomic conditions (i.e., datafication totality). Finally, they should attend to what past design decisions made the systems as they are today (e.g., if the designers decided to use skin colour as a critical feature for modelling) and whether the decisions are problematic (i.e., reflective criticism). As this hypothetical example shows, each principle has its respective concerns. They are not mutually exclusive, but complementary. For example, a combination of 'datafication totality' and 'reflective criticism' may promote an investigation on what fields are in a law enforcement database, how the data has been captured and stored, and why it was designed like that. Ideally, a datafication research should use all the three principles in combination (see Figure 17.3) for a more comprehensive and in-depth understanding of the datafication system in use and more thoughtful vision for the datafication system under design.

It should be noted that we do not rule out the opportunity for data scientists, engineering designers and quantitative researchers to act as an empathetic, holistic and critical design thinker. In fact, we would encourage them to do so. However,

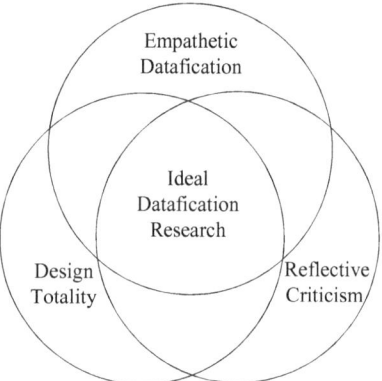

Figure 17.3 Ideal implementation of design forensics principles

our main point is that ethnographic research is a key skill that (ethnographic) qualitative researchers have been practising and refining for a long time. With an empathetic, holistic and critical mindset, and a focus on design history, qualitative researchers with this ready skill set can complement data scientists and engineering designers. Such qualitative researchers-as-design-thinkers do not have to retreat to the second position even in a highly technical datafication research project, but may engage actively, making full use of their ethnographic skills to shape the initial conditions towards a more desirable end.

17.5 Discussion and Conclusions

Datafication is a theoretically and practically important phenomenon in research and practice. There is no doubt that as more data are accumulated, further insights can be extracted and new benefits can be obtained. However, at the same time, new problems of datafication are also emerging and causing concerns. Against such a background, we propose a design ethnography approach for studying the complexity of datafication, especially in its extreme forms. In this chapter, we propose 'datafication momentum' as a concept that sheds light on the risk that datafication systems may be biased because of social forces in their earlier stages and, in turn, amplify these biases in their latter stages as they shape our social systems. Especially when the inscribed biases root in the dark side of a society, being inattentive to datafication momentum may lead to adverse social outcomes. Hence, we call for researchers and practitioners to carefully consider this social shaping aspect of datafication and its momentum.

To this end, we believe that qualitative researchers may play an active role in datafication research by tapping into their qualitative research toolkit, especially the ethnographic method. The method is not only useful for helping engineering designers better understand targeted users and appreciate what engineering designers are doing (Baskerville and Myers, 2015). It is also useful to allow qualitative researchers to actively engage in shaping the current situation to a more desirable end (Baskerville and Myers, 2015). More importantly, it helps data scientists and engineering designers to keep reflective awareness of their practice and the development history of the datafication systems (Barab et al., 2004). This last feature of design ethnography is particularly useful for qualitative researchers not only to understand, but also influence, a datafication research project even if they are not directly making design decisions.

To better perform such a role, we propose a 'qualitative researchers as design thinkers' research mindset and a 'design forensics' research practice. The former encourages qualitative researchers to take every research project as an opportunity to redesign the future for bettering human conditions by approaching past and ongoing design with empathetic, holistic and critical thinking. The latter further recommends to them to apply the mindset in design ethnography with a particular focus on uncovering and communicating with the actors, past design decisions and their effects on human conditions.

17.5.1 Implications for Research

This chapter has several implications for research. First, it sheds light on the social shaping aspect of datafication. Although the mutual shaping of social systems and technological systems has long been argued (e.g., Orlikowski, 2000; Leonardi, 2011), the discourse on datafication, especially in data and engineering disciplines, is dominated by

overoptimistic enthusiasm. Here, we do not intend to pour cold water on it. Rather, we seek to complement it with a reflective attitude. The 'qualitative researchers as design thinkers' research mindset and the 'design forensics' research practice are proposed as complements to achieve sustainability for healthier and more prudent development of datafication.

Second, it also sheds light on the fact that no matter how great the volume and variety of data are, they are partial representations of the world. Therefore, while advancing datafication systems allows increasingly rapid accumulation of data and pattern recognition, it is less likely to capture the depth of understanding comparable to intensive participant observations in a locus where data is generated. Well-trained qualitative researchers are adept at achieving such deep understanding that may offer useful insights into the design and use of datafication systems. In addition to the input of richer information by tapping into the advantages of their toolkits (e.g., ethnographic method), they may also stimulate data scientists and engineering designers to maintain self-reflexivity for careful use of given datafication systems and strive for constant betterment of their design of new datafication systems.

This chapter also has implications for research evaluation in terms of ethics. As datafication is causing large-scale fundamental transformations, including in areas related to people's lives such as social surveillance and wars, ethics is a vital concern for all datafication projects. Although ethics has been approached with various ontological stances (Clegg et al., 2007), we approach it as a performance and contend that an ethical datafication research project should at least make the best effort for the most possible in-depth understanding of the past and ongoing design decisions. We highlighted several limitations of datafication systems. In particular, because data is only a partial representation of a dynamic and complex world, people may be under- or over-represented, and systematic biases can easily be inscribed in datafication systems. We, IS researchers, have to strive to understand and address such risks. This is also why we argue that the three principles of design forensics proposed above should be an integral part of datafication research.

17.5.2 Implications for Practice

In this chapter, we argue that qualitative researchers are well suited to identifying the risks of datafication. This argument may go beyond an academic research setting to a practical setting, especially in terms of the creation of new roles for balancing datafication momentum in practice.

While envisioning the coming future of ubiquitous AI transformation, Wilson et al. (2017) anticipate the rise of three new occupations: trainers, explainers and sustainers. Under the category of explainers, they propose *algorithm forensics analysts* as a job responsible for uncovering the rationale behind results produced by 'black-box' AI systems. *Algorithm forensics* is *reactive* as it seeks to understand backwards why an algorithm gives out certain results. However, as we have already seen in many scandals, sometimes it is too late even if the reasons for results are explained.

In contrast, design forensics can be *preventative*. It keeps design decision-making attentive and reflective to the needs of stakeholders and environments. Its detailed insights into the design logic of a datafication system can help prevent problematic design outputs. It can also be reactive as it unveils and records past design decisions that can be retrieved later for, at least partially, understanding why mistakes happen. In comparison with algorithm forensics that mainly resorts to external information, design forensics complements algorithm forensics as it offers inside information for understanding why a datafication system leads to certain results. In this regard, we propose *design forensics analysts* as an occupation responsible for making the design of a datafication system transparent and enhancing the traceability of responsibilities. In addition to the benefit for diagnosis and prevention of technical problems, we suspect the presence of such a job will also be helpful for gaining stakeholders' trust, which is most critical in the current environment.

References

Agrawal, A., Gans, J. and Goldfarb, A. (2018). *Prediction Machines: The Simple Economics of Artificial Intelligence*. Boston, MA: Harvard Business Press.

Atkinson, P. and Hammersley, M. (2007). *Ethnography: Principles in Practice*. London: Routledge.

Barab, S. A., Thomas, M. K., Dodge, T., Squire, K. and Newell, M. (2004). Critical design ethnography: Designing for change. *Anthropology & Education Quarterly*, 35(2), 254–268.

Baskerville, R. L. and Myers, M. D. (2015). Design ethnography in information systems. *Information Systems Journal*, 25(1), 23–46.

Baumer, E. P. and Silberman, M. S. (2011). When the implication is not to design (technology). Proceedings of the SIGCHI Conference on Human Factors in Computing Systems, Vancouver, Canada.

Beckman, S. L. (2020). To frame or reframe: Where might design thinking research go next? *California Management Review*, 62(2), 144–162.

Boland, R. J., Collopy, F., Lyytinen, K. and Yoo, Y. (2008). Managing as designing: Lessons for organization leaders from the design practice of Frank O. Gehry. *Design Issues*, 24(1), 10–25.

Boland, R. J. and Lyytinen, K. (2004). Information systems research as design: Identity, process, and narrative. In B. Kaplan, D. P. Truex, D. Wastell, A. T. Wood-Harper and J. I. DeGross (eds), *Information Systems Research*. Boston, MA: Springer, pp. 53–68.

Boyd, D., Levy, K. and Marwick, A. (2014). The networked nature of algorithmic discrimination. In S. P. Gangadharan (ed.), *Data and Discrimination: Collected Essays*. Washington, DC: Open Technology Institute, pp. 53–57.

Buchanan, R. (2015). Worlds in the making: Design, management, and the reform of organizational culture. *She Ji: The Journal of Design, Economics, and Innovation*, 1(1), 5–21.

Buchanan, R. (2001). Human dignity and human rights: Thoughts on the principles of human-centered design. *Design Issues*, 17(3), 35–39.

Buchanan, R. (1992). Wicked problems in design thinking. *Design Issues*, 8(2), 5–21.

Cao, L. (2017). Data science: A comprehensive overview. *ACM Computing Surveys*, 50(3), 1–42.

Carlsson, S. A., Henningsson, S., Hrastinski, S. and Keller, C. (2011). Socio-technical IS design science research: Developing design theory for IS integration management. *Information Systems and E-Business Management*, 9(1), 109–131.

Carvalho, T. P., Soares, F. A., Vita, R., Francisco, R. D. P., Basto, J. P. and Alcalá, S. G. (2019).

A systematic literature review of machine learning methods applied to predictive maintenance. *Computers & Industrial Engineering*, 137, 1–10.

Chander, A. (2017). The racist algorithm. *Michigan Law Review*, 115(6), 1023–1046.

Churchill, E. F. (2017). Data, design, and ethnography. *Interactions*, 25(1), 22–23.

Clegg, S., Kornberger, M. and Rhodes, C. (2007). Business ethics as practice. *British Journal of Management*, 18(2), 107–122.

Cossins, D. (2018). Discriminating algorithms: 5 times AI showed prejudice. *New Scientist*, www .newscientist.com/article/2166207-discriminating-algorithms-5-times-ai-showed-prejudice/.

Davis, D. (1992). Technological momentum, motor buses, and the persistence of Canada's street railways to 1940. *Material Culture Review*, 36, 6–17.

Foucault, M. (1977). *Discipline and Punish: The Birth of the Prison*. London: Allen & Lane.

Friendly, M. (2008). A brief history of data visualization. In C.-H. Chen, W. Härdle and A. Unwin (eds), *Handbook of Data Visualization*. Berlin and Heidelberg, Germany: Springer, pp. 15–56.

Gitelman, L. and Jackson, V. (2013). Introduction. In L. Gitelman (ed.), *Raw Data Is an Oxymoron*. Cambridge, MA: MIT Press, pp. 1–14.

Haenlein, M. and Kaplan, A. (2019). A brief history of artificial intelligence: On the past, present, and future of artificial intelligence. *California Management Review*, 61(4), 5–14.

Hamilton, M. (2019). The sexist algorithm. *Behavioral Sciences & the Law*, 37(2), 145–157.

Harvey, L. J. and Myers, M. D. (1995). Scholarship and practice: The contribution of ethnographic research methods to bridging the gap. *Information Technology & People*, 8(3), 13–27.

Hassan, N. R. and Mingers, J. (2018). Reinterpreting the Kuhnian paradigm in information systems. *Journal of the Association for Information Systems*, 19(7), 568–599.

Hauskeller, C. (2020). Care ethics and care contexts: Contributions from feminist philosophy. *East Asian Science Technology and Society – an International Journal*, 14(1), 153–161.

Heymann, M. and Nielsen, K. H. (2013). Hybridization of electric utility regimes: The case of wind power in Denmark, 1973–1990. *RCC Perspectives*, 2, 69–74.

Hovorka, D. S. and Germonprez, M. (2010). Reflecting, tinkering, and tailoring: Implications for theories of information system design. In H. Isomäki and S. Pekkola (eds), *Reframing Humans in Information Systems Development*. London: Springer, pp. 135–149.

Hughes, J., King, V., Rodden, T. and Andersen, H. (1994). Moving out from the control room: Ethnography in system design. Proceedings of the 1994 ACM conference on Computer Supported Cooperative Work, Chapel Hill, NC.

Hughes, T. P. (1994). Technological momentum. In M. R. Smith and L. Marx (eds), *Does Technology Drive History? The Dilemma of Technological Determinism*. London and Cambridge, MA: MIT Press, pp. 101–113.

Hughes, T. P. (1969). Technological momentum in history: Hydrogenation in Germany 1898–1933. *Past & Present*, 44(1), 106–132.

Ingold, T. (2015). Design anthropology is not and cannot be ethnography. Research Network for Design Anthropology, https://kadk.dk/sites/default/files/08_ingold_design_anthropology_network.doc.

Kelly, S. and Noonan, C. (2017). The doing of datafication (and what this doing does): Practices of edification and the enactment of new forms of sociality in the Indian public health service. *Journal of the Association for Information Systems*, 18(12), 872–899.

Kim, P. T. (2016). Data-driven discrimination at work. *William & Mary Law Review*, 58(3), 857–936.

Kimbell, L. (2012). Rethinking design thinking: Part II. *Design and Culture*, 4(2), 129–148.

Kitchin, R. (2014). *The Data Revolution: Big Data, Open Data, Data Infrastructures and Their Consequences*. London: Sage.

Lambrecht, A. and Tucker, C. (2019). Algorithmic bias? An empirical study of apparent gender-based discrimination in the display of stem career ads. *Management Science*, 65(7), 2966–2981.

Langley, A., Smallman, C., Tsoukas, H. and Van de Ven, A. H. (2013). Process studies of change in organization and management: Unveiling temporality, activity, and flow. *Academy of Management Journal*, 56(1), 1–13.

Ledford, H. (2019). Millions of black people affected by racial bias in health-care algorithms. *Nature*, 574(7780), 608–610.

Lee, J. K. (2016). Reflections on ICT-enabled bright society research. *Information Systems Research*, 27(1), 1–5.

Leonardi, P. M. (2011). When flexible routines meet flexible technologies: Affordance, constraint, and the imbrication of human and material agencies. *MIS Quarterly*, 35(1), 147–167.

Li, M. and Sadler, J. (2011). Power and influence in negotiations. In M. Benoliel (ed.), *Negotiation Excellence: Successful Deal Making*. Singapore: World Scientific Publishing Co., pp. 139–160.

Liakos, K. G., Busato, P., Moshou, D., Pearson, S. and Bochtis, D. (2018). Machine learning in agriculture: A review. *Sensors*, 18(8), 1–29.

Lomborg, S. (2020). Disconnection is futile – theorizing resistance and human flourishing in an age of datafication. *European Journal of Communication*, 35(3), 301–305.

Mayer-Schönberger, V. and Cukier, K. (2013). *Big Data: A Revolution that Will Transform How We Live, Work, and Think*. Boston, MA: Houghton Mifflin Harcourt.

Mehlenbacher, B. (2010). *Instruction and Technology: Designs for Everyday Learning*. Cambridge, MA: MIT Press.

Mejias, U. A. and Couldry, N. (2019). Datafication. *Internet Policy Review*, 8(4), 1–10.

Merry, S. E. (2016). *The Seductions of Quantification: Measuring Human Rights, Gender Violence, and Sex Trafficking*. Chicago, IL: University of Chicago Press.

Monteiro, E. and Parmiggiani, E. (2019). Synthetic knowing: The politics of the internet of things. *MIS Quarterly*, 43(1), 167–184.

Myers, M. D. (1999). Investigating information systems with ethnographic research. *Communications of the Association for Information Systems*, 2(23), 1–19.

Myers, M. D. (1997). Critical ethnography in information systems. In A. S. Lee, J. Liebenau and J. I. DeGross (eds), *Information Systems and Qualitative Research*. New York, NY: Springer, pp. 276–300.

Neyland, R. (2017). HPE: Stay on the cutting edge with software defined OT. CFOtech Australia, https://cfotech.com.au/story/hpe-stay-cutting-edge-software-defined-ot.

Norman, D. (2013). *The Design of Everyday Things*, revised and expanded edition. New York, NY: Basic Books.

Orlikowski, W. J. (2000). Using technology and constituting structures: A practice lens for studying technology in organizations. *Organization Science*, 11(4), 404–428.

Owen, C. (2007). Design thinking: Notes on its nature and use. *Design Research Quarterly*, 2(1), 16–27.

Press, G. (2013a). A very short history of big data. *Forbes*, www.forbes.com/sites/gilpress/2013/05/09/a-very-short-history-of-big-data/#11cf6ff765a1.

Press, G. (2013b). A very short history of data science. *Forbes*, www.forbes.com/sites/gilpress/2013/05/28/a-very-short-history-of-data-science/#6110a89b55cf.

Razzouk, R. and Shute, V. (2012). What is design thinking and why is it important? *Review of Educational Research*, 82(3), 330–348.

Reinsel, D., Gantz, J. and Rydning, J. (2018). Data age 2025: The digitization of the world from edge to core. IDC White Paper, pp. 1–29.

Scharre, P. (2018). *Army of None: Autonomous Weapons and the Future of War*. New York, NY: W. W. Norton.

Schön, D. A. (1984). Problems, frames and perspectives on designing. *Design Studies*, 5(3), 132–136.

Sharda, R., Delen, D. and Turban, E. (2016). *Business Intelligence, Analytics, and Data Science: A Managerial Perspective*. Boston, MA: Pearson.

Thaler, R. H. and Sunstein, C. R. (2009). *Nudge: Improving Decisions about Health, Wealth, and Happiness*. New York, NY: Penguin.

Thompson, L. and Schonthal, D. (2020). The social psychology of design thinking. *California Management Review*, 62(2), 84–99.

Tsoukas, H. (1989). The validity of idiographic research explanations. *Academy of Management Review*, 14(4), 551–561.

Van de Ven, A. H. (1992). Suggestions for studying strategy process: A research note. *Strategic Management Journal*, 13(S1), 169–188.

Van der Aalst, W. M. (2014). Data scientist: The engineer of the future. In K. Mertins, F. Bénaben, R. Poler and J.-P. Bourrières (eds), *Enterprise Interoperability VI: Interoperability for Agility, Resilience and Plasticity of Collaborations*. Cham, Switzerland: Springer, pp. 13–26.

Verganti, R. (2017). *Overcrowded: Designing Meaningful Products in a World Awash with Ideas*. Cambridge, MA: MIT Press.

Viljoen, N. and Van Zyl, R. H. (2009). Design thinking – crossing disciplinary borders. *Image & Text*, 15, 66–78.

Weber, R. (2004). The rhetoric of positivism versus interpretivism: A personal view. *MIS Quarterly*, 28(1), III–XII.

Weiss, J. C., Natarajan, S., Peissig, P. L., McCarty, C. A. and Page, D. (2012). Machine learning for personalized medicine: Predicting primary myocardial infarction from electronic health records. *AI Magazine*, 33(4), 33–45.

Williams, B. A., Brooks, C. F. and Shmargad, Y. (2018). How algorithms discriminate based on data they lack: Challenges, solutions, and policy implications. *Journal of Information Policy*, 8(1), 78–115.

Williams, R. and Edge, D. (1996). The social shaping of technology. *Research Policy*, 25(6), 865–899.

Wilson, H. J., Daugherty, P. R. and Morini-Bianzino, N. (2017). The jobs that artificial intelligence will create. *MIT Sloan Management Review*, 58(4), 14–16.

What Data Sharing in Government Tells Us about the Digitalization of Government Services

Lessons from the UK Digital Economy Act

EDGAR A. WHITLEY

18.1 Introduction

Globally, governments are among the largest creators and collectors of data about their citizens, often holding the definitive records about a range of life events (births, marriages and deaths), health interactions (including vaccinations) and educational achievements, as well as data about income and taxation. In most cases, these records are held in data centres associated with different functional areas of government bureaucracy (civil registration, health, education, taxation) either at the national or local level (Phippen et al., 2011; Graham et al., 2016).

For many of the functions that citizens expect their governments to undertake, however, this functional distribution of data is sub-optimal. A citizen struggling with a loss of income as a result of the pandemic might look to the government for financial support, assistance with childcare and the opportunity to set up a new business from home. They should not be expected to understand the (often arbitrary) departmental division of labour within government and are often frustrated at needing to engage with multiple parts of government, often re-entering the same information about their circumstances time and again (Allum, 2020), particularly when government can be seen as a monopolist provider of many of these key data items (Ducuing, 2020), resulting in a situation where 'citizens feel that they live at the convenience of the state: that the government acts not as servant but as master' (Government Digital Service, 2017: 3).

Data sharing across government departments is one important way in which government as a whole can achieve its goals of providing tailored services to citizens (Dawes, 1996; Perri 6 et al., 2005). For example, a data share between the tax authorities and the welfare department might automatically trigger financial support for individuals whose income (as reported in tax records) has fallen below a specified level since the start of the pandemic. Eligibility for income support might then be shared with the education department, which might be able to arrange subsidized childcare. Finally, their details and experience might be shared with the business department, which could target them with appropriate business start-up support.

Data sharing can become politically contentious when the data being shared relate to individuals. In many jurisdictions, such data are subject to relevant data protection legislation (such as the GDPR in Europe) and, more generally, there is a growing awareness of the risks that can arise when personal data are shared (Perri 6 et al., 2005; Graham et al. 2016; Sexton et al., 2017). Fear of a public backlash against inappropriate or unexpected data-sharing activities can be one of the major constraints on effective data sharing, alongside a range of technical, organizational and legal and policy barriers (Dawes, 1996; Zhang et al., 2005; Gil-Garcia et al., 2007).

In addition to the general enhancement of computing tools to share and analyze data safely, many governments are putting in place new policies to support the use of data sharing between departments (Stalla-Bourdillon et al., 2020). While many of the initiatives address concerns that have been identified by academic research over the past twenty-five years, successful data sharing remains an all too elusive part of digital or e-government (Sexton et al., 2017). Analyzing the challenges that such policy initiatives continue to face, despite the recognition of many constraints and barriers, needs to look beyond the quantitative analysis of data sharing in terms of numbers of records shared and numbers of successful matches across records, etc. and focus on the uniqueness of the situation (see Chapter 12).

This chapter therefore presents an engaged, qualitative study representing the experiences of the author who has played a key role across a range of activities in the UK government's latest iteration of its data-sharing actions, specifically those associated with the Digital Economy Act, which became law in 2017 (Parliament, 2017). Assessing both the successful and less successful results of these activities from a qualitative perspective will enable a better understanding of the state of digitalization in the UK government.

The structure of the chapter is as follows. It begins by acknowledging the methodological considerations that shaped the research, with the next section reviewing the key academic literature about government data sharing. This helps frame the insights from the case being studied, namely a qualitative assessment of the data-sharing practices arising from the United Kingdom's Digital Economy Act (2017). These practices are the outcome of over twenty years of policy development which are summarized in the third section, followed by consideration on the examples of data sharing that have been enabled by the Act. The chapter ends with reflections on what this means both for the study of qualitative research and the digitalization of government services.

18.2 Methodological Acknowledgements

Davison (2021) notes that authors frequently 'ignore their own preparation for the research and the process that they followed to acquire relevant knowledge'. He continues by suggesting that authors should discuss how they prepared before entering the field. In Chapter 7, Chughtai and Myers continue in this vein by proposing that authors should also disclose the values they hold and acknowledge the implications of these values for the research alongside the discussion of the methodological choices they make in the study design.

My involvement in this research began as a direct consequence of my personal and academic interest in privacy and consent (Whitley, 2009; Kaye et al., 2015) and my impactful engagement with policy issues around data sharing and use (Whitley, 2014a). Upon learning of these government proposals around data sharing and the open policy-making process associated with it, I actively participated in the process, attending a large number of the open policy-making meetings. My academic expertise and engagement resulted in my being invited to become a member of an expert advisory group for the process. Additionally, as a consequence of an additional expert role advising government, I became an ex-officio member of two data-sharing review boards representing privacy and consumer perspectives on the proposals. Recognizing that data 'are performed, brought into being by social and technical processes that enact particular representations of phenomena' (see Chapter 3), my qualitative, academic perspective enables me to shape public policy by questioning the extent to which the data being shared are truly referential, natural, foundational and objective (see Chapter 3) and the implications of this for evaluating proposals for data sharing in government.

Methodologically, this research reports on a qualitative, interpretive field study based on my role as a participant observer and my analysis of the discourse and contents of the various documents presented throughout the whole process. In particular, the analysis presented here is tempered, in part, by the nature of the data sharing considered by the review boards, particularly the fraud and debt review board. I have taken care to draw only on publicly available documentation so as not to run the risk of my research hampering the legitimate activities of government in reducing fraud against the public sector. My interpretation of the significance of the documents (and the choice of the documents used in this chapter) is influenced by my broader views about privacy and consent and my understanding of the information systems management practicalities associated with data sharing (Whitley, 2014b, 2016).[1]

18.3 Government Data Sharing

As a way of working with data in government, data sharing is the focus of a growing academic literature in e-government. This literature often also draws on ideas from knowledge sharing or the open data/science movement (Axelsson and Schroeder, 2009; Douglass et al., 2014). It considers how organizational, technological and legal constraints may shape data-sharing practices (Stalla-Bourdillon et al., 2020), as well as the effects of data sharing on the attitudes of citizens to the government use of data. In so doing, the study of data-sharing practices can serve as a proxy for a better understanding of the limits of digitalization of government services (Department for Digital, Culture, Media & Sport, 2021).

Using information and communication technologies to share data and knowledge across different parts of an organization has been widely studied by information systems and management researchers (Blackler, 1995; Alavi and Leidner, 2001; Schultze and Leidner, 2002; Ghobadi and Mathiassen, 2017). By studying the various ways in which formal and informal mechanisms of sharing can take place as well as the growing role of computerized systems to facilitate such

activities, novel forms of knowledge creation can be identified (Nonaka, 1994; Duguid, 2005).

Analogous claims are made about the use of data sharing in government, where having more data available for research and analysis is 'a positive thing' (Axelsson and Schroeder, 2009: 216) that will 'enhance government effectiveness, efficiency, and responsiveness to constituency needs' (Fusi, 2020: 1). Specifically, data sharing allows 'different human services agencies [to] view their common clients as complete individuals of families rather than as unrelated sets of problems or needs' (Dawes, 1996: 378).

Some researchers draw parallels between data and knowledge sharing and the broader open science movement, with government-held personal data being a special case of scientific data (Axelsson and Schroeder, 2009). Similarly, there are important parallels with the openness of open source software (Feller and Fitzgerald, 2002; Weber, 2004), where the use of shared (or openly accessible) data as a means of obtaining a societal benefit becomes apparent (Ljunberg, 2000; Goldman and Gabriel, 2005; Benkler and Nissenbaum, 2006; von Krogh and Spaeth, 2007).

Key considerations from these related fields include the role of licences (for both software and data) (Turnbull and Marks, 2000; Stewart et al., 2006; Cheliotis, 2009; Tsiavos and Whitley, 2010) as a regulatory means of supporting open endeavours (Turnbull and Marks, 2000; Gruss, 2003; González, 2006; Stewart et al., 2006; Cheliotis, 2009; Tsiavos and Whitley, 2010; Douglass et al., 2014; Open Science Collaboration, 2015), as well as the take-up of open data sets (Jetzek et al., 2019; Verhulst et al., 2020).

The incentives to collaborate in data-sharing agreements have also been studied in the context of government, with the turf wars and power inequalities (Dawes, 1996) between different parties involved in sharing data being seen as an important constraint (Welch et al., 2016; Fusi, 2020). Some authors propose incentive mechanisms to encourage data sharing coupled with accountability mechanisms to minimize inappropriate data sharing which is likely to discourage further collaborations (Wang, 2018).

---

[1] Although this chapter draws on information obtained from my longitudinal involvement with the data-sharing policy process, all inferences and assessments are my own and should not be taken as inferring or implying anything regarding official UK government policy. This chapter has benefitted from suggestions provided by the relevant data-sharing review board teams. These should not be taken as an endorsement of the document or confirmation of its accuracy, but were provided in the spirit of supporting transparency in government data-sharing activities.

Government data sharing raises many of the same ethical considerations as scientific research using personal data more generally (e.g., Kalkman et al., 2019). For example, there are concerns about how data sharing might affect the attitudes of the individuals whose data is being shared (Zhang et al., 2005). Here, legal (and ethical) consideration of consent and expectations of appropriate use become particularly important (Kaye et al., 2015). For example, plans in the United Kingdom to allow extensive data sharing of medical data had to be abandoned following a groundswell of opposition to the proposed plans that seemed misaligned to expectations, consents and opt-outs of UK citizens (Whitley, 2014b; Caldicott, 2016; Vezyridis and Timmons, 2017).

Many studies of government data-sharing experiences have highlighted the need for a clear policy on how to address privacy concerns (Harris and Wyndham, 2015; Graham et al., 2016), including consideration of whether the consent of citizens is an appropriate legal basis for sharing personal data (Bellamy et al., 2005; Perri 6 et al., 2005).

At a practical level, data-sharing depends on matching records in data set X with records in data set Y and requires high quality data to avoid type 1 (spurious match) and type 2 (undetected match) errors. Ensuring high quality data is a non-trivial managerial task often involving misaligned incentives (Public Accounts Committee, 2019). If managed badly, the adage 'garbage in, garbage out' applies and fixing this can add considerable 'hidden' costs to any data-sharing activity.

Thirty years ago, Clarke (1988) highlighted the problems that can arise when data-sharing and matching is based on poor quality data. He reported that when the US Department of Health, Education and Welfare ran its welfare files against its own payroll files, 33,000 potential 'matches' were found. A year's worth of further investigation reduced this to a narrower set of 638 cases. Of these, only fifty-five were prosecuted. Moreover, when fifteen of these cases were independently reviewed, five were dismissed, six were convicted of felonies and no prison sentences resulted (Clarke, 1988: 508–509). This strongly suggests serious data quality issues with the underlying digitalization of those government services.

In 2016, a review of another data-sharing agreement revealed many similar trends. The report by the Independent Chief Inspector of Borders and Immigration examined the implementation of a data-sharing agreement that was intended to help create a 'hostile environment' for individuals who are in the United Kingdom without valid leave.

Two specific measures were examined: the refusal by the Driver and Vehicle Licensing Agency (DVLA) of applications for a UK driving licence and the revocation of existing licences for individuals not lawfully resident in the United Kingdom; and the requirement placed on banks and building societies to refuse an application for a UK current account from an individual listed as a 'disqualified person'. Both processes rely on bulk data-sharing between the Home Office, DVLA and Cifas (an independent, not-for-profit organization working to reduce fraud and related financial crime in the United Kingdom); they are based on pre-existing collaborative arrangements between the different organizations and, of course, rely on the quality of the (Home Office) data being shared.

The inspection found, however, that 'records for individuals were incomplete or had been completed incorrectly (with data placed in the wrong fields), or there were delays in updating records' (2.7). To mitigate these problems, 'the Home Office checks its records manually for new licence applicants and also to confirm that the DVLA should proceed with a revocation' (2.8).

Even in the cases where individuals were correctly identified and had their driving licence revoked, only a small proportion surrendered their revoked licence. This undermines the intended policy objectives: 'stopping illegal migrants from being able to drive lawfully, and from using a driving licence to access other benefits and services'. This latter point might have particular significance if it becomes necessary to present government-issued photo ID documents (passport/driving licence) before accessing health services and apps.

Similar data quality issues affected the bank account opening checks, with 10 per cent of a sample of 169 reviewed cases incorrectly listing people as 'disqualified persons' (i.e., who shouldn't be allowed to open a bank account), but who in fact either had leave to remain in the United Kingdom or outstanding applications/appeals (6.29).

Importantly, this report also found problems with the safeguards that had been put in place, including the memoranda of understanding about data-sharing between the various agencies (2.6). Moreover, the Inspector's concerns that the justification for the policy 'is based on the conviction that they are "right" in principle, and enjoy broad public support, rather than on any evidence that the measures already introduced are working or needed to be strengthened' (2.21) has direct parallels with Clarke's concluding point that the benefits of data-sharing 'must not be assumed, but carefully assessed' (Clarke, 1988: 511).

In summary, as noted by Dawes, 'any jurisdiction seeking the benefits of interagency information sharing must adopt policies which do more than simply make sharing possible. It needs policies which make it probable that appropriate problems will be identified and that reasonable effort will lead to success' (Dawes, 1996: 392). Specifically, while the existing research repeatedly highlights the potential benefits that arise from using larger and more diverse data sets to improve government actions, it also highlights the challenges that any such policies need to address, including addressing the incentives for different parts of government to engage in data sharing, as well as how to address risks associated with the use of personal data and data quality (and metadata) issues that can affect the quality of the outcomes from the data sharing (Mayernik, 2017). These insights are particularly helpful for contextualizing the development of data sharing in the United Kingdom over the past twenty-plus years, which is described in the next section.

18.4 Data Sharing in the United Kingdom: 1997–2021

Data-sharing plans in the United Kingdom, following the election of the Labour government in 1997, were shaped by two potentially inconsistent policy initiatives. On the one hand, the government enacted a manifesto commitment to domesticate the European Convention on Human Rights and was obliged to enact into national law the 1995 EU Data Protection Directive (Perri 6 et al., 2005). On the other hand, it launched plans for more horizontal coordination and integration of public services ('joined-up government'). The data sharing that would underpin this joining up could potentially be challenged on the basis of human rights and data protection laws. Moreover, the implementation of these initiatives would likely vary across different parts of government (Bellamy et al., 2005). For example, Bellamy et al. (2005) note that policy in the area of crime and disorder was often authorized using general police powers and changes to executive guidelines, whereas data sharing for social security was on the basis of specific legal instruments and associated codes of practice.

After three terms in government, the Labour Party lost the 2010 general election, with a new coalition government being formed by the Conservative Party and the Liberal Democrats. A key element of the election manifestos of these parties was a push to protect freedoms against concerns of the Labour government creating a surveillance state (Whitley et al., 2014), arguing that 'personal information belongs to the citizen, not the state, and where the government collects private details they are held on trust' (Conservatives, 2009).

In November 2012, the new government launched its new digital strategy (Cabinet Office, 2012). This noted that 'government's online services are not necessarily better or more convenient than other channels, meaning they will not be users' first choice to transact with us' (2012: 14), with this being both frustrating and time-consuming for users, but also costly for government. It suggested that there were a number of causes of this, including reliance on digitized versions of pre-digital business processes, legacy IT systems and 'outdated back-end systems which prevent effective data sharing' (2012: 15). Nevertheless, given its commitments to minimizing 'state surveillance', it sought to ensure that government services met a requirement to 'maintain the privacy and security of all personal information' (Cabinet Office, 2012).

In order to resolve the long-standing tensions between privacy and efficiency and produce a broader balance of trust, the government launched a multi-year open policy-making process (Involve, 2018a) that brought together, in regular meetings, representatives from central and local government, as well as academics and civil society organizations, to 'explore the potential for sharing more personal data in three specific areas of public service delivery' (Involve, 2016a). The process specifically sought to ensure 'data sharing can be done properly, with the right safeguards in place that protect privacy' (Involve, 2016b).

As noted above, on hearing about this initiative, the author became an active participant observer to this process. This involved attending as many of the workshops as possible.

These workshops were associated with the various proposed streams of data sharing that were under consideration: data sharing for research and statistics, data sharing to address issues of fraud, error and debt, and data sharing to enable tailored public services (Involve, 2018b). Participating in these meetings provided an opportunity for all attendees to improve their understanding of the practices and concerns of other stakeholders. For example, following this participation, the author fully appreciated the statutory arrangements that created Her Majesty's Revenue & Customs (HMRC) and the consequential duty of confidentiality imposed on HMRC which limits the amount of data sharing that it can initialize.

Similarly, the author was able to observe a number of instances where one body argued that it was desperate to have a data-sharing arrangement with a relevant government department, only for that department to express frustration that there was limited awareness (and hence take-up) of existing legal gateways that already permitted such data sharing to take place, echoing the concern raised by Dawes (1996) that policies must do more than simply make sharing possible.

In line with government commitments, the open policy process was founded on a number of key principles, including the avoidance of indiscriminate sharing of data within government and no weakening of existing safeguards that exist under data protection law (Involve 2018b, para. 5).

The open policy-making process produced a series of recommendations – for example, to reduce the restrictions on HMRC in terms of what data they could share for public benefit (Involve, 2018b: para. 12). In terms of fraud, error and debt, the process highlighted the need for more robust evidence on a range of issues and, in particular, it suggested that given the uncertainty about the efficacy of different forms of data sharing for this area, the best approach might be to enable a series of pilots which would be evaluated in terms of the value of the data-sharing interventions (Involve, 2018b: para. 12).

Data sharing for research and statistics was more straightforward, given the extensive experience of the UK Statistics Authority in handling personal data and the use of trusted third parties to de-identify data for statistical purposes.

Finally, the discussion around data sharing for tailored public services resulted in a proposal for broad but constrained powers, whereby a permissive power for defined public bodies to share data for the purpose of improving the delivery or targeting of public services in specific areas of social policy would be proposed (Involve, 2018b: para. 12).

Following the end of the open policy-making process, the government issued a consultation on the 'better use of data in government' (Cabinet Office and Government Digital Service, 2016). The consultation sought views on the three areas covered by the open policy process, adding consideration of sharing civil registration information (births, marriages and deaths) as part of the process of improving public services.

Continuing the spirit of the open policy-making process, the government convened an eight-person External Advisory Group as part of a process for greater transparency in government consultations (Involve, 2016c). The author was a member of the group. The initial objectives of the group were set out as:

a) Quality assuring the methodological approaches taken to analyse any responses received;
b) Quality assuring the government's findings and consultation analysis;
c) Continuing the Open Policy Making principle of external challenge. (2016c: 2)

The work of the Expert Advisory Group ended up being more limited than planned as the government had received over 280 responses (most just at the deadline for submissions), many of which did not use the consultation template, meaning that only a limited coding and thematic analysis of the responses had been undertaken before the group met.

The expert group noted that some of the issues with the consultation included questions that assume assent or that did not ask the questions that people wanted to answer (hence the large number of less structured responses), compound questions (which ask about two things, but for which only one answer is permitted) and questions where the free text answers were likely to be more informative than just a yes/no response (Involve, 2016c: 5). These complications highlight the complexity of developing policy in this area where, even after an extensive open policy-making process, there was still significant ambiguity about what was being proposed and why.

The insights from the consultation responses resulted in a set of proposals found in Part 5 of the Digital Economy Bill. The Bill as a whole introduced a wide range of measures in support of the United Kingdom's digital economy, including universal service broadband obligations and digital infrastructure, as well as provisions around intellectual property and online pornography. Part 5 sought to provide 'the necessary legal framework to enable data sharing for a public benefit' (Department for Culture, Media and Sport, 2016: 10), which would become a key enabler for the government's transformation plans.

The Digital Economy Bill received Royal Assent and became UK law on 27 April 2017 (Parliament, 2017). Alongside the legislation, Part 5 of the Digital Economy Act introduced a number of draft codes of practice that give important information about requirements that all persons who are involved in disclosing or using information under the DEA powers will need to understand if they wish to make use of these powers in Part 5 of the Digital Economy Act 2017 (Department for Digital, Culture, Media & Sport et al., 2018). These codes of practice cover the main areas enabled by data sharing in the legislation: the linking of data sets to support research purposes and data sharing by civil registration officials, as well as data sharing to support the delivery of public services and data sharing around fraud and debt (which will initially be run as pilot shares) (Department for Digital, Culture, Media & Sport et al., 2018). In July 2018, Parliament approved the draft codes and they were published on 23 July 2018, which meant that public authorities and other participants using the information-sharing powers in Part 5 of the Digital Economy Act must now have regard to the relevant code before any data is shared.

18.5 Data-Sharing Review Boards

Two of the data-sharing elements of Part 5 of the Digital Economy Act involve the creation of review boards that 'advise the relevant Ministers on proposals for new ... objectives and to ensure a consistent strategic approach to the use of the public service delivery powers' (Department for Digital, Culture, Media & Sport et al., 2018: para. 76) and 'to oversee any ... information sharing under the debt powers, and to monitor the pilots' (2018: para. 95). These boards are intended to provide some of the accountability mechanisms suggested by Wang (2018).

There are two boards under three powers in the act, one combining fraud and debt powers and pilots. The Public Service Delivery (PSD) Board makes recommendations to the relevant minister for new PSD objectives in the regulations subject to consultation and affirmative action by Parliament, effectively changing elements of the law. The Fraud and Debt Board, in contrast, makes recommendations to the relevant minister to approve pilot data-sharing projects. These pilots can be approved by the minister without further recourse to Parliament.

All proposals that seek to make use of the data-sharing powers under these parts of the Act must be submitted to the relevant review board for consideration. The author is a member of both review boards and so has sight of all proposals around data sharing for public service delivery and fraud and debt pilots.

In contrast to much of the existing literature on government data sharing, the proposals that come to the review boards are seeking to take advantage of the gateways enabled by the legislation. That is, all parties involved in the data sharing have (already) agreed to participate in the data shares and, as part of the documentation for the review boards to consider, need to provide an agreed business case, information-sharing agreement, security plan and, for those data shares that involve personally identifiable data, a Data Protection Impact Assessment (Information Commissioner's Office, 2021) that sets out the objectives of the data share. Additionally, fraud and debt data shares are initially considered as pilots and so must provide measurable objectives so that the review board can assess whether the pilot was successful, proportionate and suitable for converting to a business-as-usual data share.

The secretariat for the review boards works closely with the departments preparing the proposals to ensure that they provide the kinds of detail that members of the review board expect to see. Proposals to the review board are typically accompanied by oral presentations, which provide an opportunity for board members to ask further questions about the proposals. Initially, these interactions provided a means of better understanding the norms and approaches adopted by various parties – for example, how the estimated benefits of fraud prevention are calculated and generalized from the findings in the pilot studies. They also helped provide clarity about proposals that simply sought to explore the efficacy of particular shares to those that would use the findings from the pilot to lead to formal investigation and potential prosecution in cases where likely fraud was identified.

However, with the details of the data sharing, matching and follow-through being undertaken by the relevant departments and agencies, a key part of the review board's role was to provide an independent consideration of the overall logic behind the data-sharing proposals. Details of all approved information-sharing agreements are provided in a publicly accessible register (Cabinet Office and Central Data and Digital Office, 2021), including information specified in the Codes of Practice

(Department for Digital, Culture, Media & Sport et al., 2018: sec. 5.1).

In terms of minimizing the amount of fraud against the government, a key conceptual challenge is determining who is in a 'household' as a number of social welfare benefits may be allocated, for example, to people living alone. As the United Kingdom does not have a live population register which records where people are living, a number of proxy measures have been considered to determine this. One proxy was explored in a data-sharing agreement between the Department for Work and Pensions (DWP) and the DVLA (Cabinet Office and Central Data and Digital Office, 2021: pilot 37). This pilot involved sharing details of the registered address of a vehicle (held by DVLA) and matching these address details with data held in relation to benefits. The purpose of the pilot was to determine the utility of using vehicle-registered-address details as a source of additional data for determining household composition.

While the appeal of using this less invasive data is apparent, it also makes strong assumptions about the behaviours of individuals (including that they are conscientious in notifying DVLA of the change of registered address for their vehicle – a process that involves at least three changes [driving licence, vehicle log book and payment details for car tax]). This pilot reveals the importance of being clear about the likely quality of the data being shared, although in this case it is more about the match between accurate data in the systems and real-world behaviours than it is about possible errors in the database itself.

Another pilot (Cabinet Office and Central Data and Digital Office, 2021: pilot 57) was based on the debt powers under the DEA and sought to analyze vulnerable and overlapping debtors across a range of government departments and local authorities. In particular, it sought to better understand the extent to which the departments and local authorities had consistently flagged individuals as being vulnerable and whether they had incurred multiple debts across multiple bodies.

A key consideration by the review board in this case involved the act of flagging someone as being vulnerable. In some databases, this might be a flag indicating that the individual's characteristics match a predefined set of circumstances. However, without appropriate contextual information, sharing this data with another body might trigger a duty of care towards that individual (echoing Stamper's [1985: 59–60] example of the very different semantic meanings of a similar flag indicating that a property was 'unfit for human habitation').

A final important consideration relates to the amount of business presented to the two review boards. As of October 2021, the majority of data shares under the public service delivery power (Cabinet Office and Central Data and Digital Office, 2021) relate to assisting people living in fuel poverty (one of the four objectives written into the initial legislation). In contrast, there are seventy-two shares under the debt recovery powers and eleven under the fraud powers (see also UKSA, 2020), although this is in part because there are a number of pilots involving different local authorities and each local authority's data-sharing agreement is listed separately on the register.

The absence of significant proposals under the public service delivery powers returns to consideration of the issues identified by the existing literature in this space and highlights the differences between proposals that seek to change legislation (and need parliamentary approval) compared to pilots that simply need ministerial approval.

In recognition of the mismatch in take-up between the two powers, the government commissioned independent research into the motivations for and barriers to data sharing (Busby et al., 2020). This research included interviews with nineteen diverse stakeholders who provided their views as to why they believed use of the public service delivery powers was so limited.

Some stakeholders raised concerns with the powers under the Act, suggesting that they were both too broad in some circumstances and too specific in others (2020, sec. 1.2.1). This is particularly surprising given the detailed open policy-making process and public consultation (summarized above) alongside the scrutiny of new legislation by Parliament. The use of the powers was believed to be 'difficult and time consuming' (2020, sec. 1.2.2) (although with data sharing

under only one power having been approved, it is unclear what this perception is based on).

Other concerns raised included worries that data regulations (such as the General Data Protection Regulation [GDPR]) might be breached through the use of the powers, even though the powers were explicitly intended to provide a legal gateway to enable the sharing. Similarly, many of the stakeholders reported a culture of risk aversion that went 'beyond the practical considerations around data sharing' (2020, sec. 4.2.2), as well as awareness of 'the consequences of getting data sharing wrong' (2020, sec. 4.2.2).

Concerns about reputational risk were often associated issues about the quality of the data that might be shared. However, this doesn't necessarily explain the difference in take-up across the two powers.

18.6 Conclusion

While effective data sharing has been a common goal for many governments, the increased digitalization of government services in general (as well as the need to digitalize services further in response to the social distancing requirements arising from the pandemic) is transforming the government data-sharing environment. Although the practices of data sharing and matching have strong techno-rational and engineering components, the success or failure of data-sharing proposals is rarely grounded in just these components. Instead, historically, some of the most significant challenges have been in the broader environment within which the data sharing takes place. This might involve consideration of the power relationships between the different bodies involved in the data share or the ways in which sharing personal data by government addresses both the ethical and legal requirements that exist. Equally, data sharing might be limited by concerns about the underlying quality of the data being shared and the reputational risks that might arise if data is used out of context. Qualitative research methods, such as in-depth engagement with meetings and documents, are a particularly effective way of studying the operational processes over time. In particular, they examine the practices within the context of their use and can provide a trace of operational processes over time (see Chapter 5).

This chapter therefore contributes to our understanding of the role of qualitative research under digitalization by presenting the experiences of the author in the most recent UK data-sharing initiative. The author's access to large parts of the policy-making and -using process have enabled a qualitative analysis and reflections on this process.

An important concern highlighted by the literature concerns a (perceived) lack of legitimacy of many government data-sharing proposals. In contrast, the studied UK case sought to build and maintain legitimacy through an explicitly open policy-making process. This sought to engage with the many and varied stakeholders with an interest in data sharing, both within and without government. Nevertheless, this part of the process was still imperfect. The resulting legislation, found in Part 5 of the Digital Economy Act (2017), provided a strong enabling environment for a range of data-sharing activities. These permissive powers were intended to address many of the concerns about power relationships between different parties in the data-sharing process that had been highlighted during the policy-making process and which echo perceived concerns identified in the literature (Gil-Garcia et al., 2007; Susha et al., 2019).

Additionally, the open policy-making process highlighted the importance of transparency in the governance of the more contentious data-sharing processes by specifying the role of the two review boards in the codes of practice associated with the legislation (Department for Digital, Culture, Media & Sport et al., 2018). It is generally recognized that a strong, independent governance body can significantly aid effective data sharing (Stalla-Bourdillon et al., 2021).

Alongside their role in enhancing the legitimacy of the data-sharing process, the review boards highlight the ongoing issues with the data that is being shared. These include a growing recognition of the extent to which data are brought into being by social and technical processes that enact particular representations of real-world phenomena rather than being truly objective and referential (see Chapter 3). This is particularly evident in the comparison between the number of proposals that have been approved by the two review boards.

What is also striking is the extent to which many of the traditional concerns around data sharing are re-articulated as possible explanations for limited take-up of the public service delivery powers under the Act. This qualitative study of data sharing in the United Kingdom has revealed the efficacy of some parts of the process that have enabled digitalized government to benefit from data-sharing initiatives. Nevertheless, some significant barriers remain and allow us to reflect on the limits of the digital first/digitalization research agenda (Baskerville et al., 2020) and, specifically, the extent of digitalization of government services.

References

Alavi, M. and Leidner, D. (2001). Knowledge management and knowledge management systems. *MIS Quarterly*, 25(1), 107–136.

Allum, J. (2020). Introducing GOV.UK Accounts – Government Digital Service, GOV.UK, https://gds.blog.gov.uk/2020/09/22/introducing-gov-uk-accounts/.

Axelsson, A.-S. and Schroeder, R. (2009). Making it open and keeping it safe: E-enabled data-sharing in Sweden. *Acta Sociologica*, 52(3), 213–226.

Baskerville, R. L., Myers, M. D. and Yoo, Y. (2020). Digital first: The ontological reversal and new challenges for information systems research. *MIS Quarterly*, 44(2), 509–523.

Bellamy, C., Perri 6 and Raab, C. (2005). Joined-up government and privacy in the United Kingdom: Managing tensions between data protection and social policy: Part II. *Public Administration*, 83(2), 393–415.

Benkler, Y. and Nissenbaum, H. (2006). Commons-based peer production and virtue. *Journal of Political Philosophy*, 14(4), 394–419.

Blackler, F. (1995). Knowledge, knowledge work and organisations: An overview and interpretation. *Organization Studies*, 16(6), 1021–1045.

Busby, A., Mason, L., St Clair, C. and Williams, L. (2020). Motivations for and barriers to data sharing. Department for Digital, Culture, Media & Sport, https://assets.publishing.service.gov.uk/government/uploads/system/uploads/attach

ment_data/file/895505/_Kantar_research_publi
cation.pdf.

Cabinet Office. (2012). Government digital strategy.
GOV.UK, www.gov.uk/government/publica
tions/government-digital-strategy.

Cabinet Office and Central Data and Digital Office.
(2021). Digital Economy Act information
sharing powers and objectives register.
GOV.UK, www.gov.uk/government/publications/
register-of-information-sharing-agreements-under-
chapters-1-2-3-and-4-of-part-5-of-the-digital-econ
omy-act-2017.

Cabinet Office and Government Digital Service.
(2016). Better use of data in government.
GOV.UK, www.gov.uk/government/consult
ations/better-use-of-data-in-government.

Caldicott, D. F. (2016). Review of data security,
consent and opt-outs. GOV.UK, www.gov.uk/
government/publications/review-of-data-secur
ity-consent-and-opt-outs.

Cheliotis, G. (2009). From open source to open content: Organization, licensing and decision processes in open cultural production. *Decision
Support Systems*, 47(3), 229–244.

Clarke, R. (1988). Information technology and data-
veillance. *Communications of the ACM*, 31(5),
498–512.

Conservatives. (2009). Reversing the rise of the surveillance state: 11 measures to protect personal
privacy and hold government to account. https://
web.archive.org/web/20100328053242/http://
www.conservatives.com/News/News_stories/
2009/09/Reversing_the_rise_of_the_surveil
lance_state.aspx.

Davison, R. M. (2021). From ignorance to familiarity:
Contextual knowledge and the field researcher.
Information Systems Journal, 31(1), 1–6.

Dawes, S. S. (1996). Interagency information sharing:
Expected benefits, manageable risks. *Journal of
Policy Analysis and Management*, 15(3),
377–394.

Department for Culture, Media and Sport. (2016).
Digital Economy Bill: Explanatory notes. UK
Parliament, https://publications.parliament.uk/
pa/bills/lbill/2016-2017/0080/17080en.pdf.

Department for Digital, Culture, Media & Sport.
(2021). Increasing access to data across the
economy. GOV.UK, www.gov.uk/government/
publications/increasing-access-to-data-held-across-
the-economy.

Department for Digital, Culture, Media & Sport,
Cabinet Office, Home Office, and UK Statistics

Authority. (2018). Digital Economy Act
2017 Part 5: Codes of Practice. GOV.UK,
www.gov.uk/government/publications/digital-
economy-act-2017-part-5-codes-of-practice.

Douglass, K., Allard, S., Tenopir, C., Wu, L. and
Frame, M. (2014). Managing scientific data as
public assets: Data sharing practices and policies
among full-time government employees.
*Journal of the Association for Information
Science and Technology*, 65(2), 251–262.

Ducuing, C. (2020). Data as infrastructure? A study of
data sharing legal regimes. *Competition and
Regulation in Network Industries*, 21(2), 124–142.

Duguid, P. (2005). 'The art of knowing': Social and
tacit dimensions of knowledge and the limits of
the community of practice. *Information Society:
An International Journal*, 21(2), 109–118.

Feller, J. and Fitzgerald, B. (2002). *Understanding
Open Source Software Development*. London:
Addison-Wesley.

Fusi, F. (2020). When local governments request
access to data: Power and coordination mechanisms across stakeholders. *Public Administration
Review*, 81(1), 23–37.

Ghobadi, S. and Mathiassen, L. (2017). Risks to
effective knowledge sharing in agile software
teams: A model for assessing and mitigating
risks. *Information Systems Journal*, 27(6),
699–731.

Gil-Garcia, J. R., Chengalur-Smith, I. and Duchessi,
P. (2007). Collaborative e-Government:
Impediments and benefits of information-sharing
projects in the public sector. *European Journal
of Information Systems*, 16(2), 121–133.

Goldman, R. and Gabriel, R. P. (2005). *Innovation
Happens Elsewhere: Open Source as Business
Strategy*. London and San Francisco, CA:
Morgan Kaufmann.

González, A. G. (2006). Open science: Open source
licences in scientific research. *North Carolina
Journal of Law & Technology*, 7(Spring),
321–366.

Government Digital Service. (2017). Government
transformation strategy. GOV.UK, www.gov
.uk/government/publications/government-trans
formation-strategy-2017-to-2020/government-
transformation-strategy.

Graham, F. S., Gooden, S. T. and Martin, K. J.
(2016). Navigating the transparency–privacy
paradox in public sector data sharing. *American
Review of Public Administration*, 46(5),
569–591.

Gruss, P. (2003). Berlin declaration on open access to knowledge in the sciences and humanities. Conference on Open Access to Knowledge in the Sciences and Humanities, https://openaccess.mpg.de/Berlin-Declaration.

Harris, T. L. and Wyndham, J. M. (2015). Data rights and responsibilities: A human rights perspective on data sharing. *Journal of Empirical Research on Human Research Ethics*, 10(3), 334–337.

Information Commissioner's Office. (2021). Data protection impact assessments. https://ico.org.uk/for-organisations/guide-to-data-protection/guide-to-the-general-data-protection-regulation-gdpr/accountability-and-governance/data-protection-impact-assessments/.

Involve. (2018a). What we're doing – data sharing. https://web.archive.org/web/20180901164714/http://datasharing.org.uk/what-were-doing/index.html.

Involve. (2018b). Conclusions of civil society and public sector policy discussions on data use in government. https://web.archive.org/web/20180220012818/http://datasharing.org.uk/wp-content/uploads/sites/2/2015/03/20150327_Conclusions_OPM_paper_Data_final.pdf.

Involve. (2016a). What data should government bodies be allowed to share about us? www.involve.org.uk/our-work/our-projects/practice/what-data-should-government-bodies-be-allowed-share-about-us.

Involve. (2016b). Planning the open policy process | 31 March 2014 | Meeting note – data sharing. https://web.archive.org/web/20161220035035/http://datasharing.org.uk/2014/04/03/planning-the-open-policy-process-31-mar-2014-meeting-note/.

Involve. (2016c). Report from the External Advisory Group for the Better Use of Data in Government Consultation. https://web.archive.org/web/20161219034648/https://datasharing.org.uk/wp-content/uploads/sites/2/2016/07/External-Advisory-Group-Report-1.pdf.

Jetzek, T., Avital, M. and Bjorn-Andersen, N. (2019). The sustainable value of open government data. *Journal of the Association for Information Systems*, 20(6), 702–734.

Kalkman, S., Mostert, M., Udo-Beauvisage, N., van Delden, J. J. and van Thiel, G. J. (2019). Responsible data sharing in a big data-driven translational research platform: Lessons learned. *BMC Medical Informatics and Decision Making*, 19(1), 283.

Kaye, J., Whitley, E. A., Lund, D., Morrison, M., Teare, H. and Melham, K. (2015). Dynamic consent: A patient interface for twenty-first century research networks. *European Journal of Human Genetics*, 23(2), 141–146.

Ljunberg, J. (2000). Open source movements as a model for organising. *European Journal of Information Systems*, 9(4), 208–216.

Mayernik, M. S. (2017). Open data: Accountability and transparency. *Big Data & Society*, 4(2), Article 2053951717718853.

Nonaka, I. (1994). A dynamic theory of organizational knowledge creation. *Organization Science*, 5(1), 14–37.

Open Science Collaboration. (2015). Estimating the reproducibility of psychological science. *Science*, 349(6251), aac4716-1–aac4716-8.

Parliament. (2017). Digital Economy Act 2017. GOV.UK, www.legislation.gov.uk/ukpga/2017/30/contents/enacted/data.htm.

Perri 6, Raab, C. and Bellamy, C. (2005). Joined-up government and privacy in the United Kingdom: Managing tensions between data protection and social policy: Part I. *Public Administration*, 83(1), 111–133.

Phippen, A., Raza, A., Butel, L. and Southern, R. (2011). Impacting methodological innovation in a local government context – data sharing rewards and barriers. *Methodological Innovations Online*, 6(1), 58–72.

Public Accounts Committee. (2019). Challenges in using data across government. GOV.UK, https://publications.parliament.uk/pa/cm201719/cmselect/cmpubacc/2492/2492.pdf.

Schultze, U. and Leidner, D. E. (2002). Studying knowledge management in information systems research: Discourses and theoretical assumptions. *MIS Quarterly*, 26(3), 213–242.

Sexton, A., Shepherd, E., Duke-Williams, O. and Eveleigh, A. (2017). A balance of trust in the use of government administrative data. *Archival Science*, 17(4), 305–330.

Stalla-Bourdillon, S., Carmichael, L. and Wintour, A. (2021). Fostering trustworthy data sharing: Establishing data foundations in practice. *Data & Policy*, 3, e4.

Stalla-Bourdillon, S., Thuermer, G., Walker, J., Carmichael, L. and Simperl, E. (2020). Data protection by design: Building the foundations of trustworthy data sharing, *Data & Policy*, 2, e4.

Stamper, R. (1985). Management epistemology: Garbage in, garbage out (and what about deontology and axiology). In L. Methlie and R. Sprague (eds), *Knowledge Representation for Decision Support Systems*. Amsterdam, the Netherlands: Springer, pp. 55–77.

Stewart, K. J., Ammeter, A. P. and Maruping, L. M. (2006). Impacts of license choice and organizational sponsorship on user interest and development activity in open source software projects. *Information Systems Research*, 17(2), 126–144.

Susha, I., Rukanova, B., Ramon Gil-Garcia, J., Tan, Y.-H. and Hernandez, M. G. (2019). Identifying mechanisms for achieving voluntary data sharing in cross-sector partnerships for public good. Presented at the ACM International Conference Proceeding Series, Dubai, United Arab Emirates.

Tsiavos, P. and Whitley, E. A. (2010). Open sourcing regulation: The development of the creative commons licences as a form of commons based peer production. In D. Bourcier, P. Casanovas, M. D. Rosnay and C. Maracke (eds), *Intelligent Multimedia: Managing Creative Works in a Digital World*. Florence, Italy: European Press Academic Publishing, pp. 89–114.

Turnbull, B. H. and Marks, D. S. (2000). Technical protection measures: The intersection of technology, law and commercial licenses. *European Intellectual Property Review*, 22(5), 198–213.

UKSA. (2020). Mid-point report on use of the DEA powers. UK Statistics Authority, www.gov.uk/government/publications/digital-economy-act-2017-part-5-codes-of-practice/mid-point-report-on-use-of-the-dea-powers.

Verhulst, S. G., Young, A., Zahuranec, A. J., Aaronson, S. A., Calderon, A. and Gee, M. (2020). The emergence of a third wave of open data. Open Data Policy Lab, https://opendatapolicylab.org/images/odpl/third-wave-of-opendata.pdf.

Vezyridis, P. and Timmons, S. (2017). Understanding the care.data conundrum: New information flows for economic growth. *Big Data & Society*, 4(1), Article 2053951716688490.

von Krogh, G. and Spaeth, S. (2007). The open source software phenomenon: Characteristics that promote research. *Journal of Strategic Information Systems*, 16(3), 236–253.

Wang, F. (2018). Understanding the dynamic mechanism of interagency government data sharing. *Government Information Quarterly*, 35(4), 536–546.

Weber, S. (2004). *The Success of Open Source*. Cambridge, MA: Harvard University Press.

Welch, E. W., Feeney, M. K. and Park, C. H. (2016). Determinants of data sharing in U.S. city governments. *Government Information Quarterly*, 33(3), 393–403.

Whitley, E. A. (2016). Can data-sharing improve public services? Lessons for Parliament. LSE blog, http://blogs.lse.ac.uk/politicsandpolicy/can-data-sharing-improve-public-services-some-lessons-for-parliament/.

Whitley, E. A. (2014a). REF impact case study: Scrapping costly and controversial proposals for identity cards. London School of Economics and Political Science, www.lse.ac.uk/Research/research-impact-case-studies/scrapping-costly-controversial-proposals-identity-cards.

Whitley, E. A. (2014b). The Privacy Impact Assessment undertaken for care.data isn't clear on what opting out would mean for our data. LSE blog, http://blogs.lse.ac.uk/politicsandpolicy/the-impact-of-privacy-impact-assessments/.

Whitley, E. A. (2009). Informational privacy, consent and the 'control' of personal data. *Information Security Technical Report*, 14(3), 154–159.

Whitley, E. A., Martin, A. K. and Hosein, G. (2014). From surveillance-by-design to privacy-by-design: Evolving identity policy in the UK. In K. Boersma, R. Brakel, C. Fonio and P. Wagenaar (eds), *Histories of State Surveillance in Europe and Beyond*. London: Routledge, pp. 205–219.

Zhang, J., Dawes, S. S. and Sarkis, J. (2005). Exploring stakeholders' expectations of the benefits and barriers of e-government knowledge sharing. *Journal of Enterprise Information Management*, 18(5), 548–567.

Index

Page numbers in **bold** refer to content in tables; those in *italics* refer to content in figures.